Building English Skills

Purple Level

Building English Skills

PURPLE LEVEL

Yellow Level

Blue Level

Orange Level

Green Level

Red Level

Gold Level

Silver Level

Aqua Level

Brown Level

Plum Level

Pink Level

Cherry Level (K)

THE McDOUGAL, LITTELL ENGLISH PROGRAM

Building English Skills

Purple Level

Joy Littell, EDITORIAL DIRECTOR

McDougal, Littell & Company
Evanston, Illinois
New York   Dallas   Sacramento

Prepared by the Staff of
THE WRITING IMPROVEMENT PROJECT

Joy Littell, Editorial Director, McDougal, Littell & Company

J. A. Christensen, East High School, Salt Lake City, Utah

Stephen G. Ham, New Trier Township High School East, Winnetka, Illinois

Patricia Phelan, Chairperson, English Department, Hale Jr. High School, San Diego, California

Marcia Baldwin Whipps, East High School, Salt Lake City, Utah

The Staff wishes to thank the more than 1500 students who contributed samples of their writing for analysis.

Consultants

Dr. Patsy M. Davis, Assistant Professor, College of Education, Department of Curriculum and Instruction, University of Tennessee, Knoxville, Tennessee

Beth Johnson, English Department Chair, Polk County School District, Lakeland, Florida

Karen Kutiper, Language Arts Coordinator, Alief Independent School District, Houston, Texas

Adrian W. McClaren, English Consultant, Memphis City Schools, Memphis, Tennessee

Julia S. Nichols, English Department Chair, North Area II, Memphis, Tennessee

Harry H. Raney, Teacher, Memphis School District, Memphis, Tennessee

Carolyn C. Walter, Educational Consultant and Writer, Chicago, Illinois

ISBN: 0-86609-323-0   TE ISBN: 0-86609-324-9

Acknowledgments: Time, Inc.: For "Signs of an Angry Goddess," from *Time* Magazine, February 27, 1984; copyright © 1984 Time, Inc., all rights reserved; reprinted by permission of *Time.* Macmillan Publishing Company: Chapters 1 and 3–6 and the Handbook contain, in revised form, some materials that appeared originally in *English Arts and Skills, Grade 12,* Ronald J. Wilkins et al., copyright © 1965, 1961 by The Macmillan Company. Used by arrangement.   (Acknowledgments are continued on page 813)

Contents

Chapter 14   The Library and Its Reference Materials   305

Chapter 15   Critical Thinking and Language   328

Chapter 18 Public Speaking and Debate 398

Handbook

8.0 Adjective and Adverb Usage 645

9.0 The Right Word 664

10.0 Capitalization 682

11.0 End Marks and Commas 698

12.0 The Semicolon, the Colon, the Dash and Parentheses 720

17.0 Good Manuscript Form 784

18.0 Outlining 802

Chapter 1

Vocabulary Development

Words are often called "the building blocks" of communication. To some people, this means that words are the basic units of language from which all sentences, paragraphs, speeches, and novels are built. To others, however, the phrase implies that words are also the simplest, most easily mastered elements of language. This last interpretation could not be further from the truth. The acquisition of a powerful vocabulary is a lifelong task. You may learn everything there is to know about development, organization, and form, but without the right words to express your ideas, you will never be able to communicate effectively.

In this chapter, you will learn how to increase your vocabulary by unlocking the meanings of the unfamiliar words you encounter. With a more powerful vocabulary, you will find that you can present ideas with new force and increased effectiveness. You will also be able to add a sophistication to your writing that will set you apart in school, on the job, and in every other situation where you communicate with others.

1

Part 1　Expanding Your Vocabulary

You have four distinct vocabularies. Two contain words that you understand when others use them. These are your **passive vocabularies** of listening and reading. Two contain words that you understand well enough to use yourself. These are your **active vocabularies** of speaking and writing.

Each of your four vocabularies grows over time. You first encounter a new word in the speech or written work of others. Once you find out what the new word means, there follows a period of time in which you recognize and understand the word in context but do not use it yourself. Eventually, when the word becomes familiar, you will begin to use it on your own. At this point you can truly be said to understand the new word, and it becomes part of your active vocabulary.

In order to increase the rate at which you acquire new words, you must take charge of this process. When you encounter a new word, always attempt to determine its meaning by using one or more of the techniques discussed in this chapter. This will enable you to add the new word to your passive vocabularies, and eventually to use it in your own speech and writing.

Exercise Expanding Your Vocabularies

Read the passages below. Then follow the directions given after these passages.

> Late in the *autumn* of 1887, a *rural* Wisconsin newspaper briefly noted that a baby girl had arrived two days before on Tuesday, November 15, in the farmhouse of Ida and Francis O'Keefe. . . The twenty-three-year-old Ida named her infant Georgia Totto for her *patrician* Hungarian grandfather, George Totto. Georgia, it appeared, would have Ida's dark hair, and her round face was pure Irish, like her father's. The *variegated pigment* of her eyes suggested the *mingled* bloodlines of brown-eyed *maternal forebears* and blue-eyed *paternal* ones.—LAURIE LISLE

John Brennan loved to take things apart. His idea of fun was to *dismantle* something that worked perfectly well and try to put it back together. He particularly enjoyed *fiddling* with the television set. He would go to the roof of the six-story *tenement* that the family lived in for several years, at Ninety-seventh and Lexington, and *jiggle* the *antenna*. Mickey and Paddy had the job of *monitoring* the *situation* in the living room. Mickey would sit behind the set and control the *fine* tuning while Paddy watched the screen. An *intercom* *rigged* from a telephone *enabled* them to communicate with their father, *aloft. Inevitably,* this *ritual* developed a certain *tediousness*. The day that Micky and Paddy both fell asleep on the job was the same day that their father, who was not a *wispy* man, fell into the chimney and was stuck there for a while.—MARK SINGER

1. Make five columns on a sheet of paper. Label these columns as follows: *Word, Unknown, Understood in Listening/Reading, Used In Speaking/Writing,* and *Definition*.

2. Enter the italicized words from the passages given above in the column marked *Word*.

3. Indicate whether each word is unknown to you, understood in listening and reading, or used in speaking and writing.

4. Write a complete definition for each word in the column marked *Definition*. If you have marked *Unknown* for a given word, you will have to consult a dictionary.

5. Reread the passages, paying particular attention to any words previously marked *Unknown*.

6. Write a sentence of your own using each word.

Part 2 Getting Meaning from Context

In the exercise for Part 1, you used the dictionary to ascertain the meaning of unknown words. Sometimes, however, you can get a clue to the meaning of an unfamiliar word from its **context,** the words with which the unfamiliar word is used.

Using context clues is a simple but powerful method for increasing your listening and reading vocabularies. Five common types of context clues are definition, restatement, example, comparison, and contrast.

Definition. The most obvious and straightforward type of context clue is direct definition. Clues of this type are usually signaled by a form of *to be (am, is, are, was, were, be)*:

> A *sycophant* is someone who tries to win favor by using flattery.

Restatement. Sometimes a writer will explain a term by restating it in other words. Be alert to such words or phrases as *in other words, that is, to put it another way, or*, and *this means*, which often signal restatements. The demonstrative pronouns *this, that, these*, and *those* may also indicate restatements. Finally, a restatement may be signaled by commas, parentheses, or dashes. Such restatements are called *appositives*. (See Section 2.17 in the Handbook.)

> Sara was *ambivalent* about Jack; that is, her feelings about him were conflicting and contradictory.
>
> Irv was getting a degree in *topology*. This branch of mathematics deals with those properties of geometric figures that do not change even when the figure is distorted.
>
> Many metals are *malleable* (capable of being hammered into sheets) and *ductile* (capable of being drawn into wire).
>
> The symbols etched on the magnificent sword were *runes*, characters from an ancient Germanic alphabet.

Example. Sometimes a writer will give one or more examples to show the meaning of a word. Words that signal examples include *such, such as, like, other, especially, particularly, for example*, and *for instance*.

> All *crustaceans*—crayfish and shrimp, for example—have hard outer skeletons.

Comparison. Occasionally a writer will make a comparison that enables you to grasp the meaning of an unfamiliar word.

Words often used to signal comparisons include *similar, like, the way,* and *as*.

> He approached his work *meticulously,* like a landscape painter who must render every leaf in precise detail.

Contrast. Sometimes a writer will supply a contrast that allows you to determine the meaning of a word. Such contrasts may be signaled by words such as *but, although, unlike, on the contrary, on the other hand,* or *as opposed to*.

> As work of all kinds becomes more specialized, the amateur and the *dilettante* have less chance of making important contributions. The day of the passionate tinkerer working in a garage is gone; today, inventions come from teams of professionals working in multi-million-dollar laboratories.

Inferring Word Meanings

The five types of context clues that you have just studied provide direct information concerning the meanings of words. Sometimes, however, context clues are much more subtle. In such contexts you must **infer** the meaning of an unfamiliar word.

To infer is to draw a conclusion from specific facts. When you encounter an unfamiliar word, search the context to see what information is provided. Then try to determine what the connection is between those facts and the unknown word.

Study the following example. Do you understand the reasoning that leads to a definition of the italicized word?

> He kept the *talisman* on a chain around his neck at all times. Once he had gone skiing without it, and he had fallen and broken his arm. It didn't pay to take chances with a thing like that.

The context tells you that the object called a *talisman* is something that can be worn around the neck, and that it is apparently supposed to bring good luck, since going out without it brought bad luck. Therefore, you can infer that a talisman must be something like a good luck charm.

ExercisesGetting Meaning from Context

A.Use context clues to determine the meaning of the italicized words in the following sentences. Identify the method by which the context reveals the meaning.

1. The movement of soil by water, wind, and ice is called *erosion*.

2. Charlene did not resist the suggestion. On the contrary, her *acquiescence* was immediate and enthusiastic.

3. Louis Pasteur investigated *rabies*, the disease that makes dogs go "mad".

4. Marlowe's "To His Coy Mistress" describes a scene from the simple, pleasant lives of shepherds. Marlowe's poem can thus be called an *idyll*.

5. The points at which bones make contact or unite with one another are called *articulations*.

6. The rooms of the hotel were wonderfully *commodious*, quite unlike the cramped quarters to which she had become accustomed.

7. The fact that the lower vertebrates do not depend very much on the *cerebrum* can be demonstrated by removing that part of the brain and observing the general behavior of the animal.

8. The young people of the tribe were no longer *devotees* of the ancient religion. In fact, they often expressed the desire to tear down the idols and temples and begin anew.

9. To understand the principles involved in the treatment of cataract, it is first necessary to understand its *etiology*, or causes.

10. Many *Porifera*, including the elephant ear sponge, are used commercially for cleaning and cosmetic purposes.

11. The *marine* fishes respond only to notes of low frequency; freshwater species are sensitive to frequencies of several thousand cycles per second.

12. In my home town there is a law against smoking in public, but the law has fallen into *desuetude*. Until recently, people have not felt it was their concern whether another person was smoking or not, and the law has not been used in forty years. Now people are beginning to ask that the law be enforced.

B. In the following sentences you are to infer the meaning of the words in italics. Be ready to explain to the class what clues in the context led you to your definition. Afterwards, compare a dictionary definition for each word with the definition you have constructed.

1. Eleanor, who has always suffered from *acrophobia,* could not be induced to go to the top of the Washington Monument.

2. Of the American artists of the thirties and forties, some were traditionalists following *canons* of taste well formulated in the past; others were audacious innovators.

3. Americans have extended their high standard of living to more citizens since the days of the Poverty Program of President Johnson, and yet it is still possible to find people living in *destitution* in the land of plenty.

4. An *indefatigable* worker, Thomas Edison often spent days and nights on his experiments, not even taking time to eat and sleep.

5. Moths and butterflies are the insects to which budding *entomologists* are first attracted.

6. Roots may extend both much farther downward into the soil and much wider *laterally* than most people realize.

7. In 1921 the Soviet government turned against modern art, and Wassily Kandinsky thought it wise to leave his native land for good, settling again in Germany which, in turn, he left after the Nazis came to power. According to Kandinsky, since the artist's first loyalty is to the satisfaction of an inner need, these displacements, despite their sadness, were *peripheral* to the actual work of the artist.

8. Each of the pianists is an erstwhile *prodigy.* Gould is supposed to have been able to read notes before he could read the printed word. He started playing the piano at the age of three, and gave his first recital at fourteen.

9. People's response to the decline in fish harvest has been to try harder—an action more suicidal than *sapient.*

10. The first national parks were established because people feared that commercial development of all lands in the *public domain* would eventually destroy the magnificent scenic wealth of the continent.

C. Examine the following passages, paying special attention to the italicized words. What is the special meaning of each word *in this context?*

1   Although it is difficult to generalize, too many of our universities have become huge circuses in which the side-shows overshadow the main attraction. "When a university president makes a speech calling for intellectual leadership," writes Dr. Hutchins, "he cannot be heard over the din his publicity man is making about the newest campus queen." Our colleges have involved themselves in activities that have only the most *tenuous relation* to the *academic function.*—MARTIN B. MARGOLIES

2   Languages die but words tend to be *immortal*. Catchwords, slang, and technical terms often disappear after a *brief run*, but many become established parts of the language, and once so established they persist. *Hosts* of Greek and Latin words are in use in dozens of the world's present-day languages.—JOHN CIARDI

3   The English language is an unpredictable medley, but no other can communicate such subtle shades of thought and feelings, such fine discriminations of meaning. The riches of its *mingled derivations* supply a multitude of synonyms, each with its own *distinction of implications.*

— ELIZABETH DREW

4   One of the great *visionaries* of the architectural world is Paolo Soleri, who came to the United States from Italy thirty-one years ago. Soleri's fame does not rest on the structures he has actually built, for these are few in number: a striking glass-domed house, a ceramics factory on the Amalfi coast, and the so-called earth colony where he and his followers lived in Arizona. His impact on the world of design has been made almost entirely through his *intricate,* detailed drawings for the city of the future—in which he fully intends to live. These drawings have astonished and *mesmerized* visitors to museum shows around the country.—JOSEPH J. THORNDIKE, JR.

5   Certainly, some amount of criticism of the *bathos* and
sentimentality that constitutes so great a part of our theatre fare today is justifiable. Serious students of literature
should indeed maintain a *skeptical* attitude toward the
commercially successful *floss;* they should be wary of
gulping down uncritically the *mawkish sentiments* of the
few who, by gently patting their audience on the head,
comfort them with cheap and empty solutions.

—LEONARD FLEISCHER

Part 3   Analyzing Word Parts

You have already learned how to use context clues to determine the meanings of unfamiliar words. Another technique
that you can use for this purpose is the analysis of prefixes,
suffixes, base words, and roots—the parts from which words
are made. The following chart describes these parts.

Word Parts	
prefix	a word part that is added to the beginning of another word or word part
suffix	a word part that is added to the end of another word or word part
base word	a complete word to which a prefix and/or a suffix can be added
root	a word part to which a prefix and/or a suffix can be added. Roots cannot stand alone

Prefixes

Every word part has a meaning or function of its own. When
word parts are combined, therefore, their meanings also combine to form a new word with a unique meaning. A careful

reader or listener can use this fact to unlock the meanings of many unfamiliar words.

When you use this technique, keep in mind some of the special characteristics of each type of word part. For example, many of the prefixes used to form English words have more than one possible meaning. If you encounter an unfamiliar word with such a prefix, you will have to decide which of the possible meanings fits the context. If this fails, you will have to consult a dictionary. The following is a list of common prefixes in English:

Common English Prefixes

Noun Prefixes		
Prefix	**Meaning**	**Example**
bene-	good	benefit
circum-	around	circumscribe
con-	with	consequence
dis-	the opposite of, away	disapprove, dispense
equi-	equal, even	equidistant
in- **il-** **im-** **ir-**	not, in	impossible input
intra- **inner-**	within	innermost
inter-	between	interplanetary
intro-	into	introspection
mal-	bad	malnutrition
mis-	wrong	mismatched
non-	not	nonflammable
pre-	before	prejudge
re-	back, again	return, review
sub-	under, less than	subsoil, substandard
super-	above, beyond, more than	supernatural supersonic

Suffixes

Suffixes affect the function as well as the meaning of a word. **Noun suffixes,** for example, are used to create nouns from other parts of speech; **adjective suffixes** create adjectives.

Common English Suffixes

Noun Suffixes		
Suffix	**Meaning**	**Example**
-age	act, condition, collection, home, result	marriage peerage parsonage
-an	belonging to, born in	American
-ary	member, doer	missionary
-archy	form of government	monarchy
-cide	killer, killing	insecticide
-dom	state, condition	freedom
-ee	receiver of an action	employee
-eer	doer, maker	puppeteer
-er	doer, maker	winner
-ery	place, occupation, act, product, collection, quality	robbery pottery
-hood	order, condition, rank	priesthood
-ician	doer	dietician
-ics	science, skill	mathematics
-ism	doctrine, ideology	Romanticism
-ist	doer, maker	violinist
-itis	inflammation	tonsillitis
-ment	result, means, agency, act, process, state, condition	disappointment
-ness	quality	happiness
-or	doer	director
-ster	doer, member	youngster
-tion -ion -sion	state, condition	inflation
-tude	state, quality	quietude

Adjective Suffixes

Suffix	Meaning	Example
-able -ible -ble	able, capable	washable
-al	like or suited to	musical
-ar	of, pertaining to	solar
-en	made of	wooden
-fic	causing or producing	honorific
-fold	specified number of times	threefold
-ful	having qualities of	wonderful
-ic	pertaining to	volcanic
-ive	tending to or toward	instructive
-ish	like, similar to	impish
-less	without	penniless
-like	similar to	lifelike
-ose	full of, having	verbose
-ous	full of, having	nervous
-some	like, given to, showing	worrisome
-ward	in the direction of	homeward

Exercise Using Word Parts

Each of the following words consists of a base word plus a prefix, a suffix, or both. Identify these word parts. Then, give the meanings of the word parts and of each whole word.

1. mismanagement
2. distasteful
3. non-democratic
4. irreplaceable
5. extraterritorial
6. presupposition
7. superphysical
8. reinvigorate
9. intermolecular
10. prankster
11. suborbital
12. circumnavigate

Roots

Sometimes, if the prefix and suffix are removed from a word, you are left with a word part that will not stand by itself. Such a word part is a **root**. A root has a specific meaning that can help you to determine the meaning of an entire word.

The following chart lists some commonly used Latin roots.

Roots Derived from Latin		
Root	**Meaning**	**Example**
alius	other	alien
amicus	friend	amity
animus	mind, life	animate
bellum	war	rebel
cor, cordis	heart	discord
corpus, corporis	body	corporeal
credere, creditus	believe	creed
dicere, dictus	say, tell	dictate
dormire	sleep	dormant
errare, erratus	wander	errant
facere, feci, factus	do, make	manufacture
fluere	flow	fluid
gratia, gratus	kindness, favor	gratitude
grex, gregis	flock	segregate
jus, juris	law, right	injury
lumen, luminis	light	illuminate
mandare	command	reprimand
manus	hand	manipulate
pendere, pensus	hang	depend
rumpere, ruptus	break	rupture
sequor, secutus	follow	sequence
solus	alone	solitaire
tempus	time	temporary
tenere, tentus	hold	tenuous
terminus	end, boundary	terminate
unus	one	universe
videre, visus	see	visit

The following chart lists some of the most commonly used Greek roots.

Roots Derived from Greek		
Root	**Meaning**	**Example**
anthropos	human	anthropology
autos	self	automobile
biblos	book	Bible
bios	life	biography
chronos	time	chronic
cryptos	secret, hidden	cryptic
demos	people	democracy
dynamis	power	dynamo
ge, geos	earth	geology
graphein, gramma	write, writing	graphic
homos	same	homogenous
logos	word, thought	dialogue
logy	study of	biology
metron	measure	metric
micro	small	microscope
monos	alone, single	monotone
neos	new	neoclassic
onyma	name	anonymous
orthos	right	orthopedic
pathos	suffering	sympathy
philos	love	philharmonic
phobos	fear	phobia
phone	sound	microphone
pneuma	air, breath	pneumonia
polis	city	police
psyche	breath, soul, mind	psychic
scope	seeing, look at	oscilloscope
sophos	wise, wisdom	sophisticated
syn, sym	with, together	symphony
tele	far	television
techne	art	technique
therme	heat	thermometer

Word Families

Sometimes a root serves as a basis for many longer words. If you compare an unfamiliar word with other words built on the same root, you can often get an idea of the meaning of the unknown word. For example, the word *symmetry* belongs to a related group of words, or **word family,** that includes *metric, metronome, diameter, perimeter, thermometer, speedometer,* and *kilometer.* Each of these words has a meaning that includes the idea "measure." Therefore you can begin with the meaning "measure," and by adding the meaning of the word part *sym-* arrive at the definition "same measure." This approximates the real meaning of *symmetry,* which is "a similarity of form or arrangement on either side of a dividing line or plane."

Exercises Analyzing Word Parts

A. Each of the words given below contains two or more of the following: a prefix, a base word, a suffix, or a root. Identify these word parts. Write a definition for each whole word based on the meaning of its parts. Finally, look up the word and write the actual definition.

1. credible	6. supervision	11. prologue
2. ingratitude	7. inconsequential	12. cryptography
3. injurious	8. chronological	13. pathology
4. manual	9. demographic	14. symmetrical
5. contemporary	10. technician	15. geometer

B. Follow the directions for Exercise A.

1. inalienable	6. geopolitical	11. integral
2. benefactor	7. nonconformist	12. pathology
3. superfluous	8. germicide	13. pneumatic
4. extragovernmental	9. bibliographer	14. telegraph
5. unsympathetic	10. synchronous	15. gregarious

Words for Vocabulary Study

1. abstruse	35. exigency	69. overt
2. acquisitive	36. façade	70. paltry
3. acuity	37. fatuous	71. paucity
4. adversity	38. frenetic	72. pedantry
5. aesthetic	39. gainsay	73. penchant
6. allay	40. germane	74. portend
7. anachronism	41. histrionic	75. propitious
8. avid	42. ignominy	76. pusillanimous
9. banal	43. impeccable	77. quintessence
10. cacophonous	44. impecunious	78. raze
11. coalition	45. importune	79. rebuff
12. celerity	46. incongruous	80. rectitude
13. chronic	47. incumbent	81. recumbent
14. collusion	48. inexorable	82. rudiments
15. congeal	49. laconic	83. sequester
16. conjecture	50. manifest	84. somnambulist
17. countermand	51. mélange	85. sporadic
18. counterpart	52. mendacious	86. taciturn
19. credence	53. mesmerize	87. temporize
20. decimate	54. misanthrope	88. tirade
21. delineate	55. monotheism	89. tyro
22. demur	56. moot	90. unequivocal
23. deprecate	57. multiform	91. unremitting
24. derogatory	58. mundane	92. unscathed
25. dilettante	59. moribund	93. unwonted
26. disarray	60. murky	94. utopian
27. dismantle	61. mutable	95. vacillate
28. dissident	62. myopic	96. verbiage
29. ebullient	63. nadir	97. viscous
30. eclectic	64. neologism	98. visionary
31. efficacy	65. *non sequitur*	99. witless
32. errant	66. nuance	100. zealot
33. ethereal	67. obtuse	
34. evince	68. onerous	

SUMMARY AND APPLICATIONS

1. Practicing various vocabulary development techniques will increase your ability to understand the ideas of others and improve the clarity and precision of your own speaking and writing.

2. Develop your passive vocabularies of listening and reading by determining the meanings of unfamiliar words that you encounter. Develop your active vocabulary of speaking and writing by using new words yourself.

3. To determine the meaning of an unfamiliar word, study context clues such as restatement, example, comparison, and contrast. If no such clues are given, try to infer the meaning from facts provided by the context.

4. You can also determine the meaning of an unknown word by analyzing its parts: its prefixes, suffixes, base words, and roots.

5. Using these methods of vocabulary analysis and development will help to prepare you for the vocabulary sections of standardized tests.

Applications in Other Subject Areas

All Subjects. When you study for your classes, it is a good idea to keep lists of vocabulary items encountered in readings, discussions, and lectures. One way to do this is to keep a vocabulary notebook that is divided into sections for each of your classes. The more detailed this notebook is, the more it can help you develop a powerful vocabulary.

Business / Science / Fine Arts. Many areas of business, science, and the fine arts develop their own specialized vocabularies. These vocabularies, sometimes called *jargon*, allow people within the same field to communicate efficiently with one another. Choose one of the areas listed above and then limit it to a specific field, such as computer science. Using an encyclopedia, textbook, or other authoritative source, compile a list of at least twenty terms that have special meanings in that area.

Chapter 2

Combining Ideas in Sentences

Good writers are aware that there are many different ways to express any idea. Therefore, they experiment with such elements as word choice, level of language, and tone until they find the sentence or paragraph that best communicates their ideas to a specific audience.

One important factor that a writer considers is how several ideas might be expressed in relation to each other. For example, someone who is writing for children might present ideas in short, simple sentences such as this:

> We bundled up in warm clothing. We wanted to protect ourselves from the north wind. It was icy. We set out for Park Hill.

A writer who is composing for adult audiences, however, would want to express the same ideas in a more sophisticated manner. This new version could show the relationship between the ideas while avoiding the choppiness of the first example.

> We bundled up in warm clothing to protect ourselves against the icy north wind, and then we set out for Park Hill.

By learning the sentence combining techniques in this chapter, you will be able to tailor your own writing to a specific level and a particular audience. You will also be able to add more precision and variety to your sentences.

Part 1   Joining Sentences and Sentence Parts

When two sentences or sentence parts express ideas that are of equal importance, they can usually be joined by using a coordinating conjunction such as *and, or,* or *but.* When complete sentences are joined in this way, a comma is placed before the conjunction.

Similar ideas of equal importance can usually be joined by using the word *and.* When such ideas are joined, repeated ideas, such as the word given in italics in the second group of sentences, can be deleted.

> The First Continental Congress met on September 5, 1774. Its members deliberated for seven weeks.
> The First Continental Congress met on September 5, 1774, and its members deliberated for seven weeks.

> Rachel Carson took a required undergraduate course in biology. *She* went on to get a Master's degree in genetics.
> Rachel Carson took a required undergraduate course in biology and went on to get a Master's degree in genetics.

Contrasting ideas of equal importance can usually be joined by using the word *but.*

Many ancient harvest customs have disappeared. Traces of these customs survive in Thanksgiving celebrations.

Many ancient harvest customs have disappeared, but traces of these customs survive in Thanksgiving celebrations.

Montezuma tried to bribe the Spanish to leave his empire. *He* could not persuade them to do so.

Montezuma tried to bribe the Spanish to leave his empire but could not persuade them to do so.

A choice between ideas of equal importance can usually be expressed by using the word *or*.

Did Van Gogh receive any recognition in his lifetime? Did he remain unknown?

Did Van Gogh receive any recognition in his lifetime, or did he remain unknown?

Scientists believe that some varieties of schizophrenia may be caused by vitamin deficiencies. *They may also be caused* by chemical imbalances in the brain.

Scientists believe that some varieties of schizophrenia may be caused by vitamin deficiencies or by chemical imbalances in the brain.

Exercises Joining Sentences and Sentence Parts

A. Join related sentences or sentence parts by using the appropriate conjunction. Eliminate any italicized words, and add a comma if necessary.

1. The subway is faster. It is not as comfortable.
2. Our class will study water. *We will also study* solar energy.
3. Do you think we can go ahead and replace the alternator? Will we first have to purchase some metric tools?
4. The President's limousine arrived at the airport exactly on time. Air Force One was an hour late.
5. Karen found a defect in the wiring. *She* couldn't complete the repair because of the danger of electrical shock.
6. You can stake the tomato plants. *You can* string them to an overhead wire.

7. The Lilly Library at Indiana University displays a letter written by Edgar Allan Poe. Inside the envelope is a lock of Poe's hair.

8. Frank prepared baked ham for the team's victory dinner. *He also prepared* sweet potatoes.

9. The ancient Greeks were great thinkers. They lacked the desire or inclination to put their thoughts to practical use.

10. W.C. Fields began his career as a juggler. *The odd-looking man* eventually became a great movie comedian.

B. Join each of the following pairs of sentences in one of two ways. You may join complete sentences using **, or**, **, and**, or **, but**, or you may join related sentence parts by eliminating unnecessary words and using conjunctions.

1. Annie Sturges Daniel was a physician. She was also a public health reformer.

2. Typical Colonial towns were located by coastal harbors. *They were* also found by river junctions.

3. The noise from the road work outside was deafening. Rosa tried to shout over it.

4. The nature preserve can try to save the young condors itself. It can send them to a zoo with better medical facilities.

5. The critics loved the film. The moviegoers ignored it.

Part 2   Adding Words

As you have seen, sometimes a word or group of words is unnecessarily repeated. In such cases, the repeated material can often be deleted and the remaining ideas combined.

Adding Single Words

You may be able to delete all but one word in a sentence. This one important word is then added to another sentence.

First we removed the paint. *It was* peeling.
First we removed the peeling paint.

You may be able to add several single words to a sentence in this manner.

> Dr. Clark demonstrated her discovery to the scientists. *The discovery was* amazing. *It was* new. *The scientists were* skeptical.
>
> Ms. Clark demonstrated her amazing new discovery to the skeptical scientists.

Sometimes you may want to join the words with *and*.

> I was impressed by Donna's serve. *It was* smooth. *It was also* powerful.
>
> I was impressed by Donna's smooth and powerful serve.

Often you will have to use a comma when you add more than one word to a sentence. See Sections 11.14 and 11.15 for discussions on the use of commas.

> Tim Reed ran an inn on the edge of town. *It was* small *and* quiet.
>
> Tim Reed ran a small, quiet inn on the edge of town.

In the above examples, words were added without any changes in their form. Occasionally, however, the form of the important word must be changed slightly before it is added to the other sentence. Sometimes this means adding *-ing*.

> The sound of the motor annoys me. *It* whines.
>
> The sound of the whining motor annoys me.

At other times, you may have to change the word so that it ends with *-ly*.

> Adalita performed the ballet routine. *Her performance was* perfect.
>
> Adalita performed the ballet routine perfectly.

Often, the word ending in *-ly* can be placed in any of several positions in the sentence.

> Josh knocked over a can of paint. *It was an* accident.
>
> Josh accidentally knocked over a can of paint.
>
> Accidentally, Josh knocked over a can of paint.

Adding Groups of Words

As you look for ways to combine a series of sentences, you may find that one sentence contains an important group of words that can be added to another sentence. The group may be added in one of several ways.

1. When the group of words gives more information about someone or something, it should be added near the words that identify the person or thing.

> A case stood on the pier in the hot sun. *It was* filled with dozens of cheeses.
> A case filled with dozens of cheeses stood on the pier in the hot sun.
>
> I was surprised by a shaggy, gray dog. *I was* rounding the corner.
> Rounding the corner, I was surprised by a shaggy, gray dog.

In some cases where the group of words describes a person or thing, you will have to separate the added group of words from the rest of the sentence with a comma or a pair of commas. This is necessary when the added group of words is an **appositive,** a restatement of an idea contained in the sentence to which you are adding material.

> The recipe calls for saffron. *Saffron* is an expensive spice.
> The recipe calls for saffron, an expensive spice.
>
> The Grand Canyon is located in Arizona. *It is* the earth's largest gorge.
> The Grand Canyon, the earth's largest gorge, is located in Arizona.

2. When the added group of words describes an action, it should be added near the words that name the action.

> The crowd had been waiting for hours. *They had been waiting* outside the theater.
> The crowd had been waiting outside the theater for hours.

3. When the group of words adds more information concerning the entire main idea of the other sentence, it may be added at the beginning or at the end.

> The snow had disappeared. *It had disappeared* by the time the sun set.
> By the time the sun set, the snow had disappeared.
> The snow had disappeared by the time the sun set.

4. Sometimes you will have to change the form of one or more of the words in the added group by adding *-ing*.

> The leading man revived the interest of the audience. *He tripped* over a stage brace and *fell* through a wall.
> Tripping over a stage brace and falling through a wall, the leading man revived the interest of the audience.

Notice that the words *tripped* and *fell* were changed to *tripping* and *falling* and that the word *He* was eliminated. Notice also that the resulting phrase, *Tripping over a stage brace and falling through a wall,* is used to modify the word *man*.

5. Sometimes one word in a sentence refers to the whole idea expressed in another sentence, as does the word *this* in the following example:

> *He* packed only the essentials. *This* enabled him to travel easily.

In such cases the pair of sentences can often be combined by substituting a phrase beginning with *-ing* for the word that refers to the whole idea.

> Packing only the essentials enabled him to travel easily.

The word *packed* was changed to *packing,* and the italicized words were eliminated. Here is another example of two sentences combined by using *-ing*.

> *She had* had her meals brought to her every day. When she left the hospital, Sara missed *that*.
> When she left the hospital, Sara missed having her meals brought to her every day.

Notice that the word *had* was changed to *having*, and that the italicized words were eliminated.

6. In some cases, the necessary changes are a bit more complicated. Notice the changes that must be made in the following example.

> Mr. Judson volunteered to coach the soccer team. *That* meant we would be able to start the season on schedule.
>
> Mr. Judson's volunteering to coach the soccer team meant we would be able to start the season on schedule.

The word *volunteered* has been changed to *volunteering*, and *Mr. Judson* has been changed to *Mr. Judson's*. If the words *Mr. Judson's* had not been included in the combined sentence, an important part of the original meaning would have been lost. Notice the similar changes in the following example.

> She hummed the same tune over and over again under her breath. *That* drove me crazy.
>
> Her humming the same tune over and over again under her breath drove me crazy.

The word *hummed* has been changed to *humming*, and *She* has been changed to *Her*. Notice that, if the word *Her* were not included in the combined sentence, the meaning would be different from what was originally intended.

Exercises Adding Words

A. Combine each of the following pairs of sentences by adding the important words. Eliminate the italicized words, and follow any special directions given in parentheses.

1. Anne glanced at the line of clouds. *The clouds looked* threatening.

2. *Mr. Denby* used a high-speed drill. *That* made Mr. Denby's work more efficient. (Combine with **-ing**.)

3. The commission presented the governor with a summary of the proposed changes in fish and wildlife regulations. *The summary was* detailed. *It was* accurate. (Use a comma.)

4. Gretchen was resting. *She was resting* on the sofa.

5. Maureen visited the Museum of Modern Art. *Her visits were* frequent. (End the important word with **-ly.**)

6. Sylvia worked on her report until three in the morning. *She* polished it to perfection. (Combine with **-ing.**)

7. The finance committee reached its decision after a debate. *The debate was* long. *The debate* bored *everyone.* (Combine with *-ing* and *and.*)

8. *I was* looking through current magazines. I discovered four articles. *They were* about nutrition.

9. Clark sang. *That* made the people in the front rows wince. (Combine with **-s** and **-ing.**)

10. *You can* read about a sunset. *You can* see a sunset. *The first* can never take the place of the *second.* (Combine with **-ing.**)

B. Combine each of the following pairs of sentences by adding the important word or group of words. Decide on your own what changes, if any, must be made in the added material.

1. People should get some exercise every day. That is an important part of being physically fit.

2. Margaret Sterns introduced the cast. This occurred during the intermission. She is the play's director.

3. The ship's guidance computer began to buzz. This was ominous.

4. The music calmed Russell's nerves. The music was soothing. Russell's nerves were shattered.

5. Kate found her glasses under a pile of papers. She had misplaced them.

6. We spotted a flock of ducks. We were walking near the Wabash river.

7. The Mariana Trench is the deepest known spot in the world. It is in the Pacific Ocean.

8. Maria noticed a girl on the bus. She was nervous and distracted.

9. He designed the Imperial Hotel in Tokyo, Japan. That brought Frank Lloyd Wright international acclaim.

10. I read a fascinating book. It was about the greatest years of American clipper ships. I read it during the summer.

Part 3   Adding Groups of Words Used as Nouns

A clause is a group of words that contains a subject and a verb. A clause may be used to take the place of a single noun or pronoun in another sentence.

> *We are uncertain about* who invented chess. *It* remains a mystery to this day.
> Who invented chess remains a mystery to this day.

Notice that the group of words *who invented chess* replaces the pronoun *It*.

Sometimes a clause can be used as an appositive, repeating the meaning of a word in the sentence to which it is added.

> *It was proposed* that we hold an art fair. The city council adopted the proposal.
> The city council adopted the proposal.
> The city council adopted the proposal that we hold an art fair.

A clause can also be placed after the verb in another sentence. Some of the words, or their position in the clause, may have to change slightly.

> What the speaker was saying *was unclear*. No one understood *him*.
> No one understood what the speaker was saying.

> Where had she gone? The detective couldn't even guess.
> The detective couldn't even guess where she had gone.

Sentences can also be combined by placing a clause after a preposition.

> The judge's decision will depend upon *one major factor. She will decide based upon* who presented the best case.
> The judge's decision will depend upon who presented the best case.

Exercises Adding Groups of Words Used as Nouns

A. Combine each of the following pairs of sentences by adding the important words. Eliminate the italicized words.

1. *No one can tell* what the future will bring. *This* is the biggest question of all.

2. Who will win the scholarship this year? Only the awards committee knows.

3. What would the divers find in the old wreck? *This* was the subject of much speculation.

4. A good detective conducts his or her investigation according to *the evidence. He or she depends upon* whatever evidence is available.

5. Why did Sheila leave her job at the restaurant? Phillip asked *that*.

6. Who would replace the President? *This* was the major concern of the cabinet members.

7. The campaign workers tried harder after *that. They were influenced by* what the candidate said.

8. Where Atlantis was located is *unknown. The location is* what we are trying to determine.

9. *We all believed* that Courtney would win the state championships. *This* seemed unquestionable.

10. *The lecture was about* how glaciers form. The teacher explained *this*.

B. Combine each of the following sentences by adding the important group of words. Decide on your own what changes need to be made in these sentences.

1. Where had his youth gone? Martin often wondered that.

2. Who will win the next Olympic hockey competition? This is anyone's guess.

3. Where the extra oxygen was stored was our immediate concern. We were very worried about it.

4. What would the world look like if he rode on a beam of light? When he was fourteen, Einstein asked himself that.

5. Carlotta already knows that. She knows whose paintings received the first place prize.

Part 4   Adding Groups of Words Used as Modifiers

In some cases, a clause can be added to a sentence and used as a modifier. In such situations, the clause may serve several different purposes.

1. It may supply additional information about a person, place, or thing in the sentence to which it is added.
2. It may show one of the following relationships:

time	cause	condition
place	result	purpose

Combining with *Who, That,* and *Which*

When you add a group of words to provide information about a person, place, or thing, you often must begin the group with *who* or *that*.

> The tall man must have taken the plans. *He* slipped out the side door.
>
> The tall man who slipped out the side door must have taken the plans.
>
> The plans reveal every detail of my invention. The tall man took *them.*
>
> The plans that the tall man took reveal every detail of my invention.

In the first example, the word *who* takes the place of the word *he.* The word group *who slipped out the side door* is then added to the first sentence in the example as a modifier of the word *man.*

In the second example, the word *that* takes the place of the word *them.* The word group *that the tall man took* is then added as a modifier of the word *plans.*

In the two preceding examples, the added groups of words are necessary to the meaning of the sentence. They are needed to show which man and which set of plans are meant. In some sentences, however, the added group of words is not absolutely necessary to the meaning. It merely adds additional information. When the group of words merely adds additional information, combine with *,who* or *,which*.

> The coach let me play in every game. *He* happens to be my father.
> The coach, who happens to be my father, let me play in every game.
> That comedienne's first record has become a collector's item. *It* originally sold only a few thousand copies.
> That comedienne's first record, which originally sold only a few thousand copies, has become a collector's item.

Combining To Show Relationships

One of the most common reasons that sentences are combined is to show relationships between ideas. The following methods of combining are among the most useful.

1. Events usually occur in some sort of sequence. Combining sentences can help make this sequence clear.

To add a group of words that shows a relationship in time, begin the group with *as, after, before, since, until, when, whenever,* or *while*.

> The Y.M.C.A. opened its new basketball court. We began to hold our games there.
> After the Y.M.C.A. opened its new basketball court, we began to hold our games there.

In order to combine sentences effectively in this sort of situation, you must sometimes make other changes. For example, you may have to use an *-ing* ending with one of the words.

> Be sure that the first coat is dry. Apply the second coat.
> Be sure that the first coat is dry before applying the second coat.

2. To add a group of words that shows the place where something occurs, begin the added group of words with *where* or *wherever*.

> The stage crew placed the piano *there*. It could be seen more clearly from the stands.
> The stage crew placed the piano where it could be seen more clearly from the stands.

3. To add a group of words that explains a cause, begin the added group with *because* or *since*.

> The price of oranges went up. I stopped buying them.
> Because the price of oranges went up, I stopped buying them.

4. To add a group of words that describes a result or an effect, combine with *; consequently, ; as a result,* or *; therefore*. Notice that each of these words is preceded by a semicolon.

> The price of oranges has gone up; therefore, I have stopped buying them.

5. To add a group of words that expresses a condition, begin the added group with *if, although, though, unless, provided*, or *provided that*.

> The track was muddy. The coaches decided not to cancel the meet.
> Though the track was muddy, the coaches decided not to cancel the meet.

6. To add a group of words that explains a *purpose*, begin the added group with *so that* or *in order that*.

> N.A.S.A. developed its battery-powered jet pack. Astronauts can leave their vehicles and maneuver about in space by themselves.
> N.A.S.A. developed its battery-powered jet pack so that astronauts could leave their vehicles and maneuver about in space by themselves.

Exercises Adding Groups of Words Used as Modifiers

A. Combine each of the following pairs of sentences. Eliminate any italicized words, and follow any directions in parentheses.

1. The cat toppled the vase. I had left *the vase* on the piano. (Combine with **that.**)

2. The northern part of the state hadn't had any rain for weeks. The farmers cheered the line of clouds on the horizon. (Begin the second sentence with **; therefore.**)

3. Kevin was the pitcher. *He* walked four batters in the first inning. (Combine with **who.**)

4. Leave the manuscript *there. That is* where you found it.

5. Marilyn wore the green skirt. She bought it in Mexico. (Combine with **that.**)

6. I always enjoy visiting my uncle. He owns an automobile dealership. (Combine with **, who.**)

7. A new theater complex will be constructed on this site. *It will be constructed* if sufficient federal funding is granted.

8. You must use a circuit tester to make sure that the circuit is dead. You can safely replace the switch. (Begin the second sentence with **before.**)

9. The Jacksons didn't want to lose touch with their old friends and neighbors. They continued to subscribe to our local paper after they moved away. (Begin the first sentence with **since.**)

10. One side of the termite mound was cut away. People could observe the inside. (Begin the second sentence with **so that.**)

B. Combine the following sentences. Decide what words should be added and what words, if any, should be deleted.

1. This paint must be thinned with turpentine. Turpentine is a highly flammable solvent.

2. Denise spilled coffee on her first three customers. She decided to try another line of work.

3. The moon passes through the earth's shadow. A lunar eclipse occurs.

4. The archaeologists used tiny picks and brushes. With these they could clean the fragile pottery without breaking it.

5. Lillian Hellman wrote many award-winning plays. She was a close friend of mystery writer Dashiell Hammet.

Part 5 Using Combining Skills for Revision

You have learned several ways to combine related ideas in sentences. These skills can be used to eliminate choppiness, monotony, and vagueness in your writing. Study the following paragraph.

> The island of Mahalo is a place of beauty. It is a place of wonder. Streams run down from the mountains. The streams are crystal-clear. They cascade through the forests. They empty into the ocean. The ocean is blue. The forests are filled with wonderful plants. They are also filled with exotic animals. Everyone on the island lives in happiness. No one ever goes hungry. No one can visit Mahalo. That is unfortunate. It exists only in my dreams.

Notice how this paragraph can be improved by combining:

> The island of Mahalo is a place of beauty and wonder. Crystal-clear streams run down from the mountains, cascading through the forests and emptying into the blue ocean. The forests are filled with wonderful plants and exotic animals. Everyone on the island lives in peace and happiness, and no one ever goes hungry. Unfortunately, no one can visit Mahalo because it exists only in my dreams.

When you read something that you have written, think about how it could be improved. Remember that there are many ways to express any idea; but one way may be more effective than another. Good writers choose the way that communicates an idea most clearly.

Exercise Applying Combining Skills

Use the combining skills you have learned to revise the following paragraphs. Be prepared to explain your revisions.

Hank Dekker is a sailor. In 1983, he sailed from San Francisco to Honolulu. He sailed in a 25-foot sloop. He traveled alone. The trip was unusual. It was unusual because Hank Dekker is not your typical sailor. He is blind.

Dekker is a former race-car driver. He began to lose his sight in 1972. He lost his sight from glaucoma. At first, the loss of vision drove him to despair. He would sit for hours and grieve. Finally, he decided to take charge of his life again. He stopped feeling sorry for himself. He went to work. Finally, he taught himself to sail. This was in 1981.

The trip was his crowning achievement. He wanted to show other handicapped people something. He wanted to show them that "they can do new things, learn to sail, learn a new trade, a new skill." He set out on his journey. He was in high spirits. He carried with him a 100-day water supply. He brought canned and dried food. He also brought special equipment. He did this to compensate for his inability to see. Among the special equipment were Braille charts and a Braille compass. There was also a talking clock and a special navigational system. The system reads his position out loud.

Dekker completed his journey successfully. It was a triumph for him. It was also a triumph for handicapped people everywhere.

SUMMARY AND APPLICATIONS

1. Sentence combining techniques can help you to eliminate monotony and choppiness in your speech and writing. They can also help you express relationships between ideas more clearly.

2. Combine sentences or sentence parts of equal importance by using *and, or,* or *but*.

3. Eliminate unnecessary repetition by adding single words or groups of words to sentences. When adding words, you may have to insert additional punctuation or add *-ly* or *-ing*.

4. A single noun or pronoun can sometimes be replaced by a clause, a group of words containing a subject and a verb.

5. Clauses can also be added to a sentence to provide information about a person, place, or thing or to show time, place, cause, result, condition, or purpose.

Applications in Other Subject Areas

Physical Education / Speech / Mass Media. If you listen to a live sports event, you will notice that the announcers generally use short and simple sentences. In contrast, a description of the same event in a sports magazine will contain sentences that are longer, more varied, and more interesting.

Choose a sporting event that you enjoy, and write a brief play-by-play description of the action as it might be described by a sports announcer. Then, rewrite your description, using the sentence combining techniques presented in this chapter to make your language suitable for a magazine article.

Science. Occasionally you may want to use your knowledge of sentence combining techniques in reverse, breaking down complicated sentences into simpler ones.

Find a complex explanation of some process or idea in one of your science texts. (Photosynthesis, the digestive process, or the structure of an atom or molecule are some possibilities.) Rewrite the sentence so that a sixth grade student could understand it.

Chapter 3

Effective Sentences

Whenever you revise your writing, you should attempt to eliminate errors in grammar or mechanics. This step is important because such errors can muddle your meaning and confuse your readers. However, eliminating these problems is not enough to ensure good writing. It is possible to produce perfectly grammatical sentences that are nonetheless unsatisfactory due to their content. Sentence improvement is therefore treated at length in this book. Empty, overloaded, wordy, repetitious, and awkward sentences make writing uninteresting or difficult to read. In this chapter you will learn how to identify and correct such sentences. Following chapters will cover other ways of improving what you write. Learning how to revise your sentences will help you develop a writing style that is simple, graceful, and direct.

Part 1 Avoiding Empty Sentences

The function of a sentence is to convey facts, ideas, or feelings.

Writing cannot be done well in haste. It cannot be done well without thought. **Empty sentences** like the following result from haste and from failure to think before beginning to write.

> In cities and everywhere else there is too much traffic because there are too many cars and trucks and many of the cars and trucks take up too much room because they are so big.

This sentence starts out well: *"In cities and everywhere else there is too much traffic because . . ."* The writer promises to explain why there is too much traffic. This is worth hearing about. What reason is given? ". . . there are too many cars and trucks . . ." The writer clearly does not know any reason. The sentence simply says, "There is too much traffic because there is too much traffic."As an afterthought, the writer added something about the size of cars.

This point about the size of many automobiles is a good one. It is related to traffic conditions in city streets. The writer's problem was to *think through* the relationship and to express it clearly. With a little thought, the writer might have produced a sentence like this:

> The existence of many full-size luxury cars is increasing the tangle of traffic in our city streets.

Here is another example of an empty sentence:

> I think it is unfair to charge higher automobile insurance rates for men under twenty-five because it is not fair to charge men higher rates than women.

This sentence says only that higher insurance rates are unfair because they are unfair. Why are they unfair? The word "because" leads the reader to expect reasons. However, the writer does not supply these reasons. Instead, he or she simply repeats the original idea. That this idea is an unsupported opinion becomes obvious if the unnecessary repetition is deleted:

> I think it is unfair to charge men higher rates for automobile insurance than women.

Exercise Avoiding Empty Sentences

Rewrite the following empty sentences. Add any facts or ideas that you think will improve them.

1. I want to go to college because going to college will satisfy my long-felt desires.

2. Going to college is a necessity for entering the profession that I want to enter, for my chosen profession requires a college education.

3. I thoroughly enjoyed the concert at the Auditorium because I liked the music.

4. The world is beautiful in the early morning, for everything takes on added beauty when the sun is just coming up.

5. My teachers are not what I expected because they are not as I thought they would be.

6. Having planned for a long time to buy a car, I was finally able to buy one as a result of my planning over a long time.

7. Athletics of all kinds should be provided in high school because all high schools need athletic teams to develop school spirit among the high school students.

8. If you're just starting, a Gibson guitar would be just right for a beginner.

9. Everyone who drives should drive carefully because reckless driving is dangerous.

10. Everyone needs a large vocabulary if he or she wishes to be successful in the future, for a large vocabulary is necessary for the person who wishes to go to the top in his or her career.

11. I believe in always trying my best in volleyball because I think that in that sport one must always really try.

12. The excitement of the final quarter became so unbearable that I could hardly stand it any more.

13. *Mrs. Dalloway* was the most interesting novel I have ever read because it kept my interest up more than any other I have encountered.

14. Being a paramedic is a worthwhile and vital job because what a paramedic does is really important.

15. Once you have learned to swim and ride a bike, you can always swim or ride a bike because they are skills that stay with you and you can't forget them.

Part 2 Avoiding Overloaded Sentences

The guides to writing effective sentences are few and simple:

1. Say one thing at a time.
2. Say it clearly and directly.

Everyone has the experience of writing sentences that try to say too much. They become so crowded that the writer cannot remember what he or she started to say, and the reader becomes fatigued from trying to follow the thought. Such sentences are **overloaded sentences.**

When you find an overloaded sentence in your own writing, examine it carefully. Look for the main idea. Start over again with this subject-verb combination. Drop irrelevant details. If the leftover details are important, start a second sentence.

OVERLOADED: Everyone should learn a second language today because in a shrinking world we need to know what is going on in other countries where there are many opportunities for young people to find interesting work.

IMPROVED: Everyone should learn a second language today because in a shrinking world we need to know what is going on in other countries. A second language will open opportunities for young people to find interesting work.

OVERLOADED: I prefer a large university because there you can meet many kinds of people with different interests from many parts of the world where there are different ideas, and a wide experience with many kinds of people is an important part of education.

IMPROVED: Experience with many kinds of people is an important part of education. In a large university you can meet people from many parts of the world and people with different interests. I prefer a large university because it provides this experience.

Exercise Avoiding Overloaded Sentences

Rewrite the following overloaded sentences. There is no one right way to improve them. You may add words and details.

1. Coeducational colleges are best because there men and women can work together with respect for each other and interact socially as well as academically by being together on campus.

2. Everyone wants to be a success, and this means making enough money to fulfill material needs and to pursue the goals that will make a person happy, which is the greatest thing in the world.

3. I like winter better than any other season of the year, for in winter I can skate and ski without getting too hot and too tired as I do in the summer, and I like to go to parties in the winter, and even school is exciting and interesting in the winter.

4. Hobbies can be a source of pleasure and relaxation, and they can even lead to success in a vocation, and a student who enjoys designing, drawing, or even building aircraft models may become a pilot or an executive in an aircraft company.

5. Participation in one or two extracurricular activities in high school can be enjoyable and beneficial to the student if he or she doesn't join too many and neglect classwork, but maintaining good scholastic standing is necessary for a future vocational or college career.

6. A satisfying job is one of the ingredients of a happy life, so when you choose a career, be sure that it is something you will enjoy doing and that it will give you a feeling of fulfillment, self-worth, and achievement.

7. Trying to be an amateur painter, musician, or writer is better than simply studying art appreciation, music appreciation, or literature, though these have their rewards, too, but trying to paint or write will make a person even more appreciative of the arts.

8. Juanita was chairperson of the committee, and under her leadership more was accomplished than ever before, including an all-day educational forum and a fund-raising dance, both of which attracted many new members and brought the group much favorable publicity.

9. On the first day of our trip we drove as far as Chicago, and just as we were about to stop for the night the car gurgled and died, and we learned from the mechanic that it would take a day or two to repair the motor and we'd have to stay over in Chicago.

10. A tunnel under the English Channel would be a good thing because it would make travel between England and the continent easier and more convenient and cheaper and many people cannot afford the passage now but would be able to drive from England to the continent and back.

Part 3 Avoiding Wordiness

A sentence that uses more words than necessary is boring. The extra words smother the meaning. The writer with a sharp eye can spot excess words and delete them during revision.

One kind of wordiness arises from needless repetition of a word or from needless use of words with similar meanings.

> We thought we had an *adequate* supply of *food* with *enough* for everyone to *eat*.
> Hard work *alone* is not the *only* thing you need.
> Jack is an *honest* person who *never tells a lie*.
> Carlene is the *kind* of person of the *sort* you can trust.

Wordiness also arises from the repetition of *that*.

> I thought *that* if I came *that* I might be able to help.
> We knew *that* Matt felt *that* he had been cheated.

In the last two sentences, the second *that* may be dropped.

Wordiness often results from using a group of words when a single word will suffice. (Methods of avoiding and correcting wordiness are discussed in Chapter 4, on pages 58 and 59.)

WORDY: In the case of physics, you would probably agree that physics is too hard for most young people in the tenth grade.

IMPROVED: You would probably agree that physics is too hard for most tenth-grade students.

WORDY: A year after we graduated we could look back and see that the attitude that we observed on Ms. Stein's part of being very severe and very demanding prepared us well for the rigors of college.

REVISED: When we looked back a year after graduation, we could see that Ms. Stein's severe and very demanding attitude prepared us well for the rigors of college.

Awkward Repetition

Sentences lose their effectiveness and become awkward if a word or a phrase is repeated unnecessarily. Awkward repetition can be corrected by replacing the repeated word with a synonym, by using pronouns in place of nouns, or by rewriting the sentence or group of sentences containing the repeated word.

AWKWARD: I have chosen a *topic* that is a frequent topic of conversation today. My *topic* is exploiting our natural resources.

IMPROVED: I have chosen a topic frequently heard in conversation—exploiting our natural resources.

AWKWARD: Too much *emphasis* is placed *on college educa-tion,* and this *emphasis on college education* makes many people go to college who do not need or want a *college education.*

IMPROVED: Because too much emphasis is placed on college education, many people who do not need or want to go to college do so anyway.

AWKWARD: *Hamilton and Jefferson* had entirely different ideas about government, but *Hamilton and Jefferson* both contributed much to our government.

IMPROVED: Hamilton and Jefferson had entirely different ideas about government, but they both contributed much to our country.

Exercise Avoiding Wordiness

The following sentences are wordy or needlessly repetitive. Revise them to eliminate these faults.

1. The mirror was round in shape.
2. Maya Angelou wrote an autobiography of her life.
3. The League of Women Voters is a non-partisan organization and is not in favor of any one political party or candidate.
4. A play that is very interesting and that is very unusual is the play *The Effect of Gamma Rays on Man-in-the-Moon Marigolds* by Paul Zindel.
5. I think that it could be possible that the United States will launch an orbiting space lab into space within a short period of time.
6. It is my belief that the greatest invention since the wheel is, I think, the television.
7. Albert Einstein wrote in the journal that was kept by him that creative thinking of the sort that is fresh and new is a variety or type of play.
8. Annie Dillard is a woman author who writes very, very interesting articles and books about subjects and things in nature and the like.

9. Many nations in the world are anxious to improve their economic conditions to increase the general wealth and standard of living of people living in them.

10. The graduating class heard much good advice and counsel from the commencement speakers on the occasion of their commencement exercises.

11. Since my parents spoke two languages, my mother speaking German and my father speaking French, I grew up learning both French and German from them and English in school.

12. The pamphlet that was sent to me discussed not only the problems of water conservation but also the problems of water pollution and the wastes that are poured into water from industrial plants.

Part 4 Avoiding Awkward Beginnings

The normal, easily readable pattern of English sentences is subject—verb—complement. A great many awkward sentences occur when this pattern is abandoned. Certain expressions create awkwardness when used at the beginnings of sentences. They delay the thought, and they add nothing to it. Usually, they are not needed at all. The most common of these offending expressions are *The fact that, What I believe is, What I want is, Being that*, and *The reason is*.

AWKWARD:	*The fact that* Mary was sick should be taken into account.
BETTER:	Mary's sickness should be taken into account.
AWKWARD:	*What I believe* is that no one should be compelled to go to school.
BETTER:	I believe that no one should be compelled to go to school.
BEST:	No one should be compelled to go to school.
AWKWARD:	*What Terry needs* is a little encouragement.
BETTER:	Terry needs a little encouragement.

AWKWARD: *Being that* there was no school yesterday, we have no homework assignments.

BETTER: Since there was no school yesterday, we have no homework assignments.

AWKWARD: *The reason* I chose this book *is* because of its title.

BETTER: I chose this book because of its title.

Exercise Revising Sentences with Awkward Beginnings

Revise these sentences to remove their awkward beginnings.

1. Being that he was a new student in the high school, Bob felt lonely and apprehensive.

2. What I think is that everyone should work a ten-hour day and a four-day week in order to conserve our resources.

3. The fact that too many extracurricular activities are often too time-consuming should be considered by the student before he or she joins too many campus organizations.

4. The reason I liked my summer work was because the work itself was pleasant.

5. What the stock market crash in 1929 did to many people was to make them bankrupt.

6. Being unhappy about losing my job, I lost my appetite too.

7. The reason there are so many accidents on the highways today is because people drive too fast.

8. What all Americans should do is to take part in the political process.

9. The fact that the wolves in this region were exterminated led to a population explosion among the deer and the rabbits.

10. The main reason that Valerie has been studying Russian, German, and Spanish is because she wants to go into the diplomatic service.

11. What every diplomat needs is to be able to speak several languages.

12. The fact that the weather looked threatening made us postpone our picnic.

SUMMARY AND APPLICATIONS

1. To write effective sentences, correct errors of style as well as errors in grammar and mechanics.

2. To correct an empty sentence, delete or replace any repeated material.

3. To correct an overloaded sentence, begin again with the subject and verb of the sentence. Drop any irrelevant details, and place important but less closely-related details in another sentence.

4. To correct a wordy sentence, delete unnecessary words or replace groups of words with single words. Then, recast the rest of the sentence as necessary.

5. To correct awkward repetitions, replace repeated words with synonyms, use pronouns in place of nouns, or rewrite the sentence or sentences containing the repeated material.

Applications in Other Subject Areas

All Subjects. Whenever you write for a class, use the techniques studied in this chapter to revise your sentences. Study a composition, report, or research paper that you have done for one of your classes. Identify and correct any sentences that are empty, overloaded, awkward, wordy, or repetitious.

Speech. In general, prepared speeches tend to be less wordy and awkward than ones that are given impromptu, without preparation. This is why it is generally a good idea to think through any public statement that you wish to make before making it.

Test yourself by asking a friend to give you a topic for a short impromptu speech. Without stopping to plan what you are going to say, speak your impromptu comments into a tape recorder. Then, play the tape back, and write out what you said. How many of your comments were awkward or wordy? Revise the speech to eliminate any such errors. Use the sentence revision techniques discussed in this chapter.

Chapter 4

Sentence Revision

The Welsh poet Dylan Thomas left over sixty versions of a short poem that he was working on at the time of his death. After all of these revisions, Thomas apparently still felt that the poem was not quite "right." Thomas's reputation as one of the greatest poets of the twentieth century is largely due to the meticulous care he took with his writing. Thomas knew that good writing is often synonymous with careful revision. He took advantage of the opportunity that all writers have to re-organize and adapt their material until it takes an effective form.

No one expects you to revise your writing as extensively as Dylan Thomas did, but you must always try to produce writing that reflects your best possible efforts. When you write a paper for school or when you write a résumé or a letter of application, you will want your work to be polished, impressive, and professional. To make this possible, you must apply the various techniques of sentence revision discussed in this chapter.

Part 1 Omitting Unrelated Details

The function of a sentence is to state an idea, to present facts, or to describe feelings. When unrelated details appear in a sentence, they interrupt the flow of thought.

In sentence revision, keep your mind on the main idea. Delete any detail that is not closely related to this idea.

> I would like to be an engineer like my brother, *who has a Mercedes* and works on big construction jobs all over the world.

Clearly, the Mercedes has nothing to do with being an engineer. It has a great deal to do with "my brother's" success as an engineer, but his success is another matter. It belongs in another sentence.

> It was so foggy over New York, *where we expected to spend two weeks,* that our plane could not land.

The expectation of spending two weeks in New York has nothing to do with the fog over the airport. If it is important at all, it belongs in another sentence.

Exercise Omitting Unrelated Details

Rewrite these sentences, omitting details that are not related to the main idea.

1. We spent our vacation in Virginia, where George Washington lived, and we liked the state very much.
2. We usually go shopping on Saturday, which is the last day of the week, and buy our groceries for the next week.
3. The truck, which had burned on the highway and which was a Ford truck, was being dragged away by a crew of men who wore red shirts and caps.
4. Reading good books, which can fill our leisure time, is helpful in acquiring knowledge and an extensive vocabulary.
5. The new magazines, which came yesterday, are filled with articles on foreign policy and international affairs.

6. Important problems in American history are discussed by a panel of experts, one of whom is a friend of ours, on a weekly television program.

7. I had been absorbed in a television program, which was about the forthcoming election, and I had failed to notice that someone had entered the room.

8. The students at Roosevelt High School, located in the center of the city, can choose courses from a varied curriculum.

9. The most beautiful scenes in Europe, which we visited last summer, are the lakes and mountains in the Alps.

10. TV weather forecasts, which are usually part of a news program, are based on scientific observation and knowledge.

11. Tourists love Florence, Italy, the home of the Medici, where Sue lost her purse when we were there last summer.

12. Ryan, who last year won the soccer award, went skiing.

13. Much of the poetry of seventeenth century England, which suffered from great plagues, fires, and political revolutions, is called metaphysical.

14. They were afraid that the cold front, which was moving southward, would damage the orchards, located in Orlando where I was born.

15. San Francisco, where my sister lives, is one of the most colorful cities I have ever visited.

Part 2 Keeping Related Sentence Parts Together

In effective English sentences, the verb is closely tied to the subject; it is also closely tied to the complement. Similarly, the parts of a verb phrase are tied closely together. When these related sentence parts are widely separated by intervening words, the sentence is difficult to read.

AWKWARD: The *fog*, after closely hugging the ground all day long, *lifted* at last.
(subject and verb separated)

REVISED: After closely hugging the ground all day long, the fog lifted at last.

AWKWARD: Jack *had* never in the four years of his high school career *received* such poor marks. (parts of a verb phrase separated)

REVISED: Jack had never received such poor marks in the four years of his high school career.

AWKWARD: You *have had,* whether you know it or not, your last chance. (verb and object separated)

REVISED: Whether you know it or not, you have had your last chance.

Exercise Keeping Related Sentence Parts Together

Revise these sentences to bring related parts closer together.

1. The newest discoveries in science are to the average person awe-inspiring.

2. The refugees, after having been shunted around from one camp to another, were finally settled into homes of their own.

3. The TV announcer began, after a few opening remarks, her usual morning broadcast of the news.

4. The team had never, in all the games it had played, been so lucky as in this last game.

5. The family had, after a long vacation at the beach, returned to their home in the city.

6. The Student Council had, after much weighing of pros and cons, gone to the convention.

7. The foreign ministers' conference will be, everyone hopes, of great significance.

8. The program committee has, even though several members believe it is not feasible, voted to give the choral concert on the night before graduation.

9. The house across the street has, for the last four years, been unoccupied.

10. Computer programming is, according to an article I read, extremely complicated.

11. Because United States Presidents had fewer obligations, they often vacationed for whole summers early in the nineteenth century.

12. Gary volunteered to give the oral presentation in history because he frequently enjoyed attention.

13. She regretted only having two hands.

14. The Breitzmans were, having planned to go to Sweden after the Christmas season, disappointed that they were not granted their visas.

15. Because there was a fuel shortage, many big businesses were forced to close down this winter.

Part 3 Avoiding Faulty Coordination

When ideas are closely related, they can be read together with ease. One idea seems to complete the other; in fact, the second idea may help to explain the first. A compound sentence helps the reader to see a close relationship.

If unrelated ideas are joined in a compound sentence, the reader is confused, and the writer's point is lost. Sometimes the fault of joining unrelated ideas occurs because the writer has omitted something essential to the sense.

> CONFUSING: The airport was closed in by fog, and we missed the game.
>
> IMPROVED: The airport was closed in by fog. *We were four hours late in arriving* and missed the game.
>
> CONFUSING: I took the aptitude tests last spring, and I am not going into engineering.
>
> IMPROVED: The aptitude tests I took last spring *showed that I am weak in mathematics*. I am not going into engineering because it requires mathematical skill.

Exercise Avoiding Faulty Coordination

Revise the following sentences to avoid faulty coordination.

1. Six inches of snow fell, and we were late to school.

2. The cost of living has risen sharply during the past few years, and personal incomes have risen too.

3. The admission requirements of the colleges have become more stringent, and the number of students entering college has increased.

4. The new Music Center cost six million dollars, and the city has increased the tax rate.

5. The sky is overcast, and we cannot go on our picnic.

6. The experts had predicted that Barlow would never get into office, and she ridiculed them in her acceptance speech.

7. Mother had completely forgotten to take the turkey out of the freezer, but fortunately the shrimp was delicious.

8. The last-minute camping trip was fun, and Jane and I needed an extra blanket.

9. Jack auditioned for the band yesterday, and he will choose a different activity.

10. Our team won the state tournament, and school was canceled the next day.

11. Jason won first place in the photography competition, and he is now our newspaper photographer.

12. Megan's car broke down, and we still arrived at the airport on time.

13. Illinois is called "The Land of Lincoln," and President Lincoln spent much of his life there.

14. The sky was dark and threatening, and the cross country meet was postponed.

15. Alex Haley spoke about his ancestry to a large crowd in Texas, and he is the author of the highly publicized *Roots*.

Part 4 Avoiding Stringy Sentences

Some sentences become overloaded because the writer strings a number of ideas together, placing an *and* between each idea. The result is that no one idea stands out; there seems to be no organization. You can revise stringy sentences in two ways.

1. Choose the conjunction that will show the real relationship between the ideas you are presenting.
2. Divide the sentence into two or more sentences.

STRINGY: There is a water shortage in many parts of the country, and this shortage is causing concern, and the U.S. Department of the Interior is trying out methods of changing sea water to fresh water.

REVISED: The water shortage in many parts of the country is causing concern; *consequently,* the U.S. Department of the Interior is trying out methods of changing sea water to fresh water.

STRINGY: Scientists today are working in an invisible world, and they are dealing with genes, atoms, ions, and electrons, and no one has ever seen them, and some of them may not exist, but to understand modern science, we must understand the scientists' ideas of these invisible things.

REVISED: Scientists today are working in an invisible world of genes, atoms, ions, and electrons. No one has ever seen them; *indeed,* some of them may not exist. To understand modern science, however, we must understand the scientists' ideas of these invisible things.

Exercise Revising Stringy Sentences

Revise the following sentences. In each case, you will need to make two or more sentences.

1. Many scientists have dreamed of transmitting power through the air without the use of wires, and they have experimented for many years, trying to develop their ideas, and at last they seem to have come near the realization of their dream.

2. Recently the small colleges have been sorely pressed financially, and they need more money for salaries for their teachers, and they do not want to raise the costs of tuition to supply the needed funds.

3. Students nowadays may want to learn such languages as Arabic, Russian, and Hindustani, and these are not taught in many schools, and students may have to wait until they are graduate students to learn them.

4. They were to entertain their family that night, and they decided to go on with it and try it and make the best of it.

5. She was a scholarly and accomplished book critic for a large newspaper and when she decided to write her own novel and had to quit the job, her co-workers wondered who could replace her successfully.

Part 5 Subordination

The main clause is the basic structure in any sentence. It states the main idea of the sentence. Modifying clauses and phrases are used to add details or to explain the conditions that define or limit the meaning of the main clause.

The writer alone knows what the main idea is in each sentence he or she writes. If he or she writes only compound sentences, or only main clauses, the writer gives the reader no guidance; hence, the effectiveness of the writing is lost.

MAIN IDEA	LIMITING, EXPLAINING, OR DEFINING DETAILS
We can go to the concert (at any time?)	if the tickets aren't sold out. (under this condition)
Gary may need an assistant (why?)	to help with the filing. (explaining)
Raleigh went to his death (how?)	proclaiming his innocence. (defining details)

Ideas of less importance can be subordinated (put in their proper place) by use of clauses. Adverb clauses are introduced by subordinating conjunctions, which express a great variety of relationships. (See Section 3.5 in your Handbook.) Nothing improves a sentence quite so much as substituting the right participial phrase or subordinating conjunction for a meaningless *and* that has been inserted between two clauses.

WEAK:	Jim took the heaviest pack, *and* he staggered slowly up the hill.
BETTER:	*Taking* the heaviest pack, Jim staggered slowly up the hill. (participle)
WEAK:	Mari was dressed in tennis dress, *and* she looked like a pro at the court club.
BETTER:	*Dressed* in a tennis dress, Mari looked like a pro at the court club. (past participle)
WEAK:	Pam worked hard for Sue's election, *and* she knew all along that Sue had no chance to win.
BETTER:	Pam worked hard for Sue's election, *although* she knew all along that Sue had no chance to win. (adverb clause)

Subordination may also be used to join two related sentences smoothly and economically.

FAIR:	Peg worked all night. She wanted the job completed on time.
BETTER:	Peg worked all night to complete the job on time. (infinitive)
FAIR:	Jack LeClerc is our guidance counselor. He did personnel work in the Navy.
BETTER:	Jack LeClerc, *our guidance counselor,* did personnel work in the Navy. (appositive)
BETTER:	Jack LeClerc, *who did personnel work in the Navy,* is our guidance counselor. (adjective clause)

Upside-Down Subordination

This is the fault of placing an important idea in a subordinate clause or phrase.

FAULTY:	The sailboat capsized, *nearly drowning the crew.* (The near drowning of the crew is more important.)
REVISED:	The crew nearly drowned when the sailboat capsized.

FAULTY: Mrs. Brown was crossing at the corner *when a cyclist knocked her down.*

REVISED: Mrs. Brown was knocked down by a cyclist as she was crossing at the corner.

FAULTY: Jon lost control, *falling off the cycle.*

REVISED: Losing control, Jon fell off the cycle.

Exercises Subordinating Ideas

A. Combine these sentences, converting one into either a phrase or a clause. Be careful to avoid upside-down subordination.

1. The match suddenly came to an end. The weary challenger fell against the ropes.

2. The scaffolding had been built beside the church. A workman had fallen off the scaffolding.

3. Last Sunday we were at home. Some guests came in for dinner.

4. We will vote next Tuesday for our favorite candidates. The candidates have made no promises of patronage to their supporters and advocates.

5. These plates are replicas of the marble squares in the floor of the cathedral. The cathedral is in Siena, Italy.

6. The chairperson of the committee left the meeting. The members of the committee stayed to finish the discussion.

7. The guests had been entertained well. They thanked their host and hostess profusely.

8. The team has played well throughout the season. It will probably win the championship game.

9. Egypt became a province of Rome. Cleopatra committed suicide in 30 B.C.

10. The haiku is a Japanese poem usually on some subject in nature, and consists of three lines totalling seventeen syllables.

B. Change each of the following compound sentences by subordinating one of the clauses. You may change it to either a subordinate clause or a phrase.

1. The new books are reviewed each Sunday in *The New York Times Book Review*, and the reviewers are writers and critics.

2. The foreign ministers' conference was held in Geneva, and the ministers from many nations attended the conference.

3. Science education is encouraged by the federal government, and many grants are given to improve science instruction in the high schools.

4. Golfing requires skill and experience, and many people take up golfing as a means of getting exercise.

5. The actor forgot his lines, and he went into an impromptu performance.

6. The color of the water changed from a dull gray to a bright blue, and the sun came from behind a dark cloud and shone brightly on the lake.

7. The air feels cold, but the outside thermometer registers sixty-six degrees.

8. We picked the flowers yesterday and arranged them, but they are wilted today.

9. Cross-country skiing requires strength and stamina, and many people have found cross-country skiing a way to stay fit.

10. Newly-released movies are reviewed each week in *Time*, and the reviewers are often well-known critics.

C. Correct the upside-down subordination in these sentences.

1. He was walking in the woods when he was struck by lightning.

2. The woman who fell from the second-story window and fractured her leg was a window cleaner.

3. The book, which has caused a nationwide sensation, is a novel about a small town.

4. The orchestra had begun the last number when someone shouted, "Fire!"

5. The politician, who was never elected to office, had tried five times.

6. Words, which can often be dangerous, are in reality only sounds in air or black marks on white paper.

7. The dancers, who seemed to be poetry in motion, presented a ballet.

8. The driver, who was killed when his car crashed into a tree, had fallen asleep at the wheel.

9. The outbreak of measles, which reached epidemic proportions, affected many children.

10. The special art exhibit was at The Art Institute of Chicago which included only Van Gogh originals.

Part 6   Reduction

Reduction is the means by which bulky sentences are made compact and effective. Reduction can be achieved by changing a clause to a phrase or a phrase to a single modifier.

CLAUSE: We live in a house *which has high ceilings*.
PHRASE: We live in a house *with high ceilings*.

PHRASE: One of the players *on the Detroit team* was hurt.
WORD: One of the *Detroit* players was hurt.

CLAUSE: The people *who drive the buses* are on strike.
WORD: The *bus* drivers are on strike.

CLAUSE: The class elected José, *who is my closest friend*.
APPOSITIVE: The class elected José, *my closest friend*.

If the clauses of a compound sentence have the same subject, the compound sentence can be reduced by using a compound predicate. Similarly, two clauses with the same verb can be reduced by using a compound subject.

SAME SUBJECT: The men arrived at the camp late, *and they went right to bed*.
REDUCED: The men *arrived* at the camp late and *went* right to bed.

SAME SUBJECT: The tires are wearing thin, *and they will soon be useless*.
REDUCED: The tires *are wearing* thin and *will* soon *be* useless.

SAME VERB: The cups *broke,* and the saucers *broke.*

REDUCED: The cups and saucers *broke.*

Exercise Reducing Sentences To Make Them Effective

Rewrite each of these sentences, reducing the italicized words to a shorter construction.

1. Mr. Smith, *who is a banker and philanthropist,* gave a million dollars to Aurora College.

2. The boys and girls hiked up the mountain, *and when they were up there, they ate their supper there.*

3. The 1984 Winter Olympics, *which were held in Yugoslavia,* were televised live throughout the world by satellite.

4. Karen, *who is the valedictorian of her class,* has been accepted by several universities *that are well known.*

5. The house had been burned, and *the garage had been burned too.*

6. Then men and women in the choir sang a selection *that was very beautiful.*

7. The Student Government Association sent delegates to the annual convention, *which was meeting in Denver, Colorado.*

8. The pencils, *which are a special kind with soft lead,* are lying on the table, *which is in the living room.*

9. Canoeing on the Kankakee River, *which is in northern Illinois,* is an enjoyable summer activity.

10. Organizing a paper *that is long and difficult* requires an outline, *which may be a tentative one.*

11. Source material must be acknowledged, *and it can be acknowledged in a footnote or in the body of your paper.*

12. Questionnaires *that were long and involved* were sent to the high school seniors.

13. An analogy, *which is an extended simile or metaphor,* may be helpful in clarifying an issue.

14. The Sears Tower, *which is one of the world's tallest buildings,* is 1,454 feet high.

15. James Hoban, *who was an Irish-born architect,* designed the White House.

Part 7 Parallelism

The word *and* should be used to join sentence parts of the same kind. It may join two nouns, two adjectives, two prepositional phrases, and so on. Similar sentence parts so joined are **parallel**. If the sentence parts joined by *and* are not of the same kind, **faulty parallelism** has occurred.

FAULTY: The child needs *sleep* and *to be fed at regular hours*. (noun joined to phrase)

REVISED: The child needs sleep and food at regular hours.

FAULTY: Nancy worried about the *test* and *if she would do well*. (noun joined to clause)

REVISED: Nancy worried about how she would do on the test. (When a parallel is impossible, change the sentence.)

FAULTY: The police officer told the driver to park his truck and *that he must go to the police station*. (phrase joined to clause)

REVISED: The police officer told the driver to park his truck and go to the police station.

FAULTY: We go into town *to dance, to buy food*, or *for a movie*.

REVISED: We go into town to dance, to buy food, or to see a movie.

And Which; And Who

A special kind of faulty parallelism occurs with *which* and *who*. The *and* should never appear before these words unless *which* or *who* appears earlier in the sentence.

NONSTANDARD: Dr. Granjon was a person *and who* loved people *and who* devoted her life to their care.

STANDARD: Dr. Granjon was a person *who* loved people and *who* devoted her life to their care.

NONSTANDARD:	There is a new sign over the entrance *and which* will direct you to our studio.
STANDARD:	There is a new sign over the entrance *which* will direct you to our studio.
NONSTANDARD:	We took our problem to the old repairman *and who* had never failed us before.
STANDARD:	We took our problem to the old repairman, *who* had never failed us before.

Exercise Parallelism

Correct the faulty parallelism in these sentences.

1. She is ambitious, intelligent, and has persistence.

2. The ambitious executive wants success in business, an active social life, an active family life, and works for the community.

3. The teacher told the students to write the answers to the questions and that they must finish within the hour.

4. In the park I saw old people playing checkers, families picnicking, and students who were absorbed in reading textbooks.

5. Every town and city needs more parking space, more recreational facilities, and to have more money for these needs.

6. The class in reading learned to read faster and also reading with greater comprehension.

7. The prospectors expected to get rich and an easy life.

8. The Puritans, a brave group and who suffered many hardships, influenced greatly the character of the American people.

9. All drivers using the turnpike and who cross the drawbridge must pay a toll.

10. The class read "Chicago," a poem by Carl Sandburg and who was an American poet.

11. The university attempts to teach students to think by requiring that they study logic, and they solve problems.

12. Preparing a manuscript for publication is an arduous task and that requires care and accuracy.

13. She asked for help and that I explain the theorem again.

14. Mrs. Watkins asked for votes and to be elected.

15. This is a new book and which you can get at the library.

Part 8 The Weak Passive

The subject of an active verb is the doer of the action. The subject of a passive verb is the receiver of the action. (See Section 5.5 in your Handbook.) There are many occasions when a passive verb form is useful and desirable. Sometimes the doer of an action is unknown or cannot be named.

The old house had been torn down.
The President was warned of the conspiracy.

Sometimes the passive verb is used to describe a common or ongoing experience.

The Yankee games are played in the Stadium.
The mail is delivered at one o'clock.

Sometimes the passive verb is used to avoid giving a direct order. In your Handbook, for example, rules and usages are generally stated with passive verbs.

A participial phrase at the beginning of a sentence *is followed* by a comma.
In standard usage, *bad is always used* after linking verbs.

The *weak passive* is the use of the passive when the active verb is more natural and direct.

WEAK: A good time was had by everyone.
BETTER: Everyone had a good time.

WEAK: Much time is lost by students through poor planning.
BETTER: Students loose much time through poor planning.

WEAK: The ball was hit by Pete Rose right out of the park.
BETTER: Pete Rose hit the ball right out of the park.

WEAK: My homework is not given enough attention by me.
BETTER: I do not give my homework enough attention.

Exercise The Weak Passive

Revise these sentences to eliminate the weak passive verbs. Four of the passive verbs are acceptable as they stand.

1. The book was discussed by the senior class.
2. Many gifts were brought by Mother when she went to visit her sister.
3. Dinner is served promptly at six o'clock.
4. The car was washed by us in the morning.
5. At the end of the program, a song was played by the string ensemble.
6. A letter was written by the class to the town's mayor.
7. Litter baskets have been placed at every corner.
8. The old house was bought and remodeled by us.
9. The store window was crashed into by a runaway car.
10. Arrangements had been made by me for the club to meet at our house.
11. My tennis game is not given enough attention by me.
12. The dinner was enjoyed by all of the guests.
13. The article was printed in five languages.
14. The trailer court was destroyed during the storm.
15. A petition was written by the citizens to the governor.

SUMMARY AND APPLICATIONS

1. Use sentence revision techniques to produce writing that is clear, precise, and direct.

2. Omit details that are unrelated to the main idea in a sentence.

3. Keep related sentence parts together; avoid faulty coordination of ideas.

4. Do not string together loosely-related ideas.

5. Subordinate related ideas of lesser importance; avoid placing an important idea in a subordinate clause.

6. Whenever possible, omit or replace words or groups of words to reduce wordiness.

7. Avoid faulty parallelism and weak passives.

Applications in Other Subject Areas

All Subjects. Whenever you speak or write, bear in mind the sentence revision techniques discussed in this chapter. Find a paper that you did for a class in history, government, science, mathematics, music, art, or business. Study your sentences carefully. Can any be improved by applying sentence revision techniques? Rewrite your paper, correcting any weak or poorly-structured sentences.

History / Speech. Using proper parallelism can have dramatic effects. Study copies of the following famous documents from American history.

> "The Declaration of Independence"
> "The Gettysburg Address"
> "The Inaugural Address" of President John F. Kennedy
> President Franklin Delano Roosevelt's "Declaration of War" against Japan

Look for examples of parallelism in these famous speeches. What does the use of parallelism add to each speech?

Chapter 5

Sentence Clarity

The American novelist Richard Wright is known to have revised a single sentence hundreds of times to get it just right. Though you needn't carry sentence revision to such fantastic lengths, it is important that your writing be as clear as possible. To achieve this clarity, you must revise your sentences to eliminate any errors that might confuse your readers. Such errors include omissions of necessary words, misplaced modifiers, and sudden shifts in tense or in point of view.

All of these errors can be corrected during the revision stage of the process of writing. This chapter will help you to correct or avoid such errors, thus making it possible for you to express your ideas more clearly and precisely.

Part 1 Avoiding Omissions of Necessary Words

Omission of *That*

In some sentences the *that* introducing a noun clause must be stated to avoid confusion. When it is omitted, the sentence can be read in two different ways.

CONFUSING: We heard all transportation, even Amtrak, was halted by the snowstorm.

IMPROVED: We heard *that* all transportation, even Amtrak, was halted by the snowstorm.

CONFUSING: We heard the team members, coming off the field, were complaining about the referee.

IMPROVED: We heard *that* the team members, coming off the field, were complaining about the referee.

Omission of Part of a Verb Phrase

The subjects in the two clauses of a compound sentence often differ in number. The verb in each clause must agree with its subject. When both verbs have auxiliaries, the second auxiliary is sometimes omitted, resulting in confusion. The complete verb phrase must be used for clarity.

CONFUSING: The gas tank was filled, and the tires checked. (tank *was;* tires *were*)

REVISED: The gas tank *was* filled, and the tires *were* checked.

Omissions in Comparisons

A comparison becomes awkward and confusing if necessary words are omitted.

CONFUSING:	Pat is one of the fastest, if not the fastest, student on the team. (Pat is not one of the fastest student.)
REVISED:	Pat is one of the fastest *students* on the team, if not the fastest.
CONFUSING:	The storm will be as bad or worse than last week's blizzard.
REVISED:	The storm will be as bad *as* last week's blizzard or worse.

Omission of Words in Idioms

An idiom is a group of words with a meaning different from the literal meanings of the words taken one by one.

The fisherman *held up* his catch.
The pilot *held up* her departure.

Many idioms like *hold up* are composed of a verb followed by an adverb. Here are some examples of idioms.

Idioms with *up*	Idioms with *down*	Idioms with *for*
hold up	turn down	love for
tie up	put down	need for
break up	hold down	respect for

Idioms with *in*	Idioms with *on*	Idioms with *off*
trust in	turn on	put off
pride in	put on	hold off
interest in	take on	turn off

When two idioms are used together, there is a temptation to drop the adverb from one of them. This omission is awkward and confusing.

FAULTY:	We were putting and taking off our coats all day long.
CORRECTED:	We were putting *on* and taking off our coats all day long.

FAULTY:	Mr. Andrews had no desire or need of more money.
CORRECTED:	Mr. Andrews had no desire *for* or need of more money.

FAULTY:	Carrie had a pride and respect for her work.
CORRECTED:	Carrie had a pride *in* and respect for her work.

Exercise Avoiding Omissions of Necessary Words

Revise these sentences to correct the omissions.

1. We understood the monsoons were coming.
2. The house was empty and the windows cracked.
3. Have you heard the Stray Cats concert has been postponed indefinitely?
4. The clothes were packed, and the house turned over to its new occupants.
5. Our basketball team is one of the best, if not the best, team in the entire state.
6. The food on the sky lab will be as good or better than the food on earth.
7. Bonnie Raitt has love and pride in her music.
8. The paralegal is enthusiastic and thrilled with her new job at the Legal Aid Clinic.
9. Mary Pickford was one of the most popular, if not the most popular, motion picture star of the silent films.
10. Dr. Bryant heard her name had been mentioned for the Cabinet post.
11. Sidney is one of the most intelligent, if not the most intelligent, dog in the entire neighborhood.
12. The pilots were briefed on the flight, and the order given to proceed with the mission.
13. *As I Lay Dying*, by William Faulkner, is one of the best, if not the best, novel I have ever read.
14. The principal of the school decided the players could leave their chessboards in the cafeteria overnight.
15. The Italian pastries looked and were similar to baking powder biscuits.

Part 2 The Placement of Modifiers

Single adjectives are usually placed just before the words they modify. Adjective phrases and clauses follow immediately after the words they modify. The only exceptions occur in sentences in which a phrase and a clause modify the same word. In such situations, the phrase precedes the clause.

> We talked to the man at the hardware store whom we met yesterday.

Many adverb modifiers can be moved from one place to another in a sentence without creating a change in meaning. Occasionally, however, moving an adverb produces unexpected effects. In general, be careful to place adverb modifiers so that they express your meaning exactly.

CONFUSING: Linda was learning to drive *slowly*.
REVISED: Linda was *slowly* learning to dive.

CONFUSING: *Happily*, the play ended. (just in time!)
REVISED: The play ended *happily*. (happy ending)

CONFUSING: All the students *cannot* get into the room.
REVISED: *Not* all the students can get into the room.

CONFUSING: Amy was praised for heroism *by the mayor*.
REVISED: Amy was praised *by the mayor* for her heroism.
BETTER: The mayor praised Amy for her heroism.

Exercise The Placement of Modifiers

Revise these sentences to correct the misplaced modifiers.

1. The retired sailor sat looking at the harbor in the window.
2. The club only has fifty dollars to spend for trophies.
3. The party never hopes to lose another election.
4. The dentist looked at the small child who sat in the chair stealthily.

5. Did you see the article about the new car that runs on water in the paper?

6. All of the spectators with tickets cannot get into the stadium for the concert.

7. Pulitzer prizes are given annually for outstanding work in journalism by the Pulitzer Prize Board.

8. Coretta's gift for her sister was a book of drawings by Edgar Degas on her birthday.

9. There is a large, heavy package from your grandfather in your mailbox.

10. The thieves were arrested soon after the bank had been robbed by the police.

11. The ushers brought in folding chairs for the guests with cushioned seats.

12. Terry was praised for pitching a no-hitter by the coach.

13. Everyone should see a doctor and a dentist to stay healthy at least once a year.

14. Marcus Anderson told the assembled guests about his football experiences during dinner.

15. I saw some geese and ring-necked ducks eating my lunch at the lagoon.

Part 3 Avoiding Dangling Modifiers

When a phrase or clause is placed next to a word that it cannot modify sensibly, it is called a **dangling modifier.** Dangling modifiers often appear at the beginning of sentences.

PARTICIPLE:	Opening the door, chaos met our eyes. (This says that *chaos* opened the door.)
INFINITIVE:	To be perfectly safe, good tires are necessary. (This says that *tires* are *perfectly safe.*)
ELLIPTICAL CLAUSE:	While swinging a bat, his wrist broke. (This says the *wrist* swung a bat.)

To correct a dangling participle, supply a word for it to modify sensibly, or change the participle to a main verb and give it a subject. The phrase is thus turned into a clause.

FAULTY: Walking in the dark, my foot struck something soft and furry.

CORRECTED: As I was walking in the dark, my foot struck something soft and furry.

FAULTY: Standing on tiptoe, the inside of the room could be seen.

CORRECTED: Standing on tiptoe, *we* could see the inside of the room.

FAULTY: Hoping for an immediate reply, this letter is addressed to you.

CORRECTED: I addressed this letter to you, hoping for an immediate reply.

To correct a dangling infinitive, supply a word for the phrase to modify sensibly.

FAULTY: To see the show this season, tickets must be ordered now.

CORRECTED: To see the show this season, *you* must order tickets now.

To correct dangling elliptical clauses, supply the omitted words.

FAULTY: When frozen, place the cream in a tray.

CORRECTED: When the cream is frozen, place it in a tray.

Exercise Avoiding Dangling Modifiers

Revise these sentences to correct the dangling modifiers.

1. Eleanor said, "I smelled oysters going into the kitchen."
2. Entering the English classroom, four large windows can be seen.
3. Looking at television, the electricity went off suddenly.
4. Looking up, the brilliant stars were twinkling.

5. While walking in the park, the lake and the grove of gingko trees can be seen in the distance.

6. At the age of five, my parents sent me to camp.

7. Being rushed to the hospital, the siren of the ambulance made a weird, frightening noise.

8. After seeing Rome, other cities seem much less interesting and grand.

9. To hear well, the auditorium must be built properly.

10. When thoroughly heated, serve the entree in a shallow casserole dish.

Part 4   Avoiding Needless Shifts

If you were looking at a movie and suddenly found that the pictures were showing upside-down, you would have at least a momentary feeling of confusion. Something like this occurs when a writer begins a sentence in one tense and suddenly shifts to another. Shifts in number or person, and shifts from active to passive verb forms often produce the same confusion.

Shifts from Active to Passive

A sentence that starts out in one voice should usually continue in that voice. Remember that the subject of an active verb is the doer of the action; the subject of the passive verb is the receiver of the action. To change from active to passive is therefore a considerable change in point of view.

SHIFT IN VOICE: The district attorney *questioned* the bank president, and his files *were examined*.

IMPROVED: The district attorney questioned the bank president, and examined his files.

SHIFT IN VOICE: We *telephoned* all our friends, and even strangers *were called*.

IMPROVED: We telephoned all our friends and even called strangers.

Shifts in Tense

If a sentence begins in the present tense, it should usually continue in that tense. If it begins in the past tense, it should not shift to the present.

FAULTY: We *are standing* in the street when the door *began* to open.

REVISED: We *were standing* in the street when the door *began* to open.

ALSO ACCEPTABLE: We *are standing* in the street when the door *begins* to open.

FAULTY: The class *was studying* quietly, and suddenly Jeff *lets* out a yell.

REVISED: The class *was studying* quietly, and suddenly Jeff *let* out a yell.

FAULTY: There *were* two seconds left when Laura *makes* the basket.

REVISED: There *were* two seconds left when Laura *made* the basket.

Shifts in Person and Number

The indefinite pronoun *one* is the third person. It is referred to by the personal pronoun *he, his* and *him;* or *she, her,* and *her;* or by *he or she.* If you start a sentence with *one,* do not refer to it with the pronouns *you* or *your.*

SHIFT: If *one* hears a baseless rumor, *you* can either ignore it or try to find out how it started.

CORRECTED: If *one* hears a baseless rumor, one can either ignore it or try to find out how it started.

Many collective nouns like *group, class, club, crowd, team,* and so on, may be regarded as either singular or plural. As the writer, you may decide whether the word is to be singular or plural. Having once decided, you must abide by your decision.

SHIFT:	The club *has* (singular) decided that *they* (plural) will not elect new members this fall.
CORRECTED:	The club *has* (singular) decided that *it* (singular) will not elect new members this year.
SHIFT:	The crowd roared *its* (singular) approval, and then *they* (plural) broke up the meeting.
CORRECTED:	The crowd roared *their* (plural) approval, and then *they* (plural) broke up the meeting.

Exercise Avoiding Needless Shifts

Revise these sentences to correct the needless shifts in number, person, tense, or voice.

1. Paula prepares the food for the reception, and the banquet hall was filled with flowers.

2. The group was on its way to Riverfront Stadium and is happy to be going to a World Series game.

3. Juan thinks that if one goes to college, you should do your best to succeed.

4. United Charities sold tickets for the dance marathon, and the money was collected.

5. Koi was sitting alone in the house when suddenly someone begins to pound on the door.

6. Jefferson wrote his weekly theme by hand, but it was typed before it was given to the teacher.

7. The ski club plans a trip each year, and usually they go to some interesting place.

8. Andrea heard a step on the porch, and then the dogs, hearing it also, begin to bark.

9. The mayor campaigned hard, but the election was won by the party in favor of the Charter-Council form of government.

10. When one reads a newspaper, you should read the important news and editorials as well as the sports page.

SUMMARY AND APPLICATIONS

1. Revise your sentences to correct the following errors:
   omissions of necessary words
   misplaced modifiers
   sudden shifts in tense or point of view
   These changes will make your writing clearer and much easier to read.

2. Do not leave out the word *that* or parts of verb phrases, comparisons, or idioms when these are necessary to make your meaning clear.

3. Place adjective and adverb modifiers so that they express your meaning exactly.

4. Correct dangling modifiers by moving them, by adding words, or by doing both.

5. Correct awkward shifts in tense, voice, person, or number.

Applications in Other Subject Areas

Science. In the sciences, precise description is extremely important. To make their descriptions precise, science writers often use participial phrases and other modifiers to supply information about the qualities or the actions of the subject being described. Choose an animal or a plant and write as precise a description as you can of this organism. Use participial phrases and modifiers in your description. Check to make certain that your writing contains no misplaced or dangling modifiers.

Art. When describing a work of art, as you might in an essay or review, custom dictates that you use the present tense. Choose a painting or sculpture that you either enjoy or dislike. Describe it as vividly as you can, using only the present tense. Check your review to make sure that you have avoided awkward shifts in verb tense and other obstacles to sentence clarity.

Chapter 6

Sentence Variety

Would you want to listen to a piece of music that repeats the same patterns over and over again? Probably not. Music that does not contain variety is usually uninteresting and rapidly becomes unenjoyable. The same can be said of speech and writing. Both require variety in order to maintain interest. In speech, we can use three devices to secure interesting expression: the rise and fall of the voice, stress or accent, and rhythm. Methods for achieving variety in writing include the following:

1. Variation of sentence beginnings
2. Variation of sentence structure
3. Variation of sentence length

These methods of securing sentence variety are best used in revision. They are a means of curing monotonous or dull passages in a rough draft. If you use these methods regularly, your ability to capture and hold the attention of a reader or listener will increase tremendously.

Part 1 Variety of Sentence Beginnings

Usually when every sentence in a passage begins in the same way, the effect is monotonous. As you read the two following passages, note the points at which the writing becomes monotonous.

Sentences beginning with the same kind of phrase

Leaving the road, we plunged into the brush. *Coming to a creek*, we waded across. *Fighting our way through a tangle of vines*, we at last reached a path. *Turning left*, we climbed steadily uphill for an hour.

Sentences beginning with the same word

He was puzzled by the reaction of the crowd. *He* had tried to say something that would win their approval. *He* could not understand why they seemed hostile. *He* decided finally that it would not have mattered what he said.

Sentence variety can be achieved by beginning a succession of sentences in different ways—with adverb modifiers; infinitive, prepositional, or participial phrases; or with adverb clauses.

Jill worked conscientiously at the job until evening.
(subject-verb)
Conscientiously, Jill worked at the job until evening.
(adverb modifier)
To finish the job, Jill worked until evening.
(infinitive phrase)
Until evening, Jill worked conscientiously at the job.
(prepositional phrase)
Working conscientiously, Jill stayed at the job until evening.
(participial phrase)
Until evening came, Jill worked conscientiously at the job.
(adverb clause)

Exercises Varying Sentence Beginnings

A. Rewrite the following sentences, beginning each in accordance with the suggestion in parentheses.

1. Walter walked over to the bank in the morning to cash the check. (prepositional phrase)
2. Someone had evidently notified the Coast Guard about us. (single-word modifier)
3. Harry held the precious package in his arms and climbed into the back seat. (participial phrase beginning with *holding*)
4. Drivers' licenses are issued in some states to sixteen-year-olds. (prepositional phrase)
5. Dad drives twenty miles to work every day. (adverb modifier)
6. Linda earned a thousand dollars during the summer by working at two jobs. (prepositional phrase)
7. Beth scored high on the test and won a valuable scholarship. (participial phrase beginning with *having scored*)
8. We will hire you if there is a job open. (adverb clause)
9. The Yankee pitching staff was in a state of collapse by midsummer. (prepositional phrase)
10. The rain fell suddenly in torrents. (adverb modifier)

B. Follow the directions for Exercise A.

1. We had been afraid of fire from the beginning. (prepositional phrase)
2. Mike left the pool early and hurried home. (participial phrase beginning with *leaving*)
3. The old motor was clearly not equal to the task. (adverb modifier)
4. The little movie house closed because of poor attendance. (prepositional phrase)
5. Only one of all our neighbors has a new car this year. (prepositional phrase)
6. Virginia Woolf was among the first authors to make use of the stream-of-consciousness technique in writing. (prepositional phrase beginning with *among*)

7. William Wordsworth celebrated nature in his poetry; he felt that nature was a source of "joy and purest passion" for man. (participial phrase beginning with *celebrating*)

8. The army endured until winter set in. (adverb clause)

9. The President issued the warning sternly. (single-word modifier)

10. They do not give courses in home economics in the first semester. (prepositional phrase)

Part 2 Variety of Sentence Structure

A monotonous style often arises from the overuse of compound sentences because the rise and fall of intonation is so regular. As you read the following passage, note the points at which the writing becomes monotonous.

> The storm arose without warning, and waves started to bounce our boat around. Herb pulled in the anchor, and I reeled in our lines. It was impossible to get back to our dock, so Herb steered for the point. The wind was behind us, or we would never have made it. We got fairly close, and then we jumped into water and pulled the boat ashore.

Avoid a succession of compound sentences by changing one of the clauses into a subordinate clause or a participial phrase. Some compound sentences can be changed into simple sentences with a compound predicate.

COMPOUND SENTENCE:	We were delayed by a flat tire, and we missed the first touchdown.
PARTICIPIAL PHRASE:	Delayed by a flat tire, we missed the first touchdown.
SUBORDINATE CLAUSE:	Because we were delayed by a flat tire, we missed the first touchdown.
COMPOUND PREDICATE:	We were delayed by a flat tire and missed the first touchdown.

Exercises Varying Sentence Structure

A. Rewrite the following compound sentences, changing one of the clauses in each to the form given in parentheses.

1. The lecturer spoke about cancer, and he said that cancer could turn out to be several diseases. (compound predicate)

2. Many people do not want to go to college more than two years, and junior colleges are growing rapidly. (subordinate clause)

3. Sue has been an exchange student in France, and she speaks French fluently. (participial phrase)

4. I knew that the plane was late, and I took my time in getting to the airport. (subordinate clause)

5. We flew at an altitude of 20,000 feet, and we passed over a bad electrical storm. (participial phrase)

6. The Indian visitor was delighted by the students' knowledge of life in his land, and he stayed for three days. (participial phrase)

7. Pam Noe read the morning newspaper, and she discovered that she had not been elected after all. (subordinate clause)

8. There is plenty of rainfall in this country, but it is not evenly distributed. (subordinate clause beginning with *although*)

9. Everyone was late to work this morning, and there was a fire on the subway. (subordinate clause beginning with *because*)

10. The disassembled Statue of Liberty was brought here in 210 wooden cases, and it arrived at Bedloe's Island in June, 1885. (participial clause beginning with *brought*)

B. Rewrite the following compound sentences. Change one of the clauses in each to the form given in parentheses.

1. Pam heard about the job early, and she was first to apply. (participial phrase)

2. The American clipper ships appeared, and they swept other ships from the seas. (subordinate clause beginning with *when*)

3. The book is long, and it requires careful reading. (compound predicate)

4. News of the gold strike reached San Francisco, and there was a mad dash out of the city. (subordinate clause)

5. The band uniforms have been delivered. They are packed for the trip. (compound predicate)

6. The severe winter weather caused food and fuel shortages, and many people suffered greatly. (subordinate clause beginning with *because*)

7. The mayor spoke to the district attorney, and he urged him to proceed with the investigation. (compound predicate)

8. The crowd left, and the hall was searched thoroughly. (subordinate clause beginning with *after*)

9. Influenza vaccine is available to everyone, but we are still having epidemics. (subordinate clause beginning with *although*)

10. Pittsburgh was still a small city, and Willa Cather came there in 1910. (subordinate clause beginning with *when*)

Part 3   Variety of Sentence Length

A passage in which all the sentences are of about the same length, whether long or short, is monotonous. The insertion of a sentence of different length varies the rhythm and revives the interest of the reader. In the following passage from Hemingway's "Big Two-Hearted River," note how the short sentences are relieved by long sentences.

> He walked along the road feeling the ache from the pull of the heavy pack. The road climbed steadily. It was hard work walking uphill. His muscles ached and the day was hot, but Nick felt happy. He felt he had left everything behind, the need for thinking, the need to write, other needs.

Avoiding a Series of Short Sentences

Monotony is created especially by a succession of short sentences. There are times when a conscious use of a series of short sentences is very effective, as in narrative, when it has the effect of building up suspense. The unconscious use of a succession of short sentences, however, creates an awkward effect. The effect can be overcome by combining the sentences. As you read the two passages on the next page, note the points where the writing becomes awkward.

ORIGINAL: Quietly we walked into the hall. It was very dark. Bob found a lamp. He turned it on. We sat down to wait for Mr. Manning. We waited for an hour. He didn't come.

REWRITTEN: Quietly we walked into the dark hall. After Bob had found a lamp and turned it on, we sat down to wait for Mr. Manning. We waited for an hour, but he didn't come.

Short sentences may be combined in a number of ways:

1. By using a compound sentence.

TWO SENTENCES: The plane stopped in Okinawa for repairs. We landed in Tokyo three hours late.

COMBINED: The plane stopped in Okinawa for repairs, so we landed in Tokyo three hours late.

2. By using a simple sentence with a compound predicate.

TWO SENTENCES: I stained the cabinet. Then I coated it with shellac.

COMBINED: I stained the cabinet and then coated it with shellac.

3. By using a subordinate clause.

TWO SENTENCES: Jeff sprained his ankle. He was practicing the javelin throw.

COMBINED: Jeff sprained his ankle when he was practicing the javelin throw.

4. By using a participial phrase.

TWO SENTENCES: We were worried by some strange noises. They were coming from the engine.

COMBINED: We were worried by some strange noises coming from the engine.

5. By using a prepositional phrase.

TWO SENTENCES: The concert will take place at County Center. The date is February 10.

COMBINED: The concert will take place at County Center on February 10.

6. By using an appositive.

TWO SENTENCES: Susan Stein won first prize in the state instrumental competition. She is a soloist in our orchestra.

COMBINED: Susan Stein, a soloist in our orchestra, won first prize in the state tournament competition.

7. By using a single-word modifier.

TWO SENTENCES: Quietly we walked into the hall. It was very dark.

COMBINED: Quietly we walked into the dark hall.

Exercises Varying Sentence Length

A. Combine each of the following sets of short sentences in accordance with the suggestions in parentheses.

1. Ellen paged through the book. It was old. (single-word modifier)

2. The judge came in. (subordinate clause beginning with *when*) The spectators stood up.

3. We left Jean at home. She was watching television. (participial phrase)

4. I read about your illness in the paper. (subordinate clause beginning with *when*) I was reminded that I had not written you.

5. The engineers landed in helicopters on Ellesmere Island. It was the dead of winter. (prepositional phrase beginning with *in*)

6. The doctor decided on an operation. She realized that it might not succeed. (participial phrase)

7. I am going to Triton College in River Grove, Illinois. It is a junior college. (appositive) It specializes in technical subjects. (participial phrase)

8. We were delayed by a traffic accident. (subordinate clause beginning with *because*) We missed the first act of the play.

9. The Bayeux Tapestry is a strip of embroidered linen that depicts the incidents preceding the Battle of Hastings. The Tapestry was commissioned in 1077. (participial phrase)

10. We attended a lecture cn consumer fraud. It was informative. (one word)

11. We have been building millions of houses a year. (subordinate clause beginning with *although*) There are still not enough.

12. Grover Cleveland was elected to a second term. (subordinate clause) The country was on the verge of financial panic. People were jittery. (main clause)

13. Doctors discovered that Cleveland had cancer of the jaw. They decided on an operation. (compound predicate) They put him on a battleship. They performed the operation secretly in New York Harbor. (compound predicate)

14. Sir Georg Solti is one of the finest conductors in the world. He directs the Chicago Symphony. (appositive)

15. The play will open at the Shubert Theatre. The date is July 1. (prepositional phrase)

B. Rewrite the following paragraph. Make changes in sentence structure to create fluent, readable prose.

> Many of today's novelists write as if by rote. Their works all appear to be taken from the same pattern. Readers must be more critical in their choice of books. The shelves of bookstores are teeming with mediocre if not inferior tales. The books are praised by their publishers as being "the greatest romance of the time" or "the year's most suspenseful novel." Even the writing is poor. Many writers are interested only in making money and not in producing good, solid literature. Few writers today are interested in contributing to the growth of the novel as a literary genre. At no other time have there been so many literary works available.

SUMMARY AND APPLICATIONS   CHAPTER 6

1. By varying the sentence patterns that you use in speech and writing, you can avoid monotony and increase your ability to capture and hold the attention of an audience.

2. You can achieve sentence variety by varying the ways in which you begin sentences, by varying the structure of your sentences, and by varying the length of your sentences.

3. These techniques can be used during revision to improve passages that are monotonous or dull.

Applications in Other Subject Areas

All Subjects. Use the techniques discussed in this chapter whenever you write or speak for a class. If your language contains variety, it will be much more interesting to your readers and listeners.

Find a paper that you have written for a class in government, science, history, art, music, literature, or business. Check this paper for variety in sentence beginnings, structure, and length. How can the variety of your sentences be improved? Rewrite the paper, increasing the variety of the sentences used.

Journalism / Mass Media. Newspaper and magazine writers make frequent use of the techniques discussed in this chapter. However, some writers do a better job of achieving sentence variety than others. Look at the opening or *lead* paragraph of five or six articles from newspapers and magazines. Look in local papers and newsletters as well as in more well-known publications. Which paragraph contains the most sentence variety? Which contains the least? In what way could the worst of these paragraphs be improved?

Chapter 7

The Process of Writing

As you mature, your writing becomes increasingly involved. You gradually become aware that you have more complex ideas to sort out and a subtler kind of refining to do.

Despite the growing sophistication of your writing, however, the basic stages of the **process of writing** remain the same. There is still a pre-writing, or planning, stage. The drafting and revision stages also remain crucial.

Professional writers, especially, recognize the importance of the process. For instance, the poet Stephen Spender wrote down "as many ideas as possible, in however rough a form, in notebooks" and used those notebooks to generate topics for writing. The writer Henry Miller was always prepared to work through several drafts of his work because, as he explained, "Often I put down things which I do not understand myself, secure in the knowledge that later they will become clear and meaningful to me." For novelist Thomas Wolfe, the revision stage was a crucial one. After completing one rough draft, he wrote about an "enormous labor of revision, weaving together, shaping, and above all cutting" that remained.

In this chapter, you will review the process of writing.

Part 1 Pre-Writing

Anxious to complete a project, have you ever skipped over necessary preliminary preparations, plunged into the middle of the task, and later regretted your haste as the project collapsed around you?

The writing process, like any other process, has a beginning, a middle, and an end. These stages are called **pre-writing, writing the first draft,** and **revising.** Time spent on the pre-writing, or planning, stage is not "wasted" time. It is, instead, a valuable period of preparation that will save you time and energy in the end. During pre-writing, you select and refine your topic as well as identify your audience and purpose. At this stage you also gather ideas and organize them in a meaningful way. Each of these steps is important to a coherent, well-organized piece of writing.

Complete each of the following steps as part of the pre-writing process.

Select and Refine Your Topic

Choosing a Topic. As you continue your schooling or begin employment, you will often be writing in response to an assignment or in order to satisfy some other specific requirement. However, if you are given the opportunity to develop your own topic, you can begin to generate a list of possible subjects by using yourself as a primary source. Take an informal inventory of your ideas, interests, and experiences. You may discover a potential topic for your paper by answering questions such as these:

- –In what areas do I have special or expert knowledge?
- –What areas arouse my curiosity? Which ones would I like to investigate further?
- –What ideas do I recall from my reading and from past experience?
- –What is happening to me or around me right now? Are there details or situations I could observe and record?

The techniques listed in the chart below offer other opportunities for uncovering interesting and enjoyable subjects for writing.

Pre-Writing Techniques

Journal Writing. Use a spiral notebook to record your ideas, thoughts, feelings, impressions, and experiences. Make a practice of writing in your journal regularly. Such a book can become an invaluable source of writing ideas.

Reading. Skim magazines, books, and newspapers for intriguing topics or for stories that trigger your imagination. Compile a list of possible subjects or keep a writing file in which you save the clippings.

Discussions and Interviews. Remember that other people are a valuable resource. Every individual has a unique background of experience and knowledge. Listen attentively to what others have to say and ask questions about the opinions and stories that emerge.

Brainstorming. This technique may be done alone or with others. Begin with one general idea and then build on it by branching out from it. The topic "television" for example, could eventually lead to topics as varied and interesting as "the future of pay TV," "The effects of TV violence on children," or "my first experience in a television studio."

Clustering. Clustering is a specific type of brainstorming. Start with a word or phrase written on a piece of paper. Circle it. Now, outside this circle, write down any word or phrase that you associate with that "nucleus" word. Put each new idea in its own circle and connect it with the nucleus. Branch out from the new circles in a similar manner. When a brand-new train of thought begins, start again at the nucleus.

Limiting and Refining a Topic. In order to be of an appropriate scope for the paper you want to write, a topic may need to be narrowed or expanded. You can determine the suitability of a topic by asking yourself if it can be fully developed within the specified length.

The example below shows how one writer completed the first pre-writing steps. Throughout the chapter, you will see how the same writer handles other stages of the process of writing.

EXAMPLE: Topic

One writer was assigned "technology" as a general subject for a short paper. She realized immediately that she could not write an effective short composition on such a broad subject. To discover more specific topics, the writer tried clustering.

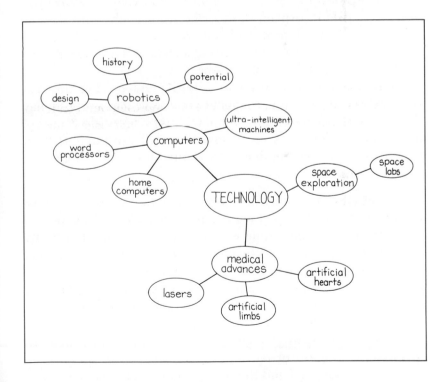

After examining her clustered list, the writer decided that "the potential of robotics" would make an interesting subject. She also realized that although this subject is much more manageable than the broad area of "technology," it can still be developed in many different ways. To focus her narrowed subject even further, the writer needed to determine her purpose and audience. This is the next step in pre-writing.

Determine Your Purpose

There is more than one way to approach any topic. If your writing arises from a personal need to express yourself, you may already have a general purpose in mind. For example, you may be writing to entertain, to inform, or to persuade your audience. However, a more specific understanding of what you want your writing to accomplish will focus your ideas even more. Consider purposes related directly to your topic. Do you want to define it, explain it, describe it, or analyze it?

Once you have determined your purpose, you may want to refine your topic further by writing a **statement of purpose.** This is sometimes called a **thesis statement.**

Many decisions in writing are interdependent. For this reason, the decisions you make about your topic and purpose may determine the types of details you will use to develop your topic as well as the types of organization that are possible. You may also begin making decisions about some of the following additional pre-writing considerations.

Point of View. You must decide whether to present your topic using the first- or third-person point of view. First-person point of view can give your writing a very personal touch. By using the pronoun *I*, you make it clear that the thoughts and ideas expressed are your own. In a fictional piece, this point of view brings a feeling of immediacy to the story. It gives your readers the sense of "being there" by allowing them to share the experiences of the first-person narrator.

Third-person point of view is somewhat more detached. In this case, the writer or narrator is not part of the action. The pronoun *I* is not used and the reader can perceive as much or as little as the writer wishes. This point of view is useful for non-fiction writing when the writer wishes to appear objective. It is also useful for narratives with many different characters and situations, or when the writer wants to avoid imposing his or her thoughts and feelings about what happens.

Tone. Tone is the attitude a writer assumes toward the subject. For instance, the tone can be light-hearted, satiric, earnest, mocking, complimentary, or critical. A writer can convey tone through careful word choice and selection of details.

Mood. Mood is the atmosphere or feeling that the reader experiences as he or she reads. For example, the writer can strive to develop a mood of humor, sorrow, peace, fear, or frustration. Again, precise word choice and the careful selection of details are important in creating a mood.

EXAMPLE: Purpose

The writer of the paper on the potential of robots considered several possible methods of developing her topic. She thought of writing an entertaining, imaginative piece in which she described a "pushbutton" future with robots doing all the work. Drawing on her own past reading, she also considered summarizing how science fiction writers such as Isaac Asimov and Ray Bradbury envisioned the use of robots in their stories. Finally, the writer contemplated a more factual, analytical approach to her subject. Pursuing this possibility, she considered two additional, more specific purposes: She could choose to inform her readers about current robotic capabilities, or she could attempt to persuade her readers of robotic benefits by giving reasons why robots should be welcomed into American industry.

After some consideration, the writer decided to adopt a persuasive approach to her topic. She had very strong, positive feelings about robotics that she wanted to convey, so the tone she would incorporate in her writing was clear. Her goal was to elicit an approval from her readers. With these points in mind, the writer also chose a possible title: "The Robot Potential."

Identify Your Audience

To increase the impact of your writing, you must clearly identify your readers, or audience. A careful analysis of your audience will help you as you develop your topic and begin to write. First, knowing your audience will help you to determine how much background material you need to provide on your topic. Secondly, an awareness of your readers' attitudes, opinions, and concerns will help you choose details that will have the greatest effect on them. Finally, your audience will also determine the type of language you use in your writing.

Choose the Correct Level of Language

The following diagram shows the different levels of language.

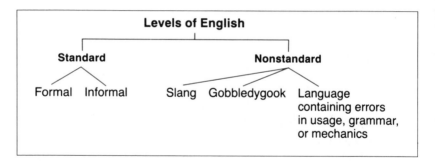

Standard English is language that is suitable at all times and in all places. It conforms to the accepted standards of grammar, usage, and mechanics. As you can see on the chart, there are two levels of standard English: formal and informal.

Formal English is language that is suited to serious, dignified, or ceremonial occasions. It is the language most often used for sermons, lectures, scholarly journals, and legal documents. Formal English is characterized by a serious tone, an advanced vocabulary, complex sentences, and an absence of contractions, clipped words, and slang.

Informal English is language that is appropriate for use in everyday situations. Also known as colloquial English, it is the language of conversation and of informal talks. It is also the kind of language most widely used in newspaper and magazine articles. Informal English is characterized by a casual tone, simpler words, a wide variety of sentence lengths, and the occasional use of contractions or clipped words.

Nonstandard English is language that does not conform to accepted standards. It is chiefly a spoken form. If it appears in print, it is usually in the dialogue of a story or play.

Two types of nonstandard English are slang and gobbledygook. **Slang** is made up of fad words and phrases that appear and disappear quickly. Because of its temporary nature, it should be avoided in all but the most informal communication.

Gobbledygook is often found in business and government publications. It is characterized by overloaded, unreasonably complex sentences and by obscure or technical words, called jargon. Because this type of language is unnecessarily confusing, it should always be avoided.

EXAMPLE: Audience

Identifying her readers was an easy task for the writer of "The Robotic Potential." The audience included anyone who opposed the development and use of robots. However, *analyzing* this audience was a crucial step for the writer. She needed to give careful thought to several questions:

How much does my audience know about robotics?
What do they believe the future of robotics should be?
What reasons do they have for holding these beliefs?
Are their reasons valid?
Can I effectively answer the opposition's arguments?

Answering these questions helped the writer to develop a clear picture of her audience's knowledge, beliefs, and attitudes. With this knowledge in mind, she also decided to use informal, nonthreatening language in her composition. Finally, the writer's awareness of her audience gave her ideas for the next step of the pre-writing process, gathering supporting information.

Gather Supporting Information

To some extent, your topic, purpose, and audience direct you to the type of additional material you will gather for writing. Supporting information can be classified in four ways.

Sensory details appeal to the readers' senses of sight, hearing, touch, smell, and taste. These details increase the readers' sense of involvement, much as carefully designed sets and costumes involve the audience of a play. For example, vivid descriptions of all the sounds, smells, and visual and tactile experiences one would experience while canoeing through rapids would help readers to re-create the ideas, feelings, and observations in their own imaginations.

Facts and statistics are verifiable statements and numbers. Because they provide concrete data about a topic, they are an effective way to support an idea or opinion.

Incidents or anecdotes are very short stories that illustrate a point. Effective in informal, artistic, or personal compositions, they often help readers to relate to unfamiliar or abstract ideas.

Specific examples also provide clear illustrations of a general concept or term. They give the reader a familiar basis for understanding new ideas.

To gather additional material, use resources and techniques similar to those you used to identify a topic. Details can come informally from your own knowledge and experience, or from outside sources such as other people and the library. You can also generate supporting details through brainstorming, discussing, reading, interviewing, and observing.

EXAMPLE: Pre-Writing Notes

The writer of "The Robot Potential" relied on background reading, her own thoughts, and ideas gathered from discussions with others to generate her list of possible supporting details. She recorded these details, along with other decisions she made during pre-writing, in the following pre-writing notes.

Possible Topics: *the potential of robots
  history of robots   robot design
Purpose: to persuade opponents of
  robotics that robots are necessary
  —use positive tone
  —answer arguments of the opposition
Audience: those who oppose robotics

Details:
  robots expensive
  robots make industries more
    economically competitive
  robots will raise the quality of life
  robots work as partners
  robots will disrupt present-day society
  robots do dangerous jobs
  robots are inflexible; not adaptive
  people find meaning in work
  robots cause job displacement
  robots never get sick or tired
  robots cause unemployment
  people find meaning outside work
  machines run people (?)

Evaluate and Organize Information

Writing is an act of communication. Your pre-writing lists
and notes contain material that is significant to you, but you
need to consider the best method for presenting this information so that it makes sense to your readers. Before composing
your ideas in a first draft, take time to evaluate your material.
Look for gaps in your information and add details that would
clarify your ideas. Check also for material that is unrelated to
your topic or purpose, and delete those references.

Once you are satisfied with the information you have gathered, you must decide how your material can most effectively

be organized. First, consider once again your purpose, audience, and the particular type of supporting information you are using. Then look for relationships among your ideas.

Sorting out your ideas is easier if you make organizing a multi-step process. As a preliminary step, group together supporting details that seem to fit naturally with one another. In larger papers, such groupings may suggest possible paragraph divisions. Identify the main idea that unifies each group and write this idea down in your notes.

Once your initial groupings are complete, decide on a specific method of organization for your major points. To make a decision, consider what order would be easiest for your readers to follow. Also try to consider what order would most effectively serve your purpose. You may choose from among these possible types of organization:

Chronological Order. With this order, you arrange your details in the order in which they happened or should happen. This organization is particularly useful for narrative writing, writing that is developed by an incident or anecdote, or for writing that explains a process.

Spatial Order. This type of organization presents details in the order in which they are arranged in space. Spatial order might proceed from side to side, from top to bottom (or the reverse), or from near to far (or the reverse). Spatial order is most effective in presenting visual details.

Order of Importance. When using this technique, you usually organize ideas so that the strongest is last. Thus, you can build to a climax or emphasize an important idea. This type of organization is useful when you are trying to persuade your audience or make a point. Sometimes, however, you may wish to capture your readers' attention by beginning with the strongest point, and then support that point with the other ideas.

Order of Familiarity. With this method of organization, you first present ideas with which your readers are most familiar or comfortable. You then move from this base to new concepts. This order is extremely useful in persuasive writing.

Comparison or Contrast. This type of organization works well whenever you want to point out the similarities or differences between two or more things.

EXAMPLE: Evaluation and Organization

Realizing that she would have to take the arguments of the opposition seriously, the writer of the sample composition began by grouping her ideas under the headings "Pro" and "Con." This gave her a chance to evaluate the reasons of both sides and to match her arguments with those of the opposition. Grouping her details in this manner led the writer to consider organization by comparison and contrast. However, after additional thought, the writer felt that this method of organization might focus too much attention on the arguments of the opposition.

After looking at her notes again, the writer realized that her details concerning robots fit into three categories of changes: changes in lifestyle, changes in employment, and economic changes. These suggested possible paragraph groupings. She reorganized her ideas within these three categories and then organized the categories from most to least familiar idea.

This last decision was a very deliberate one. The writer reasoned that the opposition's argument concerning job displacement was the most familiar one, and was also a valid point that she could not ignore. However, it would be hard for anyone to oppose the use of robots for dangerous jobs. By mentioning first the problem most familiar to her readers and then providing a solution to it, the writer would put her audience in a more receptive state of mind for her later arguments.

The reworked notes on the following page reflect the thinking of the writer at the pre-writing stage. The arrows indicate paired arguments. The numbers represent the three paragraph groupings. In addition to organizing her notes, the writer also deleted some details that she felt were inappropriate, and added others that she thought strengthened her arguments. This process of adding, deleting, and reorganizing ideas is an ongoing one in the process of writing.

③ lifestyle changes
① employment changes
② economic changes

Pro	Con
①robots do dangerous jobs-auto body painting ⟶	robots take over jobs
① robots do impossible jobs ↗	
~~people find meaning outside work~~ ↔	~~people find meaning in work~~
② robots make industries more economically competitive ↔	robots will cause unemployment and depression
~~robots never get tired or sick~~ ↔	~~robots are not flexible, adaptive~~
③ robots will raise the quality of life ↔	robots will disrupt present-day society
② robots becoming less expensive, more sophisticated − decreasing cost of microcomputers ↔	robots expensive
① retraining for those replaced by robots ↤	~~machines control people~~

⟮ save for conclusion ⟯

Order of Details
most to least familiar − overall
comparison and contrast − within ¶'s

Exercise Pre-Writing: Preparing to Write

Make a pre-writing plan similar to the one on page 95. You might begin by brainstorming to generate possible topics for a general category such as "The Future." Once you have chosen a topic, consider your purpose, audience, tone, and mood. Gather supporting details in your notes. Finally, rework these notes as shown above.

Part 2 Writing the First Draft

Once you have a well-organized set of pre-writing notes, you are ready to begin converting these notes from a simple list to an actual piece of writing. At this stage, simply write to get your ideas down on paper in sentence and paragraph form. Postpone your concern about details such as spelling and punctuation. You can correct these errors during the revision stage.

Writing the rough draft is often a process of discovery. You may suddenly discover new ideas, arguments, details, and considerations that never occurred to you before. Feel free to experiment with these ideas. Change your tone or organization if necessary. If an idea is important enough, you may even decide to change your topic and start over with a new plan.

EXAMPLE: First Draft

Here is the first draft of the composition on robotics.

The Robot Potential

I believe that robots should be welcomed into the American home, industry, and marketplace. There are those who oppose the use of robots and say they should not be welcomed. These opponents raise concerns about widespread unemployment. They are wrong for three reasons.

For one thing, most robots have taken over jobs that are unpleasant, dangerous, or even an impossibility for humans to do. Anyway, there can be retraining for those who are replaced by robots. Robots now do a dangerous job for humans, auto body painting, which was probably also not all that pleasant although it paid well. Robots replace equipment exposed to great heat, surrounded by dangerous gases, or underwater.

With the decreasing cost of microcomputers, which are continually coming down in price, the development of inexpensive, sophisticated robots is an increasing economic reality Anyone who does not step on the bandwagon of technology will be deservedly left behind in the dust. This could result in even greater unemployment and job loss from bankrupt industry than the use of robots.

It is simple. Robots come as the next step in technological development. With robotics, the future can hold more time for individuals to spend with their families or leisure activities. Shouldn't we adapt to and welcome this change?

The Age of Robotics is here. Its advent will mean changes. One change will be the loss of jobs for many people, but this is a small price to pay compared to the three great advantages that I have explained.

Compare this rough draft to the pre-writing notes in Part 1. The writer has strengthened her first argument by adding specific examples. She has also deleted other details that did not seem appropriate to her developing ideas. Although there is definite potential in this first draft, the composition needs a great deal more work before it becomes a smooth and effective piece of persuasion.

Exercise Writing a First Draft

Compose a rough draft using your pre-writing notes from the exercise in Part 1. Save this draft for later use.

Part 3 Revising

By this stage in the writing process, your original ideas have already undergone quite a transformation. You have incorporated changes or revisions in both your pre-writing notes and your rough draft. Through the addition, deletion, and reorganization of details, you have shaped and refined your ideas.

Now, at the revising stage of the process, you must think even more critically about what you have written. Revision is the stage of refinement, of careful attention to detail.

To simplify revision, read your paper several times asking only a few of the following questions during each reading:

1. Am I satisfied with what I have written? Will it get the response I want? Is my writing alive or static?
2. Have I accomplished my **purpose?**

3. Have I incorporated **adequate detail?** Can further additions make my ideas clearer or more complete?
4. Is the writing **unified?** Do all details relate to the topic and purpose of the paper, as well as to each other?
5. Is the writing **coherent?** Do my ideas flow smoothly? Are they clearly expressed? Is the writing organized logically?
6. Do I have a consistent **tone, mood,** and **point of view?**
7. Is the language appropriate to the audience? Have I used terms that are too formal, too informal, or too technical?

In addition to these points, make use of your knowledge of sentence construction to improve your writing further. (See Chapters 2 through 6.)

All good writers are concerned with these and other aspects of writing during revision. They know revision develops the potential of their first drafts.

Proofreading

As you work through successive drafts, you will correct many spelling and punctuation errors automatically. However, after you have finished your content revisions, proofread your paper specifically to correct any remaining mistakes in grammar, usage, capitalization, punctuation, and spelling. The proofreading symbols on page 107, as well as the Sections on grammar, usage, and mechanics in this book, will be helpful aids.

EXAMPLE: Revision

Study the rewritten, or revised, model composition on the following page. Notice how the tone of the writing has changed. To avoid alienating her audience, the writer softened her tone, which is still positive but less hostile. The language has become more formal. The writer has also made several changes to improve coherence. For instance, a fuller explanation in paragraph four makes the point of the paragraph clearer. Transitional words and phrases such as "for instance" and "in fact" have also been added to help the reader make logical connections between ideas.

~~THE ROBOT POTENTIAL~~

~~I believe that~~ (robots) should be welcomed into the American home, industry, and marketplace. ~~There are~~ those who ~~oppose the use of robots and~~ say they should not ~~be welcomed. These opponents~~ raise concerns about widespread unemployment [and job displacement. While] ~~They are wrong for three reasons~~ [these concerns cannot be denied, there is more to be gained than lost].

[At present,] ~~For one thing,~~ most robots ~~have taken~~ [benefit society by taking] over jobs that are [from welcoming the Age of Robotics] unpleasant, dangerous, or even ~~an~~ impossibl[e]~~ity~~ for humans ~~to do.~~ ~~Anyway, there~~ can be retraining for those who are [move idea to conclusion] replaced by robots. [For instance,] Robots [are used to] now ~~do~~ a dangerous job for humans, [who would constantly inhale fumes.] (auto body painting) ~~which was probably also not all~~ [also perform humanly impossible tasks such as] ~~that pleasant although it paid well.~~ Robots replac[ing]~~e~~ equipment exposed to great heat, surrounded by dangerous gases, [located] or underwater.

With the decreasing cost of microcomputers, ~~which are essentially coming down in price~~, the development of inexpensive, sophisticated robots is an increasing economic reality. [If our country or industries ignore this developing technology, they will be left behind] ~~Anyone who does not step on the bandwagon of technology will be deservedly left behind in the dust.~~ [by those countries and industries that do not. In fact, if we do not use robots,] ~~This could~~ [there could be] ~~result in~~ even greater unemployment and job loss from bankrupt industry than ~~the use of robots.~~ [from robotics.]

[The coming of robots is simply] ~~It is simple. Robots come as~~ the next step in [society's] technological development. [Just one century ago, everyone worked fourteen and sixteen hour days to earn a subsistence living. Now, with the aid of technology, the typical workday is eight hours.] With robotics, the future can hold even more time for individuals to spend with their families or [on] leisure activities. ~~Shouldn't we adapt to and welcome this change?~~

The Age of Robotics is here. Its advent will mean changes, [including] ~~One change will be~~ the loss of jobs for [some] ~~many~~ people[,] ~~but this~~ [who will need to be retrained.] [While American society must acknowledge these problems, it cannot ignore the even] ~~is a small price to pay compared to the three great advantages that I have explained.~~ [greater advantages of robotics. We humans must move over and make room for our new partners!]

Exercises Revision

A. Look at the revised composition on page 102. Compare it with the first draft. Some of the changes made in this composition were revisions of sentence structure. Identify these changes. Explain why they were made. In what other ways have the sentences been improved?

B. Use the guidelines outlined in this part to revise the content of the rough draft you wrote for the exercise in Part 2. Proofread your paper for errors in grammar, usage, and mechanics.

Part 4   Preparing the Final Copy

When you are satisfied that your writing is clear and correct, write it in its final form. Write carefully. Make your work as neat as possible. Be sure to follow the manuscript form that your teacher requires, including a proper heading and proper margins. For additional information about manuscript form, see Section 17 in your Handbook.

When you have finished your final copy, proofread again. Read your writing aloud to identify any remaining problems.

EXAMPLE: Final Copy

Now look at the final version of the sample composition.

Robots: Enemies or Friends?

Should robots be welcomed into the American home, industry, and marketplace? Those who say they should not raise concerns about widespread unemployment and job displacement. While these concerns cannot be denied, there is more to be gained than lost from welcoming the Age of Robotics.

At present, most robots benefit society by taking over jobs that are unpleasant, dangerous, or even impossible for humans. For instance, robots are now used to do auto body painting, a dangerous job for humans who would constantly inhale fumes. Robots also perform humanly impossible tasks such as replacing equipment exposed to great heat, surrounded by dangerous gases, or located underwater.

With the decreasing cost of microcomputers, the development of inexpensive, sophisticated robots is an increasing economic reality. If our country or industries ignore this developing technology, they will be left behind by those countries and industries that do not. In fact, if we do not use robots, there could be even greater unemployment and job loss from bankrupt industry than from robotics.

The coming of robots is simply the next step in society's technological development. Just one century ago, everyone worked fourteen and sixteen hour days to earn a subsistence living. Now, with the aid of technology, the typical workday is eight hours. With robotics, the future can hold even more time for individuals to spend with their families or on leisure activities.

The Age of Robotics is here. Its advent will mean changes, including the loss of jobs for some people who will need to be retrained. While American society must acknowledge these problems, it cannot ignore the even greater advantages of robotics. We humans must move over and make room for our new partners!

Exercise Preparing the Final Copy

Prepare a final copy of the writing that you have been developing throughout this chapter.

Guidelines for the Process of Writing

Pre-Writing

1. Select a topic that interests you.
2. Refine the topic until it can be well developed in a specific length.
3. Decide on your purpose, audience, point of view, tone, and mood.
4. Consider the language you will use. Will it be formal or informal?
5. Gather and list details that you could use to develop your topic. Consider the following types of details:

   sensory details   incidents and anecdotes
   facts and statistics   specific examples
6. Evaluate and organize your list of details. Delete unrelated ideas. Add new ones that would develop your ideas. Put your details into a logical order, such as one of the following:

   chronological order   least to most important idea
   spatial order   most to least familiar idea
                         comparison or contrast

Writing the First Draft

1. Keeping your audience and purpose in mind, begin to write.
2. Let your thoughts flow freely. Modify your initial plans for content and organization if necessary.

Revising

Read what you have written. Answer the following questions:

1. Did you stick to your topic?
2. Did you include everything you wanted to?
3. Are there any unnecessary or unrelated details?
4. Is each idea clearly expressed and thoroughly developed?
5. Do tone, mood, and level of language remain consistent?
6. Is your writing unified and coherent?
7. Is your writing organized logically, with a beginning, a middle, and an end? Are the ideas presented in an order that makes sense?
8. Is your writing interesting and lively? Is there variety in the type and structure of your sentences?
9. Is your word choice vivid and precise?
10. Do the language and content suit your audience?
11. Have you accomplished your purpose?

Revise, then proofread your work, using the Checklist on page 106.

Proofreading Checklist

Proofread your paper by answering the questions below. Additional instruction on each concept may be found in the indicated Sections.

Grammar and Usage

Are compound and complex sentences written and punctuated correctly? (Sect. 3)
Are there any sentence fragments or run-ons? (Sect. 4)
Have you used verb tenses correctly? (Sect. 5)
Do all verbs agree with their subjects? (Sect. 6)
Have you used the correct form of each pronoun? (Sect. 7)
Have you used adjectives and adverbs correctly? (Sect. 8)

Capitalization

Did you capitalize first words and all proper nouns and adjectives? (Sect. 10)
Are titles capitalized correctly? (Sect. 10)

Punctuation

Does each sentence have the proper end mark? (Sect. 11)
Are marks such as commas, colons, semicolons, apostrophes, hyphens, and quotation marks used correctly? (Sect. 12, 13, 14)

Spelling

Are plurals and possessive forms spelled correctly? (Sect. 13, 16)
Did you check all unfamiliar words in the dictionary? (Sect. 15)

Form

Were corrections made neatly? (Sect. 17)
In your final copy, is the writing legible?
Have you used the proper heading and margins?
Did you follow the manuscript form required by your teacher?

Proofreading Symbols

SYMBOL	MEANING	EXAMPLE
∧	insert	would ∧gone *(have inserted above)*
≡	capitalize	United states
/	make lower case	our club President
∾	transpose	their
ℰ	delete	finished the (the) race
¶	make new paragraph	. . . be complete. ¶ Another reason
⌢	close up space	head⌢line
⊙	period	. . . and stop⊙ Before going . . .
∧	add comma	Once that was settled∧the next
ᵛ ᵛ	add quotation marks	the poem ᵛAutumnᵛ
ᵛ	add apostrophe	the childrenᵛs needs
/=/	add a hyphen	the co/=/pilot
⌐	connect sentences	To finish your statue, you must complete this final step.⌐ Take a brush and dip it in

1. No matter how sophisticated your writing becomes, one thing remains the same: the process of writing. The process consists of three stages: pre-writing, writing the first draft, and revising. This process is essential to good composition. It is also a means of training yourself to think through problems thoroughly and logically.

2. The time and thought put into the pre-writing steps make actual writing much easier. Pre-writing includes choosing a topic; deciding on the audience, purpose, and tone for the writing; and gathering and organizing ideas.

3. The first draft is the writer's opportunity to experiment with the ideas developed during prewriting. Attention to mechanical details is not important at this time.

4. Revising and proofreading are the final stages of the process of writing. The writer checks for complete coverage; a consistent tone, mood, and level of language; sound organization; and a precise vocabulary. Finally, the writer proofreads for errors in grammar, capitalization, punctuation, and spelling.

Applications in Other Subject Areas

Science / Math. The process of writing requires the ability to use many different critical thinking skills such as analysis, organization, evaluation, and application. These same skills are crucial to solving problems in other subject areas, especially science and math. The next time you are assigned a project in one of these classes, try to apply the general stages and skills of the process of writing to it. Then write a short paper in which you present a process that would be a useful guideline to similar situations. For example, you might write "Guidelines for Conducting Experiments" or "Guidelines for Solving Equations."

Chapter 8

Writing the Paragraph

In Chapter 7, you learned about the three main stages of the process of writing. This process provides the framework for creating a unique, polished piece of writing. As you continue to develop your writing skills, the study of more sophisticated composing techniques will help you to reach your full potential as a writer.

You have already learned about some of the subtler aspects of writing, such as sentence variety and word choice. In this chapter you will continue to develop your skills by focusing on the paragraph, which is the building block of compositions, articles, stories, and books. To begin, you will review the basic characteristics of a good paragraph. Then you will explore the finer points of language selection and paragraph construction that can give your writing a unique character.

Part 1 Defining the Paragraph

"A paragraph is a group of sentences that develop a single idea." This is a definition that you have probably heard since you were a child. A more precise way of stating the same idea is to say that a paragraph is a group of sentences that demonstrate both unity and coherence. **Unity** is achieved when each sentence within a paragraph states or develops a single main idea. **Coherence** is shown when each sentence within a paragraph relates logically to the others. Without these two characteristics, a good paragraph cannot exist.

Most paragraphs are composed of two main parts. The first is the **topic sentence,** which states the main idea. The second is the **body** of the paragraph, which is made up of related sentences that explain, support, illustrate, or prove the idea in the topic sentence. The body should always be long enough and complete enough to develop the main idea adequately.

Like most definitions, this definition of an ideal paragraph has some exceptions. They are introduced later in the chapter, but for the present, the discussion that follows is based on the criteria set forth in the preceding definition.

Now read the following paragraphs and their analyses.

Analysis 1

Herbert Hoover established the image of himself as an Iowa farm boy steeped in the traditions of rural America. He spoke of the swimming hole under the willows, of trapping rabbits in cracker boxes in the woods down by the Burlington track, and of belly-whopping down Cook's Hill on winter nights. He recalled being taught by a neighboring Indian boy how to bring down pigeons and prairie chickens with a bow and arrow. Fishing, wrote Hoover, was "good for the soul," for everyone was equal before fishes. He sang the praises of "the willow pole with a butcher'd-string line, fixed with hooks ten for a dime, whose compelling lure is one segment of an angleworm and whose incantation is spitting on bait." When he wrote his letter accepting the Republican nomination in 1928, Hoover referred to himself as "a boy from a country village, without inheritance or influential friends."—WILLIAM E. LEUCHTENBURG

This is a well-constructed paragraph. The topic sentence tells the reader that Hoover represented himself as a simple farm boy. The rest of the sentences illustrate, or enlarge upon, this idea. The final sentence restates Hoover's view of himself, the subject introduced in the first sentence. Thus, unity is maintained.

Analysis 2

Recently the peasants of Transylvania, a mountainous Rumanian province, discovered that they harbor a considerable tourist attraction. For the past few years visitors have been coming round to inquire the whereabouts of Castle Dracula, home of the celebrated literary and cinematic vampire. These tourists don't understand that although there really was a Dracula, he was not the vampire of Bram Stoker's novel nor the refined ghoul portrayed by Bela Lugosi. The confrontation between the tourists and the peasants is interesting though. It is a sort of mismeeting between a surviving folk culture and a thriving mass culture.

This paragraph has serious flaws. While it opens with a strong topic sentence, the body never develops the main idea. It strays into tangents that concern the monster and the conflict between peasants and tourists. It lacks unity and coherence.

Analysis 3

Winter memories are the best memories of all. To sit before a roaring fireplace when the snow is on the ground and to remember the laughter of summer is to remember joyously. The wind howls but doesn't penetrate your warmth or security. Yes, winter memories are the best of all.

This paragraph is not only inadequately developed, but it also contains a sentence that strays from the main idea of winter memories. In addition, the paragraph concludes with a sentence that can be best described as a "space filler."

Exercise Analyzing Paragraphs

Examine the following paragraphs. Identify those that are well developed, unified, and coherent, and those that are not. Write a sentence or two giving reasons for your decisions.

1   If you relish paradoxes, consider the career of Horatio Alger, Jr. He made his fame writing books in which boys rose "from rags to riches"—yet he himself did not begin life in rags and did not die rich. The boys in his books got ahead by outwitting thieves and sharpers—yet he himself, a mild and generous little man who gave freely of his earnings to newsboys and bootblacks on the New York streets (the sort of boys who were his favorite heroes)—was an easy mark for impostors. His books were, and are, generally regarded by the critical as trash, yet their sales mounted into the millions. He was one of the most popular of all American authors, if not of all authors of all time; and there can be little doubt that he had a far-reaching influence upon the economic and social thought of America—an influence all the greater, perhaps, because it was innocently and naïvely exerted.

2   At the risk of stating the obvious, it is worth remarking that success of communication depends upon the charm (I use the word in its most serious sense) of the narrative. "Writings are useless," declared Theodore Roosevelt, "unless they are read, and they cannot be read unless they are readable."

3   Skiing demands strong legs. As all professional athletes know, it is the legs that go first as the body ages. Skiers can't count on many years in the sport and must start very young if they are to put in much time at the sport. Women have entered skiing in ever-increasing numbers. Children also are appearing on the slopes with greater frequency. Boxers need

strong legs, too. When you see a fighter's legs turn "rubbery," you know that he no longer has full body control.

4   While "instant" cameras offer you "no muss, no fuss" convenience, they all have limitations. Cartridge-loading cameras are simple to handle, but they raise your film costs. Cameras that process a picture seconds after you've shot it have a very high film cost, don't give you the best possible prints, and cause problems when you want duplicates or enlargements. Cameras with automatic exposure prevent mistakes, but they can also prevent you from experimenting and improving your skill. In short, if you want the most for your money, don't buy convenience alone.

5   Lassie was the greatest dog on earth, a collie like no other collie, a canine like no other canine. She first became known in a book by Eric Knight. Modern audiences know her from a TV show. On the show she lived with the Millers on a farm and she was the best friend of their son, Jeff. Later she lived with a forest ranger. Many was the time she would disappear from the farm, only to return barking frantically and turning in a particular direction. The whole family would drop whatever they were doing, and follow her to where their best friend had fallen out of a tree while he was trying to save his neighbor's cat. At the end of each show, Lassie would be hugged. Lassie was also a movie star.

Part 2   Pre-Writing: Choosing and Refining a Topic

In Chapter 7, you learned that pre-writing involves a series of decisions concerning topic, scope, audience, and purpose. Because these choices affect the rest of the writing process, it is important for you to consider them carefully. One way to do this is to work on developing a good topic sentence. Writing a topic sentence forces you to focus on these pre-writing considerations and make some definite decisions about them.

Using the Topic Sentence To Clarify Ideas

A topic sentence may appear at the beginning, in the middle, or at the end of a paragraph. It can also operate in various ways within a paragraph. As you are aware, its most important function is to present the main idea of the paragraph. The topic sentence should also reflect the following pre-writing decisions.

1. *Topic*. The topic sentence must present a general statement about the topic of the paragraph. It must lend itself to being supported by other, more specific ideas, examples, and details.
2. *Scope*. The topic sentence should present an idea that is neither too broad nor too narrow to be developed within a given length.
3. *Audience*. The topic sentence must capture the reader's attention and create an incentive to read further.
4. *Purpose*. The topic sentence should suggest the writer's purpose. A clear indication of purpose helps readers to focus their attention and expectations.

Using the Topic Sentence To Establish Tone

In addition to these important characteristics, the topic sentence may signal the tone of the paragraph. That is, it may suggest the writer's attitude toward the subject. The tone, as part of the general statement, must lend itself to being explained or supported.

The significance of tone in writing is illustrated by the following sentence.

December is a month of many holidays.

While the sentence has a subject, December, it neither lends itself to support nor does it contain a word or phrase that reveals the writer's attitude toward the subject. Furthermore, there is nothing in the statement that could capture audience interest.

Suppose, though, that the sentence were revised as follows:

December is a magical month of holidays.

The sentence now expresses a tone conveyed by the word *magical*. The reader will continue on to find out *why* this statement is so. The idea of magic can be developed with details about colorful window displays, the dreams and wishes of little children, the sudden appearance of good will, and the thrill of giving and receiving gifts.

The following topic sentence has the same subject, but a completely different tone.

Despite its many holidays, December can be the most sorrowful month of the year.

Because tone is one of the factors that determine which details are included in a paragraph, a paragraph developed from this topic sentence would be entirely different from one developed from the preceding example. The body of this paragraph might describe the loneliness of elderly people with no families, or children whose families are too poor to buy gifts. Readers are likely to continue beyond the topic sentence to discover why the writer has this unusual attitude.

Exercises Working with Topic Sentences

A. Here are ten sentences that would make good topic sentences. Each has both a subject and an expressed tone. Rewrite each sentence, retaining the subject but changing the tone.

1. Dancing is superb conditioning for your body.
2. I enjoy listening to the sound of a storm outside.
3. Do you believe everything you read in the newspapers?
4. Ann is a whiz at finding unusual solutions to problems.
5. Cable TV is turning us into television slaves.
6. Recent developments in music are alarming.
7. Referees often make unfair or inaccurate decisions.
8. Golf is boring, a game to be played only as a last resort.
9. Dave is an unusually grave and somber two-year-old.
10. Comic book collecting can be a fascinating hobby.

B. Find the topic sentence in each of these paragraphs. Note whether it is at the beginning, in the middle, or at the end. Explain why you think the writer chose that particular position.

1   My mother used to tell me how once a prairie wolf had stalked her as she walked home alone from school. I always felt cheated when I looked at the faded photograph of my father sitting on a horse, his hat higher than some telephone wires. He had ridden that horse right to the top of a gigantic snowbank, packed so hard that the horse's hoofs hardly dented its crust. There was usually a bank in our yard that reached to the top of the clothesline pole, but this was hardly satisfying. Why couldn't something happen *after* I was born, I wondered.

2   It was a wonderful, sleepy afternoon, tinted with crimson and gold. The air was laden with the sweet scent of multicolored flowers. Leaving the Hotel Raffles, the scene of so much literary international intrigue, I walked to the Singapore General Hospital where I was to meet its director. The flowering gardens spread out like peacocks' tails. The azure sky resembled a Fabergé Easter egg. Ships' sirens in the harbor sounded distant but fascinating, like the songs of Nausicaä in the *Odyssey*. Rickshaws, automobiles, and bicycles competed with the eager procession of pedestrians. When I arrived at the hospital, I was told I would have to wait a few minutes for my colleague. And while I waited on the sun-drenched patio, I watched some birds singing near a bed of flowers—whether they sang in Malay or in the universal language of birds, I do not know.—FELIX MARTI-IBAÑEZ

3   Charles Bedou, at the age of forty, stands four and a half feet tall. When the towheaded Bedou was born, he weighed nearly nine pounds and was the size of any normal baby. Five years later, however, he was less than two feet tall; at ten, he was three feet; when he celebrated his eighteenth birthday, he was four-foot-six; and in the ensuing twenty-two years, he did not grow another inch. His head and torso are the size of a much taller person; his arms and legs are too small. He is what is known as a dwarf. —SONNY KLEINFIELD

4   Pink was moving around in the bedroom. William cocked his head on one side, listening to her. He could tell exactly what she was doing, as though he were in there with her. The soft, heavy sound of her stockinged feet as she walked to the dresser. The dresser drawer being pulled out. That meant she was getting a clean slip. Then the thud of her two hundred pounds landing in the rocker by the window. She was sitting down to comb her hair. Untwisting the small braids she'd made the night before. She would unwind them one by one, putting the hairpins in her mouth as she went along. Now she was brushing it, for he could hear the creak of the rocker; she was rocking back and forth, humming under her breath as she brushed.—ANN PETRY

5   It was a bucket of bolts and barnacles. The staterooms were little more than cramped closets with iron bunks. The debris and litter of countless voyages were scattered about its deck. The *Vulcania* was a tired old ship. Her engines broke down in mid-voyage. Her third-class travelers had only one rusty shower room, its plumbing obsolete and its floors covered with fungus.

C. Pre-Writing. Generate a list of ten topics and write a topic sentence for each of them. Make certain that you have a specific audience and purpose in mind. Also be sure that each sentence states a main idea, is interesting, and implies a tone toward the subject. Save your sentences to use later in this chapter.

Part 3   Pre-Writing: Gathering Information

By establishing your topic and tone, the topic sentence "sets the stage" for the body of your paragraph. The information included in the body may come from **primary sources,** such as your own knowledge, experiences, or observations, or from **secondary sources,** such as books, magazines, and newspapers. The types of information you use to develop the main idea of the topic sentence might include any of the following, either alone or in combination:

sensory details
facts or statistics
examples
incidents or anecdotes

See Chapter 7, Part 1 for a more detailed explanation of this part of the writing process.

The body of the following paragraph is developed using specific examples.

> That dragonflies can adapt is obvious. Their failures to adapt, however, are dazzling. It is hard to believe that nature is partial to such dim-wittedness. Howard Ensign Evans tells of dragonflies trying to lay eggs on the shining hoods of cars. Other dragonflies seem to test a surface, to learn if it's really water, by dipping the tips of their abdomens in it. At the Los Angeles la Brea tar pits, they dip their abdomens into the reeking tar and get stuck. If by tremendous effort a dragonfly frees itself, Evans reports, it is apt to repeat the maneuver. Sometimes the tar pits glitter with the dry bodies of dead dragonflies.—ANNIE DILLARD

The second sentence of the paragraph is the topic sentence. It states the general topic of the paragraph, which is the failure of dragonflies to adapt. It also conveys the writer's attitude toward the topic through the word *dazzling,* which in this case means "astounding." The rest of the paragraph supports the topic sentence by citing specific examples of the ways in which dragonflies have not adapted to their environment. In addition, the absurdity of the dragonflies' actions justifies the writer's tone. Thus, the body supports the main idea and tone presented in the topic sentence, thereby creating unity.

The above example illustrates the key to successful paragraph development. Regardless of the type or types of development you choose, maintain the unity of your writing by checking all your details to make sure that they support the main idea and reflect the purpose for which you are writing.

Exercises Gathering Supporting Information

A. In each of the following paragraphs, identify the main idea that is expressed in the topic sentence. Next, identify the types of supporting information—sensory details, facts and statistics, examples, incidents, or anecdotes—that are used in the body of each paragraph. (Remember that more than one type may be used.) Explain how this information develops the main idea.

1   Whenever we children came to stay at my grandmother's house, we were put to sleep in the sewing room, a bleak, shabby, utilitarian rectangle, more office than bedroom, more attic than office, that played to the hierarchy of chambers the role of a poor relation. It was a room seldom entered by the other members of the family, seldom swept by the maid, a room without pride; the old sewing machine, some castoff chairs, a shadeless lamp, rolls of wrapping paper, piles of cardboard boxes that might someday come in handy, papers of pins, and remains of material united with the iron folding cots put out for our use and the bare floor boards to give an impression of intense and ruthless temporality. Thin white spreads, of the kind used in hospitals and charity institutions, and naked blinds at the windows reminded us of our orphaned condition and of the ephemeral character of our visit; there was nothing here to encourage us to consider this our home.—MARY MCCARTHY

2   The nuclear industry started off small: in 1957 the Government beached a submarine reactor at Shippingport, Pennsylvania, and converted it into a power station with an output of 60 megawatts. The earliest American nuclear facilities were built by private companies, such as General Electric and Westinghouse, as loss leaders to convince utilities that atomic power was the future. They needed little convincing. By the end of 1967 the United States had 28 times as much nuclear capacity on order as it did in operation. The capacity of plants under construction increased from 300 megawatts in 1962 to 700 megawatts in 1965 and 1,150 megawatts in 1972. "It is clear," said NRC Commissioner Victor Gilinsky, a

frequent critic of the industry, "that we got ahead of ourselves in expanding and scaling up the applications of nuclear power as fast as we did."—PETER STOLAR

3   The forest was the source of life and every Iroquois was comfortable in it. The forest provided the Iroquois with deer, moose, beaver, bear, and every sort of fowl to hunt. Wild turkeys sometimes ran to forty pounds and pigeons numbered in the millions. Cod, sturgeon, mackerel, and salmon were available in inland waters or in the nearby ocean. Children and women could gather lobsters, crabs, clams, and other shellfish along the beaches; or they could enter the forest to get maple sugar, birds' eggs, and berries. As a guarantee that they would never be hungry, the Iroquois used clearings among the trees to plant corn, beans, and squash, which they called the Three Sisters.

—DAN GEORGAKAS

4   Everywhere we turn, we see the symbolic process at work. Feathers worn on the head or stripes on the sleeve can be made to stand for military rank; cowrie shells or rings of brass or pieces of paper can stand for wealth; crossed sticks can stand for a set of religious beliefs; buttons, elks' teeth, ribbons, special styles of ornamental haircutting or tatooing, can stand for social affiliations. The symbolic process permeates human life at the most primitive and the most civilized levels alike. Warriors, medicine men, police officers, door attendants, nurses, cardinals, and kings and queens wear costumes that symbolize their occupations. American Indians collected feathers, college students collect membership keys in honorary societies to symbolize victories in their respective fields. There are few things that people do or want to do, possess or want to possess, that have not, in addition to their mechanical or biological value, a symbolic value.

—S. I. HAYAKAWA

5   Jim was a Jellybean. I write that because it has such a pleasant sound—rather like the beginning of a fairy story—as if Jim was nice. It somehow gives me a picture of him with a round, appetizing face and all sorts of leaves and vegetables

growing out of his cap. But Jim was long and thin and bent at the waist from stooping over pool tables, and he was what might have been known in the indiscriminating North as a corner loafer. "Jellybean" is the name throughout the undissolved Confederacy for one who spends his life conjugating the verb *to idle* in the first person singular—I am idling, I have idled, I will idle.—F. SCOTT FITZGERALD

6   These student-recital audiences were the best in the world. The audience loved every performer; that is, each family loved its own, but applauded sympathetically for all. The program was longer than a Wagnerian opera as originally scored, without intermission. It usually opened with "Flow Gently, Sweet Afton" performed on the violin by Paul Berkowitz, age nine, six months' instruction. The music flowed neither gently nor sweetly. He started without waiting for the piano introduction, covered the Afton in thirty seconds flat, and tore the house down when he bowed so low that his head touched the floor. He then exited the wrong way and bumped into a young cellist coming on stage. Grand ovation for both.—SAM LEVENSON

B. Pre-Writing. Look at the list of topic sentences you composed for Exercise C on page 117. Select one sentence and develop complete pre-writing notes for it. Be sure to identify your audience and purpose and to develop a full list of specific details. Refer to Chapter 7, "The Process of Writing," for help with each of these steps.

Part 4   Pre-Writing: Organizing Information

After gathering information for your paragraph, your next step is to organize this information. This step ensures coherence once you begin to write.

The idea of logical order does not mean that there is only one "correct" arrangement of details. A paragraph developed by facts, examples, or sensory details does not have to follow any particular order if all of the details are of equal importance. For example, if you wish to describe a party, you can write about the food first and the band second, or you can reverse the order. If you were describing a raging storm, it would not matter if you first described the rain or the wind.

In contrast, other subjects, by their very nature, are developed with details that must be organized in specific ways in order to demonstrate coherence or to achieve a desired effect. There are five frequently used ways of ordering ideas.

chronological order order of familiarity
spatial order   comparison and contrast
order of importance

Chronological Order

The Greek word *chronos* means "time." From this word comes the word *chronological,* which means "in the order of occurrence." Paragraphs that explain processes and those that relate incidents are almost always arranged in chronological order. For example, in a paragraph that presents the steps in assembling an engine, these steps would be listed in sequence.

The ideas in the following paragraph are arranged chronologically. The writer traces the melting of the polar ice caps in seasonal time, from early spring until midsummer.

> Easily the most conspicuous feature of the planet is the white caps that cover its polar regions. They display a fascinating rhythm of advance and retreat. At the end of winter in each hemisphere, the polar cap covers some four million square miles. As spring comes, it begins to diminish—rather slowly at first, then at an increasing rate. Near the middle of spring, dark rifts appear. They grow steadily and soon split the cap into several sections. Disintegration of the fragments then proceeds rapidly. The cap never disappears completely; however, even in midsummer a tiny, dazzling spot remains near the pole.—GERARD DE VAUCOULEURS

Spatial Order

Spatial order, the order of things as they are arranged in space, is used most often in descriptive writing. When planning a description in which the details will be arranged in spatial order, a writer must choose either a central focus or a position from which to view the object or scene. He or she then can begin the description by picking out the most striking or imposing feature that is visible from that position. Next, the writer presents other details relative to that feature.

For example, a writer wishing to describe a country church must decide whether to describe it from the outside or from the inside. If the position chosen is inside, he or she must decide whether to describe the interior by moving from the unusual altar to the front door, from the magnificent ceiling to the parquet floor, or in some unique order that fits the particular content of the paragraph.

The writer of the following paragraph has chosen to view the lobby of her apartment building from a position at the entrance. She begins by describing the size of the lobby, which first captures her attention, and then lets her gaze travel methodically through the lobby, describing in details each prominent feature.

At that time we were living in a second-floor apartment on West 10th Street. The lobby was an asset to the tenants; large, faintly grand, a polished place that smelled strongly of Liquid Veneer and dimly of cats. It was illuminated by paired bracket-lamps, each with one eye blinded by economy, and the melting hues of their Tiffany glass shades reminded me of half-sucked candy. Two staircases—one for the tenants on the east side of the building and one for the tenants on the west—opened out and upward with expansive, old-fashioned gestures; and in each French window stood a twirled iron tripod holding a pot of those plants that somehow cling to life through all: spitting radiators, north light, neglect of janitors. For me, the lobby had a soothing elegance; it brought to mind the baronial halls in illustrations by Reginald Birch.—ELIZABETH ENRIGHT

Order of Importance

The order of importance is usually used in paragraphs of explanation, argument, and persuasion. Most often a writer moves from the least important to the most important idea, thus ending on a strong note. A writer may, however, use the reverse order, starting with the most important idea in order to catch the reader's immediate attention.

In the following paragraph, the writer begins with simple, almost humorous reasons. She then progresses to reasons that are more alarming and therefore more important to her.

> I distrust the forest, or any wilderness, as a place to live. Living in the wilderness, you may well fall asleep on your feet. Without the stimulus of other thinkers, you handle your own thoughts on their worn paths in your own skull till you've worn them smooth. The contents of your mind are so familiar you can forget about them. You glide through your days even calmer; when you talk, you whisper. This is the torpor of deprivation. Soon your famished brain will start to eat you. Here is some excitement at last: you are going crazy.—ANNIE DILLARD

Order of Familiarity

The order of familiarity is another method of organization that is useful in paragraphs of explanation, argumentation, and persuasion. With this method, the writer first presents the idea or concept that is most familiar or comfortable to an audience. After establishing a base of common understanding or agreement with readers, the writer moves on to more controversial ideas or new concepts. This increases the likelihood of a reader understanding and accepting less familiar ideas.

The writer of the paragraph on the following page begins with a commonly held belief concerning modern civilization, which he supports with examples. In the middle of the paragraph, he uses these initial ideas to support a further, less accepted, conclusion about how we humans have lost our understanding of what and who we are.

As civilization becomes more complicated, humankind has less and less to do with the living things which are on our side. We live in cities surrounded by dead things. We deal far more with machines than we do with animals. The principal context of our lives has come to be dead matter, not living matter. And under these circumstances we tend more and more to lose sight of what we are and what we are like. Even the graphic and plastic arts are forsaking nature so that the wheel and the lever are more familiar than the flower or the leaf. An attitude which became fully explicit at the Renaissance seems to be in the process of disappearing.

—JOSEPH WOOD KRUTCH

Comparison and Contrast

Comparison and contrast can be used to show how persons, things, or events are alike or different. A paragraph organized by comparison highlights the similarities between subjects by placing them side by side. A paragraph organized by contrast uses this same strategy to emphasize differences. It is also possible to combine these two strategies in order to include both similarities and differences within one paragraph.

The following paragraph is developed by first employing a comparison and then a contrast of examples.

By the summer of A.D. 79, life in Pompeii and Herculaneum must have been very pleasant. Set in a fertile countryside with a warm climate, both towns could offer visitors delicious fruits in abundance and a variety of delicate wines from the vineyards that flourished on the slopes of Vesuvius. Pompeii, with its shops, offices, and busy market, its amphitheatre, public baths, and taverns, had all the bustle of a typical Roman country town. Herculaneum was smaller, quieter, and more secluded. There were no chariots rattling through its cobbled streets as they did through the streets of Pompeii, and its inhabitants—mainly wealthy people—were content to live away from the hurly-burly of commerce. Life was carried on in quiet dignity.—HENRY GARNETT

Combination of Orders

Many writers use a combination of orders. The following example combines spatial and chronological order.

> These days our back porch was piled with baskets of peaches and grapes and pears, bought in town, and onions and tomatoes and cucumbers grown at home, all waiting to be made into jelly and jam and preserves, pickles and chili sauce. In the kitchen there was a fire in the stove all day, jars clinked in boiling water; sometimes a cheesecloth bag was strung on a pole between two chairs, straining blueblack grape pulp for jelly. I was given jobs to do and I would sit at the table peeling peaches that had been soaked in the hot water, or cutting up onions, my eyes smarting and streaming. As soon as I was done I ran out of the house, trying to get out of earshot before my mother thought of what she wanted me to do next.—ALICE MUNRO

Exercises Understanding the Order of Ideas

A. Each of the following paragraphs is developed using one of these types of organization: chronological order, spatial order, order of importance, order of familiarity, comparison or contrast, or a combination of two of these orders. Determine the order of ideas in each paragraph and be ready to explain your choice.

1 He heard footsteps and crawled quickly into the coalbin. Lumps rattled noisily. The footsteps came into the basement and stopped. Who was it? Had someone heard him and come down to investigate? He waited, crouching, sweating. For a long time there was silence; then he heard the clang of metal and a brighter glow lit the room. Somebody's tending the furnace, he thought. Footsteps came closer and he stiffened. Looming before him was a white face lined with coal dust, the face of an old man with watery blue eyes. Highlights spotted his gaunt cheekbones, and he held a huge shovel. There was a screechy scrape of metal against stone, and the old man lifted a shovelful of coal and went from sight.

—RICHARD WRIGHT

2   There are at least three good reasons for the study of Indian authors and themes in the English classroom. First, the
Indian is an essential part of our American history and literature. At the time that the Pilgrims arrived, Indian tribes
had an oral tradition of storytelling and ceremony that inte-
grated all of life. Only recently have the rest of us begun to
realize the richness of this literature. Secondly, the Indian
has always furnished inspiration and characters for the standard writers and works from American literature—from Fre-
neau to Faulkner. Unfortunately, some of these writers have
helped to create about the Native American certain stereotypes and generalizations that need to be dispelled. Finally,
American Indians, with their spiritual oneness, their concept
of the sacred hoop, have much to teach modern youth, many
of whom find their own world dreary and materialistic. The
Indian's problem of trying to live in two worlds also strikes a
responsive chord in teenagers who are trying to find out who
they are.—ANNA LEE STENSLAND

3   Wit is a lean creature with a sharp, inquiring nose, where
humor has a kindly eye and comfortable girth. Wit, if it be
necessary, uses malice to score a point—like a cat it is quick
to jump—but humor keeps the peace in an easy chair. Wit
has a better voice in a solo, but humor comes into the chorus
best. Wit is as sharp as a stroke of lightning, whereas humor
is diffuse like sunlight. Wit keeps the season's fashions and is
precise in the phrases and judgments of the day, but humor
is concerned with homely, eternal things. Wit wears silk, but
humor in homespun endures the wind. Wit sets a snare,
whereas humor goes off whistling without a victim in its
mind. Wit is sharper company at table, but humor serves
better in mischance and in the rain. When it tumbles, wit is
sour; but humor goes uncomplaining without its dinner. Humor laughs at another's jest and holds its sides, while wit sits
wrapped in study for a lively answer. But it is a workaday
world in which we live, where we get mud upon our boots
and come weary to the twilight. It is a world that grieves and
suffers from many wounds in these years of war; and there-

fore, as I think of my acquaintances, it is those who are humorous in its best and truest meaning, rather than those who are witty, who give the more profitable companionship.—CHARLES S. BROOKS

4   There is a photo of the two of us on the second page. There's Maggie in Minnie Mouse shoes and a long, polka-dot affair with her stocking rolled up at the shins, looking like muffins. There's me with nothing much at all on, in her arms, and looking almost like a normal, mortal, everyday-type baby—raw, wrinkled, ugly. Except that it must be clearly understood straightaway that I sprang into the world full wise and invulnerable and gorgeous like a goddess. Behind us is the player piano with the spooky keys. And behind that, the window outlining Maggie's crosshatched face and looking out over the yard, overgrown even then, where later I lay lost in the high grass, never hoping to be found till Maggie picked me up into her hair and told me all about the earth's moons.—TONI CADE BAMBARA

5   You have heard it repeated, I dare say, that scientists work by means of induction and deduction and that, by the help of these operations, they wring from nature certain other things (which are called natural laws and causes), and that out of these, by some cunning skill of their own, they build up hypotheses and theories. And it is imagined by many that the operations of the common mind can be by no means compared with these processes. To hear all these large words, you would think that the mind of a scientist must be constituted differently from that of other human beings. However, if you will not be frightened by terms, you will discover that you are quite wrong, and that all these terrible apparatus are being used by yourself every day of your life.
—THOMAS HENRY HUXLEY

6   She dressed her tiny self carefully, donning a clean white camisole and her black Sunday frock. After she had drunk her tea and eaten a slice of thinly margarined toast, she washed her cup and saucer in some water she had drawn

from the bathroom the evening before and put them away on her "kitchen" shelf in the clothes closet. Then she tiptoed down the steep stairs to the bathroom and washed her face and hands—"a lick and a spit" as she called it.

—HUGH GARNER

B. Pre-Writing. Determine a logical method of organization for the list of details that you prepared for Exercise B, page 121. First group details that seem to relate to each other naturally. Then number your details in the order you would present them in a paragraph. If necessary, add additional material that might aid in the development of the topic. Delete any details that seem to detract from your main point or destroy the coherence.

Part 5   Writing the First Draft

After taking time to explore your topic and develop its potential, you are ready to write your first draft. Use your pre-writing notes as a guide. Do not halt the flow of your writing by stopping to check spellings or correct mechanical errors. There will be time for that later, during revision.

As you write, remember that the drafting stage is the time to experiment with ideas and presentation. The act of writing may also stimulate the discovery of new ideas and details. You may then find yourself reconsidering decisions made in the pre-writing stage. For example, if your material changes enough, you might decide to alter your organization, modify your topic, or select a different tone. Allow yourself to improvise. Sometimes accidental decisions lead to exciting results.

Exercise Writing the First Draft

Use the pre-writing notes that you developed and organized in Exercise B above to write a rough draft of a paragraph. Keep your topic, tone, audience, and purpose in mind and use them as a point of reference for adding, deleting, and rearranging details.

Part 6 Revision: Incorporating Adequate Detail

Revision is a crucial stage in the writing process. During revision, you refine the rough material of your first draft. You can combine or subordinate ideas and add variety to your sentences. You can search for that precise word to convey just the right shade of meaning. You can continue to add, delete, clarify, reword, and reorder ideas.

Revision involves the final crafting of your product. Think of yourself as an artist adding the final details of color, shadow, and line to a painting. Complete your revision in several steps. Concentrate on only one aspect of the paragraph at each step.

One important concern during revision is adequate detail. Sufficient detail allows the reader to share the writer's thoughts and experiences. It helps the reader to visualize people, places, and things, and to understand clearly the concepts that a writer is attempting to convey.

One way writers can weave details into the textures of their paragraphs is by selecting strong, specific verbs and nouns. They can add richly connotative adjectives and adverbs, alone or within descriptive phrases. They can also use figurative language to express feelings and ideas.

Some writers create a paragraph with a profusion of details.

> Edinburgh is a city of pure drama. It sits on a natural terrain of ridges, hills, ravines, and stupendous rocks as sharp-edged as a piece of crumpled steel. An amalgam of light and shadow, brightness and gray mist, it joins two separate parts: an Old Town, whose craggy skyline is one of the most dramatic in the world, and a New Town, an eighteenth-century concept of fine residences that is Europe's largest stretch of Georgian houses. A subtle, somber, yet exciting city, it can thrill or chill a visitor, for its striking townscapes—its Castle, its sky-piercing churches, its superb crescents—are marvelously thrilling to the eye; but its inner life is pulled back out of sight. At night the city becomes a tomb, the yellow streetlamps flickering in the mist.—FRANCES KOLTUN

Other writers subordinate their details to the flow of ideas in their paragraph. The following paragraph exemplifies this approach. Although the paragraph contains plentiful details, they are woven unobtrusively into the fabric of the narrative.

The soldiers were forbidden to leave the train, but at every station they pushed the windows down so that they could call to girls on the platform or buy chocolate bars from a barrowman or jeer in transparent asides at the striding guard. When the train was still for a few minutes in this way, the bugler would begin to play—always the same air, an antiquated, sentimental tune that belonged, perhaps, to a regimental song. This wistful music filled the train and floated out on the cold dark station of every town they stopped at. The song never reached its conclusion, for the train would always start up again with the last refrain and the instrument would be violently shaken in the musician's mouth and grasp. But after each such departure, for a little while, the bugler tried to keep playing, to reach the end of the song; and these last notes, wobbling and swaying, persisted until the train, gathering speed, made it impossible to play any longer.—SHIRLEY HAZZARD

Still another option is to write deceptively simple prose in which the details are spare but highly effective. Notice, in the following example, the striking use of such simple words as *dry, white, clear, blue, dust,* and *bare.*

In the late summer of that year we lived in a house in a village that looked across the river and the plain to the mountains. In the bed of the river there were pebbles and boulders, dry and white in the sun, and the water was clear and swiftly moving and blue in the channels. Troops went by the house and down the road, and the dust they raised powdered the leaves of the trees. The trunks of the trees too were dusty and the leaves fell early that year, and we saw the troops marching along the road and the dust rising and leaves, stirred by the breeze, falling, and the soldiers marching, and afterward the road bare and white except for the leaves.—ERNEST HEMINGWAY

Exercises Supplying Adequate Details

A. Here are some ideas for paragraphs. Choose one of them and generate a list of details that you could use in developing a paragraph. By each detail, jot down two or three vivid, specific words that would bring your details to life.

1. The snow and cold of winter complicate my life.
2. Somehow, there doesn't seem to be enough time to read.
3. Saturday is the busiest day of my week.
4. I have many weaknesses.
5. I was completely exhausted after our picnic.
6. The program was wonderful.
7. The garbage at the camp site was scattered all over.
8. I received an unusual birthday present.
9. The car was loaded, and we were ready to start our trip.
10. The man who entered the kitchen looked emaciated.
11. The sky to the west was an ominous black.
12. The year 19— was an exciting year for cars.

B. Revision. Reread the rough draft of the paragraph you wrote for the exercise on page 129. What details can you add to create a more vivid word picture or to foster more complete understanding? After your analysis, revise your first draft. Use one of the techniques described in this part to incorporate the details.

Part 7 Revision: Achieving Unity

Unity is an ongoing concern in all good writing. Your attempts at achieving unity began as you reviewed your prewriting notes and deleted any details that did not seem appropriate. They continued as you wrote your first draft and gained a fuller sense of how your ideas were developing. Revision offers further opportunity to scrutinize each sentence for its contribution to the topic, purpose, and tone of the paragraph.

In attempting to explain an idea clearly, to examine all sides of a question, or to express many thoughts and feelings on a subject, a writer may unintentionally violate the unity of a paragraph in an early draft. He or she may include ideas that relate only indirectly to the main idea of the paragraph or may shift the discussion away from that idea.

Look for the unneeded sentences in this paragraph.

> In 1850, Pinkerton founded the country's first private detective agency, whose insomnolent logo (an open eye) and motto ("We Never Sleep") gave birth to the phrase "private eye." Of course, other people used Pinkerton's idea to start agencies of their own. Many made a great deal of money in those days because police officers were very limited in number. A few agencies, though, failed and went bankrupt. The Pinkertons pursued Jesse James, spied for Lincoln (himself a detective-fiction fan), and smashed the heads of striking steelworkers for Andrew Carnegie before settling down to become a reputable multimillion-dollar corporation which now has some 37,000 employees. Only about five percent of Pinkerton's work today is investigative, but that still requires close to 1,000 detectives nationwide.

The writer of this paragraph made a common mistake. Although he started out to deal with one subject, the Pinkerton Agency, in sentence two he introduced the idea that other people set up agencies of their own. He then went on in sentences three and four to speak of the money made by many of these companies and of the bankruptcy of some of them. These three sentences do not develop the main idea. To achieve unity within the paragraph, the writer would have to delete the three intruding sentences in revision.

Exercises Achieving Paragraph Unity

A. The following three paragraphs lack unity because they contain sentences that do not support or explain the idea in the topic sentence. Revise each paragraph, deleting sentences that violate unity and, if necessary, adding sentences.

1   I used to think I was a person, but I'm really just a bunch of numbers. In English class I sit in row 4, seat 2. If I'm not in that chair, I am marked absent—even though I may be

somewhere else in the room. The teacher doesn't know me; he merely knows if the chair is occupied. I'm a number on a driver's license. I'm an ID number, and I'm a locker number. I had a combination lock that was numbered. However, I changed to a lock that opens with a key. That kind of lock is much safer than a combination lock. Mine cost only a dollar.

2   I enjoy being a joiner. My days and evenings are filled, and I avoid boredom. I belong to a stamp club, I play in the school orchestra, I am a member of the chef's club, and I belong to the city's drum and bugle corps. I get a lot of companionship and pleasure from being in these organizations, and I have made many friends. Friendship is a valuable thing. Everyone needs friends. You need someone in whom to confide, and you need friends when you are depressed. I love being a member of active groups.

3   We made an exciting trip to the West last summer. It was thrilling to observe what I had always been told—that America is as scenic as any country in the world. We saw the Rocky Mountains, which are huge masses on the landscape. They were surprisingly green. I had expected them to be solid rock. We saw lakes that we had never seen before except in travelogues. A highlight of our trip was seeing the Pacific Ocean. I will never forget the fun we had on that trip.

B. Revision. Reread the rough draft of the paragraph you wrote for Part 4. Examine every idea, sentence, and word for its contribution to the main idea, purpose, and tone of the paragraph. Make additions and deletions to achieve unity within your paragraph.

Part 8   Revision: Reinforcing Coherence

A good paragraph contains ideas that are arranged in a logical order and are clearly related to each other. Such a paragraph enables the reader to follow the writer's train of thought with ease. Since writing is, above all, an act of communication, the importance of coherence cannot be overestimated.

Concern for coherence begins at the pre-writing stage. Determining your method of organization is a major step in creating coherence. Now, at the revision stage, check your draft to make certain that your organization is effective. It is still possible to reorder your ideas if another method of organization seems better suited to your audience or purpose.

In addition to achieving coherence by arranging the ideas in a paragraph in logical order, a careful writer reinforces that coherence by adding **transitional devices** that help the reader to follow the line of thought from one idea to another.

Transitional Devices

Some transitional words and expressions are identified with particular logical orders; for example, words such as *next, then, soon,* and *later* are associated with chronological order. Words and phrases such as *above, below, next to,* and *across from* are associated with spatial order.

Other linking devices have more general applicability. For example, by referring to persons, places, things, and ideas in preceding sentences and clauses, pronouns help to join together the ideas in a paragraph.

In the following paragraph, note how each word in color refers to a previously mentioned person, place, or thing.

> Of course I had to live somewhere, and the somewhere turned out to be Montrouge, a worker's quarter, just beyond the Porte d'Orléans; for a friend sublet **me** **his** apartment there, in the Place Jules Ferry, where there were a few blocks of modern apartment buildings. **My** place, in one of these, was like that whole winter, curiously empty and curiously crowded. **It** was chiefly a studio, empty except for a large, glass bottle made into a lamp, a mattress on the floor beside **it**, a phonograph, and some records—**my** friend was a dancer. The living quarters were on a small balcony above this chill vacuum, and **they** were extremely crowded, containing as **they** did a bed, a desk, bookshelves, chairs, a fireplace, all in

a small place. A tiny kitchen and bath opened off on one side of this balcony, and on the other side it gaped draftily onto the unheated studio. This strange apartment was on the ground floor, and I lived there, acutely aware of every footstep on the pavement outside. I was lonely at first, and frightened.—MAY SARTON

Linking expressions, or connectives, also help to clarify the relationships among the ideas in a paragraph. These expressions move the reader smoothly from sentence to sentence. Here are some commonly used linking expressions.

Commonly Used Linking Expressions

TO ADD IDEAS

also	in addition	and then
too	likewise	further
besides	again	furthermore
in the second place	nor	as a result
equally important	moreover	in the same fashion

TO LIMIT OR CONTRADICT

but	however	at the same time
yet	although	on the other hand
and yet	nevertheless	on the contrary
still	otherwise	nonetheless

TO ARRANGE IN TIME OR PLACE

first	at this point	afterward	here
second	meanwhile	at length	nearby
presently	eventually	beyond	opposite to
finally	sooner or later	there	adjacent to

TO EXEMPLIFY

for example   for instance   in fact   in other words

TO SUM UP

in short	on the whole	for the most part	in any case
in brief	to sum up	in any event	as I have said

In the following paragraph, note how the transitional expressions, shown in color, show the relationships between ideas.

I don't live in the past very much. In fact, I hardly live there at all. My memory is just awful for things that happened last week, let alone what happened fifteen, twenty, or twenty-five years ago. I've never kept a diary or journal or even a scrapbook. I don't know exactly; there just never seemed to be time. Every now and then, though, I'll run across an old newspaper clipping my parents saved, or maybe a school yearbook, and that'll trigger the memory of some experience or feeling I had many years ago. I rarely remember details—what I was wearing or what somebody said to me or whether the sun was shining—and I'm sure that the few things I do remember vividly are colored by the way I feel about them now, today. Still, certain incidents stand out, and they're important to me, at least right at this moment. How important they were to me when they actually happened, I don't really know.

Finally, repeating words or phrases from a previous sentence is another means of providing coherence. Consider this and all of the above methods whenever you write or revise.

Exercises Reinforcing Coherence

A. Read the following paragraph carefully. Identify the pronouns and other transitional devices that help to make the paragraph coherent. Copy them in order, numbering each with the number of the sentence in which it appears. Some sentences have more than one linking word or expression; others do not contain any pronouns or connectives.

1. Animals talk to each other, of course; there can be no question about that; but I suppose there are very few people who can understand them. 2. I never knew but one man who could. 3. I knew he could, however, because he told me so himself. 4. He was a middle-aged, simple-hearted miner who had lived in a lonely corner of California among the woods and mountains a good many years, and had studied the ways

of his only neighbors, the beasts and the birds, until he believed he could accurately translate any remark that they made. 5. This was Jim Baker. 6. According to Jim Baker, some animals have only a limited education and use only very simple words and scarcely ever a comparison or a flowery figure; whereas certain other animals have a large vocabulary, a fine command of language, and a ready and fluent delivery. Consequently, these latter talk a great deal, they like it, they are conscious of their talent, and they enjoy "showing off."—MARK TWAIN

B. Revision. Check the rough draft of your paragraph for coherence. Do your ideas and sentences flow together logically? Is there recognizable progression of thought? Can you add transitional devices to enhance coherence?

Part 9   Revision: Achieving Emphasis

Whenever you write, you consciously or unconsciously make a decision to emphasize certain ideas within a paragraph. In the pre-writing stage, for example, you may have selected a specific organizational method, such as order of importance, in order to stress a particular idea. In writing your first draft, you may have expanded a detail that you sensed was particularly meaningful to your audience. Now, in this stage of your revision, you have further opportunities to highlight your ideas.

Many devices are available to the writer who wishes to emphasize an idea or ideas within a paragraph. The following paragraphs exemplify the most common of these devices.

EXAMPLE 1

The orchard to the east of the house was full of gnarled old apple trees, worm-eaten as to trunks and branches, and fully ornamented with green and white lichens, so that it had a sad, greenish-white, silvery effect in moonlight. The low outhouses, which had once housed chickens, a horse or two, a cow, and several pigs, were covered with patches of moss as to their roof; and the sides had been free of paint for so long that they were blackish gray as to color, and a little spongy. The picket fence in front, with its gate squeaky and askew, and the side fences of the stake-and-rider type were in an equally run-down condition. As a matter of fact, they had aged synchronously with the person who lived here, old Henry Reifsneider and his wife Phoebe Ann.

—THEODORE DREISER

In this paragraph, each detail is presented in relation to the house, the implied central focus of the scene. This emphasizes its importance.

EXAMPLE 2

About half way between West Egg and New York the motor road hastily joins the railroad and runs beside it for a quarter of a mile, so as to shrink away from a certain desolate area of land. This is a valley of ashes—a fantastic farm where ashes grow like wheat into ridges and hills and grotesque gardens; where ashes take the forms of houses and chimneys and rising smoke and, finally, with a transcendent effort, of ash-gray men who move dimly and already crumbling through the powdery air. Occasionally a line of gray cars crawls along an invisible track, gives out a ghostly creak, and comes to rest, and immediately the ash-gray men swarm up with leaden spades and stir up an impenetrable cloud, which screens their obscure operations from your sight.

—F. SCOTT FITZGERALD

In this paragraph, the words *shrink* and *desolate* are keys to the writer's tone. By repeating the word *ashes* several times, along with the related word *gray,* the writer emphasizes his feelings about the lifeless, foreboding nature of his subject.

EXAMPLE 3

Who is there who isn't peddling himself to the devil in some way? There are those who do it according to the tradition: for knowledge and power. There are those who do it for fame and money. There are those who do it to maintain the *status quo* and those who do it for the sake of revolution. There are those who do it to keep their children fed, to quiet their own consciences, to make the sun rise tomorrow morning, or to torment their heirs. There are those who do it for what most of us might agree are sufficiently good reasons, and others whose reasons, well, leave something to be desired. Why do I do it? I do it for a .368 batting average.

—ALVIN GREENBERG

In this paragraph, repetition is the stylistic device used to emphasize the final, most important sentence in the paragraph. By opening the five supporting sentences with "There are those who do it," the writer creates a comfortable rhythm that brings the reader up to the concluding questions and answers. At this point, the cadence of the paragraph changes, and the approach shifts from objective to subjective, sharply contrasting the conclusion with the rest of the paragraph.

EXAMPLE 4

It is a compressed Vietnamese morning, hot, bright, and steamy. I feel the weight of air and sunlight. Flies buzz solidly. Odors have earthy textures. Everything in the shade rots and smells. Everything in the sunlight bakes and shimmers. The surrounding jungle resembles impervious, shiny, hot green vinyl.—DAVID GRINSTEAD

This writer skillfully emphasizes his feelings by employing a very subtle repetitive technique. Rather than repeat *hot*, *bright*, and *steamy*, the words in the topic sentence that convey his tone, he uses words and phrases that extend the same idea to all five senses.

EXAMPLE 5

His legs pump. His eyes are wild. His brows work fiercely. His hands are helpless fists. He leans against a wall, seeking the cool plaster. He darts to a chair, perches on its edge with hands clasped, as if imploringly, between his

knees. He jumps up, fills his pipe, sets it down, lights a cig-
aret, puffs twice; it goes out; it remains between his lips. He
nibbles his fingernails. He rubs his head. He explores a dental cavity. He pinches his nose. He plunges his hands into his
jacket pockets. He kicks a chair. He glances at the headline
of the morning newspaper on his desk but glances away
heroically. He goes to the window and soon becomes interested in the scientific aspects of a fly crawling upon the
screen. He fingers the tobacco grains in his right pocket,
rolls a grain in a wad of lint, places the wad in a piece of
paper that happens to be in the same pocket. He folds the
paper around it, takes the paper out, glances at it.

—ELLERY QUEEN

The emphasis here is the staccato style in which the details of
the paragraph are presented. This style parallels the nervous,
disjointed movements of the character being described.

Exercise Achieving Emphasis

Consider both the subject and the tone of the paragraph that
you are revising. What do you feel are the most important ideas or
details? How can these be highlighted? Use one or more of the
methods illustrated in this section to revise your writing.

Part 10 Revision: Developing Tone

The tone of a piece of writing reveals the writer's attitude
toward the subject. This attitude might be angry, joyous, dis-
gusted, formal, amused, satirical, flippant, naive, bored, or sar-
castic. In the pre-writing stage, the subject matter of the paragraph, combined with the writer's background and personal
experiences, influences the writer's selection of a tone.

In revising, a writer must make sure that the tone is consistent throughout the paragraph. The writer can also refine the
tone through the skillful use of a varying array of techniques.
These include the careful choice and placement of words, the
use of figurative language, the selection of appropriate details

and their arrangement within the paragraph, the creation of rhythm, and the conscious manipulation of sentence constructions. By employing these techniques, a writer can control the tone, or coloration, of a paragraph. Notice how tone is achieved in the following paragraph.

> The lazy, sinister summer evening thickened with dust and petrol fumes, and the weariness of homeward-turning human beings drifted over Notting Hill like poison gas. The perpetual din of the traffic diffused itself in the dense light, distorting the facades of houses and the faces of men. The whole district vibrated, jerked, and shifted slightly, as if something else and very nasty were trying, through faults and knots and little crazy corners where lines just failed to meet, to make its way into the ordinary world.
>
> —IRIS MURDOCH

The words *sinister, fumes, weariness,* and *poison* in the opening sentence set the tone for the entire paragraph. Through the careful selection of words and details with negative connotations, the writer creates a paragraph that reveals her aversion to the place called Notting Hill. It is the aversion of an observer who is in a position to generalize about the district.

Consistency of tone within a paragraph is as important as consistency or unity of idea. Good writers maintain the same tone from the beginning to the end of their paragraphs. They avoid the inclusion of sentences written in a tone incompatible with the rest of the paragraph; for example, the placement of a humorous statement within an otherwise serious paragraph. Following is a paragraph with completely consistent tone.

> Our Southern springs are filled with quiet noises and scenes of growth. Apple buds laugh into blossom. Honeysuckles creep up the sides of houses. Sunflowers nod in the hot fields. From mossy tree to mossy tree—oak, elm, willow, aspen, sycamore, dogwood, cedar, walnut, ash, and hickory—bright green leaves jut from a million branches to form an awning that tries to shield and shade the earth. Blue and pink kites of small boys sail in the windy air.
>
> —RICHARD WRIGHT

The writer of this paragraph lovingly describes the beauty, joy, and richness of the Southern spring. There is no mistaking his attitude of wonder and appreciation for the many signs of rebirth, an attitude uncompromised by any element in the paragraph.

Exercises Developing Tone

A. Determine the tone of each of the following paragraphs and be able to explain how the tone is created.

1   On December 20 there flitted past us, absolutely without public notice, one of the most important, profane anniversaries in American history—to wit: the seventy-fifth anniversary of the introduction of the bathtub into these states. Not a plumber fired a salute or hung out a flag. Not a governor proclaimed a day of prayer. Not a newspaper called attention to the day.—H. L. MENCKEN

2   It is sometime before dawn, in the late spring, as I write this. The seagulls have more than an hour before it will be their moment to fly in from the river, screeching and crying, and then fly back. After them, the pigeons will murmur, and it will be day, perhaps a hot and sticky day. Right now the air is deliciously cool, but I find myself shivering. I find myself imagining the cold, the bitter cold, of that morning when Death came in full panoply, like one dressed for dinner. That morning so very long ago.—AVRAM DAVIDSON

3   It was a beautiful college. The vines and the roads gracefully winding, lined with hedges and wild roses that dazzled the eyes in the summer sun. Honeysuckle and purple wisteria hung heavy from the trees and white magnolias mixed with their scents in the bee-humming air. I've recalled it often, here in my hole: How the grass turned green in the springtime and how the mocking birds fluttered their tails and sang, how the moon shone down on the buildings, how the bell in the chapel tower rang out the precious, short-lived hours; how the girls in bright summer dresses promenaded the grassy lawn. —RALPH ELLISON

4   It's a story they tell in the border country, where Massachusetts joins Vermont and New Hampshire. Yes, Dan'l Webster's dead—or, at least they buried him. But every time
there's a thunderstorm around Marshfield, they say you can
hear his rolling voice in the hollows of the sky. And they say
that if you go to his grave and speak loud and clear, "Dan'l
Webster—Dan'l Webster!" the ground'll begin to shiver and
the trees begin to shake. And after a while you'll hear a deep
voice saying, "Neighbor, how stands the Union?" Then you
better answer the Union stands as she stood, rock-bottomed
and copper-sheathed, one and indivisible, or he's liable to
roar right out of the ground. At least, that's what I was told
when I was a youngster.—STEPHEN VINCENT BENÉT

5   These are the times that try men's souls. The summer soldier and the sunshine patriot will, in this crisis, shrink from
the service of his country; but he that stands it NOW, deserves the love and thanks of man and woman. Tyranny, like
hell, is not easily conquered; yet we have this consolation
with us, that the harder the conflict, the more glorious the
triumph. What we obtain too cheap, we esteem too lightly:
'tis dearness only that gives everything its value. Heaven
knows how to put a proper price upon its goods; and it would
be strange indeed, if so celestial an article as FREEDOM
should not be highly rated. Britain, with an army to enforce
her tyranny, has declared that she has a right (*not only to*
TAX) but "to BIND *us in* ALL CASES WHATSOEVER," and
if being *bound in that manner,* is not slavery, then is there
not such a thing as slavery upon earth. Even the expression
is impious, for so unlimited a power can belong only to
God.—THOMAS PAINE (1776)

6   A clear, racy day with the wind smelling of leaves. Even
grubby sparrows in the gutter showed not uniformly sooty
but brown-capped and blackthroated. Content to be alone,
Anna walked toward the lake, a blanket over her arm and a
book Leon had pressed on her—an interpretation of Blake he
claimed was his theory of film—tucked in her cow of a
purse. As she passed under the echoey railroad viaduct, she
wondered in which lakeside tower Leon was lunching with

his mother, in these blocks almost entirely white and largely vertical. The managers, the lawyers, and middle echelon administrators lived over here in grandiose, well kept apartment hotels or new glass-walled skyscrapers. Cliffs of money on the lake.—MARGE PIERCY

7   Sometimes at evening I sit, looking out on the big Missouri. The sun sets, and dusk steals over the water. In the shadows I seem again to see our Indian village, with smoke curling upward from the earth lodges; and in the river's roar I hear the yells of the warriors, the laughter of little children as of old. It is but an old woman's dream. Again I see but shadows and hear only the roar of the river, and tears come into my eyes. Our Indian life, I know, is gone forever.

—BUFFALO BIRD WOMAN

B. Look at one of the paragraphs in Exercise A. Identify a tone that is *opposite* to the one demonstrated in that paragraph. How would adopting this opposite tone affect the paragraph? If you were rewriting the paragraph, what details would you change? How would you change them? How would you alter your use of language and word choice?

C. Revision. Reread the paragraph that you are revising to see if you have maintained a consistent tone throughout. Utilize the techniques you have learned to develop your tone further.

Part 11   Revision: Creating a Mood

Maintaining a clear distinction in your mind between *tone* and *mood* is helpful as you revise. Tone is the writer's attitude toward a subject; mood, on the other hand, is the attitude evoked in the reader. This paragraph illustrates the difference.

Michael Lowes hummed as he shaved, amused by the face he saw—the pallid, asymmetrical face, with the right eye so much higher than the left, and its eyebrow so peculiarly arched, like a "v" turned upside down. Perhaps this day wouldn't be as bad as the last. In fact, he knew it wouldn't be, and that was why he hummed. This was the bi-weekly day of escape, when he would stay out for the evening and play bridge with Hurwitz, Bryant, and Smith. Should he tell Dora at the breakfast table? No, better not. Particularly in view of last night's row about unpaid bills. And there would be more of them, probably, beside his plate. The rent. The coal. The doctor who had attended to the children. Jeez, what a life. Maybe it was time to do a new jump.

—CONRAD AIKEN

The paragraph describes a self-satisfied man. He is "amused" by his face. He is somewhat upset about unpaid bills, but they are little more than passing annoyances. Uppermost in his mind is that evening's card game, which he decides to keep secret from his wife. The thought passes through his mind that he should duck out on his wife and his bills. The writer does not judge Lowes. His tone is one of acceptance.

The reader, on the other hand, responds to the writer's revelations with feelings of dislike toward Lowes. The mood of the paragraph, then, is sinister.

What mood is created in the following paragraph?

Aristide Valentin, Chief of the Paris Police, was late for his dinner, and some of his guests began to arrive before him. These were, however, reassured by his confidential servant, Ivan, the old man with a scar, and a face almost as gray as his moustaches, who always sat at a table in the entrance hall—a hall hung with weapons—Valentin's house was perhaps as peculiar and celebrated as its master. It was an old house, with high walls and tall poplars almost overhanging the Seine; but the oddity—and perhaps the police value—of its architecture was this; that there was no ultimate exit at all except through this front door, which was guarded by Ivan and the armory. The garden was large and elaborate, and there were many exits from the house into the garden. But there was no exit from the garden into the world outside; all round it ran a tall, smooth, unscalable wall with special spikes at the top; no bad garden, perhaps, for a man to reflect in whom some hundred criminals had sworn to kill.

—GILBERT K. CHESTERTON

The writer of this paragraph presents many bizarre details in a completely matter-of-fact tone. The reader, though, suspects that the guests should be far from reassured by Ivan's presence and that their evening will be anything but ordinary. The mood is one of expectation and of curiosity.

Exercises Creating Mood

A. Turn back to Exercise A at the end of Part 9. Identify the mood of each paragraph and explain how that mood is created.

B. Revise your paragraph so that it elicits a specific mood from your readers. Select just the right vocabulary and keep in mind that the mood can be similar to the tone or quite different from it.

Part 12 Making a Final Copy

In the process of a thorough, conscientious revision, you will have caught and corrected many errors in grammar, usage, and mechanics. When you are satisfied with the content of your paragraph, check your most recent rough draft for any remaining errors of this type. The Proofreading Checklist on page 106 is a helpful guide for this step.

After you have corrected any lingering errors, make your final copy. Follow proper manuscript form and remember to proofread.

Exercise Making the Final Copy

Check the most complete rough draft of the paragraph you have been revising for errors in spelling, grammar, usage, and mechanics. Correct any errors and make a neat, final copy. Proofread this copy one last time.

1. The skills involved in writing a good paragraph are the same ones necessary to all good writing. It is essential, therefore, that you learn to create strong paragraphs that demonstrate unity and coherence.

2. Paragraphs usually begin with a topic sentence that states the main idea, catches the reader's interest, and sets a tone for the rest of the paragraph.

3. Paragraphs may be developed using sensory details, facts, statistics, incidents, or anecdotes. This information may be organized in chronological order, spatial order, order of importance, order of familiarity, or by comparison and contrast.

4. Revision often determines the final quality of a piece of writing. Handle revision in several stages, checking only one or two aspects of it at a time. These aspects include adequate detail, unity, coherence, emphasis, tone, and mood.

Applications in Other Subject Areas

Mass Media. In any type of mass communication, *audience* is an important factor. Television shows, for example, are designed for specific audiences. Newspapers are slanted toward a certain type of reader. Advertisements are written for a particular market.

Assume, for a moment, that you are a writer of commercials. Choose a product and write a paragraph of advertising copy for each of four different audiences: children, teenagers, parents, career-oriented adults.

Fine Arts. When critics evaluate any piece of art, they often use many of the same terms that are used in a discussion of a good paragraph. They may, for example, speak of the *mood* of a painting, the *unity* of elements in a dance, and the *development* of a piece of music. Find a review or critique in a magazine or newspaper. Make a list of the criteria by which the subject was judged. Which criteria are similar to those used to judge writing? Which are different?

Chapter 9

Different Types of Paragraphs

Paragraphs rarely exist in isolation. Instead, they work together to achieve a certain goal. For instance, your ultimate purpose in writing a paper may be to convince your readers to adopt a new recreation program in your town. In order to do this, you may have paragraphs *giving reasons* why such a program is needed, but you might also have a paragraph that *describes* how the program you propose has worked successfully in other communities. If your proposed program has some unique features, you may also include a paragraph that *defines* the program or *contrasts* it with others. Knowing the types of paragraphs that you can use will help you make intelligent, decisions about how best to present your opinions and ideas.

Part 1   The Paragraph of Narration

A narrative paragraph is a short account of an event that actually happened or that the writer imagined. In this type of writing, a writer relates an event or brief series of events and concentrates on the unfolding of the story line.

Following is an example of a paragraph of narration. Note how simply and directly it is written.

> During the night we had already prepared our rescue net, and when with a rising sea Skipper Mees brought the *Insulinde* alongside the wreck, four persons were able to jump into the net. At the second attempt, three succeeded in jumping across. In the meantime the day had fully dawned. Again we tried. Everything cracked and creaked as we touched the wreck, but we got nobody across. We tried anew for the fourth time. The *Insulinde* thumped against the doomed ship, seeming to tear everything on board from its moorings, but no one jumped. The fifth attempt—again in vain. The sixth: no one saved. Six attempts in the furious surf in a raging storm—and five sailors still aboard the lost ship! Six times hurled against the wreck, again seeking space, again up and through the breakers to the waiting sailors, again alongside the ship. Six times under almost impossible circumstances, through ground swells and a treacherous surf, each time the *Insulinde* scraping the hard sand of the reef. I can assure you that it wasn't much fun.
>
> —KLAAS TOXOPEUS

Applying the Process of Writing

As you continue to present your ideas in writing, there will be many times when your topic and your purpose will suggest the narrative form. If you wish to recount an entertaining story, write a personal letter, or make journal entries, you will most likely use narrative writing.

You should also be aware that the narrative form is common in business and professional writing. Historians, for example, use the narrative form to record oral histories. Sociologists and psychologists use it for writing up their case studies. Narrative can even be used to record official information for an insurance claim or an accident report. In each case, the process of writing a narrative paragraph remains basically the same.

Pre-Writing. Whenever you do use the narrative form, make sure that your topic would be interesting to your reader, or that it has some special significance to you. Once you have your topic and purpose clearly in mind, you will need to make decisions concerning tone, mood, and point of view. Depending upon your specific purpose and audience, these decisions will vary greatly. For instance, if you are retelling the events of an accident for an official report, you will want to adopt a very **objective,** or impersonal, tone. On the other hand, if you are relating the same incident in a letter to a friend, your tone is likely to be **subjective,** full of the specific feelings you associate with the event. Refer to Chapters 7 and 8 for a more in-depth discussion of these writing choices.

Once you have made these initial decisions, you are ready to focus on gathering and organizing your details. Recall or create all of the actions, sensory details, and details of setting and character that make up the incident. Make sure you include enough information to make the scene or story as vivid as possible for your readers. Emphasize those details that strengthen your tone and mood. Omit other details that do not contribute directly to your story.

Chronological order is frequently used in organizing the details of a narrative. However, you may wish to experiment with this order and adapt it to your needs by utilizing a variation such as the **flashback** technique. In a flashback, you present a scene that occurred before the present action, but which has some bearing on it. Choose transitional devices carefully so that your reader is not confused by the switch in time.

First Draft and Revision. Using your pre-writing notes as a guide, try to recreate the story or experience on paper. The act of writing may trigger additional details from your memory or imagination. Add these if they are consistent with your other pre-writing decisions of purpose, tone, and mood. Remember, though, that unnecessary details will detract from the unity and coherence you are working to create.

After you have completed a first draft, ask yourself these questions as you revise your work:

> −Does every detail contribute to my purpose in telling the story? (Unity)
> −Are the details arranged logically so that they are easy for my readers to follow? Can transitional devices be added to clarify the relationships among details? (Coherence)
> −Are there enough details so that the reader can visualize, or mentally recreate, the experience?
> −Do vivid, specific adjectives and verbs help to create a strong mood?
> −Are the tone, mood, and point of view consistent?

Exercise Writing a Paragraph of Narration

Develop a topic for a paragraph of narration. You may choose to recount a personal experience, or you may want to write an historical account or an objective report. Once you have chosen your topic, complete the following steps:

Pre-Writing: Narrow your topic by determining the special significance of the event or the peak point of interest. Select a tone that reflects the attitude that you want to convey to your readers, and choose a mood that you wish to create for them. Also choose an appropriate point of view.

Having made these decisions, write a strong topic sentence that clearly reflects your choices. Then generate a list of details to support and develop your narrative. Organize your details logically.

First Draft: Use your pre-writing notes as a guide and begin to write. Experiment with new ideas, but refer to your earlier decisions as a point of reference for adding, deleting, and reorganizing material. Employ transitional devices as a means of enhancing the development of the narrative.

Revision: Go over your rough draft several times. During each reading, have a specific revision objective in mind. Finally, refer to the Guidelines on pages 105, 106, and 176 for further help with revision and proofreading.

Part 2   The Paragraph of Description

Persons, places, and things are the subjects for paragraphs of description. Usually, a writer describes more than just the external characteristics of the subject. He or she also attempts to capture its essence, or internal qualities. For example, in describing a woman, a writer might indicate that she is five feet six inches tall, that she is Caucasian, and that she has blue eyes and black hair. These facts reveal nothing about the kind of person she is. The writer might go on, though, to note that she has a shy smile, that her hands and eyes are in constant motion, and that she always looks away from the person who talks to her. These details provide the reader with a glimpse of the woman's inner qualities.

Depending upon the purpose, descriptions of places and things can go beyond inventories of external facts. For example, a writer describing the Statue of Liberty might convey the idea that the immigrants who sailed into New York harbor were heartened by the symbolic strength of her welcoming smile and thrilled by her quiet dignity and uplifted torch of freedom. In contrast, the writer of an encyclopedia article would be careful to include only observable, verifiable facts.

Describing a Person

Read the following description of a person. Note how the writer uses physical details to reveal inner qualities.

Before the prisoner left for Texas, the police took the traditional mug shots of him. In these photographs, Abel looks something like an unfrocked monk who had been caught blaspheming. A scowl clouds his ascetic face, and the sparse fringe of brownish-gray hair around his ears and the back of his head is disarranged. He is looking down an aquiline nose with tired eyes, and his receding chin is darkened by a one-

day growth of beard. The collar of his white shirt is unbut-
toned, and his striped tie is askew. Looking at this face, one
might think immediately of a clerk who has worked too long
in the same department. The photograph brings to mind an
observer's remark: "He has a genius for the inconspicuous."
The foreman of the Abel jury, John T. Dublynn, exclaimed
when he first saw the defendant: "He could be walking down
the street and he could be anybody."—SANCHE DE GRAMONT

The writer concentrates almost exclusively on Abel's unpleasant
characteristics, noting his scowling expression; sparse, disarranged hair; tired eyes; receding, unshaven chin; and rumpled
clothing. If Abel has attractive features, such as a pleasant
smile, or an easy self-assurance, you would not know it from
this description. By maintaining such a consistent tone, the
writer communicates his own dislike for the man and arouses a
similar mood in the reader.

Describing a Place

You have five senses—touch, taste, smell, hearing, and
sight—and ideally a description will appeal to at least one of
the five. In other words, a description paragraph will enable
you to "feel," "taste," "smell," "hear," or "see" whatever the
writer is describing. Many descriptions include details that
appeal to several senses as well. These details work together to
develop the tone of the paragraph and to recreate the scene for
the reader. In a description of a place, the details convey the
feeling or atmosphere that imbues the place, as in the following description.

It was a lovely morning. The last stars withdrew while we
were waiting, the sky was clear and serene, but the world in
which we walked was somber still, and profoundly silent.
The grass was wet; down by the trees where the ground
sloped, it gleamed with the dew like dim silver. The air of
the morning was cold; it had that twinge in it which in
Northern countries means that the frost it not far away.
However often you make the experience—I thought—it is

still impossible to believe, in this coolness and shade, that the heat of the sun and the glare of the sky, in a few hours' time, will be hard to bear. The gray mist lay upon the hills, strangely taking shape from them; it would be bitterly cold on the Buffalo if they were about there now, grazing on the hillside as in a cloud.—ISAK DINESEN

The words *serene, somber,* and *silent* capture the feeling of the place in the hours before the heat and glare of the day. This tone is expanded with details that appeal to the senses of touch, hearing, and sight—"profoundly silent," "wet grass," "dim silver," "coolness and shade," "gray mist."

Describing a Thing

Describing a thing is much the same as describing a place. In this kind of description, a writer utilizes details with sense appeal to communicate an attitude toward an object. A writer might also make use of similes and metaphors. For example, he or she might describe a stone as looking like a plump little pillow embroidered in tiny black stitches.

Read the following description of a thing, noting the sense appeal of the details and any comparisons used by the writer.

The object that most drew my attention, in the mysterious package, was a certain affair of fine red cloth, much worn and faded. There were traces about it of gold embroidery, which, however, was greatly frayed and defaced; so that none, or very little, of the glitter was left. It had been wrought, as was easy to perceive, with wonderful skill of needlework; and the stitch (as I am assured by ladies conversant with such mysteries) gives evidence of a now forgotten art, not to be recovered even by the process of picking out the threads. This rag of scarlet cloth—for time and wear and a sacrilegious moth had reduced it to little other than a rag—on careful examination, assumed the shape of a letter. It was the capital letter *A*. By an accurate measurement, each limb proved to be precisely three inches and a quarter in length.—NATHANIEL HAWTHORNE

The "thing" described in the paragraph is the famous "A" worn by the heroine of *The Scarlet Letter*. Notice how the writer invests it with mystery. There is something strange and compelling about the letter that fascinates him.

Applying the Process of Writing

You already understand how description can be crucial to effective creative writing. However, many circumstances of everyday life also call for strong descriptive talents. If you write up a lab report for science, for example, you must closely observe and accurately describe the results of your experiments. If you are ever asked to write a letter of recommendation, description can help you to convey not only outward appearances but also inner personality traits. In business, the copywriter or the travel consultant who is about to launch an advertising campaign must create exciting and enticing descriptions for the new product or cruise. All of these situations dictate specific purposes and potential topics. All require the careful construction of a paragraph of description.

Pre-Writing. No matter what the situation, identifying your topic and purpose for writing will still be your first step. These decisions, in turn, will help you to clarify other pre-writing decisions concerning audience, mood, and tone. If, for instance, you are writing up a lab experiment, you might describe the compound you created as a "dark blue precipitate." Your language would be technical, and your tone, detached. On the other hand, if you were a traveler trying to record in a journal the beauty of the Aegean Sea, you would be likely to write about the horizon as "the point at which the sparkling azure water meets the misty blue sky."

As the previous example shows, your initial pre-writing decisions will help you to identify the appropriate type of detail to generate. If your tone is objective, you may want to rely more on facts and statistics. If your tone is subjective, you will want to use sensory detail. After all, a carrot can be described as "an orange, conical object" or as a "crisp, cold crunch."

Organization, of course, is the final pre-writing step. If your details are primarily visual, you may want to use spatial order. However, consider other options that might better suit your purpose. If you are writing about two types of cars, for instance, comparison and contrast might work best. If you are writing a recommendation, order of importance might be more effective in creating a strong impression of your candidate's traits.

First Draft and Revision. In writing your first draft, keep your pre-writing decisions concerning purpose, tone, and mood clearly in mind. Also consider the dominant impression you wish to create. These are all your points of reference as you develop and expand your ideas on paper. If the changes you make at this stage are consistent with these pre-writing decisions, you will still maintain unity and coherence in your writing.

After you have completed your first draft, check for the following concerns during revision:

- –Does every detail relate directly to my purpose? (Unity)
- –Does the method of organization work well to convey these details logically? (Coherence)
- –Do precise, vivid words highlight the most important parts of my description? Do they work together to create a specific impression? (Emphasis)
- –Is enough detail provided to help the reader recreate, visualize, or understand the subject? (Adequate Detail)
- –Are the tone and mood consistently developed?

Exercises Writing Descriptive Paragraphs

A. Write a paragraph describing someone you know, like, or find fascinating or create a totally imaginary character. Include details that reveal your subject's inner qualities and your own attitude toward that person. Complete the following steps:

Pre-Writing: Once you have a specific subject in mind, identify the dominant impression that your character creates or reveals. Determine your own attitude toward your subject, as well as the response you wish to elicit from your readers. Finally, generate details that are appropriate for your topic, purpose, and tone. Arrange these details logically.

First Draft: Use your pre-writing notes to get your ideas down on paper. Develop a topic sentence that prepares the reader for the description that is to come. Add and delete details in order to shape and focus your impressions. Use transitional devices to help relate your details.

Revision: Go over your rough draft several times. Add vivid, specific language to reinforce the impression you are trying to create. Omit details that do not contribute directly to the image you want to convey. Check to see that your details are consistent with your purpose and tone. When you are satisfied with your content, proofread your paper for errors in spelling, grammar and mechanics. Use the checklist on page 106.

B. Write two paragraphs that describe the same place, but which each convey a different tone or mood. In one description include details that reveal a fondness for the place; in the other description present details that reveal intense dislike. Follow the stages outlined in Exercise A. In revision, check carefully to make sure your tone is consistently developed.

C. Write a paragraph describing a thing that has some unusual qualities. You may, for example, want to choose an item you saw in a museum. Follow the steps outlined in Exercise A. In developing your list of details, try to include at least one comparison and details that appeal to two or more senses. As you revise, check to make sure you have emphasized your subject's unusual qualities.

Part 3   The Expository Paragraph

The **expository,** or explanatory, paragraph is a broad classification that includes a variety of paragraph forms. While all expository paragraphs are written to explain something or to convey information, the distinctions among the various forms are based on the differences in their purposes and in their methods of development.

The Paragraph That Explains a Process

To explain how to do something or how something works, you must develop a logical, usually chronological, presentation of ideas. You also need enough detailed information to enable the reader to duplicate or to understand each step in the process. The following paragraph is an explanation of how a dictionary editor goes about writing a definition.

> To define a word, the dictionary editor places before himself the stack of cards illustrating that word. Each of the cards represents an actual use of the word by a writer of some literary or historical importance. He reads the cards carefully, discards some, rereads the rest, and divides up the stack according to what he thinks are the several senses of the word. Finally, he writes his definitions, following the hard-and-fast rule that each definition *must* be based on what the quotations in front of him reveal about the meaning of the word. The editor cannot be influenced by what *he* thinks a given word *ought* to mean. He must work according to the cards or not at all.—s. i. HAYAKAWA

The Paragraph That Explains an Idea

A common kind of explanation is one in which details—in the form of facts, statistics, examples, and anecdotes—are used to develop the idea presented in the topic sentence of the paragraph. Following is an example of this type of explanation.

> A unique idea that pervades all Hindu thinking and forms . . . is the concept of *karma*. *Karma* is literally "action" and the concept may be described as the law of consequences. Every action, good or bad, has its consequence or fruit. The consequence comes back to the individual, the fruit must be plucked or the crop reaped, by a law from which there is no escape. This idea is closely linked with that of transmigration of the soul, or reincarnation, since the fruits of one's actions clearly cannot all be experienced in a single physical existence. These two ideas are intimately interwoven into the

texture of the Hindu mind, from the prince to the peasant, from the philosopher to the worldly wise merchant. They serve as a justification of the whole system of caste, justifying both the claims of the privileged and the disabilities of the lowly.—PERCIVAL SPEAR

After reading this paragraph, you can understand why explaining ideas can sometimes be a difficult undertaking. Considering that the topic is philosophical in nature and foreign to our culture, the writer has achieved a truly fine explanation.

The Paragraph That Defines

Some words can be defined within the context of a sentence. Their definitions are brief, often consisting of a synonym or a short descriptive phrase, and are tangential to the ideas being presented in the paragraph. Other terms, though, must be defined more completely. This may be due to the complexity of their meanings, their openness to misinterpretation, their unusual use by a writer, or because a writer chooses to explain them in some detail. When the need for an extended definition occurs, a writer can develop a paragraph of definition.

The paragraph of definition may be developed in many ways. The use of examples is one technique available to a writer wishing to define a term. Other techniques are the inclusion of a dictionary definition, the discussion of connotations, the exploration of a word origin, the discussion of synonyms and their differing connotations, and the identification of inappropriate interpretations of a word.

The following paragraph page exemplifies a highly subjective, or personal, approach to defining a term. The writer makes no attempt to construct an objective definition of the word *reservation*, but rather, explains the meaning of the concept in her own life.

To me, *reservation* means a wide network of related people through time. I have relatives through blood and marriage on all the South Dakota reservations, mainly the Standing Rock Sioux where I am enrolled, and the Cheyenne River

Sioux. At the moment, my here and now is New York City, but I can return to the reservation at any time, and I do. I return to the reservation for strength and direction, to find what I am seeking, which enables me to "keep going on." I know that I am in the midst of a wide circle of a journey. I knew when I was able to come into the world again and I will know when I am to leave it. I am young enough to have many challenges yet to meet, and things to accept which are not all of my own making. But I feel a wholeness in the relationship between reservation and urban people; I respect the link; it sustains me.—DAWN KATHLEEN GOOD ELK

The Paragraph That Gives Reasons

A fourth kind of expository paragraph gives reasons for something that happened once or that happens regularly, or for a conclusion that you have reached. For example, you can explain why your football team lost, why you were late for an appointment, why you forgot to return a phone call, why you failed a test, why hurricanes occur at certain times of year, why presidential primaries are held, or why corn grows well in the Midwest. Explanations of this kind can be drawn from your own experience, from general knowledge, or from research.

The following paragraph is an explanation of why the writer considers herself lucky.

I'm one of the lucky people. My Otoe-Pawnee-Wyandot parents and ancestors endowed me with a sureness of identity I will never lose. The Wyandots have been terminated as a tribe, and there are indeed no fullblood Wyandots now. Even so, enrolled Wyandots, if called upon to do so, would have no problem identifying as a definite tribe. Their history even today is distinct. The beauty of their heritage is still to be felt and seen in the early morning mists that refresh the luxuriant greenery of the Wyandot countryside in Oklahoma and Kansas. And I, blessed one, can still know firsthand the strengths and beauties of my seventy-nine-year old Wyandot mother.—MIFAUNWY SHUNATONA HINES

Applying the Process of Writing

Whenever your general purpose is to create order or understanding, you will find yourself using the expository mode. You may be writing something as personal as a statement of belief, or you may be writing policy and procedure manuals for a corporation. You may be giving reasons why you should be elected to an office, or you may be justifying the expenditure of thousands of dollars. In every case, your topic and purpose will direct you to a paragraph in the expository mode.

Pre-Writing. Once you have established your topic and purpose, it is important that you identify your audience. Determine what your audience already knows, what they need to know, and how they might best absorb the new information. Considering these issues will help you to identify the types of details you need to develop your paragraph.

The organizational method that you use will depend on both your specific purpose and the types of detail you use. Paragraphs that explain a process are usually developed chronologically; however, paragraphs that give reasons are often organized from least to most important idea. On the other hand, the information in a paragraph that defines or one that explains an idea might be arranged from most familiar to least familiar idea, or from general concept to specific details.

First Draft and Revision. As you incorporate the ideas from your writing plan into your first draft, keep your audience in mind. Add details that will further clarify understanding. Delete or rearrange details that confuse the logical development of your ideas. Use transitional devices for coherence.

In revising your first draft, refer frequently to your pre-writing decisions. Make sure that these decisions are consistently and thoroughly implemented in your writing. Ask yourself the following questions:

–Does my topic sentence clearly indicate my subject and purpose?

–Does every detail directly contribute to my readers' understanding? (Unity)

−Do the details ensure that the directions will be followed or the concept understood? (Adequate Detail)

−Are the details presented in a logical manner? Do transitional devices establish links between the ideas presented? (Coherence)

Exercises Writing Expository Paragraphs

A. Write a paragraph that explains a process. For example, explain how a helicopter can stay in the air, how a tornado develops, how to grow tomatoes, or how to bowl. When you are choosing a subject, be certain that it can be developed as an expository paragraph. Complete the following steps as you write:

Pre-Writing: Narrow your subject so that it can be thoroughly explained in a paragraph. Have your purpose clearly in mind and then determine the knowledge and concerns of your audience. Generate a list of details that will fully develop your topic. Decide on an appropriate method of organizing these details.

First Draft: Use your pre-writing notes to get your ideas down on paper. Add precise and specific details to your developing ideas in order to make them as informative as possible.

Revision: Go over your rough draft several times. Check to see that your topic and purpose are clear. To guarantee that your explanation is complete, review your main points to make sure that each is adequately developed. To ensure coherence, check to see that each detail is logically related to the topic in general and specifically linked to the points that come before and after it. Make necessary additions and deletions in order to improve your readers' understanding. When you are satisfied with your content, carefully proofread your paper. Use the Guidelines on pages 105, 106, and 176.

B. Choose an abstract concept such as brotherhood or sisterhood, charity, respect, prejudice, or self-denial and write a paragraph explaining that idea. Follow the steps outlined in Exercise A. In the pre-writing stage, be sure to limit and focus your subject sufficiently so that it can be handled in a single paragraph.

C. The following subjects are starting points for expository paragraphs that involve giving reasons. Choose one of these, or one of your own, and write an explanatory paragraph. Follow the steps outlined in Exercise A. In organizing your details, check to make sure that your reasons are logically sequenced.

1. He was unable to keep up with the rest of the class.
2. Clothing styles no longer seem to follow any set rules.
3. The rights of victims are now being recognized.
4. Even over-the-counter pills can have harmful side effects.
5. Automobile insurance is costly.
6. Many people take their dogs to obedience school.
7. Knowledge of a foreign language is a useful asset.
8. The ocean is our next frontier.
9. As we get older, we need the release of "play" even more.
10. We must never forget the past.

Part 4   The Paragraph of Argument or Persuasion

Paragraphs of argument and persuasion are essentially the same form of writing. In each, reasons are presented to support an idea that is open to question or debate. The distinction between these two kinds of paragraphs lies in their intent. In a paragraph of argument, the writer explains one side of an issue without expecting the reader to act upon or to embrace his or her way of thinking. For example, Ellen attacks Maria for being a conservationist. Maria then writes a paragraph in which she argues in favor of practicing conservation. She does not attempt to persuade Ellen to buy soft drinks in reusable bottles or to organize a car pool. She does try to get Ellen to acknowledge the validity of her stand on the issue.

In a paragraph of persuasion, the writer's purpose is to convert the reader to his or her way of thinking. Paragraphs of persuasion are much more common than paragraphs of argument because writers seldom argue without also trying to persuade. For example, a writer is not likely to write an editorial for the student newspaper arguing the case for shorter school days or less homework without also trying to persuade someone to take action on these issues. Following is an example of a paragraph of persuasion.

In our day the Constitution has been used to shield racketeers, gangsters, and those suspected of radicalism from the necessity of testifying about their activities before courts and legislative investigating committees. It has prevented the censorship of books, magazines, and movies offensive to many groups; upset the convictions of criminals found guilty by juries; and blocked religious instruction in the public schools. Constitutional restraints (Fourth Amendment) on police make warrants necessary for searches of homes and offices for evidence of crime and forbid the police to use intensive interrogation or drugs to get confessions from persons accused of crimes. As a result, some citizens believe that the courts are soft on criminals and that constitutional rights that protect enemies of society and members of despised political minorities should be abolished or, at least, limited. The ordinary law-abiding citizen has no need of such protection, they argue. With crime rising in our major cities, with juvenile delinquency spreading among youth, with the spread of illegal gambling, drug addiction, and sex offenses, with the competition between the United States and the Soviet Union for world leadership, should we not strengthen the powers of government and law-enforcement officers?

The writer introduces his opinion concerning constitutional rights by citing several controversial applications of the Constitution. These facts gain the attention of the reader and arouse curiosity as to the purpose of the paragraph. The writer then describes the desire of some citizens to abolish or limit constitutional rights and the current social and political situation. He ends with a question that invites the reader to agree with his idea that the powers of government and law enforcement officers should be strengthened.

Although the writer relies heavily on facts, he also uses many words and phrases that appeal to a reader's emotions; for example, "racketeers," "gangsters," "soft on criminals," "despised political minorities," "ordinary law-abiding citizen," "juvenile delinquency," "illegal gambling," "drug addiction," "sex offenses," "competition between the United States and the Soviet Union." Such words and phrases play on the readers' fear of crime and criminals, their desire to be considered law-abiding citizens, and their patriotic feelings.

Remember that although the use of emotionally charged language is a common persuasive device, you should not rely on it too heavily. Instead, support your ideas with solid factual evidence. (See Chapter 15, "Critical Thinking and Language.")

Applying the Process of Writing

You may be familiar with the phrase, "the powers of persuasion." The ability to use persuasion does constitute a form of power, especially in a democratic society founded upon the idea of freedom of choice. The persuasive paragraph is used by the private citizen writing a letter to the editor of a local newspaper, by the lawyer writing an appeal, and by the ecological activist writing a pamphlet urging the control of environmental pollution. Whenever your convictions are strong and your purpose is to convince others to subscribe to your cause, opinion, or candidate, the paragraph of persuasion is the form you should use.

Pre-Writing. After establishing your topic and purpose, consider both the tone and mood that you wish to create. Do you want to convey an emotional or a dispassionate tone? Do you want to elicit a mood of calm agreement from your readers, or do you wish to inspire outrage, indignation, or alarm? To develop your position, you will need to analyze your audience thoughtfully. Are they neutral about the subject, or do they presently hold opinions that are opposed to yours? If your readers do hold opposing opinions, what are their reasons?

Once you have your audience clearly in mind, determine which reasons will be most appealing or convincing to them. A solid, well-reasoned case buttressed with concrete examples and verifiable facts is your most effective means of making an impact. Indeed, it is much more sound and effective than emotionally charged language or deceptive reasoning.

Consider your organizational options carefully. A strong organization can enhance your arguments. There are five basic ways to organize a persuasive paragraph:

1. Begin with your weakest argument and build to your strongest argument in order to leave your reader with a forceful conclusion in mind.
2. Gain your reader's attention and approval by mentioning your strongest argument first. Then follow it up with other supporting arguments.
3. Begin with the argument that is most acceptable to your readers and then gradually introduce them to those ideas with which they are more likely to take exception.
4. Utilize a form of comparison and contrast to highlight the weaknesses of the opposing side and the strengths of your own. Begin by answering the arguments of your opposition and then introduce your own arguments.
5. Reverse the order of the comparison and contrast outlined above. Present your case first and then pinpoint weaknesses within the arguments of the other side.

First Draft and Revision. The topic sentence for a paragraph of persuasion is a statement of belief. It should leave no doubts concerning the issue you are discussing and the opinion you hold regarding it. This statement should then be followed by your supporting arguments. Remember that the quality of your arguments is more important than the quantity, and that specific facts and examples are more persuasive than empty generalizations or slanted and emotional language.

In revising, keep the following concerns in mind:

–Does every reason support the stated opinion? (Unity)
–Will your reasons and language inspire the desired mood?
–Have you provided enough information for your readers to make an informed decision? (Adequate Detail)
–Are your arguments arranged to have the greatest impact on your audience? (Coherence)

Exercise Writing the Paragraph of Persuasion

Write a paragraph of persuasion in which you develop your opinion on some controversial issue, such as nuclear power or an issue in your local community. Complete the following steps:

Pre-Writing: Once you have selected a specific issue, write a topic sentence that clearly indicates both the topic and your opinion. Identify your audience and their opinions. Develop and select reasons that would be convincing to your readers. Support these reasons with verifiable details. Organize your reasons.

First Draft: Develop your pre-writing notes into the fuller form of a draft. Use reasons and language that are consistent with your tone and mood. Try to appeal to logic rather than emotion.

Revision: Go over your rough draft several times. Strengthen your reasons with appropriate details. Delete any details or reasons that relate only superficially to your opinion. Make sure there is a logical progression to your ideas. When you have fully developed your content, proofread for mechanical correctness.

Part 5 The Paragraph of Comparison and Contrast

Certain paragraphs do not fit into one general category. Although they have unique characteristics, they may be used for any of several different purposes, including explanation, description, or persuasion. One such paragraph is the paragraph that compares or contrasts details.

Using Comparison

In a paragraph of comparison, a writer shows the similarities between two or more people, places, or things. The primary purpose of such a paragraph can be the comparison itself. To achieve this purpose, a writer would present several points of similarity, along with supporting details. For example, a writer setting out to compare Earth and Mars might note similarities in temperature, pressure, atmospheric gases, and topography.

Comparison can also play a secondary role. In the following paragraph the writer's purpose is to describe the surface of Mars, a purpose achieved largely through comparison.

> In appearance, at least, Mars is not so different from the Earth. Many regions of the Earth must resemble Mars so closely that you could not tell which was which from a photograph. An artist friend of mine who has made a name for himself depicting planetary scenes tells me that Mars is his hardest subject. Editors balk at paying for a picture supposedly representing Mars when their readers are likely to mistake it for the country around Reno or Las Vegas, for Mars is practically all dry land and most of that land is desert.
>
> —ROBERT S. RICHARDSON

The writer of this paragraph used a brief anecdote to develop the comparison between Earth and Mars. Other techniques include the use of one or more examples and the presentation of facts and statistics.

Using Contrast

In using contrast, the writer shows how two things differ. The writer of the following paragraph contrasts the inspiring and the challenging aspects of Indian history.

> The history of India provides both an inspiration and a challenge to the historian. It inspires by its vast range and scope, its color, its variety, its rich cluster of personalities; it challenges with its complexities, its long periods of obscurity, its unfamiliar movements, and its stark contrasts between luxury and poverty, between gentleness and cruelty, creation and destruction. For the few with gorgeous processions and rainbow pageantry there were the many with mud huts and a handful of rice or millet a day, with the burning heaven for a canopy and the stifling dust for perfume.—PERCIVAL SPEAR

This paragraph captures the duality of Indian life through three contrasts: the contrast of broad generalizations (its variety versus its complexities), the contrast of narrower ideas (luxury versus poverty), and the contrast of specific information (the few with gorgeous possessions versus the many with mud huts). The paragraph exemplifies writing in which broad concepts are distilled into a few descriptive sentences.

The writer of the following paragraph focuses on a much more limited topic.

> How does one determine whether a law is just or unjust? A just law is a man-made code that squares with the moral law or the law of God. An unjust law is a code that is out of harmony with the moral law. To put it in the terms of St. Thomas Aquinas: An unjust law is a human law that is not rooted in eternal law and natural law. Any law that uplifts human personality is just. Any law that degrades human personality is unjust.—MARTIN LUTHER KING, JR.

The writer presents criteria for judging the justice of a law with definition-like clarity. Each statement about just laws is contrasted with a corresponding statement about unjust laws.

Combining Comparison and Contrast

Often, writers combine comparison and contrast in the same paragraph. In the following example, the writer first presents the similarities between the experiences of the Indian and the white person, then draws a contrast between their value systems.

> At the time of the Creation, the Cherokee say, the white person was given a stone, and the Indian a piece of silver. Despising the stone, the white person threw it away. Finding the silver equally worthless, the Indian discarded it. Later the white person pocketed the silver as a source of material power; the Indian revered the stone as a source of sacred power. This prophetic story underscores the profound differences in Indian and white value systems. In time, the Indian would be forced to use the white person's currency as

a medium of exchange, but the white person would never appreciate the Indian's sense of the cosmic power invested in an ordinary pebble.—PETER NABOKOV

The writer of the following example takes a different approach to organizing a paragraph of comparison and contrast.

It is to be assumed that if people were to live this life like a poem, they would be able to look upon the sunset of their lives as their happiest period, and instead of trying to postpone the much feared old age, be able actually to look forward to it, and gradually build up to it as the best and happiest period of existence. In my efforts to compare and contrast Eastern and Western life, I have found no differences that are absolute except in this matter of the attitude toward age, which is sharp and clearcut and permits of no intermediate positions. The differences in our attitude toward sex, toward women, and toward work, play, and achievement are all relative. The relationship between husband and wife in China is not essentially different from that in the West, nor even the relationship between parent and child. Not even the ideas of individual liberty and democracy and the relationship between the people and their ruler are, after all, so different. But in the matter of our attitude toward age, the difference is absolute, and the East and the West take exactly opposite points of view.—LIN YUTANG

Applying the Process of Writing

Whenever there are decisions or evaluations to be made, comparison and contrast provides a useful format for presenting ideas. This type of writing may be an informal note to a friend comparing two movies, or it may someday appear as an official document detailing the pro's and con's of a corporate merger. In either case, the purpose will be to put the facts before your readers so that they may either draw their own conclusions or see how you reached your decision.

Pre-Writing. As you begin to write, it is important to have your topic and purpose clearly in mind so that you can determine an adequate focus for your paragraph. There may be many similarities or differences between two subjects, but your task will be to identify those that are major, significant, or pivotal. These will provide the focus for your writing.

Developing a focus will help you to generate a list of specific details. It will also guide you in eliminating details that are only tangential. Finally, focus and purpose will influence your choice of organization. For instance, you may compare or contrast your subjects point by point or you may develop one subject completely before discussing the other.

First Draft and Revision. In writing your first draft, begin by crafting a topic sentence that clearly states both the subjects to be compared and the point you are trying to establish through this comparison. This topic sentence serves as a reference for you in developing your ideas and later for your reader in absorbing the complex content of this form. As you write, try to enhance the logical flow of your supporting ideas. Depending on your topic, your organization might be spatial, order of importance, or order of familiarity.

Once you have completed a first draft, consider the following points as you revise:

- Do all of the details relate specifically to the main point of the paragraph? (Unity)
- Do the points of comparison or contrast move easily from one to another? (Coherence)
- Have transitional words and phrases such as "in the same fashion" or "on the contrary" been used to highlight the points being made? (Emphasis and Coherence)
- Have both subjects been developed with adequate detail?

Exercise Writing Paragraphs of Comparison and Contrast

Write a paragraph in which you compare or contrast two places or people you know well. Complete the following steps:

Pre-Writing: Identify your two subjects and develop a list of specific details for each. Compare the two lists in order to identify significant similarities or differences. Then, considering your topic and purpose, add to and delete from your list of details. Experiment with different methods for organizing these points.

First Draft: Translate your pre-writing decisions into a first draft. Write a topic sentence that states your subjects and the main point you are trying to make about them. Add specific details that will further clarify the differences or similarities.

Revision: First determine if your paragraph achieves its purpose in making the comparison. Make sure that your points are easy to follow and sufficiently developed. To improve coherence, add appropriate transitional words. After you have completed your content revisions, proofread for mechanical correctness.

Part 6   The Paragraph of Analogy

An analogy is a comparison in which something unfamiliar is compared with something similar but more familiar to the reader. Like the paragraph of comparison and contrast, the paragraph of analogy can be used for several purposes. Often, an analogy is used to classify an abstract concept that would otherwise be difficult to explain. In the following paragraph of analogy, the participants in the agricultural system in California's San Joaquin Valley are compared with the human body.

> The backbone of the valley's prosperity is the farmer who grows the many fruits and vegetables. But if the farmer, or grower, is the backbone, the blood and sinew are supplied by the farm worker, usually a migrant, who labors long and hard to make the dream of a "Golden State" a reality. Without farm workers, there would be no four-billion-dollar-a-year agribusiness. Without them, the soil, perhaps, would revert to its condition of 150 years ago—an arid, wind-sucked land covered with sagebrush and inhabited mainly by the coyote, bobcat, and ring-tailed pheasant.—JAMES SANTIBAÑEZ

The analogy in this paragraph is a detail, used along with other details to support the main idea: the farm worker is essential to California's agriculture. In the next example, the analogy between the art of war as practiced by human beings and by ants *is* the main idea, which is explained by the details that are included in the paragraph.

> It is a curious phenomenon of nature that only two species practice the art of war—human beings and ants, both of which, ironically, maintain complex social organizations. This does not mean that only humans and ants engage in the murder of their own kind. Many animals of the same species kill each other, but only humans and ants have practiced the science of organized destruction, employing their massed numbers in violent combat and relying on strategy and tactics to meet developing situations or to capitalize on the weaknesses in the strategy and tactics of the other side. The longest continuous war ever fought between countries lasted thirty years. The longest ant war ever recorded lasted six-and-a-half weeks, or whatever the corresponding units would be in ant reckoning.—NORMAN COUSINS

Applying the Process of Writing

Because understanding is broadened by relating the familiar to the unfamiliar, analogy is a very effective teaching tool. At some point, everyone assumes the role of "teacher," and you will discover opportunities to use analogy not only in the classroom, but also in speeches, in descriptions of a new product or idea, or in explanations detailing the procedures of a job.

Pre-Writing. After you have identified your purpose for writing the paragraph of analogy, you will employ many of the same procedures you followed in writing a paragraph of comparison. Since one of your subjects will be less familiar to your readers than the other, it is very important for you to identify the points of comparison carefully and to generate enough specific detail to make the correspondence clear to others. For clarity, you may decide to organize your comparisons point by point.

First Draft and Revision: Begin your first draft by writing a topic sentence that introduces your two subjects and the correspondences you have identified between them. As you write, include any further details that will make your comparisons clearer. Try to maintain a direct, uncomplicated style of presentation. When you have worked through a first draft, make revisions by considering the following points:

—Are the points of correspondence between the two subjects clearly highlighted? (Emphasis)

—Is there a logical development in the order of the points' presentation? (Coherence)

—Is enough detail provided to make the unfamiliar concept easily understood? (Adequate Detail)

Exercise Writing a Paragraph of Analogy

Select two subjects for comparison and develop them into a paragraph of analogy. Complete the following steps:

Pre-Writing: Having selected a topic, keep in mind that your purpose is to clarify an unfamiliar or abstract idea by comparing it with one that is more familiar or concrete. (Generate a list of specific details for each subject.) Focus your analogy by identifying the points of correspondence between your two subjects. Select a method of organization that will facilitate your readers' understanding of the unfamiliar concept.

First Draft: Write a topic sentence that states your subjects and the similarities between them that you plan to develop. As you write, try to balance your purpose with your development. You may need to devote more attention to the unfamiliar concept.

Revision: Read through your first draft several times. Make sure that the intention of your paragraph is clearly stated. Check to see that each point of comparison is adequately identified and carefully developed. Delete any distracting details. Reinforce your coherence with the addition of transitional words and phrases. When your analogy is fully developed, proofread your work for any remaining errors in spelling, grammar, or mechanics.

Guidelines for Writing and Revising Paragraphs

These Guidelines will help to remind you of the qualities necessary for good paragraphs. However, your writing procedure should also follow the steps in the Guidelines for the Process of Writing on page 105.

1. Does the paragraph deal with only one main idea?

2. Does the paragraph have a topic sentence that states the main idea?

3. Does the topic sentence have a subject? Does it express some tone or attitude toward the subject?

4. Does the body of the paragraph support or explain the main idea in the topic sentence? Does the paragraph demonstrate unity?

5. Is the paragraph coherent? Are the ideas presented in a logical order and clearly linked to one another? Is the order of ideas appropriate for the subject of the paragraph?

6. Are there transitional words and expressions that reinforce coherence by showing relationships among the ideas in the paragraph?

7. Are there enough details to engage the reader's interest?

8. Does the paragraph work to evoke the desired mood?

9. Are tone, mood, and point of view consistent?

10. Does the paragraph have a carefully determined emphasis?

11. If it is a paragraph of narration, does the story or anecdote achieve the purpose of the paragraph?

12. If it is a paragraph of description, does it capture the essence of what is being described? the atmosphere of a place? the quality of a thing?

13. If it is a paragraph of definition, does it clarify a concept or a term?

14. If it is an expository paragraph, do the details adequately explain the main idea? If explaining a process, does the paragraph follow a step-by-step order? If explaining something that happened, are the reasons convincing? If supporting an opinion, are the reasons logical and valid?

15. If it is a paragraph of persuasion, is it developed by the kinds of information that would effect your purpose?

16. If it is a paragraph of comparison, does it compare similarities? If contrast, does it show differences?

17. If it is a paragraph of analogy, does it compare something unfamiliar with something familiar?

SUMMARY AND APPLICATIONS

1. Several different types of paragraphs are available to you as a writer. The unique characteristics of each type allow you to suit the writing you do to any particular situation.

2. Narrative paragraphs are used to relate stories or anecdotes. They are generally organized in chronological order.

3. Descriptive paragraphs recreate an image or situation through the use of sensory details. These details are usually organized in spatial order. Good descriptive paragraphs reveal the internal, as well as the external, characteristics of their subjects.

4. Expository, or explanatory, paragraphs can explain a process, give definitions, or offer reasons to support an idea. The most common methods of organization for expository writing are order of familiarity and order of importance.

5. Paragraphs of comparison or contrast point out the similarities or differences of two or more people, places, or things. Comparison is usually done in order to point out some striking link between the two subjects.

Applications in Other Subject Areas

Science. Researchers such as Jacques Cousteau and Carl Sagan have made us aware that science need not be discussed in a dry or technical manner. A subject can instead be presented using a narrative or descriptive style that emphasizes its wonder and beauty. Choose one of the following subjects. Write a paragraph on that subject which departs from the more traditional expository style.

a nova	cell division	a molecule
a coral reef	migration	tides

Business. Choose two of the situations described below. Write paragraphs that meet the needs of each one as effectively as possible. Choose your paragraph types carefully.

1. You have developed a way to streamline one of the procedures where you work. Present your idea in a memo.

2. You are writing a letter of recommendation for a friend.

3. You are evaluating the effectiveness of two similar businesses.

Chapter 10

The
Composition

You now understand the steps of thinking and composing that are called the process of writing. You have seen how the techniques of the process can be applied to many different types of paragraphs. Now you will apply all this knowledge to a different situation—the development of a composition.

A composition is a piece of writing that develops an idea or expands a topic in a coherent and unified manner. Any of the paragraph types you studied in Chapter 9 can be used to develop different aspects of the idea, thus making possible an in-depth treatment. The writer need only be certain that the paragraphs adequately develop the topic or idea, are logically connected, and form a unified whole.

In this chapter you will trace the development of a composition through all three stages of the writing process—pre-writing, writing the first draft, and revising. You will also apply the process yourself to create a composition of your own.

Part 1   The Definition of a Composition

A composition is a larger piece of writing than those you have dealt with up to this point, but you are already familiar with its structure. This is because a composition can be thought of as an expanded paragraph. Both types of writing develop a single main idea, and both should demonstrate unity and coherence. Even the types of compositions parallel the types of paragraphs—narrative, descriptive, and expository. The main difference between paragraphs and compositions is that a paragraph is a group of sentences with a main idea, while a composition is a group of paragraphs.

A composition can be divided into three main parts. The **introductory paragraph** presents the main idea of the composition. The **body paragraphs** explain or support the main idea. Body paragraphs may be developed in different ways. For example, an expository composition might include one paragraph that describes the subject, one that makes a point by narrating an incident, and several other paragraphs that simply explain supporting points in a very straightforward manner. Lastly, the **concluding paragraph** restates the main idea, summarizes the information that has been presented in preceding paragraphs, or makes a final comment.

Read the following example of an expository composition. Try to identify the types of paragraphs that are used.

SIGNS OF AN ANGRY GODDESS

Even though it is named for the mythic goddess of love, there is nothing very fetching about the planet Venus. It is veiled in a dense atmosphere of carbon dioxide, laced with corrosive clouds of sulfuric acid, and its surface temperatures hover around 900° Fahrenheit. Liquid water, if it ever existed, has long since vanished. Nothing, not even the hardiest microbes, could survive for long in this cauldron.

Yet Venus, the second planet from the sun . . ., shares significant characteristics with its neighbor, Earth. It is nearly the same size and density, and by astronomy's vast measures, is a similar distance from the sun (67 million miles versus 93 million for the earth). Now it appears that Venus resembles the earth in still another way. Scientists recently announced that Venus seems to be pockmarked with giant volcanoes, at least one of which erupted as recently as five years ago.

The evidence comes from a remarkable automated observatory called Pioneer Venus. Since late in 1978 the 810 pound machine has been circling Venus, probing it with a battery of instruments, including radar. The devices, said Pioneer Venus scientists meeting at NASA's Ames Research Center near Mountain View, California, have revealed that under Venus' clouds is a landscape almost as dramatic as the earth's: sprawling plateaus, mountains as high as Everest and great chasms similar to terrestrial rift valleys.

Analyzing data from Pioneer's ultraviolet spectrometer, . . . scientists found that 1978 sulfur dioxide levels in the Venusian atmosphere were fifty times as high as expected. Since then, the sulfur dioxide levels have been slowly tapering off, just as they drop after a major volcanic eruption on earth. Another investigator . . . disclosed that an on-board instrument called a plasma-wave detector had recorded repeated lightning discharges over two mountain regions. On earth, such electric activity commonly accompanies volcanic outbursts.

Still more tantalizing, the lightning was detected above two mountainous regions called Beta and Atla, which sit astride the Venusian equator. These areas appear to be supported by younger, denser rock, a characteristic of terrestrial volcanoes. . . . In addition, radar reconnaissance showed material radiating from Beta that looked uncannily like recent lava flows.

The researchers are elated about their long-distance snooping, but not simply for scholarly reasons. They note that a planet like Venus provides a real-life laboratory for understanding such essential questions as global weather patterns and the spread of acid rain, whose most corrosive ingredient is sulfur dioxide. Venus is also valuable for studying the buildup of carbon dioxide in the atmosphere, which increases global temperatures. Says the U.S. Geological Survey's Harold Masursky of the . . . Venus findings: "These are not just nice things to know. They may be vital to our survival."—*Time*

This composition deals with one main idea—the discovery of volcanoes on Venus. The title and introductory paragraph introduce the reader to the subject with a familiar allusion to ancient mythology and then present a vivid image of the harsh planet that is to be the subject of the written piece. The body paragraphs develop the main idea in a variety of ways. Comparison is used in the first paragraph, description in the second, and facts and statistics are utilized throughout. This variety adds a great deal of interest to what might otherwise be a rather dry discussion of a recent discovery. Finally, the conclusion summarizes the main idea and pinpoints its significance.

Part 2   Choosing Your Subject

The first step in writing any composition is to decide on a subject. What is worth writing about? It is anything worth thinking about. What is a worthwhile subject for your composition? It is anything that interests you. Remember, however, that you must develop your subject in a coherent and unified manner. Therefore, you must ask yourself whether you know enough about your subject to discuss it in some depth. If you do not, are you willing to research the subject enough to allow you to develop it more fully? Will you be able to do the required research? Is the information available?

Limiting Your Subject

The composition you will write for this chapter will consist of five paragraphs and will total approximately 500 words. Because you will not be able to develop any broad or general subject within those limits, you will have to limit or narrow the scope of your subject. You will recall that there are several techniques you can use in the narrowing process. If you are writing about a personal subject, you can use brainstorming and clustering to generate some topics. If your subject requires more objective treatment, read some general articles or scan the table of contents of a book on the subject.

To see how this narrowing process works, consider the subject of communication. It is a vast subject, and adequate treatment of it would fill many volumes. To limit it, you might do some preliminary reading in an encyclopedia. You could then follow a process similar to the following, continually dividing each large subject into two smaller ones. In each pair, the subject in boldface type is the one chosen for further subdivision.

UNLIMITED:	Communication
SLIGHT LIMITATION:	History of Communication
	Modern Communication
2000-WORD LIMITATION:	Postal Service Today
	Television Today
1000-WORD LIMITATION:	Television Entertainment Today
	Informative Television Today
500-WORD LIMITATION:	Consumer Information *via* Television
	Network News

Exercises Choosing and Limiting the Subject

A. The subjects on the following list are too large for adequate treatment in a 500-word composition. Within each subject, find three narrow subjects suitable for a composition of that length. Keep your list of subjects for a later exercise.

1. Energy
2. Government
3. Superstition
4. Cities
5. Transportation
6. Sports
7. Art
8. Rivers
9. Stars
10. Literature

B. Choose and narrow a subject for your own five-paragraph composition.

Determining the Purpose

Each decision you make during the pre-writing stage has an impact on every other element you consider. As you select and limit your subject, for example, you automatically make other preliminary decisions about how you want to treat that subject, and about what your purpose in writing the composition is. You may decide that you simply want to present your reader with a clear explanation of your subject. If so, you would write an expository composition. On the other hand, you may want to create a vivid description of your subject or to tell an amusing story concerning it. If so, you would write a descriptive or narrative composition.

There are also other elements you would consider at this time. For example, you would have to identify your audience and make some initial decisions about the tone and mood you want to convey. Your audience, you remember, helps to determine the type and amount of background information and supporting details you will need to provide. It also guides you as to how formal and technical your language can be. The tone is your attitude toward the subject, an attitude you may want to communicate to your reader. The mood is the feeling or atmosphere you want your reader to experience.

Once these pre-writing decisions have been made, you should have a fairly clear idea of the controlling purpose of your composition. It is important to write down a clear statement of the purpose and to keep it in front of you through all stages of your composition. This is because your composition and your controlling purpose must work hand in hand; your composition should achieve what your controlling purpose says you are setting out to do.

In a statement of controlling purpose, often called a **thesis statement,** the most common verbs are *to explain, to show, to analyze, to demonstrate.* For example, if you chose to write on the subject of network news, your controlling purpose might be stated like this:

> The controlling purpose of this composition is to analyze whether TV news programs adequately inform the public.

This statement will not appear in your composition, at least not in the form of a statement of purpose, nor will it be your title. It is intended for your own use as a way of controlling your thinking and writing.

Additional Pre-Writing Choices

The decisions described above must be considered no matter what type of composition you write. However, you will also have to make some other pre-writing choices based on the specific type of composition you decide to develop.

The Narrative Composition. To enjoy a narrative, a reader must be able to visualize every detail. This means that you, the writer, must provide those details. Consider and write down ideas for the following aspects of a narrative:

CHARACTER: the people or animals in the story

SETTING: the place where the events in a narrative occur and the time frame of the story

CONFLICT: the struggle or problem that is central to the narrative

THEME: the dominant impression or idea the writer wants to convey to the reader

POINT OF VIEW: the eyes and mind through which the story is told. The writer may choose to use **first-person point of view,** where the narrator is a part of the action and refers to himself or herself as *I*, or **third-person point of view,** where the narrator is outside the action of the story.

The Descriptive Composition. To create a vivid picture in the "mind's eye" of your reader, consider the following points:

DOMINANT IMPRESSION: the feature of the subject that affects you the most. This is the detail that would be the center of emphasis in the composition.

the position from which you will view the scene, object, or person. Details must be limited to those things that can be seen, heard, touched, tasted, and smelled from that vantage point.

The Expository Compositon. Each type of expository composition—the composition that explains a process, the composition that defines, the composition that gives reasons, and the composition that persuades—has its own particular purpose. Make certain that you clearly identify the type of composition you are developing, and make appropriate pre-writing choices. See Chapter 9 for more information on expository writing.

Exercises Determining the Controlling Purpose

A. In the exercise on page 182 you limited each of ten broad subjects to three possible subjects for compositions of 500 words. Choose three of these limited subjects and write for each a statement of the controlling purpose that you would follow in developing the composition. Save your statements for later use.

B. Write a one-sentence controlling purpose for your own composition.

Part 3   Pre-Writing: Writing Down Your Ideas

You have chosen a subject and limited it. You have also established a controlling purpose for your composition. Your next step is to write down your ideas on the subject you have chosen. These details may include sensory impressions, facts and statistics, examples, incidents, or anecdotes.

The purpose of this step is to get as many ideas as possible down on paper. If your subject is personal, details may be generated through brainstorming. If the subject is more objective, you may need to do some research. You will organize and polish those ideas later, so do not concern yourself with order, relative importance, or phrasing. At the top of your paper, write your title if you already have one. If not, leave the space blank, to be filled in later. Write your controlling purpose below your title space so that you can use it to guide your thinking. Then begin to jot down whatever ideas come to mind. Write quickly, in note form, so that you do not interrupt the flow of ideas.

As you begin to write down ideas, you may find that you do not have as many ideas on your subject as you thought you had. You may have to do more extensive reading or research in the subject you have chosen. You may find that you are not certain of the accuracy of some points. If so, you will have to check these points in reference books or other source material. (See Chapter 14, "The Library and Its Reference Materials.") When you have completed any additional research, you can add to your list of ideas.

Your first list of ideas might look something like this:

TENTATIVE TITLE:

CONTROLLING PURPOSE: The controlling purpose of this composition is to analyze whether TV news programs adequately inform the public.

a half hour of news is too short

television too dependent on visual stories

everybody watches television

television polls have an undue influence

oversimplification in TV news

shallowness

depth possible in newspapers

television dependent on brief stories

paternal newscasters

newspapers more idea-oriented

television more personality-oriented

Jefferson's notion of an informed populace

uninformed or misinformed public will act foolishly

intrusive commercials

rise in newspaper cost

decline in newspaper readership

dependence on TV news

economics of television

emergency programing

famous newscaster

famous reporters

portable cameras

history of TV news

ratings of news shows

When you have finished your list, carefully evaluate your details. Is each one related to your topic? Will every detail fit the type of composition you are writing? Does the information fit the controlling purpose? Can more details be added to support the main idea?

A review of the preceding list of ideas will show you that some are not closely related to the topic or controlling purpose of the composition. The following unrelated ideas should be eliminated so that the focus of the composition remains clear and well-defined. As you continue to write, however, you may also delete or add other ideas.

everybody watches television	rise in newspaper cost
television polls have an undue influence	emergency programing
	famous reporters
	portable cameras

Two additional ideas are too broad to be treated within the limit of 500 words. The unmanageable ideas should also be eliminated.

economics of television	history of TV news

As you develop your composition further, you may find that some of the remaining ideas are not so appropriate to your purpose as they had seemed earlier, or that some ideas cannot be adequately developed within the limits of your composition. If so, do not hesitate to eliminate those ideas. Your composition will be further improved by the elimination of every inappropriate or unmanageable idea.

After you have reviewed your list of ideas and eliminated all those that are unrelated or unmanageable, study those that remain in search of ideas for your tentative title. Try to write two or three possible titles at this time. They will also help to focus your work as you write, and you can eliminate two later. Possible titles for this subject include the following:

What's the Use of Network News?
Sorry, Mr. Jefferson
Network News Is Not Enough

Exercises Writing Down the Ideas

A. In Exercise A on page 185, you wrote a controlling purpose for each of three limited subjects. Select two of these controlling purposes and list under them all the ideas that come to your mind for developing that subject. After studying your lists, (1) eliminate every idea that is irrelevant to the topic or controlling purpose, and (2) eliminate every idea that cannot adequately be developed in a 500-word composition. Save these lists for later use.

B. Do the same as above for the subject you have chosen for your composition.

Part 4 Pre-Writing: Organizing Your Ideas

You have eliminated those ideas that are unmanageable within the 500-word limit of your composition and those that are not directly relevant to your topic or controlling purpose. The ideas that are left are those that are manageable and relevant. It remains now to order them into a coherent pattern.

First, examine your remaining list of ideas for related details that could be grouped together into idea clusters. Then try to identify the major point that each cluster represents. Sometimes, one of the ideas within the cluster will be general enough to fulfill this function. At other times, you will have to develop a statement of the main point and add it to your notes.

In the ideas on network news programs, notice that "oversimplification in TV news" is a major point in support of the controlling purpose. The ideas below are related to this point.

> a half hour of news is too short
> television too dependent on visual stories
> shallowness
> television dependent on brief stories
> paternal newscasters
> intrusive commercials

A second major point is "depth possible in newspapers," and the following ideas are directly related.

newspapers more idea-oriented
television more personality-oriented
decline in newspaper readership
public dependence on TV news

The third major point seems to be "Jefferson's notion of an informed populace," with the related idea that an "uninformed or misinformed public will act foolishly."

There are now three major ideas to be developed.

oversimplification in TV news
depth possible in newspapers
Jefferson's notion of an informed populace

Two other ideas—*ratings of news shows* and *popular newscasters*—do not fit into any of the three categories. Therefore, they can be deleted at this point. This can also be a good time to adjust your controlling purpose. For example, given the information that has been generated for this composition, a better purpose might be "to show that network news programs do not adequately inform the public."

Choosing an Effective Order

The first job of organization has been accomplished: grouping into three major categories. The second job is to determine in what order each of the major points should be developed to enable you to present the reader with a logical progression of ideas. You may, of course, use one of the orders described in earlier chapters. These include chronological order, spatial order, order of importance, most familiar to least familiar, simple to complex, or comparison and contrast. All of these organizational methods are just general guidelines, however. You must also rely on your own common sense in order to determine an organization.

Begin by asking yourself which of the major points, if any,

cannot be understood without the others. Clearly these must follow the others. This technique can be applied to the composition on the subject of television news as follows: First, review the purpose of the composition.

> The controlling purpose of this composition is to show that TV news programs do not adequately inform the public.

Since the composition will be building to the conclusion that network news programs do not adequately inform the public, it seems logical that the major idea of oversimplification in television news should come last. Jefferson's notion of an informed populace would logically come first, since it establishes a reason for concern over the inadequacy of television news. The comparison of the depth possible in newspapers can fall between the two, partly as a link between the past—the informed populace that Jefferson had in mind—and the present—the ill-informed public of the television age. Thus the final order of ideas in developing the composition will be

> Jefferson's notion of an informed populace
> depth possible in newspapers
> oversimplication in TV news

The groups of subordinate ideas can now be organized into a logical order of development under their respective major points. New ideas are almost certain to come to you at this time. Do not hesitate to add or eliminate at this stage.

At this point in the organization it was necessary to do some additional reading on Jefferson's notion of an informed populace because that idea lacked sufficient supporting ideas. The grouped ideas for the composition on the subject of television news programs might now resemble the list on the following page. This completed, organized list becomes the writing plan for the composition.

> Jefferson's notion of an informed populace
>> vital to democracy
>> political decisions based on reason
>> uninformed public would focus on personality
>> fear of demagogues

depth possible in newspapers
　　long, careful analyses of issues
　　declining newspaper readership
　　increasing dependence on television

oversimplification of TV news
　　television too dependent on visual stories
　　intrusive commercials
　　dependence on brief stories
　　shallowness
　　paternal newscasters

You may wish to put your writing plan into outline form. See Section 18 in the Handbook for a discussion of outlines.

Exercises Organizing the Ideas

A. Refer to the lists of ideas you developed for two subjects in Exercise A on page 188. Organize each set of ideas into three major points and related subordinate ideas. Then order the ideas in the sequence in which you would expect to develop them in a 500-word composition. Save this work for use in a later exercise.

B. Do the same as above with the ideas for your composition.

Part 5　Writing the First Draft

You now have a statement of controlling purpose and a writing plan for the body of your composition to work from. You have also identified your audience and made other pre-writing decisions. You are now ready to begin the actual writing of a first draft, which will include all the information in your plan and also an introduction and a conclusion.

While the work you have already done will serve as a base for the writing itself, you may find that you have a difficult time beginning. If you find it so, begin with the second paragraph, which is the first paragraph that appears on your outline. The information for this paragraph is already at hand, and therefore ready to be put in your first draft. The introduction can be written later, even as the last writing you do.

Keep in mind that you are writing a first draft. This is simply your first opportunity to work with the material you have developed. You will still be able to explore new ideas and experiment with different approaches. For now, concentrate on getting your ideas expressed in a logical manner, and do not worry too much about sentence structure, word choice, or punctuation. These matters can be adjusted during revision.

Remember that the composition will have three parts—the introduction, the body, and the conclusion. The composition will be only as strong as the weakest of these parts.

The Introduction

The introduction to a composition serves two purposes: it *introduces* the reader to the subject, and it *interests* the reader in the subject. In a five-paragraph composition, the introduction should be limited to a single paragraph. Sometimes this paragraph begins with a statement of the main idea and then outlines the information that is to follow. More often, however, the paragraph leads the reader from a more general idea to the specific topic. Many different techniques can be used to construct an effective introduction of the second type. For example, a writer may choose to use a quotation, startling statistics, or an interesting anecdote.

The composition on the subject of television news programs might begin with any of the following introductions:

QUOTATION: Mails from the North—the East—the West—the South—whence, according to some curious etymologists, comes the magical word NEWS.—THOMAS DE QUINCEY

STATISTIC: According to a recent survey conducted by The Center for the Study of Public Information, a full sixty percent of American voters get all their information about political issues from nightly television news programs.

ANECDOTE: Over lunch one day last week, I asked a friend of mine whether she thought the water control bill should pass. "I don't know anything about it," she said. "Was it on TV?"

Each of these introductions goes beyond merely getting the reader's attention; each tells the reader what the subject of the composition will be: specifically, the news. But two of the three, the final two, are stronger because they raise the key issue of the composition: the question of the adequacy of television news as the public's primary source of information. The first might be strengthened as follows:

It is certainly true that news comes from all directions, but if we get our news solely from television, it might be said that we are getting more magic than fact.

Regardless of the device used to open a composition, the introduction should never be merely a lifeless restatement of the controlling purpose such as the following:

This composition will discuss the shortcomings of television news programs.

Remember that the controlling purpose is a device used to keep the composition focused on a single purpose; it will never serve the two functions of an adequate introduction—to introduce the subject and to interest the reader.

Exercises Writing an Effective Introduction

A. Choose three of the following introductions. Rewrite them in order to make them both informative and interesting. Use a quotation, a statistic, or an anecdote.

1. It seems to me that the invention of the camera changed our understanding of cultures around the world.

2. Everyone should know something about the history of his or her local community.

3. We really know very little about this small and fragile planet we live on.

193

4. Many people underestimate the skill required to train animals to perform in films.

5. The Nobel Prizes have an interesting history.

B. Write a first paragraph for your composition. Remember that it should both introduce the subject and interest your reader. Review your introduction to decide whether it completely covers the controlling purpose of your composition. The first sample introduction by Thomas de Quincey, for example, would have been misleading without the additional statement. The reader would have expected the composition to treat news in general rather than television news specifically.

The Body

The body of the composition is the longest section. Here the points are made, the issues raised and discussed. In a five-paragraph composition, the body consists of the three paragraphs in the middle, and the writer must accomplish his or her purpose within that body.

1. Use your writing plan, or outline, as a guide. The plan is developed as an aid to establishing a clear and appropriate pattern of development. If you do not follow this plan, you may lose the logical structure that it was designed to provide. However, do not be afraid to modify the plan somewhat as new ideas or insights strike you. Remember, the rough draft is your opportunity to experiment.

2. Keep your purpose and audience in mind. Make the body of your composition accomplish what your controlling purpose promises you will accomplish. Also keep your language and material suitable to your audience.

3. Divide your writing into paragraphs. Develop each main topic in your writing plan into a single paragraph in your composition. Begin each paragraph with a topic sentence and support each topic sentence with the information you have included in your subtopics. Develop each topic and subtopic fully.

4. Provide clear transitions.   Transitional devices at the beginning of paragraphs indicate how each idea is logically related to the ideas in preceding paragraphs. It is crucial that your reader be able to follow the development of your thoughts if he or she is to be able to understand them.

Using Transitional Devices

Transitional Words and Phrases.   Just as the linking expressions or connectives in Chapter 8 are used to achieve coherence within a paragraph and to help the reader move smoothly from one idea to another, certain words and phrases are used to help the reader move smoothly from one paragraph to another. The following transitional words and phrases are the ones most often used in the first sentence of a new paragraph.

TO INDICATE TIME RELATIONSHIPS

before	earlier	once	sooner or later
during	later	then	at this point
after	soon	in time	at the same time
afterward	first	eventually	until
at last	next	finally	recently

TO INDICATE LOGICAL RELATIONSHIPS

since	besides	furthermore
therefore	consequently	and then
because	inevitably	as a result

TO INDICATE SIMILARITY

as	also	similarly	in the same way
like	again	another	equally important
and	likewise	moreover	
too	equally	in addition	

TO INDICATE CONTRAST

but	however	otherwise
yet	although	in contrast
nor	nevertheless	on the contrary
still	nonetheless	on the other hand

Each of the following sentences is the first sentence of a paragraph. Notice how the transitional devices serve, in each case, to link the new topic to that of the preceding paragraph. You can even guess what the preceding paragraph was about.

Still, solar power will never totally eliminate the need for other sources of energy.

Later, the Romans established an outpost of the empire near what is now the border of England and Scotland.

His attitude toward NATO was *equally* contemptuous.

Pronouns. The use of a pronoun to refer to an idea in the preceding paragraph can also create a link in the mind of the reader. The words *this, that, these,* and *those* are frequently used as trasitional devices, sometimes as pronouns and sometimes as adjectives. Great care must be taken in the use of these words as adjectives. They must be followed by a noun that makes the reference clear. Consider the sentence "This cannot continue indefinitely." The reader would be justified in wondering, "This *what* cannot be continued indefinitely?"

Other pronouns can also function as transitional devices. The following sentences, which could serve as opening sentences of paragraphs, demonstrate how the technique works.

That attitude soon changed, however.

Never before have *these* issues seemed so critical or *their* resolution so important.

This procedure has been effective in the past, but stronger measures are required today.

Repetition. The flow of meaning from one paragraph to the next can be smoothed by the repetition of a key word in the opening sentence. Notice the following examples.

1   Mass production has made it possible for a great number of people to own reproductions of significant works of art. It is now only a matter of taste that determines whether a person hangs an inexpensive reproduction of a lithograph by Picasso or a cat calendar on that blank spot on the wall.

But taste is not the only consideration for collectors of high-priced original prints.

2   The people who wonder about such things predict that the next boom in home entertainment will not be better washing machines or microwave ovens but computers.

     The typical home computer setup will be no larger than a component stereo system and will serve equally well as an accountant, a family nutritionist, or a chess opponent.

Repetition need not be limited to a single word; sometimes a writer will use a single word or phrase in the second of two paragraphs to refer to the whole idea developed in the first. Here, the repetition serves the same purpose as the use of a pronoun. See how this works in the following examples.

3   To the manufacturers, the recall rate for American cars is startling testimony to the ability of the industry to turn out a product that does what it is supposed to do in a dependable manner. To the owner of a car recalled for a defective seat belt, however, the recall rate is shocking.

     Reliability, it seems, is in the eye of the beholder.

4   On an increasingly large number of golf courses in the winter, one can see lines of weekend skiers gliding along without fear of broken legs or the price of a lift ticket.

     However, safety and economy are not the only reasons for the rise in popularity of cross-country skiing.

Exercises The Body of the Composition

A. Find a magazine article on a subject that interests you and examine it for transitional devices. Write down the opening sentences of ten paragraphs that make use of the transitional devices discussed in this section. Explain how the devices work.

B. The body of your composition will consist of three paragraphs. Write the body now, keeping the following in mind:

1. Test your ideas against your controlling purpose.
2. Use your writing plan as your guide.
3. Develop the ideas in each paragraph completely.
4. Provide clear transitions between paragraphs.

The Conclusion

As its name implies, the conclusion of the composition should bring matters to a close. The reader should be left with a sense that what should have been said has been said. It is always a good technique to return in the conclusion to the ideas you used in your introduction. This reiteration of the key ideas leaves a feeling of completeness.

If the paragraphs in your composition have adequately developed your topics and are logically connected, your concluding paragraph will form the complete whole, making the structure complete and stable.

The model composition might have a conclusion like the following:

> The situation is deplorable, but what are people to do? People cannot be forced to read newspapers. People cannot be forced to study political and economic issues in detail. The power of the television image will remain, no matter what people do, but television news programs might be improved to the point where they provided more of the substance of information. Network news programs could be expanded to an hour. The focus of the programs could be directed to larger issues, not just to the events of the day. Instead of one or two paternal newscasters, the public could be offered a variety of men and women, reporting from a variety of political perspectives. These changes are small, but they would go a long way toward making television news contribute to a truly informed populace.

Notice that the conclusion begins with the use of the word *situation* as a repetitive device, providing the transition from the preceding paragraph. The writer offers suggestions for improvement of the situation and returns to a key idea of the introduction and the composition as a whole: that an informed public is essential to a democratic society. The reader has, in the course of reading the composition, learned why an informed public is necessary, why dependence on television news has made for an inadequately informed public, and now learns in the conclusion what might be done about it.

With the draft of the entire composition complete, the writer is at last in a position to select a final title for the work. The title, like the introduction, should both inform and interest the reader. It should not be clever without substance, but neither should it be accurate without life.

Exercises Writing an Effective Conclusion

A. Write the concluding paragraph of your composition, including in it an echo of the ideas and techniques you used in your introduction. Refer again to your controlling purpose and try to include all its essential ideas in your conclusion.

B. Choose a title for your completed composition.

Part 6 Revising the Composition

The best compositions are largely the products of work done in this final stage of the process of writing. It is in revision that your ideas will achieve their best and most succinct expression. Work through your rough draft several times, concentrating on only one or two of the following aspects of revision during each reading.

1. Read your composition aloud. The importance of this step cannot be overemphasized. Nothing else will show you so clearly where your ideas were not fully developed or where your thinking was fuzzy or where your sentences were awkward. Reading aloud will also make you more aware of the rhythm and variety of your sentences.

2. Revise for content. Is your purpose clear from the outset? Have you said enough to accomplish your purpose? Is your information accurate? Are your ideas laid out clearly?

3. Revise for unity. Does each paragraph relate directly to the topic and controlling purpose of the composition? Do the details within each paragraph support the topic sentence?

4. Revise for coherence. Have you organized your composition clearly and logically? Have you given each main idea its own paragraph and introduced it with a topic sentence? Is each individual paragraph coherent? Are all your ideas clearly related to each other? Have you made connections between ideas by using transitional devices?

5. Check for a consistent tone, mood, and point of view. Once you have chosen the way you want to present your material, make sure that there is no shift from one paragraph to the next.

6. Revise for wording. Is your level of language appropriate? Have you used the most precise words to express your ideas? Use a dictionary or thesaurus to check the meanings of key words in your composition and to locate synonyms for them. If you find synonymous words with meanings closer to what you had intended, revise the wording.

7. Proofreading. Check grammar, usage, and mechanics. If necessary, consult Sections 10-16 in the Handbook.

Sample Revision

On the following page is a body paragraph from the composition on network news. Try to analyze what the writer has done in this revision.

Notice the improvements that were made in this paragraph:

1. Unity was improved with the deletion of the unrelated idea in line 7.
2. Coherence was strengthened by moving the ideas about Jefferson's informed public closer together. The substitution of the pronoun *his* for the possessive noun *Jefferson's* also provides a transition between ideas.
3. Word choice was improved throughout the paragraph. The resulting sentences are much more mature and precise.
4. Sentence structure was revised throughout to be more varied and sophisticated.
5. Errors in grammar, usage, and mechanics were identified and corrected.

The importance of ~~good~~ (solid) information (to a democracy) did not escape Thomas Jefferson, He felt (who) that a democracy (only could) survive ~~(most strongly)~~ when the public ~~knew what was going on in the world.~~ (was well informed about current affairs.) He feared a public that received (false or) inadequit (ate) information. They ~~will~~ (would) be unable to ~~decide things well.~~ (make intelligent decisions; instead) They (would) ~~might~~ focus on ~~people instead of ideas,~~ (personalities, not issues,) and would be likely to follow ~~rabble-rousers.~~ (demogogues.) ~~The same is true today.~~ In Jefferson's (his) view, an informed public would have the ability to ~~look at political things~~ (evaluate issues and make political decisions) on the basis of reason ~~,~~ (not on preconception or whim.) Jefferson could not have ~~known~~ (forseen) about (∧) television, but he clearly ~~saw what it could mean.~~ (anticipated its impact.)

Final Copy: A Model Composition

Following is the revised composition based on the writing plan in this chapter. Read the composition critically.

NETWORK NEWS
IS NOT ENOUGH

According to a recent survey conducted by the Center for the Study of Public Information, a full sixty percent of American voters get all their information about political issues from nightly television programs. A democracy that gets most of its news from such shows is a democracy in great jeopardy, for half-hour news programs provide the public with the illusion of information, not the substance. This insubstantiality is the result not of a conspiracy to misinform or underinform; it is an inherent shortcoming of

The introduction offers a statistic and asserts the purpose of the composition: to show that television news programs, as currently organized, are not a sufficient means of informing the citizens of a democracy.

television as an information medium, at least as currently organized.

The importance of solid information to a democracy did not escape Thomas Jefferson, who felt most strongly that a democracy could survive only when the public was well informed. In his view, an informed public would have the ability to evaluate political issues and make political decisions on the basis of reason, not on preconception or whim. He feared a public that received false or inadequate information. They would be unable to make intelligent decisions; instead they would focus on personalities and would be likely to follow demagogues. Jefferson could not have foreseen television, but he clearly anticipated its impact.

Until recently, the main source of information in America has been the newspaper. By its very nature—the fact that it is in print and can be read at the reader's own pace—a newspaper can provide long and careful analyses of issues and events. However, recent polls show a sharp decline in newspaper readership. Each year, more Americans get most of their information not from a newspaper, but from television.

Television, however, unlike a newspaper, is by its very nature an inadequate medium for communicating information. Because it is a visual medium, relying on stories that can be filmed, it cannot probe the complexity and interrelatedness of the issues that confront the citizens of a complex world. Television news programs are

The first paragraph of the body of the composition corresponds to the first section of the writing plan. The first sentence is the topic sentence; the rest of the paragraph develops the statement it makes.

Repetition of the key word *information* serves as a transition from the introduction.

Again, the key word *information* is repeated, linking this paragraph to the preceding one and to the introduction. The words *until recently* locate the paragraph in time. The paragraph corresponds to the second section of the writing plan.

Two words, *however* and *unlike,* provide a transition from the preceding paragraph and indicate a contrast between its topic and the topic discussed here. The paragraph corresponds to the third section of the writing plan.

prisoners of time, dominated by periodic commercial breaks and dependent on brief stories that can never provide the depth that is possible in newspapers. The visual image encourages a focus on personalities rather than issues, a focus that is demonstrated by the attitude of the newscasters themselves, who adopt a wise and paternal manner. This focus on personalities is exactly what Jefferson feared from an ill-informed public.

The situation is deplorable, but what are people to do? People cannot be forced to read newspapers. They cannot be forced to study political and economic issues in detail. The power of the television image will remain, no matter what people do, but television news programs might be improved to the point where they provided more of the substance of information. Network news programs could be expanded to an hour. The focus of the programs could be directed to larger issues, not just to the events of the day. Instead of one or two paternal newscasters, the public could be offered a variety of men and women, reporting from a variety of perspectives. These changes are small, but they could help make television news contribute to a truly informed populace.

The final paragraph constitutes the conclusion of the composition. The writer returns to the problems posed in the introduction, echoes a phrase from the Introduction in the words *the substance of information,* and returns to Jefferson's concerns in the closing words. As a whole, the conclusion is prescriptive, offering the reader a possible solution.

Exercise Revising a Composition

Revise your composition, following the suggestions in this section. Prepare a clean, final version, carefully proofread.

Guidelines for Writing and Revising Compositions

As you write a composition, follow the steps in the Guidelines for The Process of Writing on page 105. Use the Guidelines below after you have written your first draft.

1. Has the subject been narrowed to a topic that can be covered in a few paragraphs?

2. Does the composition deal with a single topic or idea?

3. Does the composition follow your writing plan? Have you used your major topics as the main idea of each paragraph? Have you used the subtopics to develop the main idea of each paragraph? Does the composition have an introduction, a body, and a conclusion?

4. Does the introduction present the main idea of the composition? Does it catch the reader's interest?

5. Does the body explain or support the main idea?

6. Does the conclusion restate the main idea, summarize the information, or comment upon it? Does it leave the reader with a sense of completeness?

7. Do the paragraphs work together to develop the single topic or idea that is the subject of the composition?

8. Is the composition appropriate for the audience for which it is intended? Is the purpose clear? Is the level of language suitable?

9. Does the composition have unity? Are the supporting ideas in each paragraph related to the topic sentence? Is each paragraph directly related to the main idea in the introductory paragraph? Does the composition relate directly to the idea set forth in your controlling purpose?

10. Is the composition coherent? Are the ideas presented in a clear, logical order?

11. Are there transitional devices that tie the paragraphs together?

12. Are the tone, mood, and point of view consistent?

13. Could any words or phrases be replaced with more vivid or precise language?

14. Is the title meaningful and interesting?

15. Are there any errors in grammar, usage, and mechanics?

1. A composition is a group of paragraphs that develops a single idea and exhibits unity and coherence. There are three main types of compositions: narrative, descriptive, and expository.

2. A composition has three main parts. The introduction tells what the composition will be about. The body paragraphs develop this idea. The final paragraph, or conclusion, summarizes the information or comments on it.

3. Limit the subject of the composition to an idea that can be covered within the specified limits of the paper.

4. By writing a statement of your controlling purpose, you can clarify your topic even more. Also, identify your audience and select a tone, mood, and point of view.

5. Generate and organize information by brainstorming or taking notes, identifying main ideas, grouping details under these main ideas, and putting the material in logical order.

6. Revise for content, unity, and coherence. Check for a consistent tone, mood, and point of view. Proofread your material when the content changes are complete.

Applications in Other Subject Areas

Science / History. Choose a topic that might normally be considered "dry" by a reader. By using vivid language and a great deal of variety in your development, make the topic seem exciting. Refer to the article on Venus in this chapter for a good example.

Mass Media. Most of the news and magazine articles you read can be considered expanded compositions. However, the subject, tone, language, and other elements are carefully matched to the particular audience at which the publication is aimed. Select two popular magazines directed at widely different audiences. Now choose a general subject and narrow it to two specific topics, each one suitable for one of the audiences you have identified. Then compose your articles, suiting all the elements of the piece to the audience for which it is being written.

Chapter 11

Language and Techniques of Literary Criticism

Whenever you are confronted with a new and unfamiliar situation, you must attempt to make sense of it. To do so, you must observe the situation carefully, analyze and interpret what you have observed, and then make any necessary decisions or judgments. This process of analysis and interpretation is called **criticism.**

Whether you continue your education or enter the business world, the situations that require precise criticism will increase. The purpose of this chapter is twofold. First, it will equip you with a vocabulary to use in analyzing and interpreting everything from people and things to current events. Second, it will show you how to apply these skills to formal, written discussions of literature.

Part 1   Developing a Vocabulary of Criticism

Every day you analyze and make judgments about everything from people, clothes, food, and books to news accounts and traffic conditions. For each of these analyses and judgments, there are specific words that can be used to state your conclusions. These words—the vocabulary of criticism—will help you to describe your perceptions and reactions more precisely. What can be said, for example, about another person? How can the person's personality, manner, intelligence, or character be described? Here are some possibilities:

Words Useful for Describing People

Personality	Manner	Intelligence	Character
cold	forthright	quick	strong
aloof	outspoken	keen	reliable
reserved	frank	sharp	selfless
retiring	candid	agile	dependable
restrained	straightforward	fine	trustworthy
cool	debonaire	incisive	spotless
warm	ingratiating	acute	determined
vibrant	patronizing	brilliant	certain
buoyant	charming	bright	sure
bubbly	devil-may-care	nimble	selfish
vivacious	carefree	alert	demanding
outgoing	footloose	astute	thoughtless
attractive	brusque	clever	driven
compelling	curt	ingenious	calculating
charming	rude	creative	egoistic
magnetic	surly	slow	self-serving
appealing	blunt	dull	vain
fascinating	abrupt	dim	weak
beguiling	short	limited	sheepish
adorable	sullen	ignorant	helpless

Similarly, an objective judgment of a motion picture or TV program can go far beyond the vague, subjective judgments that underlie *great*, *dull*, or *poor*. The characters can be discussed in the terms listed above. But what about the acting, the pace, the story, or the sound effects? Another sample of possibilities is shown below.

Words Useful for Criticism of Motion Pictures and TV Programs

Acting	Pace	Story	Sound Effects
inspired	brisk	contrived	complementary
natural	quick	artificial	supportive
realistic	lively	unbelievable	appropriate
relaxed	breakneck	calculated	jarring
truthful	hasty	maudlin	annoying
melodramatic	abrupt	clever	distracting
overblown	slow	bewildering	inappropriate
exaggerated	lethargic	baffling	intrusive
affected	leisurely	surprising	intricate
unbelievable	relaxed	realistic	
unnatural	indolent	creative	
wooden	halting		
uninspired	measured		
clumsy	irregular		
thoughtless	jerky		

Attempting to be objective in your judgments will have more than one benefit.

1. An objective criticism is precise and informative.
2. Making an objective criticism will require you to look at what you are criticizing with an open mind.
3. Searching for words to relay an objective criticism with precision and clarity will help you *think* more precisely and more clearly.
4. An objective criticism will earn the respect of your audience not only for the judgment you express but also for the critical effort that underlies it.

Exercises Developing a Vocabulary of Criticism

A. Substitute a precise judgment word for each of the italicized words in the following sentences.

1. It was a *good* game.
2. Michael Jackson is a *wonderful* dancer.
3. *Stories from the Twilight Zone* is a *great* book.
4. The music at the party was *poor*.
5. The movie was *funny*.
6. The weather was *terrific*.

B. Think about a motion picture you have seen recently. What judgments can be made about it? What can you say more specifically than *great, dull,* or *poor?* What about the acting, costumes, sound effects? You might think of the aspects of a motion picture for which Oscars are awarded.

C. Below are ten subjective criticisms. Write a paragraph of objective criticism for two of the items.

EXAMPLE: a good audience

The audience was familiar with the music and became involved with the soloist's interpretation of the sonata. When the program was over, the audience rose for a standing ovation and demanded an encore, which the violinist obligingly gave.

1. an ideal vacation	6. nice hair
2. a weak performance	7. a comfortable house
3. a good book	8. soothing music
4. an elegant dinner	9. an appetizing meal
5. a friendly dog	10. the perfect gift

D. What can be said about a piece of clothing? Make a list of judgment words that convey precise information. These will be nouns as well as adjectives. Avoid words like *lovely, sharp, adorable,* or *nice.* Consult fashion pages of newspapers and magazines for suggestions.

Part 2 The Language of Literary Criticism

As you react with greater maturity and sensitivity to the world around you, you will become increasingly aware of the importance of a vocabulary of criticism—a vocabulary that will help you describe and evaluate people, places, and things.

In your study of books, plays, motion pictures, and so on, you may already have become aware of the need for such a vocabulary. You need words to analyze the characters you encounter—their words, actions, and motives. You need words to evaluate the style or form of a piece of writing.

For these purposes, you need more than just an understanding of the connotations of common words and a knowledge of common synonyms. You need a vocabulary with depth and scope, a store of words from which you can take the *one* word that best conveys the *precise meaning* you have in mind.

If, for example, you are criticizing a scene from a novel in which a character describes a childhood of suffering and deprivation, a scene which moves the reader to a feeling of pity, will you characterize the scene as one that contains *pathos* or *bathos?*

If you are discussing a protagonist who is roguish and appealing and appears in a series of humorous or satiric adventures, will you classify the character as a *romantic idealist* or as a *picaresque hero?*

If a writer includes a passage that is intended to represent the thoughts of a character, a passage that mixes memories, anxieties, and everyday concerns, will you say that the writer has used a *stream of consciousness technique* or *stark realism?*

If you are reading a novel described as a *Gothic novel*, will you expect it to be about the ancient Goths, to be set in a Gothic cathedral, or to have a mood of horror?

A good dictionary will answer these questions for you, but terms such as those italicized above must become your stock in trade if you are to achieve that depth and breadth of language necessary to the understanding and enjoyment of literature.

Exercises The Language of Literary Criticism

A. The following sentences contain words that will be useful to you in expressing judgments about books, motion pictures, plays, and so on. Examine carefully each underlined word and be able to tell the class exactly what each sentence means. If you are not sure, consult your dictionary.

1. The atmosphere of Poe's "The Fall of the House of Usher" is one of mystery.

2. The mood of Barry's *Joyous Season* is not really one of joy at all but rather of a happiness that shows the leading character in tears at the final curtain.

3. Susan Glaspell builds up suspense in *Trifles* by skillfully introducing obstacles that the women must overcome to gain their ends.

4. Some people hold that Holden Caulfield in *Catcher in the Rye* is not fully believable.

5. The imagery of Keats's poems is very rich.

6. The dialogue in Hemingway's short stories is racy and pungent.

7. Robert Frost relies less upon metaphor than upon tone to achieve his effects.

8. The most important aspect of poetry is sound, and therefore a poem must be read aloud to be fully appreciated.

9. "The Purloined Letter," by Edgar Allan Poe, was the first of a new genre, the detective story.

10. Bernard Shaw was regarded by his contemporaries as an iconoclast.

11. Tennessee Williams frequently used the South and its people as his milieu.

12. Because of the sensational action of the new play, critics classified it as outright melodrama.

13. *Oedipus Rex* contains numerous ironies.

14. The climax of *The Bridge of San Luis Rey* comes at the beginning of the book with the collapse of the bridge and justifies the telling of the tale.

15. In "Stopping by Woods on a Snow Evening," the horse, without losing its identity as a horse, also becomes a symbol.

B. A comprehensive knowledge of the words that describe people, places, and events is indispensable to good writing. Examine the italicized words below. Define each exactly and use each correctly in an original sentence. If you are not sure of any word, use your dictionary. Also, master the pronunciation of the word.

1. *lethargic* disposition	11. *sanguinary* nature
2. *dour* expression	12. *vacillating* character
3. *vicarious* enjoyment	13. *genteel* manner
4. *mendacious* personality	14. *malodorous* atmosphere
5. *stentorian* tones	15. *pertinacious* individual
6. *scurrilous* remarks	16. *sophisticated* manner
7. *didactic* literature	17. *morbid* obsession
8. *auspicious* beginning	18. *abject* poverty
9. *impeccably* attired	19. *ironic* situation
10. *indefensible* conduct	20. *poignant* ending

C. Supply the name of a person—fictional or historical—whom you feel would fit each adjective given below.

EXAMPLE: procrastinating: Hamlet

1. garrulous	11. senile
2. ambitious	12. naive
3. cunning	13. suave
4. magnanimous	14. egotistical
5. obsequious	15. humble
6. quixotic	16. sagacious
7. compassionate	17. steadfast
8. treacherous	18. irrational
9. subservient	19. unsavory
10. implacable	20. fickle

D. Select a short story or play that you have read recently. Describe the following as clearly and specifically as possible:

1. the character of the protagonist
2. the character of the antagonist
3. the nature of the conflict
4. the style of writing
5. the effect of the piece upon you

Part 3   Writing About Literature

Now that you have sharpened your vocabulary of criticism, you are ready to apply that knowledge to the actual process of literary criticism. Writing about literature is an important way of studying literature. It forces you to read more carefully and more critically. In order to find a focus for an analysis, you must understand the structure of a piece of literature. You must sort out the elements that the writer has used to achieve the meaning.

Once you have determined your focus and the general point you want to make about it, you will find that the process of writing about literature is similar to other composition work you have done. As in all expository writing, you develop your main idea with specific details. When your subject is a literary work, your supporting details come from the work itself.

Most often, you will be asked to write this type of composition about a story or poem you have just read. Although the subject of your writing may affect some of the decisions and choices you make as you work through the writing process, the same basic writing techniques can be applied to any situation.

Pre-Writing: Analysis and Interpretation

When you analyze a piece of literature, you take a role similar to that of a detective. You begin by isolating the different bits of information you have been presented with. You then study this information in order to find identifiable patterns, meaningful relationships, and an overall logic or purpose to the material taken as a whole. You will find it helpful to follow much the same process in analyzing literature. You must break a story or poem down into its elements in order to examine how these parts are related. Follow these steps:

Step 1. Read the story or poem.

Step 2. Take notes on the elements of the story or poem. These elements will be discussed in Parts 4 and 5.

Step 3. Choose a topic and determine a purpose. Once you have taken notes, decide whether you wish to analyze *what* the writer has written or the *way* in which he or she has presented the material. The first type of paper would require you to analyze the elements that make up the story or poem. The second type would mean that you would concentrate more on the writing techniques and strategies of the author. You could also present your opinion on how successfully the writer achieved his or her purpose.

No matter what focus you give your writing, however, you must limit your topic to one you can analyze thoroughly. Begin by deciding which aspect of the piece interests you most. Sometimes you will decide to deal with just one of the elements. For instance, you might write about the theme of the piece, the way the writer creates a certain atmosphere, or the development of a character. At other times, you might want to discuss the effect of one or more elements on another. For instance, you might write about how a character resolves a conflict, what the relationship is between the form and meaning of a poem, or how the point of view affects understanding.

Step 4. List the points you wish to cover. Once you have decided on your topic and purpose, identify the points you will need to make in order to convey your ideas to a reader. Also gather support for each idea by carefully selecting details, lines, or passages from the piece you are analyzing.

Step 5. Organize your ideas. Look for relationships among your ideas and arrange the material in a logical order. As with other types of writing, your topic will often help you determine the most logical method for organizing your material. For example, if your topic is the impact of two characters on each other, a logical order might be comparison-contrast. However, you could use chronological order to show how the relationship changed throughout the story.

The pre-writing steps of analyzing and interpreting literature are very important to a successful paper. Take your time with this stage. Remember that it is through analysis that you find all of the details that you need to begin writing a first draft.

Writing and Revising the Analysis

Write your first draft to get your ideas down on paper. As always in the process of writing, you will develop and refine your ideas as you write. You will be adding, deleting, and rearranging ideas to fit your topic and purpose in your first draft as well as in subsequent revisions.

In later revisions, check your writing for unity, coherence, and thorough development. Make certain that you do not leap from idea to idea without logical transitions. Each major point should have a clear relationship to the ideas that directly precede and follow it. The paper as a whole should flow smoothly and reflect a meaningful thought process on the part of you, the writer. Also check to see that you have used the most effective vocabulary to describe your impressions of the various elements or techniques you are discussing. Finally, as always, proofread for errors in grammar, usage, and mechanics.

Part 4 Writing About a Short Story

The process described in Part 3 is essential to successful writing about a short story. First, read and reread the story carefully, taking notes as you read. Next, decide upon a focus for your composition. Your focus will probably be one or more of the elements of the short story—plot, character, setting, point of view, theme, and style. The final step is the development of a controlling purpose and the selecting of specific details from the story to develop it. After you have completed these three steps, you are ready to organize your paper.

Elements of a Short Story

Here is a brief review of the elements of a short story.

Plot. A short story shows characters living through a single experience or several closely related ones. This action is the plot of the story. It need not be exclusively physical. Sometimes the writer is primarily concerned with the thoughts of the characters and the insights they gain. The plot begins with the presentation of a situation that needs to be resolved. As the characters act and react, the plot moves to its resolution.

Character. The characters in a story are the persons who initiate or go through the experiences of the plot. Their qualities emerge and your understanding of them develops as the story progresses. Sometimes a character is more universal than individual, representing a basic human type.

Setting. Setting is the environment in which the characters live and move. It may include such things as time of day, natural surroundings, elements of weather, and even sounds and smells. Sometimes setting is incidental to the story; it serves as a mere location for events. In other stories, setting is essential to the action.

Point of View. This refers to the position from which the writer views his subject. Two different points of view are common in short stories.

1. *First-person narrator.* The story is told by an "I." The action is seen through the eyes and mind of this character.
2. *Third-person limited.* The writer uses *he, she,* and *they,* not *I* in telling the story. The narration is limited, however, to the observations, feelings, and behavior of one character. Most short stories use this third-person limited point of view.

Theme. Short stories do more than show characters in action in a particular place and time. Most serious stories develop a theme, a deeper meaning underlying the human experience of the story. Discovering thematic significance is one of the most satisfying aspects of reading fiction.

Style. Style refers to the way in which a writer uses language. It includes qualities of word choice, sentence structure and variety, imagery, rhythm, repetition, coherence, emphasis, and arrangement of ideas. It also includes the use of irony and the surprise ending.

Analyzing a Short Story

Step 1. Read the following story and then work through the procedures that follow it. The first reading will give you the story line, the incidents that lead to the climax, and the resolution.

THE SNIPER

The long June twilight faded into night. Dublin lay enveloped in darkness, but for the dim light of the moon that shone through fleecy clouds, casting a pale light as of approaching dawn over the streets and the dark waters of the Liffey. Around the beleaguered Four Courts the heavy guns roared. Here and there through the city, machine guns and rifles broke the silence of the night, spasmodically, like dogs barking on lone farms. Republicans and Free Staters were waging civil war.

On a rooftop near O'Connell Bridge, a Republican sniper lay watching. Beside him lay his rifle, and over his shoulders were slung a pair of field glasses. His face was the face of a student—thin and ascetic, but his eyes had the cold gleam of the fanatic. They were deep and thoughtful, the eyes of a man who is used to looking at death.

He was eating a sandwich hungrily. He had eaten nothing since morning. He had been too excited to eat. He finished the sandwich, and taking a flask of whiskey from his pocket, he took a short draft. Then he returned the flask to his pocket. He paused for a moment, considering whether he should risk a smoke. It was dangerous. The flash might be seen in the darkness and there were enemies watching. He decided to take the risk. Placing a cigarette between his lips, he struck a match, inhaled the smoke hurriedly and put out the light. Almost immediately, a bullet flattened itself against the parapet of the roof. The sniper took another whiff and put out the cigarette. Then he swore softly and crawled away to the left.

Cautiously he raised himself and peered over the parapet. There was a flash, and a bullet whizzed over his head. He dropped immediately. He had seen the flash. It came from the opposite side of the street.

He rolled over the roof to a chimney stack in the rear, and slowly drew himself up behind it, until his eyes were level with the top of the parapet. There was nothing to be seen— just the dim outline of the opposite housetop against the blue sky. His enemy was under cover.

Just then an armored car came across the bridge and advanced slowly up the street. It stopped on the opposite side of the street fifty yards ahead. The sniper could hear the dull panting of the motor. His heart beat faster. It was an enemy car. He wanted to fire, but he knew it was useless. His bullets would never pierce the steel that covered the grey monster.

Then round the corner of a side street came an old woman, her head covered by a tattered shawl. She began to talk to the man in the turret of the car. She was pointing to the roof where the sniper lay. An informer.

The turret opened. A man's head and shoulders appeared, looking toward the sniper. The sniper raised his rifle and fired. The head fell heavily on the turret wall. The woman darted toward the side street. The sniper fired again. The woman whirled round and fell with a shriek into the gutter.

Suddenly from the opposite roof a shot rang out, and the sniper dropped his rifle with a curse. The rifle clattered to the roof. The sniper thought the noise would wake the dead. He stooped to pick the rifle up. He couldn't lift it. His forearm was dead. "I'm hit," he muttered.

Dropping flat on to the roof, he crawled back to the parapet. With his left hand he felt the injured right forearm. The blood was oozing through the sleeve of his coat. There was no pain—just a deadened sensation, as if the arm had been cut off.

Quickly he drew his knife from his pocket, opened it on the breastwork of the parapet and ripped open the sleeve. There was a small hole where the bullet had entered. On the other side there was no hole. The bullet had lodged in the bone. It must have fractured it. He bent the arm below the wound. The arm bent back easily. He ground his teeth to overcome the pain.

Then, taking out his field dressing, he ripped open the packet with his knife. He broke the neck of the iodine bottle and let the bitter fluid drip into the wound. A paroxysm of pain swept through him. He placed the cotton wadding over the wound and wrapped the dressing over it. He tied the end with this teeth.

Then he lay still against the parapet, and closing his eyes, he made an effort of will to overcome the pain.

In the street beneath all was still. The armored car had retired speedily over the bridge, with the machine gunner's head hanging lifeless over the turret. The woman's corpse lay still in the gutter.

The sniper lay for a long time nursing his wounded arm and planning escape. Morning must not find him wounded on the roof. The enemy on the opposite roof covered his escape. He must kill that enemy, and he could not use his rifle. He had only a revolver to do it. Then he thought of a plan.

Taking off his cap, he placed it over the muzzle of his rifle. Then he pushed the rifle slowly upwards over the parapet, until the cap was visible from the opposite side of the street. Almost immediately there was a report, and a bullet pierced the center of the cap. The sniper slanted the rifle foward. The cap slipped down into the street. Then, catching the rifle in the middle, the sniper dropped his left hand over the roof and let it hang, lifelessly. After a few moment he let the rifle drop to the street. Then he sank to the roof, dragging his hand with him.

Crawling quickly to the left, he peered up at the corner of the roof. His ruse had succeeded. The other sniper, seeing the cap and rifle fall, thought that he had killed his man. He was now standing before a row of chimney pots, looking across, with his head clearly silhouetted against the western sky.

The Republican sniper smiled and lifted his revolver above the edge of the parapet. The distance was about fifty yards—a hard shot in the dim light, and his right arm was paining him like a thousand devils. He took a steady aim. His hand trembled with eagerness. Pressing his lips together, he took a deep breath through his nostrils and fired. He was almost deafened with the report and his arm shook with the recoil.

Then, when the smoke cleared, he peered across and uttered a cry of joy. His enemy had been hit. He was reeling over the parapet in his death agony. He struggled to keep his feet, but he was slowly falling forward, as if in a dream. The rifle fell from his grasp, hit the parapet, fell over, bounded off the pole of a barber's shop beneath, and then cluttered onto the pavement.

Then the dying man on the roof crumpled up and fell forward. The body turned over and over in space and hit the ground with a dull thud. Then it lay still.

The sniper looked at his enemy falling and he shuddered. The lust of battle died in him. He became bitten by remorse. The sweat stood out in beads on his forehead. Weakened by his wound and the long summer day of fasting and watching on the roof, he revolted from the sight of the shattered mass of his dead enemy. His teeth chattered. He began to gibber to himself, cursing the war, cursing himself, cursing everybody.

He looked at the smoking revolver in his hand and with an oath, he hurled it to the roof at his feet. The revolver went off with the concussion, and the bullet whizzed past the sniper's head. He was frightened back to his senses by the shock. His nerves steadied. The cloud of fear scattered from his mind and he laughed.

Taking the whiskey flask from his pocket, he emptied it at a draft. He felt reckless under the influence of the spirits. He decided to leave the roof and look for his company commander to report. Everywhere around was quiet. There was not much danger in going through the streets. He picked up his revolver and put it in his pocket. Then he crawled down through the skylight to the house underneath.

When the sniper reached the laneway on the street level, he felt a sudden curiosity as to the identity of the enemy sniper whom he had killed. He decided that he was a good shot, whoever he was. He wondered if he knew him. Perhaps he had been in his own company before the split in the army. He decided to risk going over to have a look at him. He peered around the corner into O'Connell Street. In the upper part of the street there was heavy firing, but around here all was quiet.

The sniper darted across the street. A machine gun tore up the ground around him with a hail of bullets, but he escaped. He threw himself face downwards beside the corpse. The machine gun stopped.

Then the sniper turned over the dead body and looked into his brother's face.—LIAM O'FLAHERTY

Step 2. Reread the story. As you read, take notes on anything that seems significant, whether related to plot, character, setting, theme, or style.

Notes on "The Sniper" might look like this:

a. Setting is one of contrasts: peaceful scene and guns.
b. The Republican sniper has the look of a student, but he has grown accustomed to death.
c. He provokes danger by lighting his cigarette. He seems excited by the war.
d. The story is told in the third person from the point of view of the sniper. Thus we see through his eyes and share his feelings.
e. The enemy sniper is similar to the Republican sniper. He, too, keeps undercover on a rooftop.
f. The enemy sniper is alert and quick. He sees the light of the match and fires immediately.
g. Neither man is given a name by the writer.
h. The Republican sniper kills both the soldier in the armored car and the old woman who betrayed his hiding place.
i. He seems to do this with little feeling.
j. The major character shows great courage, endurance, and ingenuity.
k. He dresses his own wound after he is shot.

l. He carries out a clever ruse, despite his pain.

m. The real death of the enemy parallels the fake death of the sniper. The dead man's rifle falls to the ground.

n. The sniper is revolted by his enemy's death. He curses the war and feels an identity with his fallen enemy.

o. He almost kills himself.

p. The ending is ironic. The sniper turns over the dead body and finds it is his brother.

q. The theme seems to be that in civil war brother kills brother.

Step 3. Read over your list. Look for related ideas and notice any patterns that emerge. This is a story about courage under duress, about the brutalizing effect of war on a city's inhabitants, about the self-destructive quality of civil war. Important in the development of these themes is the technique of the writer.

A critical analysis cannot deal with every aspect of the story. Nor can it tell its entire plot. A good analysis must be sharply focused and should include only such details as support and develop the main idea. Never include comments about your own experiences when writing about a piece of literature. Always draw your ideas from the work itself.

Look through the list and find a group of items that are related and that interest you. Suppose, for example, that you choose letters a, b, e, g, m, n, p, and q. For these items, an appropriate controlling purpose would take note of the structure of the story as it develops and reinforces the idea of the self-destructiveness of civil war. A workable controlling purpose might be stated like this:

> The controlling purpose of this critical analysis is to examine the techniques that Liam O'Flaherty uses in his short story, "The Sniper," to reinforce the theme of the self-destructiveness of civil war.

Step 4. Plan the organization of your analysis, using the items you have chosen. You do not need to follow the sequence of your notes. Some items can be incorporated into others, giving you major topics and supporting details.

Sample Outline

The following is a sample outline for a critical analysis paper. At this point, you may not have formulated your idea for your introductory paragraph. Remember, however, that the introduction that you eventually write must present your controlling purpose.

    I. (Introduction—to come)

    II. Difference versus similarities
        A. Contradictory quality of setting
        B. Similarities of snipers

    III. Critical point of story
        A. Republican's feigning of death
        B. Republican's killing of enemy
        C. Republican's revulsion toward killing

    IV. Ironic ending
        A. Republican's descent to street
        B. Republican's recognition of brother

    V. Conclusion of story
        A. Both men nameless
        B. Universal meaning in anonymity

Step 5. Write the first draft of your critical analysis. Keep your controlling purpose in front of you as you write. Note how each major division of the outline becomes a paragraph and the subdivisions act as supporting details. Note, too, that letter g in the notes, the anonymity of the snipers, has been used to create a concluding idea that extends the meaning of the story. As you write, remember that a work of literature is always discussed in the present tense.

Step 6. Rewrite, or revise, your paper. Refer to the guidelines for revision given in Chapter 7, page 105. Then, proofread your paper carefully, referring to the proofreading checklist on page 106. Finally, title your paper appropriately.

Critical Analysis of the Short Story

Here is a final version of the critical analysis.

STYLE AND STRUCTURE IN "THE SNIPER"

In Liam O'Flaherty's "The Sniper," style and structure reinforce the theme of the unnatural and self-destructive quality of civil war. The initial description of the contradictory aspects of the setting sets the tone for the events that follow. The parallel actions in the structure of the story, along with the irony of the conclusion, serve to emphasize the dehumanization of war.

The language of the opening paragraph emphasizes the contradiction between a peaceful, natural setting and the sounds of war. O'Flaherty talks of "June twilight" and of the moon shining through "fleecy clouds." Violating the serenity are the sounds of roaring guns and of rifles "like dogs barking on lone farms." A "Republican sniper," a young man with the "face of a student," watches over this scene. He is not at his studies, however; he is armed with a rifle, a revolver, and field glasses. On a neighboring roof, similarly armed, is another young man, also on the alert for enemy attack. Here, their seeming kinship ends. They are enemies, stalking each other in the environs of a great city.

The critical point of the story is reached when the Republican sniper, shot at by his enemy, feigns death and lets his rifle fall to the ground. Off his guard, the Free State sniper stands up and is killed by the Republican with a single shot. What follows is a scene that parallels the action moments before the deception. The Free Stater's rifle, too, falls to the ground, but not in pretense. He has been killed, and his body crumples and falls over the parapet of the roof. At this point, the Republican sniper has a moment of revelation. He recognizes how easily he himself could have been the victim, and he is revolted by his murderous act.

Total insight, however, comes only at the end. The Republican sniper descends to the street and turns over the dead body. He looks "into his brother's face." The ironic ending clarifies the theme suggested throughout the story: In nations torn by civil war, brother destroys brother.

The reader may carry this insight a step further. The author leaves the snipers unnamed, thus giving the story universal application. Not just civil wars but all wars deny humanity and turn man against his brother man.

Exercises Writing About a Short Story

A. Look over the list of notes again and find a different focus. Two mentioned earlier were the brutalizing effect of war and the courage and strength shown by the young sniper despite his pain and danger. You might also consider, as a topic for analysis, the effect of the point of view on the reader. Because you experience the story only as the Republican sniper experiences it, your sympathies are with him. The third-person narration, however, provides a kind of detachment that affects your perception.

Follow the step-by-step pattern, ending with an analysis of about 250 to 350 words. Bear in mind that a critical analysis does *not* retell the story. Include only such details as are necessary to develop your main idea. Be careful not to move outside of the story in your analysis. Write an appropriate title.

B. Choose a story you like. Using the techniques you have learned, formulate a controlling purpose and then write. Complete the following steps:

Pre-Writing: Identify the various elements of the story. What is the major conflict? Who are the characters? How would you describe them? What is the mood of the story? the point of view? Identify the elements that interest you and determine your topic and purpose. What method of organization best suits your topic?

First Draft: Use your pre-writing notes to get your ideas down on paper. Use details from the story to support your ideas. Look for new insights.

Revision: Go over your rough draft several times. Is your main idea clearly stated? Are your reasons convincing? What story details can you add to support your ideas?

Part 5 Writing About a Poem

Writing about a poem is similar to writing about a short story. However, poetry is shorter and more concentrated than prose. Because the poems are short, you can read each one many times before writing about it. Because they are concentrated, you must read very carefully, paying close attention to each stanza, line, and word. Vital meaning and power can be packed into a single word.

As you analyze poems, you will notice that they often contain many of the same elements of short stories. For example, a poem usually has a specific purpose, theme, and focus. It may contain characters, a setting, and even a plot and conflict. Point of view, mood, and tone are also utilized.

Poetry has additional elements as well. One of these is form. Poets often set up their ideas in recognizable patterns of syllables and lines. Often, these patterns have some effect on the impact of the poem. Therefore, an understanding of such terms as *stanza, couplet, sonnet, free verse,* and *blank verse* can be quite useful during analysis.

The language of poetry is also a crucial element. This is because the poet uses words for their sounds as well as their meanings. Rhythm, rhyme, and other sound effects bring poetry close to music. In order to analyze a poem successfully, you must familiarize yourself with sound devices such as *alliteration, assonance, consonance,* and *onomatopoeia.*

Finally, you must be aware of the visual appeal of poetry. Images, or word pictures, are often central to the appeal of a poem. Devices such as *metaphor, simile,* and *personification* help the poet to achieve vivid imagery and therefore must be considered in any thorough analysis.

When you write about a poem, be sure to consider its poetic devices as well as more familiar elements. Although prose uses poetic devices, too, they are usually incidental to the other elements of the story. In poetry, they are central. Any of them can serve as the focus of a critical analysis.

The poet uses words for their sounds as well as their meanings. Rhythm, rhyme, and other sound effects bring poetry close to music. Poetry has visual appeal as well, creating word pictures through its imagery. Prose uses poetic devices, too, but in prose they are often incidental. In poetry they are central.

When you write about a poem, be sure to consider its poetic devices and the feeling it evokes, as well as its theme. In fact, you might choose any one of these three as the focus for a critical analysis.

Analyzing a Poem

Here is a step-by-step analysis of a poem. First, read the poem carefully several times. Then follow the procedure as it leads you to a final analysis.

OZYMANDIAS

    I met a traveller from an antique land
    Who said: Two vast and trunkless legs of stone
    Stand in the desert . . . Near them, on the sand,
    Half sunk, a shattered visage lies, whose frown,
5   And wrinkled lip, and sneer of cold command,
    Tell that its sculptor well those passions read
    Which yet survive, stamped on these lifeless things,
    The hand that mocked them, and the heart that fed:[1]
    And on the pedestal these words appear:
10 "My name is Ozymandias, king of kings:
    Look on my works, ye Mighty, and despair!"
    Nothing beside remains. Round the decay
    Of that colossal wreck, boundless and bare
    The lone and level sands stretch far away.

                 —PERCY BYSSHE SHELLEY

Can you see how this fourteen-line sonnet falls naturally into separate sections? The first eight lines introduce remnants of a mammoth statue, the legs and shattered face of a once-powerful king. The last six lines break into two parts. The first three

---

[1]Lines 6-8: The *passions* of Ozymandias *survive* (outlast) the hand of the sculptor and the *heart* of Ozymandias.

lines present the proud king's boast. The last three lines show how time has dealt with it.

"Ozmandias" is a poem with a strong central idea. To find this idea, look at the elements that the poet presents.

1. *A king who boasted of his power and supremacy.* The character of Ozymandias lives on in "lifeless things." What do "wrinkled lip" and "sneer of cold command" reveal? What "passions" fed his heart? What do the words he chose for his pedestal show about him?

2. *The sculptor who created an awesome monument to the king.* The sculptor lives on through his art. His observations were keen and his skill considerable. What did he observe in the face of the king? What did his hand mock?

3. *Time and its effects.* Time is a major element in this poem. Consider how time has destroyed the power of Ozymandias and altered the meaning of his boast. Originally, his words were backed by the magnitude of his works. Ozymandias was a "king of kings," capable of causing the mighty to despair. Now, surrounded by empty sand, they proclaim a different message. You might express it like this: Worldly greatness—and the tyrant's power—will not outlast time. The monuments man builds to vanity all fall to dust.

However, the poem is more than this simple statement of truth. Reread the words of Ozymandias in lines 10 and 11. Notice the following:

1. The heavy, tramping sound of the one-syllable words
2. The harsh effect of repeated *k* sounds
3. The commanding second sentence
4. The powerful final word *despair*

Now contrast the quiet effect of the three-word sentence that follows: "Nothing beside remains."

Finally, notice how the *sound* of the last lines helps to describe endless desert sand. The repetition of *s* sounds mirrors the shifting of sands. The word *boundless* stretches out in both sound and sense. The following vowel sounds emphasize length: long *o* in *lone,* broad *a* in *far,* and long *a* in *away.*

Because the theme is so important to an understanding of this poem, a good controlling purpose might be this:

> The controlling purpose of this analysis is to discuss the theme that world greatness will not outlast time in Shelley's poem "Ozymandias."

However, a good analysis must have a sharp focus. It must include more than a restatement of its theme. Your main idea, stated in the topic sentence might read as follows:

> Shelley's sonnet "Ozymandias" gives poetic force to the idea that wordly greatness will not outlast time.

Sample Outline

Here is a sample outline.

I. Poetic force of theme
   A. Language
   B. Irony

II. Details of wrecked statue
   A. "Trunkless legs"
   B. "Shattered visage"

III. Character of tyrant
   A. "Wrinkled lip"
   B. "Sneer of cold command"

IV. Irony of boast
   A. Contrast between wrecked statue and desolate sands
   B. Contrast of intended meaning to deeper truth

V. Poetic effects
   A. Quiet, matter-of-fact beginning
   B. Booming boast
   C. Slow, musical close

A Sample Critical Analysis

Here is a final version of the critical analysis.

THE ELEMENT OF TIME IN "OZYMANDIAS"

Shelley's sonnet "Ozymandias" gives poetic force to the idea that worldly greatness will not outlast time. The poem is basically a story told by an unnamed traveler about a strange scene he has come upon in the desert. The force of the irony, however, and the power of the language give universal significance to the story.

The poem presents a vivid picture—the remnants of a mammoth statue half-buried in desert sand. "Two vast and trunkless legs" still stand in the empty desert. Nearby, lies a "shattered visage." These two legs and a shattered face are all that remain of a monument to a once-proud king. The grotesque scene seems out of time and out of place.

The arrogance of the king lives on, however, in the "frown," the "wrinkled lip," and the "sneer of cold command" on the lifeless face. The sculptor seems to have understood this king well. His art has made a mockery of vanity. The art of the poet has recreated the mockery through the power of his language.

Paralleling the haughty face of the king are the boastful words on the pedestal.

My name is Ozymandias, King of Kings.
Look on my works, ye Mighty, and despair!

In the contrast between this boast and the endless, surrounding sand, the poet has created the basic irony of the poem. He uses time as the major element that destroys the power of Ozymandias and alters the meaning of his boast. The mighty ones will despair, not because they see Ozymandias's works, but because they see the devastation of them. So must we all despair if we hope to build lasting monuments to vanity and power.

The sonnet moves from a quiet, story-telling beginning to the booming boast of the king. The poetic language is powerful and compressed. The images build in force and power. The element of time is at work, however, on both the power of the king and the statue that was erected to honor him. Time has eroded all. "Nothing beside remains." The image is a "colossal wreck." The poem quickly falls away to a last line whose long vowels convey the feeling of endless waste.

Exercises Writing About a Poem

A. Read the following poem carefully. Work through the questions on it and then write a critical analysis, as directed in question 5.

RICHARD CORY

Whenever Richard Cory went down town,
We people on the pavement looked at him:
He was a gentleman from sole to crown,
Clean favored, and imperially slim.

5   And he was always quietly arrayed,
And he was always human when he talked;
But still he fluttered pulses when he said,
"Good-morning," and he glittered when he walked.

And he was rich—yes, richer than a king—
10   And admirably schooled in every grace:
In fine, we thought that he was everything
To make us wish that we were in his place.

So on we worked, and waited for the light,
And went without the meat, and cursed the bread;
15   And Richard Cory, one calm summer night,
Went home and put a bullet through his head.

             —EDWIN ARLINGTON ROBINSON

1. Like the surprise ending of "The Sniper," the ending of this poem makes a generalization about human nature. State the theme of the poem in a single, clear sentence.

2. Like the "people on the pavement," the reader sees Cory from the outside. This view is shown by images of royalty.

a. The use of *crown* instead of *head* in line 3

b. The word *imperially* in line 4 and *glittered* in line 8
Find the word in line 9 that is a key to all these images,
giving them coherence.

3. The words *meat* and *bread* (line 14) are used symbolically to show the people's view of themselves in relation to Cory. What do the words stand for?

4. Consider the ironic contrast between the people's view of Cory and the surprise ending of the poem. Your statement of theme in question 1 should focus on this contrast.

5. Write a controlling purpose that relates the meaning of the poem to its surprise ending and effective imagery. Organize your material in outline form. Then refine your controlling purpose into a topic sentence with a sharp focus and develop it into a critical analysis of the poem. Be sure to support your main idea with specific details from the poem.

B. Select a favorite poem of your own and complete an analysis of one aspect or element. Follow the process of writing as presented in Part 3 of this chapter.

SUMMARY AND APPLICATIONS

1. A strong vocabulary of criticism can help you to make specific and objective judgments about people, places, things, and events. A precise vocabulary will also help you to think more precisely.

2. To analyze a piece of literature, follow all of the steps in the process of writing.

3. During the pre-writing stage, complete a thorough analysis and interpretation of the various elements in the poem or story you are writing about. Focus your paper by concentrating on one or two of these elements.

4. Remember that a poem is likely to contain several devices of sound and imagery that have a great deal of impact on the reader. Be aware of these devices during analysis.

5. During your drafting and revising stages, work to make sure that each concept is thoroughly developed with details from the piece you are analyzing. Also make sure that the presentation of your ideas is coherent.

Applications in Other Subject Areas

Fine Arts. The type of criticism with which we are all most familiar is the review. Most reviews deal with something in the arts, such as a movie, play, TV show, dance, choral production, painting, or sculpture. Choose an area of the arts in which you have a particular interest. Write a review of one particular performance or piece of art. Use a precise vocabulary to present objective judgments.

Business / Physical Education. A different type of criticism is the evaluation. Supervisors evaluate the work of employees, teachers evaluate the work of students, and coaches or judges evaluate the performance of athletes. Try to recall a specific job you had or a competition you were involved in. Now take on the role of someone evaluating your performance. Write up a report, using a precise, objective vocabulary.

Chapter 12

The Paraphrase and the Summary

How often have you described a speech or article to another person by relating only the most important concepts and ideas? This ability to identify and present the significant aspects of written or spoken material is very valuable. By using this skill, you can communicate the ideas of others in a precise and efficient manner. When these altered versions take a written form, they are called **paraphrases** and **summaries.**

You will find both the paraphrase and the summary, or **précis,** extremely useful as tools for research and study. Not only can they be used to record essential information contained in a reading passage, they can also be used to adapt material for presentation in a research paper or report. Learning to write proper paraphrases and summaries can therefore be of enormous value to you both in your studies and in the future.

Part 1 The Paraphrase

Paraphrasing is putting the ideas of others into your own words. A paraphrase can help you to understand a difficult passage you are reading. It can also provide an excellent basis for reviewing ideas. Finally, paraphrases are useful as a means for adapting material for inclusion in a research paper or report. Whenever you use paraphrased material in a research paper or report, the source of the material must be credited in a footnote or in the text of the paper. Not crediting a paraphrased source is a variety of plagiarism.

The paraphrase requires a careful reading and rephrasing of the original material. The paraphrase simplifies; it does not necessarily shorten the selection.

How To Write a Paraphrase

I. Pre Writing

   a. Read the selection through once to get the central meaning.

   b. Look up any words you do not understand.

   c. Reread the selection at least twice more. Think of simple words to substitute for any long or difficult ones.

2. Writing

   a. Follow the same order that the writer uses in presenting the ideas.

   b. Put the material into your own words. Shorten long sentences. Use simple vocabulary.

3. Revision

   a. Check your paraphrase to be sure that it expresses the ideas of the original. Revise as necessary.

   b. Proofread your revised paraphrase for errors in spelling, grammar, usage, and punctuation. It is especially important that names and unfamiliar terms have been spelled correctly and that numbers have been copied accurately.

A Sample Paraphrase

Read the paragraph below. Then work through the steps that lead to a finished paraphrase.

> On the weekend of the Kennedy assassination, Walter Cronkite's sober mien—his natural strength—reflected the mood of the country. His earnest, almost reverent approach, often criticized as being stuffy, now struck many viewers as solid and reassuring. This was the start, for Cronkite, of a new persona or, to be more precise, what was perceived as a new persona. In the years ahead, as the country continued to reel through difficult times (a despised war, urban riots, more political assassinations), Cronkite always seemed to be there, on the TV screen, in moments of crisis or travail. Thus the image of solid integrity was steadily reinforced until, eventually, his reputation grew so immense that it extended well beyond the limits of broadcast journalism.
>
> —GARY PAUL GATES

Applying the Techniques

Step 1. Reread the selection for the main idea. Usually the key sentence comes first in a paragraph. Here, it is the third sentence. This sentence summarizes the preceding two and prepares us for what follows. The writer is showing how Cronkite's handling of a crisis changed the public's view of him.

Put into your own words, the idea of the paragraph might read like this:

> The country's view of Walter Cronkite as a journalist of integrity and strength began as a result of his sober, earnest handling of the Kennedy assassination.

This sentence may not appear in your finished paragraph, but it is helpful to keep it in front of you as you work. It will give focus and coherence to your writing.

Step 2. Several words in the paragraph need defining. The dictionary will give you more than one synonym for each.

Select the one that is best for the context. Whenever possible, choose the word with which you are familiar and comfortable.

For example, *travail* is defined as (1) toil (2) drudgery (3) agony (4) effort. Clearly, what the writer has in mind is the mental agony of the nation.

Following is a list of the more difficult words in the selection and their appropriate synonyms.

sober	serious
mien	manner
reverent	deeply respectful
persona	image
perceived	viewed
reel	stagger
integrity	honesty

Step 3. As you reread, substitute the synonyms above. Look for other words and phrases that can be simplified or even omitted.

Writing the Paraphrase

Step 1. Structure your paragraph in the same way the writer does. Begin with Cronkite's TV handling of the Kennedy assassination. Contrast this view with what had been the view of Cronkite as a stuffy person. Conclude with the new view in the years that follow.

Step 2. Here is the completed paraphrase:

> On the weekend of the Kennedy assassination, Cronkite's serious manner mirrored the feeling of the country. Although viewers had once seen him as stuffy, they were now reassured by his serious, deeply respectful approach. This was the beginning of a changed view of him—a new image. As the country staggered through its times of crisis and agony (a hated war, unrest in the cities, more assassinations), Cronkite was reassuringly present. Thus the sense of his honesty was strengthened and expanded into areas beyond TV broadcasting.

Exercises Practice in Writing Paraphrases

A. Paraphrase this selection. Follow the pre-writing steps that are outlined after the selection. Then, write your paraphrase.

> Bats are obliged to make sounds almost ceaselessly, to sense, by sonar, all the objects in their surroundings. They can spot with accuracy, on the wing, small insects, and they will home onto things they like with infallibility and speed. With such a system for the equivalent of glancing around, they must live in a world of ultrasonic bat-sound, most of it with an industrial, machinery sound. Still, they communicate with each other as well, by clicks and high-pitched greetings. Moreover, they have been heard to produce, while hanging at rest upside down in the depths of the woods, strange, solitary, and lovely bell-like notes.
>
> —LEWIS THOMAS

Step 1. Here the key sentence is the first one. Rephrase it.

Step 2. Do any words need defining? What synonyms can you substitute for the more difficult words?

Step 3. Reread the selection and in your mind substitute the synonyms you have selected. Now rewrite the paragraph.

B. Using the same procedure, paraphrase each of the following.

1   For a great tree, death comes as a gradual transformation. Its vitality ebbs slowly. Even when life has abandoned it entirely, it remains a majestic thing. On some hilltop a dead tree may dominate the landscape for miles around. Alone among living things, it retains its character and dignity after death. Plants wither; animals disintegrate. A dead tree, however, may be as arresting, as filled with personality, in death as it is in life. Even in its final moments, when the massive trunk lies prone and it has moldered into a ridge covered with mosses and fungi, it arrives at a fitting and a noble end. It enriches and refreshes the earth. And later, as part of other green and growing things, it rises again.—EDWIN WAY TEALE

2   The lion tamer's will must be stronger than that of his or her beasts. How often has one been to the circus and suddenly felt a certain tension in the cage when a beast is proving difficult? There is clearly a battle of wills going on. The most observant in the audience will watch fascinated; the rest will sense that a moment of crisis is upon them, and the trainer must impose both will and mastery on the recalcitrant animal. The trainer may turn quickly upon it as though making quite clear that it has earned his or her displeasure, and, if not careful, will earn some chastisement; the trainer may merely look in the direction of the animal or may point imperiously with a whip—not that that would prove any real protection should the animal attack—it is more an instrument for instruction. Then with a snarl, or with a whimper, or with defiance, the beast will do as it should have done, and everyone will sigh with relief. The battle of wills is over; the human has won, and the other animals in the act will be as aware of that all-important fact as the wayward beast itself.

—PETER VERNEY

3   Of the great American popular singers, Bing Crosby has been among the most profoundly and decisively influential. It might be more accurate to say that he has been among the most immediately influential. The impact of earlier innovators, notably Al Jolson, Bessie Smith, and Ethel Waters, was indirect, filtered to a considerable extent through Bing—and the microphone. The two elements contributing to a new, distinctive vocal idiom—an Afro-American approach to phrasing, and radio, bringing with it the microphone—met in him. They were synthesized in his singing, and passed on to all who came after him. —HENRY PLEASANTS

Part 2   The Summary, or Précis

Unlike the paraphrase, the summary, also known as the précis, cuts a selection down to about one-third of its original length. Its purpose is to condense without losing the basic meaning of the original. Being able to summarize material will be particularly helpful in your research paper. In most cases, you will have to condense material from your reading in order to prepare your note cards. In addition, summaries can be used, like paraphrases, to rework material contained in complex reading assignments.

The summary is not new to you. Radio and TV broadcasts summarize important events of the day. The last paragraph of a textbook chapter often summarizes the main points of the chapter. In fact, you read and listen to summaries daily.

How To Write a Summary

1. **Pre-Writing**

   a. Read the selection carefully. There usually is a key sentence that expresses the main point. Sometimes a topic sentence will summarize a whole paragraph for you.

   b. Note the important ideas, the order in which they occur, and the way the writer has connected them. You may want to write these ideas briefly in your own words.

2. **Writing**

   a. Omit unnecessary details, examples, anecdotes, and repetitions.

   b. Rephrase the material. You may want to retain some of the key words or technical language of the original, but the bulk of the summary should be in your own words.

3. **Revision**

   a. Check your first draft to see that it includes all the important ideas of the original. Any unnecessary or repetitious details should be omitted.

   b. You may need to revise and rewrite. Your final summary should be about one-third the length of the original. It should give all the essential information in a way that the reader can use without referring to the original.

   c. Proofread your summary for errors in grammar, usage, and mechanics.

A Sample Summary

Read the paragraph below. Then work through the steps that lead to a finished summary.

About a hundred years ago, Thomas Henry Huxley, the English biologist, could say with confidence: "I believe that probably all the great sea fisheries are inexhaustible; that is to say that nothing we do seriously affects the numbers of fish." Huxley, of course, did not foresee the technological advances that would be made and applied within a century to fishing, as well as to every other aspect of man's activities. Sadly, Huxley's prediction has proved wrong. Today's fishing fleets consist of entire flotillas equipped with electronic devices and include floating ships that process the catch at sea. Planes are used as spotters to locate schools of fish. Radio telephones direct the boats to the fish. Radar and echo sounders find schools that cannot be seen from the air or on the water's surface. Moreover, oceanic sciences have determined the conditions of salinity and temperatures required for various species to thrive. Today, thermometers and salinometers are used by fishing fleets. These ultramodern fishing fleets can stay in the open water almost indefinitely, sweeping the sea of much of its life. The herring population in the Atlantic, the most heavily fished area of the world, is decreasing. Haddock may have been wiped out. Similarly, modern whaling methods have all but eliminated several types of whales from the face of the earth. Helicopters and swift, engine-driven catcher boats with sounding equipment spot the whales. Explosive harpoons fired from guns mounted on the catchers find their mark. Humans have become by far the greatest predators of all time.

—JACQUES COUSTEAU

Applying the Techniques

Step 1. The writer begins this paragraph with a quotation from the past, reflecting an optimism about the abundance of nature. The rest of the paragraph refutes this optimism with a hard-headed look at the present reality. Two things have worked to deplete the resources of the ocean: technology and scientific advancement. The writer develops each of these points with examples and then cites specific kinds of fish that are either threatened or extinct. His concluding sentence places the responsibility squarely on humans.

Step 2. By omitting unnecessary details, examples, and repetitions, you can reduce long phrases and even whole sentences to short phrases or single words.

Original	Summary
Sentence 1. Lengthy quotation from Huxley.	brief paraphrase
Sentence 10. "These ultramodern fishing fleets can stay in the open water almost indefinitely."	year-round fleets
Sentences 4, 5, 6, 7.	electronic detectors, radar, echo sounders, and spotter planes
Sentences 8, 9.	Advances in oceanic sciences have further improved their efficiency.
Sentences 11, 12, 13.	As a result, the herring population has been seriously decreased; haddock and several kinds of whales have been almost wiped out.

The final sentence of this paragraph indicts humans.

Following is a finished summary. It is eighty-six words compared with the original two hundred and fifty-five. Does it include all of the important ideas of the original?

A hundred years ago, the English biologist Thomas Henry Huxley predicted that despite anything we might do, our supply of fish would remain inexhaustible. Technological and scientific advances have proved him wrong. Today's year-round fleets are aided by electronic detectors, radar, echo sounders, and spotter planes. Advances in oceanic sciences have further improved their efficiency. As a result, the herring population has been seriously decreased; haddock and several kinds of whales have been almost wiped out. Humans are the greatest destroyers of all time.

Exercises Practice in Writing Summaries

A. Summarize the following selection. Follow the steps that are outlined after the selection.

You can make computers that are almost human. In some respects they are superhuman; they can beat most of us at chess, memorize whole telephone books at a glance, compose music of a certain kind and write obscure poetry, diagnose heart ailments, send personal invitations to vast parties, even go transiently crazy. No one has yet programmed a computer to be of two minds about a hard problem, or to burst out laughing, but that may come. Sooner or later, there will be real human hardware, great whirring, clicking cabinets intelligent enough to read magazines and vote, able to think rings around the rest of us.

Well, maybe, but not for a while anyway. Before we begin organizing sanctuaries and reservations for our software selves, lest we vanish like the whales, here is a thought to relax with.

Even when technology succeeds in manufacturing a machine as big as Texas to do everything we recognize as human, it will still be, at best, a single individual. This amounts to nothing, practically speaking. To match what we can do, there would have to be three billion of them, with more coming down the assembly line; and I doubt that anyone will put up the money, much less make room. And even so, they would all have to be wired together, intricately and delicately, as we are, communicating with each other, talking incessantly, listening. If they weren't *at* each other this way, all their waking hours, they wouldn't be anything like human, after all. I think we're safe, for a long time ahead.

—LEWIS THOMAS

Step 1. Reread the selection.

a. Look for the sentence that expresses the basic idea. You will find that in this selection it is the topic sentence of paragraph three.

b. Note the structure of the selection and list the important ideas in the order in which they occur. In paragraph one, Thomas somewhat humorously warns us that computers may be developing superhuman qualities. In paragraph two, he reassures us about the unlikelihood of such a development. In paragraph three, he explains why we may feel safe.

Step 2. Summarize the selection in your own words, keeping to the structure outlined above.

a. Omit unnecessary details.

b. Read your summary and check for accuracy. Revise as necessary.

B. Using this same procedure, summarize each of the following selections.

1   Nearly all four-legged predators have extremely good senses of smell, but more than that is required from a domesticated dog. The modern dog has a genetic history of sociability. Wolves, dingos, and other wild dogs live in highly social pack structures in which each member knows who the boss is, what the territorial limits are, and where to stand in line at suppertime. These social concepts have been carried over, and in many cases even enhanced by selective breeding, so that your dog is usually very well adjusted to the basic concepts of teamwork and obedience. Most dogs will usually make a distinct effort to let you know when they smell something worth bringing to your attention.—DENNIS G. WALROD

2   We have an abiding impression of the outlaw as a low-life renegade, a violent fool who lived off luck and the gun. We view him as one of society's misbegotten, who had to be hunted down like an animal by morally superior men in white hats. That was not so, however. In truth, the line

between the "good guy" and the "bad guy" in the West was often blurred, and many of the outlaws, in spite of their errant and often violent natures, were men of extraordinary skill and cunning, who by comparison made lawmen look pathetic.—ROBERT REDFORD

3   Members of a dreamer's family constitute a fairly high percentage of dream characters. For younger dreamers, those in their late teens and early twenties, mother and father are dreamed about more often than any other family members, while among middle-aged dreamers, the dreamer's mate and his children play important roles. Why should we dream about our family? We believe that people who enter our dreams are ones with whom we are emotionally involved. The emotion may be one of love, fear, or anger, or a mixture of these feelings. For young people who are not married and do not have children, the most significant members of the family and the ones with whom they are emotionally involved are their parents. Young people are trying to break family ties and assert their independence, yet they are apprehensive about leaving the security of home for the hazards of the world. Moreover, they often feel guilty about deserting their parents. On the other hand, older dreamers, having resolved these particular conflicts, find themselves involved with their husbands or wives and with their children. It is rather ironical that while children are dreaming about parents, parents are dreaming about children, and while husbands are dreaming about wives, wives are dreaming about husbands. It might be said that if anyone wants to know who is dreaming about him or her, one will find the answer by consulting one's own dreams. The people in one's dreams are likely to be those who are dreaming about him or her.—RALPH L. WOODS AND HERBERT B. GREENHOUSE

SUMMARY AND APPLICATIONS CHAPTER 12

1. The paraphrase and the summary may be used to adapt material for inclusion in a research paper or report. They may also be used to help you to understand difficult or complex reading assignments, or to provide an aid for review.

2. A paraphrase is a simplified, but not necessarily shortened, version of ideas originally presented by another person in different words.

3. A summary, or précis, is a shortened or condensed version of a written or spoken selection. It reflects both the order and the content of the selection on which it is based.

4. A paraphrase or summary must accurately reflect the content of the selection from which it is drawn.

Applications in Other Subject Areas

Science / Journalism. The paraphrase is often used to simplify difficult or complex material. Authors of articles in popular science magazines often use paraphrases to simplify the results of scientific reports so that these can be read by general audiences. Find such a science magazine and choose a short article that interests you. Imagine that you are preparing a science bulletin for use in grammar school classes. Paraphrase the article, simplifying the language so that it can be read by children.

Speech. One way to conclude an informative or persuasive speech is to write a summary of the information presented in the rest of the speech. Choose an issue that is currently being debated in your school or community. Write a persuasive speech presenting your opinions on this subject. Conclude the speech with a summary of the facts used to support your opinions.

Chapter 13

The Research Paper

A research paper is a formal report that presents an in-depth study of a specific topic. It is based upon information that is gathered from reliable sources and organized according to the judgment of the writer. As you probably know, research papers are often required of students in high schools and colleges. In addition, workers in many fields, including science, business, health, and the civil services, frequently prepare research papers in order to present large amounts of information to others in a concise form.

A typical research paper takes weeks to prepare and requires careful planning on the part of the writer. Therefore, whenever you are assigned to write a research paper, you should begin by making a time schedule that contains specific deadlines for completing each step in the process of writing the paper. These steps may be summarized as shown on the next page.

1. Choose and limit your subject.
2. Prepare a working bibliography.
3. Prepare a preliminary outline.
4. Read and take notes.
5. Organize your notes and write the final outline.
6. Write the first draft.
7. Revise the first draft.
8. Write the final draft with footnotes.
9. Write the final bibliography.

Writing a research paper is one of the most ambitious and demanding tasks that you will undertake as a student. It can also be one of the most rewarding. If you follow the guidelines presented in this chapter and apply what you have already learned about writing compositions and reports, you should have little difficulty.

Part 1 Pre-Writing: Choosing a Subject

One key to the success of a research paper is choosing an appropriate subject. Your choice of subject determines what sources you will use, what information you will gather, and how this information will be organized and presented to your readers. It is therefore important that you choose your subject with care. The following guidelines will help you:

1. Choose a subject that interests you. Choose a subject that you want to learn more about. If your subject does not really interest you, your paper will probably not be interesting to the reader either.

2. Choose a subject for which a wide range of source materials is readily available. Subjects that are too recent in development, or too technical in nature, will have few, if any, source materials. If you have doubts about source materials for a subject, consult your school librarian to find out how much information the library has. Also check the card file, the vertical file, and the *Readers' Guide to Periodical Literature*.

3. Choose a subject of some significance.   A subject of lasting interest will be challenging and gratifying to pursue. After all, you will be spending much time and effort on this assignment, and what you learn should be a significant addition to your store of knowledge as well as that of the reader.

4. Choose a subject that can be presented objectively.   Your purpose is to sift through and reshape an accumulated body of information, not to indulge in arguments and persuasion. Argument and persuasion are right for debates, but not for a research paper. Your paper should be an objective presentation.

5. Avoid straight biography.   Biography requires long, intensive research, involving letters, interviews, and unpublished material not available to the average person. If the person is well known, biographies already exist and using them as resource material, even if they are in unusual quantity, results merely in a rehashing of already published information. If you do wish to write about some interesting figure, try to choose an unusual angle or viewpoint.

As you know from previous chapters, limiting your subject is important whenever you write.

One way to begin limiting your subject is to do some general reading in reference works. By doing this, you can learn what topics lie within the broader subject that you have chosen. A list of reference works that are useful for this purpose may be found in Chapter 14, pages 311-320. In addition to consulting these sources, you may wish to glance at indexes or tables of contents in books on your subject. These will show you how other people have broken down the subject in the past.

When limiting your subject, bear in mind that your paper should serve a definite purpose. The purpose may be **to inform** your audience about a topic. It may be **to analyze** the topic. It may be **to compare or contrast** one topic with another. Keeping a specific purpose in mind will help you to narrow the topic prior to doing your research. It may also provide an interesting angle or approach to the actual writing of the paper.

Here is an example of a subject for a paper on literature. Suppose you were interested in the works of Stephen Crane. The process of limiting your subject might proceed like this:

1. Stephen Crane
2. The works of Stephen Crane
3. The realism of Stephen Crane
4. *The Red Badge of Courage*

You have worked your way down to what seems to be a manageable subject: one book. However, the subject is still too general because there are countless ways in which to discuss a book. You need to focus on a particular aspect of the book that you feel will lend itself to a wide variety of source materials. Bearing in mind that your subject should reflect a specific purpose, you might decide on the following:

> Realism in the portrayal of Henry Fleming in Stephen Crane's *The Red Badge of Courage*

This subject is ideal for a research paper that informs.

Exercise Limiting Your Subject

Bring to class three subjects that interest you as possible choices for a research paper. Limit them properly, and be sure that each one can be adequately researched. You will probably have to work in the library to complete this assignment.

Part 2 Pre-Writing: Compiling a Working Bibliography

Once you have decided on a subject and have had this subject approved by your teacher, the next step is to locate relevant sources of information. Begin by consulting reference works that contain entries on your general subject. For example, if you are planning a paper on *The Red Badge of Courage*, you might read an encyclopedia article that discusses the works of the book's author, Stephen Crane. You might also read a selection in a book of literary biographies. Finally, you could check the *Readers' Guide to Periodical Literature* to find an article that deals with your subject in a general way. Consulting such reference works will give you an overview of the subject. It may also suggest possible modifications in the subject you have chosen. If you do decide to modify your subject, consult your teacher.

Recommended Sources

At this point, you may wish to review Chapter 14 so that you can use your library time wisely. The following sources are the most important for a research paper.

1. The card catalog.   Suppose you are doing a paper on William Faulkner. You would first look at all the subject cards with his name. In addition to all the books Faulkner has written, you will find major biographies and works of criticism mainly concerned with him. However, many books that may have informative chapters on Faulkner may not be entered under the heading *Faulkner*. Therefore, you should also look at "American Literature," "Twentieth Century Literature," "Literature of the South," "The Novel," "Literary Criticism," and any other general subjects related to Faulkner and his work. The description of the book on the card will tell you whether the book is worth investigating.

2. The *Readers' Guide to Periodical Literature*.   This source will list current magazine articles on your subject. For most subjects, past articles are as useful as present ones, and the library has cumulative bound volumes of past years.

3. Specialized reference books.   Turn to Part 3 in Chapter 14 and review the list of reference books. If any of them relate to your subject, consult them.

In preparing a working bibliography, your object is to accumulate as many books and articles as you think might be helpful. Because you cannot always tell whether the information on a catalog card or in the *Readers' Guide* or in a bibliography will be worthwhile, it is wise to include sources you may be doubtful about at the moment. If some sources turn out to be of little help, you can later drop them from your bibliography.

4. Other sources.   Do not neglect interviews, television programs, radio shows, recordings, graphic aids, and other possible sources of information. These often provide unique insights that can add considerably to the freshness of a paper.

Guidelines for Selecting Source Materials

These guidelines will help you in selecting source materials:

1. **Is the author an authority on the subject?** While you may not know this at the beginning, an author who has written several books on your subject or whose name is included in various bibliographies may be an authoritative source. As you read, be on the alert for writers whose opinions are frequently mentioned or quoted.

2. **Is the source reliable, unbiased, and up-to-date?** A book on a well-known politician, written by a friend or relative, may not be as accurate as one written by an authority on scientific thinking. A book on computers published in 1968 may not be as accurate as one published in 1984. A third edition of a book would be more valuable than the first or second edition. Recent material is especially important for those topics on which research is still being done.

3. **If a magazine article looks promising, what kind of magazine does it appear in?** Many popular interest magazines are not suitable sources for a research paper.

4. **If a book looks promising, for what audience is it intended?** Many interesting books are actually intended for younger readers. Because they present information in an overly-simplified form, they are not suitable for research papers. Books of a highly technical nature are also usually unsuit-

able. They are too detailed or too complex to be useful to the average reader.

5. **Are additional books or articles included in any of the bibliographies you have consulted?** In addition to the bibliographies in reference books, you may be able to find bibliographies in many of the books listed in the card catalog. When you find such a bibliography, examine its entries closely. If the same books or authors appear in several bibliographies, they are probably worth investigating.

Bibliography Cards

1. To record all the information needed to find the reference in the library.
2. To record the information needed to prepare the footnotes for your paper.
3. To record the information needed to prepare the final bibliography for your paper.

For each bibliography entry, use a 3″ x 5″ card or slip of paper. Here are the correct forms for bibliography cards from three different kinds of sources: a book, a magazine article, and an encyclopedia article.

BOOK

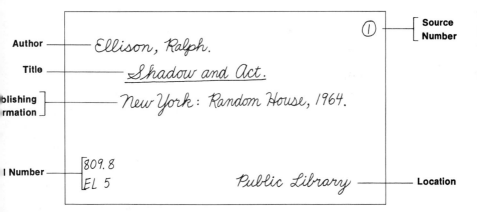

MAGAZINE ARTICLE

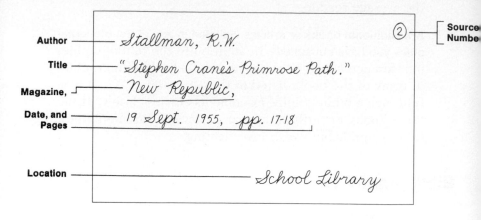

Author — Stallman, R.W.

Title — "Stephen Crane's Primrose Path."

Magazine, — New Republic,

Date, and Pages — 19 Sept. 1955, pp. 17-18

Location — School Library

② Source Number

ENCYCLOPEDIA ARTICLE

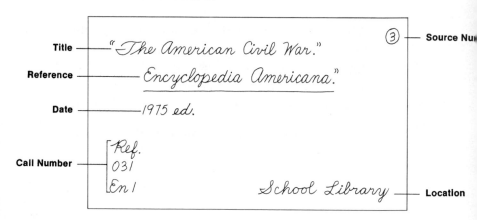

Title — "The American Civil War."

Reference — Encyclopedia Americana."

Date — 1975 ed.

Call Number — Ref. 031 En 1

School Library — Location

③ Source Number

On these sample bibliography cards, note that the titles of books are underlined and the titles of articles are enclosed in quotation marks. Note also the correct abbreviations and punctuation.

Here is some additional information that will be helpful in preparing bibliography cards.

1. When you first locate a source, find the correct bibliography form for this source by checking the sample bibliogra-

phy entries on pages 281-288. Then write a bibliography card, making certain that you include all the information that you will need in your final bibliography entry.

2. If a book has an editor rather than an author, use ed. (editor) or eds. (editors) after the name: Bloom, Harold, ed.

3. If no publication date is given, use the copyright date.

4. If neither publication nor copyright date is given, use the abbreviation *n.d.* (no date).

5. Information such as the above is usually found on the title page. Sometimes pamphlets have the information on front or back covers or on the last page. Magazines may have the information on the front cover or on one of the first pages.

6. The source number in the upper right-hand corner of your card will save you a great deal of time when you are writing your first draft. Instead of having to write out all the information on the bibliography card every time you use information from the source, you can merely jot down the number of the card after the paraphrased or quoted material in your draft. Later, you can use these numbers to locate the cards that you need to write your footnotes.

Exercise Preparing a Working Bibliography

Using all available facilities, prepare a working bibliography for your chosen subject.

Determining the Controlling Purpose of Your Paper

Now that you have chosen your subject, prepared your working bibliography, and done some background reading, you are ready to formulate a controlling purpose for your paper. This is a formal, exact statement of what your paper is going to be about. You began this process when you limited your subject. Now, based upon the reading you have done, you can refine your controlling purpose until it is clear and precise. You can use this purpose to direct your note-taking and to help you write a good outline and paper.

It is possible that you will want to revise your controlling purpose, but stating it as clearly as possible now will help you select the right material for your note-taking. Material that does not relate directly to your controlling purpose does not belong in your paper or in your notes.

You will recall that on page 250, the student interested in Stephen Crane decided to write a paper on "realism in the portrayal of Henry Fleming in Stephen Crane's *The Red Badge of Courage*." While this statement may be suitable as a title, it is not sufficiently focused for a statement of controlling purpose. Clarifying how it is going to be demonstrated that Fleming is a realistic character would help. The statement must be recast as one that requires proof, such as the following:

> CONTROLLING PURPOSE: to demonstrate that Henry Fleming, the protagonist of Stephen Crane's *The Red Badge of Courage*, is an accurate portrayal of a Civil War soldier by comparing him with actual soldiers through their letters and diaries

As you begin to write your report, you may want to include a revised version of this statement in your introductory paragraphs. Such a sentence is sometimes called a **thesis statement**.

Exercise Stating the Controlling Purpose

Write out the controlling purpose for your paper, stating it as exactly as you can.

Part 3 Preparing a Preliminary Outline

Once you have determined your controlling purpose and know what materials are available to you, the next step is to prepare a preliminary outline. This outline will function as a general guideline for your reading. It is only tentative, and will probably change considerably as you learn more.

Begin by listing major divisions suggested by the background reading you have done. Then fill in any subdivisions that come to mind. As you read and gather information, revise and extend your outline as necessary. If you find that your sources do not contain enough information to develop a major topic thoroughly, you may have to delete this topic and substitute another. If you find that your sources contain material that you did not know about when you wrote your preliminary outline, you may want to alter or replace one of your major divisions. Your research will doubtless suggest subdivisions to be added beneath the major divisions on your outline. As you pursue your research, revise your outline regularly. This will help considerably when it comes time to prepare the final outline of your paper. Keep the following guidelines in mind:

1. Make sure that all divisions are related to your subject.
2. Make sure that all divisions help to serve the stated purpose of your paper.
3. Follow the guidelines for outline form presented in Section 18 of the Handbook.

Here is an example of how a rough preliminary outline of the paper on Stephen Crane might look.

The Realism of Henry Fleming in Stephen Crane's
The Red Badge of Courage

CONTROLLING PURPOSE: to demonstrate that Henry Fleming, the protagonist of Stephen Crane's *The Red Badge of Courage*, is an accurate portrayal of a Civil War soldier by comparing him with actual soldiers through their letters and diaries.

I. (Introduction—to come)

II. Soldiers in battle
   A. Risks
   B. Fears

III. Change in attitude
   A. Urgency
   B. Rage
   C. New Purpose

IV. Desertion
   A. Mental problems
   B. Physical problems
   C. Excuses

V. Expectations versus realities of battle

VI. Soldiers mature

VII. (Conclusion—to come)

Exercise Preparing a Preliminary Outline

Prepare a preliminary outline for your paper in the following form:

1. Put the title of your paper at the top.
2. Below the title, write your controlling purpose.
3. Follow standard outline form. (See Section 18.)
4. Keep the details of your outline to a minimum so you can revise and expand more easily as your reading progresses.

Part 4   Pre-Writing: Reading and Taking Notes

Once you have located your sources and prepared a preliminary outline, you are ready to begin your actual research. To do this, you must take notes on specific information related to your controlling purpose and to the divisions on your preliminary outline.

Take notes on 4"x6" cards in order to distinguish these from your 3"x5" bibliography cards. Use a separate card for each note. Avoid putting unrelated facts or many facts on a single card. Remember that you will have to group your cards under separate topics before you can write your final outline and rough draft. If you have two different ideas on one card, you may need one idea for the beginning of your paper and the other for the end of your paper. Having separate ideas on one card will make sorting your material almost impossible.

A Sample Note Card

Here is a sample note card containing both a paraphrased idea and a direct quotation and showing the position and spacing for each part of a note card.

Sample Note Card

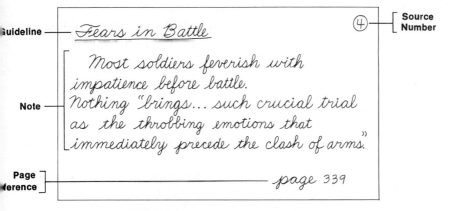

Here is an explanation of the parts of a sample note card.

1. The guideline is a heading that identifies the note on the card. It corresponds to a topic or subtopic on your preliminary outline. Include on the card only ideas pertaining to the guideline and use a different card for each source. If your reading does not yield enough information for your guideline, you may need to delete the topic from your outline and discard the corresponding note cards. If your reading yields new or different information, revise your outline and your guideline.

As you work, you will probably want to keep cards with similar guidelines grouped together. You may even want to try to put cards with similar guidelines in a logical order. Of course, this order may shift as you learn more about your subject, but making the attempt to organize your notes as you work will simplify the task of ordering your material later on.

2. The source number corresponds with the number of your working bibliography card and is the source from which the note was taken. By checking the card in the working bibliography, you can obtain all the information on the source whenever you need it.

3. The page reference must be exact for two reasons: (1) You may want to refer again to the source to verify the facts, and (2) you may need the page reference for footnotes.

4. The note, of course, is the most important part of the card because it is this part that you are going to use in writing your paper. Except for direct quotations, all notes should be paraphrased in your own words (See Chapter 12, "The Paraphrase and the Summary.")

The purpose of paraphrasing is twofold. First, it helps you to take notes more quickly and efficiently. Second, it helps you to avoid plagiarism.

Plagiarism

Because plagiarism is intellectually dishonest and therefore a form of stealing, it is an extremely serious offense and can result in severe penalties, even no credit for the course. The following forms of plagiarism are the most frequent:

1. Failure to document with quotation marks any material copied directly from other sources.

2. Failure to acknowledge paraphrased material (someone else's ideas).

3. Failure to provide a bibliography.

4. Use of others' work as one's own, particularly in the creative arts.

5. Use of others' ideas as one's own for themes, poems, musical compositions, or artwork.

Improving Your Skill at Taking Notes

Here are some ways to improve your skill in taking notes.

1. Keep your topic, purpose, and audience in mind at all times. Do not bother recording material that is unrelated to your topic, that will not help you accomplish what you want to in your paper, or that is too basic or too technical for your audience.
2. Use indexes, tables of contents, glossaries, appendices, and other parts of books to help you to locate specific information. (See Chapter 14, pages 309-310, for instructions on finding information in a book.)
3. Be accurate. Double-check statistics and facts to make sure you have them right. When you summarize or paraphrase a writer's words, be sure you do not misinterpret or distort the meaning.
4. Distinguish between fact and opinion. (See Chapter 15 for an in depth discussion of fact and opinion.) Label opinions: "Dr. Graves thinks that . . ." or "According to Grace Jackson, . . ." Be careful to note differences in opinion and to point out such differences in your notes.
5. Take notes as quickly as possible. Omit all words or phrases not essential to meaning; use abbreviations. Be careful, however, not to take notes so brief that when you need to use them you cannot understand what you have written.
6. Copy a direct quotation exactly, including punctuation, spelling, and grammar. Be sure to use quotation marks both at the beginning and at the end of the quotation so that you can easily separate the quotation from paraphrased material.
7. Any words inserted by the writer in the text of a quotation must be enclosed in brackets. (See Section 12.13 in your Handbook.) Parentheses must not be used. Insert brackets in ink if your typewriter does not have them.
8. Indicate the omissions of nonessential parts of a quotation by ellipses. (See Section 12.14 in your Handbook.)
9. If you can't get all the information on one side of a card,

write *over* in parentheses at the bottom of the card, flip the card over, and continue on the back. If you have more than two more lines, you probably have too much material for one card.

Exercise Reading and Taking Notes

Complete your reading and your note cards. Adjust or revise your preliminary outline as you do your research, and make any final revisions of your controlling purpose.

Part 5 Pre-Writing: Organizing Your Material

A research paper is longer and more complex than a short composition, and your outline will be correspondingly so. Remember, however, that much of your work has already been done. The guidelines on your note cards reflect the divisions and subdivisions of your outline which you have been modifying as you did research. Your next step is to organize these note cards so that you can write your first draft by referring to them.

Put each note card with the same guideline into a separate pile. You may already have begun this process during your research. Each of these piles of cards should relate to one of the major or minor divisions of your preliminary outline. Study these piles of cards to see what information each contains. Also determine the extent to which the information conforms to the information on your preliminary outline. Refer to your controlling purpose often as you study your cards.

Gradually, some groups of ideas will emerge as major divisions of your subject, some as subdivisions, and others as sub-subdivisions. This part of the organization process is exactly the same as in shorter compositions except that you are dealing with more material. If some cards reveal insufficient material on a subdivision but you feel that the subdivision is important, you may have to do more reading. If the subdivision is not important, you can either combine it with another closely related subdivision or delete the information and the card entirely.

This is the point at which you decide exactly what you are going to include in your paper and what you are going to leave out. Keep checking your controlling purpose to see that all your usable material is relevant to your subject. Do not be afraid to delete information that is not relevant. The decisions you make at this point will be reflected in your paper.

Finally, when you have chosen your main topics and subtopics and tested each note card for relevance to your controlling purpose, begin to organize the topics for your final outline. Try to decide in what order your topics would move most logically toward the conclusion you have determined in your controlling purpose. Feel free to move an entire main topic from one place to another or to shift the note cards within a group to different positions. See Chapters 7 and 8 for a review of possible types of organizations.

Write down your main topics in various orders and study them, thinking about how logically you can make transitions between topics. If a transition from one topic to another seems forced, something is probably wrong. Either you need to rearrange your topics or you need to revise the emphasis or the direction of one of them.

When you are finally satisfied with the order of your material, test it once more against your controlling purpose in the following ways.

1. Does it begin at the beginning and move logically to the conclusion?
2. Are the main topics the most important ideas?
3. Do the subtopics relate specifically to the main topics?
4. Is there unnecessary duplication of topics or subtopics?
5. Do all main topics relate clearly to the controlling purpose?
6. Will the transition from one topic to the next be logical?
7. Will the conclusion correspond to the controlling purpose?
8. Is there too much information on any one idea that upsets the balance of the paper?
9. Is enough information included to develop each idea?

When you are satisfied with the answers to these questions, you are ready to write your final outline. Include all of the major groupings and subgroupings in the order you have devised. If you have any doubts about standard outline form, see Section 18 in the Handbook. Remember that a good outline is not necessarily a long, elaborate one. Try to keep it within reasonable bounds.

Exercise Organizing Notes and Writing the Final Outline

Organize your note cards and write your final outline.

Part 6 Writing the First Draft

Writing a final outline is the last step in the pre-writing stage of writing a research paper. You are now ready to begin work on your first draft. In this draft, do not worry about achieving an elegant style or about eliminating all errors in grammar, mechanics, and spelling. Simply attempt to get your ideas down in a form that you will be able to follow when you are ready to make revisions.

Follow your outline, and keep your controlling purpose in mind. Begin a new paragraph for every topic and subtopic on your outline, and make some attempt at transitions between and within paragraphs, though you can work these out more carefully later.

Write your entire paper in the third person. Never use *I, me,* or *my* because you will be in danger of injecting your own opinion, and personal opinion has no place in a research paper. The only opinions you should use are those of authorities. These opinions, as was mentioned earlier, should be attributed to the authorities either directly or through a footnote. Use the information on your note cards as you write, and be sure to follow this information with the source number from the upper right-hand corner of your note card. You will need these sources for your footnotes. To save time, you can write only the first few words of a direct quotation in your rough draft. The source numbers will help you to locate the quotations quickly when you need to copy them carefully onto your final draft.

Stay alert to the possibility of using maps, charts, diagrams, and other graphic aids as a concise way to present some of your information. You can reproduce a graphic aid from one of your sources, or you can create one of your own. Just be certain to credit your source to avoid plagiarism.

As you write, keep in mind that the first paragraph of your paper will constitute your introduction, in which you set forth your controlling purpose. Your final, or concluding, paragraph should round up all your ideas in a restatement of your controlling purpose.

Exercise Writing the First Draft

With your controlling purpose and your outline before you, write the first draft of your paper. Use the information from your note cards as your write.

Part 7 Revising the First Draft and Adding Footnotes

Before writing your final draft, review the section on Revising in Chapter 7, "The Process of Writing." Also review the recommendations for manuscript form in Section 17 of your Handbook. Taking the time to review these materials will help you to produce a final draft that reflects the time and effort that you have put into planning and writing your paper.

Long Quotations

As you write your final draft, you will be including the complete form of the direct quotations you are using. If direct quotations are more than three typed lines long, indent them five spaces from both the left and the right margins. Single space each line, and do not use quotation marks. If the quotation is the beginning of a paragraph in the source, indent the first word an additional two spaces.

Footnotes

Uses

1. To indicate the source of material that is directly quoted
2. To give credit for other people's ideas even though you write them in your own words
3. To give the sources of graphic aids, figures, or statistics

Numbering

Number footnotes consecutively throughout the paper, beginning with number 1. Use Arabic numerals placed in the text of your paper, usually after the last word of a sentence or direct quotation. The footnote number should be placed slightly above the line in which it appears, as follows:

This same feeling was expressed by many Federals and Confederates. Bruce Catton, the Civil War historian, wrote that ''the instinctive loyalty of all these men went . . . to the army.''[1]

Position

Footnotes may appear in a paper in one of two ways: at the bottom of each page or on a separate page at the end. The actual form of each is the same.

If footnotes are to appear on each page, you must be careful to allow enough room at the bottom of each page for all the footnotes on that page. This will also include a one-inch margin of blank space at the bottom of each page.

When you have typed the last line of text on a page, skip a line. Then type a line that extends across the page, from the left margin to the right. Skip another space, and then type your first footnote. The bottom of your page will look like the example below.

This same feeling was expressed by many Federals and Confederates. Bruce Catton, the Civil War historian, wrote that ''the instinctive loyalty of all of these men went . . . to the army.''[1]

---

[1]Bruce Catton, This Hallowed Ground: The Story of the Union Side of the Civil War. (Garden City, New York: Doubleday and Co., 1956), p. 360.

Form

1. Number each footnote with an Arabic numeral to correspond to the material in the text. (See above.)
2. Indent each footnote five spaces, just as you do for paragraphs. Observe the text margin at the right. If the footnote runs to a second or third line, bring those lines back to the left margin.
3. Single space each footnote, but double space between footnotes.
4. Place a period at the end of each footnote.

The guidelines that follow contain all the information that you need to write footnotes of your own. Refer to these models as you write footnotes for your paper. Keep in mind that underscores are used to identify books, magazines, and other long works or collections of works. Quotation marks are used for chapters, stories, and other short pieces or parts within longer works. (See Section 14 of the Handbook.)

Basic Forms for Footnotes

A. One author:

[1]Margaret Mead, Blackberry Winter: My Earlier Years (New York: William Morrow and Co., 1972), pp. 175—76.

B. Two authors:

[2]Sandra M. Gilbert and Susan Gubar, The Madwoman in the Attic: The Woman Writer and the Nineteenth Century Literary Imagination (New Haven, Conn.: Yale University Press, 1979), p. 607.

C. Three authors:

[3]Bertram L. Linder, Edwin Selzer, and Barry M. Berk, A World History: The Human Panorama (Chicago: Science Research Associates, 1983), pp. 276—77.

D. Four or more authors:

[4]Gaston Wiet and others, The Great Medieval Civilizations, Vol. III of History of Mankind: Cultural and Scientific Development (New York: Harper and Row, 1975), p. 524.

Instead of the words *and others*, you may use the Latin abbreviation *et al*.

E. No author given:

[5]Literary Market Place: The Directory of American Book Publishing, 1984 ed. (New York: R.R. Bowker, 1984), p. 76.

Basic Forms for Footnotes

F. An editor, but no single author:

⁶Charles G. Duffy, ed., Ballad Poetry of Ireland (Delmar, N.Y.: Scholar's Facsimiles and Reprints, 1973), p. 3.

G. Two or three editors:

⁷James A. Emanuel and Theodore L. Gross, eds., Dark Symphony: Negro Literature in America (New York: Macmillan, 1968), pp. 350–51.

⁸James Camp, X.J. Kennedy, and Keith Waldrop, eds., Pegasus Descending: A Book of the Best Bad Verse (New York: Macmillan, 1971), p. xv.

H. Four or more editors:

⁹Willard Thorp and others, eds., The American Literary Record (Chicago: J.B. Lippincott, 1961), p. 472.

Instead of the words *and others*, you may use the Latin abbreviation *et al.*

I. A translator:

¹⁰Albert Camus, The Plague, trans. Gilbert Stuart (New York: Modern Library, 1965).

J. Author, editor, and translator:

¹¹Andreas Capellanus, The Art of Courtly Love, trans. John J. Parry, ed. Frederick W. Locke (New York: Frederick Ungar, 1976), p. 42.

Basic Forms for Footnotes

K. A particular edition of a book:

¹²Donald Hall, <u>Writing Well</u>, 4th ed. (Boston: Little, Brown and Co., 1982), pp. 120—21.

L. A book or monograph that is part of a series:

¹³Marguerite C. Rand, <u>Ramón Peréz de Ayala</u>, Twayne's World Authors Series, Vol. 138 (New York: Twayne Publishers, 1971), pp. 95—97.

M. A particular volume of a multi-volume book:

¹⁴Francis James Child, ed., <u>The English and Scottish Popular Ballads</u> (New York: Dover, 1965), II, pp. 17—19.

N. A volume with its own title that is part of a work of several volumes under a different title:

¹⁵George Holmes, <u>The Later Middle Ages: 1272—1485</u>, Vol. III of <u>A History of England,</u> eds. Christopher Brooke and Denis Mack Smith (Edinburgh: Thomas Nelson and Sons, 1962), p. 57.

Parts Within Books

A. A poem, short story, essay, or chapter from a collection of works by one author:

¹⁶Randall Jarrell, ''The English in England,'' <u>The Third Book of Criticism</u> (New York: Farrar, Straus and Giroux, 1969), p. 287.

Basic Forms for Footnotes

When the name of the author of the work appears in the title of the collection, you may omit the first mention of the author's name:

[17]''Hamlet and His Problems,'' Selected Essays of T.S. Eliot (New York: Harcourt, Brace and World, 1964), p. 122.

B. A poem, short story, essay, or chapter from a collection of works by several authors:

[18]Alberto Rubio, ''Portrait of a Little Girl,'' in New Voices of Hispanic America: An Anthology, eds. Darwin J. Flakoll and Claribel Alegría (Boston: Beacon Press, 1962), p. 94.

C. A novel or play from a collection of novels or plays published under one cover:

[19]Rod Serling, Requiem for a Heavyweight, in Twelve American Plays, eds. Richard Corbin and Miriam Balf (New York: Charles Scribner's Sons, 1973), p. 300.

If the author of the collection is mentioned in the title of the collection, omit the first mention of the author's name:

[20]Cannery Row, The Short Novels of John Steinbeck (New York: The Viking Press, 1963), p. 356.

D. An introduction, preface, foreword, or afterword written by the author of a work.

[21]Fernand Braudel, Preface to the English Edition, The Mediterranean and the Mediterranean World in the Age of Phillip II (New York: Harper and Row, 1976), I, pp. 13—14.

Basic Forms for Footnotes

E. An introduction, preface, foreword, or afterword written by someone other than the author of a work:

[22]Harry T. Moore, Preface, <u>Palimpsest</u>, by Hilda Doolittle (Carbondale: Southern Illinois University Press, 1968), p. viii.

Magazines, Encyclopedias, Reports, Pamphlets, and Newspapers

A. An article from a quarterly or monthly magazine:

[23]Mary Batten, ''Life Spans,'' <u>Science Digest</u>, Feb. 1984, p. 49.

B. An article from a weekly magazine:

[24]Douglas Davis, ''Art in the Marketplace,'' <u>Newsweek</u>, 30 Jan. 1984, p. 67.

C. A magazine article with no author given:

[25]''Challenging Mount Etna's Power,'' <u>Time</u>, 30 May 1983, p. 48.

D. An article from a daily newspaper:

[26]Noah James, ''The Comedian Everyone Loves to Hate,'' <u>The New York Times</u>, 22 Jan. 1984, p. 23, col. 1.

If no author is given, begin with the title. If the paper is divided into sections, include the section number or letter before the page number. (See sample footnote E.)

E. An editorial in a newspaper:

[27]''The Politics of Arms Control,'' Editorial, <u>The Chicago Tribune</u>, 29 Jan. 1984, Sec. 5, p. 2, cols. 1-2.

Basic Forms for Footnotes

F. An article in a journal that has continuous page numbers throughout the annual volume:

²⁸Mary R. Leftkowitz, ''Patterns of Fiction in Ancient Biography,'' <u>The American Scholar</u>, 52 (1983), pp. 209—10.

G. An article in a journal that numbers the pages of each issue separately:

²⁹Emily P. Aumiller, <u>''Lord of the Flies</u> as a Musical,'' <u>The English Journal</u>, 71, No. 8 (1982), p. 32.

The volume number, the number of the issue, the date, and the page number(s) follow the title of the journal.

H. An encyclopedia article:

³⁰''Architecture,'' <u>The World Book Encyclopedia</u>, 1983 ed., pp. 566—593.

I. A signed review:

³¹Arthur Lubow, ''Glass Houses,'' rev. of <u>Rolling Breaks and Other Movie Business</u> by Aljean Harmetz, <u>The Movies</u>, Aug. 1983, p. 76.

J. An unsigned, untitled review:

³²Rev. of <u>Harry and Son</u>, dir. Paul Newman, <u>American Film</u>, March 1984, p. 78.

If the review is unsigned but has a title, use the form for a signed review, but delete the author's name.

K. A report or a pamphlet:

³³American Medical Association, <u>Medical Relations Under Workmen's Compensation</u> (Chicago: American Medical Association, 1976), p. 3.

If the report is by an individual author rather than by an association or committee, begin with the author's name.

Basic Forms for Footnotes

A. An interview:

[34]Personal interview with E. Talbot Donaldson, Distinguished Professor Emeritus, Department of English, Indiana University, 26 Sept. 1978.

B. A letter that has not been published:

[35]Letter from Hon. Jimmy Carter, President of the United States, Washington, D.C., 22 May 1977.

C. Information in private files:

[36]Of Our Lives: A History of the 1960's and 1970's, by the students of Paul D. Schriener, Munster High School, Munster, Indiana, 3 May 1981 (in the files of the Department of Social Studies).

D. A thesis or dissertation:

[37]Daniel M. Dunn, The Acceptance and Rejection of the American Dream: 1960–1975, (unpublished Ph.D. dissertation, Department of Speech Communication and Theatre, Wayne State University), p. 38.

E. A quotation:

[38]Robert Benchley, as quoted in Alistair Cooke, America (New York: Alfred A. Knopf, 1973), p. 273.

F. A film:

[39]Richard Attenborough, dir., Gandhi, with Ben Kingsley, Columbia Pictures, 1982.

Basic Forms for Footnotes

G. A work of art:

⁴⁰Paul Klee, <u>Twittering Machine</u>, Museum of Modern Art, New York.

H. A television or radio program:

⁴¹''A Desert Blooming,'' writ. Marshall Riggan, <u>Living Wild</u>, dir. Harry L. Gorden, prod. Peter Argentine, PBS, 29 April 1984.

I. A musical composition:

⁴²Chopin, Waltz in A–flat major, op. 42.

Subsequent Reference Footnotes

To refer to sources already cited, use a shortened form.

A. In most cases, the author's last name, followed by the relevant page numbers is sufficient.

⁴³Susan Sontag, <u>Illness as Metaphor</u> (New York: Farrar, Straus and Giroux, 1978), p. 50.

⁴⁴Sontag, pp. 79–80.

B. If references by other authors with the same last name are used, include the author's first name or initials.

⁴⁵Edmund Burke, <u>Reflections on the Revolution in France</u>, ed. Thomas H.D. Mahoney (Indianapolis: Bobbs–Merrill, 1955), p. 30.

⁴⁶Kenneth Burke, <u>The Philosophy of Literary Form: Studies in Symbolic Action</u> (New York: Random House, 1957), p. 21.

⁴⁷Kenneth Burke, p. 77.

Basic Forms for Footnotes

C. If more than one work by the same author has been referred to, you should write the author's last name and the title. The title may be in shortened form.

[48]Will Durant, The Pleasures of Philosophy: A Survey of Human Life and Destiny (New York: Simon and Schuster, 1953), p. 179.

[49]Will Durant, The Story of Philosophy: The Lives and Opinions of the Great Philosophers of the Western World (New York: Simon and Schuster, 1961), p. 209.

[50]Durant, Story of Philosophy, p. 49.

Reference Words and Abbreviations Used in Footnotes

Here are some of the more common reference words and abbreviations used in footnotes. Some of these words and abbreviations are no longer used in writing footnotes and bibliography entries, but are provided here for reference.

bk., bks.	book or books
ca. (or c.)	*circa*, "about" or "near." Used with approximate dates: *ca*. 1776; "*ca*." is preferable to "*c*.," which can also mean "chapter" or "copyright."
cf.	*confer*, "compare." Used, for example, when you wish to have your reader compare footnotes 22 and 23, which follow: *cf*. footnotes 22 and 23 or *cf*. *Ernest Hemingway, The Sun Also Rises*, p. 15.
c., ch., chs., (or chap., chaps.)	chapter(*s*)
col., cols.	columns(*s*)
comp.	compiled or compiler
ed., eds.	editor(*s*), edition(*s*)
e.*g*.	*exempli gratia*, "for example"
esp.	especially (as in "pp. 208–232, esp. p. 220")
et al.	*et alii*, "and others"
et seq.	*et sequens* and *et sequentes*, "and the one following," "and those that follow." But cf. "f.," "ff."
ex., exs.	example and examples
f., ff.	and the following page(s) or line(s). These abbreviations are replacing *et seq*.
fig., figs.	figure(s)

fn.	footnote (Cf. "n.")
ibid.	*ibidem,* "in the same place"; i.e., the single title cited in the note immediately preceding.
idem	(no period; sometimes *id.*) "the same." Used in place of *ibid.* when the footnote is to the same source on exactly the same page as that referred to in the note immediately preceding.
i.e.	*id est* "that is"
illus.	illustrated, illustrator, illustration(s)
l., ll.	line, lines
ms.	manuscript
mss.	manuscripts
n. or nn.	note or notes (as "p. 48, n. 2")
n.b., N.B.	*nota bene,* "note well"
n.d.	no date
no., nos.	number(s)
op. cit.	*opere citato,* "in the work cited." If several different items have come between the first mention of a book and a subsequent reference to it in a footnote, the last name of the author is repeated, followed by *op. cit.* and the page number.
p. or pp.	page(s)
par., pars.	paragraph(s)
passim	"throughout the work, here and there" (as pp. 79, 144, *et passim*)
pref.	preface
pseud.	pseudonym, a pen name: e.g., Mark Twain, pseud.
rev.	review, reviewed; revised, revision

sec. (or sect.), secs.	section(s)
ser.	series
sic	"thus, so." If the word *"sic"* in brackets [*sic*] is inserted in a quotation, it shows that you are recognizing and pointing out an error or a questionable statement. For example: "There were nine [*sic*] men on the bench at that time." Your own additions to quotations are shown by bracketing those words added: "He [Wouk] was a member of the New York Writers' Club."
st.	stanza
trans. (or tr.)	translator, translation, translated ("by" understood in context)
vol., vols.	volume(s)
vs.	*versus*, "against"; also verse

Exercise Writing the Final Draft with Footnotes

Write the final draft of your paper with the footnotes. Leave a three-inch margin at the top of your first page and number each page beginning with page two. Reread your paper several times to check the following:

1. Does your introductory paragraph engage the reader? Is it well developed? Does it set forth the controlling purpose?

2. Does your paper follow your outline exactly? Is it well paragraphed? Do your ideas flow logically?

3. Are your paragraph transitions natural and logical?

4. Does your conclusion sum up your ideas and restate your purpose? Is it a logical result of what you set out to prove?

5. Have you numbered all the ideas and direct quotations in the text and footnoted them correctly?

6. Have you tested the force and accuracy of specific words? Do you have interesting sentence variety?

7. Have you checked spelling, punctuation, and usage?

Part 8 Writing the Final Bibliography

Research papers usually end with a **bibliography.** This is a list of sources that were cited in the text of the paper, provided for the benefit of those who wish to investigate the subject on their own. Sources that were not actually cited in the paper should not be included in the bibliography.

Bibliography entries generally contain the same information that is found in footnotes. However, this information appears in a different form. The following guidelines contain all the information you need to write entries for your own papers.

General Guidelines

1. Arrange all bibliography entries alphabetically by the last name of the author or editor.

2. If you wish to do so, you may divide your bibliography into separate sections for books, magazines, and other sources. If this is done, each section should be numbered separately and should begin with a centered subheading reading, in upper and lower case letters, *Books, Magazines,* or *Other Sources.*

3. If no author or editor is given, alphabetize each entry by the first word of the title. If the first word of the title is *A, An,* or *The,* begin with the second word of the title.

4. Begin the first line of each entry at the left margin. If the entry runs to a second or third line, indent those lines five spaces.

5. Single space each bibliography entry, but double space between entries.

6. Place a period at the end of each entry.

7. Bibliography entries contain page numbers only when they refer to parts within whole works. For example, an entry for a chapter in a book or an article in a magazine should contain page numbers for the complete chapter or article.

Basic Forms for Bibliography Entries

Whole Books

A. One author:

Mead, Margaret. Blackberry Winter: My Earlier Years. New York: William Morrow and Co., 1972.

B. Two authors:

Gilbert, Sandra M., and Susan Gubar. The Madwoman in the Attic: The Woman Writer and the Nineteenth Century Literary Imagination. New Haven, Conn.: Yale University Press, 1979.

C. Three authors:

Linder, Bertram L., Edwin Selzer, and Barry M. Derk. A World History: The Human Panorama. Chicago: Science Research Associates, 1983.

D. Four or more authors:

Wiet, Gaston, and others. The Great Medieval Civilizations. Vol. III of History of Mankind: Cultural and Scientific Development. New York: Harper and Row, 1975.

Instead of the words *and others,* you may use the Latin abbreviation *et al.*

E. No author given:

Literary Market Place: The Directory of American Book Publishing. 1984 ed. New York: R.D. Bowker, 1984.

Basic Forms for Bibliography Entries

F. An editor, but no single author:

> Duffy, Charles G., ed. <u>Ballad Poetry of</u>
> <u>Ireland</u>. Delmar, N.Y.: Scholar's Fac-
> similes and Reprints, 1973.

This form may be used when you have cited several works from a collection. Instead of writing separate bibliography entries for each work, you may write one entry for the entire work, listing the editor or editors first.

G. Two or three editors:

> Emanuel, James A., and Theodore L. Gross,
> eds. <u>Dark Symphony: Negro Literature</u>
> <u>in America</u>. New York: Macmillan, 1968.

> Camp, James, X.J. Kennedy, and Keith Wal-
> drop, eds. <u>Pegasus Descending: A Book</u>
> <u>of the Best Bad Verse</u>. New York: Mac-
> millan, 1971.

H. Four or more editors:

> Thorp, Willard, and others, eds. <u>The Ameri-</u>
> <u>can Literary Record</u>. Chicago: J.B.
> Lippincott, 1961.

Instead of the words *and others*, you may use the Latin abbreviation *et al.*

I. A translator:

> Camus, Albert. <u>The Plague</u>. Trans. Gilbert
> Stuart. New York: Modern Library, 1965.

J. Author, editor, and translator:

> Capellanus, Andreas. <u>The Art of Courtly</u>
> <u>Love</u>. Trans. John J. Parry. Ed. Fred-
> erick W. Locke. New York: Frederick
> Ungar, 1976.

Basic Forms for Bibliography Entries

K. A particular edition of a book:

Hall, Donald. <u>Writing Well</u>. 4th ed. Boston: Little, Brown and Co., 1982.

L. A book or a monograph that is part of a series:

Rand, Marguerite C. <u>Ramón Peréz de Ayala</u>. Twayne's World Authors Series, Vol. 138. New York: Twayne Publishers, 1971.

M. A particular volume of a multi-volume book:

Child, Francis James, ed. <u>The English and Scottish Popular Ballads</u>. New York: Dover, 1965.

Note that in such cases the bibliography entry is for the entire work, not for a particular volume. This is true even if only one volume was cited in footnotes.

N. A volume with its own title that is part of a work of several volumes under a different title:

Holmes, George. <u>The Later Middle Ages: 1272–1485</u>. Vol. III of <u>A History of England</u>. Eds. Christopher Brooke and Denis Mack Smith. Edinburgh: Thomas Nelson and Sons, 1962.

Parts Within Books

A. A poem, short story, essay, or chapter from a collection of works by one author:

Jarrell, Randall. ''The English in England.'' <u>The Third Book of Criticism</u>. New York: Farrar, Straus and Giroux, 1969, pp. 279–92.

Basic Forms for Bibliography Entries

When the name of the author of the work appears in the title of the collection, you may omit the first mention of the author's name. In such cases, alphabetize the entry by the title, ignoring *A, An,* or *The.*

''Hamlet and His Problems.'' Selected Essays of T.S. Eliot. New York: Harcourt, Brace and World, 1964, pp. 121–26.

B. A poem, short story, essay, or chapter from a collection of works by several authors:

Rubio, Alberto. ''Portrait of a Little Girl.'' In New Voices of Hispanic America. Eds. Darwin J. Flakoll and Claribel Alegría. Boston: Beacon Press, 1962, p. 94.

C. A novel or play from a collection of novels or plays published under one cover.

Serling, Rod. Requiem for a Heavyweight. In Twelve American Plays. Eds. Richard Corbin and Miriam Balf. New York: Charles Scribner's Sons, 1973, pp. 299–327.

Cannery Row. The Short Novels of John Steinbeck. New York: The Viking Press, 1963, pp. 355–469.

D. An introduction, preface, foreword, or afterword written by the author of a work:

Braudel, Fernand. Preface to the English Edition. The Mediterranean and the Mediterranean World in the Age of Phillip II. New York: Harper and Row, 1976, pp. 13–14.

Basic Forms for Bibliography Entries

E. An introduction, preface, forward, or afterward written by someone other than the author of a work:

Moore, Harry T. Preface. <u>Palimpsest</u>. By
    Hilda Doolittle. Carbondale: Southern
    Illinois University Press, 1968, pp.
    vii–ix.

Magazines, Encyclopedias, Reports, Pamphlets, and Newspapers

A. An article from a quarterly or monthly magazine:

Batten, Mary. ''Life Spans.'' <u>Science Di-
    gest</u>, Feb. 1984, pp. 46–51; 95.

B. An article from a weekly magazine:

Davis, Douglas. ''Art in the Marketplace.''
    <u>Newsweek</u>, 30 Jan. 1984, pp. 66–67.

C. A magazine article with no author given:

''Challenging Mount Etna's Power.'' <u>Time</u>,
    30 May 1983, p. 48.

D. An article from a daily newspaper:

James, Noah. ''The Comedian Everyone Loves
    to Hate.'' <u>The New York Times</u>, 22 Jan.
    1984, p. 23, col. 1.

If no author is given, begin with the title. If the paper is not
divided into sections, omit section information.

E. An editorial in a newspaper:

''The Politics of Arms Control.'' Editori-
    al. <u>The Chicago Tribune</u>, 29 Jan. 1984,
    Sec. 5, p. 2, cols. 1–2.

Basic Forms for Bibliography Entries

F. An article in a journal that has continuous page numbers throughout the annual volume:

Lefkowitz, Mary R. ''Patterns of Fiction in
    Ancient Biography.'' The American
    Scholar, 52 (1983), pp. 209–10.

The volume number, the date, and the page numbers follow the title of the journal.

G. An article in a journal that numbers the pages of each issue separately:

Aumiller, Emily P. ''Lord of the Flies as a
    Musical.'' The English Journal, 71,
    No. 8 (1982), p. 32.

The volume number, the number of the issue, the date, and the page numbers follow the title of the journal.

H. An encyclopedia article:

''Architecture.'' The World Book Encyclo-
    pedia. 1983 ed.

I. An unsigned, untitled review:

Rev. of Harry and Son, dir. Paul Newman.
    American Film, March 1984, p. 78.

If the review is unsigned but has a title, use the form for a signed review, but delete the author's name.

J. A report or a pamphlet:

American Medical Association. Medical Re-
    lations Under Workmen's Compensa-
    tion. Chicago: American Medical Asso-
    ciation, 1976.

If the report is by an individual author rather than by an association or a committee, begin with the author's name.

Basic Forms for Bibliography Entries

K. A signed review:

> Lubow, Arthur. ''Glass Houses.'' Rev. of
> <u>Rolling Breaks and Other Movie Business</u>, by Aljean Harmetz. <u>The Movies</u>,
> Aug. 1983, p. 76.

Other Sources

A. An interview:

> E. Talbot Donaldson. Distinguished Professor Emeritus, Department of English,
> Indiana University. Personal Interview. 26 Sept. 1978.

D. A letter that has not been published:

> Letter from Hon. Jimmy Carter, President of
> the United States, Washington, D.C.,
> 22 May 1977.

C. Information in private files:

> <u>Of Our Lives: A History of the 1960's and
> 1970's</u>. The Students of Paul D.
> Schriener, Munster High School, Munster, Indiana. 3 May 1981. In the
> files of the Department of Social
> Studies.

D. A thesis or dissertation:

> Dunn, Daniel M. ''The Acceptance and Rejection of the American Dream: 1960 to
> 1975.'' Unpublished Ph.D. dissertation, Department of Speech Communication and Theatre, Wayne State University.

Basic Forms for Bibliography Entries

E. A quotation (See footnote number 38.):

> Cooke, Alistair. <u>America</u>. New York: Alfred
>   A. Knopf, 1973.

F. A film:

> Attenborough, Richard, dir. <u>Gandhi</u>. With
>   Ben Kingsley. Columbia Pictures,
>   1982.

G. A work of art:

> Klee, Paul. <u>Twittering Machine</u>. Museum of
>   Modern Art, New York.

H. A television or radio program:

> ''A Desert Blooming.'' Writ. Marshall Rig-
>   gan. <u>Living Wild</u>. Dir. Harry L. Gord-
>   en. Prod. Peter Argentine. PBS, 29
>   April 1984.

I. A musical composition:

> Chopin. Waltz in A-flat major op. 42.

Exercise Writing the Final Bibliography

Following the correct form for your entries, prepare your final bibliography. Assemble your research paper in the following order:

1. Title page, in whatever form your teacher requires
2. Page containing title at top, statement of controlling purpose beneath it, followed by your final outline
3. The text of your paper
4. The final bibliography

THE REALISM

OF

HENRY FLEMING

IN

STEPHEN CRANE'S

THE RED BADGE OF COURAGE

by

Craig Pirrong

[The following is a high school
student's complete research paper.
Use it as a model for preparing
your own paper.]

3 English H
Mrs. Ichkoff
March 8

The Realism of Henry Fleming
in Stephen Crane's <u>The Red Badge of Courage</u>

<u>Controlling Purpose</u>: to demonstrate that Henry Fleming, the
protagonist of Stephen Crane's <u>The Red Badge of Courage,</u> is
an accurate portrayal of a Civil War soldier by comparing
him with actual soldiers through their letters and diaries.

 I. A comparison of war experience
  A. Memoirs of actual Civil War soldiers
  B. Experiences of soldiers in <u>The Red Badge of</u>
   <u>Courage</u>
 II. Soldiers' attitudes toward battle
  A. Risks of combat
  B. Fear of cowardice
  C. Nervousness before battle
 III. Soldiers' change in attitude during battle
  A. Sense of urgency
  B. Feeling of rage
  C. Emergence of unity of purpose
   1. Abandonment of self
   2. Loyalty to army
 IV. Problems of desertion
  A. Mental struggle
  B. Physical exhaustion
  C. Rationalizations
 V. Differences between expectations and actualities
  of battle
  A. Physical
  B. Mental
 VI. Growing maturity of soldiers
  A. Coping with stress
  B. Attitude toward death
 VII. The reality of war experience
  A. In the Civil War
  B. In <u>The Red Badge of Courage</u>

Stephen Crane's The Red Badge of Courage was the first novel to explore the real feelings of a soldier going into action for the first time. Before The Red Badge, American fiction concerning the Civil War concentrated on the heroic deeds of soldiers and was marked by over-glorification and inaccuracy. However, the letters and diaries of actual Civil War soldiers reveal that these soldiers were more concerned with their feelings than their deeds. By examining the memoirs of Civil War soldiers and comparing them with experiences in The Red Badge, one can see that Stephen Crane's novel is an accurate portrayal of the reality of a soldier's emotions and resulting actions during the war.

Henry Floming, the protagonist in The Red Badge, like many actual Civil War soldiers, feared the consequences of an impending battle. Henry thought that "as far as war was concerned he knew nothing of himself."[1] He also thought that "the only way to prove himself was to go into the blaze, and then figuratively to watch his legs to discover their merits and faults."[2] Many Civil War soldiers had the same feelings as Henry. Bell Wiley, a historian who has done extensive research on the Common Private of the Civil War, wrote that soldiers were more concerned with the question of how they would stand up in battle than they were over the chance of being wounded or killed.[3] One private wrote, "'I have a marked dread of the battle field, for

---

[1]The Red Badge of Courage, The Complete Novels of Stephen Crane, ed. Thomas A. Gullason (New York: Doubleday and Co., 1967), p. 206.

[2]The Red Badge of Courage, p. 209.

[3]Bell Irvin Wiley, The Life of Billy Yank (Indianapolis: Bobbs-Merrill, 1951), p. 68.

I...have never seen a person die...& I am afraid
that the groans of the wounded & dying will make me shake
nevertheless I hope & trust that strength will be given me
to stand & do my duty.'"[4]

The methods that soldiers devised to avoid battle or
to alleviate their doubts about their courage were many.
Some would self-inflict wounds; others would leave the front
on the pretense of a broken musket, helping a wounded
comrade, being ordered to do some special task by an
officer, illness or a "call of nature." Many never
returned.[5] Like Henry, some soldiers tried to relieve their
fear of battle by calculating the odds of their being hit
or their chances of running. Officers, as well as common
soldiers, computed the risks of combat. Before the Battle
of Perryville, three brigade commanders discussed the
chances of their getting hit and of their troops' running.
The generals predicted that their troops would stay and
fight and that they themselves would not be hit, but all
three were killed and their brigades were routed.[6] Like
Henry's own calculations, the officers' calculations
were wrong.

Some soldiers tried to hide their fear and go into the
fight as bravely as possible. One of these real soldiers
was Elbridge Capp. Like Henry, who felt that he had to "go
into the blaze," Elbridge said to himself, "'I must face the
danger.'"[7] Others resolved to let death solve their

---

[4] Bell Irvin Wiley, The Common Soldier of the Civil War
(Gettysburg: Historical Times, 1973), p. 56.

[5] Wiley, Billy Yank, p. 86.

[6] James M. Hillard, "'You Are Strangely Deluded':
General William Terrill," Civil War Times Illustrated,
1975, p. 18.

[7] Elbridge Capp, Reminiscences of the War of the
Rebellion (Nashua, N.H.: Telegraph Publishing, 1911), p. 135.

problems. One of these soldiers said, "'I'm willin ter die
...but I don't want ter be no coward.'"[8] Another private,
Sam Watkins, said, "I had made up my mind to die."[9] Henry
had these same feelings, thinking "that it would be better
to get killed directly and end his troubles."[10] He thought
it better to "fall facing the enemy, than to play the
coward."[11]

The descriptions of Henry's feelings immediately before
and during battle were consistent with the accounts of both
Federal and Confederate soldiers. Before facing fire for the
first time, Henry was "in a fever of impatience."[12] Most
soldiers experienced this same feeling. One wrote that
nothing "brings...such crucial trial as the throbbing
emotions that immediately precede the clash of arms."[13]
Another private said that "the knowledge of an impending
battle always sent that thrill of fear and horror."[14]

Once the firing started, however, Henry's feelings, as
well as those of most soldiers, changed. Henry had been
advised that a man changed in battle, and he found it was
true.[15] Before he went into action, Henry's main concern
was for himself. After the battle opened in earnest,
however, his outlook changed: "He suddenly lost concern

---

[8]William Hinman, Si Klegg and His Pard (Cleveland: N.G.
Hamilton, 1892), p. 400.

[9]Sam R. Watkins, Co. Aytch (New York: Macmillan, 1962),
p. 234.

[10]The Red Badge of Courage, p. 220.

[11]Wiley, Billy Yank, p. 68.

[12]The Red Badge of Courage, p. 219.

[13]Hinman, p. 339.

[14]Capp, p. 140.

[15]The Red Badge of Courage, p. 219.

for himself, and forgot to look at a menacing fate."[16]
He became an automaton.

> He was at a task. He was like a carpenter who
> has made many boxes, making still another box,
> only there was furious haste in his movements. . .
> Following this came a red rage. He developed the
> acute exasperation of a pestered animal, a
> well-meaning cow worried by dogs. His impotency
> appeared to him, and made his rage into that of a
> driven beast.[17]

Civil war veterans' reminiscences echo Henry's change from
fear to indifference, rage and urgency. One private wrote,
"'Strange as it may seam to you, but the more men I saw
killed the more reckless I became.'"[18] Henry Morton Stanley,
the famous explorer, also described this feeling of urgency.
He wrote, "We plied our arms, loaded, and fired, with such
nervous haste as though it depended on each of us how soon
this fiendish uproar would be hushed."[19] Oliver Norton, a
Pennsylvania infantryman wrote, "I acted like a madman....
The feeling that was uppermost in my mind was a desire to
kill as many rebels as I could."[20] A third soldier, like
Henry, wished to grapple face to face with his enemies:
"'I was mad...;how I itched for a hand-to-hand struggle.'"[21]
Gradually a feeling of unity—oneness—with the army,

---

[16] The Red Badge of Courage, p. 225.

[17] The Red Badge of Courage, pp. 225-226.

[18] Wiley, Billy Yank, p. 71.

[19] Henry Morton Stanley, "Henry Stanley Fights with
the Dixie Grays at Shiloh," The Blue and the Gray, ed.
H.S. Commager (Indianapolis: Bobbs-Merrill, 1950), I, 354.

[20] Oliver Norton, Army Letters (Chicago: O.C. Deming,
1903), p. 91.

[21] Wiley, Billy Yank, p. 72.

the corps, the regiment manifested itself in both the
average Civil War private and in Henry Fleming. Throughout
The Red Badge Henry calls himself "part of a vast blue
demonstration."[22] When he first came under fire, Henry
thought that

> He became not a man but a member. He felt that
> something of which he was a part—a regiment, an army,
> a cause, or a country—was in a crisis. He was welded
> into a common personality which was dominated by a
> single desire. For some moments he could not flee,
> no more than a little finger can commit a revolution
> from a hand.
> There was a consciousness always of the presence of
> his comrades about him. He felt the subtle battle
> brotherhood more potent even than the cause for which
> they were fighting. It was a mysterious fraternity
> born of the smoke and danger of death.[23]

This same feeling was expressed by many Federals and
Confederates. Bruce Catton, the Civil War historian, wrote
that "the instinctive loyalty of all of these men went...
to the army."[24] Henry Morton Stanley wrote that, "there were
about four hundred companies like the Dixie Greys, who
shared our feelings."[25] Sergeant Thomas H. Evans, a member
of the regular army, said that an "abandonment of self"[26]
emerged in battle. At the surrender of the Army of Northern
Virginia, one private, "unwilling to outlive his army,"[27]

---

[22]The Red Badge of Courage, p. 205.

[23]The Red Badge of Courage, p. 225.

[24]Bruce, Catton, This Hallowed Ground (Garden City, N.Y.:
Doubleday and Co., 1956), p. 360.

[25]Stanley, p. 354.

[26]Thomas H. Evans, "There Is No Use Trying to Dodge
Shot," Civil War Times Illustrated, Aug. 1967, p. 43.

[27]William C. Davis, "The Campaign to Appomattox,"
Civil War Times Illustrated, Aug. 1975, p. 40.

shouted, "'Blow, Gabriel, blow!'"[28] These loyalties became "more potent even than the cause for which they were fighting."[29]

On the other hand, flight from the field of battle was not uncommon to Civil War soldiers. In fact, "there was a considerable amount of malingering, skulking, and running in every major battle."[30] Henry's own reasons for running were similar to those of many who fled from an actual battle. When the Confederates charged for the second time, Henry ran. He saw "a revelation."[31] When he fled, "There was no shame on his face."[32] A soldier in the Twelfth Connecticut was much like Henry. William DeForest described the soldier in these terms: "He did not look wild with fright; he simply looked alarmed and resolved to get out of danger;... he was confounded by the peril of the moment and thought of nothing but getting away from it."[33]

Soldiers who fled from the field of battle were generally beset with a conflict between their bodies and their souls. When the Rebels charged for the second time, Henry was exhausted and dismayed. "He seemed to shut his eyes and wait to be gobbled."[34] William Hinman echoed Henry's feelings, saying that a soldier had to

---

[28] Davis, p. 40.

[29] The Red Badge of Courage, p. 225.

[30] Wiley, Common Soldier, p. 26.

[31] The Red Badge of Courage, p. 230.

[32] The Red Badge of Courage, p. 230.

[33] John William DeForest, A Volunteer's Adventures, (New Haven, Conn.: Yale University Press, 1946), p. 63.

[34] The Red Badge of Courage, p. 230.

> ...go through the struggle...between his mental and
> physical natures. The instinct of the latter at such a
> time—and what soldier does not know it?—was to seek
> a place of safety, without a moment's delay. To fully
> subdue this feeling by the power of will was not...
> such an easy a matter as might be imagined....Some
> there were who could never do it.[35]

Soldiers who ran usually tried to rationalize their actions.
Henry thought that he had been right in running because he

> ...was a little piece of the army. He considered the
> time, he said, to be one in which it was the duty of
> every little piece to rescue itself if possible. Later
> the officers could fit the little pieces together
> again, and make a battle front. If none of the little
> pieces were wise enough to save themselves from the
> flurry of death at such a time, why, then, where would
> be the army? It was all plain that he had proceeded
> according to very correct and commendable rules.[36]

Henry again tried to demonstrate to himself that he was
right by "throwing a pine cone at a jovial squirrel."[37]
When the youth saw that the squirrel fled rather than let
the missile strike him, Henry felt that, "Nature had
given him a sign."[38]

Actual combatants who ran from battle gave somewhat
less symbolic and complicated, yet similar, excuses. George
Townsend, a hospital steward, stumbled on a group of
skulkers at the Battle of Cedar Mountain and recorded:

> Some of these miserable wretches...muttered that they
> were not to be hood-winked and slaughtered.
> "I was sick, anyway," said one fellow, "and felt
> like droppin' on the road."

---

[35] Hinman, p. 398.

[36] The Red Badge of Courage, p. 233.

[37] The Red Badge of Courage, p. 234.

[38] The Red Badge of Courage, p. 235.

"I didn't trust my colonel," said another; "he ain't
no soldier."
"I'm tired of the war, anyhow," said a third, "and
my time's up soon; so I shan't have my head blown
off."[39]

One soldier who deserted his comrades at the Battle of
Corinth said on his return that he had not run, but had been
detailed to guard a water tank. His comrades never let him
live it down.[40] Another soldier, nicknamed "Spinney," said
he had run because he thought that the bullets were calling
his name.[41]

Henry found battle time to be very different from what
he had conceived it would be. At first, he "had the belief
that real war was a series of death struggles with small
time in between for sleep and meals."[42] He learned later,
however, that battle took up very little time in a soldier's
life.[43] He also thought that "Secular and religious
education had obliterated the throat-grappling instinct."[44]
However, when the Confederates were attacking for the first
time, and Henry "wished to rush forward and strangle with
his fingers,"[45] he realized that this thought was wrong,
too.

---

[39]George A. Townsend, "A Camp of Skulkers at Cedar
Mountain," The Blue and the Gray, I, 493.

[40]Wiley, Billy Yank, pp. 87-88.

[41]Warren Lee Goss, "Yorktown and Williamsburg,"
Battles and Leaders of the Civil War, ed. Robert U.
Johnson and Clarence C. Buel (New York: Thomas Yoseloff,
1956, II, 197.

[42]The Red Badge of Courage, p. 205.

[43]The Red Badge of Courage, p. 205.

[44]The Red Badge of Courage, p. 205.

[45]The Red Badge of Courage, p. 225.

Many actual soldiers also experienced a difference
between their expectations and the realities of battle.
Henry Morton Stanley wrote, "It was the first Field of
Glory I had seen in my May of life, and the first time that
Glory sickened me with its repulsive aspect, and made me
suspect it was all a glittering lie."[46] Sam Watkins wrote,
"I had heard and read of battlefields...but I must confess
that I never realized the 'pomp and circumstance' of the
thing called glorious war until I saw this."[47] Some were
so naive about the realities of war that they were surprised
that the enemy was firing bullets.[48] This difference
between the untrained soldiers' image of war and the
realities of combat was well portrayed in The Red Badge
of Courage.

Under the stress of combat, both Henry Fleming and
many actual Civil War soldiers rapidly matured. Henry's
attainment of maturity was both quick and dramatic. Early
in The Red Badge, Henry felt the need to make excuses to
escape the reality of his cowardice, but by the end of the
book, Henry was able to look upon his feats, both bad and
good, objectively. He thought that "He could look back upon
the brass and bombast of his earlier gospels and see them
truly."[49] Earlier, when Henry had been walking with a
wounded soldier called the tattered man, Henry felt guilty
and embarrassed because he himself had no wound, while
everyone around him had a "red badge of courage."[50] To
escape his guilt and embarrassment, Henry ran from the

---

[46]Stanley, p. 357.

[47]Watkins, p. 42.

[48]Watkins, p. 42, and Stanley, p. 353.

[49]The Red Badge of Courage, p. 298.

[50]The Red Badge of Courage, p. 240.

tattered man, feeling that he "could have strangled"[51] his
wounded companion. By the end of The Red Badge, however,
Henry realized that the tattered man had actually been
trying to help him, and he felt guilty for deserting this
man who had cared for him and aided him.[52] When Henry had
outgrown the selfishness of immaturity, he could finally
say of himself that "He was a man."[53]

Henry's attainment of maturity was common to many
adolescent soldiers. Bell Wiley wrote, "One of the most
interesting things about the boy soldiers was the speed
with which they matured under the stress and strain of army
life."[54] Sam Watkins, a Confederate private, wrote that
early in the war "we wanted to march off and whip twenty
Yankees. But we soon found that the glory of war was at home
with the ladies, not upon the field of blood and...death....
I might say the agony of mind were very different indeed
from the patriotic times at home."[55] One soldier wrote:

> With the new troops, they have not been called on to
> train or restrain their nerves. They are not only
> nervous, but they blanch at the thought of danger....
> What to them, on joining the service, was a terrible
> mental strain, is soon transformed into indifference.[56]

This view of the experience of war is also similar to
Henry's. Before Henry had attained his maturity, he was
nervous and afraid of how the strain of battle and the

---

[51] The Red Badge of Courage, p. 245.

[52] The Red Badge of Courage, p. 297.

[53] The Red Badge of Courage, p. 298.

[54] Wiley, Billy Yank, p. 301.

[55] Watkins, p. 21.

[56] Frank Holsinger, "How It Feels To Be Under Fire,"
The Blue and the Gray, I, 308.

thought of death would affect him. After he had "become a man," however, Henry could say matter-of-factly that "He had been to touch the great death, and found that, after all, it was but the great death."[57]

Henry's final understanding of the meaning of life and death has emerged from his experiences during war. His diverse emotional experiences, his growth to maturity, and his eventual feeling of unity with his comrades all parallel the experiences that actual Civil war soldiers have recorded in their letters and diaries. These parallel experiences reveal that The Red Badge of Courage is an accurate representation of real life under the conditions of the Civil War.

---

[57]The Red Badge of Courage, p. 298.

BIBLIOGRAPHY

Books

Capp, Elbridge. Reminiscences of the War of the Rebellion.
    Nashua, N.H.: Telegraph Publishing, 1911.

Catton, Bruce. This Hallowed Ground. Garden City, N.Y.:
    Doubleday and Co., 1956.

Commager, Henry S., ed. The Blue and the Gray.
    Indianapolis: Bobbs-Merrill, 1950.

DeForest, John William. A Volunteer's Adventures. New
    Haven, Conn.: Yale University Press, 1946.

Hinman, William. Si Klegg and His Pard. Cleveland: N.G.
    Hamilton, 1892.

Norton, Oliver. Army Letters. Chicago: O.C. Deming,
    1903.

The Red Badge of Courage. The Complete Novels of Stephen
    Crane. Ed. Thomas A. Gullason. Garden City, N.Y.:
    Doubleday and Co., 1967, pp. 155-299.

Watkins, Sam R. Co. Aytch. New York: Macmillan, 1962.

Wiley, Bell Irvin. The Common Soldier of the Civil War.
    Gettysburg: Historical Times, 1973.

Wiley, Bell Irvin. The Life of Billy Yank. Indianapolis:
    Bobbs-Merrill, 1951.

Periodicals

Davis, William C. "The Campaign to Appomattox." Civil War
    Times Illustrated, April 1975, p. 40.

Evans, Thomas H. "There Is No Use Trying to Dodge Shot,"
    Civil War Times Illustrated, Aug. 1967, p. 43.

Hillard, James M. "'You Are Strangely Deluded': General
    William Terrill," Civil War Times Illustrated,
    Feb. 1975, p. 18.

1. A research paper is a formal report that presents an in-depth study of a particular topic. It is based upon information gathered from diverse sources and organized according to the judgment of the writer.

2. When writing a research paper, you must complete each of the following steps.

    Choose and limit your subject.
    Prepare a working bibliography.
    Prepare a preliminary outline.
    Read and take notes.
    Organize your notes and write a final outline.
    Write the first draft.
    Write the final draft with footnotes.
    Write the final bibliography.

3. Always check your paraphrases and quotations for accuracy. Avoid plagiarism by documenting your sources in footnotes.

4. Follow proper form for bibliography cards, note cards, final outlines, footnotes, and final bibliographies.

Applications in Other Subject Areas

Science. Writers in scientific and technical fields often use a special method to document sources of quoted or paraphrased material. If, for example, a psychologist wishes to refer to a report of an experiment conducted by another psychologist, he or she might say something like the following:

> Recent studies (Smith, 1983; Robbins, 1984; and Salk, 1984) indicate that the right hemisphere section of the brain corresponding to Warnecke's Area shows increased activity among some schizophrenic patients.

Find a report of a scientific experiment. Study the methods of documentation used. How do these differ from the methods presented in this chapter?

Chapter 14

The Library and Its Reference Materials

Learning how to use library resources efficiently is an asset. Whether you do research in literature, history, science, or other disciplines, the library is an indispensable tool.

To make effective use of the library, it is necessary for you to know (1) how books are classified and arranged, and (2) how to use the card catalog. It is also important for you to learn how to locate and use such reference works as dictionaries, encyclopedias, almanacs, catalogs, atlases, and magazines. Finally, you should become familiar with many other valuable resources for specific subject areas, such as literature and biography.

In this chapter you will learn how to gain access to the information contained in libraries. By learning to use libraries well, you will greatly increase your prospects for success both in high school and in college.

Part 1 The Classification and Arrangement of Books

To find any book in the library, you must first locate that book in the card catalog. Every book is listed on at least three cards: the **author card,** the **title card,** and the **subject card.** Once you have found the card for the book you are interested in, you must then find that book on the library shelves. A knowledge of how books are classified and how they are arranged will help you locate the material you need.

The Classification of Books

Fiction. Works of fiction (novels and anthologies of short stories) are usually arranged in alphabetical order by author. When there are two or more books written by the same author, you would find them shelved alphabetically by title. For example, Ray Bradbury's books would be found under *B*. His *Dandelion Wine* and *Fahrenheit 451* would be followed by *The Martian Chronicles*.

Nonfiction. Most libraries—including high school libraries— use the Dewey Decimal System, named for its originator, the American librarian, Melvil Dewey. There are ten major classifications in the Dewey Decimal System; all books fit into one of these classifications.

THE TEN MAJOR CLASSIFICATIONS ARE THESE:

000–999 **General Works** (encyclopedias, handbooks, almanacs, etc.)

100–199 **Philosophy** (includes psychology, ethics, etc.)

200–299 **Religion** (the Bible, mythology)

300–399 **Social Science** (sociology, economics, government, education, law, folklore)

400–499 **Language** (languages, grammars, dictionaries)

500–599	**Science** (mathematics, chemistry, physics, biology, etc.)
600–699	**Useful Arts** (farming, cooking, sewing, nursing, engineering, radio, television, gardening, inventions)
700–799	**Fine Arts** (music, painting, drawing, acting, photography, games, sports, amusements)
800–899	**Literature** (poetry, plays, essays)
900–999	**History** (biography, travel, geography)

As you can see from the major categories of the Dewey Decimal System, each discipline has a classification number. For example, all books on the fine arts are classified between 700 and 799, and all history books will be found between 900 and 999. The system becomes more detailed as each of these major groups is subdivided. The table below subdivides works in literature as follows:

800–899 **Literature**	810 **American literature**
810 American literature	811 Poetry
820 English literature	812 Drama
830 German literature	813 Fiction
840 French literature	814 Essays
850 Italian literature	815 Speeches
860 Spanish literature	816 Letters
870 Latin literature (classic)	817 Satire and Humor
880 Greek literature (classic)	818 Miscellany
890 Other literature	819 Canadian-English literature

The numbers in a particular classification combined with the letter of the author's last name make up the **call number**. The call number helps you locate the book on the shelf once you have found it in the card catalog.

Arrangement of Books on the Shelves

You can see that books are arranged numerically on the library's shelves in order of classification. Most libraries prominently mark their shelves with the numbers indicating the books to be found in each particular section. Like fiction books, nonfiction books are arranged alphabetically by authors' last names under their subject classification.

Biographies are one of the most popular kinds of books in libraries. The Dewey Decimal System division for them is 920. However, large libraries will often place biographies in a separate section because of the large number of these books. In this case, they will have a "B" on the spine of the book and on the catalog card. If you are looking for a particular biography and are unable to locate it, ask the librarian for assistance.

Reference Books are located in the library's reference room or area. They are categorized in the Dewey Decimal System, often with the letter "R" or "Ref" above the classification number. Usually, a reference book may not be checked out.

Exercise The Classification and Arrangement of Books

Using the Dewey Decimal Classification summary on pages 306 and 307, assign the correct classification number to each of the following books.

1. *The Book of Jazz,* by Leonard Feather
2. *Ancient Greece,* by Roger Green
3. *Economics and the Public Purpose,* by John Kenneth Galbraith
4. *The Concise Oxford Dictionary of Current English,* ed. J. B. Sykes
5. *The Treasury of House Plants,* by Rob Herwig
6. *Law and Everyday Life,* by Elinor Swiger
7. *Decisive Battles of the Civil War,* by Joseph Mitchell
8. *Fireside Book of Humorous Poetry,* ed. William Cole
9. *The Teenager and Psychology,* by Robert Gelinas
10. *Camping and Woodcraft,* by Horace Kephart
11. *Masters of the Drama,* by John Gassner
12. *Handbook of the World's Religions,* by A. M. Zehavi
13. *Explorations in Chemistry,* by Charles Gray
14. *Highlights of the Olympics,* by John Durant
15. *Tomorrow's Math,* by C. Stanley Ogilvy

Part 2 Using Books for Research

When you conduct research, only certain sections or passages in a book may be relevant to your topic. To find these sections, you must familiarize yourself with the parts of a book.

Parts of a Book

The **title page** usually gives the complete title of the book, the names of authors or editors, the name of the publisher, and the place of publication.

The **copyright page** gives the copyright dates, the names of copyright holders, the dates of editions or printings of the book, and the Library of Congress catalog number.

The **forword, preface,** or **introduction** is a written commentary that supplies necessary background information.

The **table of contents** is a summary or outline of the contents of the book, arranged in order of appearance.

The **text** is the body of the book. It may be divided into chapters or sections.

The **appendices** contain additional information, often in the form of maps, charts, tables, illustrations, or graphs.

The **notes** section contains footnotes to works cited or explanations of statements made in the text.

The **bibliography** is a list of sources that were used in preparing the book or that may be of interest to readers who wish further information on the subject.

The **glossary** is a dictionary of unusual or technical terms used in the text of the book.

The **index** is an alphabetical list of subjects covered in the book. Each entry is followed by page numbers that enable you to locate specific information.

Not all books will contain all of the preceding parts. Before you start to look for the information that you need from a book, glance through it to see what parts the book contains. Then, use these parts to locate the information that you need.

Exercise Using Books for Research

Answer the following questions. For questions 1–4, refer to the appropriate parts of this textbook.

1. According to the index, what pages of this book will give you information on applying to colleges? writing résumés?
2. According to the table of contents, what pages of this book will give you information on inductive and deductive reasoning?
3. What is the copyright date of this book?
4. What company publishes this book?
5. Suppose that you encounter the term *conference committee* in a political science textbook. What section of the book might you turn to in order to find a definition of this term?
6. Imagine that you are doing a research paper on the later plays of Eugene O'Neill. You have found a book by John Gassner entitled *Masters of the Drama*. In what two places could you look to find out whether or not the book contains information about O'Neill's plays?
7. Imagine that you are doing a report on economic conditions in America during the early 1920's. You find a source entitled *The American Economy: A History*. Where in the book might you find charts and graphs showing economic trends during the period that you are researching?
8. Suppose that you are reading a book entitled *Our Oriental Heritage*. Where might you find a list of books that were used as sources by the author of the book that you are reading?
9. While reading a book about contemporary American poetry, you come across an interesting quotation by Gwendolyn Brooks, followed by a footnote number. You want to find out the source of this quotation. Where might you look?
10. You are reading a collection of essays by the science writer Loren Eiseley. Where might you look for information on Eiseley's life and work?

Part 3 Using Reference Materials

One of the best ways to obtain information on a particular topic is to consult a reference work. Libraries have either a reference section or a reference room. It is here that you will find just about everything you want, from a *Newsweek* article that reviews a recently published novel to a college catalog from a local junior college.

Reference works include the following: dictionaries; encyclopedias; pamphlets, handbooks, and catalogs; almanacs and yearbooks; atlases; biographical reference books; literary reference books; and magazines.

Reference works are tools, and like tools, should be used in definite ways. Most reference works have prefaces that describe how information is arranged, show sample entries, and explain the symbols and abbreviations used in the book. Before using any reference work for the first time, you would be wise to skim the preface.

The basic reference books are described in this section.

Dictionaries

The most widely used reference books in the library are the general dictionaries. General dictionaries fall into three major categories:

1. **Unabridged** dictionaries are dictionaries with over 250,000 entries.
2. **"College"** or **"desk" dictionaries** generally carry 130,000 to 150,000 entries.
3. **Concise** or **"pocket"** dictionaries are those with a smaller number of entries.

Unabridged Dictionaries. An unabridged dictionary may contain up to 500,000 words. It gives uncommon as well as common meanings of many words and explains in detail how they are used. The best known unabridged dictionaries are listed on the following page.

Webster's Third New International Dictionary
The Random House Dictionary of the English Language,
   Unabridged Edition

You will find at least one—if not both—of these in your school or community library.

College or Desk Dictionaries. A college or desk dictionary is a quick and convenient reference. It provides information you would normally need about definitions, spellings, pronunciations, and matters of usage. It usually contains a special section that gives biographical information, and articles on such topics as pronunciation, spelling, and dialects.

Your school or local library probably carries several different college dictionaries. The best known are these:

The American Heritage Dictionary of the English Language
The Macmillan Dictionary
The Random House Dictionary of the English Language,
   College Edition
Thorndike-Barnhart Dictionary
Webster's New Collegiate Dictionary
Webster's New World Dictionary of the American Language

Dictionaries About Language. Each of these deals with a specific aspect of our English language: synonyms and antonyms, rhymes, slang, Americanisms, etymology, and so forth.

As a young writer, you need to be concerned with precision in your writing. A help in finding the precise word you are looking for is a **thesaurus,** or a dictionary of synonyms.

A thesaurus should be used only as a "memory-jogger," to help you find words that are already in your vocabulary. You are treading on dangerous ground if you select from a thesaurus a word you do not know in place of a word you do know. A list of reliable thesauruses follows:

Roget's International Thesaurus
Roget's Thesaurus in Dictionary Form
Roget's Thesaurus of English Words and Phrases
Webster's Collegiate Thesaurus
Webster's Dictionary of Synonyms

Additional dictionaries dealing with our language are the following:

> *Abbreviations Dictionary: (Abbreviations, Acronyms, Contractions, Signs and Symbols Defined)*
> *Acronyms, Initialisms, and Abbreviations Dictionary*
> *Brewer's Dictionary of Phrase and Fable*
> *A Dictionary of American Idioms*
> *Dictionary of American Slang*
> *Dictionary of Literary Terms*
> *A Dictionary of Slang and Unconventional English*
> *A Dictionary of Word and Phrase Origins (3 volumes)*
> *Harper Dictionary of Contemporary Usage*
> *Mathews Dictionary of Americanisms*
> *The Oxford Dictionary of English Etymology*
> *Wood's Unabridged Rhyming Dictionary*

Special-Purpose Dictionaries. Finally, there are special-purpose dictionaries that deal exclusively with music, medicine, foreign language, and many other subjects. These include the following:

FOREIGN LANGUAGE

> *Cassell's Dutch Dictionary*
> *Cassell's French Dictionary*
> *Cassell's German Dictionary*
> *Cassell's Italian Dictionary*
> *Cassell's New Latin Dictionary*
> *Cassell's Spanish Dictionary*

HISTORY

> *Concise Dictionary of American History*
> *Dictionary of American History*
> *A New Dictionary of British History*

LITERATURE

> *Dictionary of Fictional Characters*
> *Dictionary of Literary Terms*
> *Dictionary of World Literary Terms*
> *Webster's Dictionary of Proper Names*

Compton's Illustrated Science Dictionary
Dictionary of Biology
Dictionary of Science and Technology
The International Dictionary of Applied Mathematics

MUSIC AND ART

Grove's Dictionary of Music and Musicians (10 volumes)
Harvard Dictionary of Music
Bryan's Dictionary of Painters and Engravers (5 volumes)
McGraw-Hill Dictionary of Art (5 volumes)

Encyclopedias

General Encyclopedias. An encyclopedia (from the Greek *enkyklios paideia,* which means "general education") is a collection of articles, alphabetically arranged in volumes, on nearly every conceivable subject. It is designed for quick reference and provides you with general information on various fields or branches of learning.

Guide letters on the spine of each volume and guide words at the top of the pages assist you in finding information. It is best, however, to check the general index. It may list several good sources. For up-to-date information on a topic, check the yearbook that many encyclopedias include.

Never use an encyclopedia as your only source. Use it only to obtain a general survey of your subject. The library is a storehouse of information; an encyclopedia should be used only as a door to that storehouse.

Most libraries include the following encyclopedias in their reference section:

GENERAL ENCYCLOPEDIAS

Collier's Encyclopedia (24 volumes)
Publishes *Collier's Yearbook;* Volume 24 includes a Bibliography and Index
Encyclopaedia Britannica (30 volumes)
Publishes *Britannica Book of the Year;* includes separate Index and Atlas for the set (more details follow)

Encyclopedia Americana (30 volumes)
  Publishes *Americana Annual*
World Book Encyclopedia (22 volumes)
  Publishes annual supplement; Volume 22 includes Research Guide and Index

The *Encyclopaedia Britannica* is unique in its organization. In dealing with the great amounts of knowledge known to humankind, the *Britannica* is broken down into three parts: the *Propaedia* (*pro* meaning "prior to"), the *Micropaedia* (*micro* meaning "small"), and the *Macropaedia* (*macro* meaning "big").

The *Propaedia,* or Outline of Knowledge and Guide to the *Britannica,* presents more than 15,000 different topics, arranged according to fields or areas of knowledge. For each topic in the Outline, there are references to the *Macropaedia* of three kinds: (1) whole articles, (2) sections of articles, (3) other references. These references make possible systematic study or reading on any subject in the encyclopedia.

The *Micropaedia,* consisting of 10 volumes, is a ready reference and index to the entire encyclopedia. As a ready reference, it is a short-entry encyclopedia. Its more than 100,000 entries, arranged in alphabetical order, give the most important and interesting facts about their subject. Often this is all you will want to know. When a subject is also treated in depth in the *Macropaedia*, the *Micropaedia* becomes an index.

The *Macropaedia,* which contains knowledge in depth, is the main body of the *Britannica.* The *Macropaedia's* 19 volumes contain 4,207 long articles by world-renowned contributors.

Encyclopedias on Specific Subjects. Encyclopedias on a wide variety of specific subjects fill library shelves. To give you some idea of the diversity of encyclopedias, here is a partial list:

ENCYCLOPEDIAS ON SPECIFIC SUBJECTS

ART

Encyclopedia of Modern Art
LaRousse Encyclopedia of Byzantine and Medieval Art
LaRousse Encyclopedia of Prehistoric and Ancient Art
LaRousse Encyclopedia of Renaissance and Baroque Art

An Encyclopedia of World History
Encyclopedia of World History

Encyclopedia of Gardening
The Illustrated Encyclopedia of World Coins
The International Encyclopedia of Cooking

The Concise Encyclopedia of English and American Poets and Poetry
The Concise Encyclopedia of Modern Drama
LaRousse Encyclopedia of Mythology
McGraw-Hill Encyclopedia of World Biography (12 volumes)
McGraw-Hill Encyclopedia of World Drama (4 volumes)

Encyclopaedia of Occultism
Encyclopaedia of Religion

The Concise Encyclopedia of Archeology
The Encyclopaedia of Chemistry
Grzimek's Animal Life Encyclopedia (13 volumes)
The Illustrated Encyclopedia of Aviation and Space
International Encyclopedia of Social Sciences (17 volumes)
Universal Encyclopedia of Mathematics

The Baseball Encyclopedia
Encyclopedia of Auto Racing Greats

Pamphlets, Handbooks, and Catalogs

The Vertical File. Pamphlets, handbooks, booklets, and clippings on a variety of subjects are available in most libraries. These subjects include information about vocations, travel, census data, and program schedules. It is here that you may find college catalogs, too. All this information is kept in a set of file cabinets called the **vertical file.**

A main feature of the vertical file is that the information in it is current. This file can be an invaluable source to you when writing a report on a contemporary topic, seeking current statistics, or looking up information on careers.

Information About Vocations, Colleges, and Universities. The reference section of the library can be a starting point in seeking information about careers and about colleges. Here is a list of some resources you might use:

Encyclopedia of Careers and Vocations
Barron's Guide to the Two-Year Colleges
Barron's Profiles of American Colleges
Lovejoy's College Guide

The 300 section of your reference area will provide related material. Many libraries also have college catalogs.

Almanacs and Yearbooks

Published annually, almanacs and yearbooks are useful sources of facts and statistics on current events, as well as on matters of historical record in many fields.

Guinness Book of World Records
Information Please Almanac, Atlas and Yearbook
Statistical Abstract of the United States
Women's Rights Almanac
World Almanac and Book of Facts

Atlases

We usually think of an atlas mainly as a book of maps, but it also contains interesting data on a number of subjects. The excellent *National Geographic Atlas of the World,* for example, lists some of the following topics in its table of contents: "Great

Moments in Geography," "Global Statistics," and sections on population, temperature, oceans, and place names. Below is a list of other widely used atlases.

> *Atlas of World History*
> *Atlas of World Wildlife*
> *The Britannica Atlas*
> *Collier's World Atlas and Gazetteer*
> *Goode's World Atlas*
> *Grosset World Atlas*
> *The International Atlas from Rand McNally*
> *The Times Atlas of the World*

Biographical References

There are brief biographical notations in dictionaries and longer biographical articles in encyclopedias. Often, however, a better source is one of the specialized works listed below.

Current Biography. Biographies of currently newsworthy individuals are published here monthly. Each issue is indexed. All copies are bound in an annual volume with a cumulated index of people in that particular volume as well as previous annual volumes. Also listed in the annual volumes are the names of the people in *Current Biography* according to their professions. Biographies of internationally known persons are found here, but Americans are well represented throughout.

Dictionary of American Biography. This is the most famous and most reliable of all American biographical dictionaries. Alphabetically arranged, this twenty-two-volume work carries articles on the lives and accomplishments of prominent deceased Americans. The work contains 14,870 biographies of Americans from the colonial days to 1940. It is kept up-to-date by supplements.

Dictionary of National Biography. This multi-volume dictionary is the most famous and the most reliable of British biographical dictionaries. Its accurate and concise information makes it a most valuable source. It includes only English people who are no longer living.

The International Who's Who. This source provides brief biographical sketches of prominent living people of all nations. The publication includes thousands of personalities and provides a valuable source for current biographies.

Webster's Biographical Dictionary. This is a source of biographical facts about past and present noteworthy people. More than 40,000 individuals are listed alphabetically, and pronunciation keys are given for each name.

Who's Who. Principally concerned with British personalities, this source provides a very brief description of the life and accomplishments of each individual included. You would probably need to refer to another source if you needed more information.

Who's Who in America. This volume provides biographical sketches, listed alphabetically, of prominent Americans who are known either for their positions or their accomplishments. Published every two years, this book can guide you to other sources in seeking detailed information about a particular person.

Who's Who in America also has regional editions: *Who's Who in the East (and Eastern Canada), Who's Who in the Midwest, Who's Who in the South and Southwest,* and *Who's Who in the West.*

Who's Who in American Women. Unusual in its title, this book not only lists outstanding American women, but women of international acclaim.

Books About Authors. For biographical information about authors and critical evaluations of their works, the following sources are especially useful:

> *American Authors: 1600–1900*
> *British Authors Before 1800*
> *British Authors of the Nineteenth Century*
> *Contemporary Authors*
> *Cyclopedia of World Authors*
> *Twentieth Century Authors*
> *Twentieth Century Authors: First Supplement*
> *World Authors: 1950–1970*

Literary Reference Books

The following are valuable reference books on the history of literature, on quotations and proverbs, for locating poems and stories, and for finding information about writers.

Bartlett's Familiar Quotations
Book Review Digest
Contemporary Poets
Cyclopedia of Literary Characters
Encyclopedia of World Drama
Granger's Index to Poetry and Recitations
Illustrated Encyclopedia of the Classical World
A Literary History of England
A Literary History of the United States
Mencken's *A New Dictionary of Quotations*
The Oxford Companion to American Literature
The Oxford Companion to Classical Literature
The Oxford Companion to English Literature
The Oxford Companion to the Theatre

From the above list, three widely used reference works are:

Bartlett's Familiar Quotations. This is one of the best known of the dictionaries of quotations. Its completeness and accuracy have made it notable for over a century.

Quotations are arranged chronologically by author in the main section of the book. A shorter section of passages from the Bible, Koran, and the Book of Common Prayer follow. To find the complete source of a quote, you should use the main index in the back of the book.

For example, study this quotation from a poem by the American poet, Walt Whitman:

"I hear America singing, the varied carols I hear."

You may find a reference to this quotation in three places:

1. under"Walt Whitman"entries in the main index of the book
2. in the index under the first line of the quote
3. under the subject heading "America"

Whatever your recollection or your need for a quotation on a subject, *Bartlett's Familiar Quotations* is an excellent source.

Book Review Digest. Arranged alphabetically by author of the book reviewed, this monthly digest gives short quotations from selected reviews from many popular American and English periodicals. If a work of fiction has had four or more reviews or a work of nonfiction has had two or more reviews, and if the book is hard-bound and has been published in the United States, it will appear in this digest.

You will find this to be a good source in finding both unfavorable and favorable reviews of particular books.

Granger's Index to Poetry and Recitations. This source includes an index of first lines as well as an index of authors to assist you in finding a poem if its title is unknown to you. By using this reference book, you will also be able to locate not only a quotation but also an entire short work. For example, suppose you need to find an anthology or book containing the poem "The Love Song of J. Alfred Prufrock" by T.S. Eliot. You would look up this title in the *Index* and under the title of the poem you will find listed a number of books containing this poem. The titles, however, are coded, and you will find the code explained in the front of the book.

Granger's Index to Poetry and Recitations is a standard, worthwhile source for any student of literature.

Magazines

The *Readers' Guide to Periodical Literature* lists the titles of articles, stories, and poems published during the preceding month in more than 100 leading magazines. It is issued twice a month from September through June and once a month in July and August. An entire year's issues are bound in one hard-cover volume at the end of the year. Articles are listed alphabetically under *subject* and *author* (and *titles* when necessary). You will find the *Readers' Guide* invaluable when looking for articles on a subject for a composition.

The excerpt from the *Readers' Guide* on the following page illustrates how articles are listed.

Excerpt from the *Readers' Guide*

LEADERSHIP
Leadership [address, November 2, 1979] N. D. Potter. Vital
Speeches 46:103-8 Ja 1 '80
Where have all the leaders gone? [Canada: with editorial — **title of article**
comment by P.C. Newman] R. MacGregor. il Macleans — **name of magazine**
93:3, 16-19 Ja 28 '80
LEADERSHIP (periodical)
Message from the publisher. H. L. Myra. il Chr Today 24:3 — **volume number**
Ja 25 '80
LEAFLETS. See Pamphlets
LEARNING, Psychology of
Degree of success while learning and academic achievement.
E. J. Schneider. Educ Digest 45:21-3 Ja '80
LEARNING and scholarship — **subject entry**
See also
Education
Student achievements
LEARNING theory. See Learning, Psychology of
LE CARRE, John, pseud. See Cornwell, David John Moore
LECKEY, Delores R.
Mixed & ambiguous. Commonweal 107:49:50 F 1 '80 — **page reference**
LEDERER, Esther Pauline (Friedman) See Landers,
Ann, pseud
LEDFORD, Cawood
Wildcats come in loud and clear. W. F. Reed. il por Sports
Illus 52:46 F 18 '80 — **date of magazine**
LEE, M. Owen
More than an opera. il Opera News 44:14+ F 2 '80
Lee, Milton L. and others
Dimethyl and monomethyl sulfate: presence in coal fly ash
and airborne particulate matter. bibl f il Science 207:186-8
Ja 11 '80
LEE, Robert, and Mar, Frank — **author entry**
Reopening church doors in China. il Chr Cent 97:105-7
Ja 30 '80
LEEHRSEN, Charles
Jump: anatomy of the top Olympic spectacle. il Pop Mech
153:91-5+ F '80
LEEWARD Islands
See also
British Virgin Islands — **"see also" cross referen**
LEFEVER, Ernest W.
Nuclear arms in the third world: options for the future. il — **illustrated article**
Futurist 14:68-70 F '80
LEFOURNIER, Phillippe
France: where consumers will suffer the most. il Bus W p70-1
F 4 '80
LEG exercises. See Exercise — **"see" cross reference**
LEGAL fees. See Lawyers—Salaries, fees, etc.
LEGGETT, William
Horse racing [cont] Sports Illus 52:56+ Ja 28 '80

Microfilm and Microfiche

Today's students can take advantage of several sources of information made possible by modern technology. Two such sources are **microfilm** and **microfiche**. These are types of film on which printed materials are reproduced in miniature. To read these materials, you must place the film into a projector to enlarge the miniature print. Newspapers, magazines, pamphlets, and even whole books are often available in one of these forms. Contact libraries in your area to find out whether they make use of microfilm or microfiche. Then, ask a librarian to show you how to use a microfilm or microfiche projector.

Computers

Recently, several computer companies in the United States have begun marketing special information services. If you have a home computer that has a modem—a device for communicating with other computers via telephone lines—you can make use of these services. Through them, you can gain access to reports on current events and to information from encyclopedias. To learn more about these information services, talk to a dealer in home computer software or to a reference librarian.

Exercises Using Reference Materials

A. Dictionaries and Encyclopedias. Using the dictionaries and encyclopedias listed on pages 311–316, indicate the best source for answers to these questions. Include the page reference.

1. Where did the phrase "ugly duckling" originate?
2. Find a short article on cryogenics.
3. In what epic is Hector an important character?
4. How did Currier and Ives become famous?
5. What are the basic steps in computer data processing?
6. What were the "Jim Crow" laws?
7. Compare Miltonic sonnets with Shakespearean sonnets.
8. Describe "op art."
9. What are the four main blood groups?

10. What was the original meaning of the word *flivver*?
12. Who wrote the ballet "Slaughter on Tenth Avenue"?
12. Was Robin Hood a real or legendary character?
13. What is existentialism?
14. Find an illustration and description of a lute.
15. What is the story of Scylla and Charybdis?

B. Almanacs, Yearbooks, and Atlases. Using the almanacs, year-books, and atlases listed in this chapter, indicate the best source for answers to these questions. Include the page reference.

1. Find a list of the major North American turnpikes.
2. How is a patent issued?
3. What are the major land uses in the United States?
4. Who is the mayor of Los Angeles?
5. What are the warning signs of a heart attack?
6. What is the law on succession to the presidency?
7. Whose portrait is on the $20 bill?
8. Compare the number of American participants in World War II and the Vietnam War.
9. How many times has the United States won the Olympic Games since 1900?
10. Find a map showing climates of the world.
11. What is the National Guard?
12. Find a list of the state compulsory school attendance laws.
13. What play has had the longest Broadway run?
14. Which states have a sales tax?
15. What are some of the endangered species of birds?

C. Biographical References. Using the biographical references listed in this chapter, give the best source for answers to these questions. Include the page reference.

1. What series of novels did Upton Sinclair write?
2. Find a list of Isaac Bashevis Singer's works in English.
3. What is the setting of Joseph Heller's novel *Catch-22*?
4. What made Bill Mauldin, the cartoonist, famous?
5. What part did Charlotte Corday play in the French Revolution?
6. Which novel of Jessamyn West's became a popular movie?

7. How has Jacques Cousteau graphically shared his experiences as a marine explorer?

8. What were some of Clarence Darrow's famous cases?

9. Where can you find a picture of Geoffrey Chaucer?

10. What is the background of many J. P. Marquand novels?

11. What was Henrik Ibsen's contribution to drama?

12. What story influenced William Golding in the development of his novel *Lord of the Flies*?

13. What honor was Gwendolyn Brooks given by the state of Illinois?

14. What was the ultimate success of Clarence Day's family sketches?

15. What handicaps made drawing difficult for James Thurber?

D. Literary Reference Books. Use the literary reference books listed in this chapter to answer the following questions. After each answer write the name of the reference book you used.

1. What is a morality play?

2. What influence did the McGuffey readers have on American education?

3. Find a poem on freedom.

4. On what occasion did John F. Kennedy say, "Let us never negotiate out of fear, but let us never fear to negotiate"?

5. In what century was the Tower of London built?

6. What is the "theater of the absurd"?

7. What are some of the treasures in the British Museum?

8. Who wrote the poem "Renascence"?

9. What was meant by Manifest Destiny?

10. What forced the magazine *Literary Digest* to cease publication?

11. Who are the main characters in the musical comedy *Of Thee I Sing*?

12. What are the Leatherstocking Tales?

13. How favorable were the reviews of John Steinbeck's *The Grapes of Wrath*?

14. Where was Tin Pan Alley?

15. What is the plot of Frank Norris's novel *The Pit*?

E. Readers' Guide to Periodical Literature. Use the excerpt from the *Readers' Guide* on page 322 to answer the following questions.

1. On what page in *Christianity Today* will you find a message from the publisher on leadership?
2. Give the complete magazine title of the following abbreviations:

Educ Digest	NY
Sprts Illus	Bus W
Chr Cent	Pop Mech

3. What is Ann Landers' real name?
4. Who has delivered an address on leadership?
5. Who has written a continuing article on horseracing?

F. Using Reference Materials for a Research Paper. The American novelist, Sinclair Lewis, is best known as a satirist of the American middle class. In a study of his major novels, *Main Street* and *Babbitt,* some background knowledge of his life and writings would be valuable. From the reference sources listed in this chapter, find the specific books that will answer these questions. Include the page references.

1. Locate comprehensive biographical information.
2. Find reviews of *Babbitt* and *Main Street*.
3. What Minnesota town is the locale for *Main Street?*
4. What was Lewis' reason for declining the Pulitzer Prize in 1926?
5. Compare Sinclair Lewis with Willa Cather as an interpreter of small town life in America.
6. What is the entry under "babbitt" in the unabridged dictionaries?
7. On what occasion did he say, "Our American professors like their literature clear and cold and pure and very dead"?
8. What is the plot of *Arrowsmith?*
9. What was the title of his address in Stockholm on receiving the Nobel Prize for Literature?
10. Were the critics justified in accusing him of romanticism?

1. Mastering library skills will help you to do research efficiently. It will also help you to find books and other materials to read for pleasure.

2. Works of fiction are arranged on library shelves in alphabetical order, according to the last names of their authors.

3. Works of nonfiction are usually arranged according to the Dewey Decimal classification system.

4. Card catalogs contain alphabetically-organized cards that can be used to locate specific materials. Most card catalogs contain author cards, title cards, and subject cards.

5. When conducting research, locate specific information in books by making use of the table of contents, index, and other parts of a book.

6. Make use of dictionaries, encyclopedias, magazines, and other reference works when doing research. Libraries usually mark reference works with an "R" and keep them in a special reference section.

Applications in Other Subject Areas

Computer Science. Rapid change is characteristic of such high technology fields as computer science. To keep up with changes in this field, people who use computers must read about recent developments in computer-related magazines. Go to the library and locate two or three articles devoted to computers. Do a written report describing recent developments in computer technology.

Science / Language / Music / Fine Arts. The following people all made revolutionary contributions to their fields. Choose any two of these people, and do some research on them in the library. Find information in as many different sources as possible.

Albert Einstein	Sigmund Freud
Noam Chomsky	Arnold Schönberg
Claude Lévi-Strauss	Pablo Picasso

Chapter 15

Critical Thinking and Language

It is easy to think of reading and listening as passive pursuits. This is because people engaged in these activities are generally quiet and still. However, good readers and listeners do not simply absorb information. Instead, they continually analyze and evaluate what they read and hear to determine whether particular statements are true or false, reasonable or unreasonable. Such an active approach to reading and listening requires sound critical thinking.

In this chapter you will learn how to use critical thinking skills to analyze and evaluate ideas encountered in written and spoken sources. You will also learn how to use the principles of critical thinking to test the truth or reasonableness of ideas presented in your own speech and writing. Once you have mastered these skills, you will find that it is easier for you to recognize weak or dangerous ideas. You will also find yourself better equipped to communicate your own ideas persuasively.

Part 1   Statements of Fact and Opinion

In any written or spoken work, some statements are more important than others. Such statements include the following:

Sentences that express a main or controlling idea
Topic sentences of paragraphs
Sentences that express a conclusion or summary

Whenever you read or listen to informative or persuasive language, you should isolate important statements and evaluate them to determine whether they are probable or true. You should also attempt to evaluate the arguments used to support these important or essential statements. The first step in evaluating a statement is to determine whether it is a fact or an opinion.

Distinguishing Facts and Opinions

The statements that you encounter in such sources as speeches, advertisements, and editorials may be either facts or opinions. It is important to be able to distinguish between the two, since facts may be used as solid evidence, while opinions are simply one individual's beliefs or views on a subject.

A **fact** is a statement that can be proved by one of the following methods:

Personal observation of the subject
Reference to a human authority or expert
Reference to an authoritative written source such as an encyclopedia or dictionary

For example, the following statement is a fact: "Mahatma Gandhi led the movement for Indian independence from British rule." The statement can be proved by talking to people who personally observed the Indian revolution or by reading about this revolution in a history text.

An **opinion** is a statement that cannot be proved. However, it may be possible to support a given opinion with facts that can themselves be proved by one of the methods mentioned above. Opinions may take one of three forms:

A **prediction** is an opinion about the future. It cannot be proved because the events that it describes have not yet taken place. The following is an example of a prediction:

> By the middle of the next century, America's coal reserves will be depleted.

A **judgment** is an opinion that expresses an attitude toward a subject. Such opinions usually contain judgment words such as *good, excellent, poor, fine, wonderful,* or *boring.* Judgments cannot be absolutely true or false because attitudes differ from person to person. The following are examples of judgments:

> Anne Sexton was a wonderful poet.
> The 1970's was one of the most uneventful decades of this century.

A **statement of obligation** is an opinion about what *ought to be* the case. Such statements usually contain the words *must, should,* or *ought to.* The following are statements of obligation:

> You must water that plant.
> Parents should be selective about the television programs that they allow their young children to watch.

Evaluating Facts and Opinions

It is not enough simply to isolate the important statements in a work and determine whether these statements are facts or opinions. A conscientious reader or listener will also evaluate them to determine how well they support the arguments or ideas they refer to. The procedures that you should follow depend upon whether the statements are facts or opinions.

Evaluating Facts. If a statement is a fact, evaluate it by asking the following questions:

Guidelines for Evaluating Facts

1. Can the statement be proved by personal observation or by reference to an authoritative source? That is, can you or an expert verify the truth of the statement based upon what you have seen or heard?
2. Has the speaker or writer offered evidence to support the statement? If so, how convincing is this evidence?
3. Does the statement come from a reliable, unbiased source, or does the statement represent a slanted or prejudiced view? For example, facts on the consequences of expanding a local airport might be open to question if they came from the president of an airline that would benefit from the proposed expansion.
4. Is the source of the statement up-to-date? Remember that a statement that was true in 1950 may not be true now.
5. Is the statement consistent with other known facts? Contradictory evidence must be taken into consideration. For example, the statement that "there are no unexplored territories on earth" contradicts the fact that the oceans and certain arctic territories remain mysteries to us.

Evaluating Opinions. If a statement is an opinion, evaluate it by determining whether it can be supported by facts. A **sound opinion** is one that is supported by facts. An **unsound opinion** is one that is not supported by facts, or that is supported by facts that have been distorted through an error in reasoning. (See Parts 2 and 3.) Consider the following examples:

SOUND OPINION: People who wish to become doctors should study chemistry.

UNSOUND OPINION: People who wish to become doctors need not study chemistry.

The first is a sound opinion because it is supported by facts such as the following:

Medical programs in colleges require chemistry of their applicants.

Knowledge of chemistry is necessary to understanding bodily processes and functions.

Knowledge of chemistry is necessary to understanding how various medicines and treatments affect the functioning of the human body.

The second example is an unsound opinion because it is not supported by facts such as these.

Once you have identified the facts supporting a given opinion, you can further check the soundness of the opinion by evaluating these facts. An opinion that is supported by statements of fact that turn out to be false is not a sound opinion.

Exercises Evaluating Statements of Fact and Opinion

A. Determine whether the following statements are true by referring to the source indicated in parentheses.

1. You can obtain a passport by contacting your local post office. (Contact the post office.)

2. Alan Shepard was the first American astronaut in space. (Refer to an encyclopedia.)

3. The average rainfall in Hawaii is thirty-two inches per year. (Refer to an almanac.)

4. Andrew Jackson and Richard Nixon were forced to resign from the Presidency of the United States. (Refer to an encyclopedia or to a textbook.)

5. The Cadillac was named after the founder of Detroit. (Refer to an encyclopedia.)

6. *The Canterbury Tales* were written by John Donne. (Refer to an English literature anthology or textbook.)

7. Teachers in your state are required by law to obtain a Master's degree. (Ask one of your teachers.)

8. The word *camera* derives from a Greek word for a type of *room*. (Refer to a dictionary.)

9. Robert Frost, the poet of New England, was born in San Francisco. (Refer to a biography or to a literary reference work.)

10. Germany is the largest country in Western Europe. (Refer to an atlas.)

B. Determine whether the following statements are facts or opinions. If a statement is an opinion, tell whether it is a prediction, a judgment, or a statement of obligation; then write two statements of fact that support or contradict the opinion.

1. FORTRAN is a computer language used by engineers.
2. Prospective engineers should learn FORTRAN.
3. By the mid 1990's, the National Aeronautics and Space Administration will have launched its proposed orbiting space laboratory.
4. In the vacuum of space, astronauts are able to mix together elements that cannot be combined on earth.
5. Science and engineering offer many fascinating possibilities for study and research.

C. Statements used to support ideas presented in a report or research paper should be facts, not opinions. Which of the following statements would be appropriate as supporting evidence in a research paper on George Washington Carver?

1. George Washington Carver won international fame for agricultural research.
2. Carver developed hundreds of products from such crops as peanuts, sweet potatoes, and pecans.
3. Carver will be remembered forever as a man of great spirit and industry.
4. He made more than three hundred products from the peanut.
5. Carver earned his way through Iowa State College by cooking, taking in laundry, and working as a janitor.
6. His most outstanding discovery was how to make synthetic marble out of wood shavings.
7. George Washington Carver was a professor at Tuskegee Institute in Alabama for many years.
8. Carver's example should be followed by all science students.
9. In 1939 Carver received the Roosevelt medal for his many contributions to science.
10. The George Washington Carver National Monument is located on the Missouri farm where he was born.

Part 2 Evaluating Inductive and Deductive Arguments

Neither facts nor opinions are likely to appear in isolation. Instead, they are commonly found as supporting statements in formal and informal arguments. A **formal argument** is a group of statements that have a logical relationship to one another. The two most common types of formal argument are induction and deduction.

Inductive Reasoning

Induction is the process of drawing general conclusions from specific observations. Imagine that you try to start your car, and the motor won't turn over. You turn on the light switch, but the light doesn't come on. You turn on the car radio, and nothing happens. By combining all this evidence, you can come to the conclusion that something is wrong with the car's battery. This conclusion is the result of inductive reasoning.

Preparing an inductive argument involves three steps:

1. You note several specific facts, called the **sample.**
2. You examine the facts carefully, looking for a relationship between them.
3. You reach a general conclusion, or **generalization.**

Inductive Reasoning

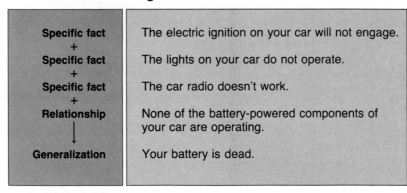

Specific fact +	The electric ignition on your car will not engage.
Specific fact +	The lights on your car do not operate.
Specific fact +	The car radio doesn't work.
Relationship ↓	None of the battery-powered components of your car are operating.
Generalization	Your battery is dead.

As the example shows, a conclusion reached through inductive reasoning is probable, but not absolutely certain. There may be other explanations for the facts given in the example, but the conclusion that the battery is dead is probable given the evidence. To test a conclusion reached through inductive reasoning, check to see if the conclusion is consistent with other known facts. The conclusion drawn in the example may be tested by charging the battery and observing whether this corrects the problem with the car.

Although inductive reasoning is not a "perfect" means of reasoning, it can be quite dependable if you avoid the following errors:

1. Overgeneralization. Generalizations, or conclusions reached through inductive reasoning, are statements about whole groups or classes of things. Sometimes a person makes the error of jumping to a generalization that is too broad. The jump may be the result of an insufficient or inaccurate sample, or it may simply be because of hastiness or indifference on the part of the person making the statement. This error in reasoning is known as **overgeneralization.**

Some overgeneralizations are harmless exaggerations. For example, the statement "There's never enough time to get all my work done" can be translated to mean "I wish I had more time." The speaker or writer probably does not mean for the statement to be taken literally. Instead, he or she is exaggerating the actual facts to convey a strongly-felt emotion.

Some overgeneralizations, however, can be very harmful. For example, suppose that a sensational crime were to occur in a small town. If this crime were publicized nationwide, people might begin to think of the town as "crime ridden" or "dangerous." These overgeneralizations might well have devastating effects. Businesses could decide not to locate their operations in the town; families could decide not to move there. In short, the overgeneralization could destroy the reputation of the community.

The most harmful sort of overgeneralization is the **stereotype,** a broad generalization made about members of particular ethnic, racial, political, social, or religious groups. Stereotypes are based upon a small number of observations of particular people within groups and do not reflect the actual qualities or characteristics of group members. Because they are based upon poor evidence, stereotypes are unscientific and illogical. They create barriers to communication and foster division and misunderstanding.

One way to combat stereotypes is to recognize and reject them whenever you encounter them in advertising, in jokes, and in everyday speech. A second way is to come to know and respect individuals from various backgrounds. When people learn to see each other as individuals—not primarily as members of groups—stereotypes tend to be destroyed.

2. Improper Sampling. Most errors in inductive reasoning are caused by basing an inductive conclusion on **improper samples.** A sample is improper if it does not represent the whole group or population being referred to. In order to guarantee a sound inductive conclusion, the sample must be large enough and random enough to represent the group or population adequately.

The randomness of the sample ensures the accuracy of the evidence. If you watch only the television shows on one network, for example, you cannot draw a conclusion about television programming in general. You would have to evaluate a random sample of shows from every network and channel before you could make an accurate judgment about television shows as a whole.

In general, then, to avoid making errors in inductive reasoning, keep the following guidelines in mind:

1. Avoid making statements that refer to whole groups of people or things unless you can prove these statements conclusively.
2. Keep your sample—the facts on which you base your conclusion—as large and as representative as possible.
3. Avoid making statements that contain such absolute words as *never, always,* and *every time.* Instead, qualify your statements by using words such as *sometimes, occasionally,* and *a few.*

Deductive Reasoning

Induction begins with a series of specific facts and moves to a general conclusion, or generalization. **Deduction,** on the other hand, begins with a general statement, adds a related statement, and moves to a specific, more limited conclusion.

Deductive arguments can be presented in a series of three statements. This series is called a **syllogism.** The first statement in the syllogism is the major premise; the second is the minor premise; and the third is the conclusion.

MAJOR PREMISE: Dumping sewage into lakes destroys plant and animal life.
MINOR PREMISE: Sewage was dumped into Lake Oswego.
CONCLUSION: Plant and animal life were destroyed in Lake Oswego.

Errors in Deductive Reasoning. In deductive reasoning two conditions must be met for the conclusion to be true: Both of the premises must be true, and the argument must follow a valid or logical form. One untrue or weak premise may result in a false conclusion. Consider the following argument:

Everyone loves canoeing.
The Forensics Club is planning a canoe trip.
Everyone in the Forensics Club will love it.

Even though the second premise is true, the major premise is false. Therefore, the conclusion has not been proved.

An **invalid form** is equally destructive to a deductive argument. The major premise must be true of *all, every, no,* or *none* of the persons, objects, or events that it describes. Therefore, the major premise should never contain a qualifier such as *some, most, occasionally, a few,* or *many.*

MAJOR PREMISE: Some novels are based on myths.
MINOR PREMISE: *1984* is a novel.
CONCLUSION: *1984* is based on a myth.

Though both premises are true, the conclusion has not been proved because the argument does not follow proper logical form. In other words, the argument is invalid.

Exercises Using Inductive and Deductive Reasoning

A. Using the inductive method, draw general conclusions from the following groups of related facts. Word your conclusions so that they avoid the error of overgeneralization.

1. *The Professor*, the first of Charlotte Brontë's novels, was autobiographical.

   Sons and Lovers, the first of D. H. Lawrence's novels, was autobiographical.

   A Portrait of an Artist as a Young Man, the first of James Joyce's novels, was autobiographical.

2. Coretta was interested in purchasing a new car. She checked the advertisements of several local car dealers.

   One ad said, "No one can beat our prices."

   Another ad said, "Lowest prices in town."

   Yet another said, "We will never be undersold."

3. Nazi Germany was a centralized state, one in which all power resided in the government. The heads of this government ordered the destruction of all non-realistic artwork.

   The Soviet Union is also a centralized state. Soviet government officials discourage the production of non-realistic artworks.

4. In Shakespeare's *Henry IV, Part I*, nobles such as King Henry speak in poetry. Commoners such as Mistress Quickly speak in prose.

   In Shakespeare's *Macbeth*, nobles such as Macbeth speak in poetry. The porter, a commoner, speaks in prose.

   In Shakespeare's *Hamlet*, nobles such as Hamlet speak in poetry. The gravedigger, a commoner, speaks in prose.

5. Alexander the Great conquered most of the Mediterranean, Northern Africa, and the Middle East. His soldiers made use of a new invention, the stirrup, which allowed them to fight from horseback without being thrown.

   In 1346, the English troops at the battle of Crécy were able to defeat their French opponents because of the introduction of squads of archers using longbows.

   The victory of the Allies in the First World War was partially due to the use of new inventions such as tanks and fighter planes.

B. Rewrite the following overgeneralizations, making them into valid generalizations by using qualifying words.

1. The most important invention of the twentieth century is the computer.
2. Young adults love comedies more than any other type of movie.
3. America's electronic products are the best in the world.
4. Jane Austen was the greatest writer who ever lived.
5. Everyone should study a foreign language in college.

C. Study the following deductive arguments. Identify the conclusions of these arguments as *True, False Due to False Premises,* or *False Due to Invalid Form.*

1. MAJOR PREMISE: All subjects taught in college require computer skills.

   MINOR PREMISE: Football is a subject taught in college.

   CONCLUSION: Football requires computer skills.

2. MAJOR PREMISE: All mammals have internal mechanisms that regulate the temperatures of their bodies.

   MINOR PREMISE: Whales and people are mammals.

   CONCLUSION: Whales and people have internal mechanisms that regulate the temperatures of their bodies.

3. MAJOR PREMISE: Some languages have no means of expressing action in the future.

   MINOR PREMISE: English is a language.

   CONCLUSION: English has no means of expressing action in the future.

4. MAJOR PREMISE: Viewers learn nothing from television programs.

   MINOR PREMISE: News shows are television programs.

   CONCLUSION: Viewers learn nothing from news shows.

5. MAJOR PREMISE: Some third world countries do not have the technology to produce energy through nuclear power.

MINOR PREMISE: India is a third world country.

CONCLUSION: India does not have the technology to produce energy through nuclear power.

D. Study the following paragraphs. Explain the type of reasoning being used in each paragraph, and tell whether the conclusion of each argument is proved.

1. In her English literature class, Maria read a poem by Thomas Hardy called "Channel Firing." It told about a group of corpses who were awakened one night by gunnery practice. In the poem, the corpses discuss the foolishness of war. Later, in the library, Maria ran across a second poem by Hardy called "The Man He Killed." This was also an anti-war poem. Maria decided that all of Hardy's poems must be about the evils of warfare.

2. A U.S. government study reports that most productive workers are not easily distracted from their duties. Yesterday, the normally-quiet routine of our office was interrupted by the sounds of construction going on outside. These sounds caused many of our workers to be distracted. Therefore, our workers must not be very productive.

Part 3 Common Fallacies in Argument and Persuasion

A **fallacy,** or error in reasoning, results in confusion and invalid conclusions. In Part 2 you learned about several common fallacies in reasoning, including overgeneralization, stereotyping, argument from false premises, and invalid logical form. The fallacies described on the following pages are also common in argument and persuasion. Learn to recognize these fallacies and to avoid using them in your own speech and writing.

Fallacies of Reasoning

The Either/Or Fallacy. An argument that offers only two alternatives may contain the **either/or fallacy.** Such an argument ignores the possibility of alternative solutions or choices.

> The county prison is dangerously overcrowded. It contains almost two thousand prisoners in a building designed to hold a maximum of one thousand. Either we must build a new prison in this county, or we must release at least one thousand prisoners.

A more sound conclusion to this argument would be "We must find some way of relieving this overcrowding." In most situations there are many possible options, not just two. Whenever you are faced with a problem to solve, it is a good practice to list as many solutions as possible.

False Analogy. An **analogy** is a comparison in which two dissimilar things are shown to have at least one quality in common. When such a comparison is weak or misleading, it is called a **false analogy.**

> An ideal human society would be like the societies of bees. Every individual would have a job to do, know what that job is, and perform it well. There would be no waste, no doubt, no insecurity.

Human society cannot be compared meaningfully to life in a bee colony, where individuals have no choice regarding the roles they perform. The colony is dominated by a single individual—the queen bee—and worker bees live for only six weeks. Would people be happy in a society that provided no opportunity for individual initiative or creativity? Of course not. Therefore, the analogy is false.

Circular Reasoning. The fallacy known as **circular reasoning** or **begging the question** occurs when someone argues that a conclusion is true without providing evidence or proof. In such arguments, the conclusion is simply a restatement of the premises. For example, a person might argue that "Shakespeare is a greater writer than Sidney Sheldon because people with good taste in literature prefer Shakespeare." If asked how you can tell who has good taste in literature, the person might reply that such persons can be identified by the fact that they prefer Shakespeare to Sheldon. This argument is begging the question and going in circles.

Post hoc, ergo propter hoc (after this; therefore, because of this). The **post hoc, ergo propter hoc** fallacy occurs when one event is said to be the cause of a second event simply because the events occurred in sequence. The following is an example of *post hoc* reasoning:

EVIDENCE: The Great Depression occurred after Herbert Hoover became President.
CONCLUSION: Herbert Hoover caused the Great Depression.

Notice that no evidence is offered to show that these two facts are related. Therefore, one fact cannot be considered the cause of the other, and the conclusion has not been proved.

The Single Cause Fallacy. The **single cause fallacy** occurs when an event with more than one cause is said to have only one. For example, the statement "Erosion is caused by running water" is not completely true because it attributes a result that has many causes, including wind and the stripping of vegetation, to a single cause, water.

Similarly, the statement "Jim is irritable because he has a headache" may be only partially true. Jim's irritability may also be the result of other factors combined with the headache. Human behavior usually is the result of many causes, some biological, some social, some internal, some external. Therefore, it is usually necessary to identify more than one cause when explaining human actions.

Transfer. Speakers or writers sometimes attempt to move their audiences to associate feelings about one thing with another, unrelated thing. This technique is called **transfer.**

Advertisers use the transfer device when they show their product being used by an appealing personality or in an appealing setting. For example, a soft drink manufacturer may show his or her product being consumed by a crowd of high-spirited, fun-loving people engaged in a pleasurable activity in an interesting or exotic place. Of course, none of these trappings have anything to do with the quality of the product, but they do affect the emotions of the manufacturer's intended audience.

Unreliable Testimonial. A testimonial is an endorsement of a person, product, or idea. **Unreliable testimonial** occurs when the person making the endorsement is unqualified to do so. For example, political candidates often ask celebrated sports figures or movie stars to endorse them during elections. The sports figure or movie star may know nothing at all about politics, economics, or government, but such an endorsement nonetheless leads some people to vote for the candidate.

Bandwagon. The fallacy of accepting something as true or right simply because it is believed or done by many other people is called **bandwagon.** An advertiser who says. "Everyone is hurrying down to our fantastic sidewalk sale" is using this technique. The opposite of bandwagon is the fallacy known as **snob appeal,** in which people are encouraged to do or believe something because this thing is done or believed by a select few.

Fallacies of Meaning

Sometimes errors in reasoning occur because of the misuse of individual words. To recognize errors of this kind, you must familiarize yourself with the various kinds of word meaning.

Symbol and Referent. Every word is a **symbol** that stands for something beyond itself. The thing for which a word stands is called its **referent.** Thus the referent of the word *dance* is a particular group of actions performed by people. The referent of the word *tree* is a particular group of organisms in the outside world. This meaning of a word—what the word stands for—is its **denotation,** or primary meaning.

In addition to referring to things, many words also convey particular attitudes toward the things they name. These attitudes or associations that a word carries in addition to its denotative meaning are its **connotations,** or secondary meanings.

Consider the following pairs of words:

perspiration	sweat	antique	old
friend	buddy	unique	odd

Each word in each pair has the same denotative meaning. However, the connotations of these words are quite different and cause people to respond to them in different ways. Speakers and writers often choose words with particular connotations in order to influence their audiences.

Vague or Undefined Terms. When a writer or speaker employs a term that has no clear denotation, he or she commits the fallacy of using **vague or undefined terms.** Statements that include such terms are usually themselves unclear or even meaningless. Judgment words (See Part 1, page 330, of this chapter) often fall into this category.

Suppose, for example, that a senator tells his or her colleagues that "This legislation will do irreparable *harm*." Unless further clarification is offered by the speaker, this statement is improper because the word *harm* has no clear referent. Does the speaker mean that the legislation will result in physical damage to people or to property? Does he or she mean that people will suffer emotional distress if the legislation is passed? It is impossible to tell. The speaker does not say clearly what *harm* means in this context, and this is particularly confusing since what is *harm* to one person may be a positive act or idea to another.

As you evaluate people's ideas, remember to watch for vague terms. Often these words or phrases are used unconsciously. However, writers and speakers sometimes use them purposefully in an attempt to sway or mislead their audiences.

Equivocation. Sometimes errors occur because a particular word has more than one referent. When a speaker or writer intentionally causes his or her audience to misinterpret a word, he or she is committing the fallacy of **equivocation.** Suppose, for example, that you read the following headline:

PRESIDENT CONSULTS WIZARD WHO FORETELLS FUTURE

You then read the article and find out that the President has been discussing plans for future space shuttle flights with a "wizard" in aerospace engineering. The writer of the headline has taken unfair advantage of the fact that the words *wizard* and *foretell* have several meanings.

Loaded Words. Sometimes a word carries such powerful connotations that its denotative meaning is all but lost. Such **loaded words** are used to manipulate people's feelings, often in lieu of presenting genuine evidence. For example, someone who dislikes televised productions of ballet, opera, and classic theater might say that these are "geared to pseudo-intellectual snobs."

In the above example, the speaker is using **snarl words,** words that have powerful negative connotations, to sway his or her audience. On the other hand, someone who enjoys televised ballet and the like might say that such programming "makes high culture accessible to everyone." In this case, the speaker is attempting to sway his or her audience by using a **purr word,** one that has powerful positive connotations. Such terms as *pseudo-intellectual, snob,* and *high culture* mean very little, but are nonetheless extremely effective because of their emotional content. Whenever you read or hear material containing such loaded words, remember that emotional outbursts are often used to disguise ignorance of facts and the inability to reason.

Exercises Avoiding Errors in Reasoning

A. Identify the fallacy in each of the following statements by choosing its name from among those provided in parentheses.

1. People who oppose the space program are just like people who opposed the first railroads. They are attempting to stop progress. (circular reasoning, post hoc, false analogy, bandwagon)

2. The violence in our society is due to the violence on television. (post hoc, either/or, single cause, unreliable testimonial)

3. The best furs, for all the best people, are at Courier's Furriers. (either/or, false analogy, single cause, transfer, snob appeal)

4. I saw a shooting star just before I found my wallet. The shooting star must have brought me good luck. (circular reasoning, post hoc, either/or, false analogy)

5. Safe Soap is the best brand of laundry detergent because it is better than any other brand on the market. (circular reasoning, post hoc, either/or, single cause)

6. As Dr. Sandra Marcus, the star of your favorite daytime soap opera, I often have to deal with crisis situations. Crises occur in real life, too, and, when they become more than I can bear, I turn to Regal Brand Aspirin. (circular reasoning, either/or, unreliable testimonial, bandwagon)

7. There's no point in my telling you about the movie, because you either love science fiction or you hate it. (post hoc, false analogy, either/or, single cause)

8. Bring the simple elegance of Colonial America into your home with a new colonial dining set from Franklin Furniture. (post hoc, either/or, unreliable testimonial, transfer, bandwagon)

9. If you haven't tried our new Action Arcade home computer game, you're one of the very few people who have not found out just how exciting home entertainment can be. Get back into the game! Join the stampede down to Eric's Electronics and Hobbies. (circular reasoning, single cause, transfer, bandwagon)

10. Writing is a lot like parachuting. If you can't get it right the first time, you had better take up some other activity. (circular reasoning, post hoc, false analogy, snob appeal)

B. Study this political advertisement. Then, write a review of the ad in which you identify its fallacies of meaning: vague or undefined terms, equivocation, snarl words, and purr words.

Will Wentworth, candidate for United States Senator, understands your problems. He knows how tired you are of the petty backroom bureaucrats and political lackeys who daily assail your liberties and pilfer your pocketbook. Will Wentworth wants to do something about this, but he'll need your help. Please send a five dollar donation for your free copy of "How to Keep the Liberty Bell Ringing," the book that sets forth Wentworth's program for the revitalization of America. All contributions are tax-deductible.

SUMMARY AND APPLICATIONS

1. Applying the principles of critical thinking will help you to recognize weak or dangerous ideas. It will also improve your ability to speak and write persuasively.

2. Statements of fact can be proved by observation or by reference to an authoritative source. Statements of opinion cannot be proved, but can be supported by facts.

3. Inductive reasoning makes general conclusions based upon specific observations.

4. Deductive reasoning draws a specific or narrow conclusion from a general observation.

5. The following are some common fallacies in reasoning that you should learn to recognize and avoid:

unsubstantiated opinions	false analogy
overgeneralization	circular reasoning
stereotyping	*post hoc, ergo propter hoc*
improper or limited sampling	the single cause fallacy
argument from false premises	vague or undefined terms
invalid deductive argument	equivocation
the either/or fallacy	loaded words

Applications in Other Subject Areas

History / Political Science. An awareness of the methods of inductive and deductive reasoning can help you to understand opposing sides of historical or contemporary issues. Identify such an issue in the news or in a history text. Weigh the arguments on all sides of the issue. What sorts of arguments are used by people on opposing sides? How good are these arguments? Can you detect any fallacies of reasoning or meaning in them?

Mathematics. In deductive reasoning you take a general hypothesis, add a related premise, and arrive at a specific conclusion. Find examples of deductive reasoning in a mathematics textbook. How does the statement of the mathematical problem and its solution compare to the premises and conclusion of a deductive argument?

Chapter 16

College Entrance Examinations and Other Standardized Tests

Whether your next goal is college or a job, achieving it will often depend on your satisfactorily completing a test of knowledge or skill. In this chapter you will learn how to prepare for and take college entrance examinations and other standardized tests. These strategies will increase your chances of receiving acceptable scores. They will also enable you to view these tests, not as obstacles or burdens, but as opportunities to demonstrate just how much you know.

Part 1   Taking Standardized Tests

A **standardized test** is one that is given to groups of people under strictly-controlled conditions to ensure equal chances of success. These tests are used for purposes of evaluation by schools, businesses, and government agencies.

If you are planning to go to college, the chances are that you have taken or plan to take one or more of these tests:

The Preliminary Scholastic Aptitude Test/National Merit Scholarship Qualifying Test (the P.S.A.T./N.M.S.Q.T.)

The Scholastic Aptitude Test (the S.A.T.)

The Test of the American College Testing Program (the A.C.T.)

Advanced Placement or Achievement Tests

The following guidelines will help you to prepare for and take standardized tests of all kinds:

Taking Standardized Tests

Before the Test

1. Prepare for aptitude tests such as the A.C.T. or S.A.T. well in advance by reading and writing often, by developing your vocabulary, and by devoting much time and energy to study in the following areas: English grammar, usage, mechanics, and composition; mathematics; the natural sciences; and the social sciences.

2. Make use of practice materials, including the sample tests supplied by testing organizations, and commercially-prepared test-taking manuals.

3. Study the types of questions asked on the test that you plan to take, and learn specific strategies for answering them.

4. Rest and eat well before the test.

5. Cope with anxiety by thinking of the test as an opportunity, not an obstacle. If possible, do some light exercise before taking the test to relieve tension. If you are nervous, relax your body and breathe slowly and deeply.

Getting Started

During the Test

1. Equip yourself with the necessary materials. These are detailed in the informational booklet accompanying your registration form. Typically, you will need several sharpened pencils, your properly-completed admission ticket, a recognized form of personal identification, and a watch to aid you in budgeting your time.

2. Arrive at the test center approximately half an hour before the test is scheduled to begin. Settle into your assigned seat and accustom yourself to the surroundings. Relax by closing your eyes, taking ten deep breaths, and imagining yourself in a tranquil environment.

3. Listen carefully to the oral instructions of the test supervisor. Be alert to announcements explaining how and where to supply the requested information on the answer form. Further announcements will direct you to the appropriate page in the examination booklet. Before the test begins, you will be given an opportunity to ask questions.

4. Wait for the command to begin and do so upon hearing it.

Using the Answer Key

1. The answer key will look something like this:

1. Ⓐ Ⓑ Ⓒ Ⓓ Ⓔ

2. Ⓕ Ⓖ Ⓗ Ⓘ Ⓙ

2. Indicate your answer by darkening the circle on the answer key that corresponds to the correct answer in your test booklet. Check regularly to make sure that you are marking the correct spaces on the answer sheet.

3. Make sure that circles are completely darkened. Erase any stray marks on the answer sheet. These marks may be interpreted as answers by the scoring machine.

4. If you change an answer, be sure to erase completely.

1. S.A.T. scores reflect the number of questions answered correctly minus a penalty for questions answered incorrectly. Therefore, it is not in your best interest to guess unless you can eliminate two or three incorrect answers.

2. A.C.T. scores do not reflect a penalty for guessing.

3. As you begin the test, note the number of questions and the time available. Check your watch regularly to make certain that you are not wasting time on difficult questions. Remember that you are not expected to answer every question correctly.

4. Read quickly over the entire section of the test and answer easy questions as you come to them.

5. Place a "+" on your answer sheet next to any question that seems answerable but would require a great deal of time.

+ 3. Ⓐ Ⓑ Ⓒ Ⓓ Ⓔ

6. Place a "−" on your answer sheet next to any question that appears to be too difficult to answer.

− 4. Ⓕ Ⓖ Ⓗ Ⓘ Ⓙ

7. After answering all the easy questions, go back to the ones marked with a "+" and answer them. Then attempt to answer the ones marked with a "−."

8. Make sure that you save time to erase your "+" and "−" marks. Otherwise, these may be read by the computer as answers.

Part 2 Strategies for Standardized Tests

Standardized tests typically contain questions of the following types: antonyms, analogies, sentence completion, sentence correction, reading comprehension, and usage. The best way to prepare for taking college entrance examinations and other standardized tests is to learn specific strategies for answering questions of each kind.

Antonyms

Antonyms are words that are opposite in meaning. A typical antonym question provides a single word and asks you to choose its clearest opposite from a list of words, as follows:

EXAMPLE: Antonyms

FERMENTING: (A) improvising   (B) stagnating
(C) wavering   (D) plunging
(E) dissolving

Use the following strategies when answering antonym questions:

1. Look only for words with *opposite* meanings. Do not be thrown off by synonyms—words that have the same meaning as the given word.
2. Make sure that you know the meaning of the given word before you look at the choices. Define this word using any of the following methods:

   a. Think of other words with the same meaning.
   b. If this does not work, create one or more sentences that use the word. Then try to arrive at its definition.
   c. If the meaning of the word is still unclear, try analyzing any prefixes, suffixes, base words, or roots that the word contains. See Chapter 1 for more information on using word parts to determine meaning.

3. After you have arrived at the meaning of the given word, study the choices. Few words have exact opposites, so you must find the word that is most nearly opposite. You might also try either or both of the following strategies:

a. Eliminate any obviously incorrect answers.

b. Think of other possible meanings of the given word. Many words have more than one meaning.

The answer to the sample question is B.

Exercise Antonyms

Each question in this and the following Exercises is from an S.A.T. preparation guide put out by the C.E.E.B. Each example below consists of a word in capital letters, followed by five lettered words or phrases. Choose the word or phrase that is most nearly *opposite* in meaning to the word in capital letters. Since some of the questions require you to distinguish fine shades of meaning, consider all the choices before deciding which is best.

1. VERSATILE: (A) unadaptable (B) mediocre
   (C) impatient (D) egocentric (E) vicious

2. FRAUDULENT: (A) rather pleasing
   (B) extremely beneficial (C) courteous
   (D) authentic (E) simplified

3. PROTRUSION: (A) mirage (B) indentation
   (C) deceleration (D) disorder (E) fruitlessness

4. BOLT: (A) cleanse (B) slide (C) look upon
   (D) move sluggishly (E) exhibit proudly

5. ANTIQUATED: (A) fake (B) flat
   (C) modern (D) secret (E) applied

6. SNIPPET: (A) vague response (B) bargain
   (C) sudden plunge (D) fantasy
   (E) large amount

7. IMPUGN: (A) speak well of
   (B) describe in detail (C) forget to complete
   (D) disassociate (E) stimulate

8. RECANT: (A) reduce (B) ridicule
   (C) prevent delivery of (D) reaffirm belief in
   (E) accept remuneration for

9. DEPRAVITY: (A) talent (B) certainty
   (C) noble behavior (D) successful venture
   (E) elaborate decoration

10. EPHEMERAL: (A) lasting (B) inhumane
    (C) contemporary (D) destructive
    (E) appropriate

Analogies

Analogies are comparisons that are made in order to show how two things are related. In analogy questions, you are given two words that are related. You are then asked to compare the words to determine what this relationship is. Finally, you choose a second pair of words that have the same relationship to one another. The following is a typical analogy question:

EXAMPLE: Analogies

TERRESTRIAL: LUNG:: (A) marsupial: pouch
                    (B) floral: root
                    (C) aquatic: gill
                    (D) perennial: seed
                    (E) canine: mouth

Use the following strategies when answering analogy questions:

1. Do not look at the choices until after you have determined the relationship between the first pair of words. Determine this relationship by creating a sentence containing both of the words.

   Terrestrial creatures breathe by means of their *lungs*.

2. Then, find a pair of words among the choices that you can put in the places of the original pair in your sentence:

   Aquatic creatures breathe by means of their *gills*.

3. The following relationships are often found in analogy questions.

Type of Analogy	Example
object to its function	scissors: cutting
object to its material	memorial: granite
cause to effect	acid: etching
action to object	fire: cannon
part to whole	brick: wall
item to category	Iliad: epic
item to characteristic	diamond: hard
worker and tool	dentist: drill
worker and creation	composer: score
word to antonym	haughty: meek
word to synonym	guard: sentry

Exercise Analogies

Each of the following questions consists of a related pair of words or phrases, followed by five lettered pairs of words or phrases. Select the lettered pair that *best* expresses a relationship similar to that expressed in the original pair.

1. PAINTING:CANVAS:: (A) drawing:lottery
   (B) fishing:pond (C) writing:paper
   (D) shading:crayon (E) sculpting:design

2. VOLUME:SPHERE:: (A) altitude:triangle
   (B) diagonal:square (C) area:circle
   (D) angle:rectangle (E) length:cube

3. RAMSHACKLE:COLLAPSE::
   (A) intact:explode (B) threadbare:hem
   (C) waterlogged:sink (D) dilapidated:repair
   (E) flammable:quench

4. TRICK:ROGUE:: (A) stratagem:friend
   (B) sentence:criminal (C) accident:witness
   (D) conspiracy:traitor (E) novel:reader

5. CALIPERS:MEASURING:: (A) nails:hammering
(B) crops:harvesting (C) glasses:polishing
(D) decisions:weighing (E) scissors:cutting

6. WHEEDLE:FLATTERY:: (A) inspire:creations
(B) intimidate:threats (C) scrutinize:clues
(D) accuse:denials (E) appreciate:offers

7. CACOPHONY:SOUND:: (A) beauty:vision
(B) stench:smell (C) decadence:age
(D) radiance:illumination (E) ignorance:knowledge

8. LECHER:LUSTFUL::
(A) glutton:surly (B) fanatic:ungodly
(C) skinflint:miserly (D) disciplinarian:unruly
(E) spendthrift:homely

Sentence Completion

Sentence completion questions measure your knowledge of vocabulary and your ability to recognize relationships between parts of a sentence. A sentence is provided from which one or two words have been removed. You must choose words to complete meaning of the sentence. Sentence completion questions typically look like this:

EXAMPLE: Sentence Completion

Although Spalding . . . the importance of the physical necessities of life, her most successful endeavor was the . . . of the condition of the impoverished.

(A) deprecated . . alleviation
(B) emphasized . . investigation
(C) accentuated . . amelioration
(D) epitomized . . delineation
(E) disregarded . . desecration

When answering sentence completion questions, use the following strategies.

1. Read the incomplete sentence carefully, noting any key words. In particular, look for words that indicate contrast (but, however) or similarity (and, another).
2. Try each choice in the sentence, eliminating any choices that are nonsensical or grammatically incorrect.
3. Some choices may contain one word that fits well into the sentence and one word that doesn't. In the example, the second word in answer "C" makes sense, but the first word does not. Do not be misled by choices of this kind.
4. Grammar will often provide clues. Decide what part of speech the answer should be. If a verb is required, what should the tense of this verb be?

The answer to the sample question is "A."

Exercise Sentence Completion

Each of the following sentences has one or two blanks, each blank indicating that something has been omitted. Beneath the sentence are five lettered words or sets of words. Choose the word or set of words that *best* fits the meaning of the sentence.

1. In the North Pacific, the number of whales has been so drastically reduced that the sighting of even one is ___ event.

   (A) a newsworthy   (B) a treacherous
   (C) an everyday   (D) an elaborate
   (E) an expected

2. Musicians' salaries have risen so much faster than concert admission prices and donations that some famous ___ are threatened with ___.

   (A) composers . . silence
   (B) orchestras . . bankruptcy
   (C) works . . oblivion
   (D) conductors . . strikes
   (E) soloists . . taxation

3. In view of the ___ value of the new treatment for this complicated case, ___ with another physician is advisable.

   (A) questionable . . a consultation
   (B) necessary . . an interlude
   (C) accepted . . an exploration
   (D) impossible . . a confrontation
   (E) presumed . . an argument

4. Parental devotion, especially if too solicitous, has its ___,
   one of which is ___ a child's progress toward maturity.

   (A) delusions . . envisioning
   (B) excesses . . abetting
   (C) targets . . ensuring
   (D) rewards . . ameliorating.
   (E) pitfalls . . protracting

Sentence Correction

   In **sentence correction** questions part or all of a sentence is
underlined. If the underlined material contains no errors, you
mark "A," the answer that repeats the underlined material ver-
batim. If the underlined material does contain one or more
errors, you choose the word or group of words that corrects the
error or errors. Sentence correction questions typically look
like this:

EXAMPLE: Sentence Correction

Dolphins have a basic social organization, a system of
communication, *and* their brains are highly developed.

   (A) and their brains are highly developed.
   (B) and highly developed brains.
   (C) with highly developed brains.
   (D) while their brains are developed highly.
   (E) but their brains are developed highly.

---

1. Find the error, if there is one, before looking at the answers. Look for errors in grammar, word choice, punctuation or capitalization, awkwardness, and ambiguity.

2. Check your answer by inserting it into the sentence and then reading the entire sentence through.

Choice "B" is the correct answer to the sample question.

Exercise Sentence Correction

In each of the following sentences, part or all of the sentence is underlined. Below each sentence you will find five ways of phrasing the underlined part. Select the answer that produces the most effective sentence. This sentence should be one that is clear and exact, without awkwardness or ambiguity. In choosing answers, follow the requirements of standard written English. Also choose the answer that best expresses the meaning of the original sentence.

1. Issued in Great Britain in 1840, the first gummed postage stamp in history was known as the "Penny Black."
   (A) the first gummed postage stamp in history was known as
   (B) they called the first gummed postage stamp in history
   (C) history refers to the first gummed postage stamp as
   (D) was the first gummed postage stamp in history,
   (E) the first gummed postage stamp in history being known as

2. A number of parents are concerned about the protection of high school athletes and the many injuries being reported.
   (A) athletes and the many injuries being reported
   (B) athletes and numerous reports of injuries
   (C) athletes because of reports of numerous injuries
   (D) athletes, but many injuries are being reported
   (E) athletes, numerous injuries have been reported

3. <u>Many inferior films earn</u> a great deal of money for their producers, some extremely good ones do not.

   (A) Many inferior films earn
   (B) Many an inferior film earns
   (C) With many inferior films which earn
   (D) However, many inferior films earn
   (E) Although many inferior films earn

4. Gas rationing would force consumers to use their cars less, use public transportation more, <u>while conserving</u> gas.

   (A) while conserving
   (B) as well as conserving
   (C) conserving
   (D) and thereby conserve
   (E) to conserve

Usage Questions

Usage questions test the ability to recognize writing that is not standard. Usage questions usually contain four words or phrases that are underlined and lettered. You must identify the underlined part that contains an error or mark the choice labeled *no error*. Usage questions look like this:

EXAMPLE: Usage Question

Idealists are <u>not always</u> <u>as ignorant of</u> realities as <u>his</u>
          A   B   C

critics would <u>like to</u> believe. <u>No error</u>
           D   E

Use the following strategies when answering usage questions:

1. Read the entire sentence, not just the underlined parts.
2. Look for errors in word choice; punctuation errors; capitalization errors; errors in grammar; improper, awkward, or unclear sentence structure.

3. Grammatical errors commonly found in usage questions include incorrect verb tenses, improper agreement of pronoun and antecedent or of subject and verb, improper form of the pronoun, and improper use of adjectives and adverbs. Common errors in sentence structure include fragments, dangling modifiers, improper parallelism, and run-ons caused by comma faults. For information, see your Handbook.
4. Remember that if there is an error, it will be in one of the underlined sections. The correct answer to the sample question is "C." The object pronoun "his" does not agree with its antecedent, "idealistic."

Exercise Usage Questions

The following sentences contain problems in grammar, usage, and word choice. One sentence is correct. No sentence contains more than one error. In choosing answers, follow the requirements of standard written English. If there is an error, select the *one underlined part* that must be changed to make the sentence correct. If there is no error, select choice E.

1. During the early Middle Ages, before the development of
      A
   the printing press, virtually the only books were those
           B   C
   that are laboriously copied by monks. No error
       D   E

2. The decision that has just been agreed with by the com-
                A   B
   mittee members should serve as a basis for their work in
                                   C
   the years to come. No error
      D   E

3. People who dislike cats sometimes criticize them
                 A
   for being aloof and independent; people who are fond of
    B   C
   cats often admire them for the same qualities. No error
             D   E

Reading Comprehension

Reading comprehension questions are designed to measure the ability to understand reading passages of various kinds. Passages are taken from such fields as the humanities and the biological, physical, and social sciences. A passage may be biographical or it may tell all or part of a story. It may also analyze a topic, provide information, or attempt to persuade you to take some action or adopt some point of view. The passage is followed by a list of questions on its content, form, and style. Reading comprehension passages generally look like this:

EXAMPLE: Reading Comprehension

Some words which were once neutral but low in the social scale have sunk much lower because they acquired moral and even aesthetic connotations. A person would have to be bitterly angry to call someone a *boor,* a *churl*, and a *villain*. But, going by the original meaning of the words, you would only be saying that this individual was a farmer. A boor is the same as the German *Bauer* and the Dutch *Boer*. A *churl* is a commoner, a member of the lowest class of free men in Anglo-Saxon England, a peasant drifting gradually into servitude. A *villain* was a person attached to a villa, which in the Dark Age was a country estate; later it began to mean somebody who was virtually a serf tied to his lord's land. Since the Middle Ages and the Renaissance were predominantly aristocratic, one of the worst fates that could befall anyone was to be born a peasant. Therefore, *villain* and *churl* and *boor* became words of bitter contempt.

According to the passage, the words *villain, churl,* and *boor* originally meant

  (A) low   (C) country villa

  (B) aesthetic   (D) farmer

To answer reading comprehension questions, use the following strategies:

1. Expect questions on the following subjects:
   a. specific details in the passage
   b. the central thought of the passage
   c. the meanings of words in the passage
   d. the mood of the passage
   e. conclusions that can be made based upon information provided in the passage
   f. relationships between ideas mentioned in the passage
   g. specific techniques used by the writer of the passage

2. Identify the main idea as you read. Pay attention to transitions and words that show relationships.

3. Read all the choices before you select your answer.

4. Base your answer on information provided by the passage, not on your own knowledge or opinions.

5. A choice may be a true statement and yet not be an answer to the question being asked.

6. Do not be misled by answers that are partially correct.

The correct answer to the sample question is "D".

Exercise Reading Comprehension

Answer the questions following this passage.

My grandmother's notorious pugnacity did not confine itself to the exercise of authority over the neighborhood. There was also the defense of her house and her furniture against the imagined encroachments of visitors. With my grandmother, this was not the gentle and tremulous protectiveness of certain frail people who infer the fragility of all things from the brittleness of their own bones and hear the crash of mortality in the perilous tinkling of a teacup. No, my grandmother's sentiment was more autocratic: she hated having her chairs sat in or her lawns stepped on or the water turned on in her sinks, for no reason but pure administrative efficiency, she even grudged the mailman his daily promenade up her sidewalk. Her home was a center of power, and she would not allow it to be insulted by easy or democratic usage. Under her jealous eye, its social properties had withered and it functioned in the family structure simply as a political headquarters. Family conferences were held there, consultations with the doctor and the clergy; unruly grandchildren were brought there for a lecture or an interval of thought-taking; wills were read and loans negotiated. The family had no friends, and entertaining was held to be a foolish and unnecessary courtesy required only by the bonds of a blood relationship. Holiday dinners fell, as a duty, on the lesser members of the organization: sons and daughters and cousins respectfully offered up baked alaska on a platter, while my grandparents sat enthroned at the table, and only their digestive processes acknowledged the festal nature of the day.

1. The author's main purpose in this passage is to

    (A) review childhood impressions and fears
    (B) mourn the vanishing unity of the nuclear family
    (C) create a vivid portrait of a strong personality
    (D) revive the memory of a dimly recalled ancestor
    (E) commend some of a grandmother's firmly held principles

2. It can be inferred from the passage that all of the following are characteristic of the author's grandmother EXCEPT

    (A) desire for order
    (B) pride in authority
    (C) disdain for sentiment
    (D) reluctance to compromise
    (E) jealousy of youth

3. The tone of the passage is best described as

    (A) sympathetic and sentimental
    (B) restrained and cautious
    (C) apathetic and aloof
    (D) satirical and candid
    (E) bitter and loathing

SUMMARY AND APPLICATIONS

1. Standardized tests are tests given under strictly controlled conditions. They are used widely by various organizations and institutions.
2. Commonly-used standardized tests include the following:
    The Scholastic Aptitude Test (The S.A.T.)
    The Preliminary Scholastic Aptitude Test (The P.S.A.T/N.M.S.Q.T.)
    The test of the American College Training Program (the A.C.T.)
    The Achievement Tests of the College Entrance Examination Board
    The Advanced Placement Tests in particular subjects
3. Preparation for taking standardized tests should include vocabulary study; frequent reading and writing; and classwork in English, mathematics, social studies, and science.
4. Before taking a standardized test, make use of practice materials, eat and sleep well, and learn specific strategies for answering different types of test questions.

Applications in Other Subject Areas

Business / Health / Vocational Arts. To enter many vocational and professional fields you must first pass a standardized test to demonstrate your competence and to obtain the necessary licensing or certification. The following is a partial list of job titles from fields in which such standardized tests are usually required:

Radiologist	Stockbroker
Nuclear Medicine	Certified Public Accountant
Technologist	Registered Nurse
Physical Therapist	Airplane and Power Plant Mechanic
Real Estate Broker	

Choose any two of the above professions and do some research to determine the nature of the examination that must be passed before entering this field.

Chapter 17

Using Language Skills To Plan Your Future

During your years in high school you have exercised and sharpened your skills in speaking, listening, reading, and writing. Soon you will begin to put these skills to practical use as tools for shaping your future. Whether you choose to enter college or begin a career, your success will depend a great deal upon how well you apply your skills to such practical matters as writing business letters, preparing résumés, and completing interviews.

In this chapter you will learn how to use your language skills for these and other purposes related to your future. You will also learn how to choose a college or career path that is consistent with your particular talents and goals.

Part 1 Writing Business Letters

Whatever your plans for the future, you will doubtless write many business letters during the coming years. Some of these letters will serve routine purposes, such as conveying or requesting information, placing orders, or registering complaints. Others, such as letters of application to colleges and employers, will serve more important purposes. They may even be decisive factors in determining what opportunities will be made available to you. Because so much depends upon the ability to create positive impressions through letters, it is important that you learn the commonly-accepted guidelines for form and content in business letters of all kinds. These guidelines, along with sample letters, will be found in the following pages.

The Form of a Business Letter

Business letters may be organized in block or modified block form. In letters written in block form, all information is aligned at the left margin. In letters written in modified block form, the heading and closing are moved to the right, and the paragraphs of the letter are indented. For examples of both styles, see pages 369 and 370. A discussion of the content of those letters can be found on page 372.

Whether you choose to write your letter in block or modified block form, it must contain the following information:

1. The **heading** is made up of three lines:

   LINE 1: Street address
   LINE 2: City, state, and ZIP code
   LINE 3: Date

A comma is always placed between the city and the state, but never between the state and the ZIP code. A second comma should be placed between the day and the year.

2. The **inside address** contains the following information:

LINE 1: Name and title of person to whom you are writing (or the name of the department, if you are not writing to a specific person)

LINE 2: Name of the organization

LINE 3: Street address

LINE 4: City, state, and ZIP code

3. The **salutation** follows the inside address. Leave one blank space before the salutation and one blank space after it. The following are some commonly used salutations:

FOR A DEPT. OR COMPANY	FOR A SPECIFIC PERSON, NAME UNKNOWN
Gentlemen:	Dear Sir:
Ladies and Gentlemen:	Dear Madam:
Dear Sir or Madam:	Dear Sir or Madam:

4. The **body** states the message of the letter. It should be clear, concise, polite, and business like. Say what you have to say without including unnecessary information. Single space the body unless it is very short, in which case double spacing is acceptable.

5. The **closing** should be preceded by a single blank space. Keep the closing simple and direct. Capitalize the first word and follow the last word with a comma. Then, skip four spaces and type or print your name. Always choose a closing that is appropriate to the audience and occasion of your letter. Some common closings are as follows:

FORMAL: Yours respectfully,
Respectfully yours,
Yours very respectfully,
BUSINESSLIKE: Yours truly,
Very truly yours,
LESS FORMAL: Sincerely,
Yours sincerely,
Sincerely yours,

6. The **signature** should be written in the space between the closing and your typed name.

Glenn Everson
223 Harvest Way
Austin, Texas 78712
January 3, 1985

Catalog Department
Starbuch's Hobby and Crafts
889 American Street
Cleveland, Ohio 44144

Dear Sir or Madam:

Please send me the following items from
your Winter, 1985 catalog:

1	model helicopter propeller		
	style: B646-A		
	color: white		
	catalog #7732		
	price		$32.95
4	wheel bearings		
	size 3m		
	catalog #2435		
	price	@ $2.00	8.00
		Total	$40.95

Enclosed is a check for $40.95. The catalog
states that your prices include postage and
handling.

Yours truly,

Glenn Everson

Glenn Everson

MODIFIED BLOCK FORM

Cynthia Marx
P. O. Box 68
White Hill, Alabama 36624
November 16, 1985

Jason Woemack, Service Manager
Woemack Motors
467 Main Street
Mobile, Alabama 36601

Dear Mr. Woemack:

The paint job completed by your company on my 1982 Plymouth is inadequate. Your paint shop supervisor, John Singer, will verify that the job was not completed satisfactorily.

The instructions on my order and on invoice number 6634-P state that both the hood and the right front quarter panel were to be repainted. However, when I arrived to pick up the car, only the hood had been done. Unfortunately, I was unable to leave the car at the shop because I needed it for work.

I have enclosed a copy of the invoice. As you will note, I did pay for the completed job, which totalled $184.36. Therefore, I expect that the quarter panel will be painted at no additional charge.

Please contact me as soon as possible to arrange a date for completion of this job. I may be reached at home after 3:00 p.m. The telephone number is 555-9743.

Sincerely,

Cynthia Marx

Cynthia Marx

The Content of a Business Letter

As you have just learned, the body of a business letter contains its primary message. The specific content of this message depends on the audience and purpose for which the letter is intended. However, a few general guidelines should be followed:

1. **Make certain that your message is well-organized.** Good business letters have a definite beginning, middle, and end.

   a. Begin by stating your purpose simply and concisely.

   b. Follow this introduction with any necessary information or details related to the purpose of the letter.

   c. End the letter by asking the reader to take whatever action will accomplish your purpose.

2. **Be brief and to the point.** Before writing, make an outline listing the major points that you wish to communicate. After writing, revise to eliminate unnecessary information. Remember, your reader may be extremely busy.

3. **Establish a polite and businesslike tone.** Make certain that you remain courteous, even if you are writing a letter of complaint. If your letter is written in a pleasant manner, your reader is more likely to take positive actions.

Types of Business Letters

There are several different types of business letters, each with its own particular purpose. The following guidelines will help you when writing each kind.

Letters Requesting Information.   These letters are used to gain information about schools, employment opportunities, and specific products or services. In addition, they are often used to gather information for research projects.

When you write a letter requesting information, begin by stating specifically what information you need and why you need it. You may wish to include an itemized list of this information in the body of the letter.

Letters Ordering Merchandise. In letters of this kind, you need to provide the reader with specific catalog numbers, sizes, colors, names of items, and prices. In addition, check to determine whether you or the company must pay postage and sales tax. Include the correct amount in your enclosed payment. Keep a carbon or duplicate copy of the letter in case mistakes are made in fulfilling your order. (See the sample letter on page 369.)

Letters of Complaint. Occasionally you may have to write a letter to resolve a conflict or settle a claim. Address your letter to the correct person or department. Keep your tone objective and reasonable. Remember that in most cases the reader was either not directly responsible for the mistake or did not make the error intentionally. (See the sample letter on page 370.)

Letters of Application. Letters of this kind are written to apply for jobs or for admission to schools. If the letter is to a college, it will probably be accompanied by a form containing most of the essential application information. Therefore, the letter itself may be very brief:

Dear Sir or Madam:

Please consider me a candidate for admission to the DeVry Institute of Technology this fall. Enclosed you will find my application form, transcripts, and letters of recommendation. The College Board will send my S.A.T. scores directly to your office.

Thank you for considering my application. Please let me know if you need additional information.

Sincerely,

A letter of application to an employer should state the position for which you are applying and your related experience and skills. Your language should reflect an enthusiastic attitude. Refer the employer to your résumé for specific information. If you have not listed references on your résumé, do so in your letter. Be sure to ask these people if you may use their names first and provide their telephone numbers and addresses. In your application letter, request that the employer send you an application form or set up an interview. State where and when you may be contacted by mail or by telephone. (See pages 392-393 for further information.)

Interview Follow-up Letters. After completing any interview, you should write a short follow-up letter. This letter thanks the interviewer for his or her time and reminds the interviewer of your continued interest in the job or school. The letter also gives you an additional opportunity to provide information that may enhance your chances of being accepted.

Dear Mr. Thomas:

I appreciate your taking the time to interview me last Friday for the position of part-time clerk-typist. You may be interested to know that I have been appointed to the student receptionist position in the principal's office at our school. This job will involve typing, filing, answering the phone, and scheduling appointments during my free periods at school. It will not interfere with my after-school commitments.

I am still very interested in working for you. Thank you again for your time.

Respectfully,

Exercise Writing Business Letters

Choose one of the following subjects and write a letter using your own return address and a block or modified block form.

1. Write to a company in your area asking for information about summer employment. Let them know your age, qualifications, and previous experience.

2. Write to a college or university requesting information regarding its facilities or programs.

3. Write a request for information to the Chamber of Commerce in some city. Be specific as to why you need this information (you are planning to move to the city, you are interested in vacationing there, or you are researching the city as part of an assignment).

4. Write a letter of complaint to the manufacturer of some defective product that you have recently purchased.

5. Write a letter to a magazine, ordering a subscription.

Part 2 Making Choices for the Future

The next few years will be a time of discovery and decision-making. Your most important decisions will concern schools and careers. In Part 1 you learned about one tool, the business letter, that you can use to gather the information required to make informed choices. Now you will learn about the various sources of college and career information and how to use them.

Assessing Your Interests and Skills

One of the most important sources of information about your future is you. Careful self-assessment can help you to decide which college or career paths are best suited to your particular strengths. Professional academic and career counselors make such assessments by holding interviews, studying records of past performance, and examining the results of various tests. You can do a similar evaluation by carefully analyzing your skills, interests, and abilities.

You can begin your self-assessment by determining what occupational skills you are now good at or could become good at with experience or further training. Study this list carefully to determine where your strengths and weaknesses lie.

Basic Occupational Skills

Acting	Driving	Painting
Analyzing	Entertaining	Persuading
Building	Experimenting	Playing
Calculating	Extrapolating	Proving
Classifying	Hypothesizing	Questioning
Computing	Imagining	Reading
Cooking	Inferring	Repairing
Counseling	Leading	Researching
Dancing	Listening	Selling
Decorating	Managing	Speaking
Deducing	Measuring	Teaching
Designing	Operating	Typing
Drawing	Organizing	Writing

Another self-assessment that you can perform is to examine your own interests. One way to do this is to complete an **interest inventory,** a list of questions designed to measure differences in the occupational or academic preferences of individuals. The following questions are taken from such an inventory. To determine the types of jobs that are suited to you, rank yourself on a scale of one to five in regard to each of the following questions. An answer of 3 means that you are not committed to either of the two alternatives presented. An answer of 2 or 4 means that you lean toward one of the two alternatives. An answer of 1 or 5 means that you are strongly committed to one of the two alternatives.

A Sample Interest Inventory

1. Which do you prefer more, mental labor or physical labor?	mental 1 2 3	physical 4 5
2. Which do you prefer more, working with other people or by yourself?	by myself 1 2 3	with others 4 5
3. Which do you prefer more, working with words or with numbers?	words 1 2 3	numbers 4 5
4. Which do you prefer more, outdoors or indoors?	outdoors 1 2 3	indoors 4 5
5. Which do you prefer more, working with people or with objects (including machines)?	people 1 2 3	objects 4 5
6. How important is making a great deal of money to you?	very important 1 2 3	not important 4 5
7. Do you like lots of variation in your daily activities, or do you prefer things to remain stable from day to day?	like change 1 2 3	prefer stability 4 5
8. Do you prefer being your own boss or working under a leader?	being my own boss	working under a leader 1 2 3 4 5

See your school counselor for information on how you can complete such an inventory.

Obtaining Additional Information

Once you are familiar with your own interests and skills, you are ready to do some research to determine which fields of work or study are appropriate for you. The following are some valuable sources of information about schools and occupations:

1. College catalogs or bulletins.
2. Employers and school admissions personnel.
3. Your school counselor or a professional career counselor.
4. Parents, guardians, and friends who have attended schools and pursued various careers.
5. *The Federal Occupational Handbook.* (Available in most counseling offices and libraries.)
6. *Barron's Guide to Colleges.* This source lists major and minor U.S. colleges and universities.
7. *Comparative Guide to American Colleges.* (Available in most counseling offices and libraries.)
8. *Life Plan: A Practical Guide to Successful Career Planning.* (Available in most counseling offices and libraries.)
9. *What Color Is Your Parachute?* This is a guide to further skills and interest assessment. It is available in many bookstores and libraries.
10. In addition, check the vertical files and card catalogs in libraries for other sources of information. Pay particular attention to sources that describe specific fields of endeavor in which you are interested.

Exercises Making Choices for the Future

A. Make a list of skills that you are now good at or wish to develop in the future. These could include calculating, computing, managing, organizing, repairing, researching, or teaching. Can you draw any conclusions about some possible college majors or career choices? (Remember that this exercise is only a sample. Ask your school counselor to provide you with more in-depth analysis techniques.)

B. Answer the questions shown in the interest inventory on page 376. Then, write a short paragraph that summarizes what you find out about yourself.

C. Write down three careers in which you are interested. Research each one by consulting sources such as those listed on page 377. Then, answer the questions given below.

1. What skills are required in the job?
2. What special training or education must a person receive before entering this career?
3. What is the typical work environment of someone working in this job?
4. What financial return can someone working in this job expect to receive?
5. Is there currently a demand for new workers in this field?
6. Is this job consistent with your own interests and skills?

Part 3 Résumés and Interviews

As you work toward your goals in school or business, you will find that many of the decisions others make about you are based on the impression you create during short, highly structured screening procedures. In order to make these procedures work to your advantage, you should become as familiar with them as possible. The two that you will encounter most often are the résumé and the interview.

Organizing a Résumé

Almost any application procedure involves your submitting a résumé. A résumé is a list of your experience, education, skills, and references. Its purpose is to make a good impression on an employer or admissions officer. A résumé should follow the rules of effective composition, including proper punctuation, grammar, and spelling. It should also present the following specific information, organized in an accepted manner.

Personal Data.   Include your full name, address, and telephone number (including the area code).

Objective.   State your purpose (obtaining employment, gaining admission to college). If you are going to use the résumé to apply for several different types of jobs, your objective will have to be fairly general. However, if you are preparing the résumé to help you obtain a specific job, the objective may be more specific.

GENERAL OBJECTIVE: Position in retail sales that will provide
an opportunity to use my
considerable sales experience

SPECIFIC OBJECTIVE: Employment as a groundskeeper at the
Cincinnati Zoo

If you are writing a résumé to accompany a college application, your objective may state when you wish to enter school and the field of study that you wish to pursue:

Admission to the certificate program in Dental Hygiene, beginning Fall 1985

Experience.   Include all paid and significant volunteer experience that you have had. Begin with your most recent job and work backward. List the following information about each job:

Period employed   Position held
Name and address of employer   Duties performed

If you have had little work experience, expand the skills section described below.

Education.   List all schools you have attended, dates of attendance, and special courses of study. Also identify any honors or awards you have received, including special recognition for projects and activities. Begin with the most recent school, and work backward.

Personal Qualifications and Skills.   This section is optional, but can be useful if you have had little or no work experience. List any additional information that may be of interest to the admissions officer or employer. Such information may include:

1. Curricular or extracurricular activities
2. Languages that you speak
3. Professional memberships
4. Community or group activities
5. Hobbies or special interests
6. Health
7. Other special qualifications, experiences, or skills

The following is a sample entry from such a skills section:

CLERICAL: Type 80 wpm; two years' experience on CRT (Lanier); operate various duplicating machines, including IBM and Xerox 220; as secretary of senior class, recorded and transcribed minutes of weekly meetings.

References. List the names, titles, and addresses of three people who will give you good references. Request permission of these people before listing them on the résumé. Previous employers, teachers, principals, advisors, and family friends may be listed here.

Writing the Résumé

Begin by listing the information needed for each section of the résumé. Plan to write at least two drafts of your résumé, following one of the models given on pages 382 and 383 and keeping in mind the following general guidelines.

1. Use action words that describe specific skills and duties you have performed in the past. Do not use complete sentences or personal pronouns referring to yourself.

   WRONG: I was in charge of the pet department. I also selected and ordered merchandise.
   RIGHT: Managed pet department. Selected and ordered merchandise.

2. Use language that conveys positive attitudes. Avoid negative, dull, vague statements.

3. Do not make reference to your sex, weight, height, age, race, or religious affiliations.
4. Do not refer to salary or wage expectations.
5. If your résumé is for submission to a college, emphasize your skills, academic achievements, and extracurricular activities.

When preparing the final copy of the résumé, use white, 8½" x 11" paper. Type the résumé yourself or have it typed. Proofread the typed copy for neatness, consistency of format, and correct capitalization, punctuation, and spelling. The final résumé should be limited to one page, if possible, and should never be more than two pages long.

The sample résumés on pages 382 and 383 demonstrate two accepted formats. The first résumé was written by a teenager with little work experience. It therefore highlights this person's skills and personal qualifications. The second résumé was written by a teenager who has had significant part-time work experience. Therefore, the skills section has been deleted, and the work experience has been emphasized. When you write your own résumé, employ the format that is most effective given your own qualifications and experience. Remember, your résumé is the only impression an employer or admissions officer will initially have of you. Make sure that it is as positive as possible.

Exercise Writing a Résumé

Choose one of the following objectives or one of your own and write a résumé. Follow one of the formats shown on pages 382 and 383. The objective stated on your résumé may be general or specific.

1. Part-time employment in a local office
2. Full-time employment in a local manufacturing firm or retail store
3. Admission to a vocational or trade school
4. Admission to a two-year college
5. Admission to a four-year college or university

CHARLES PAGONE

234 First Avenue   Telephone: 603-555-6200
Freemont, NH 03044

OBJECTIVE

A part-time position in retail sales with opportunity for advancement to full-time after graduation.

SKILLS

Supervisory/Leadership: acted as co-captain for
high school baseball team for three years; coordi-
nated activities of a youth group at camp during past
two summers; sports editor of school newspaper.

Sales/Marketing: have taken Introduction to Marketing, an elective course at my school; have participated in drives to raise funds for various charities.

Teaching/Training: acted as assistant coach for
Little League baseball team for two years; tutor in
the computer lab at South High School.

PERSONAL QUALIFICATIONS

* Marketing abilities proved through school and
  fund-raising activities
* Learning abilities demonstrated by maintaining
  a ''B'' average throughout high school
* Capacity for logical organization shown by success in various computer programming projects

EDUCATION

South High School, Freeport, N.H. 1981-present.
Will graduate in June, 1985.

REFERENCES

Ms. Judith R. Cranst,   Mr. Norman Alsworth,
Principal   Baseball Coach
South High School   South High School
Freemont, NH 03044   Freemont, NH 03044

Résumé

MARY LIANOS   6642 W. Water Street
Denver, Colorado 80201
Telephone: (303) 555–8842

OBJECTIVE   Position as Assistant Office
Manager, Merton Construction Company

EXPERIENCE

June, 1984
to
Present

Assistant Ticketing Agent, Acme Travel Agency, Denver, Colorado. Duties include answering phones, researching flight information through microcomputer, billing, ticket write-ups.

June, 1983
to
June, 1984

Office Assistant, Bartlett Construction, Aurora, Colorado. Duties included filing, typing, invoicing, answering phones, greeting customers, general office work.

June, 1982
to
August, 1982

Counselor's Aide; Wee Ones Pre-School and Youth Camp; Denver, Colorado. Duties included organizing activities (handicrafts, sports, and nature hikes).

SKILLS

1. Familiar with basic office procedures
2. Typing, 80 wpm
3. Familiar with construction business
4. Familiar with most office machines

EDUCATION

1980
to
Present

Lakeland High School, Denver, Colorado. Courses in typing, shorthand, office procedures; B+ grade point average

REFERENCES

Janice Dalton, Ticketing Agent
Acme Travel Agency
Denver, Colorado

William A. Bartlett, President
Bartlett Construction
Aurora, Colorado

Interviewing

If you are required to go to an interview for a job or for admission to a school, this means that your letter and résumé have already made a good impression. Keep this fact in mind to help you to control any nervousness you might feel.

Spend the time before the interview preparing information about your qualifications and skills. When you are at the interview, answer any questions honestly and confidently, emphasizing your most important skills and experiences. Also keep in mind the following criteria used by interviewers to evaluate applicants.

Appearance.   Wear comfortable clothes that are appropriate to the interview situation. You can make a positive impression simply through attention to general good grooming and neatness.

Promptness.   Arrive at the interview on time or a few minutes early. Get directions to the interview site if you need them. Remember, promptness can be interpreted by the interviewer as meaning you are courteous and reliable.

Courtesy.   Answer questions in a polite manner and react positively toward the interviewer. Your opening and closing statements are especially important. Begin with a handshake and a friendly introduction. When the interview is over, thank the interviewer for his or her time. Follow up the interview with a thank-you call or letter.

Communication Skills.   Listen closely to the questions and comments made by the interviewer. Maintain good eye contact, sit up straight, and avoid nervous hand gestures. When you speak in response to a question or to ask a question of your own, take a few moments to think about your answer. Then make sure that you speak clearly and use correct grammar. Avoid being too soft-spoken or too boisterous. Answer questions thoroughly, but concisely. Also be prepared to answer questions such as the ones shown in the charts on the next two pages.

Types of Interviews

Some colleges and other schools hold **college admission interviews** as part of the application process. Even if the school or college to which you are applying does not require an interview, you may want to arrange one on your own to learn more about programs, facilities, housing, financial aid, and other matters.

Prepare for the interview by studying the college catalog. This will help you determine what questions to ask the interviewer. Admissions officers expect to be asked questions about programs, facilities, housing, dining, recreation, costs, financial aid, and policies and regulations of the school. The admissions officer, in turn, will probably ask you questions such as the following:

**Questions Often Asked in
College Admissions Interviews**

In what subjects did you receive your best grades?

In what subjects did you receive your worst grades?

What subjects do you like best? Why?

What subject do you like least? Why?

What extracurricular activities have you participated in?

What is your class rank?

What are your hobbies and interests?

How do you spend your free time?

What books have you read recently besides those required for your classes? Tell me about them.

What courses do you wish to take in college?

What field of study do you wish to pursue?

What are your future goals?

The **job interview** is usually the final step in the application process. Generally, a job interview occurs only after an employer has decided to consider you a likely candidate for a job. The decision to grant you an interview is usually based upon your initial contacts by letter or telephone, your completed application form, and your résumé.

To make a good impression during a job interview, come prepared with any materials that might further your application. Such materials include written letters of recommendation and, if you haven't already sent one, a résumé. You might also do some research into the company to which you are applying. An employer is always impressed by an applicant who is serious enough about the position to do some groundwork first.

During the interview, demonstrate your interest in the job and in the company by asking well thought-out questions. Stress the skills and qualifications that make you a good candidate for the job, and avoid negative references to yourself or to other people, particularly to former employers or co-workers. Finally, be prepared to answer questions such as the following:

Questions Often Asked in Job Interviews

Why are you interested in the job?

Why do you think that you could handle the job?

What experience do you have?

Tell me a little about yourself—your hobbies and interests, for example.

What do you like most about yourself? What do you like least?

Describe a good work experience that you have had.

Describe a poor one.

Why did you leave your last job, or why do you want to leave your present one?

Exercises Interviewing

A. Look at the list of questions on page 385. Pretend that you are going for a college interview. Write out your answer to each of the questions on this list.

B. Look at the list of questions on page 386. Choose a job that you might be interested in and pretend that you are going to an interview for this job. Write out your answers to each of the questions on the list.

C. Obtain a college catalog for your school or public library. Study the contents and make a list of questions that you might ask an admissions officer.

Part 4 Applying to Colleges and Other Schools

There are several excellent methods for choosing a college, and an equal number of poor ones. For example, how often have you heard someone say that he or she is applying to a college because a parent went there, or because it is in a certain state, or because it has a good football team? These reasons might have some merit, but they are no substitute for the careful evaluation that can lead you to the school that will best prepare you for your future.

Evaluating Your Prospects for College

When assessing your potential for college, consider the following factors: your grades in high school, your scores on entrance examinations (See Chapter 16), and the possibility of obtaining good recommendations. If college does not seem a realistic alternative for you now, but you still want to attend college eventually, consider entering a junior college or trade school. Once you have demonstrated your ability to succeed academically in one of these schools, you can then apply to the college of your choice.

Choosing a College

If you decide that college is the best choice for you, you must then choose the colleges to which you wish to apply. To do so, you must consider such factors as the following:

Guidelines for Choosing a College

ACADEMICS

What is the academic reputation of the college?
Does the college offer programs in your fields of interest or need?
Is the college accredited?
Are there any subjects that you would like to study that are not offered by the college?
Does the college offer any special services or opportunities?

COSTS

What is the cost of tuition, fees, and housing at the college?
Does the college offer work study programs or other financial aid opportunities?

LOCATION

Do you wish to attend college close to home or not?
Is the college located in an area that is suitable to your interests, tastes, and experience?

SIZE

Are students given individual attention?
What are the class sizes like?
Would you be comfortable with the number of people at the school?

FACILITIES

Does the college have a good library?
Do the departments in your areas of interest have the special facilities that they need, such as laboratories or a studio theater?
What is the quality of the housing available at the college?
Does the college have ample recreational facilities?

Two publications are extremely useful in making comparisons between colleges. These are *The College Handbook* and *Barron's Guide to Colleges*. Both should be available in the library or guidance office of your school. These publications contain information on both two- and four-year schools and can help you to answer the questions on the preceding chart. They will also provide you with addresses of college admissions offices. Any further information that you need can be obtained by contacting colleges directly.

Writing for Information

Once you have chosen the colleges to which you wish to apply, write to the admissions offices of these schools to obtain catalogs and application forms. (See the sample letter on page 391.) State in your letter when you plan to attend. If you need financial aid or plan to live in student housing, request information about these subjects as well.

The college catalogs that you receive will contain information on entrance requirements, tuition, costs, types of financial aid available, and deadline dates for admissions and financial aid applications. These catalogs also contain descriptions of the facilities, programs, and courses offered by the college, as well as information about the members of the faculty and staff.

Meeting Entrance Requirements

Study the college catalog carefully to determine what requirements you must meet for admission. Colleges may require any combination of the following:

1. A completed application form. (Refer to Part 5 pages 394-395, for information on filling out forms and applications.)
2. Transcripts of courses and grades from your high school.
3. A report of your scores on the S.A.T., A.C.T., or other college entrance examinations. (See Chapter 16 for information on college entrance examinations.)

4. An application fee.
5. An essay written to demonstrate your writing abilities.
6. Letters of recommendation.
7. An interview. (Refer to Part 3, pages 384–385, for information on interviewing.)
8. A résumé. (Refer to Part 3, pages 380-381, for a discussion of résumé-writing techniques.)

A formal letter of application should accompany your completed application form and any other required material.

During your final year of high school, you should be prepared to begin taking the necessary steps to apply to colleges. If you have not already gathered information on various schools, do so at the beginning of the year. If you have not already taken the necessary college entrance examinations, discuss this with your guidance counselor. It is important that you begin the application process early so that you can meet deadlines for submitting test scores, application forms, and other required information.

Exercises Applying to Colleges and Other Schools

A. Consult one of the following guides to colleges and universities. Then, write a letter to a college requesting a college catalog and any other relevant information. Make sure that your letter follows proper business letter form.

1. *Barron's Profiles of American Colleges*
2. *The College Handbook*
3. *Comparative Guide to American Colleges*

B. Using a college catalog, answer the following questions concerning any college of your choice.

1. What is the amount charged per credit hour for tuition?
2. Does the college offer courses in Women's Studies?
3. Are applicants to the college required to take the S.A.T? The A.C.T? Other college entrance examinations?
4. Does the college provide student housing? What types?
5. When is the deadline for applications to the undergraduate program for the fall term?

336 South Main Street
Tampa, Florida 33602
February 9, 1985

Director of Admissions
Admissions Office
Northwestern University
Evanston, Illinois 60201

Dear Sirs:

I am a senior at Central High School in Tampa,
Florida, interested in attending a university
that offers a strong program in Speech and Theater. Please send me the following information:

1. A catalog describing your programs and
   facilities in Speech and Theater.
2. Information on admissions and financial
   aid.
3. Information on the types of housing
   available both on and off campus.

I would appreciate receiving this information as soon as possible, as I am planning a
trip to visit colleges early this spring.

Thank you for your time and attention.

Yours truly,

Debbie Grossman

Debbie Grossman

Part 5   Using Language Skills To Find a Job

In the near future, it is possible that you may decide to look for a full- or part-time job. If so, you should determine the type of employment that is best suited to you. The next step is to assess your skills and interests to find the type of work for which you are best suited. (See Part 2, pages 374-377.)

Once this assessment is complete, you can begin to examine the job market.

Contacting Employers

Contacting Employers by Phone.   If you choose to call an employer for your initial job contact, keep in mind that you may be interrupting a busy work day. During the phone conversation, state your name and the purpose of your call. Inform the employer of any skills related to the job and briefly summarize your experience. Ask politely for an interview, for a job application, or for permission to send a résumé.

Contacting Employers by Letter.   Instead of calling, and particularly if you are applying for a long-term job or for a position with a large company, you may wish to write a letter.

1. *A statement of the purpose of the letter.* If you are applying for a specific position, say so. Refer to the ad or person that told you about the job and mention the type of employment you are seeking.

2. *A description of your qualifications and references.* If you are enclosing a résumé, this section may be limited to a few comments about those qualifications that make you right for the job. If you are not enclosing a résumé, make sure to list your references in your letter.

3. *A request for an application and/or an interview.* When requesting either of these, be sure to provide your phone number and to tell the employer exactly where and when you can be contacted.

Mark Feldman
6682 East Seventh Street
Lakewood, Ohio 44107
February 26, 1985

Ms. Susan Steel, Manager
Sunnyside Family Resort
The Dells, Wisconsin 53965

Dear Ms. Steel:

I am responding to your ad for hotel, grounds, and restaurant personnel for this summer's vacation season at Sunnyside Family Resort. I am interested in the position of groundskeeper.

You will notice as you review my enclosed résumé that I have spent the past three summers working as an assistant greenskeeper at a local golf course. This experience has taught me the basics of lawn and garden management. I feel that my experience, training, and capacity for hard work will make me a true asset to your staff.

I will be available to begin working during the first week in June. If you wish to interview me prior to that time, I can arrange a trip to Wisconsin during spring break, the week of March 26.

Please send me an application form and contact me for an interview at your earliest convenience. My phone number is (216) 555-2309.

Respectfully yours,

Mark Feldman

Mark Feldman

Completing Job Applications

Complete a job application carefully, completely, and neatly. Keep in mind that this may be the first sample of your work an employer sees, and it may tell him or her something about your work habits. Be sure to read the entire application form before filling out anything. Read and follow all directions, and proofread your application once you have completed it.

If you have not filled out an application form prior to going to an interview, take with you to the interview the information you will need to complete the form. Most application forms require the following information.

Job Application Forms

Personal Data	Name, address, phone, date of birth, social security number
Schools Attended	Names, cities and states, dates of attendance, subjects studied, activities
Employment History	Names, places, supervisors, dates, job titles, duties, reasons for leaving previous jobs, previous wages or salaries
Skills and Achievements	Job-related skills, honors or awards, volunteer positions (Examples: word processing skills, National Merit finalist, French tutor)
References	Names, titles, addresses, relationship to you, telephone numbers

Completing Other Work-Related Forms

You may have to complete several other work-related forms after accepting a job offer. One such form is the application for a social security card. Other forms commonly required include work permits, W-2 forms, and health permits.

1. **Social Security Applications.** Before you can begin working, you must apply for a social security number at your local office of the Department of Labor.

2. **Work Permits.** Most states require that teen-agers obtain work permits and present these to their employers before beginning to work. To obtain a permit, check with your employer or your school counselor. To apply for the permit, you will need a birth certificate and, in some states, a physician's statement of health.

3. **W-2 Forms.** These forms are used for tax purposes. Your employer will provide you with a W-2 form after you have accepted a position.

4. **Health Permits.** Some jobs in food service require a permit certifying your state of health. Again, your employer will be able to tell you where to obtain one.

When completing any job application, college application, or work-related form, keep the following basic guidelines in mind:

Completing Forms and Applications

1. Read the entire form before filling it in.
2. Gather all the information that you need to complete the form.
3. Reread the directions for each section of the form as you complete it. Make certain that you follow all directions precisely. Notice special directions, such as "Please type."
4. If a section of the form does not apply to you, write "N.A.", or "not applicable" in the space provided.
5. Proofread the form for accuracy and for correct spelling, punctuation, and capitalization.

Exercises Finding a Job

A. Read the following employment ads and determine your suitability for the positions. Write a short paragraph explaining why you would or would not apply for each job based upon your experience, skills, interests, and personal qualifications.

SWITCHBOARD OPERATOR	SHIPPING/RECEIVING CLERK
Part time, some weekends. Immediate opening for an individual who can deal with a heavy volume of calls in a congenial manner. Experience is not as important as having a pleasant voice and being articulate.	20-hour week, including some nights. Diversified duties and opportunity for growth with this manufacturer of a well-known humidifier line.

AIRFREIGHT	NURSING ASSISTANT
Part-time warehouse person. Experience in inventorying preferred.	Start fresh in the medical field. No experience necessary, only a willingness to serve and help others. St. Anne's Hospital. Some 3-11 shifts available for part-time students.

B. Write a letter to an employer in your area requesting a part-time job now, or a full-time job upon graduation. Include the job you are seeking, the hours that you can work, information on your skills, and a request for an interview.

C. Pretend you are an employer in a company or business. After determining the type of business you operate, devise an application for employment to be used by your business. Then, ask one of your classmates to fill out the form and to provide you with suggestions for improving it.

SUMMARY AND APPLICATIONS

1. Well-written business letters can help you to obtain information, settle claims, order merchandise, apply to schools, and gain employment.

2. Business letters may be in block or modified block form and should contain the following parts: heading, inside address, salutation, body, closing, signature.

3. Carefully assess your interests and skills before choosing a career or field of study. Then gather information about the options and opportunities available to you.

4. A résumé is designed to highlight your particular strengths by presenting, in positive language, your experience, skills, education, and references.

5. To apply to colleges or other schools, determine the type of school best suited to your needs and consider the following: academics, reputation, costs, location, size, and facilities. Then, obtain catalogs and applications forms, and follow the admissions procedures detailed in these sources.

6. To find a job, determine your interests and skills and then survey the job market, contact employers, set up interviews, and provide employers with your résumé and completed job application forms.

Applications in Other Subject Areas

Computer Science. Computer science is one of the fastest growing fields in the business world. Do some research in this field, and list at least ten possible careers. Determine the types of training and skills that are needed for each position.

All Subjects. List three classes from high school in which you were reasonably successful. Then, for each class, describe what skills or knowledge you have acquired in it. Do some research to identify careers and/or areas of specialization in college that require the skills and knowledge that you obtained in these classes. Refer to college catalogs and to the sources of information listed on page 377.

Chapter 18

Public Speaking and Debate

Public speaking is an important part of many careers in business, law, politics, and education. Even if you choose not to enter such a field, you will still find it necessary to speak in public from time to time. You may be asked, for example, to make an introduction or announcement, to give a demonstration, to deliver a report, or to state your opinions on an issue. You may even find yourself engaged in a discussion or debate, upholding one side of an argument, offering evidence to support your position, and analyzing opposing views.

In this chapter you will learn how to write and deliver speeches. You will also learn how to participate in discussions and debates. These skills will be useful to you whenever you engage in public or group activities as a student, as an employee, or as a citizen participating in the process of political decision-making.

Part 1 Public Speaking

Many people feel nervous when they are called upon to speak in public. A certain degree of nervousness is quite natural in such circumstances. It may even contribute to the quality of a speaker's delivery by adding energy to what might otherwise be a dull presentation. However, nervousness, or stage fright, should not be allowed to get out of hand. Instead, it should be held in check by proper preparation and practice of the sort discussed on the following pages.

Preparing a Speech

The procedure you must follow to prepare a speech is similar to the one followed in the process of writing. (See Chapter 7.) The three basic stages of speech preparation are as follows:

Pre-Writing. In the pre-writing stage, you must complete the following steps:

1. Choose and narrow your topic.
2. Define your purpose.
3. Identify your audience.
4. Develop a statement of your main idea.
5. Gather information.
6. Organize your information in a logical manner.

When you **choose your topic,** pick a subject that you know well or wish to learn about. Remember that unless you are interested in and well informed about your topic, you will not be able to make it seem fresh and exciting to your listeners. Once you have chosen a general topic, you must narrow it to suit the time allotted for your speech.

Once you have chosen your topic, you must **define your purpose.** Will you inform, persuade, or entertain? Bear in mind that a single speech may, at various times, fulfill all three of these purposes. However, every speech must have a single, controlling purpose that determines its overall content and tone.

Now you must take the time to **identify your audience.** Remember, the topic, purpose, and content of your speech will depend a great deal on your listeners. You will, for example, want to choose a topic in which your audience has some interest. You will then want to include material that takes into account their knowledge of the subject and their attitudes toward it. Your audience will also determine the level of language that you use in the speech.

After you have identified your topic, your purpose, and your audience, the next step is to **write a statement of your main idea.** This statement, usually a single sentence, will determine what information you will gather. In the speech itself, this sentence may appear as a thesis statement.

The next pre-writing step is to **gather information** to support your main idea. Gather enough material to develop your topic thoroughly. Remember, too, that an oral presentation can proceed very rapidly, and you want to have enough information to make your speech of a substantial length.

The final step in preparing a speech is to **organize your information.** Information in a speech may be organized as for any composition. (See Chapters 7 and 8 for more information.)

Writing. A speech should contain an introduction, a body, and a conclusion. The introduction should gain the attention of your audience and state the main idea of your speech. To make your introduction interesting, you may begin with a story or anecdote, a question directed to the audience, a startling fact, or an exhibit. The body should develop the main idea of the speech by providing supporting facts, details, or examples. The conclusion, if your speech is informative or persuasive, should summarize major points made in the body. If you are speaking to entertain, the conclusion may be a high point of amusement rather than a summary.

At this point, you must also consider the manner in which you want to write the speech. You might choose to write it out completely, as you would a composition. Some speakers, however, are comfortable simply recording the main points of the speech in outline form or on note cards. Let your own instincts and level of confidence guide you in this decision.

Revision. When you revise your speech, make sure that your main idea is clear and well-supported. Use the revision techniques discussed in Chapters 2-6 to correct any errors in sentence structure, clarity, or variety. Check your paragraphs for clear topic sentences, logical transitions, unity, and coherence. Finally, check your draft by referring to the chart on evaluating speeches given on page 403.

Practicing Your Speech

Because the success of a speech depends largely upon its delivery, it is important that you practice thoroughly.

Practicing a Speech

1. If possible, listen to a recording of your speech to check the vocal elements of your delivery. Pay particular attention to pace, pitch, pauses, emphasis, variation in volume and intensity, and appropriateness of tone.

2. Practice your speech before a mirror to check the nonverbal elements of your delivery. Make sure that you maintain correct but relaxed posture, and use facial expressions and gestures that reflect the content of the speech.

3. Invite friends or family members to listen to your delivery and ask for suggestions for improvement.

4. Evaluate the verbal and nonverbal elements of your delivery. Refer to the chart on page 403.

Delivering Your Speech

When delivering your speech, act confident even if you do not feel confident. Talk in your natural speaking voice, but be sure to project so that all members of your audience can hear you quite easily. Try not to read or recite your speech. Instead, refer to your written material only occasionally and deliver your material in a more conversational manner. Enunciate your words more clearly than you would in ordinary conversation and speak just a bit more slowly. Vary your pace, volume, pitch, and tone. Maintain proper eye contact by looking directly at your audience or slightly above the heads of audience members. You can also make contact with your audience by using appropriate facial expressions and gestures. Above all, be enthusiastic and excited about your subject. Such enthusiasm is contagious.

Listening to and Evaluating Speeches

When you listen to a speech delivered by someone else, make the speaker feel at ease by communicating your receptiveness through appropriate body language. Maintain eye contact with the speaker, remain still, and avoid making unnecessary noises.

If you are called upon to evaluate a speech given by a classmate, be constructive in your approach to the evaluation. Comment on the speech itself and on specific aspects of the speaker's delivery. Do not make personal comments about the speaker. The guidelines on the following page will help you when evaluating speeches by other people and when rehearsing speeches of your own.

Exercises Public Speaking

A. Imagine that you are a broadcaster for an in-school news program. Write a two-minute speech highlighting the important events of a week in your school. Practice and deliver this informative speech.

B. Choose a topic of your own. Following the steps described in this chapter, write a five-minute informative, persuasive, or humorous speech. If your teacher directs you to do so, deliver this speech to your class.

Guidelines for Evaluating Speeches

CONTENT:

Introduction

_____ arouses interest

_____ is brief and to the point

_____ is appropriate to the topic

Body

_____ supports thesis or main idea

_____ contains no irrelevant material

_____ has clear main ideas are clear

_____ develops main ideas

Conclusion

_____ is brief

_____ provides a summary of major points or
draws attention back to thesis

PRESENTATION:

Nonverbal

_____ speaker has good posture

_____ speaker is relaxed and confident

_____ speaker has good eye contact

_____ gestures and facial expressions are natural

Verbal

_____ speaker is not too quiet or too loud

_____ speaker's articulation is good

_____ speaker's pace is not too slow or too rapid

_____ speaker's pitch is not too high or too low

_____ speaker varies volume, pace, and pitch

_____ speaker expresses appropriate emotions

_____ speaker uses pauses effectively for emphasis

Part 2 Discussion

Your skills in formal speaking can be used to great advantage any time you communicate with others. One situation in which these skills are useful is in discussion. When you exchange ideas with others, the way you present your own thoughts and respond to those of others can have a great effect on the success of the discussion as a whole.

There is more to a discussion than good speaking and listening skills, however. A discussion has a definite format, and its participants have specific responsibilities. The more familiar you are with these, the greater will be your contribution.

The Organization of Discussion

To be effective, a discussion must have a purpose that is clearly identified from the outset. Groups may hold discussions for any of the following reasons:

1. To explore ideas
2. To exchange information
3. To resolve mutual problems
4. To plan a course of action

The chairperson, or leader, of the discussion usually begins by making a statement that specifies the topic and purpose. Once the entire group understands the goal that the group is attempting to accomplish, they confirm their understanding of any key terms that will be used in the discussion. This will help the group avoid needless arguments and misunderstandings. At this point, group members may also wish to narrow the discussion topic to avoid irrelevance or vagueness.

Once the participants have agreed on the basic terms, the group discusses and analyzes the discussion topic in detail. What happens during this step varies according to the nature of the topic and the purpose of the group.

Finally, as the discussion draws to a close, one group member, usually the chairperson or the secretary, summarizes the major points made during the discussion.

Duties of the Participants

The chairperson of a discussion group has several duties that are crucial to the orderly exchange of ideas. If you are selected to perform this role, the following guidelines will help you to fulfill your responsibilities.

The Responsibilities of a Chairperson

1. Prepare for the discussion with research and thoughtful planning.
2. Introduce the topic and state the goal of the discussion.
3. Allow time for the introduction, the discussion, and a short summary of the conclusions reached.
4. Maintain order in the discussion group.
   a. Allow only one person to speak at a time.
   b. Insist that members of the group ask to be recognized and remain respectful toward one another.
5. Encourage everyone to contribute to the discussion.
6. Ask stimulating questions to keep the group interested in the topic. Encourage creative and critical thinking. Remember that your role is to guide participants toward conclusions, not to impose conclusions of your own on the group.
7. Keep the discussion on track by guiding the group toward a generally-accepted conclusion, or consensus. Do not allow the discussion to wander into unimportant or irrelevant matters.
8. Take notes and be prepared to summarize the key points at the end of the discussion.

The chairperson's role is important, but no more so than that of the rest of the participants. Without thoughtful input from its members, a discussion group cannot accomplish anything worthwhile. As a participant, therefore, it is your duty to prepare mentally for a group discussion by researching the topic, formulating some ideas or opinions about it, and preparing a list of major points you think should be covered. Once the discussion begins, you should follow these guidelines:

1. Speak only when the leader recognizes you.
2. Voice your ideas. You are there because your opinion is as important as that of anyone else.
3. Support your statements with concrete evidence.
4. Speak correctly and distinctly.
5. Listen carefully and politely to others. Take notes on what is said by other group members, and refer to these when you speak.
6. Be courteous and tactful, especially when voicing disagreement.
7. Try to understand the viewpoints of other group members. Ask questions to clarify points that you do not understand.

Exercise Group Discussion

Several possible discussion topics are listed at the top of the following page. Select one that interests you. First, identify and define any key terms. (You may also find yourself narrowing your topic as you define the terms.) Next, do some research on the topic. List the key points that you think should be covered, as well as any specific information that you would use in a discussion of these points. If your teacher directs you to do so, participate in a discussion with others that share an interest in the topic.

1. Are the benefits of the space program worth the cost?
2. What steps can we take while still in high school to prepare ourselves to choose the right career?
3. What are the main priorities of our generation, and are they good ones?
4. What is the state of television programming?
5. Is the voting age too high/low?
6. Should the United States increase its dependence on energy derived from nuclear power?

7. How can we best prepare for "life after high school"?
8. Have the news media lost their credibility?
9. What are the rights of a terminally ill patient?
10. Is the nuclear family becoming a thing of the past?
11. Should scientific research be restricted in any way by government regulation?
12. Are videos, computer games, and other new forms of electronic entertainment having a positive or negative effect on the young?

Part 3 Debate

A **debate** could be considered an extremely structured discussion. It consists of two opposing sides arguing a controversial subject. The subject being debated is called the question, or **proposition**. It is a precisely worded statement that advances an opinion, a solution, or a course of action.

In a formal debate, the proposition is stated as a **resolution**. That is, it begins with the words "Resolved, that . . .," and then makes a positive statement. A typical proposition might be: "Resolved, that Puerto Rico should become the fifty-first state."

The speakers in a debate are always divided into two teams. The **affirmative team** argues that the resolution should be upheld and accepted. The **negative team** argues that the resolution should be rejected. The aim of both teams is to persuade the audience to side with them, that is, to accept or reject the resolution being debated. Each team tries to collect enough reasons and evidence to prove that its stand is the correct one.

The Debate Proposition

Debates may be held on almost any subject. However, all debates concern one of three types of propositions, as follows:

Propositions of fact make a claim that a particular state of affairs exists and can be proved to exist by making certain observations.

> Resolved, that America's supplies of fossil fuels are sufficient to meet the current demand for energy.
>
> Resolved, that large cars are safer than small cars.

Propositions of value state that something is good, ethical, worthwhile, or desirable.

> Resolved, that public employees should have the right to strike.
>
> Resolved, that reporters are justified in maintaining the confidentiality of their sources under any circumstances.

Propositions of policy recommend particular actions.

> Resolved, that grades should be abolished in elective courses.

Every debate proposition, whatever its kind, must also have the following characteristics:

Characteristics of Debate Propositions

1. The proposition should be stated in the affirmative. That is, it should make a positive rather than a negative statement. For example, a proposition might state that "Warren High School should abolish its dress code," but would never state that "Warren High School should not have a dress code."
2. The proposition should state only one main idea.
3. The proposition should be arguable. There should be two valid sides to the issue. Neither side should be obviously right or wrong.
4. The proposition should be clearly worded. The language should be precise and specific so that the debate does not become a quibble over the meaning of a single word.

Exercises Wording Debate Propositions

A. Decide whether each of the following statements is a proposition of fact, of value, or of policy.

1. Resolved, that our school should increase the budget of the theater department.

2. Resolved, that violence on television creates violence in real life.

3. Resolved, that the knowledge gained from the space program is of inestimable value.

4. Resolved, that theater studies are of great value to all.

5. Resolved, that stricter controls should be placed on the programming of violent television shows.

6. Resolved, that space-related research and development is important and necessary to our daily lives.

7. Resolved, that our theater facilities need renovation.

8. Resolved, that many television programs are unfit for viewing by children.

9. Resolved, that the United States should continue to fund the space program at current levels.

10. Resolved, that the television industry should contribute money to crime prevention efforts in major citites.

B. Decide whether each of the following statements is a valid, well-worded proposition. If not, explain why and write one possible revision.

1. Resolved, that presidential candidates spent more money in 1980 than in 1984.

2. Resolved, that TV debates do not change the opinions of the voters.

3. Resolved, that campaign spending by politicians running for election should be limited.

4. Resolved, that presidential elections should be held every six years, and foreign-born citizens should be eligible to run for the office.

5. Resolved, that the electoral college is a good means of reflecting the voting mood of the public.

C. Write a proposition of fact, of value, and of policy about one of the following subjects:

final exams	the use of computers
energy sources	education in the arts
year-round school	foreign policy

The Debate Format

Formal debates follow a definite structure. One traditional debate format is as follows:

Organization of a Formal Debate

1. Both the affirmative and negative teams have the same number of debaters and the same amount of time to speak.
2. Members of the two sides alternate speaking. The affirmative team opens and closes the debate.
3. Each speaker gives an opening speech called the **constructive speech** and a closing speech called the **rebuttal.**
4. A chairperson presides and maintains order during the debate.
5. Either a panel of judges or the audience may vote to decide which team wins the debate.

Preparing for Debate

A debate itself may take only an hour or so, but many hours of studying, planning, and practicing must come first. You will need to complete a great deal of library research, take notes, analyze issues and information, and organize your evidence into a proper form for presentation to others. The chart on the following page describes these steps as they relate to debate preparation.

Researching the Proposition. The first step in preparing for debate is to learn as much as possible about the subject. The more you know, the better you can argue your side of the proposition. To gather your information intelligently, you need a plan. This will ensure that your research is systematic and thorough. The following guidelines will help you to gather sufficient information about your debate topic:

1. Do preliminary reading to gain background information on the proposition. Find out both its history and its current status. Consult encyclopedias, yearbooks, atlases, almanacs, textbooks, current magazines, newspapers, and other reference works.
2. Prepare a bibliography on your topic. A bibliography is a list of books, articles, pamphlets, government reports, and other printed or spoken sources on a given subject. Use the card catalog at your library and any bibliographies given in books that deal with the debate topic. Also consult such indexes as the *Readers' Guide to Periodical Literature,* the Vertical File Index, and the Monthly Catalog of U. S. Government Publications. (See Chapter 13 for more information on preparing a bibliography.)
3. Collect as much material on your topic as you can find.
4. Read and study the material you have collected. Take notes on 3″ × 5″ cards. Record any facts that you can use to support your argument. (See Chapter 13 for more information on taking notes.)
5. Organize your note cards by topic so that you can gain ready access to the information that they contain.

Planning Your Case. Once you have researched and studied your subject, you are ready to plan your case. That is, you are ready to build an argument. Proceed according to the guidelines presented in the following chart:

Building an Argument

1. **Analyze the proposition.** You have already studied the background of the proposition. Now study the proposition itself. You must know exactly what you are to defend or reject. Go over every important word of the proposition to make sure you know what you are to prove or disprove. Look for any words or phrases that your opponent might interpret differently.

---

2. **Determine the issues.** The issues are the main differences between the affirmative and the negative positions. To determine the issues, list all the reasons you have for supporting your side of the proposition. Then list what you feel your opponent's contrasting reasons might be, based on the reading you have done. To help you determine the issues, you might list the answers to the following questions.

Affirmative	Negative
a. Why does the current state of affairs need changing?	a. Why is there no need to change?
b. Why will the proposed change improve conditions?	b. Why will the proposal not improve conditions?
c. What other advantages will the change bring?	c. What bad effects will occur if the proposal is adopted?
d. Why is the negative team wrong to attack this proposition?	d. What more desirable idea could be suggested?

3. **Choose your contentions, or main points.** Once you have listed the reasons you have for supporting your position, choose the ones you will use to build your case. Remember, your aim is to make your audience believe you. Therefore, choose the points that make the strongest case for your position. Your main points will be short, definite statements of belief that you can support with strong evidence.

4. **Find and choose your evidence.** Go over the notes from your reading. Select items of evidence that support each of your points. If you have not already done so, record each item of evidence and its source on a separate note card. If your evidence to support any point is weak, reexamine your bibliography for additional sources of evidence. You may also conduct interviews to obtain quotes from knowledgeable sources. Whatever your sources, your case will appear stronger if you use various types of evidence, including statistics, examples from past experience, quotations from recognized authorities, and analogies to similar situations.

5. **Prepare an outline.** Follow the same process used to prepare an outline for a research paper. Separate your note cards according to topic. Let your main points become the main topics of your outline. Let your pieces of evidence become your subtopics. Order the arguments in your outline in a way you think would have the greatest impact on your audience. Follow this outline as you prepare your constructive or rebuttal speeches.

Constructive Speeches. Once you have a working outline, you can write and practice your constructive speech. This process is the same as for any persuasive speech. The constructive speech should include an introduction, a body, and a conclusion. The introduction should arouse the interest of the audience by presenting questions, startling facts, illustrations, or anecdotes. It should also state the debate proposition as clearly and precisely as possible.

The following is a sample introduction to an affirmative speech. Notice how this author of this introduction arouses audience interest through the use of visual details and statistics before stating the proposition itself:

> Picture in your mind the carpet of land lying between Hollister and Clifton Avenues. This is the last remaining open, green pasture in our small valley. Do you realize what one out-of-state company is planning for this tranquil piece of property? The Fremont Development Corporation wants to crowd fifteen hundred houses and a sprawling motel onto this land. Such a development would increase the population of the area by three thousand. This increase, in turn, would generate over eleven thousand daily car trips, resulting in added traffic, congestion, and pollution. More importantly, to complete their project, the Fremont Developers will have to divert tons of water from our already overtaxed, rapidly dwindling water supply. This community already bears the scars of growing too large, too fast, and, until now, no community agency has been willing to take the responsibility for controlling this growth. It is because the very quality of our lives here is threatened that we urgently wish to support the following proposition: Resolved, that the Saulito Valley Water District should have the authority to limit new residential and industrial development.

The body of an affirmative or negative speech states the main points of the argument and presents evidence to support each point. However, affirmative and negative speeches differ in the following ways:

1. The constructive speeches of an affirmative team show the need for change, the way to change, and the advantages of change.
2. The constructive speeches of a negative team defend the current conditions, show how proposed changes will be harmful, and suggest possible counterplans.

The conclusion of a constructive speech should simply summarize the main points listed in the body of the speech. It should not be too detailed, it should never introduce new material, and it should not repeat the evidence used to support the main points. Following the summary points should be a restatement of the main position. This concluding statement does not have to be in the exact words of the debate proposition. It may contain a rewording of the resolution or a quotation from an expert who has expressed the position concisely.

Rebuttal Speeches. In rebuttal or refutation, one side attacks the opponents' constructive arguments and defends its own arguments after they have been attacked. Rebuttal speeches follow constructive speeches. They do not include new issues, but they may introduce new evidence. Constructive speeches are completely written and practiced many times before the debate begins. Rebuttal speeches, on the other hand, must be prepared while the debate is in progress. Of course, the well-prepared debater anticipates what arguments he or she will have to answer. The debater has on hand the evidence necessary to answer opposing arguments and practices making rebuttal speeches before the debate. Each debater listens carefully to the opponents' constructive speeches and prepares the exact wording and details of the rebuttal on the spot.

The purpose of rebuttal is to counter the opponents' arguments. This can be done in the following ways:

1. Prove that the opponents' evidence is not sufficient.
2. Prove that the opponents' evidence is inaccurate.
3. Prove that the source of the opponents' evidence is unreliable.
4. Prove that the opponents' evidence could lead to a different conclusion.

In many cases the attack on the opponents' evidence is actually an attack on their reasoning. In other words, the facts given by your opponents may be true, but the reasoning that leads to their conclusions may be faulty. To prepare to attack such faulty reasoning, you need to train yourself to listen critically and to recognize the errors in clear thinking described in Chapter 15.

The following is a sample selection from a speech made in rebuttal to the constructive speech excerpted on page 414. Study this speech to determine what affirmative statement is being refuted and how this is being done.

Did I hear my opponent say that the Fremont Plan would generate eleven thousand daily car trips? How did he arrive at such a figure? Notice that he did not cite any authority nor give the source of this statistic. Can anyone reliably predict how many daily car trips will be made from houses not yet built by people not yet identified?

My opponent has also failed to point out that bus service already exists to the area in question. In addition, the two largest employers in the neighborhood, Simco Electronics and Saulito Research Center, insist that their employees use car pools. Moreover, both schools and a shopping center are already within walking distance of the proposed development. Obviously, the eleven thousand figure is a gross exaggeration. Surely you are entitled to more reliable evidence before you begin to feel threatened.

Exercises Preparing for Debate

A. Choose one of the following propositions. Prepare to debate this proposition, taking either the affirmative or the negative side. Research the proposition, gather evidence on note cards, and write a constructive speech. Make sure that your introduction states the proposition and arouses interest. Also make sure to support the main points made in the body of your speech.

Resolved, that steps should be taken to limit the sales of foreign-made goods in this country.

Resolved, that a greater emphasis should be placed on science and math in our schools.

Resolved, that military service should remain voluntary.

B. Make a list of opposing arguments that might be expressed by opponents of the position that you took in Exercise A. Then, write a rebuttal speech in which you counter these arguments.

SUMMARY AND APPLICATIONS

1. Preparation in public speaking and debate will help you to share your ideas in public forums of all kinds.

2. To prepare a speech, follow steps similar to those of the process of writing.

3. Before writing your speech, make sure that you have a well-defined topic, a specific purpose, and a definite audience in mind. Speeches may inform, persuade, or entertain.

4. In delivering or evaluating a speech, stay aware of the following elements: eye contact, posture, facial expressions, gestures, volume, articulation, pace, pitch, pausing, variation, and tone.

5. For a discussion to be successful, all participants must use good speaking and listening skills. In addition, each group member must understand his or her special responsibilities in a discussion.

6. In debate, an affirmative team and a negative team argue opposing sides of a proposition of fact, value, or policy. Such a proposition is called a resolution.

7. Both constructive speeches—in which main arguments are presented—and rebuttal speeches—in which the arguments of the opposition are attacked—should be supported by evidence drawn from careful research.

Applications In Other Subject Areas

Science/Business. Many innovations in scientific research have raised controversial issues of policy. One such innovation is the use of robots in place of human workers in factories. Another is the development of nuclear power sources. Yet another is the use of computers by telephone companies, banks, grocery stores, and other businesses to handle routine inquiries and transactions with customers. Choose one of these issues, or one of your own, and write a resolution of policy. Then, conduct research and prepare arguments for a debate.

Handbook

A detailed Table of Contents of the Handbook appears in the front of this book.

How To Use the Handbook

This Handbook is your reference book. In it the concepts of grammar, usage, and mechanics are organized so that you can study them efficiently and refer to them quickly.

To use the Handbook well, you should first leaf through it to become familiar with its organization and contents. Note especially the following:

Organization of the Handbook

Grammar Sections 1–4 define and explain the elements of English grammar. Refer to these pages when you have questions about grammar in your speaking or writing.

Usage Sections 5–9 are a guide to English usage. When you are puzzled about which form of a word to use in your writing, turn to the appropriate part of these Sections.

Forms and constructions marked STANDARD are accepted as standard usage—the kind of usage that is appropriate at all times and in all places. Forms and constructions marked NON-STANDARD are not.

Mechanics Sections 10–16 give rules for capitalization, punctuation, spelling, and the formation of plurals. Use these Sections when proofreading or when you have questions about mechanics.

Good Form Sections 17 and 18 present the accepted forms for manuscripts and outlines.

The Handbook includes exercises that test your understanding of the concepts explained. These exercises are the first step in putting what you learn here to practical use. The next step is to apply the concepts in your own writing and speaking.

1.0 The Classification of Words

The words in our language have been classified into eight large groups according to the jobs they perform in a sentence. These eight groups are called the eight **parts of speech.**

nouns	adjectives	conjunctions
pronouns	adverbs	interjections
verbs	prepositions	

In addition to the parts of speech, there are three kinds of words, formed from verbs, that are used as various parts of speech. These words are called **verbals.** The verbals are the *infinitive*, the *participle*, and the *gerund*.

This section defines the different parts of speech and the verbals and explains the function of each.

1.1 The Noun

Some of the words in our language can be used as labels with which to identify people, places, things, and ideas.

A noun is the name of a person, place, thing, or idea.

Most nouns are labels for the people, places, and objects that we can perceive through our five senses. Such nouns name concrete things, like *trees, buildings,* and *rocks.* Nouns, however, can also label things that cannot be perceived by any of the senses. Ideas, emotions, thoughts, and beliefs fall into this category.

PERSONS	PLACES	THINGS	IDEAS
Thomas Jefferson	Salem	desk	curiosity
architect	library	barn	health
salesperson	continent	boot	eternity

A **common noun** is a name common to a whole group of persons, places, or things. It does not name a specific member of that group.

A **proper noun** is the name of an individual person, place, or thing.

A proper noun always begins with a capital letter.

COMMON NOUNS	PROPER NOUNS
singer	Lionel Ritchie
tunnel	Lincoln Tunnel
river	Columbia River
cemetery	Arlington National Cemetery
building	John Hancock Building

As the items in this list show, a noun may consist of more than one word. Each word in a proper noun is capitalized.

If a word can be immediately preceded by *the,* it is a noun: *the* cake, *the* river, *the* language. Many proper nouns, but not all of them, can also be preceded by *the: the* Black Hills, *the* San Diego Zoo, but not *the* Robert Goddard or *the* Canada.

Exercise A: Find all the nouns in the following sentences.

1. Glass is made of melted sand mixed with soda and lime.
2. Grasshoppers and crickets "sing" by rubbing their legs together.

3. Frogs lay eggs that look like a mass of dark-centered tapioca.
4. The raccoon has a sharp nose, dainty feet, and a long, ringed tail.
5. Snakes move by a wavelike motion along the body.
6. Katharine Hepburn usually played characters who were intelligent and outspoken.
7. Geckos are lizards that can cling to smooth surfaces.
8. Dr. Alexander Fleming discovered penicillin while working as an obscure researcher in a hospital.
9. The anthropologist studied the Aztecs—their physical structure, their social customs, and their artifacts.
10. The atmosphere is not a calm ocean of air, but a tossing sea laced with swift currents.

Exercise B: In the sentences below, substitute proper nouns for the words in italics.

1. My favorite food originated in *a foreign country*.
2. *A mayor* was elected for the third time this year.
3. *A queen* ruled in England when Shakespeare wrote his early plays.
4. The latest release by that musician is *a song*.
5. Shrimp boats go out into *a gulf* each morning before dawn.
6. We saw paintings and sculptures in *a museum*.
7. Fred was able to point out *a constellation* in the eastern sky.
8. Kris is preparing a report on the novels of *an author*.
9. A popular tourist spot can be found in *a Southern state*.
10. We went to *a national park* in *a summer month*.

1.2 The Pronoun

A **pronoun** is a word used in place of a noun. By using pronouns to refer to people, places, things, and ideas, we can avoid the awkward repetition of some words.

A pronoun is a word used in place of a noun.

The noun for which the pronoun stands and to which it refers is its **antecedent.**

> *Kim* said *she* would call the airport. (*Kim* is the antecedent of *she*.)

> The *artists* displayed *their* skill. (*artists* is the antecedent of *their*.)

> Mr. Carter is the *counselor* with *whom* I discussed my plans for college. (*counselor* is the antecedent of *whom*.)

The antecedent of a pronoun may appear in a preceding sentence.

> The *candidate* was asked about *foreign aid*. *She* said *it* was necessary for the security of the United States. (*She* refers to the antecedent *candidate; it* refers to *foreign aid*.)

There are six kinds of pronouns.

personal pronouns	demonstrative pronouns
compound personal pronouns	interrogative pronouns
indefinite pronouns	relative pronouns

Personal Pronouns

A pronoun that takes the place of a person's name is a **personal pronoun.** Personal pronouns may also take the place of nouns that refer to things.

> Mr. Aldritch is our chemistry teacher. *He* also coaches gymnastics.

> Buy these tomatoes; *they* are the ripest.

> Monica is a wonderful dancer. *She* has a lead in the school musical.

Personal pronouns may be classified in several different ways.

Person. When a pronoun refers to the speaker or writer of a sentence, it is a **first person** pronoun. When the pronoun refers to the person being spoken to, it is a **second person** pronoun. When a pronoun refers to a person, place, thing, or idea that is being spoken about, it is a **third person** pronoun.

First Person (the person speaking)
I, me, my, mine
we, us, our, ours

Second Person (the person spoken to)
you, your, yours

Third Person (the person, place, thing, or idea spoken about)
he, him, his, she, her, hers, it, its
they, them, their, theirs

Number. Pronouns are **singular** if they refer to one person, place, thing, or idea. Pronouns are **plural** if they refer to more than one person, place, thing, or idea.

SINGULAR: Ravi bought a flower and gave *it* to *me*.
PLURAL: Ravi bought flowers and gave *them* to *us*.

Gender. A pronoun is **masculine** in gender if it refers to a male. A pronoun is **feminine** in gender if it refers to a female. A pronoun is **neuter** in gender if it refers to an object or an idea.

MASCULINE: *He* wished to earn *his* living as an actor.
FEMININE: *She* hoped to see one of *her* stories in print.
NEUTER: *It* was the oldest house on *its* block.

Feminine pronouns are often used to refer to countries, ships, and airplanes. Neuter pronouns are used to refer to animals unless the gender of a particular animal is known.

Case. A personal pronoun may change its form depending on how it functions in a sentence. This change in form is called the **case** of the pronoun. There are three cases: *nominative, possessive,* and *objective.*

NOMINATIVE: *They* photographed the ruined citrus orchards.

POSSESSIVE: *Their* photographs were printed in a national magazine.

OBJECTIVE: The editor quickly offered *them* another assignment.

The following table shows person and number for the three cases of personal pronouns.

Personal Pronouns

SINGULAR		
Nominative	Possessive	Objective
FIRST PERSON: I	my, mine	me
SECOND PERSON: you	your, yours	you
THIRD PERSON: he, she, it	his, her, hers, its	him, her, it

PLURAL		
Nominative	Possessive	Objective
FIRST PERSON: we	our, ours	us
SECOND PERSON: you	your, yours	you
THIRD PERSON: they	their, theirs	them

Possessive Pronouns. Personal pronouns have one or two special forms that show ownership or belonging. These pronouns are called **possessive pronouns.**

Joan put the thermos in *her* backpack. (ownership)
Jules likes to spend time with *his* family. (belonging)

Some personal pronouns are used in place of a noun: *mine, yours, hers, his, ours, theirs*.

Carrie lost the stopwatch and had to borrow *mine*.
Most of the pottery on display is *theirs*.

Other possessive pronouns are used as modifiers before nouns: *my, your, her, his, our, their*.

Carrie had to borrow *my* stopwatch.
Their pottery is on display.

Exercise: In the following sentences find the personal pronouns. Find the antecedent of each pronoun.

1. Leona designed her model carefully before she constructed it.
2. Barb and Jim had their lunch after they tied up the canoe.
3. Claire has two careers, and she says they are compatible.
4. Her friends in Madison are giving Janet a farewell party.
5. Elliot said, "I recently cut my best time by .3 seconds."
6. Beth, have you made your decision yet?
7. The technician gave her supervisor the report, and he studied it carefully.
8. Armand bought a sweater, but he returned it the next day.
9. After Sarah had sanded the chairs, she painted them.
10. The rancher eyed the stallion warily.

Compound Personal Pronouns

Certain personal pronouns may be combined with the suffix *-self* or *-selves* to form **compound personal pronouns.**

FIRST PERSON:	myself, ourselves
SECOND PERSON:	yourself, yourselves
THIRD PERSON:	himself, herself, itself, oneself, themselves

There are no other acceptable compound personal pronouns. Forms such as *hisself* and *theirselves* are nonstandard.

Compound personal pronouns are used *intensively* for emphasis or *reflexively* to refer to a preceding noun or pronoun.

> The mayor *herself* inspected the slum buildings. (intensive)
> Barry hurt *himself* in the scrimmage. (reflexive)

Never use a compound personal pronoun unless it has an antecedent.

> INCORRECT: A reporter interviewed Nan and myself.
> CORRECT: A reporter interviewed Nan and me.
> CORRECT: I myself was interviewed.

Exercise: Supply the correct compound personal pronoun in each of these sentences. Underline its antecedent.

1. Roy injured _____ while using the band saw.
2. Darlene taught _____ how to play folk guitar.
3. You _____ should have delivered the message.
4. The car _____ somehow seemed sinister.
5. The cheerleaders exhausted _____ by the end of the third quarter.
6. By abusing his rivals, Ed defeated _____ in the election.
7. Lincoln _____ heard the woman's complaint.
8. They took the responsibility upon _____.
9. Brace _____ against the back of the seat.
10. I found _____ in a strange predicament.

Indefinite Pronouns

Some pronouns do not refer to a specific person or thing. They are called **indefinite pronouns.** Sometimes an indefinite pronoun has an antecedent.

> The *players* practiced in the rain. *Some* got sick.
> (*players* is the antecedent of the indefinite pronoun *some*)

Usually, however, there is no antecedent for the indefinite pronoun.

> *Everything* you say is true.

An indefinite pronoun may itself be the antecedent of a personal pronoun.

> *Both* of the boys look like *their* father.
> (the indefinite pronoun *both* is antecedent to the personal pronoun *their*)

There are two main groups of indefinite pronouns.

SINGULAR INDEFINITE PRONOUNS

another	anything	either	everything	no one
anybody	one	everyone	neither	someone
anyone	each	everybody	nobody	somebody

PLURAL INDEFINITE PRONOUNS

both   many   few   several

The pronouns *all, some, none, most,* and *any* may be singular or plural, depending upon their meaning in the sentence.

> *All* of the research *was* completed. (singular)
> *All* of the supplies *were* donated. (plural)
>
> *None* of the corn *has* been harvested. (singular)
> *None* of the officers *have* resigned. (plural)
>
> *Has any* of the publicity helped? (singular)
> *Have any* of the risks been considered? (plural)

Note: Sometimes an indefinite pronoun is used to modify a noun: *most* listeners, *few* performers. When used in this way, these words are functioning as adjectives.

Some pronouns, like *this, that, these,* and *those,* are used to point out the thing to which they refer. These pronouns are called **demonstrative pronouns.** The noun or nouns they point to may come later in the sentence, or they may appear in a separate sentence.

This is the *poem* I wrote. (*poem* is the word referred to.)

On the ship were two Bengal *tigers*. *These* were headed for the St. Louis Zoo. (*tigers* is the word referred to by *These*.)

Note: The demonstrative pronouns *this, that, these,* and *those* are also used as adjectives: *this* hammer, *that* book, *these* shoes, *those* albums.

Interrogative Pronouns

Pronouns that are used to ask questions are called **interrogative pronouns.** Such pronouns include *who, whose, whom, what,* and *which*.

Who won the game?
Whom did she vote for?
Those skis are John's. *Whose* are these?
What did he say?
Which should I choose?

Relative Pronouns

Some pronouns are used to relate one idea to another. They are called **relative pronouns.** *Who, whose, whom, which,* and *that* are sometimes used in this way. At these times they help combine two ideas as in the example below.

IDEA 1:	Zenobia conquered Egypt in the third century.
IDEA 2:	Zenobia declared herself Queen of the East.
IDEAS COMBINED WITH A RELATIVE PRONOUN:	Zenobia, *who* conquered Egypt in the third century, declared herself Queen of the East.

Exercise A: List the pronouns in these sentences. Tell whether each is an indefinite, demonstrative, interrogative, or relative pronoun.

1. Are those hermit crabs? They don't look like whelks.
2. This is my radio. Is that yours?
3. Everyone took the driving test except him.
4. Which of the Frisbees in that stack is yours?
5. Someone with an appreciation of fine food is a gourmet.
6. All of the moviegoers who attended the festival love Hitchcock's mysteries.
7. In spite of the fence, several of the rabbits ate everything in the garden.
8. None of the spectators could hear his cries for assistance.
9. I should have allowed myself more time.
10. Is this the book you asked for?
11. Here is the record you wanted to borrow.
12. Who is planning to come to the movies with us?
13. Anyone who wants to join us for dinner is welcome.
14. Who besides yourself is going on the trip?
15. The man who is painting our house does not like the color we have chosen.

Exercise B: Follow the same directions as for Exercise A.

1. Those are your cassettes, and these are mine.
2. Few are better educated than she.
3. The vice-president who served under Buchanan was Hamlin.
4. A few of the short stories are by Eudora Welty.
5. She asked me to give the book to him, but he decided not to read it.
6. I wish you had given them a more definite answer.
7. The dog that rescued the swimmer was mine.
8. Everybody went out of his way to be nice to Rob.
9. Emily Dickinson's poem begins, "I'm nobody. Who are you?"
10. Who told everyone to wear costumes?

1.3 The Verb

The verb is the key part of every sentence. It tells what is happening in the sentence.

A verb is a word that expresses action, condition, or state of being.

To understand the grammatical structure of a sentence, it is helpful to locate the verb first. The other parts of the sentence will be easier to identify once the verb has been located.

Verbs are the only words that change their form to show past and present time. This change in form can help you recognize the verb in a sentence.

> Summer jobs *were* very scarce last year. (past)
> Summer jobs *are* very scarce this year. (present)

> The rank and file *demanded* a voice in government. (past)
> The rank and file *demand* a voice in government. (present)

Most verbs also change their form to show the difference between singular and plural in the third person.

> The President *meets* many people in his travels. (third person singular)
> Travelers *meet* many interesting people. (third person plural)

There are two main categories of verbs: **action verbs** and **linking verbs**.

Action Verbs

Action verbs tell what the subject of the sentence is doing. The action of an action verb may be a physical action that is visible, or it may be a mental action that is not visible.

> The cars *collided*. (visible)
> Shirley *shoveled* snow. (visible)
> We *enjoyed* the comic effects. (not visible)
> Eileen *decided* to wait. (not visible)

Linking Verbs

Not all verbs express action. Some verbs link the subject of the sentence with a noun, pronoun, or adjective. They are called **linking verbs.**

> Pat *is* a writer. (*is* links the subject *Pat* to the noun *writer*)
> Tina *seemed* upset. (*seemed* links the subject *Tina* to the adjective *upset*)

Linking verbs fall into three categories: forms of the verb *be* (*be, am, are, is, was, were, been, being*), verbs having to do with the senses, and verbs that express condition or placement.

Linking Verbs

FORMS OF TO BE	SENSORY VERBS
Sam *was* perplexed.	She *sounds* nervous.
I *am* a senior.	Mike *looks* proud.
The trees *were* oaks.	I *feel* sleepy.
You *are* generous.	The soup *tastes* salty.
Butch *is* a sheepdog.	The sky *appeared* stormy.

VERBS OF CONDITION OR PLACEMENT	
The afternoon *became* cloudy.	The puppies *grew* frisky.
Uncle George *remained* a salesman.	The sign *stayed* upright.
The guard *seemed* suspicious.	

A verb that is used as a linking verb in one sentence can sometimes be used as an action verb in another kind of sentence.

> Jack *felt* a sharp blow. (action)
> Jack *felt* dizzy. (linking)

> The city *sounded* the alarm. (action)
> The record *sounded* scratched. (linking)

Main Verbs and Auxiliaries

Sometimes verbs consist of more than one word. In addition to the main verb, they also have helping verbs, or **auxiliaries.** These auxiliaries help the **main verb** to express action or make a statement. The main verb is always the last word in these verb phrases.

There are three verbs that can be used either as main verbs or as auxiliaries. Here are their forms.

DO	HAVE	BE		
do	has	is	was	be
does	have	am	were	been
did	had	are		being

AS MAIN VERB	AS AUXILIARY
He will *do* his duty.	I *do* need a new dress.
Have they a reason?	We *have* chosen our leader.
The hinges *are* rusty.	Some customers *are* arriving.
The rockets *were* powerful.	The crops *were* exported.

Other auxiliary verbs are not used alone. They are always used in phrases with main verbs. Here are the most common of these.

must	may	shall	could	would
might	can	will	should	

AUXILIARY	MAIN VERB	VERB PHRASE
has	had	has had
had	been	had been
was	doing	was doing
had	done	had done
must have	driven	must have driven
could have	gone	could have gone
might have been	seen	might have been seen
is being	improved	is being improved
shall have	finished	shall have finished

The words in a verb phrase may be separated by a modifier or modifiers that are not part of the verb.

The clerk *was* unjustly *accused*.
Don *had* quietly *assumed* control.

Exercise A: Write each verb and tell whether it is an action verb or a linking verb.

1. Both Anita and Jerry are outstanding swimmers.
2. Just leave your boots outside the door.
3. The child looked cold and hungry.
4. The child looked hungrily at the cake.
5. The freshly baked bread smelled delicious.
6. The steak tasted tender and juicy.
7. The audience grew tense with excitement.
8. Bob Summers, a cousin of mine, is a champion bowler.
9. The committee has been meeting at the home of the chairperson.
10. This rope bridge seems relatively safe.
11. Carefully, the guide led the way.
12. That stunt on one ski was breathtaking.
13. Her expression betrayed her lack of attention.
14. Laurie tasted the icing on the cupcake.
15. The runner collapsed over the finish line.

Exercise B: Write the verb in each of these sentences. Include the auxiliaries that are part of the verb phrase. Do not include any word that separates an auxiliary from a main verb.

1. Several candidates are being considered for the job.
2. The thief may still be lurking in this house.
3. I could meet you at the Guggenheim Museum.
4. I have just read some articles on solar energy.
5. Dr. Ferrera will return from her vacation next week.
6. *Moby Dick* is now regarded as a classic.
7. Heather will probably be appointed editor-in-chief.
8. Our old Buick has just been painted.

9. Is anyone using the hot water?
10. New sources of fuel are being developed every year.
11. *Romeo and Juliet*, one of the most famous of Shakespeare's plays, will always be a favorite.
12. Everything was being readied for the President's inaugural speech.
13. We probably should have taken the train.
14. Termites have practically consumed the beams on our porch.
15. The mayor would undoubtedly have been defeated anyway.

Exercise C: Writing Write two sentences for each verb. In one, use the verb as an action verb. In the second, use the verb as a linking verb. You may also add auxiliaries if you wish.

1. felt
2. looked
3. smell
4. appear
5. sound
6. remain
7. grew
8. taste

Transitive and Intransitive Verbs

There are two kinds of action verbs. A **transitive verb** transfers the action from the subject to an object. The object is the word that comes after the verb and tells *who* or *what* receives the action. (See Section 2.8.) When a verb has an action that is complete and requires no object, it is an **intransitive verb.**

TRANSITIVE	INTRANSITIVE
Cindy *liked* the **novel.**	The experiment *succeeded.*
The debaters *argued* the **point.**	The non-thinkers *conformed.*
The country *faced* a **crisis.**	The game *started* late.
Diane *bought* the **radio.**	We *walked* to the lake.

Note: Sometimes intransitive verbs are followed by adverbs or other modifiers that tell *where, when, why, how,* or *to what extent.* Do not mistake these modifiers for objects.

Many verbs may be transitive in one sentence and intransitive in another.

TRANSITIVE	INTRANSITIVE
Chico *moved* the **car.**	No one *moved*.
Did they *pass* the **law?**	*Did* they *pass?*
The pilot *could* not *see* the **runway.**	The pilot *could* not *see*.

Exercise A: Identify each verb as transitive or intransitive. If it is transitive, write down the object of the verb.

1. Tara breathlessly rushed to basketball practice.
2. Beatrix Potter wrote children's books.
3. Porpoises can communicate through sounds.
4. Polo players on horseback drive a wooden ball with mallets.
5. An investigative reporter will speak next week in assembly.
6. Even ancient Egyptians and Romans wore makeup and perfumes.
7. Some students receive programmed instruction from computers.
8. Shirley Temple Black served as ambassador to Ghana.
9. In recent decades, photography has developed into a highly respected art form.
10. Satellites transmit radio and television signals between points on earth.

Exercise B: Writing Tell whether the verb in each of the following sentences is transitive or intransitive. Then write new sentences, using the transitive verbs as intransitive verbs and the intransitive verbs as transitive verbs.

1. Michael Jackson sang on the American Music Awards special.
2. One of the Karamazov brothers juggled a bowling ball, a torch, and an egg.
3. The panther moved silently through the jungle.

4. I can pack a suitcase in five minutes flat.
5. The electrician ran a wire into our attic.
6. The ranchers hunted the dangerous wolf all night.
7. Drop your entries into the bowl by the door.
8. One trail drops steeply toward the edge of the cliff.
9. The trapper paddled swiftly through the rapids.
10. A huge flock of geese circled overhead.

1.4   The Adjective

Words called **modifiers** are used to describe nouns and verbs and make them more precise. They can add clarity and vividness to our speech and writing. One kind of modifier is the **adjective,** which describes nouns and pronouns.

An adjective is a word that modifies a noun or pronoun.

Adjectives are used to tell *which one, what kind, how many,* or *how much* about nouns and pronouns.

WHICH ONE: this, that, these, those
WHAT KIND: large, sweet, dull, anxious
HOW MANY: some, all, several, six, eleven
HOW MUCH: little, much, abundant

A *red, juicy* apple was hanging on the branch.
We ordered *twenty* cases of that shampoo.
Little benefit resulted from our *strenuous* efforts.

Notice that demonstrative pronouns can also be used as adjectives.

The Articles

The three articles *a, an,* and *the* are classified as adjectives because they modify the nouns they precede. The article *the* is called a **definite article** because it often points to a specific person, thing, or group.

Give *the* bronze cup to *the* third-place winner.
The cheerleaders renewed the spirit of *the* wet and shivering
   crowd.

The articles *a* and *an* are called **indefinite articles.** These articles can only be used with singular nouns. They usually express
the idea that a noun is not unique, but one of many of its
kind.

We took *a* train to *an* unknown destination.

The article *a* is used before nouns that begin with a consonant sound. The article *an* is used before nouns that begin with
vowel sounds. It is the sound, not the spelling, that counts.

a hasty decision	*a* new car	*an* onion
an honorable person	*an* NBA game	*a* one-time offer

Proper Adjectives

An adjective formed from a proper noun is a **proper adjective.**
Proper adjectives are capitalized.

NOUN	ADJECTIVE	NOUN	ADJECTIVE
Poland	Polish	North	Northern
Chaucer	Chaucerian	President	Presidential
Africa	African	Hawaii	Hawaiian
Italy	Italian	Shakespeare	Shakespearean

Predicate Adjectives

An adjective may come after the noun or pronoun it modifies. The two words are linked by a linking verb.

The cat seems *hungry*.   The boys were *angry*.

**An adjective that follows a linking verb and modifies the subject is
a predicate adjective.**

Exercise A: Find each adjective and tell which word it modifies. Ignore the articles.

1. The acoustics in the new auditorium are excellent.
2. The irate skunk sent off a pungent odor.
3. Fifty governors met to discuss critical urban problems.
4. Police conducted a thorough investigation of the brutal crime.
5. She was frank with congressional investigators but uncooperative with the press.
6. The first electric light burned for forty hours.
7. The northern part of Canada is a vast Arctic waste.
8. In a full orchestra there are four families of instruments.
9. Jellyfish are boneless animals with long, stringy tentacles.
10. The traffic was terrible during the late afternoon and early evening.

Exercise B: Follow the same directions as for Exercise A.

1. There were only twenty people in the huge auditorium.
2. Amy gave the dog fresh water and some food.
3. The dance, colorful and sprightly, delighted the large audience.
4. Picasso was one of the major artists of modern times.
5. Some people have a strange antipathy for cats.
6. Aunt Carol is both musical and artistic.
7. The weary hikers tried to ignore their intense hunger.
8. There are several books on architecture on the second shelf.
9. Editorial cartoons are humorous as well as persuasive.
10. The vehicular intersection by the bridge is congested and dangerous.

Exercise C: Writing Write a short paragraph describing an interesting place or person you have seen recently. Then revise the paragraph, adding modifiers to make the image more vivid for your reader.

1.5 The Adverb

Another kind of modifier is the **adverb**. Like an adjective, it can add precision and interest to your writing. Adjectives, however, modify nouns and pronouns; adverbs modify verbs, adjectives, and other adverbs.

An adverb modifies a verb, an adjective, or another adverb.

MODIFYING A VERB: She voted *wisely*.

MODIFYING AN ADJECTIVE: Information is *readily* available.

MODIFYING AN ADVERB: He felt criticism *very* keenly.

Adverbs tell *where, when, how,* or *to what extent*.

WHERE: They lingered *outside*.
WHEN: The team left *early*.
HOW: The story ended *happily*.
TO WHAT EXTENT: The writing was *totally* illegible.

Adverbs are frequently formed from adjectives by adding the suffix *-ly*.

ADJECTIVE	ADVERB
noisy	noisi*ly*
careful	careful*ly*
gracious	gracious*ly*
angry	angri*ly*
loving	loving*ly*

However, some adjectives end in *-ly* already. Be careful not to mistake adjectives such as *friendly, lovely,* and *lively* for *-ly* adverbs.

You must also be alert for adverbs that do not end in *-ly*. The negative words *no, not,* and *never,* for example, are almost always adverbs. Adverbs that express time, such as *now, ever, almost,* and *soon,* also do not have *-ly* endings.

Some words may be either adjectives or adverbs.

ADJECTIVE	ADVERB
a *hard* task	Study *hard*.
a *late* program	We arrived *late*.
a *deep* crevasse	The anchor sank *deep* into the mud.

Directive Adverbs

A **directive adverb** tells *where* (place or direction) about the verb it modifies. It usually comes after the verb.

They tiptoed *in*.	Stack the supplies *inside*.
The box slid *down*.	No one ventured *near*.

Directive adverbs in combination with verbs have added many idioms to our language, such as *put through, give up,* and *point out*. An idiom is a group of words that has an accepted meaning that is different from the meanings of the individual words.

Position of Adverbs

Adverbs can be positioned in various parts of a sentence to give special emphasis. An exception is the directive adverb, which generally follows the verb it modifies. Also, adverbs which modify other modifiers usually precede them.

DIRECTIVE: The ship sailed *away*.

ADVERB
MODIFYING MODIFIER: It was a *very* tense moment.

He left *rather* unexpectedly.

OTHER ADVERBS: *Quickly,* she opened the letter.

She *quickly* opened the letter.

She opened the letter *quickly*.

Exercise A: Find each adverb in the following sentences. Tell which word or words it modifies.

1. You drive too fast for safety.
2. The supposedly unsinkable *Titanic* had actually sunk.
3. Suddenly a loud shot rang out.
4. The paint is not quite dry yet.
5. The story is only moderately interesting to me, but some readers find it quite exciting.
6. We rose late, breakfasted slowly, and leisurely drove to Memphis.
7. You will undoubtedly hear from her soon.
8. Hemingway's *A Farewell to Arms* was first published serially.
9. The door will probably open if you push hard.
10. The weather satellite sent back clear pictures.

Exercise B: Writing Fill in the blanks in the sentences below with adverbs that answer the questions in parentheses.

1. The old man spoke _____ and _____. (how?)
2. You should check the information _____. (when?)
3. My mother took us _____ in the car. (where?)
4. I completed the job _____. (how?)
5. The runners were _____ tired. (to what extent?)
6. _____ he put the menu down and looked around. (when?)
7. Leontyne Price sings this piece _____. (how?)
8. I had _____ been _____ angry. (when? to what extent?)
9. The kittens slept _____. (how?)
10. The retriever swam _____ through the waves. (how?)

Exercise C: Writing Write a paragraph that describes some activity that you witnessed recently or in which you took part. Revise the paragraph, adding adverbs to make your descriptions of the action more vivid.

1.6 The Preposition

English sentences convey meaning through the way in which the words within them are linked together. One of the most common ways to show relationships between words in a sentence is by using **prepositions.** Prepositions are often small words, but they play an important part in communicating meaning.

There are seventeen one-syllable prepositions in English.* They are used to show the following relationships.

LOCATION:	at, by, in, on, near
DIRECTION:	to, from, down, off, through, out, past, up
ASSOCIATION:	of, for, with, like

There are also many two-syllable prepositions.

about	along	below	during
above	among	beneath	except
across	around	beside	inside
after	before	between	outside
against	behind	beyond	over
under			

A number of prepositions have been formed by combining two one-syllable prepositions.

into	upon	without
onto	within	throughout

A **compound preposition** is made by combining a preposition and a modifier, or by combining several prepositions.

according to	out of	on account of
prior to	owing to	inside of
in front of	subsequent to	because of
as to	by means of	aside from

---

*The word *but* may be used as a preposition with the meaning of *except*. The word *as* may be used as a preposition with the meaning *in the capacity of*.

Objects of Prepositions

Prepositions are not used alone in sentences. A preposition always appears with a word or group of words that is called its **object.** The job of the preposition is to express a relationship between its object and some other word in the sentence. The preposition, its object, and any modifiers of the object make up a **prepositional phrase.**

The sign *over the door* read, "Welcome."
Light filtered *into the damp subterranean passage.*
The motorcade moved slowly *through the crowded streets.*

In most sentences, the object of the preposition comes after the preposition. This usual order is often changed when the sentence has an interrogative pronoun or a relative pronoun.

What *hotel* will they have the dance *in?*
Jack asked *whom* the telephone call was *for.*
Was Sue the girl *whom* you gave the ring *to?*

The object of a preposition may be a single word or a group of words.

WORD:	The doctor hurried into the *house.*
WORD:	I went with *them* willingly.
WORD:	Upon *arriving,* Joan asked for an interview.
WORD GROUP:	After *testing the equipment,* I found it defective.
WORD GROUP:	Before *recommending the book,* read it well.
WORD GROUP:	Explain the problem to *whoever is in charge.*

Exercise: Find the prepositions. Tell the object of each one.

1. Everyone contributed to the success of the party.
2. There are several books with blue covers on that shelf.
3. Heart disease is one of the chief causes of death.
4. Most accidents in boats happen to amateurs.
5. You will find the dictionary on the bottom shelf.

6. The armistice went into effect on November 11, 1918.
7. The grizzly bear gazed into my camera with the composure of a professional model.
8. Traffic on Main Street was rerouted because of the accident.
9. The game was postponed on account of rain.
10. Whom are you going with?
11. The meteor blazed through the earth's atmosphere.
12. Over the crowd and into the top bleachers flew the Dodgers' first home run of the season.
13. Inside the cozy cabin, a roaring fire crackled in the fireplace.
14. The rain pelted the roof throughout the night.
15. In the Middle Ages, people in Europe made pilgrimages on foot to the Holy Land.

1.7 The Conjunction

Another kind of word used to show relationships between parts of a sentence is the conjunction.

A conjunction is a word that connects words, phrases, or clauses.

There are three kinds of conjunctions: coordinating conjunctions, correlative conjunctions, and subordinating conjunctions.

Coordinating Conjunctions

Words or groups of words that are used in the same way in a sentence may be joined by **coordinating conjunctions.** The coordinating conjunctions are *and, but, or, so, for,* and *yet*.

His chief interests are backgammon *and* ceramics.
A camp counselor must be patient *and* resourceful.
The marlin fought savagely *and* cunningly.

We could camp out *or* stay in motels.
It started to rain, *so* we went indoors.
We felt sorry for the puppy, *for* he looked sad.
The barn was picturesque *yet* useless.

The word *nor* may be used as a coordinating conjunction if it is preceded by another negative word.

The rookie could *not* field, *nor* could he hit well.
I have *no* tape, *nor* do I have glue.

Correlative Conjunctions

Conjunctions that are used in pairs are called **correlative conjunctions.** The correlative conjunctions are as follows: *not only . . . but (also); either . . . or; neither . . . nor; both . . . and; whether . . . or.*

Motocross racing requires *not only* skill *but* great daring.
Either chemistry *or* physics is required.
Neither the book *nor* the movie was historically accurate.
Both the organization *and* the content of the composition were excellent.
We must consider *whether* he will act responsibly *or* impulsively.

Note: There is a third type of conjunction, called the **subordinating conjunction.** Subordinating conjunctions are discussed in Section 3.5.

Conjunctive Adverbs

Some adverbs act like conjunctions and are called **conjunctive adverbs.** They connect groups of words that could stand alone as separate sentences. A conjunctive adverb is preceded by a semicolon and followed by a comma.

Both chairs were blue; *however,* one had stripes.
Do your laundry; *otherwise,* you will have nothing to wear.

A list of the most common conjunctive adverbs is given below.

accordingly	furthermore	moreover	still
also	hence	nevertheless	therefore
consequently	however	otherwise	thus

Exercise A: Find the conjunctions and conjunctive adverbs. Tell whether the conjunctions are coordinating conjunctions or correlative conjunctions.

1. We tried to hurry, but the crowd delayed us.
2. A paralyzing snowfall hit Buffalo; consequently, all transportation was halted.
3. Korea has been called "The Land of the Morning Calm"; however, it has seen turbulent days.
4. The apartment was old but charming.
5. The roads were partly flooded; nevertheless, we kept driving.
6. We did not bring our raincoats, nor did we have an umbrella.
7. Randall does five hours of homework each night, yet he is happy to be in honors classes.
8. We visited not only Disneyland but also the San Diego Zoo.
9. Boxes and cartons filled the warehouse.
10. Either the medication or the blood transfusion saved his life.

Exercise B: Find the conjunctions. Show what words or word groups they join.

1. Either he or I must go.
2. He has a stern manner but a good heart.
3. I walked across the highway and along the tracks.

4. Tanya tried to ask the librarian, but he was busy.
5. Elaine has written the report and has revised it.
6. William Jennings Bryan ran three times for the Presidency, but he was never elected.
7. She knew when to talk and when to listen.
8. Richard Pryor is not only a comedian but also a commentator on society.
9. The sign was faded yet legible.
10. The children were frightened, for the woods were growing dark.

1.8 The Interjection

An **Interjection** is a word or word group that expresses strong feeling or emotion. It is usually followed by an exclamation point. An interjection does not have a grammatical relationship to other parts of the sentence. It is interjected, or "thrown," into the sentence.

An interjection is a word or word group used to express surprise or other emotion. It has no grammatical relation to other words in the sentence.

| Wow! | Attention! | Ouch! | Terrific! |
| Watch out! | Help! | Hi! | Oh no! |

1.9 Words Used as Different Parts of Speech

Some words are always used as the same part of speech. The word *are*, for example, is always a verb. The word *you* is always a pronoun. Many other words, however, change their parts of speech depending on the roles they play in specific sentences.

The treaty was signed, *but* we had misgivings. (conjunction)
Everyone *but* the speaker noticed the incident. (preposition)

449

Will you turn on the *light?* (noun)
It needs a new *light* bulb. (adjective)
Light the birthday candles. (verb)

Verb or Noun?

To determine whether a word is being used as a noun or a verb, decide whether it names something (noun) or expresses an action or state of being (verb).

The dining hall was full of *flies*. (noun)
My uncle *flies* experimental planes. (verb)

Noun or Adjective?

To determine whether a word is being used as a noun or an adjective, decide whether it names something (noun) or modifies a noun or pronoun (adjective).

The teacher viewed *history* as the quest for human freedom. (noun)
The *history* book was old and out of date. (adjective)

Adjective or Pronoun?

The demonstrative pronouns—*this, that, these,* and *those*—may also be used as adjectives. If the word is used in place of a noun, it is a pronoun. If it modifies a noun, it is an adjective.

This is a disc camera. (pronoun)
These are more practical shoes for you. (pronoun)
That experience is hard to forget. (adjective modifying *experience*)
Those aspects of the case are clear. (adjective modifying *aspects*)

In a similar way the words *what, which,* and *whose* may be used alone as pronouns or before nouns as adjectives.

> *What* will your salary be? (pronoun)
> *What* grade did you get in history class? (adjective modifying *grade*)
> *Which* is the best route to take? (pronoun)
> *Which* play should I read? (adjective modifying *play*)
> *Whose* did you want? (pronoun)
> *Whose* skateboard is this? (adjective modifying *skateboard*)

The words *your, my, our, his, her,* and *their* are forms of the personal pronouns used to show possession. Used in this way, they perform the job of adjectives. The words *mine, yours, hers, ours,* and *theirs* are always pronouns. The word *his* may be used either as a pronoun or an adjective. (See Section 1.2.)

> That car of *his* is sporty. (pronoun)
> That hat of *hers* is colorful. (pronoun)
> The fingerprints are definitely *his*. (pronoun)
> *His* autobiography is rich in anecdotes. (adjective use)
> *His* shirt is too small. (adjective use)

Adjective or Adverb?

Some adjectives and adverbs have the same form. To tell whether a modifier is an adjective or an adverb, ascertain which word it modifies. If it modifies a noun or a pronoun, it is an adjective. If it modifies any other kind of word, it is an adverb. It is also helpful to remember that adjectives tell *which one, what kind, how many,* or *how much* about nouns and pronouns. Adverbs tell *where, when, how,* or *to what extent* about the words they modify.

> Jimmy was singing *loud*. (adverb telling *how*)
> The *loud* music kept us awake. (adjective telling *what kind*)
>
> Jets travel *fast*. (adverb telling *how*)
> Drive in the *fast* lane. (adjective telling *what kind*)

451

Adverb or Preposition?

To determine whether a word is used as a preposition or as an adverb, you must check its relationship to other words in the sentence. If the word modifies a verb, adjective, or adverb, it is an adverb. If the word is followed by a noun or pronoun that completes its meaning, then the word is probably a preposition.

> The coach rode *in* a special car. (*car* completes the meaning of *in*. *in* is a preposition.)
> The coach sent a substitute *in*. (*in* is an adverb.)
> Everyone danced *at* the party. (*party* completes the meaning of *at*. *at* is a preposition.)
> The bulb finally burned *out*. (adverb)
> The cold drove the cattle *inside*. (adverb)
> We were talking *about* the music festival. (preposition)
> The players were conversing *quietly*. (adverb)

Exercise A: Determine how the italicized word is used in each sentence.

1. The orchestra warmed up *before* the concert.
2. Neither candidate had held public office *before*.
3. The responsibility is all *his*.
4. *Those* cards are my favorites.
5. The inspector will *dog* your steps.
6. The moderator kept the discussion on the *main* topic.
7. A water *main* has burst.
8. The people who *frequent* this place are actors.
9. The woman from the nursery *pruned* the trees.
10. Roy is finding *college* algebra extremely difficult.
11. Whole-wheat bread contains greater *food* value than white.
12. The Acropolis *towers* over the city of Athens.
13. Can a hummingbird really fly so *fast*?
14. *Which* is your raincoat?
15. *Which* raincoat is yours?

Exercise B: Writing Determine how the italicized word is used in each sentence. Then write a new sentence using the word as a different part of speech.

1. Flames from the *oil* refinery illuminated the sky.
2. We admired Mr. Leonard's *rose* garden.
3. I *rose* at six this morning.
4. The crocodile sheds *no* tears.
5. The lightning had knocked the flagpole *down*.
6. We took the *through* train to Chicago.
7. My grandfather still has a *party* line.
8. Expect progress, *but* don't expect miracles.
9. They had subsisted on nothing *but* berries and water.
10. The mayor said she would not *countenance* the plan.

1.10   Verbals

Infinitives, participles, and **gerunds** are part of a classification of words called **verbals.** Verbals are derived from verbs. Like verbs they can have modifiers and complements. However, they are used as nouns, adjectives, and adverbs, not verbs.

1.11   The Infinitive

The infinitive is a verbal that is usually, but not always, preceded by *to*. *To* is called the "sign of the infinitive." The kinds of infinitives are as follows:

ACTIVE PRESENT: to invite
PASSIVE PRESENT: to be invited
ACTIVE PERFECT: to have invited
PASSIVE PERFECT: to have been invited

The infinitive may be used as a noun. Like a noun, it may be the subject or object of a verb. It may also be a predicate noun or an appositive.

To dream was still possible. (subject of *was*)
Sammy loves *to learn*. (object of *loves*)
Linda's goal is *to teach*. (predicate noun)
Leo's job, *to clean* the garage and attic, took him all day.
    (appositive)

The infinitive may also be used as a modifier. Used as an adjective, it may modify nouns and pronouns.

This is the book *to read*.   She is someone *to emulate*.

When used as an adverb, the infinitive may modify adverbs, adjectives, or verbs.

Laughter is good *to hear*. (modifying the adjective *good*)

Courtney tried too hard *to succeed*. (modifies the adverb *hard*)

They dived *to get* pearls. (modifies the verb *dived*)

See Sections 2.14 and 3.6 for additional details on the uses of infinitives.

1.12   The Participle

A **participle** is a verbal that acts as an adjective. The present participle ends in *-ing*. The past participle usually ends in *-ed, -d, -en,* or *-t*.

PRESENT PARTICIPLE:	instructing
PAST PARTICIPLE:	instructed
PERFECT PARTICIPLE:	having instructed
PASSIVE PERFECT PARTICIPLE:	having been instructed

A participle modifies a noun or a pronoun. In the sentences on the following page, the arrow points to the word modified by the participle.

Hesitating, Art questioned the wisdom of the idea.

Surrounded, the guerrilla forces capitulated.

The pilot, *having been forewarned,* prepared for an emergency landing.

The *fallen* leaves made patterns on the sidewalk.

1.13   The Gerund

A **gerund** is a verbal that ends in *-ing.* It is always used as a noun and can be used in almost every way a noun can be used.

> *Rowing* is hard work. (subject of the verb)
> Juanita enjoys *camping.* (object of the verb)
> Before *applying,* check your qualifications. (object of the preposition)
> The best treatment for a cold is *sleeping.* (predicate noun)
> Larry's favorite pastime, *talking,* ran up a huge phone bill. (appositive)

1.14   Participle, Gerund, or Verb?

Several verb forms end in *-ing.* All gerunds, all present participles, and some verbs in verb phrases use this ending. The following questions will help you distinguish among them.

1. Is the word used as an adjective? If so, it is a present participle.
2. Is the word used as a noun? If so, it is a gerund.
3. Is the word preceded by an auxiliary verb? If so, it is a verb in a verb phrase.

> PRESENT PARTICIPLE: The *drying* laundry was soaked by the sudden rain shower. (*drying* is used as an adjective. It modifies the noun *laundry.*)

GERUND: *Drying* is one way to preserve foods. (*Drying* is used as a noun. It is the subject of the sentence.)

VERB IN A VERB PHRASE: The artists have been *drying* flowers to use in their collages. (*drying* is part of the verb phrase *have been drying.*)

Exercise A: Find the verbals in the sentences below. Label them as infinitives, participles or gerunds.

1. Passengers in the sinking ship were rescued by lifeboats.
2. One of the tastiest ways to prepare food is frying.
3. Jimmy's desire to win made him practice night and day.
4. To entertain was the comedian's greatest pleasure.
5. Janet watched the V-formation of migrating Canada geese.
6. The exhausted travelers arrived too tired to eat.
7. Stumbling, the runner lost his first-place lead.
8. Phyllis got a good price on a used car by bargaining.
9. The skills you will need to complete the project are sewing and drawing.
10. We all thought Mrs. Sanchez was a woman to admire.

Exercise B: Tell whether the italicized word in each sentence is a verb, a present participle, or a gerund.

1. Mary and Katy were *thinking* of ways to repair the vase.
2. *Driving* can lead to eye strain.
3. You can prevent the sauce from *burning* by *stirring*.
4. Clarence tried to bandage his *bleeding* finger.
5. Leonard won first prize for *baking*.
6. Our family has been *hearing* strange noises at night.
7. Some people must have thought that these insects looked like *walking* sticks.
8. The effects of *aging* were discussed at the seminar.
9. *Purring,* the cat sounded like a well-oiled motor.
10. *Reupholstering* is taught in evening classes at the school.

REINFORCEMENT EXERCISES
The Classification of Words

A. Identify common and proper nouns. Write the nouns used in the following sentences. Next to each noun, write P if it is a proper noun and C if it is a common noun.

1. Ginger Rogers danced with Fred Astaire in several old musicals.
2. Liverworts exist in all parts of the world except in deserts.
3. Kevin MacLaren wore a green, red, blue, and yellow tartan.
4. Francois Rabelais published his early works under the anagram Alcofribas Nasier.
5. David O. Selznick produced *Gone With the Wind* in 1939.
6. The poet wrote using metaphors that the class could not understand.
7. Americans in different parts of the country speak various dialects.
8. A large icicle fell from the bleachers.
9. Which countries in Europe still have a monarchy?
10. The wind set off the burglar alarm in the auto.

B. Recognize pronouns. Write each pronoun in the following sentences. Then tell whether it is a personal, a compound personal, an indefinite, a demonstrative, an interrogative, or a relative pronoun.

1. Kerry wants to pay for the flying lessons herself.
2. The angry customer demanded that he be taken to the manager.
3. Rudyard Kipling, who was born in India, won the Nobel prize in 1907.
4. The diver herself presented me with a precious pearl.
5. "Which of the paintings are by Miro?" asked Susanne.
6. Both of my parents were born in Taiwan.

7. They studied Vesuvius, which is the only active volcano on the European mainland.
8. These are the baseball statistics that must be entered into the computer.
9. Many have tried to climb Mt. Everest, but few have reached the top.
10. "Would you like me to help you?" the truck driver asked the cyclist.

C. Recognize complete verbs. Write the complete verb in each sentence. Then tell whether the verb is an action verb or a linking verb. If it is an action verb, tell whether it is transitive or intransitive.

1. This illustrator has drawn for several national magazines.
2. The smell of smoke must have alerted the Labrador retriever.
3. Rod Dixon, the New Zealander, looked triumphant after the race.
4. The stationary computer will run all of the home's electrical equipment.
5. For seven years the prospector mined without success.
6. My brother is writing a paper on the dobsonfly.
7. Chandra has not yet replaced the steel blade of the lawn mower.
8. Lacrosse players must wear helmets and face masks for protection.
9. I felt ill only minutes later.
10. Harold was making a mess of the once-crisp bow tie.

D. Identify adjectives. Write the adjectives in the sentences below. Tell which word each adjective modifies. You may ignore the articles.

1. The venomous sting of the bee left a red and painful bump.
2. The runaway vehicle gained speed on that downhill grade and went over the steep cliff on a hairpin turn.
3. "I can answer the unanswerable question," said the Socratic philosopher.

4. Coriander is an annual plant whose large seeds are used as a spice.
5. Silk is durable as well as beautiful.
6. The pioneers settled there because the region had a favorable climate and fertile soil.
7. A few vigorous strokes brought the young swimmer to the yellow buoy.
8. Marissa has studied Slavic languages and Russian history.
9. The noisy siren and stark red light startled the residents of that quiet neighborhood.
10. Francis prefers practical applications of ideas over idle speculation.

E. Identify adverbs. Find the adverbs in the sentences below. Tell which word each adverb modifies. Also tell the part of speech of each modified word.

1. Guido looked at the stopwatch skeptically, then grinned broadly.
2. The leaves drifted downward and settled noiselessly in the silt.
3. "Play outside," he implored, "or you will certainly wake Dad."
4. Most pearls have very little commercial value.
5. "That story is completely false," complained the irate reader.
6. "Never walk there alone," warned the officer.
7. Marty tried repeatedly to call the airline terminal.
8. JoAnne quickly pulled the toddler out of the unusually treacherous surf.
9. Did you notice how warily he answered my perfectly innocent question?
10. The ambassador was profoundly embarrassed by the incident.

F. Use prepositions. Write a prepositional phrase to complete each sentence below. The prepositional phrase should answer the question given in parentheses.

1. The troops did not march willingly. (where?)
2. The tornado howled. (from what direction?)
3. Steffie said she would meet me. (when?)
4. Each Friday, the members of the club went fishing. (where?)
5. I gingerly placed the package. (near what?)
6. The inspector examined the scene. (what scene?)
7. Justine practiced baton twirling. (where?)
8. The computer industry will produce many exciting innovations. (when?)
9. The pioneers moved. (in what direction?)
10. New York City is famous. (for what?)

G. Identify conjunctions and conjunctive adverbs. Write the conjunctions and conjunctive adverbs in the following sentences. Label conjunctions as coordinating or correlative.

1. The nightingale has dull-colored plumage, but it has a sweet song.
2. Eastern Orthodox Churches consider Constantine a saint, for under his rule Christians gained freedom of worship.
3. My cousin could not decide between the karate course and the judo course.
4. Scottish tartans identify clans; however, few who are not Scots know how to interpret the designs.
5. Diane was exhausted, yet continued practicing.
6. Although neither unicorns nor dragons have ever existed, many stories have included them.
7. Van Gogh experienced violent seizures; therefore, he committed irrational acts.
8. Both Eva and Inge entered their works in the science fair.
9. The infant seemed quiet but observant.
10. The veterinarian could sedate the cub or try to treat it without a tranquilizer.

H. Use words as different parts of speech. Determine the part of speech of each italicized word. Then write new sentences using each word as a different part of speech.

460

1. Paul could not *park* the car on the street after the heavy snowfall.
2. The Mascarene Islands are *in* the *Indian* Ocean.
3. The floor *exercises* seemed like child's *play* to the expert.
4. Jethro bought *one loaf* of freshly-baked bread.
5. *That* is one of the *few* pieces of macramé I've ever liked.
6. *One* should try to stand *still* around a bee.
7. The *mandolin* is a *string* instrument with a pear-shaped *back*.
8. The guide moved *through* the dark *cave* passages as though he lived there.
9. Melissa set *up* the *swing* without reading the instructions.
10. The pilot flew *low* and blanketed the field with an insecticide *spray*.

I. Identify verbals. Find each verbal in the following sentences. Identify each one as an infinitive, a participle, or a gerund.

1. Emergency rations saved the stranded mountain climbers from starving.
2. Waving, the children greeted each train that passed.
3. Beth's favorite pastime, exercising, enabled her to compete in the triathalon.
4. You can learn more by listening than by talking.
5. Developing pictures is a satisfying hobby.
6. Is a flying fish any more amazing than a swimming bird?
7. The council hopes to improve safety regulations before approving the bill.
8. Snorkeling took up all of Albert's free time on weekends.
9. Standing, the audience continued to applaud the virtuoso performance.
10. Irritated by the crawling traffic, several drivers began to honk their horns.

MIXED REVIEW

The Classification of Words

A. Identify the italicized words in these sentences as noun, pronoun, verb, adjective, adverb, preposition, conjunction, interjection, infinitive, gerund, or participle.

1. Denise applied *for* a patent on her *new* invention.
2. The audience gave the *veteran* actress a standing *ovation*.
3. *Although she* enjoys Scrabble, Maria prefers *playing* Trivial Pursuit.
4. *Aha!* The thief entered *through* this *rear* window.
5. The Electoral College *chooses* the *President* and Vice-President of the United States.
6. Ramona whistled and the horse turned and *galloped to* her side.
7. *With flawless* grace, the pianist played a concerto by *Mozart*.
8. Frannie *routinely* deposits her *weekly* paycheck into a savings account.
9. Al's Restaurant, *which* is *often open* all night, serves pancakes and waffles.
10. The centerfielder *and* the shortstop collided as *they* raced for the ball.
11. The control tower *soon gave* the pilot clearance *to land*.
12. Brian *created* a unique animated cartoon by *photographing* clay figures.
13. *Anyone who* wants *to work* during the summer should apply in the spring.
14. The ski slopes *near* Aspen *have accumulated* a forty-inch snow base.
15. The curator *bluntly declared* that the painting was a *fake*.
16. Deborah made a *family* tree *showing* all of her ancestors for *five* generations.
17. Graves *vehemently* denied the *charges* of espionage against *him*.
18. *Oh*, those cars are *very* sleek, *but* they gobble fuel!
19. *Exhausted, Mark* limped *painfully* toward the finish line.

20. *Some* areas, such as the Greenland ice cap and northwest Siberia, are *still* virtually *inaccessible*.

B. In each sentence below, identify the part of speech of the italicized word. Then list the other word in the sentence that is the same part of speech. Do not be misled by similarities in word type.

1. Oh! *Stop!* I forgot the tickets.
2. Diode tubes eventually replaced *crystal* detectors in radios.
3. Seeing is not always *believing*.
4. The hat *spun* down the street and landed in a puddle.
5. Aunt Sylvia brought back *German* marzipan and delicious chocolate from Holland.
6. The *perplexed* hikers studied the confusing trail maps.
7. *Elkhounds* are Norwegian hunting dogs.
8. Kent had never ridden his horse *bareback*.
9. The plastic ball bounced off the table and *into* the potato salad.
10. Sean *and* I agreed to sweep the cabin or wash the dishes.

C. Each of the words listed below can be used as more than one part of speech. Write two sentences for each of the words, using them as the parts of speech given in parentheses.

1. table (verb, noun)
2. those (adjective, pronoun)
3. off (adverb, preposition)
4. plant (noun, verb)
5. monitor (noun, verb)
6. sample (adjective, verb)
7. football (noun, adjective)
8. one (pronoun, adjective)
9. register (noun, verb)
10. live (adjective, verb)

USING GRAMMAR IN WRITING
The Classification of Words

A. Language grows in many ways. Sometimes, new nouns or verbs are created as labels for new products, processes, and items of technology. The words for innovations such as the telephone, X-ray, microfilm, and videotape, for example, entered the language as both nouns and verbs. Try to think of other examples of recent inventions and developments that have added nouns to our language. See if any of these words are used as both nouns and verbs. (You may use specific product names, like Xerox, if they apply.) Write an essay in which you discuss these additions to the language. You may also speculate about other nouns that may eventually become verbs. Will people, for example, someday say, "I am going to holograph you?"

B. Details make the difference between dull writing and exciting prose. Try to isolate the most exciting or fascinating event that you have witnessed or taken part in during the last year. Write an account of that event. As you revise your writing, add precise nouns, strong verbs, and vivid modifiers, to make your subject "come alive" for the reader. Remember that participles and prepositional phrases can also be used to add detail.

C. You are probably beginning to plan for your future. Why not include running for the office of governor or President among these plans? Write a list of the ten points of your program if you were to run for elective office. Use infinitives for all items on the list. (For example, *"To establish* full employment," *"To limit* federal spending.") Then write a list of the ten ways you would go about accomplishing these points. Use gerunds and participles in the second list whenever possible. (I would limit federal spending by cutting unnecessary departments.)

CUMULATIVE REVIEW
The Parts of Speech

Recognizing the Parts of Speech and the Verbals. Number your paper from 1 to 25. Identify each italicized word in the following paragraphs as a *Noun, Pronoun, Verb, Adverb, Adjective, Conjunction, Preposition, Gerund, Infinitive,* or *Participle*.

No one *really* knows *how* Valentine's Day *originated*. The holiday was named after St. Valentine, a figure who *survives* in name alone. No records exist to tell *who* St. Valentine was or why he is associated with this particular *holiday*. *However*, it is known that in the Middle Ages people believed that *this* was the day in which the birds of the woods met *to choose* their partners. Geoffry Chaucer, *one* of the *earliest* and greatest of English poets wrote a curious work entitled "The Parliament of Fowls" *to describe* this annual convention of *feathered* suitors. How Chaucer's *mythical* spring ritual became associated with St. Valentine remains a mystery.

In recent years, Valentine's Day has developed into a business of *quite* staggering proportions. *Buying* becomes the *most* important goal of the day. Not only are millions of greeting cards, flowers, and boxes of candy bought on this day, *but* thousands of rings, necklaces, bracelets, and other pieces of jewelry are purchased as well. In fact, some florists and jewelers do *more* business on this one day in February than during any entire month of the *remaining* year. Shopkeepers seem not in the least *upset* that the *singing* of birds has given way almost *entirely* to the ringing of their *cash* registers. Perhaps this is to be expected in our modern, commercial age.

2.0 The Parts of a Sentence

There are times when a single word may express a complete idea. A sign that says *Exit* or *Yield* does not require further explanation to be understood. Most of the time, however, words are used in groups such as *during the game, singing a song,* or *Doug ran.* These groups of words are organized into specific patterns to express meaning.

Speakers of every language know how to organize word groups into sentences even if they have never given much thought to how they do it. For example, no one who speaks English would make the mistake of saying *My twice dog a year coat sheds his.* In order to convey meaning, the sentence would have to be arranged *My dog sheds his coat twice a year.*

In this Section you will study the various types of sentences and their parts. Understanding how groups of words are organized into sentences will help you speak and write effectively.

2.1 The Sentence

A sentence expresses a complete thought or idea. This thought or idea may be expressed as a statement, as a question, or as a command. The first part of the definition of a sentence is given below.

A sentence is a group of words that expresses a complete thought.

You can tell if an expression is incomplete because it leaves you asking questions such as *what? what about it? what happened? who did it?*

INCOMPLETE: The player on the sidelines (What about her?)
COMPLETE: The player on the sidelines was injured.
INCOMPLETE: Jack Allen, a sophomore (Did what?)
COMPLETE: Jack Allen, a sophomore, placed first in public speaking.
INCOMPLETE: Building a boat (Who did what?)
COMPLETE: Building a boat, they were happily occupied.

Exercise A: Which of the following groups of words are sentences?

1. Easily the best dancer in the troupe
2. Sleek, high-stepping horses parading around the track
3. A book about the history of Chicago
4. Eugene O'Neill, possibly the greatest playwright of the century
5. Representing the United States in the Olympic Games
6. An expert performer on the parallel bars
7. An interesting article about exchange students
8. Two men on base and Ken Giffey at bat
9. Speleologists explore caves
10. Has the yearbook gone to press

Exercise B: Writing Some of the following groups of words are not complete sentences. Identify these and make them into complete sentences. Write *Sentence* if the group is already a complete sentence.

1. Under a seven-foot snowdrift
2. By using a makeshift lever
3. Tapping his foot and moving his body in time to the music
4. Four flamingos stood in the yard
5. October, once considered the eighth month of the year

6. Documents filed in the drawer marked "Top Secret"
7. Water clocks, astrolabes, and sundials
8. Turn right at the corner of Main and Elmwood
9. Is the auditorium available on weekends
10. Sid Caesar and Imogene Coca, a comedy team

2.2 Kinds of Sentences

Sentences are classified in two ways. They are classified according to their structure* and according to their purpose.

1. The **declarative sentence** makes a statement of fact, intent, desire, or feeling.

   Plans for celebrating the millenium will be made throughout the 1990's.
   I wanted to read *The Discoverers* by Daniel Boorstin.

2. The **imperative sentence** is used to give a command, make a request, or give directions. Usually the subject of an imperative sentence is not expressed but is understood to be the pronoun *you*. An imperative sentence is usually followed by a period.

   (You) Take Route 88 for nine miles.
   (You) Get bedrest and drink plenty of liquids.

3. The **interrogative sentence** is used to ask a question. It is followed by a question mark.

   Who wrote *Billy Budd?*
   What is the temperature of the earth's interior?

4. The **exclamatory sentence** is used to express strong feeling. It is followed by an exclamation point.

   What a wonderful day that was!
   I was so mad!

---

*For classification of sentences by form, see Section 3.

Exercise A: What kind of sentence is each of the following?

1. Poe's life was short and tragic.
2. Go to the next corner and turn right.
3. Was the speed-reading course effective?
4. Help yourself to some pretzels.
5. How small these calculators are!
6. The first tourists to arrive will receive souvenirs.
7. Do exactly as I tell you.
8. It can't be midnight already!
9. This is a book you would enjoy.
10. What events are included in the decathlon?

Exercise B: Writing Identify the type of each sentence. Then rewrite each sentence to be the type indicated in parentheses.

1. The Olympic Games help promote international understanding. (interrogative)
2. Hand in the quizzes in five minutes. (declarative)
3. Leave the building by the nearest door. (exclamatory)
4. The new sports stadium may be reached by the interstate highway. (interrogative)
5. Will you throw off the mooring rope? (imperative)
6. Silica is a compound of silicon and oxygen. (interrogative)
7. Throw the swimmer a line. (exclamatory)
8. Is the Roman goddess Venus equivalent to the Greek goddess Aphrodite? (declarative)
9. Is this a good movie? (exclamatory)
10. Put that microphone back where you got it. (declarative)

2.3 Subject and Predicate

Every sentence can be divided into two parts. The **subject** is the person, place, thing, or idea about which something is said. The **predicate** is the idea expressed about the subject.

Every sentence contains a subject and a predicate.

The subject of the sentence is the person, place, thing, or idea about which something is said.

The predicate tells something or asks something about the subject of the sentence.

The predicate of a sentence proclaims, declares, affirms, denies, or asks something about the subject. The subject and the predicate together express a complete idea. Our definition of a sentence may now be expanded to include these points.

A sentence is a group of words expressing a complete thought by means of a subject and a predicate.

SUBJECT	PREDICATE
Water	evaporates.
Water	evaporates quickly in the hot sun.

2.4   The Simple Predicate

The most important word in the predicate is always the verb.

The simple predicate of a sentence is the verb.

The simple predicate, or verb, is sometimes a single word, such as *dance, brought, were.* At other times it is a phrase made up of a main verb and its auxiliaries: *will dance, have been brought, could have been.* If the words in the verb phrase are interrupted by a modifier, the modifier should not be considered part of the verb.

have probably *gone*   *had* just *eaten*
was never *questioned*   *had* almost *finished*

Two or more verbs may be joined by conjunctions, such as *and, but,* or *or.* Two verbs joined in this way are called a **compound verb.** The conjunction is not part of the verb.

They **stood** up *and* **cheered** spontaneously.
The union members **may** *either* **accept** *or* **reject** the contract.

2.5 The Simple Subject

To find the subject of a sentence, first identify the verb. Then form a question by placing *who* or *what* before the verb. The subject is the word or words that the verb tells about.

<table>
<tr><td>The sled crashed.</td><td>Scientists use nuclear energy.</td></tr>
<tr><td align="right">*Verb:* crashed</td><td align="right">*Verb:* use</td></tr>
<tr><td align="right">*What crashed?:* sled</td><td align="right">*Who uses?:* scientists</td></tr>
<tr><td align="right">*Subject:* sled</td><td align="right">*Subject:* scientists</td></tr>
</table>

Just as the most important word in the predicate is the simple predicate, so the most important word in the subject is called the **simple subject**. The complete subject includes the simple subject and its modifiers. The modifiers are not part of the simple subject.

Many passenger planes carry freight as well as people.

<table>
<tr><td align="right">VERB:</td><td>*carry*</td></tr>
<tr><td align="right">COMPLETE SUBJECT:</td><td>*Many passenger planes*</td></tr>
<tr><td align="right">SIMPLE SUBJECT:</td><td>*planes*</td></tr>
</table>

The inside of that shell looks like pearl.

<table>
<tr><td align="right">VERB:</td><td>*looks*</td></tr>
<tr><td align="right">COMPLETE SUBJECT:</td><td>*the inside of that shell*</td></tr>
<tr><td align="right">SIMPLE SUBJECT:</td><td>*inside*</td></tr>
</table>

In the second example, notice that *inside*, not *shell*, is the subject of the sentence. A subject is never found within a prepositional phrase.

Two or more subjects may be joined by a conjunction and share the same predicate. When subjects are joined in this way, they are called a **compound subject**.

Mood, rhythm, *and* **harmony** are aspects of music.

Television *and* **radio** are mass communication media.

Both **meaning** *and* **form** should be considered in analyzing a poem.

Diagraming. The simple subject and verb of a sentence are diagramed as follows.

Stars twinkle.

Stars | twinkle

Single-word modifiers are written on slanted lines below the words they modify.

Those tiny stars twinkle brightly.

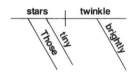

Exercise A: Find each verb and its simple subject. Watch for compound parts.

1. Morton High School, in Lowood, will soon be celebrating its centennial.
2. One comedian in that group always tells that old joke about the electric grape.
3. Both Jan and Bob work on the fourth floor of that office building.
4. Newsstands and bookstores throughout the country sell the book.
5. A good newspaper reporter checks the accuracy of all the facts of a story.
6. You can either come along or stay here.
7. Neither the young nor the old should be left out of family decisions.
8. Medical supplies and canned food were rushed to the blizzard area.
9. Yellow and red balloons filled the air after the team's victory.
10. Our retriever loves swimming in the lake and playing in the snow.

Exercise B: Write the complete subject and the complete predicate for each sentence on separate lines. Then underline the simple subject and the simple predicate (verb). Watch for compound parts.

1. Both philodendrons and palms need indirect sunlight.
2. The old model-A Ford sputtered, wheezed, and finally stopped cold.
3. A huge crowd and fair weather turned the first track meet into a big success.
4. A single drop of swamp water is teeming with microscopic life.
5. This television and that radio may be used with a nine-volt battery.
6. A professor of physics at the state university lives next door.
7. The make-up crew supplied the cast members with cold cream.
8. Several runners in the marathon injured themselves.
9. Jeans, sweaters, and hiking boots are sensible clothes for the trip.
10. Miriam and Teddy repair or replace defective bicycle parts.

2.6 Subjects in Unusual Positions

In most English sentences, the subject comes before the verb. There are, however, some common exceptions to this.

Questions. In most questions the subject appears between the words making up the verb phrase.

VERB	SUBJECT	VERB
Did	he	forget?
Has	she	returned?
Will	they	understand?

The subject also appears between parts of the verb phrase in questions that begin with the interrogative words *where, when, why, how,* or *how much.*

How much *do* I *owe* you?   When *shall* we *leave?*

When the interrogative pronoun *who* or *what* functions as the subject of the sentence, the subject precedes the verb.

Who thinks the answer is number 3?
What rhymes with "orange"?

Sentences Beginning with *There* and *Here*. In sentences that begin with *There* or *Here* followed by some form of *be, Here* and *There* are introductory words used to get the sentence started. They are never the subject of the verb. In this kind of sentence, the subject follows the verb.

Here is my idea. (*idea* is the subject.)
There are complex issues involved. (*issues* is the subject.)
There will be a flower show today. (*show* is the subject.)

Note: Not all sentences beginning with *Here* and *There* follow the above pattern: *Here we can build a campfire. Here he is. There he goes.* In these sentences, *Here* and *There* are adverbs modifying the verb.

Sentences in Inverted Order. A writer may place the subject after the verb to add variety.

Toward the cliff ran the frightened *boy.*
From his mistakes emerged my *victory.*

Finding the Subject of the Verb. To find the subject of a sentence, first identify the verb. Then form a question by placing *who* or *what* before the verb. If the sentence is in inverted order, rephrase it in normal order first.

INVERTED: Up from the field flew a family of pheasants.
NORMAL: A family of pheasants flew up from the field.

Exercise A: Find each verb and its simple subject.

1. There is an urgent need for dedicated volunteers.
2. Where is the school greenhouse located?
3. High into the air leaped the shortstop.
4. Here the embattled farmers stood.
5. How many gold medals did Eric Heiden win?
6. At 10 Downing Street lives the Prime Minister.
7. How do you make this dessert?
8. From all over the world came congratulatory telegrams.
9. There in front of us was an impassable ravine.
10. High above the valley moved a cable car.

Exercise B: Find the verb and its simple subject.

1. Directly behind me was the mayor.
2. Where are you going after the play?
3. Along the streets of Bern were tempting pastry shops.
4. Here are the books.
5. Straight between the goalie's skates shot the puck.
6. In the back of the theater were several dozen standees.
7. There have been several rumors about the appointment.
8. In the crowd were several Secret Service agents.
9. Why have you done this to me?
10. Overhead, roared the Air Force jets.

2.7 Complements

Words that come after the verb and complete its meaning are called **complements.**

SUBJECT	VERB	COMPLEMENT
Melanie	bought	a *trailer*
Grandfather	told	*us* the *legend*
The team	seemed	*disappointed*

These are three kinds of complements: **direct objects, indirect objects,** and **predicate words.**

2.8 The Direct Object

An action verb may transfer its action from the subject to another word in the sentence. The word to which the action is carried is called the **direct object**. The direct object completes the meaning of the verb.

The direct object is a word or group of words to which the verb carries over the action from the subject.

The direct object may either receive the action of the verb or express the result of the action.

RECEIVER OF ACTION:	The naturalist set a *trap*. (set what?)
RESULT OF ACTION:	The naturalist captured the *bird*. (captured what?)
RECEIVER OF ACTION:	Art carved the *ham*. (carved what?)
RESULT OF ACTION:	Art enjoyed the *ham*. (enjoyed what?)

The direct object may be a single word or a group of words.

SUBJECT	VERB	DIRECT OBJECT
The band	formed	a circle.
I	hope	to travel.
The tourists	enjoyed	seeing the giant redwoods.

A direct object may also be compound. In other words, it may be made up of two or more parts connected by conjunctions.

Kendra purchased *paper, books,* and *pencils*.
Tom likes *cereal* or *eggs* in the morning.

An action verb that has a direct object is called a **transitive verb.** An action verb without a direct object is called an **intransitive verb.** A verb may be transitive in one sentence and intransitive in another.

The hikers *whistled*. (intransitive)
The hikers *whistled* a merry *tune*. (transitive)

With some action verbs, the action is not visible, nor otherwise evident. However, the verb does carry the thought from subject to object, which makes the verb transitive.

> I *understand* your position. (understand what?)
> The stranger *appreciates* your help. (appreciates what?)
> Joanne *honored* my request. (honored what?)

Direct Object or Adverb? A direct object answers the question *what?* or *whom?* after an action verb. An adverb that follows an action verb answers the question *where, when, how,* or *to what extent* about the verb.

> The guerrillas crept *forward*. (where)
> Craig walked *stiffly* to the front of the room. (how)
> The elderly lady dropped the *letter* in the slot. (what)

Diagraming. A sentence with a direct objet is diagramed by writing the direct object on the horizontal line with the subject and verb. Separate the verb from the direct object with a vertical line that does *not* cross the horizontal line.

> Soldiers were peeling potatoes.

Soldiers	were peeling	potatoes

Exercise A: Find the direct objects in these sentences. Some may be compound.

1. Controllers tracked the aircraft with radar.
2. Trish liked the ending of the TV movie.
3. With five seconds left in the game, Dallas scored a touchdown.
4. This candy machine did not return my change.
5. For his term paper, Carl researched the life of Golda Meir.
6. At the beginning of each semester, students buy their books and other supplies.

7. Cars of all makes filled the lot.
8. Lynne gulped her milkshake and raced to class.
9. The local newspaper publicized our student talent show.
10. Ozone may have a damaging effect on the atmosphere.
11. Our canoe brigade followed the route of early explorers.
12. Several debaters captured top honors in the tournament.
13. Natalie likes Mel Gibson and Michael Jackson.
14. Andrea will study politics during a seminar in Washington.
15. Radio station WBEZ broadcasts programs about Hispanic culture.

Exercise B: Tell whether the italicized word in each sentence is a direct object or an adverb. Write what question each one answers about the verb.

1. The repairman arrived *late* in the afternoon.
2. The parachutist landed *inside* the marked target area.
3. Michele wrapped a *blanket* around her shoulders.
4. Henry tossed a *coin* into the wishing well.
5. Toni crossed the old bridge *carefully*.
6. The truck drove *east* all through the night.
7. Answer the *questions* in the spaces provided.
8. Talk *less* and do more.
9. The fans threw *confetti* after the team's victory.
10. Flames were leaping *up* from the basement windows.

2.9   The Indirect Object

An **indirect object** is a complement that tells *to* or *for whom* or *to* or *for what* the action of the verb was performed.

The indirect object of the verb precedes the direct object and tells *to* or *for whom*, or *to* or *for what*, something is done.

The manager promised *them* higher wages. (*to* them)
Dad bought *me* a new AM/FM radio. (*for* me)

The indirect object may be compound: I told *Jim* and *Carlotta* the truth.

The indirect object is never preceded by the words *to* or *for*. The words *to* and *for* are understood in an indirect object. If these words introduce a noun or pronoun, they are prepositions and the words that follow them are their objects.

> Lend *Bert* your compass. (*Bert* is the indirect object.)
> Ed lent his compass to *Bert*. (*Bert* is the object of the preposition.)

> The company offered *me* a job. (*me* is the indirect object.)
> The company offered a job to *me*. (*me* is the object of the preposition.)

Diagraming. An indirect object is written on a horizontal line below the verb. The two horizontal lines are connected with a slanted line.

Bret told Sarah a funny joke.

Exercise A: Find both the direct and indirect objects in these sentences. Some parts may be compound.

1. I loaned Alice a book about India.
2. My friend in Atlantic city sent me some salt-water taffy.
3. The committee gave their representative an expense account for the trip.
4. I'll give you and Emily a lift to the train station.
5. Thousands of readers send Ann Landers their problems.
6. Will the store give you a refund for the sweater?
7. The crash survivor told the reporters her story.
8. We offered Pat cash for his jeep.

9. The truck can give us a tow to the nearest gas station.
10. We mailed her pictures of our new house.
11. Sing us a song, Jean.
12. Gail Sheehy handed the reviewer a copy of her new book.
13. Mr. Briggs left his college a million dollars.
14. The coach gave us excellent training in hockey.
15. Barbara Walters asked Richard Pryor a question.

Exercise B: Writing. Rewrite each of the sentences below, changing the prepositional phrase in italics to an indirect object.

1. The country singer wrote a song *for his wife*.
2. The senior class gave a gift *to the school*.
3. Missionaries taught the Cyrillic alphabet *to the Eskimos*.
4. Grandmother was singing a Yiddish lullabye *to the baby*.
5. The principal handed diplomas *to the graduates*.
6. A research foundation gave a grant *to the young scientist*.
7. Mrs. Ramirez made a beautiful piñata *for the children*.
8. The employment service found a summer job *for Danny*.
9. My aunt sent postcards *to me* from China.
10. I told my version of the incident *to the officer*.

2.10 Predicate Words

The linking verb links its subject to a word in the predicate. The word in the predicate, so linked, is called a **predicate word.** The subject may be linked to a **predicate noun,** a **predicate pronoun,** or a **predicate adjective.**

Shakespeare was a great *dramatist*. (predicate noun)

The winner could have been *you*. (predicate pronoun)

The experiment seemed *easy*. (predicate adjective)

Because the predicate word refers back to the subject of the sentence, it is sometimes called a **subject complement.**

Diagraming. A predicate word is placed on the same line as the subject and verb. It is separated from the verb with a line that slants toward the subject.

Dad looks grim.   Pam is president.

Exercise A: Find the predicate words. Tell whether each is a predicate noun, a predicate pronoun, or a predicate adjective.

1. The Governor looked tired after his trip.
2. The idea for that scene was his.
3. These funnels are handy for pouring liquids.
4. The snow was deep in the driveway.
5. Bob will probably be an excellent teacher.
6. The Republicans' chances seemed promising.
7. Her wisdom became apparent.
8. Should this cream cheese taste so sour?
9. The Rocky Mountain bighorn is a wild sheep.
10. The best writer in our class is Barbara Brady.

Exercise B: Make five columns. Head them *Subject, Verb, Direct Object, Indirect Object,* and *Predicate Word.* Place those parts of the following sentences in the proper columns.

1. In the fog, the car hit a post.
2. She is a firm but fair disciplinarian.
3. Charles Dickens paid a visit to the United States.
4. The pizza smelled tantalizing in the oven.
5. The attendant gave us a new ping-pong ball.
6. Devora sent me a telegram from Los Angeles.
7. Dave's steer won a blue ribbon at the 4-H fair.
8. Many people regard autumn as their favorite season.
9. The pugilist dealt his opponent a savage blow.
10. Mr. Quinn paid Roseann twenty dollars for her old bike.

2.11 Compound Parts of Sentences

Subjects, predicates, verbs, objects, and predicate words may all be compound. That is, they may consist of more than one part *of the same kind*. The parts are joined by a conjunction.

COMPOUND SUBJECT:	Old *cars* and rusted *parts* clutter the junkyard.
COMPOUND PREDICATE:	Clare *turned off the television set* and *began her homework*.
COMPOUND VERB:	The sea *whirls* and *eddies*.
COMPOUND DIRECT OBJECT:	Volcanoes eject *lava* and *rocks*.
COMPOUND INDIRECT OBJECT:	Jim told *Tom* and *me* the news.
COMPOUND OBJECT OF PREPOSITION:	We talked about our *careers* and our *hopes*.
COMPOUND PREDICATE WORD:	He was *restless* and *fearful*.

Diagraming. Compound parts are diagramed as follows:

Max and Fern (*compound subject*) coughed and sneezed. (*compound verb*).

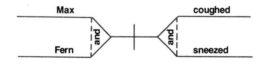

The rancher *roped* and *branded* (compound verb) the angry steer. (single complement shared by two verbs.)

The director gave Susan and I (*compound indirect object*) our scripts and costumes (*compound direct object*).

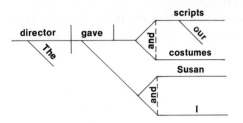

The opinions of the reporters and candidates (*compound object of preposition*) were diverse but pertinent (*compound predicate adjective*).

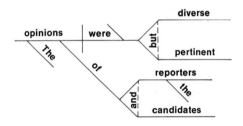

The class read the novel and evaluated the plot (*compound predicate*).

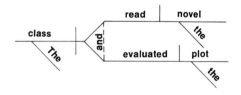

Exercise: Find the compound parts in the following sentences. Label them *Subject, Verb, Direct Object, Predicate Word,* and *Predicate*.

1. At the end of the pool were a seal and a walrus.
2. The lecturer discussed India and China.

483

3. Ann made the interception and scored the touchdown.
4. Our cheering section seemed listless and completely indifferent.
5. We were not only hungry but extremely tired.
6. Mitch tries but seldom succeeds.
7. Helping underdeveloped countries seems both charitable and practical.
8. Lee is a homemaker and a dietitian.
9. Marilyn loves golf but cannot play well at all.
10. On the table are two batteries and a new bulb.
11. Joe took the snowshoes, skis, and skates from the closet.
12. Walking toward us were the mayor and his assistant.
13. Bach, Mozart, and Beethoven were great composers.
14. A helicopter rushed food and supplies to the stranded mountain climbers.
15. The book and the pamphlets will give you information about fields of specialization.

2.12 The Phrase

A phrase is a group of words without a subject and a verb, used as one part of speech.

A verb phrase consists of two or more words that are used as a verb: *would have been, will run.* A noun phrase consists of two or more words that are used as a noun: *Yosemite National Park, Ohio Turnpike.* Groups of words may also be used as adjectives or adverbs.

2.13 The Prepositional Phrase

The prepositional phrase consists of the preposition, its object, and modifiers of the object.

Macbeth yielded to temptation *at his wife's persuasion.*
In our first football game, Carl played quarterback.

The object of a preposition is always a noun, a pronoun, or a group of words used as a noun.

The cottage is *near* the ocean. (*ocean* is the object of *near*.)

We lent our books *to* them. (*them* is the object of *to*.)

Law is a career *for* which I am qualified. (*which* is the object of *for*.)

By raising Mike's salary, Mr. Cook persuaded him to stay. (*raising Mike's salary* is a group of words used as a noun. It is the object of *By*.)

The merchants promised the plaque *to* whoever won three times. (*whoever won three times* is a group of words that functions as the object of *to*.)

Prepositional phrases act as modifiers. A prepositional phrase that modifies a noun or pronoun is an **adjective phrase.** An adjective phrase comes after the noun or pronoun it modifies.

Her car is the one *with the sun roof.* (*with the sun roof* modifies the pronoun *one*.)

The sound *of music* was heard. (*of music* modifies *sound*.)

Distrust *among nations* threatens peace. (*among nations* modifies *Distrust*.)

Note: Adjective phrases modify subjects, direct objects, indirect objects, and predicate words. Be careful not to confuse a noun or pronoun in an adjective phrase with the sentence part (subject, object, or predicate word) it modifies.

Five *of the rings* were missing. (*of the rings* modifies the subject, *Five*.)

Buy some *of these cookies.* (*of these cookies* modifies the direct object, *some*.)

When a prepositional phrase answers the question *where, when, how,* or *to what extent* it is called an **adverb phrase.** Like an adverb, it can modify a verb, adjective, or another adverb.

The letter was hidden *under some books*. (*under some books* tells *where* about the verb *was hidden*.)

The baby cries early *in the morning*. (*in the morning* tells *when* about the adverb *early*.)

The project was successful *beyond everyone's expectations*. (*beyond everyone's expectations* tells *to what extent* about the adjective *successful*.)

When two or more prepositional phrases follow each other in succession, they may modify the same word, or one phrase may modify the object in the preceding phrase.

We ate *at a diner after the show*. (Both phrases modify *ate; at a diner* tells *where* and *after the show* tells *when* about the verb.)

They analyzed the symbolism *in a novel about court intrigue in sixteenth-century England*. (*in a novel* modifies the noun *symbolism; about court intrigue* modifies *novel; in sixteenth-century England* modifies *intrigue*.)

Diagraming. Prepositional phrases are diagramed as follows:

Dom ordered a copy *of the book*. (adjective phrase)

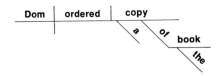

The season opens early *in the month*. (adverb phrase)

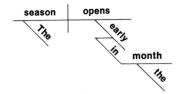

The ball went *over the fence*. (adverb phrase)

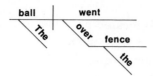

The stack *of books on China* got soaked. (adjective phrases)

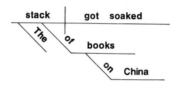

Exercise A: Write each prepositional phrase and the word or words it modifies.

1. There were newspaper clippings between the pages of the book.
2. I went to the office and got advice about my courses.
3. The manual with the green cover tells about simple home repairs.
4. Some forms of cancer have been checked.
5. Unbridled power in the hands of one person is always very dangerous.
6. The china on the shelf of the cupboard is very rare.
7. There was a feeling of unrest among the players.
8. All but one of these plants is a hybrid.
9. Cerebral palsy is high on the list of unsolved medical problems.
10. Each year in our country ten thousand children are born with injuries to the brain cells.

Exercise B: Write each prepositional phrase and the word or words it modifies.

1. Guatemala is located near Mexico.
2. Excavations at a prehistoric Mayan site began recently.
3. The excavations are in the Mayan jungle in Guatemala.
4. The area was occupied about 500 B.C.
5. Hieroglyphic writings were found on the stone slabs.
6. Most of the pottery was made between A.D. 200 and 900.
7. The Mayas excelled in astronomy and in mathematics.
8. Their pyramids tower over a cluster of smaller mounds.
9. The pyramids were used for the worship of the gods.
10. Workers in the field enjoy the mysteries of their work.

Exercise C: Writing Add prepositional phrases that supply the information asked for in parentheses.

1. The college is trying to raise funds for an archaeological excavation, or "dig." (where?)
2. A Labrador rescued the child. (where? how?)
3. Several divers searched the coral. (why?)
4. Terry Fox, a cancer victim, ran a "Marathon of Hope." (when?)
5. Construction on the new bridge should be completed. (when?)
6. The citrus crop blackened and rotted. (why?)
7. Some of the special effects were realistic. (where?)
8. The rally was canceled. (when? why?)
9. Beavers build dams and lodges. (where? why?)
10. Several artists completed the elaborate mural. (how?)

2.14 The Infinitive Phrase

You learned in Section 1 that an infinitive is a verbal that generally begins with the word *to: to laugh, to work, to appear.* Infinitives may have complements or be modified by adverbs or adverb phrases. An infinitive together with its complements and modifiers is called an **infinitive phrase.**

> to read voraciously
> to take dictation rapidly
> to find the Fountain of Youth

Adverbs or adverb phrases that modify an infinitive are part of the infinitive phrase.

> The captain had **to think** *logically.*
> I decided **to swim** *under the bridge.*

Note: Placing an adverb between the word *to* and the rest of the infinitive is an error called the **split infinitive.**

> NONSTANDARD: The class tried to profitably raise crops.
> STANDARD: The class tried to raise crops profitably.

Infinitives that are formed from action verbs may have direct objects and indirect objects. These complements are part of the infinitive phrase.

> Sandra wanted **to buy** *a new coat.*
> The school decided **to give** *Colette a scholarship.*

Infinitives that are made from linking verbs may have predicate words as complements. This kind of complement is also part of the infinitive phrase.

> Nicki resolved **to be** *a gymnast.*
> Try not **to be** *nervous.*

Infinitive phrases, like other phrases, are used as a single part of speech in sentences. When an infinitive phrase is used as a noun, it can serve as subject, object, or predicate word in the sentence.

> SUBJECT: *To establish priorities* was our purpose.
> OBJECT: The girls volunteered *to assist the elderly.*
> PREDICATE WORD: Janet's idea was *to start a company.*

Infinitive phrases may also be used as adjectives to modify nouns.

Dr. Kendall is the person *to see for contact lenses*.
What is the proper procedure *to use for this experiment?*

Infinitive phrases may also be used as adverbs to modify verbs, adjectives, and other adverbs.

We visited the aquarium *to see the coral reef exhibit*.
(The infinitive phrase modifies the verb *visited*.)

These nuts are difficult *to crack open*.
(The infinitive phrase modifies the adjective, *difficult*.)

Paula and Ken were brave enough *to go into the cave*.
(The infinitive phrase modifies the adverb, *enough*.)

Diagraming. The infinitive phrase is diagramed as follows:

Millie hoped to see a good play soon.

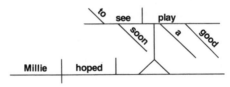

To resolve the controversial issue was very difficult.

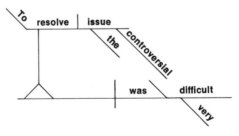

Exercise A: Find the infinitive phrases in the sentences below.

1. The man wanted to cash a check.
2. We went to see the African exhibit at the museum.
3. She visited the library to find out about her ancestors.
4. One recruit needed assistance to finish the obstacle course.

5. To work hard is to be happy.
6. The professor was happy to hear from his old student.
7. I have work to do.
8. It is too late to start over now.
9. The doctor appeared ready to leave.
10. The team went to Clinton to debate on foreign relations.
11. I asked permission to work in the library.
12. The dramatic club has decided to present *Our Town*.
13. The lead needed time to meditate about his part.
14. To be a good conversationalist is to be a good listener.
15. The need to talk to someone became overwhelming.

Exercise B: Find the infinitive phrase in each sentence below. Label each as *Subject, Direct Object, Predicate Word*, or *Modifier*. If the phrase is a modifier, indicate what word it modifies.

1. A good writer attempts to state ideas clearly.
2. Which is the best course to follow?
3. Jess has finally decided to get a haircut.
4. We could take a plane instead of the train to save time.
5. To pilot a boat safely requires practice.
6. Would you like to live in Australia?
7. Janine's instructions were to whistle three times.
8. The citizens voted for a pageant to be held on Washington's Birthday.
9. My advice is to buy new skates.
10. Grover Cleveland is the only President to serve two nonconsecutive terms.

Exercise C: Find and correct the split infinitive in each sentence.

1. To thoroughly master an instrument takes years of total dedication.
2. Katy tries to occasionally say something nice about her younger sister Janine.
3. Rusty decided to finally finish his project.
4. Mother tried to quickly hide the presents.
5. Lanie started to carefully sign her name.

2.15   The Participial Phrase

Participles are verbals that are used as adjectives. Participles usually end in *-ing, -ed, -d, -t,* or *-en:* a *whistling* kettle, a *babbling* brook, a *broken* toy, a *hurried* decision.

Participles may have complements and modifiers. A participle together with its modifiers and complements is called a **participial phrase.**

When an adverb, phrase, or clause modifies a participle, the modifier is part of the participial phrase.

> *Listening attentively,* we heard the plane approaching.
> (*attentively* is an adverb modifying *Listening.*)

> *Driving without a license,* Jim got into trouble.
> (*without a license* is a phrase modifying *Driving.*)

When a direct object, indirect object, or predicate word is used as a complement to a participle, the complement is part of the participial phrase. In the examples below, the arrows indicate the words modified by the participial phrases.

> *Having found our way,* we continued the hike.
> (*way* is the direct object of *Having found.*)

> The children sat on the front steps, *looking forlorn.*
> (*forlorn* is a predicate adjective completing *looking.*)

> *Giving her horse a pep talk,* the jockey rode toward the starting gate.
> (*horse* is the indirect object and *pep talk* is the direct object of *Giving*)

Participial phrases modify nouns, pronouns, and words used as nouns.

> *Hindered in their journey by rough terrain,* the hikers decided to camp for the night.
> (The participial phrase modifies the noun, *hikers.*)

Thrown from a horse at age six, he did not want to ride again.

(The participial phrase modifies the pronoun, *he.*)

Usually it is best to place a participle or a participial phrase as close as possible to the word it modifies. If a participle or participial phrase is misplaced, it may modify the wrong word. This error is called a **dangling participle.**

DANGLING PARTICIPLE: *Flitting merrily from branch to branch,* the old tom cat watched the brilliantly-colored cardinals.

REVISION: The old tom cat watched the brilliantly-colored cardinals *flitting merrily from branch to branch.*

Diagraming. The participle and the participial phrase are diagramed as follows:

Quickly calculating the risk, he scaled the wall.

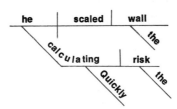

Jorge observed the full moon rising majestically in the east.

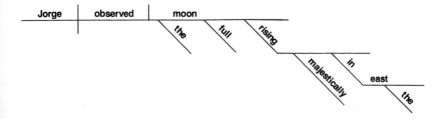

Exercise A: Find the participial phrases. Tell the word each phrase modifies. Remember that phrases may be made from past participles or present participles.

1. Pushing hard, he managed to move the trunk an inch.
2. The boy wearing the red jacket is Larry.
3. Living in Chevy Chase, she was within easy reach of the capital.
4. Guided by radar, the pilot kept in the proper lane.
5. Convinced of her client's innocence, the defense attorney worked harder than ever.
6. A film well liked by people of all ages is Disney's *Fantasia*.
7. Seen through a telescope, the sun is a ball of fiery gases.
8. Every night we could hear the waves lapping on the beach.
9. Never having eaten spumoni before, I didn't know what to expect.
10. Having conquered the world's highest peak, Edmund Hillary was knighted by Queen Elizabeth.
11. Exhausted from the climb, the hikers lay down to rest.
12. Having become more than just work clothes, blue jeans are now made to fit everyone.
13. Shut off from navigation, Africa had been difficult to explore.
14. Called "the man of the century," Albert Schweitzer gave unselfishly of himself.
15. Enriched by words from ancient and modern tongues, the English language is extraordinarily expressive.

Exercise B: Find the dangling participle in each sentence. Rewrite the sentence to correct the error.

1. Slapping its flippers against the wall, the zoo visitor held out a fish to the seal.
2. Executing a perfect swan dive from the high board, the old man watched his granddaughter with pride.

3. The Model T Ford was still being driven by its original owner, rattling and wheezing down the road.
4. Waterlogged from centuries underwater, the salvage team examined the sunken ship.
5. Lying under the refrigerator, Marian spied her lost wallet.

2.16 The Gerund Phrase

A gerund is a verbal that ends in *-ing: writing, imagining, skiing.* A gerund is always used as a noun. Like other verbals, gerunds may have modifiers or complements. A gerund together with its modifiers and complements is called a **gerund phrase.** Like a gerund, a gerund phrase is always used as a noun.

Gerunds may be modified by both adverbs and adjectives. These modifiers may be single words or groups of words. When an adjective, an adverb, or a phrase is used to modify a gerund, it is part of the gerund phrase.

> *Practicing devotedly* brought Heddie success in golf.
> (*devotedly* is an adverb modifying the gerund, *Practicing.*)
> *Deep-sea diving* was Richard's hobby.
> (*Deep-sea* is an adjective modifying the gerund, *diving.*)
> Funds were allocated for *exploring under the ice cap.*
> (*under the ice cap* is a phrase modifying the gerund, *exploring.*)

Gerunds may also have objects and predicate words as complements. These complements, too, are part of the gerund phrase.

> *Planning a career* requires foresight.
> (*career* is the object of the gerund, *Planning.*)
> Ralph enjoys *being chairman.*
> (*chairman* is a predicate word completing the gerund, *being.*)

The gerund phrase, like the gerund, is always used as a noun. A gerund phrase may be a subject, an object, or a predicate word.

SUBJECT: *Staying up all night* can make you sick.

DIRECT OBJECT: Lonnie finished *assembling the amplifier.*

PREDICATE WORD: Mary's favorite form of relaxation is *going to the movies.*

OBJECT OF THE PREPOSITION: Lloyd earned money by *mowing his neighbors' lawns.*

Diagraming. The gerund and the gerund phrase are diagramed as follows:

Sailing is great fun.

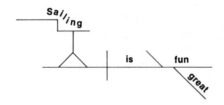

Careful checking revealed the mistake.

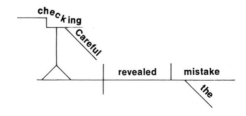

They began sorting the shells.

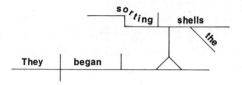

After returning from the swim, we feasted.

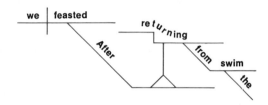

Exercise A: Find the gerund phrases.

1. Kate surprised us all by winning the athletic scholarship.
2. Directing a play is a complex job.
3. The course requires reading many plays.
4. Working in the hot sun was difficult.
5. He found excitement in using a powerful telescope.
6. Driving to the top of Mt. Palomar was interesting.
7. I enjoyed watching the sunset at Palm Springs.
8. Competing as a speaker gave Charles confidence.
9. Knowing where to look makes research easy.
10. Rehearsing the play occupies Janet's time after school.

Exercise B: Identify each gerund phrase and tell whether it is used as a subject, direct object, object of a preposition, or predicate word.

1. Before writing your essay, you should make an outline.
2. Running a summer camp requires extensive planning.
3. The marine biologist loved exploring coral reefs.

4. His alternatives were going to summer school or postponing graduation.
5. A law forbids smoking on public transportation.
6. By catching the biggest fish, Dana won the competition.
7. Candy's jobs were stacking wood and washing the dishes.
8. Standing around all day will not get the job done.
9. The Handlers offered a reward for finding their cat, Ginger.
10. I prefer making my own clothes to buying them in clothing stores.

Exercise C: Find the infinitive, gerund, and participial phrases. Label each phrase.

1. Spectators admired the sporty speedboat cutting through the water.
2. In college Beth decided to specialize in nuclear physics.
3. Several people claim to have seen the Loch Ness monster.
4. Having studied bookplates, Katy was able to design one for the school library.
5. The drama portrayed a person hardened by power.
6. The Secretary of State hopes to negotiate a Middle East peace settlement.
7. By having been alert to a previous court decision, the lawyer won the case.
8. We want to see the sunrise at Bryce Canyon.
9. This old house, defying wind and weather, has stood here for two hundred years.
10. For serving as manager of the team, Leslie received a special award.

2.17   The Appositive Phrase

An **appositive** is a word placed immediately after a noun or pronoun to identify it or further explain it. An appositive is set off by a comma or a pair of commas.

That book was written by my literary idol, *William Faulkner*.

Jodie Foster, *the actress*, began performing as a child.

An **appositive phrase** is a group of words that acts as an appositive. The phrase consists of the appositive and its modifiers, which may in turn be phrases or clauses.

The fair, *an eagerly awaited annual event*, attracts thousands of people.

The principal presented the trophy, *a tall silver cup with handles*.

Note: A compound personal pronoun, such as *myself* and *yourself*, is not an appositive and should not be set off by commas: The superintendent *herself* was not available for comment.

Diagraming. The appositive is diagramed as follows:

The author, a dynamic speaker, lectured about UFO's.

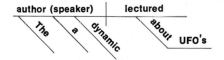

2.18   A Review of Diagraming

Sentences in English are composed according to certain specific patterns. Diagraming is a useful way to help you visualize these patterns. A diagram shows which words in a sentence are grouped together and how the various groups are related to one another.

A simple sentence consists of a subject-verb-complement arrangement. These words are placed on a base line. If there is an indirect object, it is placed on a line below the verb.

The introductory word *There* or *Here* is placed above the base line, as in the following diagram. Note the slant line after the linking verb.

The subject of an imperative sentence, *you* (understood), is placed in parentheses, as follows:

| (You) | Verb | Direct Object |

A single-word modifier is placed on a slant line below the word it modifies. An adverb modifying an adjective or adverb is placed as shown below.

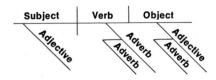

The prepositional phrase is attached to the word it modifies, as follows:

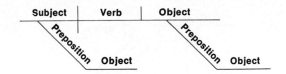

The infinitive phrase is shown in this way:

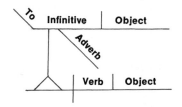

The participial phrase is shown as follows:

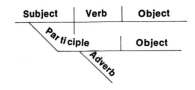

The gerund phrase is placed above the base line unless it is the object of a preposition

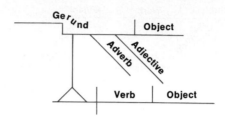

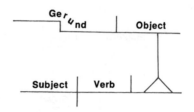

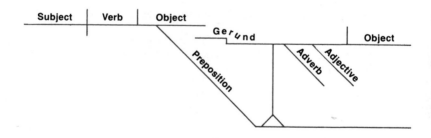

2.19   The Basic Sentence Patterns

You have seen that sentences can be made up of many different types of word groups put together in an infinite variety of ways. However, this infinite variety can be reduced to a few simple patterns from which most English sentences are derived. In fact, most sentences follow one of seven **basic sentence patterns.** Learning these patterns will help you to understand more clearly how your language works.

Pattern One

N	V	(ADVERB OR PREPOSITIONAL PHRASE)
An alarm	sounded.	
The guests	have arrived.	
A kite	sailed	overhead.
The President	responded	to our questions.
Michael Jackson	is coming	to Philadelphia.

Sentences that follow Pattern One consist of a noun *(N)* followed by a verb *(V)*. Frequently, the pattern is completed by an adverb or a prepositional phrase. Verbs in Pattern One sentences are *intransitive verbs*.

Note: In many of these patterns, you will find pronouns, gerunds, and infinitives in columns labeled *N*. Keep in mind that these words may be used as nouns.

Pattern Two

N	V	N
Juan	wrote	the poem.
We	will repair	the canoe.
Sandi	returned	the serve.
The artist	painted	a self-portrait.
Love	conquers	all.

The verbs in Pattern Two sentences are *transitive verbs*. The noun following the verb in this pattern is a *direct object*. The transitive verb carries the action in the sentence over from the subject to the object.

Most of the thousands of transitive verbs in English occur only in Pattern Two sentences. However, some transitive verbs occur in sentences that have two nouns following the verb. Such sentences are shown in Pattern Three and in Pattern Seven.

Pattern Three

N	V	N	N
The guide	gave	us	a tour.
Yolanda	loaned	Loretta	her calculator.
We	are sending	you	a gift.
The teacher	told	his students	a story.

In Pattern Three sentences, the first noun following the verb is the *indirect object;* the second noun is the *direct object.* The two nouns refer to different people or things. Remember this when you examine the Pattern Seven sentences.

Pattern Four

N	LV	N
Maria	will become	our leader.
Conifers	are	evergreens.
The play	is	a comedy.
Paul	remains	my friend.

Be, become, and *remain* are the verbs most often used in Pattern Four sentences. They are *linking verbs (LV)*. The noun following the linking verb in a Pattern Four sentence is a *predicate noun*. The predicate noun and the subject are connected by the linking verb, and refer to the *same* person or thing.

Pattern Two, which has a similar form *(N-V-N)*, uses transitive verbs and the two nouns refer to *different* people or things.

In the sentences below, notice how the noun relationship changes when a linking verb becomes a transitive verb:

> The playwright was the director. (N-LV-N)
> The playwright chose the director. (N-V-N)
> Her niece has become an architect. (N-LV-N)
> Her niece consulted an architect. (N-V-N)

Pattern Five

N	LV	ADJ
Videos	are	popular.
Nothing	is	certain.
Mr. Walters	appeared	concerned.
The salad	tasted	wonderful.

Verbs in Pattern Five sentences are also linking verbs. The most common ones in this pattern are *be, seem,* and *become.*

The adjective *(Adj.)* following the verb in this pattern is a *predicate adjective.* This word further describes the noun and is connected to it by the linking verb.

Pattern Six

N	LV	ADV
A counselor	will be	there.
The trial	was	yesterday.
They	are	at the movies.
Janet	is	in the lead.

The verb in a Pattern Six sentence is always some form of the linking verb *be,* such as *am, is, are, were, be, being,* or *been.*

The adverb *(Adv.)* or adverbial phrase that follows the linking verb refers to time or place. Adverbs such as *loudly, carefully, wildly,* never occur in this pattern (See Pattern One).

Pattern Seven

N	V	N	N
The officials	declared	the race	a tie.
Practice	will make	you	an expert.
Mike	considers	vacations	a luxury.
Our class	elected	Luis	president.
They	named	the hamster	Herman.

Both Pattern Three and Pattern Seven sentences have the same order: noun-verb-noun-noun. The difference is that the two nouns following the verb in Pattern Three sentences refer to different people or things. The first noun following the verb in Pattern Three is called the *indirect object;* the second noun is the *direct object.* The nouns following the verb in Pattern Seven sentences, however, refer to the same person or thing. The first noun following the verb in Pattern Seven is the direct object, while the second noun is an *object complement.*

With some of the verbs that occur in Pattern Seven, an adjective can replace the second noun.

> The critics made the play a success.
> The critics made the play successful.

English sentences are seldom as simple as the basic sentences listed above. In order to convey meaning adequately, we usually need to expand the basic patterns by adding modifiers and more complicated constructions. No matter how complicated or how long a sentence becomes, however, it will always have one of the basic patterns as a foundation.

Exercise A: Identify the sentence pattern in each sentence.

1. Bats were hanging from the rafters.
2. The spy remained loyal.
3. The committee appointed Mr. Sanchez chairman.
4. A priest led the procession.
5. The dog is outside.

6. The boss offered Terri a raise.
7. Adrienne waxed the car.
8. The show was a disaster.
9. We considered ourselves rich.
10. The ruins were discovered recently.

Exercise B: Write two different sentences that follow each of the sentence patterns listed below.

1. Noun   Verb
2. Noun   Verb   Noun
3. Noun   Verb   Noun   Noun
4. Noun   Linking Verb   Noun
5. Noun   Linking Verb   Adjective

Exercise C: Writing You are given a sentence that follows one sentence pattern. Identify this pattern. Then, rewrite the sentence so that it follows the sentence pattern in parentheses.

1. Andy sent a postcard. (N-V-N-N)
2. The canary was frightened by the cat. (N-V-N)
3. The trip ended tragically. (N-LV-N)
4. A jalopy passed by us. (N-V-N)
5. The symbols have meanings. (N-LV-ADJ)
6. My grandfather swam the channel. (N-V)
7. Anne is a student of chemistry. (N-V-N)
8. Our team won. (N-V-N)
9. The plan succeeded. (N-LV-N)
10. The Smiths named their child. (N-V-N-N)

REINFORCEMENT EXERCISES

The Parts of a Sentence

A. Write complete sentences. If any of the groups of words below are sentences, write *S*. If they are not sentences, make them into sentences by adding appropriate words.

1. The first heart transplant in a human
2. One boxer who earned the nickname of "Rocky"
3. Will use lasers for many specialized purposes
4. Many lives were lost in Death Valley
5. The space shuttle *Challenger* with Sally Ride on board
6. Lead ore, which is mined in Canada, the United States, and Mexico
7. Ate the pizza, ice cream, and cakes
8. A chronometer is any instrument that measures time
9. Stonewall Jackson, the Confederate General
10. Was earning less that he was worth

B. Write different kinds of sentences. Tell whether each of the following sentences is declarative, interrogative, exclamatory, or imperative. Then rewrite the sentence to be the type indicated in parentheses.

1. Fudge is the most popular of all soft candies. (interrogative)
2. Deliver the parcel today before the 3:00 conference. (declarative)
3. What a brilliant idea that music festival was! (declarative)
4. Did the committee lower the entry fees for this year? (imperative)
5. Mayan astronomers developed an accurate calendar sometime around A.D. 300. (interrogative)
6. You may use this code to gain access to my computer program. (imperative)
7. Have they discovered the secret entrance to the pyramid? (exclamatory)

8. Did Pablo Casals perform *Suites for Unaccompanied Cello* at the concert? (declarative)
9. A marionette is a string puppet with moving joints. (interrogative)
10. Cover the clay with a moist cloth when you are finished for the day. (interrogative)

C. Identify the verb and its simple subject. Find the verb and its simple subject in each of the following sentences. The verb or the subject may be compound.

1. The author wrote a novel and published it herself.
2. Eleanor Roosevelt and Betty Ford were both extremely popular First Ladies.
3. The ptarmigan is closely related to the grouse.
4. Frank Lloyd Wright and Walter Gropius developed unique architectural styles.
5. The *Hindenburg* exploded and burned in front of hundreds of spectators.
6. Deer can eat and digest lily pads.
7. The one-armed Pete Gray played baseball for the St. Louis Browns.
8. The Republic of Panama became independent in 1903.
9. The "unsinkable" *Titanic* struck an iceberg and sank.
10. King James was not the translator of the King James Bible.

D. Find subjects and verbs in unusual positions. For each sentence below, find the verb and its simple subject.

1. Was the Coast Guard started in the eighteenth century?
2. Beside Mary Decker ran her trainer.
3. From the valley below came the mysterious, shimmering lights of the ceremonial fires.
4. Beyond the reach of the spelunkers dangled the rope.
5. There had been one hundred six students in the senior class at Central High School.
6. Did Hahn and Strassmann achieve the fission of uranium?

7. Outside the circle of dancers stood the chief shaman.
8. Here are the first folios of Shakespeare's plays.
9. In plain view were the lost keys to the briefcase.
10. Are we expecting record-breaking colds this winter?

E. Identify objects and predicate words. Find direct objects, indirect objects, and predicate words in the following sentences. Label each part.

1. The supervisor gave our crew a difficult assignment.
2. Sharks store oil in their livers.
3. Chef Jean-Claude prepared the menu for the evening.
4. Fires are a common source of property damage.
5. Dad made the Friedmans their favorite dinner.
6. Harriet Beecher Stowe wrote *Uncle Tom's Cabin*.
7. The court offered the juvenile a second chance.
8. Laika was the dog who orbited in *Sputnik 2*.
9. The Academy gave Clark Gable an Oscar in 1934.
10. Sprouts are a crop even apartment-dwellers can grow.

F. Find compound parts. Find the compound sentence parts in the following sentences. Label them *Subject, Verb, Direct Object, Indirect Object,* or *Predicate Word*.

1. Percival Lowell was an astronomer and the brother of Amy Lowell, the poet.
2. The contract offered workers and management equal pay.
3. Old English and Middle English are markedly different.
4. Natives of Samoa wear Western clothing and traditional *lava-lavas*.
5. Christopher's nicknames were *Chris* and *Kit*.
6. The Highlander placed the plaid over his left shoulder and fastened it with a brooch.
7. Jeans, sweatshirts, and sneakers are what Cindy wore.
8. Walk or take the bus to the fairgrounds.
9. Lenses focus light and heat to a small area.
10. Neither San Antonio nor Lubbock is a coastal city.

G. Use prepositional phrases. To each sentence add the type of prepositional phrase indicated in parentheses. Circle the word each phrase modifies and underline any additional prepositional phrases.

1. The actress shuddered and dropped the poison into the cup. (adjective)
2. The race car spun out of control and crashed. (adverb)
3. Reverberations from the explosion were heard. (adverb)
4. A barrel of rain water stood behind the door. (adjective)
5. Contestants received a sheet of official rules and were told to meet at 10:00. (adjective)
6. School children gathered apples and brought them to the roadside stands. (adverb)
7. "You have jumped out of the fire and into the frying pan," said the witty officer. (adverb)
8. Some lithographers make pictures on stone; others print pictures with stone. (adjective)
9. Bread for sandwiches was stacked on the table. (adjective)
10. Smoke rose and warned the rangers of the forest fire. (adverb)

H. Identify verbal phrases. Find the infinitives, participial, and gerund phrases in the following sentences. Label each phrase. Some sentences may contain more than one type of verbal phrase.

1. Spectators watched the seals diving through the icy water and playing with the beach balls.
2. Nineteenth century doctors practiced bloodletting as a way of curing disease.
3. The customer was too angry to hear the saleswoman's earnest apology.
4. To photocopy multiple pages of a book could be against copyright laws.
5. Jogging five miles each day kept Mr. Nahser in shape.
6. The guide said that the Tower of Pisa, leaning at a dangerous angle, would eventually fall.
7. The sparrows, sensing the danger posed by the cat, began to chirp noisily.

8. Chad learned to compare prices by shopping without purchasing anything.
9. To become a veterinarian, you must attend college for six years.
10. Robby's idea of a perfect morning is catching trout, preparing them, and eating them for breakfast.

I. Use appositive phrases. Rewrite the sentences given below, changing the second sentence of each pair into an appositive phrase.

1. The atom bomb was tested in Bikini. Bikini is an island on the northwest end of the Ratak chain.
2. Yale College was named after a man who contributed money and books to the school. That man was Elihu Yale of Boston.
3. Aunt Jody collects albums by Bob Marley and the Wailers. They are a reggae band.
4. The train passed through Moffat Tunnel. It is one of the longest railroad tunnels in the world.
5. The Atlantic halibut may weigh four hundred pounds. The halibut is a flatfish with both eyes on one side of its head.
6. Kirstin decorated the room in Biedermeier. Biedermeier is a style of German furniture.
7. The Delaware were moved to Indian Territory. The Delaware were an Eastern Woodlands tribe.
8. The *Nautilus* and *Skate* traveled under the ice to the North Pole. They were U.S. submarines.
9. That type of goat provides wool. It is an Angora from Turkey.
10. Benjamin Disraeli wrote *Sybil*. He was a famous British statesman.

MIXED REVIEW

The Parts of a Sentence

A. Make six columns. Head them *Subject, Verb, Direct Object, Indirect Object, Predicate Word,* and *Prepositional Phrase.* Place the parts of the following sentences in the proper columns. Not every sentence will contain all six parts, but some of the parts may be compound.

1. The dragonfly has transparent wings and a slender body.
2. Giovanni de Verrazano may have named Rhode Island after the Isle of Rhodes in 1524.
3. Copyrights guarantee artists and authors control over the reproduction of their works.
4. Gullah is a mixture of English and African.
5. After the premier of his latest film, the star suddenly left.
6. Joseph Montgolfier and his brother designed the first successful hot-air balloon in 1783.
7. Photographers use dramatic lighting and unusual angles for special effects.
8. Carol Burnett told the audience a hilarious story.
9. The school cafeteria occasionally uses vegetable protein in its burgers.
10. Christy and her two brothers arranged a surprise party for their parents' anniversary.
11. The natural habitats of wolves are forests, tundra, and prairies.
12. The governor promised his constituents lower taxes and a balanced budget.
13. Professor Reising read her class excerpts from *Walden*.
14. The pronghorns leaped and ran across the dry plains.
15. The official explorers of the Northwest Territory were Merriwether Lewis and William Clark.
16. The magician performed her tricks with dexterity and humor.
17. Franklin Delano Roosevelt ran for President four times and won four times.

18. Maud and Mattie are nicknames for Matilda.
19. Uncle Marty handed my sister and me our party hats.
20. Bryce Canyon and Capitol Reef are parks in Utah.

B. Identify the verbal phrases and the appositive phrases in the following sentences. Tell what kind each verbal phrase is, and whether it functions as a subject, object, or modifier.

1. Sequoya, a Cherokee Indian, developed an alphabet to represent the spoken Cherokee language.
2. Admired for its mountains, Switzerland offers it visitors hiking, skiing, and mountain climbing.
3. The pillory, an instrument of punishment, was used by the Puritans to humiliate wrong-doers.
4. My brother Carl is too conscientious to take shortcuts in doing his homework.
5. John L. Lewis, head of the United Mine Workers, led a strike by appearing on the picket line with the miners.
6. Burt's reason for saving his pay was to attend the international peace conference.
7. Annie Dillard, the author of numerous essays, often uses vivid imagery to create a mood of beauty and serenity.
8. Launching the satellite was the major task of the shuttle crew.
9. Plugging in his word processor, Mr. Gadfrey began to work on his spy novel.
10. Loren planned to visit Kumasi, a city in the Ashanti region of Ghana.
11. Working on a proof of Fermat's last theorem was the final project of the computer club.
12. Heaving the discus, Bob Mathias went on to win a gold medal.
13. To believe in numerology or palm reading is no longer considered rational.
14. Researchers worked night and day to discover the source of the epidemic.
15. The spring garden, looking like a picture from a children's book, bloomed radiantly in the morning sun.

USING GRAMMAR IN WRITING
The Parts of a Sentence

A. Sentence variety can add excitement and interest to a piece of writing. Find a short newspaper article that describes some interesting event or incident. The article should be one that has been written objectively with short, straightforward sentences. Now rewrite the article, turning it into a more personal and subjective account. In other words, bring a dry story to life. Use as many of the following devices as possible:

> Vary sentence length
> Vary the types of sentences
> Use unusual subject-verb order
> Begin sentences with prepositional phrases
> Expand or combine sentences by using compound parts
> Add prepositional and verbal phrases
> Use appositives

B. The skeleton of a story is given below. Each of the sentences provided has a subject, a predicate, and some modifiers. Expand the sentences and finish the story by adding your own infinitive, participial, appositive, gerund, or prepositional phrases.

> The day was ending.
> Night came on quickly.
> The cyclists could not stop yet.
> Rain fell.
> The cyclists stopped.
> Each cyclist put on waterproof pants and a jacket.
> Soon the bikes were moving again.
> Home was at the end of the road.

3.0 Sentence and Clause

You have already learned about four kinds of sentences: *declarative, imperative, interrogative,* and *exclamatory.* These terms are useful for identifying the purpose that a writer had when he or she composed a sentence. These classifications also determine the punctuation at the end of the sentence.

Sentences may be classified according to form as well. In this Section you will learn about the three basic sentence forms: the *simple sentence,* the *compound sentence,* and the *complex sentence.* A fourth form, the *compound-complex sentence,* is a combination of two of the basic forms.

3.1 The Simple Sentence

A simple sentence contains only one subject and predicate. Both the subject and the predicate may be compound.

You will recall that *compound* means having two or more similar parts.

COMPOUND SUBJECT: The *designer* of the car and the *consultant* worked together for many months. (The designer worked; the consultant worked.)

COMPOUND PREDICATE: I *located* the leak and *called* the plumber. (I located; I called.)

COMPOUND SUBJECT AND PREDICATE: Faculty *advisers* and student *officers* of the various organizations *discussed the problem* and *arrived at a solution.* (Advisers and officers discussed; advisers and officers arrived.)

The examples given above are all simple sentences. The first has a compound subject and one predicate; the second has one subject and a compound predicate; the third has a compound subject and a compound predicate. A sentence can be long and still be a simple sentence in form. Simple sentences have only one subject-verb connection.

The sentence below, has two subjects and two predicates. Each subject has a separate predicate. It is not a simple sentence because there is more than one subject-verb connection.

        s.   **v.**   **s.**   **v.**

The reporters shouted questions; the President answered.

The Compound Predicate. The compound predicate is extremely useful in writing clear, smooth sentences. Two separate sentences can be combined using this construction.

The compound predicate consists of two verbs having the same subject.

> The earthquake *destroyed* the city and *left* thousands homeless.
> Both of his children *studied* hard and *won* scholarships.

Exercise A: Identify the compound subjects and compound predicates in the following sentences.

1. The roses and the carnations were in the same vase.
2. For five hours I read the material and took notes.
3. Lightning and thunder preceded the thunderstorm.
4. The young performer sang and danced his way to fame.
5. After takeoff, the airplane faltered and dove.
6. The turtle lays her eggs and never gives the next generation a backward glance.
7. The lake and the mountain behind it were beautiful.
8. Scott brought his permission slip but forgot his money.
9. Car pools always save fuel and often promote friendships.
10. Robert Redford and Woody Allen act in movies and direct them, too.

Exercise B: Writing Rewrite the following sentences making either the subject or the predicate compound.

1. In her campaign speech, Jennifer spoke of the school's problems. She promised to take action.
2. Killer whales hunt in packs. Killer whales are a threat to other creatures of the sea.
3. Decaying leaves make the soil rich. Animal matter makes the soil rich, too.
4. Ostrich eggs are as big as grapefruits. The eggs weigh two to three pounds.
5. Environmentalists object to using animal skins for fur coats. Animal-lovers object to this practice as well.
6. The Sierra Club protects wildlife. The Sierra Club also promotes ecological concerns.
7. The roller coaster swooped. It soared. It screeched around its twisting tracks.
8. The anteater rips anthills open with its powerful claws. The animal then removes the ants with its long tongue.
9. Koala bears always smell of eucalyptus. They always wear an expression of injured dignity.
10. Birds have backbones and are called vertebrates. Reptiles and mammals also have backbones and are called vertebrates.

3.2 The Compound Sentence

The compound sentence consists of two or more simple sentences put together.

The parts of a compound sentence may be put together in either of two ways: (1) with a comma followed by a coordinating conjunction (*and, but, or, for, nor*) (2) with a semicolon.

> The plan seemed feasible, *but* I still felt unsure.
> José joined the drama club; Sheila preferred the debating club.

I understood his problem, *for* I had once faced it myself.
Mary could not remember where she had left her music,
   nor could her friends help her.
Pierre knows Paris well; he was born there.
The plane made a forced landing, *and* a crowd gathered
   quickly.

The parts of a compound sentence may also be joined by a
conjunctive adverb such as *then, however, moreover, hence,
consequently,* and *therefore.* The conjunctive adverb is preceded by a semicolon and followed by a comma.

All the polls predicted a Dewey victory in 1948; *however,*
   Truman won.
Read the directions carefully; *then* begin the examination.

Diagraming. The compound sentence is diagramed on two
parallel base lines as follows:

The door was partially open, so we walked in.

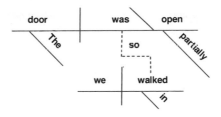

The announcer repeated the news; the story stunned us
completely.

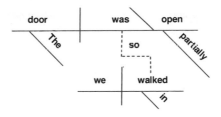

Compound Sentences and Compound Predicates. In the compound predicate every verb has the same subject. In the compound sentence, each verb has a different subject. Diagrams make this difference more apparent.

SIMPLE SENTENCE WITH COMPOUND PREDICATE:

They accepted my story and published it.

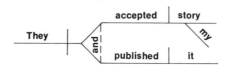

COMPOUND SENTENCE:

They accepted my story, but the editor delayed publication.

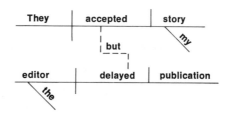

Exercise A: Decide which of these sentences are compound and which are simple. In the simple sentences identify any compound predicates.

1. Canada covers almost half of North America and is as large as all Europe.
2. Jeff commutes by train, but Vicky walks to work.
3. George Orwell's prediction was frightening, but luckily it was not fulfilled.
4. Lacrosse is fun, but it can be dangerous.
5. Giant turtles and flocks of white gulls live on that island and coexist peacefully.
6. This cars needs a muffler and new brakes, but its engine is sound.

7. Laura learned German and got a job as an interpreter.
8. Mike has played all positions on the team and is now a top-ranking player.
9. Skin diving is exciting, but there can be hazards for beginners.
10. After the game, the team lifted their coach and tossed her into the shower.

Exercise B: Writing All the following are compound sentences. Rewrite them as simple sentences. Use compound subjects or compound predicates following the example below:

EXAMPLE: The picture fell off the wall; it revealed a hidden safe.
The picture fell off the wall and revealed a hidden safe.

1. The Voice of America broadcasts to over a hundred countries; it uses thirty-six different languages.
2. Rusty missed the overture, but he heard the rest of the first act.
3. Thomas Jefferson founded the University of Virginia in 1819, and he designed some of the buildings.
4. Edgar Allen Poe wrote early science fiction tales, and Jules Verne did, too.
5. You answered all the questions in the first part right, but you made several mistakes in the second part.
6. The potato is not a vegetable; the tomato is not a vegetable, either.
7. The novels of Susan Hinton are extremely popular; several have been made into movies.
8. The Jerusalem artichoke is not really an artichoke; the Jerusalem artichoke is also not from Jerusalem.
9. We boarded the ship in New York, and we arrived in Iceland four days later.
10. Skylab was an orbiting scientific research station; Spacelab was an orbiting station as well.

3.3 The Clause

The third sentence type is the complex sentence. Before you can understand the complex sentence, however, you must have a thorough understanding of the **clause**.

A clause is a group of words containing a verb and its subject.

You have seen that a simple sentence contains a verb and its subject. Therefore, a simple sentence is a clause. You have also seen that each part of a compound sentence has its own verb and subject. A compound sentence, therefore, consists of two clauses.

Each clause in a compound sentence can be written separately as a simple sentence. Such clauses—ones that can stand by themselves as separate sentences—are called main clauses.

Some clauses cannot stand alone as main clauses. A **subordinate clause** is a group of words that has a subject and verb, but which does not express a complete thought. It cannot stand alone as a sentence.

A clause that cannot stand by itself is a subordinate clause.

Often a subordinate clause is introduced by a subordinating conjunction, such as *while* or *if*. (See Section 3.5.)

> s.　　　　 v.
> While you were talking . . . (What happened?)
> s.　　 v.
> Unless she improves her spelling . . . (What?)
> s.　 v.
> If you have the strength . . . (Then what?)

A relative pronoun can be the subject of the verb in a subordinate clause.

> Cleopatra, *who once ruled Egypt,* has been the subject of
>   many fictionalized plays. (*who* is the subject of the verb
>   *ruled* in the subordinate clause.)
> Are these the skates *that fit you best?* (*that* is the subject
>   of the verb *fit* in the subordinate clause.)

Phrase or Clause? A clause has a subject and a verb. A phrase does not.

I heard them *rehearsing*. (phrase)
  s.   v.
I heard them *when they were rehearsing*. (clause)

Students *in the caucus* did fine work. (phrase)
  s.   v.
Students *who were in the caucus* did fine work. (clause)

Exercise A: Are the italicized words phrases or clauses?

1. Jim scowls *when Jamie tells him his faults*.
2. *Because she worked nights*, she was sleepy in school.
3. The jury recessed *to eat their dinner*.
4. Kristin licked her lips *as she savored the banana split*.
5. *According to John Mason Brown*, television is chewing gum for the eyes.
6. *Unless more tickets are sold*, the dance will be canceled.
7. Some schools have classes *to teach students accounting*.
8. *In conferences with college representatives*, students get information and ask questions.
9. Interesting animals *found in South America* are the llama, the vicuna, and the tapir.
10. *Stuffed with books, coats, and old gym socks*, my locker popped open.

Exercise B: Label each main clause and each subordinate clause. Some sentences will contain only main clauses.

1. If an advertising campaign is successful, it makes people remember products and buy them.
2. Management proposed a contract that was more equitable.
3. The panda is not a bear, but it looks like one.
4. Ford was the first Vice-President who was not elected.
5. The red wolf and the Eastern timber wolf are endangered species that are native to North America.
6. When you get to Tampa, you must look me up.

7. Gertrude wrote a song, and Marge sang it.
8. A rhinocerous does not attack unless it is cornered.
9. Migrating birds can find their way even over the ocean on starless nights, and no human being knows how.
10. If you say a word over and over, it begins to sound strange.

3.4 The Adjective Clause

The adjective clause modifies a noun or pronoun. It functions like a single-word adjective or an adjective phrase.

An adjective clause is a subordinate clause used to modify a noun or pronoun.

Often, but not always, an adjective clause will begin with an **introductory word.** In the examples below, the first, second, fourth, and sixth sentences have adjective clauses with introductory words. The third and fifth sentences have adjective clauses with no introductory words.

> That is the spot *where I fell*. (*where* is an introductory word.)
>
> This is the time *when we must relax*. (*when* is an introductory word.)
>
> Legends *I read* told of his origin. (no introductory word)
> Legends *that I read* told of his origin. (*that* is an introductory word.)
>
> It's a program *I enjoy*. (no introductory word)
> It's a program *that I enjoy*. (*that* is an introductory word.)

In the first and second examples above, the introductory words act as adverbs within the adjective clause. The verb *fell* is modified by the adverb *where* in the first sentence. The verb *must relax* is modified by the adverb *when* in the second sentence. In both of these sentences the adjective clause as a whole is used to modify a noun.

Relative Pronouns. Some adjective clauses are introduced by the pronouns *who, whose, whom, which,* and *that.* When used in this way, the pronouns are called **relative pronouns.** An adjective clause introduced by a relative pronoun is sometimes called **a relative clause.**

> Tom Dooley was the doctor *who inspired him.*
> The trout season, *which opened in April,* is now over.

The relative pronoun in an adjective clause plays two roles. It modifies a noun or pronoun in the main clause. It also takes the place of that noun or pronoun in the relative clause.

> The explanation *that she* gave was not believable. (*explanation* is the antecedent for *that* and is modified by the relative clause. The relative pronoun *that* is also the direct object of the verb *gave* within the relative clause.)
>
> The letter *to which you refer* has been lost. (*letter* is the antecedent for *which* and is modified by the relative clause. The relative pronoun *which* is the object of the preposition *to* within the relative clause.)
>
> My mother is a person *who likes to work hard.* (*mother* is the antecedent for *who* and is modified by the relative clause. The relative pronoun *who* is also the subject of ·the verb *likes* within the relative clause.)

Since the relative pronoun functions as a sentence part *within* the relative clause, it must change its case to suit that function. For example, the relative pronoun *who* is used as a subject or a predicate word within a relative clause; *whom* is used as a direct object, an indirect object, or an object of a preposition. Notice that the case of the relative pronoun is *not* necessarily the same as the case of its antecedent.

> It is *he* **whom** I admire. (**whom** is in the objective case because it is the object of the verb *admire.* The antecedent *he* is in the nominative case because it is a predicate noun in the main clause.)

The pronouns *that* and *which* also have special uses. *That* introduces adjective clauses that are essential to the meaning of the sentence. *Which* introduces nonessential clauses.

> Here is the review *that irritated her.* (*that irritated her* is
> essential to the meaning of the sentence.)
> The review, which irritated her, had no real effect on the
> show. (Here, the clause is not essential to the meaning.)

Diagraming. The adjective clause is joined to the word it modifies in the main clause. A dotted line leads from this word to the introductory word. Note that the relative pronoun is placed to show its use in the clause.

The car that I borrowed belongs to Tammy.

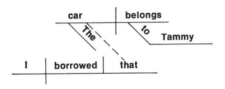

This is the building where my father works.

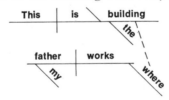

Exercise A: Find each adjective clause and the word it modifies.

1. This is the room that I decorated.
2. Springs are fed by rain, which seeps through the soil.
3. I couldn't find the place where you bought the bulbs.
4. A sharp tool was one of the first utensils that human beings needed.
5. Germany is the country where Beethoven was born.
6. I have seen the house in which Betsy Ross lived.
7. You can buy dwarf trees that will grow in your room.
8. The dog that barks the loudest usually bites the least.

9. How can we choose a play that everyone will like?
10. His father, whom he introduced as a captain, was not wearing a uniform.

Exercise B: Writing Add adjective clauses containing the material in parentheses to each of the sentences below.

1. Her conviction _____ made her unpopular. (She believed that taxes should go up.)
2. Surely the story _____ is not true. (Jerry told the story to Amy.)
3. Sugar maple _____ is the source of maple syrup. (It is also called rock maple.)
4. Manet is the painter _____. (His work is on exhibit.)
5. A diver _____ may rise to the surface too quickly. (He panics.)
6. The air _____ is mostly nitrogen. (We breathe the air.)
7. Ross and Cromarty _____ are generally thought of as one. (They are two counties in Northern Scotland.)
8. A quay _____ is a landing place where boats may moor. (It is pronounced like "key.")
9. Frankenstein _____ is the name of the scientist, not the monster. (He was a character created by Mary Shelley.)
10. Orange, Ohio, is the place _____. (James A. Garfield was born there.)

3.5 The Adverb Clause

An adverb clause modifies a verb, an adjective, or an adverb. It functions in the same way as a single-word adverb or an adverb phrase.

An adverb clause is a subordinate clause used to modify a verb, an adjective, or an adverb.

Adverb clauses tell *where, when, why, how, to what extent,* and *how much* about the words they modify.

ADVERB CLAUSES MODIFYING VERBS

We **put** the key *where we could locate it easily.* (tells *where*)

When you go to New York, **see** the Guggenheim Museum. (tells *when*)

The candidate **canceled** her speech *because she had a cold.* (tells *why*)

The dog **looked** *as if he would attack us.* (tells *how*)

ADVERB CLAUSES MODIFYING ADJECTIVES

This test is as **hard** *as the first one was.* (tells *to what extent*)

The school days are **longer** *than they used to be.* (tells *how much*)

ADVERB CLAUSE MODIFYING AN ADVERB

The dog ran **quicker** *than the sheep did.* (tells *how much*)

Subordinating Conjunctions. Adverb clauses are introduced by introductory words called **subordinating conjunctions.** These conjunctions join two clauses and make one dependent on the other. The subordinating conjunction relates the subordinate clause to the word in the main clause that it modifies.

> *If the cheerleader loses her voice,* she will go to the infirmary. (*If* is the subordinating conjunction. It relates the subordinate clause to the verb *will go* in the main clause.)

Subordinating conjunctions can be used to express many relationships between ideas. Some of these relationships are *time, place, cause, result, exception, condition, alternative, comparison,* and *purpose.* The most common subordinating conjunctions are listed below.

after	because	so that	whatever
although	before	than	when
as	if	though	whenever
as if	in order that	till	where
as long as	provided	unless	wherever
as though	since	until	while

When one of these words is placed before a clause, the clause can no longer stand by itself.

> The test scores are conclusive. (*complete*)
> If the test scores are conclusive . . . (*incomplete*)
> Whenever the test scores are conclusive . . . (*incomplete*)

A subordinating conjunction may be placed before either of two main clauses. The writer must decide which clause to make subordinate by considering the meaning of the sentence.

> *Although* Mark Twain was a great humorist, he was pessimistic.
> Mark Twain was a great humorist *although* he was pessimistic.

In addition to deciding which clause to subordinate, a writer must also choose the subordinating conjunction that most precisely expresses the relationship between the clauses.

TIME:	as, after, before, since, until, when, whenever, while
CAUSE OR REASON:	because, since
COMPARISON:	as, as much as, than
CONDITION:	if, although, though, unless, provided, provided that
PURPOSE:	so that, in order that

Using different conjunctions creates a change in meaning.

> *Before* the schedule was changed, I was upset.
> *Because* the schedule was changed, I was upset.
> *Until* the schedule was changed, I was upset.

When there is no possibility that the reader will be confused, the writer may omit words from an adverb clause. Clauses where words have been left out are called **elliptical clauses.** *Ellipsis* means "omission of a word."

> *While he was playing chess*, he was contented.
> *While playing chess*, he was contented.

Diagraming. The adverb clause is placed on a separate line:

When his friend whistled, he dashed outside.

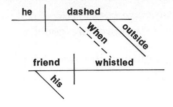

Exercise A: Find each adverb clause and the word or words it modifies.

1. The parade was postponed because it rained.
2. If we win this game, the trophy will be ours.
3. The musicians arrived after you left.
4. When she saw the rain, she ran to close the windows.
5. Class begins promptly when the bell rings.
6. They will buy the house provided they can afford it.
7. The colt ate as if it had been without food for days.
8. The children followed the kitten wherever it went.
9. Robin felt invigorated after she had swum six laps.
10. Although the film got bad reviews, it attracted huge crowds.

Exercise B: Writing Add adverb clauses containing the information in parentheses to each of the sentences below.

1. Many citizens became irate. (*Time:* Their taxes were increased.)
2. Mother cannot be disturbed. (*Cause:* She is studying.)
3. I pulled to the side of the road. (*Purpose:* The trailer truck could pass.)
4. You might win. (*Condition:* You buy a raffle ticket.)
5. The student newspaper is controversial. (*Comparison:* It was not as controversial before.)
6. Park the car. (*Place:* You can find a legal spot.)

7. I will pass the course. (*Exception:* I failed the test.)
8. That sauce is sweeter. (*Comparison:* We did not expect it to be so sweet.)
9. We always buy cheese. (*Time:* We go to Wisconsin.)
10. Please stop humming. (*Result:* I can get my work done.)

3.6   The Noun Clause

A noun clause is a subordinate clause used as a noun.

The entire noun clause is used the same way a noun is used. It may function as a subject, direct object, indirect object, predicate noun, object of a preposition, or appositive.

I understand *what the law requires*. (direct object)
The Ancient Mariner told *whoever would listen* his tale. (indirect object)
Monica was wondering about *where Maurice had gone*. (object of preposition)
The reason *that he was called* is unclear. (appositive)
Whoever told you that was wrong. (subject)
The odd part is *how Linda got the dog*. (predicate noun)

Introductory Words. The words *when* and *where* may be used to introduce noun clauses as well as adverb clauses. When they introduce adverb clauses, they are subordinating conjunctions. When they introduce noun clauses, however, they are simply introductory words used as adverbs within the clause.

Similarly, the words *who, whose, whom, which, that, when,* and *where* are sometimes used as relative pronouns to introduce adjective clauses. These words may also introduce noun clauses. When they introduce noun clauses, they serve as subjects or objects within the clause.

Luke went **where** *the fish were biting*. (adverb clause modifying *went*)
Larry explained **where** *Ann was*. (noun clause as the object of *explained*)

Who *won the election* is uncertain. (noun clause as the subject of *is*)

Holly is the one **who** *broke the record.* (adjective clause modifying *one*)

Every direct quotation preceded by words such as *I said, she asked, Eva replied* is a noun clause without the introductory word. Every indirect quotation is a noun clause preceded by the introductory word. Noun clauses in both direct and indirect quotations are direct objects of the verb.

She said, *"The road was treacherous."* (noun clause as the object of *said*)

She said *that the road was treacherous.* (noun clause as the object of *said*)

Infinitive Clauses. Unlike other verbals, an infinitive may have a subject as well as complements and modifiers. Such a construction is called an **infinitive clause.** When the subject of an infinitive clause is a pronoun, use the *objective* case.

It is advisable for *him to leave immediately.*

Since the subject of an infinitive clause sometimes follows the main verb and looks like an object, it may be mistaken for the object of the main verb. In the following sentence, the entire infinitive clause is the direct object.

The director wanted *him to look dignified.*

Gerund Clauses. A noun clause may also be made from a gerund and its subject. This type of clause includes any modifiers and complements of the gerund. When the subject of a gerund is a pronoun, use the *possessive* case.

His incessant drumming on the table unnerved the speaker.

In the sentence given above, the entire gerund clause acts as the subject of the sentence. The subject of the gerund *drumming* is the word *his,* a pronoun used in the possessive case.

The law provided for *her making one telephone call.*

In the sentence given above, the subject of the gerund *making* is the pronoun *her*. Because it is the subject of a gerund, it is in the possessive case.

Diagraming. The noun clause is diagramed as follows. The use of the noun clause determines its position in the diagram.

I think that you are improving.

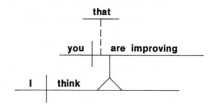

He gave help to whoever was needy.

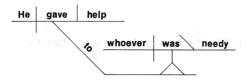

Exercise A: Identify each noun clause. Tell how each is used.

1. Lee asked what I was doing.
2. The fact that he had read about neutrons helped him.
3. What the players will do next is anyone's guess.
4. I inquired where she lived.
5. Please tell me why this movie is so successful.
6. I wonder who wrote the letter.
7. I know him to be the culprit.
8. His leaving without saying goodbye annoyed my sister.
9. We gave the book lists to whoever asked for them.
10. The photographer claimed that photography is the most truthful art.

Exercise B: Writing Add a noun clause to each sentence below, using the information given in parentheses. You will be replacing one word in the original sentence.

1. It is plain to see. (*Subject:* You are not interested in organic chemistry.)
2. The train schedule will tell you that. (*Direct Object:* When trains depart from Lloydsville.)
3. Emily would not tell us that. (*Direct Object:* Why she wears that strange hairstyle.)
4. The clue escaped everyone's notice. (*Appositive:* The stamp was British.)
5. Everyone agreed. (*Direct Object:* Summer is best.)
6. Give the person a reward. (*Indirect Object:* The person who finds my cat.)
7. Her uncle's fondest wish is this. (*Predicate Words:* Elaine will join the family business.)
8. Alfred told him that. (*Direct Object:* The thing he wanted to know.)
9. That is impossible to know. (*Subject:* Who will win the election.)
10. The fact is irrelevant. (*Appositive:* Joanne is the mayor's daughter.)

Exercise C: Find each subordinate clause and identify it as an adjective clause, an adverb clause, or a noun clause.

1. Gilda Radner portrays characters who are strange.
2. Because she excels in math, Kelly plans to become an engineer.
3. Bridal Veil Falls is at its best in late afternoon, when it forms beautiful rainbows.
4. South American monkeys have tails that are prehensile, or grasping.
5. James Madison is the person who drafted the document.
6. We took a picture of him doing a swan dive.
7. The bald eagle looks bald because it has white feathers on its head.

8. This is the meadow where I saw the deer.
9. The car she drives is an old Ford.
10. The trapdoor spider lives in a silk-lined room with a door that fits exactly.
11. Mary Harris Jones, who was known as "Mother Jones," organized labor unions and crusaded for workers' rights in the late 1800's.
12. Before child labor laws were passed, children were exploited in the work force.
13. We were in the train station when we heard the news.
14. The Bronx Zoo, which is the largest in the world, covers over two hundred acres.
15. *Macbeth* is the story of a man who suffered disaster through too much ambition.

3.7 The Complex Sentence

The complex sentence consists of one main clause and one or more subordinate clauses.

The subordinate clause or clauses in a complex sentence act either as nouns or as modifiers.

Although he did not know the answer, he raised his hand. (clause modifies *raised*)

Read the paper *while you wait.* (clause modifies *Read*)

This is the music *that I like.* (clause modifies *music*)

In the complex sentences shown above, the main clause can stand alone: *He did not raise his hand, Read the paper, This is the music.* The subordinate clauses, however, cannot stand alone because they do not express complete thoughts.

Although he knew the answer. . . (What happened?)
while you are waiting. . . (What should I do?)
that I like. . . (What do you like?)

The noun clause creates a special situation in a complex sentence. In these sentences, the noun clause functions as a sentence part *within* the main clause. Sometimes the main clause can still stand alone.

Barry could guess *who the ghost was*.

In some sentences, however, the main clause cannot stand alone without the noun clause.

What you read influences your thinking.

In this sentence, the noun clause is the subject of the verb. Because the sentence contains a main clause and a subordinate clause, it is a complex sentence. However, the main clause cannot stand alone.

Exercise A: Find the main clauses and the subordinate clauses.

1. The marathon swimmer feared that a shark was near.
2. Although the ice is thin, it is safe for skating.
3. Kendra discovered that her locker had been ransacked.
4. When a boat sails "before the wind," it follows the wind's course.
5. Mauna Loa is the largest volcano that is still active.
6. Dr. Albert Sabin developed a vaccine that prevents polio.
7. Many secretaries use shorthand whenever they take dictation.
8. Sonia threw the Frisbee to a spot where Ramon couldn't reach it.
9. Ms. Forrest asked the class who wrote the book *Jubilee*.
10. Illinois is named after the Indians who once lived there.
11. The administration finally decided where the student lounge would be located.
12. Whoever is arrested is informed of her or his rights.
13. Julio believed her to be Mrs. Sanders.
14. Alexander Solzhenitsyn is a writer who was exiled.
15. A short story is not as complex as a novel is.

Exercise B: Indicate whether each of the following sentences is simple, compound, or complex.

1. The rear tire needed no air, but the front tire did.
2. The ball circled the rim of the basket and fell in.
3. Unless Julia can obtain a scholarship, she may not go to college next fall.
4. Dad is unhappy about his golf score, which has not been improving lately.
5. Did you know that the onion is a lily?
6. At the end of the season, the team was given a banquet and presented with trophies.
7. The campers said good-bye with regret; they would not meet again for a long time.
8. The motor sputtered and then stalled.
9. The motor sputtered before it stalled.
10. You can take a side trip to Disney World at no extra cost.

3.8   The Compound-Complex Sentence

A compound-complex sentence consists of two or more main clauses and one or more subordinate clauses.

A compound-complex sentence is a combination of a complex sentence and a compound sentence. The main clauses are joined by a coordinating conjunction (preceded by a comma), a conjunctive adverb (preceded by a semicolon), or by a semicolon alone. The subordinate clause is a modifier or a noun.

MAIN CLAUSE   MAIN CLAUSE   SUBORDINATE CLAUSE

Carol entered, and she won the medal that was donated
        by the sponsor.

    MAIN CLAUSE   MAIN CLAUSE   SUBORDINATE CLAUSE

We missed the bus; however, we arrived before the others did.

Exercise: Find the two main clauses and the subordinate clause in each compound-complex sentence.

1. The window had been left open, and the papers that I had left on my desk were scattered all over the room.
2. If all modern timepieces are digital, people will forget how to use traditional clocks; then, a grandfather clock will become obsolete.
3. The team's manager was anxious to settle the contract dispute, but first he had to establish the starting line-up for the game which began in twenty minutes.
4. Beethoven, who wrote many beautiful piano sonatas, will be the subject of Tuesday's lecture; it should attract students from all the high school music classes.
5. A Christmas cactus makes a handsome houseplant, and if you take care of it properly, it will bloom once a year.
6. When the cousins get together, they like to prepare feasts; but they do not like to wash all the dishes.
7. Our advisers told us that our class could plan a trip, and they said we would earn the money as a group.
8. Elaine acted superior when she spoke to people, and that is why no one enjoyed her company.
9. Latreille was a French zoologist who was born in the 18th century; he wrote books about salamanders and apes.
10. The "ides of March," which Caesar was told to beware of, were the 15th of March; in April the ides were the 13th.

3.9 The Sentence Redefined

The complete definition of a sentence may now be given. First, we will review the difference between a phrase and a clause and between a main clause and a subordinate clause.

A **phrase** is a group of words used in a sentence as a single part of speech. A phrase may be used as a noun, verb, adjective, or adverb. It does *not* contain both a subject and verb.

PHRASE: Working on our project . . .

A **clause** is a group of words which contains a verb and its subject. It may be used within the sentence as a noun, an adjective, or an adverb.

CLAUSE: While *we were working* on our project . . .

A **main clause** can stand by itself as a sentence. A **subordinate clause** cannot stand by itself.

MAIN CLAUSE　　　　　　　　　MAIN CLAUSE

The camera was new, but the shutter did not work.

The camera was new. (*complete*)
The shutter did not work. (*complete*)

SUBORDINATE CLAUSE　　　　　　　　　MAIN CLAUSE

Although the camera was new, the shutter did not work.

The shutter did not work. (*complete*)
Although the camera was new . . . (*incomplete*)

Sentences consist of at least one main clause plus any number of additional phrases and clauses. The complete definition of a sentence is given below in three parts.

A sentence is a group of words that

1. expresses a complete thought,

2. has at least one main clause with a subject and a verb and

3. may contain phrases and subordinate clauses in addition to the main clause.

REINFORCEMENT EXERCISES
Sentence and Clause

A. Identify the subject and predicate. Copy the following sentences. Underline the subject once and the predicate twice.

1. Springsteen and Bonds recorded an album.
2. Pandora heedlessly opened the box and peeked inside.
3. *Cost-push* and *creeping* are two types of inflation.
4. Hans lost his contact lenses and then broke his glasses.
5. The president and the board of trustees argued about the budget and discussed employee benefits.
6. Wyla collects interesting rock specimens, polishes them, and displays them in lighted cases.
7. Dallas and Miami have professional football teams.
8. Elliott and Fiona play the fife in the band.
9. Queen Elizabeth II is considered a strong but temperamental ruler.
10. Either a hurricane or a tornado caused the damage.

B. Identify simple and compound sentences. Write *S* for the simple sentences and *C* for the compound sentences.

1. Buddy washed a red bathrobe with white clothes, and the whole load came out pink.
2. The audience loved Nureyev's performance and gave him twenty-three curtain calls.
3. The sun was overhead; the sundial's shadow was at XII.
4. Barbara Walters has interviewed dozens of celebrities on television but prefers to be recognized for her other journalistic abilities.
5. George Vancouver explored the Pacific Northwest; so it is only natural that a city there is named after him.
6. The ship was lost at sea; however, insurance paid for it.
7. The keyboard and the cardhopper may have been smashed by the intruders.
8. Jeremy might have the flu, or it could be more serious.

9. *Sentimentalism,* according to one writer, is "an overin-
dulgence in emotion and a failure to exercise reason."
10. There are more than seven thousand kinds of apples
grown around the world, and more than two thousand
of them are grown in North America.

C. Identify phrases and clauses. Tell if the italicized group of
words in each sentence is a phrase or a clause.

1. *When she refused to move to the back of the bus,* Rosa
Parks made history.
2. Clara, *never having seen one,* thought St. Bernards were
thin, short-haired dogs.
3. Was he the one *who wrote "Ode on a Garbage Truck"*?
4. A fisherman is not speaking about economics *when he
uses the words "net" and "gross."*
5. A team was sent to study the Masai, *the best cattle raisers
in the world.*
6. Pasteur is the man *who discovered how to heat milk to
kill bacteria.*
7. *Until Mimi saw the ocean,* she underestimated its majesty.
8. Close the disk-drive door *after you insert the disk.*
9. Who said, *"To make an omelette,* you must break eggs"?
10. *Working twenty-four hours a day* would make Dad happy.

D. Identify adjective clauses. Find the adjective clauses in the
following sentences and tell what words they modify.

1. The creature that hung from the branch was a spider.
2. It was the French explorer La Salle whom Louis de Baude
Frontenac encouraged.
3. The vizsla, which is a hunting dog, originated in Hungary.
4. The whittler, who was carving a whistle, taught his new
apprentice how to hold the chisel.
5. Yes, this is the area where Jane Goodall did her research.
6. We are trying a diet that includes whole grain foods.
7. Here is the arena where gladiators once fought.
8. Dinosaurs flourished in a time when plants grew to
gigantic sizes.

9. Plato, whose thinking has influenced all of Western culture, wrote thirty-five famous *dialogues*.
10. The part of the helmet that moved was the visor.

E. Identify adverb clauses. Find each adverb clause and tell which word or words it modifies.

1. My brother seemed hypnotized as he read the books of Barbara Tuchman.
2. The match would not light because it had a safety tip.
3. Although Edmund Burke was a great political thinker, he never held an important government position.
4. While you wait for the meat loaf to cool, make a salad.
5. The instructions for setting up the computer were not as clear as they should have been.
6. Diabetes is suspected whenever the patient has great thirst, weight loss, and feelings of weakness
7. Although she admired them, Gertrude Stein called the expatriates members of the "lost generation."
8. If you enjoy plane geometry, you may also enjoy solid geometry.
9. The coach was more nervous than her skaters were.
10. We laughed when Casey Stengel made a funny remark.

F. Identify noun clauses. Tell whether the noun clause in each sentence is used as a subject, direct object, indirect object, object of a preposition, predicate word, or appositive.

1. A remark made by his ten-year-old daughter was what started Edwin Land on his invention of the camera.
2. The laboratory assistant wondered where the hamster food was stored.
3. Senator Tsongas did not agree with what his party proposed.
4. The foundation gave whoever submitted the best proposal a grant for one year's research.
5. The belief that breaking a mirror brings bad luck is a superstition.
6. How homing pigeons navigate over unfamiliar terrain is still a mystery.

7. The reporter implied that the mayor was purposely misinterpreting her questions.
8. What Dr. Forrest meant was that heat is a form of energy.
9. The photographer agreed to do a portrait of whoever won the contest.
10. The idea that lead could be turned to gold was cherished by alchemists.

G. Identify complex and compound-complex sentences. Tell if the sentences are complex or compound-complex.

1. Since she did not identify the germ, it might have been a bacterium, a virus, or a protozoan.
2. The book was on folklore, which is the unrecorded popular beliefs and customs of people; unfortunately, the book contained examples of literature that was not folklore.
3. Many great men and women have felt like failures although the world recognized their achievements after their deaths.
4. Molasses is a by-product of the manufacturing of sugar; thus, the countries that produce sugar also produce molasses.
5. The Ford Foundation, which was established by Henry and Edsel Ford, is the world's wealthiest endowed foundation.
6. You are what you eat.
7. When *Time* first reviewed *Death of a Salesman*, it called it "No more than an altogether creditable play"; nevertheless, the play has achieved world fame.
8. Much of the richness of our language will be lost if regional dialects disappear, and some linguists say that they are disappearing rapidly in America.
9. The world's highest mountains, which have a permanent covering of snow and ice, are located in Asia and South America; but a few such peaks exist in Africa and North America also.
10. Hal enjoys what he does; therefore, he does it well.

MIXED REVIEW
Sentence and Clause

A. Indicate whether the words in italics are main clauses or subordinate clauses. Then tell whether each subordinate clause is an adjective, adverb, or noun clause.

1. The Confederate flag, *which consisted of two bars and a cross filled with stars,* was commonly referred to as the "Stars and Bars."
2. Mangrove trees send down aerial roots *that in turn send up new trunks.*
3. When we visited the natural habitat zoo, *we took pictures of the bears and the gibbons.*
4. Jack made a mistake *when he used the rain gauge to measure snowfall.*
5. Because they believed in equal human rights, *the abolitionists spoke out against slavery.*
6. *What Loretta learned in her first lesson* was how to hold the bow properly.
7. Dan Rice, *who began his career as an acrobat,* became the most famous clown of his day.
8. *Mangos, papayas, and kiwis are tropical fruits* that are now available in many Northern markets.
9. Who was the "dark lady" *to whom Shakespeare wrote several of his sonnets?*
10. *Some people own microwave ovens,* which cook with electromagnetic waves.
11. Scientists are using satellite information to determine *which planets can sustain life.*
12. *If you do not receive any further instructions,* meet us in front of the bus station at 8:00.
13. They canoed at the spot *where the white water begins.*
14. The ancient notion *that the world is flat* is still held by a few eccentrics.
15. *Jeff found an expanse of land* that is perfect for cross-country skiing.

B. Identify the following sentences as simple, compound, complex, or compound-complex. In addition, find the subordinate clauses and tell whether they are adjective, adverb, or noun clauses.

1. Cheryl used a soldering iron when she made the stained glass windows.
2. Samuel Powhatan Carter was a major general, and he was also a rear admiral.
3. After the sudden thaw, the river overflowed its banks.
4. Because I have read several of Shakespeare's plays, I recognized the allusions this modern author made.
5. The detergent came in a bottle with a squeeze spout, but the bottle was hard to squeeze.
6. John Eliot, a Puritan, was educated at Cambridge, England; he settled in Roxbury, Massachusetts.
7. Di surprised even the people who knew her.
8. Was Daylight Savings Time instituted to save fuel?
9. A story that Margaret wrote for English class was published in *Scholastic* magazine, but she has not submitted anything since.
10. Floyd has had a car since he turned seventeen.
11. The mathematicians determined that the numbers on the clay tablet were positive integers.
12. When deer meat is cooked, it is called "venison."
13. Emily and Charlotte Brontë both wrote under aliases.
14. Where to invest the company's profits was the subject of the board meeting.
15. The Norfolk Island Pine is not a pine; nor is it from Norfolk Island.
16. Parents and teachers will meet once a month and discuss common concerns.
17. For the last forty years the United States and Australia have dominated the Davis Cup matches.
18. Gina not only plays in the school band, but she also composes some of the pieces that the band performs.
19. Ann asked, "Who writes to 'Dear Abby'?"
20. Bonita learned about medical careers from the work that she did as a hospital aide.

USING GRAMMAR IN WRITING
Sentence and Clause

A. Some writers are known for their use of elaborately constructed sentences. Below is a sentence from Henry James's *The Wings of the Dove*. Read the sentence and then write a paragraph analyzing its style. Explain the effect of this style on the reader.

> She waited, Kate Croy, for her father to come in, but he kept her unconscionably, and there were moments at which she showed herself, in the glass over the mantel, a face positively pale with the irritation that had brought her to the point of going away without sight of him.

B. The acknowledged master of the short, "tough" sentence was Ernest Hemingway. The passage below is taken from his short story "Big Two-Hearted River." Read the passage and then write a paragraph analyzing Hemingway's style. What is the effect of this style on the reader?

> Nick slipped off his pack and lay down in the shade. He lay on his back and looked up into the pine trees. His neck and back and the small of his back rested as he stretched. The earth felt good against his back. He looked up at the sky, through the branches, and then shut his eyes. He opened them and looked up agian. There was a wind high up in the branches. He shut his eyes again and went to sleep.

C. Write a story in which you describe a character waiting in a room for someone or something. First write it using elaborate "Jamesian" sentences like the one in the first passage above. Then write the same scene in a "tough" Hemingway style. Compare the effects of the different types of sentences in creating an atmosphere and mood.

CUMULATIVE REVIEW
Usage (I)

Understanding How Words Are Used. A word or group of words can be used in different ways in different sentences. Study each italicized word or group of words in the following sentences. Decide whether it is being used as a *Subject, Verb, Adjective, Adverb, Predicate Word, Direct Object, Indirect Object,* or *Object of a Preposition.* Write each word and your answer next to the corresponding number.

1. John A. Wismont *set* a world record by *painting over nine thousand portraits in a single year.*
2. The investigators hadn't identified a *suspect,* but they did have several *leads.*
3. *Making music videos* is a popular *amateur* hobby.
4. *Marsha's* dream is *to become a marine biologist.*
5. The *value* of the company's stocks went *down* after the crash of one of its planes.
6. *Egg-laying* mammals are found only in *Australia, Tasmania, and New Guinea.*
7. The *success* of several movies on the subject has given *dancing* its current popularity.
8. The trilobite fossils *that Mark found in the Wabash River* are over six hundred million years *old.*
9. The moon lay *low* upon the horizon, entangled in the *branches* of an aged oak.
10. Does *anyone* know *how to get back to camp?*
11. Felicia's hobby is *collecting photographs from the 1920's and '30's.*
12. The congresswoman expresses the same ideas as her colleagues, but she *words* them very *differently.*
13. *One* insect, the walking stick, is so elaborately camouflaged that its predators almost always *mistake* it for a twig.
14. Puerto Rico is the *fourth* largest island *in the Caribbean.*
15. Lichens *are composed* of fungi and algae *living in a close relationship.*

4.0 Complete Sentences

When we speak, we sometimes use a group of words that is not a complete sentence. If the person we are speaking to is confused, he or she can ask us what we mean. When we write, however, we must use complete sentences to help the reader follow our thoughts.

There are two serious sentence errors that can create confusion in written English. One is the sentence fragment, and the other is the run-on sentence. This Section will help you identify and avoid these errors.

4.1 Fragments Resulting from Incomplete Thought

A **sentence fragment** is a group of words that is only a piece, or fragment, of a complete sentence.

> When the doctor arrives.
> Rode into the wind.
> Tired but cheerful.

A sentence fragment may occur in your writing through the simple omission of words. This often occurs when your mind is racing ahead of the sentence you are actually writing. Suppose you wanted to say something like this:

> Ted and Miriam had a loud quarrel. After the quarrel, they wondered why they had been angry. They talked about their differences the next day.

But, while hurrying to finish your thoughts, you ended up with something like this:

> Ted and Miriam had a loud quarrel. Afterwards wondered why they had been angry. They talked about their differences the next day.

The second group of words is not a sentence. It is a fragment. The reader cannot follow exactly what you meant to say.

Exercise A: Writing Find the sentence fragments. Add words or change the punctuation to make each fragment a sentence.

1. As a child, I always made decisions slowly. Especially choosing candy in the candy store.
2. After the game, a snack shop.
3. The record store had lots of albums on display. Most of them recent releases.
4. I stood in front of the glassed-in shelves. Just looked and looked.
5. Some animals are nocturnal. For example, owls and bats.
6. Especially difficult when you are seventeen.
7. They tried every door in the house. But could not get in until the windows.
8. Lynn advanced toward Sam. Offered him a lemon meringue pie and a glass of milk.
9. The missing suitcase in the cupboard under the stairs. Need it for a trip.
10. Easton, where I was born. Just across the river from Phillipsburg.

Exercise B: Writing Three of the following groups of words are sentences. The rest are fragments. Find the fragments and add words needed to make them sentences.

1. Heart disease, one of the chief causes of death.
2. How the leopard managed to escape from its cage.
3. *The Taming of the Shrew,* one of Shakespeare's most popular comedies.
4. James Madison was one of the most scholarly Presidents.
5. The pink camellia, which was especially beautiful.
6. If Martin weren't so unpredictable.
7. The many billboards along the highway.
8. The winding road, bordered by trees and the ocean.
9. Crater Lake in Oregon rests in the cone of a dead volcano.
10. Deborah Sampson, disguised as a man, fought in the American Revolution.

4.2 Fragments Resulting from Incorrect Punctuation

A complete sentence should start with a capital letter and end with a period, exclamation point, or question mark. A complete thought must be expressed between the capital letter and the end mark.

A fragment may result if the writer inserts an end mark before the sentence he or she wanted to write is actually complete. This error is called a **period fault.**

FRAGMENT: We went to the construction site. With camera and film in hand.

SENTENCE: We went to the construction site with camera and film in hand.

FRAGMENT: Slipping on an icy patch in the road. The car almost went out of control.

SENTENCE: Slipping on an icy patch in the road, the car almost went out of control.

Exercise A: Combine a fragment from Column A with an idea from Column B to make ten complete sentences.

COLUMN A

mushrooms, mildew, and molds

in Roman mythology

the nursery rhyme "Ring Around a Rosie"

was made of rhubarb, ginger, and calcined magnesia

humankind first walked on the moon

that means "naked"

needs twenty-five times longer to reach maturity than a mouse embryo

to help his father with mathematics

in a museum gallery

who won the Pulitzer prize for poetry in 1923

COLUMN B

Gregory's Mixture, my grandfather's favorite stomach medicine,

the word "gymnasium" comes from a Greek word

Edna St. Vincent Millay was an American poet

Diana was the goddess of the moon

an elephant embryo, which takes 620 days to develop

during the last decade

is actually about the bubonic plague

are familiar types of fungi

sculpture was displayed

Pascal invented a computing machine

Exercise B: Find the fragments. Correct them by changing the punctuation and capitalization.

1. Out of the cold, gray mist. Came a mournful wail.
2. You can use these coupons. To get discounts.
3. While Zachary was at the library. His friends prepared the surprise party.
4. Urania, who appears in paintings with an orb in her left hand, was the Greek muse. Of astronomy.
5. When Trish's friends slept over. They would always make apple pancakes. For breakfast.

6. A movie was made about Secaucus, New Jersey. Which is a town in Hudson County.
7. Two different birds known as the rice-bunting. Are the bob-o-link and the Mayan sparrow.
8. A quartet is a piece of music. For four instruments.
9. Stopping frequently to gather wildflowers. The children lost track of the time.
10. Jorge had to spend two weeks in the hospital. And fell behind in his work.

4.3   Phrases as Fragments

A phrase is a group of words that does not have both a subject and a verb. A phrase, therefore, cannot be a sentence.

A prepositional phrase, no matter how long, is not a sentence.

FRAGMENT: A survey showed that students favored the reorganization. *In nine out of ten cases.*

SENTENCE: A survey showed that students favored the reorganization in nine out of ten cases.

Sometimes a verbal phrase is also incorrectly used as a sentence. This occurs because a verbal looks and acts like a verb and may be mistaken for a verb. Gerunds and participles that end in *-ing* are the verbals that are most frequently confused. This confusion may be avoided by remembering this rule:

No word ending in *-ing* can be a complete verb unless it is a one-syllable word like *sing, ring,* or *bring*.

FRAGMENT: Patching his old clothes.

SENTENCE: Ernie prefers patching his old clothes. (*patching* is a gerund.)

FRAGMENT: Melissa breaking the state record.

SENTENCE: Breaking the state record, Melissa crossed the finish line. (*Breaking* is a participle.)

A participle may be part of a complete verb, however, if it is combined with *is, are, was* or some other form of *be*.

PARTICIPLE	COMPLETE VERB
reading	is reading
holding	has been holding
breaking	were breaking

A fragment may also occur when an infinitive phrase is mistaken for a complete sentence.

FRAGMENT: The Holmquist family saved for three years. *To visit their relatives in Sweden.*

SENTENCE: The Holmquist family saved for three years to visit their relatives in Sweden.

Finally, a fragment may result when a writer mistakes a noun and an appositive for a complete sentence.

FRAGMENT: This biography, *the only definitive account.*

SENTENCE: This biography is the only definitive account.

SENTENCE: This biography, the only definitive account, is a masterpiece.

Exercise A: Rewrite the following groups of words to make complete sentences. You may need to add words.

1. The loon is a brown bird. Very clumsy on the shore.
2. You can hold this microphone. Or mount it on a stand.
3. Buying a headphone and testing it instead of doing his homework.
4. Lee went to see her counselor. To discuss her problems.
5. Our sociology class invited speakers from the community. Such as police officers, social workers and doctors.
6. I found it exciting. To see the aurora borealis.
7. Vesuvius, the most famous volcano in the world.
8. Greece is still an extremely poor country. A warehouse of rocks and ruins.

9. Mike Anderson, the photographer for the local newspaper.
10. He was in a great hurry. To get to Richmond by six o'clock.

Exercise B: Follow the same directions as for Exercise A.

1. Owning a car involves a number of responsibilities. Paying for gas, insurance, and upkeep.
2. The speaker, a correspondent for *The New York Times*.
3. Red conveys certain meanings. Associated with danger.
4. Maple trees border the avenue. Bright orange, flaming red, and gold.
5. Diana Nyad, a well-known marathon swimmer.
6. Scientists hope to explore Venus. To determine whether life exists on the planet.
7. Kutztown is the scene of an annual folk festival. In the Pennsylvania Dutch country.
8. Mr. Ludwig's car was delivered today. Canary yellow.
9. Be there on Friday, March 12. At three o'clock.
10. The Declaration of Independence, one of the important documents in the struggle for human freedom.

4.4 Clauses as Fragments

A subordinate clause is sometimes mistaken for a complete sentence. A subordinate clause does have a subject and verb. However, a subordinate clause is usually introduced by a subordinating conjunction, which makes it unable to stand alone.

SENTENCE: I was trying to think of an excuse.
SUBORDINATE CLAUSE: Because I was trying to think of an excuse

A fragment results when an end mark is placed before or after a subordinate clause as if the clause were a complete sentence.

INCORRECT: Jan sold her car. Because it used too much gas.
CORRECT: Jan sold her car because it used too much gas.

Exercise A: Rewrite the word groups to eliminate fragments.

1. Few students borrow books from the school library. Although it has a wide selection.
2. When we heard the news. We rushed to the scene.
3. Jenny found time for chess, music, and debating. While she was editor of the school paper.
4. Improvements in the design of early automobiles came from Bertha Benz. Who was the wife of the inventor.
5. Jody was decorating the school gym for the dance. When she should have been writing her term paper.
6. The pilot could not communicate with the airport. Because the radio was out.
7. The two pieces of wood must be quickly clamped together. Before the glue dries.
8. The letter came in the morning mail. Just after Dad left.
9. Many people discover fascinating information. As they research their family's roots.
10. There was no fire-fighting company in Philadelphia. Until Ben Franklin formed one in 1746.

Exercise B: Writing In this exercise you will find examples of many kinds of fragments. Change them into complete sentences.

1. Leslie tried to buy glue. To mend the red dish.
2. They coasted down the hill. On the sled.
3. The game was over. The score 7-2 in our favor.
4. To get the car on Saturday night. Jennifer promised that she would mow the lawn.
5. Finding a summer job. Is difficult because of the competition.
6. Talking about life at sea. Joe excited his listeners.
7. The students presented an excellent performance of Wilder's *Our Town*. After only three weeks' rehearsal.
8. Noel won an award in photography. At the art festival.
9. There is an organization for left-handed people. Called Lefthanders International.

10. The table next to the wall. A Victorian antique.
11. Outlining can improve learning. A good study technique.
12. America would be adopting international standards of weights and measures. By converting to metrics.
13. We went to see the movie. That you recommended.
14. Dr. Power, an excellent conversationalist.
15. I plan to buy a new watch. Which will replace my old one.

4.5 Run-on Sentences

A run-on sentence is created when a writer fails to put a period or other end mark at the end of a sentence. Two or more sentences written as one are a run-on sentence.

RUN-ON:	Years ago, driving was fun there was less traffic.
CORRECT:	Years ago, driving was fun. There was less traffic.
RUN-ON:	All watched the launching excitedly it was spectacular.
CORRECT:	All watched the launching excitedly. It was spectacular.

Frequently, a writer will try to join two sentences with a comma. This is a sentence error called a **comma fault.**

COMMA FAULT:	Shari decided not to go tobogganing, she was too cold.
CORRECT:	Shari decided not to go tobogganing. She was too cold.
COMMA FAULT:	The huge crane collapsed, it crushed a car.
CORRECT:	The huge crane collapsed. It crushed a car.

Sentences like those given above are especially likely to be combined as one. They are closely related sentences, and the second begins with a personal pronoun referring to a noun in the first. Watch for this pattern in your own writing to avoid making a comma fault.

4.6   Avoiding the Run-on Sentence

It is often desirable to combine two related sentences into one compound sentence. There are three ways of doing this:

1. Use a comma and a coordinating conjunction to combine sentences.

   RUN-ON: Pat has two hobbies he spends more time on astronomy than on van art.

   CORRECT: Pat has two hobbies, but he spends more time on astronomy than on van art.

2. Use a semicolon to combine sentences.

   RUN-ON: Bob and June stayed up late watching the star shower, they missed the sunrise.

   CORRECT: Bob and June stayed up late watching the star shower; they missed the sunrise.

3. Use a semicolon and a conjunctive adverb to combine sentences.

   RUN-ON: Sandra did not choose her courses wisely she had to go to summer school.

   CORRECT: Sandra did not choose her courses wisely; consequently, she had to go to summer school.

Exercise A: Correct each of the following run-on sentences in one of these ways: (1) by using a period and a capital letter; (2) by using a semicolon; or (3) by using a comma and *and, but,* or *or.*

1. Only one paddle-wheel steamboat still operates on the Mississippi, she's the *Delta Queen.*
2. Something went wrong with the party, it just wasn't a success.
3. I overslept again, nobody woke me.
4. There must be a mistake, I didn't order any ant farms.
5. Don't be discouraged, Kerry, try to look at the bright side.

6. Some guests sat on the patio, others sat on the lawn.
7. I've been trying to close this suitcase, it's impossible.
8. I didn't finish the test, neither did Louise.
9. Mike tried to get up, he was simply unable to stand.
10. Laura and Lee were both being considered, Laura got the job.
11. The Peter Zenger case was a famous colonial trial, it established freedom of the press.
12. First we went to Sequoia, then we visited King's Canyon.
13. Tom's jokes delighted Nan, they annoyed me.
14. Laughs drowned out the speaker, we could hardly hear.
15. Hamilton wrote the Federalist Papers, he got help from Madison and Jay.

Exercise B: Writing The first part of a sentence is given on each line below. Add a second main clause, beginning it with the word in parentheses at the end of the line. If the word is a conjunctive adverb, place a semicolon before it and a comma after it. If the word is a personal pronoun, use a semicolon or use a comma with a coordinating conjunction.

1. Some of the steak was burned (nevertheless)
2. Not only did the unwelcome guests stay for dinner (they)
3. That nail should be bent back (it)
4. I know Jacques Cousteau (in fact)
5. He was advised not to use colored stationery (he)
6. In high school she learned how to take shorthand (therefore)
7. My boss wants dependable workers (she)
8. I was amazed to learn that he played in a band (moreover)
9. The blizzard lasted all day (consequently)
10. Often people believe what they want to believe (they)
11. We had planned an all-day picnic (however)
12. No sign of the crew has been found (nevertheless)
13. Playing high school sports teaches teamwork (moreover)
14. Television programs can be educational (for example)
15. The concert began with a medley of songs (then)

REINFORCEMENT EXERCISES
Complete Sentences

A. Correct fragments resulting from incomplete thoughts. Rewrite the following fragments. Make each one into a complete sentence.

1. Saccharin instead of sugar
2. When walking in the desert
3. The streamers decorating the auditorium
4. Listened to the poetry of Gwendolyn Brooks
5. Myopia, or nearsightedness
6. After the doors to the exhibit were locked at ten o'clock
7. Kerosene lamps, at one time the main source of artificial lighting
8. Wanted to become a classical musician
9. Tongue lolling and tail wagging
10. Saw the movie *Casablanca* twenty times

B. Correct fragments resulting from incorrect punctuation. Change the punctuation and capitalization of the groups of words given below to make them complete sentences.

1. Our eyes work in the same way a camera does. By bending incoming light rays.
2. Experts recommend leather jump ropes over cloth or plastic. Because leather will last longer.
3. NEPA stands for the National Environmental Policy Act. Which was passed in 1969.
4. One of the world's most famous universities. The Sorbonne was founded in the 1200's.
5. Indigo is a plant that produces a dye. Used in the woolen industry during colonial times.
6. The evening before Allhallowmas, or All Saints' Day. Eventually became known as Halloween.
7. A hamstring is either one of the two tendons. At the back of the knee in humans.

8. We spent our New England vacation hiking. And skiing in New Hampshire.
9. Related to the eagle, hawk, and vulture. The osprey is a bird of prey that lives near water.
10. Enrico Fermi was born in Rome and taught physics in Florence. Before he immigrated to the United States.

C. Correct fragments that are phrases. Correct the fragments in the following paragraph by connecting them to complete sentences.

Few people who are not mathematicians themselves have heard of Srinivasa Ramanujan. One of the greatest mathematical minds of this century. One of the remarkable things about Ramanujan's knowledge of mathematics was that he discovered much of it on his own. Having had few books from which to learn of the work of others. Although a member of the Brahman caste, Ramanujan was poor. He tried to secure scholarships and grants. To enable him to continue in his work. English mathematicians heard about the Indian genius and arranged to have him brought to Cambridge. To pursue his studies. Ramanujan maintained his Indian customs even in England. Eating only vegetables and wearing traditional Indian garments. He fell ill after a few years in England and returned to India in 1920 to die. At the age of thirty-three. All of the famous mathematicians of his day recognized in Ramanujan a unique genius for mathematics. Ramanujan's contributions to mathematics were remarkable not only for their originality and depth. But also their scope.

D. Correct fragments that are clauses. Rewrite the following groups of words to make complete sentences. You may need to add words.

1. The woolen socks did not fit my brother. After he washed them in hot water.
2. Because hailstones form in much the same way that sleet does. You can think of hail as frozen sleet.

3. Winslow Homer, famous for his sea paintings, is an artist. Who got his start painting Civil War scenes.
4. Please pass me the evidence. When I request it.
5. Yasuo Kuniyoshi, a graphic artist, was born in Okayama. Which is in Japan.
6. The nautilus lives in the South Pacific and Indian oceans. Where it feeds on crabs and lobsters.
7. Although I studied the material. I did not pass the exam.
8. Since entering college. Robert has seen us only on holidays.
9. Crystal was just filling her car with gasoline. When the truck pulled into the station.
10. Even adults seem to like the stories about Winnie-the-Pooh. Who was a creation of A. A. Milne.

E. Correct run-on sentences. Correct each of the following run-on sentences.

1. Children get vaccinations against several diseases at two months of age, they don't get the measles vaccine until they are fifteen months old.
2. One artist sold beautiful tables made from redwood slabs, another displayed clocks made from cypress trees.
3. Sylvester Stallone was once voted the top hero of young Americans the runner-up was Eddie Murphy.
4. Lech Walesa founded Solidarity in Poland, he won the Nobel Peace Prize in 1983.
5. Eisenhower was probably the last President to have been born in the nineteenth century he was born in 1890.
6. Scientists have bred a strange animal called a geep, it is a combination of a goat and an angora sheep.
7. In ancient times the birthstone for July was onyx today, however, it is ruby.
8. Oklahoma's motto is "Labor Omnia Vincit" this means "Labor Conquers All."
9. Most of the planets were named after Roman gods and goddesses, Earth, of course, is the exception.
10. Most people know a baby elephant is called a "calf" how many know that a baby shark is called a "cub"?

MIXED REVIEW
Complete Sentences

A. Rewrite the fragments and run-ons as complete sentences.

1. The American crocodile once existed in great numbers, it is now an endangered species.
2. Joyce learned how to develop film. Assisting a photographer.
3. Sometimes twins are best friends. And sometimes not.
4. That film was a success at the box office. Although the critics disliked it.
5. My brother and I often play backgammon. After we have finished our homework.
6. This restaurant has twenty toppings for hamburgers, I chose avocado.
7. Citrus crops in Florida were damaged. During the unseasonably cold weather.
8. Members of the Dance Club performed several routines. Ranging from ballet to break dancing.
9. Does meditation work, is it restful and refreshing?
10. The U.S. Weather Bureau predicted a major blizzard. Worse than last year's.
11. Yolanda exhibited her pictures in the library. Also several etchings and one woodprint.
12. Some people are extroverts, others are introverts.
13. Marcel Marceau, who revived the art of pantomime.
14. The FBI traced the ransom note. Which demanded a million dollars.
15. The magazine has many columns, one is called "Feedback."

B. Identify complete sentences, fragments, and run-ons. Rewrite any fragments and run-ons to make complete sentences.

1. Certainly the best electrical guitar in our store.
2. In 1853, the United States government sent Matthew Perry to Japan. To open relations with this nation.

3. Water is the major component of the body, it is a substance we cannot survive without for long.
4. A wooden vehicle much like a scooter, which later evolved into the modern-day bicycle.
5. Rice is actually a type of grass. That grows in water.
6. Founded in 1839, the American Liberty Party was an antislavery party.
7. The weevil, which is a type of beetle. Is among the worst insect pests that attack crops.
8. Ate eighteen grams of salt in her daily diet, which was far too much.
9. Claire had read every book. By Ngaio Marsh.
10. Bryan always used plastic goggles while swimming because they helped keep his eyes free from chlorine.

C. Find and correct the sentence fragments and run-on sentences in the following paragraph. Look for incomplete ideas, phrases or clauses used alone, complete sentences separated by commas, and sentences that are not punctuated correctly.

Ever since movies have had sound. Films have been classified according to several different types. One of these was the movie of social protest, perhaps the most famous film of this genre was the *Grapes of Wrath*. Which was produced in 1940. A second genre included the musical, this genre was extremely popular with audiences. Stars such as Fred Astaire and Ginger Rogers became famous in dancing musicals, Jeanette MacDonald and Nelson Eddy starred in other musicals. Comedies were a third genre. Which continued from the days of silent film. Early film comedies included such greats as Laurel and Hardy, Mae West, and W. C. Fields. Another film genre is escapism. Which allowed people to get away from the cares of real life through imagination or fantasy. Full-length animated films, costume drama, and science fiction movies often have escapist appeal. Although they may be part of another genre as well. Gangster movies, Westerns, war movies, detective films, and historical dramas are other popular types of movies.

USING GRAMMAR IN WRITING
Complete Sentences

A. Almost everyone is familiar with the standard comedy scene in which characters speak only in fragments and yet somehow manage to understand each other. Such a dialogue appears below. Rewrite it, completing the phrases so that someone other than the characters could know what they're talking about. Be as creative as you can. When you are done with this scene, write one of your own.

> Mr. Jones: I just heard—
> Ms. Smith: You mean the news about—
> Mr. Jones: Yes! I hadn't known—
> Ms. Smith: Neither had I, and I must say I was—
> Mr. Jones: Weren't we all! And when I also learned that—
> Ms. Smith: I know, I know! But that was nothing compared to—
> Mr. Jones: You're absolutely correct. It's the most—
> Ms. Smith: I agree entirely. Still, neither of us should repeat a word of this conversation.

B. Writers sometimes use a technique called "stream of consciousness" to present realistically the thoughts running through the mind of a character or narrator. To create this effect, the writer records ideas as they would occur naturally—in fragments and run-ons—with seemingly illogical jumps from idea to idea. William Faulkner, for example, used this technique in sections of his novel *The Sound and the Fury*.

Write a passage of your own that uses the stream-of-consciousness technique. Your character might be someone struggling with an important decision, a cashier whose thoughts keep being interrupted by customers, or a person in the middle of a daydream. When you have finished the passage, rewrite it using complete sentences. Compare the effects of the two versions.

CUMULATIVE REVIEW
The Sentence (I)

Kinds of Sentences. The paragraph below contains simple sentences, compound sentences, complex sentences, and compound-complex sentences. Number your paper from 1 to 10. Next to the number corresponding to each sentence, write *S, CD, CX,* or *CD-CX* to identify the type of sentence it is.

1. About one thousand years ago, a special class of warriors arose in Japan. 2. These aristocratic soldiers, who were known as *samurai,* served very powerful clan leaders. 3. They were the only people who were allowed to wear swords, and they became famous as the fiercest fighters on earth. 4. The code of the samurai required constant readiness for battle, but it also demanded courtesy toward opponents. 5. In fact, a samurai would often compliment a vanquished opponent's skill in battle before beheading him. 6. Now that was courtesy indeed! 7. The samurai lost their former prestige when firearms were introduced to Japan during the sixteenth century. 8. Military leaders began using common footsoldiers armed with muskets, and swordplay, no matter how skillful, was no match for weapons that operated at a distance. 9. Finally, the samurai demanded that the manufacture of firearms be forbidden. 10. However, they could not hold back modern ways forever, and eventually the courteous samurai warriors became extinct.

CUMULATIVE REVIEW
The Sentence (II)

Correcting Fragments and Run-ons. Rewrite the following passage, correcting all sentence fragments and run-on sentences. Add or omit words as necessary.

Abigail Smith Adams, wife of John Adams, the second President of the United States, and mother of John Quincy Adams, the sixth American President. Born in Weymouth Massachusetts in 1744. She was the daughter of the Reverend William Smith. Minister of the Congregational Church in Weymouth. Although she had little formal education, she was among the most influential women of her day. Especially as a fashion leader and social arbiter. She supported women's rights, opposed slavery, and made educational opportunities available to her daughter. Who was also named Abigail.

During and after the American Revolution Abigail Adams was separated for long periods of time from her husband, who was first a delegate to Congress and later a diplomat in Europe her letters to him present a vivid picture of the Revolutionary War era. In her most famous letter, written to John Adams in 1776, she urged the Continental Congress to "remember the ladies." When drafting the nation's new laws. The *Familiar Letters of John Adams and His Wife Abigail* was published, along with a memoir by their grandson, Charles Francis Adams, in 1876 the many collections of her letters show that Abigail Adams was a perceptive, warmhearted, and generous person. Worthy of her prominent place in American history and literature.

—*Funk and Wagnall's New Encyclopedia*

5.0 Verb Usage

To speak and write correctly and with confidence, you must master the various forms that verbs can take. Most of the many thousands of verbs in English do not cause difficulty. They are **regular verbs.** They follow a common pattern in the language that is familiar from constant use. There are several groups of verbs, however, that are **irregular.** Their forms are not as familiar and require special attention.

5.1 The Principal Parts of Verbs

The three **principal parts** of a verb are the basic forms from which all other forms are made. The principal parts are the **present infinitive** (or **present**), the **past,** and the **past participle.**

A **regular verb** forms its past and past participle by adding -*ed* or -*d* to the present.

PRESENT	PAST	PAST PARTICIPLE
need	need*ed*	need*ed*
bake	bake*d*	bake*d*
hear	hear*d*	hear*d*

An **irregular verb** forms the past and past participle following any one of roughly five other patterns.

PRESENT	PAST	PAST PARTICIPLE
put	put	put
lend	lent	lent
begin	began	begun
rise	rose	risen
lie	lay	lain

Another form, the **present participle,** is sometimes called the fourth principal part. It is formed by adding *-ing* to the present form. Sometimes adding *-ing* requires additional spelling changes as well.

PRESENT	PRESENT PARTICIPLE
eat	eating
save	saving
put	putting

5.2   Irregular Verbs

Irregular verbs form the past and the past participle in a variety of ways. The rule given below can help you remember which form to use.

The past tense form is used alone. The past participle form is used with forms of *be* or *have*.

> The hunter *shot* the bear. (past)
> The stores *were* all *closed*. (past participle with form of *be*)
> My father *had* already *written*. (past participle with form of *have*)

> Jennifer *jammed* the gears on her bicycle. (past)
> The soldier *was awarded* a medal for heroism (past participle with form of *be*)
> He *has* not yet *decided* on a career. (past participle with form of *have*)

To choose the correct verb form, you need only learn the past and past participle forms of the most commonly used irregular verbs.

The irregular verbs fall into five major groups. The groups are determined by the patterns according to which the principal parts are formed.

Group 1. The easiest of the irregular verbs are those that have the same form in all principal parts.

PRESENT	PAST	PAST PARTICIPLE
burst	burst	(have) burst
cast	cast	(have) cast
cost	cost	(have) cost
fit	fit	(have) fit
hurt	hurt	(have) hurt
put	put	(have) put
read	read	(have) read
set	set	(have) set
shed	shed	(have) shed

Group 2. A second group that causes little difficulty contains verbs with same form for the past and the past participle.

PRESENT	PAST	PAST PARTICIPLE
bring	brought	(have) brought
catch	caught	(have) caught
dive	dived *or* dove*	(have) dived
fight	fought	(have) fought
flee	fled	(have) fled
fling	flung	(have) flung
get	got	(have) got *or* gotten
lead	led	(have) led
lend	lent	(have) lent
lose	lost	(have) lost

*Where two forms are given, both are standard usage, but the first is more common.

say	said	(have) said
seek	sought	(have) sought
shine	shone	(have) shone
sit	sat	(have) sat
sling	slung	(have) slung
sting	stung	(have) stung
sweep	swept	(have) swept
swing	swung	(have) swung

Exercise A: In the sentences below, the present form of the verb is given in parentheses. Substitute either past or past participle, whichever the sentence requires.

1. The mayor was (sting) by the unexpected criticism.
2. Charles Evans Hughes (lose) the Presidency by only twenty-three electoral votes.
3. As the curtain rose, the audience (burst) into applause.
4. Unexpected frosts have (cost) farmers millions of dollars.
5. No one was (hurt) in the collision.
6. The epidemic has already (spread) to neighboring towns.
7. The election of 1860 (bring) Lincoln to the White House.
8. The villagers (flee) before the rising waters.
9. The shortstop (catch) the ball and tagged the runner.
10. The hurricane had (fling) street signs to the pavement.
11. Bernstein (lead) the orchestra in an all-Bach program.
12. The bank (lend) Mom some money to remodel the house.
13. The old farmer's wrinkled face (shine) with pride as he surveyed his harvest.
14. The large urban vote (swing) the election.
15. Annette (bring) me an Italian newspaper.

Exercise B: Choose the standard form from those in parentheses.

1. Ronnie blew up the balloon until it (bust, busted, burst).
2. Paula has already (caught, catched) the legal limit of trout.
3. The quarterback (hurt, hurted) his weak knee.
4. Eleanor Roosevelt once (sayed, said), "No one can make you feel inferior without your consent."

5. Alex (lent, lended) me his power saw.
6. The speedboat (swang, swinged, swung) around the buoy.
7. Dad has (losed, lost) his automobile insurance policy.
8. The cadets (flung, flinged, flang) their caps into the air.
9. The hornet (stang, stung) Dorothy on the elbow.
10. Rescuers (led, leaded) the dazed miners out of the shaft.
11. Aunt Marion (brang, brought) back slides of her trip.
12. As usual, Suzanne had (dived, dove) flawlessly.
13. The sun has not (shined, shone) for over a week.
14. The campers (fleed, fled) as the river began to rise.
15. Our trip (cost, costed) more than we had anticipated.
16. The maintenance crew (sweeped, swept) the gym floor.
17. Just as the bell rang, I realized I had (brang, brung, brought) the wrong book to class.
18. The deckhand (slang, slung, slinged) the anchor overboard.
19. The batter (swinged, swang, swung) at the fast ball but missed.
20. The weightlifter raised the barbell then (setted, set) it slowly down.

Group 3. Another group of irregular verbs adds *-n* or *-en* to the past form to make the past participle.

PRESENT	PAST	PAST PARTICIPLE
bear	bore	(have) borne*
beat	beat	(have) beaten
bite	bit	(have) bitten
break	broke	(have) broken
choose	chose	(have) chosen
freeze	froze	(have) frozen
speak	spoke	(have) spoken
steal	stole	(have) stolen
swear	swore	(have) sworn
tear	tore	(have) torn
wear	wore	(have) worn

*Note that *borne* retains the final *e*.

Exercise A: Choose the standard form from those in parentheses.

1. Somebody (broke, broken) Steve's toy pickup truck.
2. Jamie's dump truck was (broke, broken) also.
3. The company (beared, bore) all of her expenses.
4. Has the team (chose, chosen) its captain yet?
5. The Supreme Court justices (wore, weared) black robes.
6. The eggs were (beat, beaten) to make a fluffy omelet.
7. Meat that has once been thawed should not be (froze, frozen) again.
8. I could have (sweared, swore, sworn) that there were two people in that car.
9. Have you (broken, broke) your appointment again?
10. Allen has (chose, chosen) *The Bermuda Triangle* for his report.
11. The patient (bore, beared) traces of deep suffering.
12. Uncle Ben wishes he had (chose, chosen) a different profession.
13. Several diamond rings have been (stole, stolen) from Ms. Van Hoot's apartment.
14. I have just (tore, torn) my new jacket on a nail.
15. The witness was promptly (swore, sworn) in.
16. The insect repellent kept us from being (bit, bitten) by mosquitoes.
17. Sue has hardly (spoke, spoken) to me since my arrival.
18. We have (beat, beaten) Dover once in the last ten years.
19. Marsha (teared, torn, tore) the letter up and threw it away.
20. Have you ever (spoke, spoken) at an assembly?

Exercise B: The present form of the verb is given. Substitute past or past participle, whichever the sentence requires.

1. Thousands panicked when the stock market (break).
2. What book have you (choose) to read?
3. You should have (wear) your thermal sweatshirt.
4. Phil has (steal) more bases than any other player.
5. Felice has (break) the school record for the high jump.

6. The Red Sox have finally (beat) the Yankees.
7. The rock (tear) a hole in the bottom of the canoe.
8. The tribe (swear) to avenge the death of their chief.
9. The milk on the porch has (freeze) solid.
10. The carpet on the stairs was (wear) out.
11. The committee has not yet (choose) a date for the annual dinner dance.
12. The candidate (speak) earnestly and persuasively.
13. The campers were badly (bite) by mosquitoes.
14. Leslie was (beat) badly in the quarter-finals.
15. The doctor thinks Andy's wrist is (break).
16. Professor Morey (speak) about the life of Molière.
17. The deer (freeze) when it saw the on-coming headlights.
18. Even our greatest Presidents have (bear) constant criticism of their programs.
19. Our mail carrier has never been (bite) by a dog.
20. We have already (beat) Springfield once this year.

Group 4. There are only seven verbs that follow this pattern. They all have an **i** in the present that changes to an **a** in the past and to a **u** in the past participle. Memorize these seven verbs as a group.

PRESENT	PAST	PAST PARTICIPLE
begin	began	(have) begun
drink	drank	(have) drunk
ring	rang	(have) rung
sing	sang	(have) sung
sink	sank *or* sunk	(have) sunk
spring	sprang *or* sprung	(have) sprung
swim	swam	(have) swum

Exercise A: Choose the standard form from those in parentheses.

1. The choir (sang, sung) Christmas carols at the hospital.
2. Have you (began, begun) your senior project yet?
3. Colette has (swam, swum) over a hundred miles this year.
4. The players (drank, drunk) the ice water rapidly.

5. The trap was (sprang, sprung), but the bear was not in it.
6. The forward had (sank, sunk) the ball through the hoop.
7. Has the first bell (rang, rung) yet?
8. The children have (drank, drunk) all the apple juice.
9. The *Lady Elgin,* which had (sank, sunk) off the shore of Lake Michigan, was salvaged by divers.
10. Many communities (sprang, sprung) up across the country during the 1960's and 1970's.

Exercise B: The present form is given in parentheses. Substitute past or past participle, whichever the sentence requires.

1. I (ring) for the nurse.
2. I (drink) the cocoa even though it was stone cold.
3. Andrew Carnegie (begin) his career as a bobbin boy in a factory.
4. She had (sing) at La Scala before coming to the Metropolitan.
5. The fisherman (sink) a line through the hole in the ice.
6. They turned back after their rowboat had (spring) a leak.
7. We (drink) cool spring water while camping in Colorado.
8. When Claire arrived, the examination had already (begin).
9. Have you ever (drink) papaya juice?
10. All over the yard, dandelions had (spring) up.
11. The *Graf Spee* was (sink) by her own crew.
12. The telephone (ring) once and then stopped.
13. The role of Carmen has been (sing) by many opera stars.
14. Skin divers (swim) down to inspect the sunken ship.
15. The *Edmund Fitzgerald* had (sink) in the tumultuous waters of Lake Superior.
16. When Johnson missed the field goal, our hearts (sink).
17. The men (spring) out of their bunks when the captain entered.
18. Gabe must have (drink) the last container of milk.
19. At the three-quarter mark, the Navy crew had (begin) to tire.
20. Cheryl (swim) in the 50-yard free-style event.

Group 5. A large group of irregular verbs forms the past participle from the present form rather than from the past.

PRESENT	PAST	PAST PARTICIPLE
blow	blew	(have) blown
come	came	(have) come
do	did	(have) done
draw	drew	(have) drawn
drive	drove	(have) driven
eat	ate	(have) eaten
fall	fell	(have) fallen
give	gave	(have) given
go	went	(have) gone
grow	grew	(have) grown
know	knew	(have) known
ride	rode	(have) ridden
rise	rose	(have) risen
run	ran	(have) run
see	saw	(have) seen
shake	shook	(have) shaken
slay	slew	(have) slain
take	took	(have) taken
throw	threw	(have) thrown
write	wrote	(have) written

Exercise A: Choose the standard form from those in parentheses.

1. Most of the icicles have (fell, fallen) to the ground.
2. Alan (gone, went) to the basement for the brace and bit.
3. You should have (gave, given) the matter more thought.
4. I wonder who (took, taken) my scarf.
5. The officials have always (run, ran) this town efficiently.
6. I (seen, saw) an unusual television play last night.
7. This letter must have been (wrote, written) on a moving bus.
8. Many celebrities had (came, come) for the opening night.
9. The catcher (throwed, threw) the ball into center field.

10. The wind had (shaken, shook) all the apples from the tree.
11. The students (took, taken) their lunches with them.
12. I had never (ate, eaten) fried clams before.
13. The wind (blew, blowed) down several trees last night.
14. This year all the birthdays in our family have (fell, fallen) on weekends.
15. The teller was badly (shook, shaken) by the robbery.
16. Sally must have (knowed, knew, known) where we were.
17. The President must have (shook, shaken) hands with a thousand people.
18. Who (did, done) the illustrations for this book?
19. Stocks have (rose, risen) for the tenth consecutive day.
20. Have you ever (ridden, rode) in a helicopter?

Exercise B: The present form is given in parentheses. Substitute the past or past participle, whichever the sentence requires.

1. I (see) the new high school yesterday.
2. The soldiers stood at attention while taps was (blow).
3. Amy and Fran have (drive) across the continent in six days.
4. I (do) the sanding job in two hours.
5. Mr. Cross has (give) me his entire coin collection.
6. We have (grow) our own vegetables for years.
7. The judge (throw) the case out of court.
8. Archie (shake) the mop vigorously.
9. The census was (take) in 1984.
10. The price of butter has (rise) sharply.
11. Have you ever (eat) Philadelphia scrapple?
12. The new Broadway musical (draw) capacity audiences.
13. Betty has (write) a letter to *The Chicago Tribune*.
14. A stranger (come) up to us and asked for directions.
15. I should have (know) the stores would be closed.
16. Angrily the catcher (throw) her mask to the ground.
17. Bart would have (go) if he had had a coat and tie.
18. The salesperson (do) his best to sell Dad some insurance.
19. Cindy lectured while Chuck (run) the projector.
20. The tide has already (rise) two feet.

5.3 The Progressive and Emphatic Forms of Verbs

The Progressive Forms

The **progressive form** of the verb is used to show ongoing action. To make the progressive, add the present participle to a form of *be*.

They *are* talking.　　　　　Maria *has been driving*.
The clock *is working*.　　　The teacher *had been explaining*.
The actors *were rehearsing*.　I *must be dreaming*.
Joe will *be presiding*.　　　Louis *might have been sleeping*.

The Emphatic Forms

A verb may be given special emphasis by using a form of *do* with the present form of the verb.
These are examples of the **emphatic form.**

PRESENT:　Kristy *wants* to go with us.
PRESENT EMPHATIC:　Kristy *does want* to go with us.

PAST:　I *considered* it carefully.
PAST EMPHATIC:　I *did consider* it carefully.

Exercise A: Find each verb. Decide whether it is a progressive or emphatic form.

1. A guinea pig named Chester is living at our house.
2. My sister was being stubborn about our vacation plans.
3. You do agree with Burt and me, correct?
4. Mr. Randolph does lose track of his main point.
5. I will be laughing and you will be crying when the semester grades come out.
6. The mermaids were singing songs that lured sailors to their deaths.

7. The committee does make those decisions.
8. Is Flannery having a sweet sixteen party on her birthday?
9. Henry does believe that hard work pays off in the end.
10. Ten of us will be going to the state track meet.

Exercise B: Writing Rewrite each sentence, changing the italicized verb to the form indicated in parentheses.

1. I *think* good manners are still important. (emphatic)
2. A wrong guess on your answer sheet *counts* against you. (emphatic)
3. Sharon *hoped* that her cousin would be selected as spokesperson. (emphatic)
4. Chad *runs* even though there is ice on the ground. (progressive)
5. The proctor *explained* how the examination would be scored. (emphatic)
6. Shakespeare *wrote* plays as early as 1590. (progressive)
7. Time to come up with a solution ran out. (progressive)
8. Brian *turned* out the lights before he left the house. (emphatic)
9. The full moon *shines* radiantly overhead. (progressive)
10. Evidence *points* to cholesterol as a factor in heart disease. (emphatic)

5.4   Verb Tense

Verbs change form to indicate **tense,** or time. Verbs may express past, present, and future time. There are three simple tenses (present, past, and future) and three perfect tenses (present perfect, past perfect, and future perfect). The paragraphs below describe each tense and how it is used.

1. **Present tense.** The first principal part, or simple form of the verb, is used for the present tense. This tense expresses action that is occurring now, at this present time.

The swimmers *stay* near the shore. (right now)
The news *sounds* good. (at this moment)

We do not always use the simple or present forms of verbs to tell of actions that are going on at the moment. We do not say, "I listen." We are more likely to use the **progressive form** "I am listening" or the **emphatic form** "I do listen." An exception is the use of the present to describe ongoing sports events:

McAdoo *intercepts* the pass and New York *wins*.

The present forms of verbs are used to tell of repeated or regular and habitual action.

They *go* to camp every summer.
My father *parks* the car in front of the house.

The present forms of verbs are also used to tell of something that is generally true at all times.

Cream *rises* to the top in unprocessed milk.
Water *freezes* at 0° Celsius.

Sometimes we speak of an event in the past as if it were happening in the present. At these times, we use the present form of the verb and call it the **historical present tense.**

Roosevelt rises from his chair and slowly makes his way toward the podium, triumphing over the paralysis in his legs.

2. **Past tense.** The second principal part of the verb expresses action that has occurred in the past: They *wrote,* you *hammered*. Continuing action in the past is expressed with the **past progressive:** They *were writing,* you *were hammering*.
3. **Future tense.** Action that will take place in the future is expressed by combining the present form of the verb with *will* or *shall:* They *will* go, we *shall* see.
    Another way of expressing future action is to use a present tense verb with an adverb that indicates time.

We *get* our shots *tomorrow*. (*tomorrow* is an adverb telling that the verb *get* will take place in the future.)

Linda *plays* center field *from now on*. (*from now on* is an adverb phrase expressing future time.)

A third way to express future action is by combining a form of *be* with the phrase *going to* and a present tense verb.

The Parks Department *is going to redesign* the playground.

The Sadlers *are going to work* in South America next year.

4. **Present perfect tense.** The third principal part of the verb (past participle) is used with *has* or *have* to form the present perfect tense. This tense expresses action that has occurred at some indefinite time in the past.

Thousands of Americans *have viewed* the Mona Lisa.

Walter *has* already *auditioned* for the show.

The present perfect also expresses action that began in the past and continues into the present.

She *has worked* for thirty years. (She is still working.)

He *has been waiting* for a permit. (present perfect progressive)

5. **Past perfect tense.** The third principal part of the verb is combined with *had* to form the past perfect tense. This tense expresses an action completed in the past before some other past action or event.

EARLIER	LATER
I *had admired* her	before I *met* her.
He *had praised* revolution	until he *realized* its dangers.
We *had been planning* the trip	before Jim *lost* his job.

6. **Future perfect tense.** The third principal part (past participle) of the verb is combined with *will have* or *shall have* to form the future perfect tense. This tense expresses an action that will be completed in the future before some other future action takes place.

Before the musical closes, it *will have played* for five years.
The race *will have started* by the time Bill arrives.

Note: In sentences with future perfect constructions, the verb
in the present tense indicates a far future action or event. The
verb in the future perfect tense indicates future action that
will occur *before* the action of the present tense verb.

Exercise A: Find each verb and tell its tense.

1. Somebody finally heard our cries for help.
2. The rehearsal will start promptly at eight.
3. Has the bell rung yet?
4. Melinda will undoubtedly be the next class president.
5. Philip is playing a Strauss waltz.
6. Who will be at the game?
7. Shall we watch a comedian or a play?
8. The Todds had already sold their house.
9. In May, Leon will have been in the Navy two years.
10. By four o'clock the snow plows were clearing the roads.
11. Have you ever forgotten your homework?
12. The juniors arrange a class trip every year.
13. Donna will become an engineer.
14. By that time, Bob will have spent two years in college.
15. Why weren't you at the meeting last night?

Exercise B: Writing Identify the tense of the verbs in each sentence. Then rewrite each sentence so there is at least one verb in
the tense given in parentheses.

1. Tomorrow is too late. (future perfect)
2. His popularity was one reason for his victory. (past perfect)
3. Betsy Ross experimented with various designs for the
   American flag. (historical present)
4. The word *sanguine* came from a Latin word that meant
   "blood." (present)
5. Schools will be closing because the number of children in
   our town will be decreasing. (present)

6. People of all races, religions, and nationalities had equal opportunity in the New World. (future)
7. Johnny Carson was a television personality for three decades. (present perfect)
8. We go to our farm in the country when we want peace and tranquility. (past)
9. James takes care of the Nathans's pets during winter break. (future)
10. She swam a mile a day to stay in shape. (present)

5.5   Voice and Mood

Verbs have specific forms to express a variety of situations in which actions or events occur. The progressive and emphatic forms, for example, help the writer express his or her precise shade of meaning. Similarly, the six verb tenses place the action or event in time. In addition to these forms that you have already studied, there are other, more subtle, forms of the verb that can help you to express particular meanings.

The Active Voice and the Passive Voice

A verb is in the **active voice** when the subject of the sentence *performs* the action of the verb. The verb is in the passive voice when the subject *receives* the action of the verb. The passive voice is formed by using some form of *be* with the past participle of the verb.

ACTIVE: The voters *studied* the *issues* carefully.

PASSIVE: The issues *were studied* carefully by the voters.

ACTIVE: The increase in vandalism *angered* the citizens.

PASSIVE: The citizens *were angered* by the increase in vandalism.

The sentences above illustrate that the *object* of the verb in the active voice becomes the *subject* of the verb in the passive voice.

Good writers generally try to use verbs in the active voice as much as possible because they are more interesting and more powerful. Active voice constructions also make clear who is actually performing the action of the verb.

> PASSIVE: My uncle was fired. (Who did it?)
> ACTIVE: Mr. Griswold fired my uncle. (The person responsible for the action is clear.)

Be certain when you use passive voice verbs that the person or thing responsible for the action is clear. Also avoid mixing the active and passive voice in the same passage.

Exercise A: Find the verb and tell whether it is active or passive.

1. Larger contributions are needed by the National Kidney Foundation.
2. Washington buzzed with politicans and representatives of foreign governments.
3. In 1912, Arizona was admitted to the Union.
4. The trees were pruned by the owner of the nursery.
5. My sister's class elected her president.
6. A package of sunflower seeds will be mailed to you.
7. The great pyramid of Cheops covers thirteen acres.
8. The amendment was passed by a two-thirds vote.
9. The window has been broken by every storm.
10. Basketball was invented in 1891 by James A. Naismith, a Y.M.C.A. instructor.

Exercise B: Change the active verbs to passive and the passive verbs to active.

1. The first ball was thrown out by the mayor.
2. The driver of the red car hit the fire hydrant.
3. Dr. Ramsey operated on my father.

4. Lee was chosen by the group to represent them.
5. The ordinance was finally passed by the City Council.
6. The Sixth Regiment took the city.
7. The mechanic was repairing the engine.
8. The photographs have been retouched by the engraver.
9. The parade was reviewed by the governor and the mayor.
10. The famished students quickly devoured the sandwiches.

Mood

The mood of a verb expresses the writer's attitude toward his or her subject. Most sentences are in the **indicative mood.** This mood is used when the writer believes his or her subject is actually happening, or has happened, or will happen. It is used for sentences that express real, factual events and occurrences.

It is raining.
They ate seven courses.
She will compete in the play-offs.

The **imperative mood** expresses a command, directive, or request. The imperative mood is always expressed in the present tense. The subject of the verb is always the second person pronoun *you.*

(You) Tell me everything you know.
(You) Get Aunt Lucy a glass of water, please.
(You) Go left at Elm and three blocks to the stoplight.

The **subjunctive mood** expresses the writer's belief that the situation he or she is writing about is questionable or contrary to fact. The subjunctive mood is like the indicative mood in form except in the third person singular of the present tense. Here, the *s* ending is omitted.

INDICATIVE: Cassie *cleans* her half of the room regularly.
SUBJUNCTIVE: Mother insists that Cassie *clean* her half of the room regularly.

The subjunctive form of the verb *be* is a special case. With this verb, the form in the present tense for all persons and numbers is *be*.

PRESENT TENSE: I recommended that they *be* suspended.
If this *be* treason, then I am guilty.

The past subjunctive form of the verb *to be* is *were*.

PAST TENSE: I wish I *were* a musician.
If the witness *were* honest, the accused would
   be acquitted.
Do you wish he *were* your friend?

In English the subjunctive mood is used in the following situations:

1. *Were* and *be* are often used instead of other forms of *to be* . . .
   a. To express wishes

   I wish I *were* nineteen.

   b. To express conditions that are doubtful or contrary to fact. In these cases, it is used after such words as *if, as if, though,* and *although.*

   If he *were* able, Frank would join the search party.
   Helen acted as if she *were* the only one who had failed.

2. *Were, be,* and the third person subjunctive forms of other verbs are used . . .
   a. To express commands or requests after the word *that*

   The kidnappers demanded that the father *come* alone.
   The speaker asked that the audience *be* silent.

   b. In certain archaic phrases

   Heaven *be* praised
   far *be* it for me . . .
   say what he will . . .

Exercise: Tell whether each italicized verb is in the indicative, imperative, or subjunctive mood.

1. *Grab* a partner and *get* out on the dance floor.
2. The orders *required* that lights *be* out by nine o'clock.
3. If she *were* able, Sarah would run all the way to Bloomington.
4. Matthew *will be* the happiest person on earth when he graduates.
5. What would you do if you *were* king?
6. *Follow* the signs to Route 93 and then *go* south until you cross the state line.
7. Ben Jonson *wrote* plays under Tudor and Stuart rule.
8. Please *write* to Teresa and me when you are in Toronto.
9. *Be* polite when you are visiting your grandparents' house.
10. The veterinarian *asked* that all the sick animals *be fed* twice a day.

5.6 Commonly Confused Verbs

There are three pairs of verbs that look alike and have similar meanings. These verbs are frequently confused. Study their meanings and their principal parts to avoid using one when you mean to use the other.

Lay and *lie*. The verb *lay* means "to put or place something" and usually implies an action taking place. It is generally transitive and has a direct object. The verb *lie* means "to recline, to rest, or remain in horizontal position." *Lie* is intransitive. It does not take a direct object.*

The principal parts of *lay* and *lie* are as follows:

PRESENT	PAST	PAST PARTICIPLE
lay	laid	(have) laid
lie	lay	(have) lain

*There is a homonym meaning "to tell an untruth." The principal parts of that verb are *lie, lied, lied*.

Sit and *set*. The verb *sit* usually means "to rest with the legs bent and the back upright," but there are many other related meanings. *Sit* is an intransitive verb; it never has an object. The verb *set* means to "put or place something." *Set* is a transitive verb; it almost always has an object. The principal parts of *sit* and *set* are as follows:

PRESENT	PAST	PAST PARTICIPLE
sit	sat	(have) sat
set	set	(have) set

Rise and *raise*. The verb *rise* means "to go up." It is intransitive and never has an object. The verb *raise* means "to make something move upward." *Raise* is transitive; it almost always has an object. Things *rise* by themselves; they are *raised* by someone or something else. The principal parts of *rise* and *raise* are as follows:

PRESENT	PAST	PAST PARTICIPLE
rise	rose	(have) risen
raise	raised	(have) raised

Note: There are exceptions to the statements given above about the three pairs of verbs. The sentences below illustrate some of the special uses of these verbs.

> The sun *sets* early in the winter. (intransitive)
> The mixture will *set* in an hour. (intransitive)
>
> *Sit* the patient in the chair. (transitive)
> The hens are *laying* well. (intransitive)

Exercise A: Choose the standard form from those in parentheses.

1. New London (lies, lays) between New York and Boston.
2. Alonzo told the dog to (lie, lay) down.
3. The customer (lay, laid) two quarters on the counter.
4. Pat (lay, laid) on the beach and sipped lemonade.
5. The deserted bus was (lying, laying) in the ditch.

6. The foreign ministers (lay, laid) the groundwork for the summit conference.
7. Charlie is (lying, laying) in the hammock.
8. The baby was (lain, laid) on the bassinet.
9. The book that I (lay, laid) on the table has disappeared.
10. Your wallet is (lying, laying) on the floor.
11. Garrett (lay, laid) the silverware on the table.
12. Grandmother has gone upstairs to (lie, lay) down.
13. The pup is (lying, laying) the bone under the table.
14. The pup is (lying, laying) under the table.
15. Have the foundations been (lain, laid) for the new school?
16. I was (lying, laying) down when the Russells came.
17. The group (lay, laid) their plan before the City Council.
18. My purse had (lain, laid) in the breezeway all night.
19. The injured worker (lay, laid) unconscious on the ground.
20. At the foot of Mt. Vesuvius (lies, lays) Naples.

Exercise B: Choose the standard form from those in parentheses.

1. Peggy (rose, raised) quickly and answered the door.
2. The curtain was (rising, raising) as we reached our seats.
3. What time did the sun (rise, raise) this morning?
4. The elderly man (rose, raised) from his chair with difficulty.
5. The nurse (rose, raised) the patient's pillow.
6. Has the water (risen, raised) at all since last night?
7. The sun had not yet (risen, raised) above the horizon.
8. Gales of laughter (rose, raised) from the audience.
9. I am glad that these questions have been (risen, raised).
10. The supermarket will (rise, raise) the price of dairy products next week.
11. Commuter fares have (risen, raised) substantially in recent years.
12. Will everyone in favor please (rise, raise)?
13. Will everyone in favor please (rise, raise) his or her hand?
14. A heavy cloud of black smoke was (rising, raising) from the oil refinery.

15. The officers saluted as the flag was (risen, raised).
16. Our spirits (rose, raised) when our team tied the score.
17. The price of lumber has (risen, raised) sharply again.
18. Everyone (rose, raised) when the team trotted onto the field.
19. The rent cannot be (rose, raised) more than five percent.
20. Jeff's cake failed to (rise, raise).

Exercise C: Choose the standard form from those given in parentheses.

1. (Sit, Set) in the armchair if you wish.
2. I'll (sit, set) the tray on your lap.
3. Come and (sit, set) by the fire.
4. Please (sit, set) this vase on the desk.
5. We have (sat, set) in the sun for over an hour.
6. Just (sat, set) your glass on the table.
7. May I (sit, set) this wet umbrella in the kitchen?
8. From where I was (sitting, setting), it looked like a touchdown.
9. Sean was too nervous to (sit, set) still.
10. Barbara (sat, set) the lantern inside the tent.
11. My nephew scrambled over and (sat, set) on my lap.
12. Motionless, the model (sat, set) in front of the art class.
13. Did Elena (sit, set) her ticket on the mantel?
14. Antique dealers are (sitting, setting) high prices on their wares.
15. The four-year-old (sat, set) her popsicle on the bench.
16. The actress was (sitting, setting) her deck chair in the sun.
17. The actress was (sitting, setting) in the sun.
18. Everyone (sat, set) quietly during Marie's talk.
19. Just (sit, set) the trunk in the hall.
20. How long have these cartons of milk been (sitting, setting) on the step?

REINFORCEMENT EXERCISES
Verb Usage

A. Use past and past participle forms correctly. In the sentences below, the present form of the verb is given in parentheses. Substitute either past or past participle, as necessary.

1. Those two dogs have (fight) over the rubber bone before.
2. The sun (shine) on the Arctic town for the first time in months.
3. If the pranksters had not (fling) the keys into the lake, we would not have been late.
4. Last Saturday I fell and (hurt) my ankle.
5. It was the wagonmaster who (lead) the pioneers across the plains and mountains.
6. No, Larissa has never been (sting) by a wasp.
7. Samuel did not realize how much room and board (cost).
8. In 1966, scientists (catch) a live pygmy opossum, believed to have been extinct for twenty thousand years.
9. The votaries had (bring) sacrifices of grain and fruit to the altars.
10. "I have (lend) you my favorite records," said Charity.
11. "Nobody knows the burdens I have (bear)," sighed the professor dramatically.
12. Angi (break) the state record for backstroke.
13. The snake handler had never been (bite) by a snake.
14. The sturdy cloth was not (tear) by the briars.
15. Father has (speak) to me on that subject many times.
16. In our grandfather's garden, broccoli, corn, squash, and beans (grow) side by side.
17. Dr. Melinski has studied scallops, but she has never (eat) them.
18. Didn't Emily Dickinson write that the sun (rise) "a ribbon at a time?"
19. Even before the volcano erupted, the earth (shake).
20. After the winds had (blow) across the desert, the dunes changed shape.

B. Use the progressive and emphatic forms of verbs. Rewrite, changing the italicized verb to the form indicated in parentheses.

1. Yes, Kilpatrick Macmillan, a Scottish blacksmith, *added* pedals to the bicycle. (emphatic)
2. The runners *loaded* themselves with carbohydrates. (progressive)
3. The jury *believes* the second witness's story. (emphatic)
4. Kyla *writes* her report on the seven natural wonders of the world. (progressive)
5. The pharmacist *might have suggested* powdered penicillin. (progressive)
6. Brett *enjoyed* Lake Windermere, England's largest lake. (emphatic)
7. Lyn *called* her parents shortly after midnight. (emphatic)
8. She *has translated* Hawaiian proverbs into English. (progressive)
9. Many people *roller skated* during the Great Depression. (emphatic)
10. Darleen *read* about Diago Cao, the Portuguese explorer. (progressive)

C. Identify verb tenses. Find the verb in each of the following sentences and tell its tense.

1. Canada produces more than twenty million bushels of apples yearly.
2. By the end of my trip, I shall have sampled Egyptian, Indian, and Japanese cuisine.
3. One hive of bees yields over two hundred pounds of honey a year.
4. Pedro knew the answer immediately.
5. We have driven from Chicago to Atlanta many times.
6. To our dismay, boll weevils had attacked the cotton.
7. You will enjoy speleology—cave exploration.
8. One hundred fifty years ago, Americans stored large blocks of ice in their cellars all year long.
9. Our school is purchasing computers for the study area.
10. Mr David has been a volunteer firefighter for forty years.

D. Use active verbs. Rewrite each sentence below so that the passive voice becomes active.

1. The Colossus of Rhodes was destroyed by an earthquake around 200 B.C.
2. The modern theory of molecular structure was developed by Niels Bohr, a Danish physicist.
3. The land of Kentucky was granted to Virginia by Congress.
4. "My job was taken away by a robot," said the assembly line worker.
5. The gold medal was won by Mariechen Jackson.
6. Enamel was used by the potter to decorate her work.
7. Long, narrow snowshoes were worn by the Cree Indians when they hunted in winter.
8. The kangaroo was mistaken for a dog by early settlers.
9. The movie *Frankenstein* was produced by Thomas Edison in 1910.
10. The *Carl D. Bradley* was broken in half by the furious Great Lakes gale.

E. Use commonly confused verbs correctly. Choose the correct verb form from those given in parentheses.

1. When the submerged log first (raised, rose) from the lake, we thought it was an alligator.
2. The gardener (sit, set) out the cabbage and broccoli plants when the weather was still crisp.
3. The captain said jokingly that the wind had (risen, raised) in order to help him win the sailing race.
4. The new parents (set, sat) the baby in the car seat and fastened the seat belt.
5. "(Lie, lay) down and take a nap," suggested the nurse.
6. The red carpet had been (lain, laid) out for the President.
7. The dog had (lain, laid) under the table, undetected.
8. We'll have to (sit, set) the flowers in the sun.
9. Nevil's home (lied, lay) across the valley from ours.
10. One crew member was (raising, rising) the international distress signal.

MIXED REVIEW
Verb Usage

A. In the sentences below, the present form of the verb is given in parentheses. Substitute the past or the past participle to fit the meaning of the sentence.

1. The grizzly bear had (break) into our cabin and (eat) the flour, molasses, beans, and bacon.
2. Because of an overactive pituitary gland, the steer (grow) to an amazing size.
3. Captain Cook (bring) a tortoise to the King of Tonga in the eighteenth century that did not die until the twentieth.
4. The milk had (freeze) in the bottle and pushed up the paper cap.
5. Many books have been (write) about origami, the Japanese art of paper folding.
6. "I knew it!" shouted Mrs. Pillot as she (fling) the detective novel out the window.
7. Scientists concluded that the polar bear had (swim) hundreds of miles.
8. Lindsey (sit) on the porch and looked at the distant mountains.
9. Although the tiger (spring) quickly from her hiding place, the antelope managed to escape.
10. The speaker (draw) an unpleasant picture of a world without reason.

B. Choose the standard form from those in parentheses.

1. Long ago, people believed that spirits (raised, rose) from the dead at certain times of the year.
2. If we had (knew, known) how long the movie was, we would have (saw, seen) it on a weekend night.
3. Julia has never (sang, sung) a solo before.
4. Construction workers (lay, laid) the foundation for the new high-rise office building.

5. *National Lampoon* once (done, did) a parody of a high school yearbook.
6. The ship has (born, borne) the brunt of many storms.
7. Hearing a sound behind him, the guard (sat, set) the telephone receiver down and turned to investigate.
8. The reporter (rose, raised) his binoculars to watch the volcano erupt.
9. The real diamond (lied, lay, laid) among the rhinestones.
10. The wood was so heavy that it (sank, sunk) in water.
11. Unthinkingly, I (brought, brung) cake instead of popcorn.
12. The search committee believed they had (chose, chosen) the right person for the job.
13. The dress Shirley made in sewing class (began, begun) to come apart the first time she (wore, worn) it.
14. Coach Hollings has (drove, driven) the team to its limits.

C. Some of the following sentences contain errors in verb usage. Rewrite these sentences, correcting any errors. If a sentence does not contain any errors, write *Correct*.

1. The hot air balloons rose high above the balloon port and begun the race.
2. The bells in the village had rang each time a soldier had returned home to his fields.
3. Damita tore coupons out of the newspaper and saved them for her grandfather.
4. The chef had measured the dry ingredients for the cake, but he had not beat the egg yolks.
5. Three witnesses seen the suspect leave the scene of the crime on Monday night.
6. Charles had ran for Student Council every year and won.
7. You may lie your coats on the sofa in the livingroom.
8. After Angie had her operation, she lay in bed for three weeks without sitting up.
9. The instructor said, "I have spoke to you about the importance of practice too many times already."
10. The first autumn leaves were laying on the ground after the September rainstorm.

USING GRAMMAR IN WRITING
Verb Usage

A. People design clothing for warmth, for fashion, and for protection from various kinds of injury. Protective clothing, in particular, has been important in battle, sporting events, industry, and space. Write a three-paragraph essay on the subject. First, discuss protective clothing in the past and present. Then use your imagination to speculate about the types of protective clothing that may be worn in the future.

B. The paragraph below is written entirely in the passive voice. Rewrite it so that it is in the active voice. You may have to add subjects.

> Saluting is performed by soldiers around the world. Officers are saluted and flags are saluted. Saluting is considered an act of respect. It is not known exactly where or when saluting originated. It is believed by many historians of such customs, however, that saluting is derived from a prehistoric custom. That custom is believed to be the showing of an open hand. Friendliness, or at least nonaggression, is indicated by an open hand, because weapons cannot held in an open hand. Thus, a salute may have been used to show friendliness towards members of the same social group.

C. Strong verbs can help make a piece of writing much more interesting to read. For each of the following verbs, make a list of at least five synonyms that are more exact. Then write a short narrative that includes several of these words. The narrative may be original, or it may be a summary of a scene from a TV show or movie.

said   walked   moved   thought   smiled   cried

CUMULATIVE REVIEW
The Sentence (III)

Writing Good Sentences. Rewrite each sentence, following the directions given in parentheses.

1. Denise wrote a book report on a novel by Dickens, and Cara wrote a report on another novel by Dickens. (Change to a simple sentence with a compound subject.)
2. This house was designed by Frank Lloyd Wright, the founder of the Prairie School of American architecture. (Change the passive verb to an active verb.)
3. One of the most charming animals on earth is the panda. (Add an appositive phrase to describe the predicate noun.)
4. The mad scientist was a stock figure in low-budget horror films produced in the 1950's. (Add an adjective clause beginning with the relative pronoun *who*.)
5. I will drive to Hannibal to visit Mark Twain's childhood home. (Add a dependent clause beginning with *if*.)
6. The residents of Alaska paid no state income taxes in 1983. Sufficient revenue was generated by taxes related to the installation of the Alaskan pipeline. (Change these two sentences to one complex sentence.)
7. Stan had planned to paint an enormous mural. (Add a prepositional phrase.)
8. A fire engine sped across the runway. (Add a participial phrase.)
9. I will need several days to write my rough draft. (Add a dependent clause beginning with *after*.)
10. The bear tried to catch the fish. It swam too fast. The bear ate the berries that grew by the stream. (Change to one compound-complex sentence by using the words *but* and *so*.

6.0 Agreement of Subject and Verb

The subject of a sentence is said to *agree* with the verb if it is similar in number. If the subject is singular, the verb must be singular. If the subject is plural, the verb must be plural.

Sometimes a speaker will make an error in agreement and say *she don't* or *they was*. A writer may make the same kind of mistake. It is important for the writer to catch these errors and correct them during revision.

Errors in subject-verb agreement can occur when a speaker or writer does not know whether the subject is singular or plural or is unsure which word in the sentence is the subject. This Section will help you recognize the subject of a sentence and determine its number.

6.1 Subject-Verb Agreement in Number

Every sentence has a subject that is either **singular** or **plural** in number. It is singular if it refers to one person or thing. It is plural if it refers to more than one person or thing.

The verb of the sentence must agree in number with the subject. Most verbs change form to show agreement only in the present tense and only in the third person singular, where an *s* is added to the end of the verb.

$$\left.\begin{array}{l} \text{I} \\ \text{you} \\ \text{we} \\ \text{they} \end{array}\right\} \text{walk} \qquad \left.\begin{array}{l} \text{he} \\ \text{she} \\ \text{it} \end{array}\right\} \text{walks}$$

A singular verb is used with a singular subject.

A plural verb is used with a plural subject.

The subject determines whether the verb is singular or plural. The verb does not agree with any other part of the sentence.

The theorem (singular) *is* clear.
The theorems (plural) *are* clear.

The coach (singular) *works* hard.
The coaches (plural) *work* hard.

The verb *be* does not follow the usual pattern of agreement. It has different forms for the third person singular and plural, both past and present. It also has different forms for the first person singular and plural, both past and present. Since this verb is used frequently, memorize its forms, which are given below.

PRESENT TENSE		PAST TENSE	
SINGULAR	PLURAL	SINGULAR	PLURAL
I *am*	we *are*	I *was*	we *were*
you *are*	you *are*	you *were*	you *were*
he, she, it *is*	they *are*	he, she, it *was*	they *were*

Common errors with *be* are *you was, we was, they was.*

6.2 Words Between Subject and Verb

The subject of a sentence alone determines the number of the verb. If there are words between the subject and the verb, they have no effect on whether the verb is singular or plural. Be careful not to mistake a word in a phrase or clause for the subject.

> The *plane,* carrying fifty passengers, *is* landing.
> (*plane* is the subject, not *passengers.*)
> *One* of the cars *needs* a battery.
> (*One* is the subject, not *cars.*)
> The *candidates* for the Presidency *are* touring the country.
> (*candidates* is the subject, not *Presidency.*)
> The *uprisings* in small countries often *involve* violence.
> (*uprisings* is the subject, not *countries.*)

The words *with, together with, along with, and as well as* are prepositions. The objects of these prepositions have no effect upon the number of the verb.

> The trapped *miner,* together with the rescue squad, *is* safe.
> (*miner* is the subject.)
> His facial *expression,* as well as his tone of voice, conveys his meaning. (*expression* is the subject.)
> The *defendant,* with her lawyers, *enters* the courtroom.
> (*defendant* is the subject.)

Exercise: Choose the right verb from those given in parentheses.

1. Our choir with its sixty voices (is, are) very popular.
2. A bunch of grapes often (makes, make) an attractive centerpiece for a dining table.
3. The bride, with her attendants, (is, are) coming down the aisle.
4. Jack, as well as Jean, (plays, play) in the orchestra.
5. The rugs in our house (has, have) been tacked down to prevent slipping.

6. This book of poems (is, are) illustrated with photographs.
7. Bicycling trips through the countryside (makes, make) me aware of distances.
8. My towel, together with my sunglasses, (was, were) washed away by the waves.
9. Several sticks of dynamite (makes, make) a large explosion.
10. One of the most daring feats (is, are) the fifty-foot dive.
11. They (was, were) relieved when I returned home.
12. The noise of so many typewriters (was, were) deafening.
13. The teacher, not the pupils, (was, were) doing the work.
14. Frank's knowledge of the Old Masters (is, are) remarkable.
15. Her choice of words (is, are) incredible for a ten-year-old.

6.3 Indefinite Pronouns

If an indefinite pronoun is the subject of a sentence, the verb must agree with it in number. The indefinite pronouns listed below are always singular.

SINGULAR

anybody	each	everyone	anyone
anything	either	everybody	someone
everything	neither	no one	somebody
another	one	nobody	

Each of the tests *is* challenging.
Neither of your parents *was* disappointed.
Everybody in the cast *has* speaking lines.

There are four indefinite pronouns that are always plural.

PLURAL

several   few   both   many

Several of the books *were* lost.
Few of the candidates *are* under forty.
Both of the winners *have* a perfect score.

Another group of indefinite pronouns may be singular or plural, depending on the sentence.

SINGULAR OR PLURAL

some   most   all   none   any

These pronouns are singular when they refer to a quantity. They are plural when they refer to a number.

Some of the money *was* stolen. (quantity)
Some of their answers *were* wrong. (number)

Most of the sugar *is* gone. (quantity)
Most of the survivors *were* dazed. (number)

All of the food *was* donated. (quantity)
All of the tools *were* expensive. (number)

None and *any* may be either singular or plural depending on whether the writer is referring to one thing or to several.

None of the stories *was* true. (not one)
None of the stories *were* true. (no stories)

Any of these careers *is* rewarding. (any one)
Any of these careers *are* rewarding. (any careers)

Exercise: Choose the standard form of the verb for each sentence.

1. Every one of the runners (was, were) given an award.
2. Most of the cabins in the camp (was, were) repainted.
3. Not one of my shipmates (was, were) able to swim.
4. Neither of these books (interests, interest) me.
5. One of the most timid of animals (is, are) the giraffe.
6. (Does, Do) either of you play a guitar?
7. Neither of the physics experiments (has, have) been completed.
8. Several of the roads in the southern part of the state (was, were) washed away by the flood.
9. Not one of the officers (was, were) at the meeting.
10. Few of the jokes (was, were) amusing.

601

11. All of the wildlife (drinks, drink) at the waterhole.
12. Either of the motorboats (is, are) available.
13. Not one of the bulbs (was, were) working.
14. Everyone in the regiment (seems, seem) courageous.
15. Several of our best players (has, have) the flu.
16. Each of us (has, have) a perfect attendance record.
17. All of my research on runaways (was, were) fascinating.
18. One of Arthur Miller's best plays (is, are) *The Crucible*.
19. Nobody in those communities (wants, want) a sales tax but they all want more service.
20. Anyone who wants to help collect funds (is, are) welcome.

6.4 Compound Subjects

Compound subjects joined by *and* are plural.*

A watchman and a watchdog *quard* the plant.
Ms. Jansen and Mr. Sanchez *speak* highly of you.
Physical fitness and mental agility *are* necessary for athletes.

Singular words joined by *or, nor, either-or, neither-nor* to form a compound subject are singular.

Neither his sincerity nor his reliability *is* questioned.
Either their team or our team *has* a chance to win.
Ellen or Gordon *deserves* the scholarship.

When a singular word and a plural word are joined by *or* or *nor* to form a compound subject, the verb agrees with the subject that is nearer to it.

Neither the folk singers nor their agent *likes* the program.
The management or the unions *have to make* concessions.
Neither the actors nor the play *appeals* to anyone.
Shall we ask if either the folk singer or the comedians *are performing* here this evening.?

*If the words making up the compound subject are habitually used together to refer to a single thing, the subject may be used with a singular verb: *bread and butter, macaroni and cheese,* etc.

Exercise: Writing Rewrite these sentences, correcting the errors in subject-verb agreement. Two of the sentences are correct.

1. The engine and one car was derailed.
2. The governor or the mayor are usually at the ceremony.
3. Are your mother or your father going to the school play?
4. Neither the driver nor we was expecting a bump.
5. The captain or the lieutenant is always on duty.
6. Neither the swimmers nor the lifeguard were aware of the dangerous undertow.
7. Diving and ice skating calls for good judgment.
8. Were either Josie or Emily there?
9. Either Debra Winger or Karen Allen are going to star in that movie.
10. Neither illness nor loss seems to lessen her spirit.
11. Neither the Wilmington squad nor the Plainfield team were invited to the tournament.
12. Either the meat or the potatoes are burning.
13. To travel and to write a novel is Judy's ambitions.
14. A basketball court and an indoor track is in the gymnasium.
15. Neither the Wayside Inn nor the House of the Seven Gables are in Boston.

6.5 Subject Following Verb

In some sentences the verb precedes the subject. Then the writer must think ahead to the subject in order to make the verb agree in number.

The usual order of subject and verb is often inverted in sentences beginning with *There* and *Here* and in questions beginning with *Who, Why, Where, What, How.*

NONSTANDARD:	Here's the tickets for the game.
STANDARD:	Here *are* the tickets for the game.
NONSTANDARD:	There's only two possible answers.
STANDARD:	There *are* only two possible answers.

NONSTANDARD:	Who's the officers in the debating club?
STANDARD:	Who *are* the officers in the debating club?
NONSTANDARD:	What's your reasons for refusing?
STANDARD:	What *are* your reasons for refusing?
NONSTANDARD:	Down the avenue *comes* the band and the color guard.
STANDARD:	Down the avenue *come* the band and the color guard.

6.6 Predicate Words

The linking verb agrees only with its subject. The number of the predicate word has no effect on the verb.

NONSTANDARD:	New theories *is* not the answer.
STANDARD:	New theories *are* not the answer.
NONSTANDARD:	Joe's first love *are* sailboats.
STANDARD:	Joe's first love *is* sailboats.
NONSTANDARD:	Being accepted and registering *is* only the beginning.
STANDARD:	Being accepted and registering *are* only the beginning.

6.7. *Don't* and *Doesn't*

The verb *do* and its forms are often used incorrectly. When the subject of a sentence is third person singular, use *does* or its negative contraction *doesn't*. All other persons and numbers require the form *do* or its negative contraction *don't*.

DOES, DOESN'T	DO, DON'T
the boat does	the boats do
he doesn't	we don't
she doesn't	you don't
it doesn't	they don't

Exercise: Choose the standard form from the two given.

1. After the thaw (comes, come) the floods.
2. There (is, are) oranges in the refrigerator.
3. The fruit I like best (is, are) seedless grapes.
4. Why (doesn't, don't) he take the back road?
5. On the Fourth of July (comes, come) our annual picnic.
6. There (was, were) fifty people present at the meeting.
7. (Where's, Where are) the instructions for this game?
8. There (is, are) many ways to cook a lobster.
9. If she (doesn't, don't) agree, Stephanie will say so.
10. Inside the cave (was, were) many stalactites.
11. For the person who wants to advance, (there's, there are) numerous evening courses.
12. There (was, were) four students on the team.
13. On the bulletin board (was, were) a list of ten names.
14. (There's, There are) many details involved in the plan.
15. Why (is, are) they protesting the new power plant?
16. The gift I like best (is, are) books.
17. From a single plant (comes, come) dozens of flowers.
18. My only regret (is, are) the days wasted.
19. Time and a good book (is, are) all I want.
20. There (seems, seem) to be a pile of letters in the box.

6.8 Collective Nouns

A collective noun refers to a group of people or things: *flock, band, jury, crew.*

A collective noun is singular when the group is acting as a single unit. A collective noun is plural when the individuals in the group are acting separately. To make the verb agree with a collective noun, you must decide whether the noun is singular or plural in your particular sentence.

> The team *was* the winner of the play-off. (united action)
> The team *were* voting for a captain. (separate action)

Pronouns must also agree in number with collective nouns.

NONSTANDARD: The panel *has* (singular) submitted *their* (plural) findings.

STANDARD: The panel *has* submitted *its* findings.

6.9   Nouns Plural in Form

Some nouns that end in *s* are actually singular in number and should be followed by singular verbs: *molasses, measles, news*.

Nouns that end in *-ics* may be singular or plural depending on the particular sentence. These nouns are singular when they refer to a school subject, a science, or a general practice. At these times they are not preceded by *the, his, her, some, all,* or singular modifiers.

Politics *is* a field for serious study. (singular)
Her politics *are* in no way suspect. (plural)

News *is* a major attraction on television. (singular)

Not all athletics *are* right for every student. (plural)

6.10   Titles and Groups of Words

Titles of books, plays, films, musical compositions, or other works of art are used with singular verbs, even when the words in the title are plural in number. The names of countries are also used with singular verbs.

Leaves of Grass is Walt Whitman's greatest achievement.
Amahl and the Night Visitors is an opera in English.
The Potato-Eaters is a famous painting by Van Gogh.
The Netherlands *has* a colorful history.

Any group of words referring to a single thing or thought is used with a singular verb.

What our country needs *is* dedicated men and women.
"Haste makes waste" *is* sound advice.

6.11   Words of Amount and Time

Periods of time, amounts of money, fractions, weights, and measurements are generally singular in meaning and require a singular verb.

Two-thirds of the town's housing *has* been renovated.
Two yards of wire *is* enough to buy.
Three dollars *seems* like a fortune to him.
Fifty tons *is* the capacity of the freight train.
Two hours *has* sometimes seemed like eternity.

If a subject is considered a single thing, then the verb is singular. If the subject is plural, the verb is plural. If a prepositional phrase falls between the subject and verb, it has *no effect* on the verb.

Ten pounds of potatoes *is* what we ordered.
   (singular meaning)
Ten crates of sugar cane *were* piled on the floor.
   (plural meaning)

Exercise: Choose the standard form from those given.

1. The man's ethics (was, were) questionable.
2. What our magazine needs (is, are) more contributors.
3. Mathematics (is, are) Martina's favorite subject.
4. What this theater needs (is, are) two new projectors.
5. Three-fourths of our lawn (has, have) been reseeded.
6. About three-quarters of the oranges (was, were) moldy.
7. The jury (was, were) arguing heatedly.
8. Over one-half of the employees (commutes, commute).
9. Two or three feet of twine (is, are) probably enough.
10. Five dollars (is, are) too much to pay for a parking place.
11. Measles (is, are) a contagious disease.
12. Three hundred miles (is, are) a good day's trip.
13. The team (is, are) getting into their new uniforms.
14. Politics (has, have) always been my sister's main interest.

15. Two thousand pounds of paper (was, were) collected.
16. Ten weeks (is, are) the time required for the course.
17. *The Six Wives of Henry VIII* (was, were) shown on public television.
18. The Netherlands (has, have) just issued some interesting stamps.
19. Only one-half of the eligible voters (has, have) registered.
20. Ten cartons of canned goods (was, were) donated.

6.12 Relative Pronouns

A relative pronoun stands for some other noun which is its antecedent. If the antecedent is plural, then the relative pronoun is plural. If the antecedent is singular, then the relative pronoun is singular.

A relative pronoun agrees with its antecedent in number.

When a relative pronoun is used as the subject of a subordinate clause, the number of its antecedent determines whether the verb of the clause is plural or singular.

These are the *researchers* (plural) who (plural) *are* testing our new products.

Chagall is the *artist* (singular) who (singular) *has* made a free-form mosaic in downtown Chicago.

Katie is one of those *members* who always *volunteer*. (*members* always volunteer.)

He was the only *one* of the skin divers who *was* attacked by a shark. (only *one* was attacked.)

The problem of agreement arises in the last two sentences above because there are two words that *might be* the antecedent of the relative pronoun. Usually the meaning of the sentence shows which word *is* the antecedent.

Exercise A: Choose the right word from those given.

1. Only one of the girls (has, have) practiced.
2. This is one of the cars that (is, are) fully equipped.
3. The eagle is one species that (nests, nest) in a high tree.
4. This is the first of several meetings that (is, are) to be held.
5. Lisa was the one among all her classmates who (was, were) chosen to head student government.
6. Which of the students who (takes, take) math use calculators?
7. Of all the novels that (is, are) on the shelf, Pearl Buck's is the most intriguing.
8. With a bag full of books that (was, were) due at the library, Nicole trudged through the snow.
9. Ruff is one of those dogs that (does, do) somersaults.
10. He is one of those teachers who (expects, expect) the best from each student.

Exercise B: Follow the same directions as for Exercise A.

1. We found one of the kittens that (was, were) lost.
2. Which one of the counselors (advises, advise) juniors?
3. Carrie is one of those golfers who (gets, get) good scores.
4. A clarinet is one of those instruments that (needs, need) a reed.
5. Public documents are one of the sources that (reveals, reveal) one's ancestors.
6. *The Canterbury Tales* is one of those books that (defies, defy) translation into modern English.
7. Binet is one of the researchers who (has, have) studied intelligence.
8. Of all the diseases that (attacks, attack) elderly persons, hardening of the arteries is the most common.
9. Art Buchwald is one of those columnists who (uses, use) humor to make a point.
10. Peter is one of those who (has, have) a scholarship.

REINFORCEMENT EXERCISES

Agreement of Subject and Verb

A. Choose the correct verb. Identify the subject in each of the following sentences. Then choose the standard form of the verb.

1. A truckload of fresh eggs (arrive, arrives) at the farmers' market each morning.
2. Her name, as well as her mother's and his grandmother's, (is, are) Marina.
3. A plant with tendrils (climb, climbs) walls, trees, stakes, or other plants.
4. Athletes on scholarship (practice, practices) for hours each day.
5. The reproduction of the old manuscripts (was, were) barely legible.
6. Which one of your brothers (is, are) married?
7. The line of bushes (mark, marks) an ancient boundary.
8. The Grecian urn covered with dancing figures (is, are) on display at the museum.
9. Alvin, together with his five sisters, (go, goes) to the family home in Nashville for Thanksgiving.
10. Five goslings, as well as their mother, (was, were) marching comically toward the pond.

B. Choose verbs that agree with indefinite pronouns. Identify the subject in each of the following sentences. Then choose the correct form of the verb.

1. Several of the beachcombers (pick, picks) up conch shells every day.
2. All of the couriers (complete, completes) their rounds by five o'clock.
3. Each of the beautifully illustrated post cards (was, were) a collector's item.
4. Few of the students (believe, believes) in the powers of an oracle.

5. Either of the subjects (is, are) acceptable for the photography contest.
6. Some (know, knows) that Sir John MacDonald was the first prime minister of Canada.
7. (Has, Have) anyone here read Hardy's *Tess of the d'Ubervilles?*
8. Everybody on the bus (was, were) on the way to the Rose Bowl.
9. Both of the dishes (is, are) handmade.
10. Everything in the boxes (is, are) from Norway.

C. Choose verbs that agree with compound subjects. Find the errors in subject-verb agreement in these sentences. Write the sentences correctly. If a sentence is correct, write C.

1. Neither my jade tree nor my petunias bloom indoors.
2. Both Natasha and Eaton was originally born in Europe.
3. Neither the authors nor the illustrator were famous when they collaborated on that book.
4. Swallowing peanut butter and drinking vinegar are considered cures for hiccups.
5. Both the word "bungalow" and the word "dungaree" comes to us from India.
6. Mittens, ski poles, and a wool cap was packed into the box.
7. Sombreros, derbies, and a turban was seen at the festival.
8. Neither the auditors nor the actor wants any distractions.
9. This proverb and that quotation provides a good opening for this chapter.
10. Either the croquet mallet or the golf clubs is my present.

D. Choose verbs that agree with their subjects. Choose the correct form from those given in parentheses.

1. King cobra snakes (don't, doesn't) hear the music that snake charmers play because the snakes are deaf.
2. Where (is, are) camels originally from?
3. Which (is, are) the two fastest land animals ever recorded?
4. On the lunch menu (was, were) omelettes, crepes, and salads.

5. Who (was, were) the dancers we saw at Lincoln Center last spring?
6. Either pink or pale blue (become, becomes) a complexion like yours best.
7. From the sea (comes, come) foods very high in protein.
8. My telescope (doesn't, don't) allow me to see the moons of Jupiter.
9. Most Americans (doesn't, don't) approve of subliminal projection—the use of messages that we hear or see only subconsciously.
10. There (is, are) five Jennifers in my class.
11. Into the Gulf of California (flow, flows) the Colorado River and the Rio de Samora.
12. Sore muscles in his back (is, are) a problem for Jerry.
13. There (was, were) the twins waiting at the front entrance while we waited at the back.
14. Against the canyon wall (rush, rushes) the water, slowly eroding its barrier.
15. The idea of floating in a tank of salt water (doesn't, don't) appeal to me at all.

E. Make subjects and verbs agree. Choose the standard form of the verb in parentheses.

1. Two-thirds (is, are) significantly more than half.
2. *The Borrowers* (have, has) been a children's classic for many years.
3. Twenty-four hours (make, makes) a single day.
4. The United States (is, are) rich in natural resources.
5. The team (is, are) submitting their ideas for some new plays.
6. Five dollars (were, was) all Melissa had till Saturday.
7. Mr. Davis's politics (are, is) not a secret to anyone.
8. Measles (is, are) a childhood disease for which a vaccine is available.
9. The committee (adjourn, adjourns) promptly each week at lunchtime.
10. Ethics (is, are) a branch of philosophy.

F. Use correct verbs after relative pronouns. Find the antecedent of each relative pronoun. Then choose the verb that agrees with this antecedent from the two in parentheses.

1. UFO's are sighted celestial lights or objects that (have, has) not been identified.
2. This is the only one of the five original newspapers that still (exist, exists) today.
3. Sylvie is the one who (train, trains) cats for television commercials.
4. The true laurel is the only one of the laurel family that (produce, produces) bay leaves used for seasoning.
5. Which one of the cakes (contain, contains) a gold coin?
6. Phyl is the only one of the trainees who (understand, understands) what I am saying.
7. This is one of those buildings that (look, looks) well on a cliff.
8. There are the three jockeys who (want, wants) to ride your horse in the Derby.
9. Chet is one of the computer operators who (explain, explains) computer terminology to beginners.
10. Hugh is the only tumbler who (wear, wears) knee guards.

MIXED REVIEW

Agreement of Subject and Verb

A. Choose the standard form of the verb from the two forms given in parentheses.

1. Exactly eighteen ounces of water (fills, fill) this size canteen.
2. Leslie Stahl is the only one of those reporters who (is, are) based in Washington.
3. The bunch of ripe red grapes (is, are) delicious.
4. Iceland is one of those countries that (has, have) little pollution.
5. Gary's attitude, as well as his study habits, (was, were) improving.
6. Neither the fans nor the coach (approve, approves) of the referee's call.
7. Three-fourths of these diamonds (come, comes) from Africa.
8. There (is, are) several reasons for Siona's decision.
9. Everybody in the drama classes (performs, perform) in at least one play a year.
10. In my locker (sit, sits) my tennis shoes and racket.
11. *The Martian Chronicles* (describe, describes) the first settlers' adventures on Mars.
12. One of the players (is, are) going to endorse a new soft drink.
13. Onto the field (march, marches) the band.
14. There (is, are) extracurricular activities that will help new students meet each other.
15. Neither the elevator nor the escalator (go, goes) to the top.
16. The jury (have, has) adjourned to discuss its verdict.
17. Jackie's favorite dessert (is, are) fudge brownies.
18. Where (is, are) the southernmost settlements on Earth?
19. Politics (is, are) more than a hobby to Chester.
20. Toward the pink sand beach and the crystal sea (face, faces) the windows of our hotel room.

B. Correct any errors in subject-verb agreement in the following sentences. If the sentence is correct, write *Correct.*

1. Three students in the class has written on Sarah Bernhardt, the French actress.
2. The West Indies are in the Caribbean.
3. Was Charles Gordon or Judah Gordon the Russian Jewish novelist?
4. Sleet, snow, and rain was falling from northern Ohio to Iowa.
5. Pediatrics are the branch of medicine that Paul wants to enter.
6. Neither *The Lady from Shanghai* nor *The Magnificent Ambersons* are as good as *Citizen Kane.*
7. More of the tourists is with Group A.
8. The council votes the moment its meeting is convened.
9. There is the books we left behind.
10. The palace, which straddles two hills, are really two large buildings.
11. Either of those acts deserve to win the competition.
12. Either Byron or Shelley are my favorite poet.
13. The Quakers in Pennsylvania was among the first Americans to condemn slavery.
14. Some believes that cats and dogs should be fed vegetarian diets.
15. Outlining and rewriting helps make a good report better.
16. The nation of New Zealand consist of two major islands and several smaller islands.
17. Pat, as well as Harriet, thinks sailing is the perfect way to relax.
18. The phase of the moon and the season of the year concerns people interested in planting crops.
19. High on the list of fiber foods is bran, zucchini, and summer squash.
20. Who was the second and third signers of the Declaration of Independence?

USING GRAMMAR IN WRITING
Agreement of Subject and Verb

A. Your best friend has moved out of town and missed graduating with the senior class by a few months. When graduation comes, you have a lot of news to tell, and you write a long letter. To give an air of immediacy to your narrative, you write the letter in the historical present. Below are the beginnings of some of your sentences. Fill in the blanks with names and write the entire letter, being careful to make subjects and verbs agree.

It is one of those nights . . .
Neither _____ nor _____ . . .
Everyone . . .
The mixed chorus . . .
Both _____ and _____ . . .
Anyone who . . .
Several madrigals by Handel . . .
Out through the door . . .
Some of the parents . . .
Three-fourths of the seniors . . .
All . . .

B. Write a brief essay outlining the rules of your favorite game or sport. Write the rules in the present tense. Use indefinite pronouns such as *one, someone, all, each, many.* Be sure that your subjects and verbs agree.

C. Imagine that the senior class is trying to decide on a gift to give to the school. Preliminary surveys of the seniors indicate that the two favored choices are a tree to be planted on the school grounds and a large clock to be installed in the front of the building. You must write an article for the school newspaper describing these two choices and telling about a vote that will be taken in homeroom during the next week. Write the article, using compound subjects joined by coordinating and correlative conjunctions wherever possible.

7.0 Pronoun Usage

Some words like nouns, verbs, and adjectives may change form to show how they are being used in a particular sentence. This change in form is called *inflection*. Most of the time the change only affects the end of the word:

NOUN:	family—family's—families—families'
VERB:	need—needs—needed—needing
ADJECTIVE:	funny—funnier—funniest
ADVERB:	slow—slower—slowest

Sometimes, however, the spelling of the entire word is affected:

VERB:	is—was—been
ADJECTIVE:	many—more—most
PRONOUN:	we—us—our

When a pronoun changes form to show how it is being used in a sentence, the pronoun has changed **case.** There are three cases for pronouns: **nominative, possessive,** and **objective.** The cases for the personal pronouns and for *who* are given below.

NOMINATIVE	POSSESSIVE	OBJECTIVE
I	my, mine	me
we	our, ours	us
you	your, yours	you
he	his	him
she	her, hers	her
it	its	it
they	their, theirs	them
who	whose	whom
whoever	whosever	whomever

Indefinite pronouns have the same nominative and objective forms. They change form only in the possessive case.

NOMINATIVE	OBJECTIVE	POSSESSIVE
anybody	anybody	anybody's
no one	no one	no one's

There is no change at all to indicate case for the pronouns *this, that, these, those, which,* and *what*. These pronouns are not used in the possessive case.

7.1   The Pronoun as Subject of a Verb

The nominative form of the pronoun is used as subject of a verb.

The subject of a sentence is always in the nominative case. This rule of grammar does not generally cause any difficulty except when the subject is compound. When the subject includes a noun and a pronoun, or two pronouns, writers sometimes use the objective case by mistake.

NONSTANDARD: Him and me are brothers.
STANDARD: He and I are brothers.

A simple test will help you choose the right form for pronouns in a compound subject: *Try saying each part of the subject by itself with the verb.* The form that sounds right when used alone is the correct form.

Dan and (she, her) bought a new car.
(Dan bought; she bought, *not* her bought.)

Them and us are old friends.
(They are; we are, *not* us are.)

The plural forms *we* and *they* sound awkward in many compounds. They can be avoided by recasting the sentence.

AWKWARD: The referees and we have agreed.
BETTER: We and the referees have agreed.

7.2 The Predicate Pronoun

A pronoun in the predicate of a sentence is often linked to the subject by a form of the verb *be*. Such a pronoun is called a **predicate pronoun.**

The nominative form is used as a predicate pronoun.*

The nominative form of the pronoun must be used after all forms of *be: could have been, might not be, will be,* etc.

> The winner *will be* **she**. *Could* it *have been* **I**?
> The culprits *might have been* **they**.

Sometimes the nominative form sounds awkward. The awkwardness can be avoided by recasting the sentence.

> AWKWARD: It was we who made the suggestion.
> BETTER: We are the people who made the suggestion.

7.3 The Pronoun as Object of a Verb

The objective pronoun form is used as direct or indirect object.

This rule of grammar does not cause any difficulty except when the object is compound and includes a pronoun. In such a situation, a writer may use the nominative case by mistake.

> NONSTANDARD: The class elected James and I.
>   (elected James; elected me, *not* I.)
> STANDARD: The class elected James and me.

To choose the correct form for pronouns in a compound object, *say each part of the object by itself with the verb.*

> Phil showed Tad and (I, me) the experiment.
> (showed Phil; showed me, *not* I.)

---

* Standard usage permits the exception in both speech and writing of *It is me.*

Exercise A: Choose the standard form from those given in parentheses.

1. The Ford Foundation gave (she, her) and her assistant a study grant.
2. I invited Theresa and (he, him) to the party.
3. Show Larry and (I, me) the map of Long Island.
4. The only returning staff members are Terry and (he, him).
5. (She, Her) and Royko wrote the article.
6. Are you implying that it was (he, him)?
7. If I were (she, her), I would call the Better Business Bureau about the problem.
8. Wasn't it (he, him) who gave the nominating speech?
9. The workers rescued (she, her) and the other miners.
10. Lil and (he, him) have been studying the classical guitar.

Exercise B: Choose the standard form from those given in parentheses.

1. We saw Michelle and (she, her) at the science fair.
2. How many miles did you and (she, her) run?
3. If I were (he, him), I would apply for the job.
4. Why don't you meet Vinny and (I, me) on the first tee?
5. We suspect that it was (she, her) who played the practical joke at our party.
6. The bank teller spotted (he, him) and his accomplice in the getaway car.
7. Will you help Bernie and (I, me) shovel the snow?
8. Neither the Gibsons nor (we, us) have been to Sea Island.
9. I couldn't believe that it was (they, them).
10. Wasn't it (she, her) who became a famous court reporter?
11. The tallest boys in the class are Sandy and (I, me).
12. It was either Olivia or (he, him) who saw the eclipse.
13. Randy and (she, her) have been accepted at Gettysburg College.
14. The co-captains of the baseball team are Cliff and (he, him).
15. It was (they, them) who discovered the theft.

7.4 The Pronoun as Object of a Preposition

The objective pronoun form is used as object of a preposition.

This rule does not generally cause any difficulty except when the object of the preposition is compound and one or both of the parts is a pronoun. In this construction, a writer may sometimes use the nominative case by mistake.

NONSTANDARD: The librarian is reserving a book for Pam and I.

STANDARD: The librarian is reserving a book for Pam and me.

To decide which pronoun to use in a compound object of a preposition, *try each part of the object by itself with the preposition.*

The news was a surprise to Sheila and I.
(to Sheila; to me, *not* I.)

The preposition *between* causes frequent errors in pronoun usage. Use only the objective pronoun forms after *between*.

between you and him, *not* between you and he
between him and me, *not* between he and I

7.5 The Pronoun Used with a Noun

In a construction such as *we girls* or *us boys*, the use of the noun determines the case form of the pronoun.

We Republocrats are a united party.
(*Republocrats* is the subject of *are*; the nominative pronoun is therefore required.)

The lifeguard drove us surfers from the beach.
(*surfers* is direct object of *drove*; the objective pronoun is therefore required.)

To decide which pronoun form to use in a construction such as *we boys,* try the pronoun by itself with the verb or preposition.

The warning was directed mainly to (we, us) boys.
(to us, *not* to we)
They allowed (we, us) amateur photographers to compete.
(allowed us, *not* allowed we)
(We, Us) flag bearers will lead the line of march.
(We will lead, *not* Us will lead)

Exercise A: Choose the standard form from those given in parentheses.

1. (We, Us) students in the Film Club elected officers.
2. Did you hear the news about (he, him) and his brother?
3. Between you and (I, me), I regret my hasty answer.
4. There was a misunderstanding between Ed and (I, me).
5. Nobody went to the game except Denise and (I, me).
6. I wrote letters to Amelia and (he, him).
7. Dad has packed lunches for you and (I, me).
8. No one was there but Leonard and (he, him).
9. (We, Us) varsity players hope to get athletic scholarships.
10. The messages were intended for Diane and (I, me).
11. The snow sculptures were done by Meg, Tim, and (I, me).
12. None of (we, us) juniors was put on the team.
13. These plans must be kept a secret among (we, us) four.
14. Several of (we, us) sophomores were asked to attend.
15. The first ones to board the plane were (we, us) reporters.

Exercise B: Choose the standard form from those given in parentheses.

1. The coach praised (we, us) players for our teamwork.
2. Wait for Gus and (I, me) in the stationery store.
3. The gym was decorated by Don, Sandra, and (I, me).
4. The prize money will be divided between you and (I, me).
5. Directly below Pat and (I, me) sat the corps of cadets.

6. Who marches between you and (he, him) in the parade?
7. The florist talked to Peggy and (I, me) about the corsages.
8. Everyone was interested except Grace and (I, me).
9. This matter concerns no one but you and (I, me).
10. To (we, us) substitutes, the regulars looked helpless.

7.6 *Who* and *Whom* in Questions

The pronouns *who* and *whom* are used to ask questions or to introduce clauses. When they are used to ask questions, they are **interrogative pronouns.**

Who is the nominative form of the interrogative pronoun. Use this form when the pronoun is used as the subject of a sentence or as a predicate pronoun.

> *Who* is the most valuable player? (*Who* is the subject.)
> The most valuable player is *who*? (*who* is the predicate pronoun.)

Whom is the objective form of the interrogative pronoun. Use this form when the pronoun is the object of the verb or the object of a preposition.

> *Whom* does Claude respect? (*Whom* is the object of *respect*.)
> From *whom* did you receive those flowers? (*whom* is the object of the preposition *From*.)

Do not be misled by parenthetical expressions like *do you think, can you imagine, do you suppose, do you believe*. They do not determine the case of the interrogative pronoun.

> Who do you think will win the championship?
> (*Who* is the subject of *will win*.)
>
> Whom do you suppose he recommended?
> (*Whom* is the object of *recommended*.)
>
> Who do you believe is the stronger leader?
> (*Who* is the subject of *is*.)

7.7 *Who, Whom,* and *Whose* in Clauses

Who, whom, and *whose* are often used to introduce clauses. They may be relative pronouns in adjective clauses or introductory words in noun clauses. These pronouns also have roles within the subordinate clauses they introduce.

The use of the pronoun within the clause determines whether the nominative, objective, or possessive form is used.

> I did not see *whom Jed met.*
> (Noun clause; *whom* is the object of the verb *met* within the clause.)

> Our teachers are those *whom we should remember with gratitude.*
> (Adjective clause; *whom* is the object of *should remember* within the clause.)

> He is the candidate *who was not elected to office.*
> (Adjective clause; *who* is the subject of the verb *was elected* within the clause.)

> I wonder *who received the Nobel Prize.*
> (Noun clause; *who* is the subject of the verb *received* within the clause.)

> She is the person *to whom you should write.*
> (Adjective clause; *whom* is the object of the preposition *to* within the clause.)

> Janice is the worker *whose job was eliminated.*
> (Adjective clause; *whose* modifies *job* within the clause; the subordinate clause as a whole modifies *worker.*)

Whoever and *whomever* follow the same rules as *who* and *whom* when used as introductory words.

> *Whoever writes the best essay* will win a three-day trip to Washington.
> (*Whoever* is the subject of the verb *writes* within the noun clause.)

Victory comes to *whoever stands for high principles*.
(The noun clause is the object of the preposition *to; whoever* is the subject of the verb *stands* within the clause.)

It is important to cooperate with *whomever you elect*.
(The noun clause is the object of the preposition *with; whomever* is the object of the verb *elect* within the clause.)

Exercise: Choose the standard form from those given in parentheses.

1. (Who, Whom) do you think will get the leading part?
2. (Who, Whom) are those people touring the building?
3. John Hurt is the actor to (who, whom) Sid was referring.
4. (Who, Whom) are they sending to meet the train?
5. Ms. Voss is the person (who, whom) you must see.
6. (Who, Whom) do you believe is telling the truth?
7. (Whoever, Whomever) applies for the position must fill out an application blank.
8. (Who, Whom) do you suppose gave him the key?
9. She is the lawyer for (who, whom) I work.
10. Ms. Chan motivates all the students (who, whom) she teaches.
11. He is a person (who, whom) I trust implicitly.
12. (Who, Whom) did you say was elected vice-president?
13. The lecturer varied his talk depending on (who, whom) was in the audience.
14. We must support (whoever, whomever) is elected.
15. The case will come up before (whoever, whomever) is presiding at this session.
16. I'll vote for (whoever, whomever) has the qualifications.
17. You may go with (whoever, whomever) you choose.
18. Give the message to (whoever, whomever) answers the telephone.
19. There is the guidance counselor about (who, whom) you were asking.
20. (Who, Whom) does the new baby look like?

7.8 Pronouns in Comparisons

Sometimes a comparison is made by using a clause that begins with *than* or *as*.

Marie is more musical *than Lillian is*.
I have as much will power *as anyone else has*.
George trusts you more *than he trusts her*.

The final clause in the comparison is sometimes left incomplete.

Marie is more musical than Lillian (is).
I have as much will power as anyone else (has).

To decide which pronoun form to use in an incomplete comparison, complete the comparison.

Harry earned more credits than (I, me).
   (Harry earned more credits than *I earned*.)
The noise scared Phyllis more than (I, me).
   (The noise scared Phyllis more than *it scared me*.)

7.9 Pronouns with Infinitives

The objective form of the pronoun is used as the subject, object, or predicate pronoun of an infinitive.

The clerk asked *me to complete* the form. (*me* is the subject of *to complete*.)
Ray urged *her to keep* the cat. (*her* is the subject of *to keep*.)
They took *him* to be *me*. (*him* is the subject of *to be*, and *me* is the predicate pronoun following *to be*.)
His boss decided *to reward him*. (*him* is object of *to reward*.)
We expected the winner *to be her*. (*her* is the predicate pronoun following *to be*.)

7.10   Pronouns with Participles and Gerunds

Gerunds and present participles are verbals that end in *-ing*. Gerunds are always used as nouns. Participles are always used as adjectives.

A participle may be used with a pronoun in either the nominative or the objective form.

Skimming along the ice, *he* executed a perfect figure eight.
   (*Skimming* is a participle that modifies *he*.)

The spectators saw *him leaping* in the air.
   (*leaping* is a participle that modifies *him*.)

When a pronoun immediately precedes a gerund, the pronoun takes the possessive case.

The possessive form of the pronoun is used when the pronoun immediately precedes a gerund.

His daydreaming worried his parents and teachers.
   (*daydreaming* is the gerund subject of *worried; his* is the subject of *daydreaming* in the possessive case.)

The telephone company disliked *their tampering* with the lines.
   (*tampering* is the gerund object of *disliked; their* is the subject of *tampering*.)

7.11   The Pronoun as an Appositive

The form of a pronoun used as an appositive is determined by the use of the noun to which it is in apposition.

Your representatives, *Hugh* and *I*, need your help.
   (*Hugh* and *I* are in apposition to *representatives*, which is the subject of *need*. Therefore, the nominative form of the pronoun is required.)

> For both of us, *Pam* and *me,* the victory was sweet.
> (*Pam* and *me* are in apposition to *us,* which is the object of the preposition *of.* Therefore, the objective form of the pronoun is required.)

> Uncle Gino offered the newcomers, *Sophia* and *him,* good jobs.
> (*Sophia* and *him* are in apposition to *newcomers,* which is the indirect object of *offered.* Therefore, the objective form of the pronoun is required.)

To determine which form of the pronoun to use in apposition, try the appositive by itself with the verb or preposition.

> The cousins, Jerry and (her, she), had been riding in the back.
> (She had been riding; *not* her had been riding.)

> The awards were given to the juniors, Willy and (she, her).
> (The awards were given to her, *not* to she.)

7.12   Compound Personal Pronouns

Compound personal pronouns are used only when their antecedents appear in the same sentence.

STANDARD:	Jean bruised herself when she fell.
STANDARD:	It is said that history often repeats itself.
NONSTANDARD:	The decision is up to yourself.
STANDARD:	The decision is up to you.
NONSTANDARD:	The presents were for ourselves.
STANDARD:	The presents were for us.

Exercise: Choose the standard form from those given in parentheses.

1. Dan and (I, myself) are in charge of the barbecue.
2. Essie is taller than (he, him).
3. Few girls are better dancers than (she, her).

4. Irene or (I, myself) will be glad to introduce you.
5. The baby sitter must have thought Linda to be (I, me).
6. My twin, Jane, is a few minutes older than (I, me).
7. (Our, Us) missing the bus caused us to miss the show.
8. Mr. Horn didn't like (our, us) logo for the newspaper.
9. I taught Mike and (she, her) how to ski.
10. We worried about (their, them) making it home.
11. The measurements proved I was taller than (she, her).
12. Ginny and (I, me, myself) designed and built a rock garden.
13. Another girl and (I, myself) served as co-chairpersons for the election committee.
14. The final decision must be made by you and (I, me).
15. The losers, Gerald and (she, her), were good sports.
16. We praised the losers, Gerald and (she, her).
17. Anyone as young as (she, her) cannot be admitted.
18. The prize was awarded jointly to Steve and (me, myself).
19. No one can make the decision but (him, himself).
20. Mr. Moss seemed even more frightened than (we, us).

7.13   Pronouns and Antecedents

A pronoun must agree with its antecedent in number, gender, and person.

Agreement in Number. If the antecedent of a pronoun is singular, a singular pronoun is required. If the antecedent is plural, a plural pronoun is required.

Some indefinite pronouns are always singular. Use singular pronouns to refer to these indefinite pronouns.

another	anything	everybody	neither	one
anybody	each	everyone	nobody	somebody
anyone	either	everything	no one	someone

Each of the waiters wore *his* uniform.
Everyone indicated *his* or *her* preference.

The indefinite pronouns *all, some, any, most,* and *none* may be referred to by either a singular or plural pronoun, depending upon the meaning intended.

Some of the workers *have* lost *their* jobs.

Some of the cider *has* lost *its* tang.

All of the networks *are* holding over *their* best shows.

For more information on agreement with indefinite pronouns see Sections 1.2 and 6.3

Collective nouns may be referred to by either a singular or plural pronoun, depending upon the meaning intended.

The committee *has* announced *its* plans.
The committee *have* offered *their* services.

Note: In all the foregoing examples, the collective nouns and indefinite pronouns are used as subjects. The number of the verbs and the number of the pronouns referring to them must be the same.

NONSTANDARD: Some of the jury *are* giving *its* opinions.
STANDARD: Some of the jury *are* giving *their* opinions.
NONSTANDARD: None of the debaters *was* convincing *their* audience.
STANDARD: None of the debaters *was* convincing *her* audience.

Two or more singular antecedents joined by *or* or *nor* are referred to by a singular pronoun.

Neither Joni nor Rita has brought *her* guitar.
Either Jeff or Marty lost *his* jacket.

Agreement in Gender. When the antecedent of a pronoun is clearly male, use a masculine pronoun: *he, his,* or *him.* When the antecedent of a pronoun is clearly female, use a feminine pronoun: *she, her,* or *hers. It* and *its* are neuter pronouns.

The *steward* had to take *his* seat during turbulent weather. (masculine)
The *actress* was busy studying *her* lines. (feminine)
The *tree* had buried *its* roots far underground. (neuter)

Sometimes a singular pronoun refers to an antecedent that might be either masculine or feminine. Traditionally, the masculine form was used in this situation. However, many people prefer to use the phrase *his or her* to eliminate what they consider to be sexist language.

> STANDARD: No parent wishes to deny *his* child a proper education.
>
> ALSO STANDARD: No parent wishes to deny *his or her* child a proper education.

Agreement in Person. A personal pronoun must be in the same person as its antecedent. The words *one, everyone,* and *everybody* are in the third person. They are referred to by *he, his, him, she, her, hers*.

> NONSTANDARD: *One* should consider *your* hobbies an investment.
>
> STANDARD: *One* should consider *his or her* hobbies an investment.
>
> NONSTANDARD: *I* am convinced that the noise affects *your* work.
>
> STANDARD: *I* am convinced that the noise affects *my* work.

Exercise A: Find and correct the errors in agreement in these sentences. Make sure that both verb and pronoun are correct.

1. Neither Lori nor Bernadette have been in a play before.
2. Everyone plans to bring their lunch.
3. One should try to learn from your mistakes.
4. Each of the caricatures were cleverly drawn but the one of George was best.
5. No one likes to feel that they are being left out.

6. Does everyone have their art supplies?
7. Has any of the teachers dismissed their students?
8. Every citizen should exercise their right to vote.
9. Each of them hope to get a summer job.
10. I find that my geometry homework is easier to do if you do it early.

Exercise B: Follow the same directions as for Exercise A.

1. The soccer team ride on its own special bus.
2. No one should give up until you have tried.
3. Either Linda Ronstadt or Olivia Newton-John write their own songs.
4. Each of the thirty pupils raised their hand.
5. No one should try to be their own lawyer.
6. Everyone with a scientific mind should develop their potential.
7. Every player must provide their own shoes.
8. Has everyone done their homework?
9. If one doesn't know the road, you are apt to miss the cutoff.
10. We discovered that you couldn't hear a thing in the back row.

7.14　Indefinite Reference

To avoid any confusion for the reader, every personal pronoun should refer clearly to a definite antecedent.

INDEFINITE:　A statement was issued, but *they* refused to comment on its significance.

BETTER:　A statement was issued, but Pentagon officials refused to comment on its significance.

INDEFINITE:　*It* says in the paper that the senator will run for reelection.

BETTER:　The *Times* announced that the senator will run for reelection.

INDEFINITE: I want to be a doctor because *it* is rewarding.

BETTER: I want to be a doctor because helping the sick is rewarding.

INDEFINITE: Be sure to see Rome if *they* include it in the itinerary.

BETTER: Be sure to see Rome if the agency includes it in the itinerary.

The word *you* should only be used when it directly refers to the reader. Otherwise, its use is vague and confusing.

INDEFINITE: History shows that *you* must respect the dignity of the individual if *you* want *your* nation to survive.

BETTER: History shows that a nation's survival depends upon respect for the dignity of the individual.

INDEFINITE: In every contest *you* have specific rules to follow.

BETTER: In every contest there are specific rules to follow.

Exercise A: Revise the sentences below to remove all indefinite references of pronouns.

1. It says on the radio that a hurricane is coming this way.
2. When the President appeared, they played "Hail to the Chief."
3. Daydreaming can help you to relax.
4. In this exercise it says we are to eliminate indefinite references.
5. I studied hard, and I'm very confident about it.
6. In the armed services they train you for a special skill.
7. Steve Martin makes you laugh whenever he performs.
8. At our school they don't have a golf team.
9. In pioneer days you had to make the trip by horseback or covered wagon.
10. On that program they satirize television talk shows.

Exercise B: Follow the same directions as for Exercise A.

1. It says on the monument that the soldier is unknown.
2. Many people become very well educated without learning it just in school.
3. With the pocket calculators, it takes little power to operate them.
4. At the Coast Guard station they patrol the waters.
5. More and more married couples are choosing to be childless or are postponing them.
6. In the future they predict that you ll shop by computer.
7. Graduating seniors have to choose between work and school, and it is very difficult.
8. With flextime jobs, you choose your own hours.
9. In the "Help Wanted" section they tell you accountants and bookkeepers are needed.
10. Gerri likes to farm because it keeps you close to the land.

7.15 Ambiguous Reference

A pronoun should refer to a particular word or group of words. The reference of a pronoun is *ambiguous* if there are two or more words or groups of words to which the pronoun could refer. This can happen when a second noun or pronoun falls between the pronoun and its true antecedent.

AMBIGUOUS: The Red Sox and Yanks were scoreless until *their* pitcher tired.

BETTER: The Red Sox and Yanks were scoreless until the Yankees' pitcher tired.

AMBIGUOUS: Mary told Kim that *she* was going to be a great movie star.

BETTER: Mary told Kim, "I am going to be a great movie star."

AMBIGUOUS: Bob told Harry that *his* dog was found.

BETTER: Bob told Harry, "Your dog was found."

Exercise A: Revise the sentences below to remove all ambiguous pronoun references.

1. Before putting the car in the garage, Mom cleaned it out.
2. The librarian took the reference works off the shelves and labeled them.
3. Arthur told Ernie that he needed a haircut.
4. When the reporter interviewed the consumer expert, she was unfriendly.
5. Replace the gears on both engines and lubricate them.
6. Eleanor asked Kay if her cousin had arrived.
7. Mary gave Andrea a math problem she could not solve.
8. We took the screens from the windows and ran the hose over them.
9. Kelly told his father that he had been worrying too much.
10. After Ms. Nardi took the newspaper out of her briefcase, she set it on the desk.
11. Betsy told Zora that her painting had received the award.
12. Take the gloves off your hands and wash them.
13. The hockey player told the rugby player that he played rough.
14. Barry told Kevin that his camera was defective.

7.16   Vague Reference

Sometimes a writer may use the words *this, which, that,* or *it* to refer to an idea or to a chain of ideas that are not clearly identified. Such vague reference may confuse the reader. A sentence with this problem should be rephrased so that its focus is clear.

VAGUE: The organ accompaniment was very loud. *This* made the singer's voice almost inaudible.

BETTER: The singer's voice was almost inaudible because the organ accompaniment was very loud.

VAGUE:	Computers are being used to help farmers get data on selling prices. *This* helps them to know which of their operations are profitable.
BETTER:	The use of computers to get data on selling prices is helping farmers to know which of their operations are profitable.
VAGUE:	Long summer vacations are becoming boring for city high school students who are unemployed and cannot afford trips, *which* is one of the major causes of juvenile delinquency.
BETTER:	One of the major causes of juvenile delinquency is the boredom of city high school students who are unemployed and cannot afford trips.
VAGUE:	The weather was humid, and not a leaf was stirring on the few trees in the neighborhood. *It* made everyone irritable.
BETTER:	Everyone was irritable because the weather was humid and not a leaf was stirring on the few trees in the neighborhood.

Exercise A: Revise the sentences below to remove all vague references of pronouns.

1. They sailed constantly. It was their favorite pastime.
2. The mayor promised to pave the road out our way. It sounded good to us.
3. Tanya reads widely and enjoys it very much.
4. Don bought a 1970 Plymouth, which was a mistake.
5. We saw the movie twice, which made us late for supper.
6. When we left Canada and our friends, it made us sad.
7. My aunt pays me to babysit, and it has been good experience.
8. Lyn studies on her bed because she says it is comfortable.
9. Many factories and autos pollute the environment. This affects people's health.
10. We bought a house in Arizona. It was more than we had expected to pay.

Exercise B: Follow the same directions as for Exercise A.

1. Some people heat with solar energy, which is sensible.
2. The average person watches twenty-nine hours of TV per week. This means that fewer books are read.
3. College tuition is rising, which is a good reason to get a summer job.
4. Skilled labor is expensive, which makes Mr. Betts afraid to expand his business.
5. The school orchestra played each piece very well, and everyone liked it.
6. Trigonometry is a hard subject. This makes students take other courses.
7. Computers can run businesses and do housework, which allows humans to do other things.
8. The average life expectancy has increased. This should encourage awareness of the problems of the elderly.
9. The candidate says she wants to reform the prison system, and she seems sincere about it.
10. We took a left turn, which was a mistake.

Exercise C: Revise the sentences below to remove vague, indefinite, or ambiguous reference of pronouns.

1. Linda and Lauri took turns playing her guitar.
2. At camp they expect you to eat in the lodge.
3. Jim told his brother that he was in the musical.
4. Mix the gravel with the cement when it is wet.
5. Motocross is Erica's favorite pastime, and she goes to them on weekends.
6. Mr. Cross talks haltingly, which makes him hard to understand sometimes.
7. The child hit the lamp with a bottle, breaking it.
8. We arrived at the theater early, which meant we had time to read the program.
9. They tell us that the fiords of Norway are majestic.
10. The stocker took the cans from the cartons and set them in the aisle.

REINFORCEMENT EXERCISES
Pronoun Usage

A. Use pronouns as subjects, objects, and predicate words.
Choose the correct form from those given in parentheses.

1. Leona and (he, him) knew that in Egypt cats had once been worshipped as gods.
2. Couldn't it have been (she, her) who accidentally released the mice?
3. The trivia experts were (he, him) and (I, me).
4. The pollen from ragweed affects (she, her) and (I, me).
5. (They, Them) and the Claxtons reported seeing a UFO.
6. If it had been (I, me), I would have taken the left-hand fork in the road.
7. Give Leona and (she, her) your word of honor that you will keep the secret.
8. My identical twin and (I, me) have different fingerprints.
9. Uncle Art gave Sandra and (he, him) some hot chocolate.
10. The masked contestants were (she, her) and (I, me).

B. Use pronouns correctly. Choose the correct pronouns from those given in parentheses.

1. In *Treasure Island*, the struggle was between Jim Hawkins and (he, him).
2. (We, Us) mystery fans knew immediately that 221B Baker Street was the address of Sherlock Holmes.
3. Can you study with Kim and (I, me) at the library?
4. The master of ceremonies asked (we, us) contestants who Gertrude Ederle was and what she did.
5. I could not see my dinner parter because a tall flower arrangement was placed between (he, him) and (I, me).
6. It was (we, us) poets who knew that Phobos and Deimos were the moons of Mars.
7. The messages will be delivered to you and (I, me) by a special courier.

8. The guide gave (we, us) Americans a brief history of Bastille Day, France's national holiday.
9. Between Fred and (I, me), we owned every Mr. Moto title published.
10. It was for (we, us) cafeteria workers that the meeting was held.

C. Use *who* and *whom* correctly. Choose the correct pronoun from those given in parentheses.

1. (Who, Whom) will narrate the slide show on archeological discoveries in Alaska?
2. To (who, whom) did you give the formula?
3. (Who, Whom) is roasting pumpkin seeds?
4. Mr. Darnell blurted out, "The pianist is (who, whom)?"
5. (Who, Whom) did the professor hire as an assistant?
6. With (who, whom) are you taking the class in computer basics?
7. (Who, Whom) in this room has ever tasted abalone?
8. (Who, Whom) do you think the planning committee should select?
9. (Who, Whom) was the poem about sitting by the fire written for?
10. After the next election, (who, whom) do you think the President will be?

D. Use *who* and *whom* in clauses. Choose the correct pronoun from those given in parentheses.

1. Gerald Ford's adoptive father was the person for (who, whom) he was named.
2. People (who, whom) are courageous in one situation may be frightened in another.
3. Claudia was obviously the candidate (who, whom) the class stood behind.
4. A reward was offered to (whoever, whomever) could give information leading to recovery of the lost Persian cat.
5. Debbie Armstrong was one of the American skiers (who, whom) won a medal in the 1984 Olympics.

6. Seniors may invite (whoever, whomever) they please to the commencement exercises.
7. Governor-General Lord Stanley was the person for (who, whom) the Stanley Cup was named in the 1890s.
8. The writer (who, whom) wrote *One Hundred Years of Solitude* is Gabriel Garcia Marquez.
9. It was probably Agatha Christie (who, whom) most popularized the detective novel in our century.
10. The hypnotist's audience wondered (who, whom) had really become mesmerized by the performer.

E. Use pronouns correctly. Some of the following sentences contain errors in the use of pronouns. If a sentence is correct as it stands, write *Correct*. If a sentence is incorrect, change the pronoun as necessary.

1. The two painters, Picasso and her, had works on exhibit.
2. The coach criticized their breaking of the team rules.
3. It was Lana who we asked to draw the graph.
4. Antonia and myself visited EPCOT Center together in April of last year.
5. Hal and I weighed twice as much as them.
6. Steve did not anticipate them knowing that Carlos Casteneda was a writer.
7. Everyone expected the winner of the election to be he.
8. We admired the work of the underwater photographers, Dr. Katz and she.
9. Clay thinks he will be able to sell more tickets than me.
10. We decided to save the last canteen of water for us.

F. Use pronouns that agree with antecedents. Find the antecedent of the italicized pronoun in each of the following sentences. If the pronoun agrees with its antecedent, write *Correct*. If the pronoun does not agree with its antecedent, change the pronoun as necessary.

1. Everyone should be responsible for *your* own belongings.
2. Each of the contestants displayed *their* project proudly.

3. The hyena turned and seemed to laugh at *his* pursuers.
4. Neither Weldon nor Andy has offered *their* congratulations.
5. The baseball team celebrates *their* victories at Bonds Snack Shop.
6. Dolphins eat Squid as part of *its* diets.
7. Some of the ranchers knew that *their* guest was a greenhorn.
8. Mary said that computer games increase *your* eye-hand coordination.
9. Both of the sisters were expressing *her* opinion at the same time.
10. The hen was followed through the barnyard by *its* brood.

G. Correct indefinite or ambiguous reference. Rewrite the following sentences to remove all indefinite or ambiguous pronoun reference.

1. It says that the United States leads the world in the production of shrimp.
2. We asked the zookeeper whether we could stroke the mare, but she didn't seem to want us to.
3. In health class they explained that belladonna was a member of the nightshade family.
4. Ellen said that Serena actually enjoyed doing her chores.
5. In Great Britain they do not have the referendum as a method of control over lawmaking.
6. The merchant marine and battleships avoided the submarines until they reached the North Sea.
7. The article said that estivation was something like hibernation, but they didn't say what the difference was.
8. Barry took his identification tag off his badge and put it in his pocket.
9. After the farmer flooded the mole's tunnel with water, it disappeared.
10. Separate the French coins from the English coins, and give them to M. Diderot.

MIXED REVIEW

Pronoun Usage

A. Choose the standard form from those given in parentheses.

1. The training rules apply to (you, yourself) as well as to (I, me).
2. For (who, whom) was the basket of fruit and nuts intended?
3. The hippopotamus submerged and thus eluded (its, his) pursuers.
4. Everyone (who, whom) has ever given a present knows that an expression of thanks is appreciated.
5. Their parents and (they, them) raise giant schnauzers as a business.
6. One must know (your, his or her) own mind before trying to influence others.
7. Everybody believed that the judges, Danny and (he, him), would give the award to (me, myself).
8. (We, Us) fans stood in line for hours to get tickets for the concert.
9. People (who, whom) live in the Appalachian Mountains may be descendents of the Scotch-Irish.
10. We could not condone (them, their) joking about such a serious matter.
11. Nabakov wrote that every man is given (their, his) own special day.
12. Mr. Reef showed Clint and (she, her) how to make a geometric solid with twenty-four surfaces.
13. These are the archeologists, Dr. Barton and (she, her), who will speak to us about the famous excavation.
14. After the meal, we brewed herbal tea for (us, ourselves).
15. The twelve members of the jury would hear the case of (whoever, whomever) the court assigned.
16. The whisper was heard only by (we, us) three.
17. Either Sean or (she, her) must make amends for the damages.

18. (We, Us) seniors will graduate in just three weeks.
19. (Whoever, Whomever) is baking bread is going to get a visit from me soon.
20. Everyone must clean up (your, his or her) own lab area.

B. Some of the following sentences contain errors in pronouns usage. Rewrite these sentences, eliminating the errors. If there are no errors in a particular sentence, write *Correct*.

1. Try to get a seat between Francie and I.
2. It was them who suggested we visit the state legislature.
3. Sean showed Megan and me the best bike routes.
4. Zachary wiped off his coat with a rag and then shook it out.
5. Everybody seemed pleased with their test scores.
6. One must never assume that someone else is willing to do your work.
7. We consumers have begun to demand safer products.
8. Pollsters interviewed whomever answered the door.
9. The audience applauded his conducting.
10. To who do you want this package addressed?
11. Johnson has worked as a stunt driver longer than him.
12. Whom do you think is in that cat costume?
13. I would never have believed the culprit to be she.
14. Bob wanted support from Mrs. Friedman and myself.
15. In modern times they have been able to determine the size of comets.
16. Anyone with schedule problems should see your counselor.
17. The jury entered the courtroom with worried looks on its faces.
18. Most reporters get their assignments from the editors, Mr. Taylor and her.
19. Just between you and I, the Parkinsons are opening a new store in November.
20. The teacher expected we seniors to set an example for the freshmen.

USING GRAMMAR IN WRITING
Pronoun Usage

A. Deems Taylor wrote an essay in 1937 called "The Monster." In it, ten of the first eleven paragraphs begin with the pronoun "He" without ever giving an antecedent for the pronoun. Taylor's paragraphs begin with such sentences as, "He was a monster of conceit" and "He had the emotional stability of a six-year-old child." Not until the twelfth paragraph do we learn that this "monster" was Richard Wagner.

Write a description of your own that uses this clever device. In your paragraph composition, however, describe some sort of group, such as a baseball team, a rock group, a company, or an army battalion. Do not reveal the identity of the group until the last sentence.

B. You are probably familiar with the old myths and legends in which a god or other supernatural being bestows gifts upon various deserving mortals. Sometimes these gifts are money and possessions, and sometimes they are gifts of talent, looks, or other less tangible characteristics.

Imagine that you have developed the power to bestow these priceless favors to ten deserving people. Whom would you choose? What would you give each individual? Write up a list in which you describe your actions. Be sure to tell why you are awarding each person his or her particular gift. Your decisions may be serious, humorous, or satirical.

8.0 Adjective and Adverb Usage

Adjectives and adverbs sometimes are hard to distinguish from each other. These two parts of speech are used in similar ways as well. They are both used as modifiers. The guidelines presented in this Section should help you to recognize adjectives and adverbs and to distinguish between them.

8.1 Distinguishing Between Adjectives and Adverbs

Many adverbs are formed by adding an *-ly* ending to an adjective.

ADJECTIVE	ADVERB
close	closely
thorough	thoroughly
ambiguous	ambiguously

Some adverbs, however, are identical to the corresponding adjectives.

ADJECTIVE	ADVERB
a *rough* surface	play *rough*
the *first* performance	go *first*
your *left* hand	turn *left*

Most of these identical adjectives and adverbs have only one syllable. Generally, adjectives that have two or more syllables add *-ly* to form an adverb.

> Carmel is known for its *pleasant* climate.
> The class was *pleasantly* surprised by the speaker.

Several adverbs have two forms. One form has the *-ly* ending; the other does not.

> hold *tight*   fasten *tightly*
> go *wrong*   decide *wrongly*
> shine *bright*   smile *brightly*

The one-syllable adverb in each of the pairs above may also be used as an adjective: a *tight* fit, a *wrong* move, a *bright* star. To tell whether these words are adjectives or adverbs, observe how they are used in a sentence.

8.2   Using Adjectives and Adverbs Correctly

To determine whether a modifier is an adjective or an adverb, identify the word in the sentence that it modifies. Adjectives modify nouns and pronouns. Adjectives may also be used after linking verbs as predicate words. Adverbs modify verbs, adjectives, and other adverbs.

> Shakespeare wrote *comic* scenes even in his tragedies. (The adjective *comic* modifies the noun *scenes*.)

> Other plays were entirely *comic*. (The predicate adjective *comic* is linked to the noun *plays* by the verb *were*.)

> Shakespeare wrote his plays *quickly*. (The adverb *quickly* modifies the verb *wrote*.)

> His plays were *extremely* popular when he wrote them. (The adverb *extremely* modifies the adjective *popular*.)

8.3 The Placement of Adverbs

One way to identify adverbs is to notice their placement. If a modifier comes directly before an action verb, an adjective, or another adverb, it is usually an adverb.

Inventors *often* experience ridicule. (modifies the verb *experience*)

Ridicule is *terribly* demoralizing. (modifies the adjective *demoralizing*)

Inventors *very* definitely need self-confidence. (modifies the adverb *definitely*)

Sometimes an adverb is placed after the word it modifies. It is nonstandard to use an adjective in place of an adverb in this situation.

NONSTANDARD: Kevin computed the numbers *perfect*.

STANDARD: Kevin computed the numbers *perfectly*.

A word that follows and modifies an action verb is an adverb.

8.4 Adjectives with Linking Verbs

Linking verbs are followed by predicate words that are linked to the subject of the sentence. Sometimes these predicate words are adjectives.

The linking of the subject to an adjective in the predicate does not cause confusion when the linking verb is a form of *be*. However, many linking verbs can also be used as action verbs. To use the correct modifier, you must decide whether the verb is being used as a linking verb or an action verb.

The ship *appeared suddenly* out of the fog.
(action verb modified by an adverb)

The parents *appeared worried*.
(linking verb followed by a predicate adjective)

He *looked suspiciously* at my driver's license.
(action verb modified by an adverb)

Sean *looked ridiculous*.
(linking verb followed by a predicate adjective)

The following verbs are linking verbs. Most of them may also be used as action verbs.

look	feel	stay	become
sound	smell	remain	seem
appear	taste	grow	act

Exercise A: Choose the standard form from those given.

1. The young actor appeared quite (nervous, nervously).
2. Ilsa sings her solo (beautiful, beautifully).
3. I worked (steadily, steady) for five hours.
4. The child looked (envious, enviously) at her brother's candy.
5. The hikers grew (uneasy, uneasily) as nightfall approached.
6. Be sure to measure the ingredients very (careful, carefully).
7. The cherry pie smelled (delicious, deliciously) in the oven.
8. His voice sounded (harshly, harsh) on the telephone.
9. Margie's marks have improved (considerable, considerably).
10. The speaker approached the platform (nervous, nervously).

Exercise B: Decide whether the italicized modifier is standard or nonstandard. If it is nonstandard, substitute the standard form.

1. Ted has been feeling *strange* all afternoon.
2. The lemonade tasted *sour*.
3. The whole story sounds *peculiar*.
4. Be sure to put the paint on *even*.
5. Pick the baby up as *gentle* as you can.
6. This hot chocolate tastes too *sweet*.

7. I couldn't hear the signals *clear* enough.
8. The children remained *silent* throughout the concert.
9. Anna cleared the hurdle *easy*.
10. Mr. Hale sounds *abrupt* when he meets people.

8.5 This—These; That—Those

This and *that* modify singular words; *these* and *those*, plural words. *Kind*, *sort*, and *type* require singular modifiers.

NONSTANDARD: *These* kind sold immediately.
STANDARD: *This* kind sold immediately.

NONSTANDARD: *These* sort of games are tiring.
STANDARD: *This* sort of game is tiring.

8.6 Them—Those

Those may be either a pronoun or an adjective. *Them* is always a pronoun and never an adjective.

NONSTANDARD: Did you enjoy *them* stories?
STANDARD: Did you enjoy *those* stories? (adjective)
STANDARD: Did you enjoy *them*? (pronoun)

8.7 Bad—Badly

Use the adjective *bad* after linking verbs.

He felt *bad*. (*not* he felt badly)
The water tastes *bad*.

Use the adverb *badly* to modify action verbs, adjectives, and adverbs.

Ron injured his knee *badly*.
The doctor helped the *badly* burned patient.

8.8 Good—Well

The word *good* may only be used as an adjective. It modifies nouns and pronouns and is a predicate word after linking verbs.

> Barry has a *good* serve.
> Are these *good* for you?
> The movie was *good*.

The word *well* is sometimes an adjective and sometimes an adverb. When it is an adjective, *well* means "in good health."

> Mr. Longman still looks *well* at ninety.

When it is an adverb, *well* means "properly or expertly performed."

> Mr. Longman plays golf *well*.

If you cannot decide whether a verb is being used as a linking verb or an action verb, try substituting a form of *be*. If the sentence still makes sense, the verb is a linking verb.

> The infection appears (serious, seriously).

In the sentence above, substitute *is* for *appears*. It does not make sense to say *The infection is seriously*. However, it does make sense to say *The infection is serious*. Therefore, *appears* is a linking verb in the sentence, and the predicate adjective *serious* is the correct choice. If it had made sense with neither modifier, the adverb would have been the correct choice.

8.9 Fewer—Less

Fewer is used to describe things that can be counted. *Less* refers to quantity or degree.

> Careful driving results in *fewer* accidents.
> Use *less* heat for that dish.
> I have *less* respect for him now.

Exercise A: Decide whether the italicized words are standard or non-standard usage. Substitute a standard form for each nonstandard usage.

1. Jeff feels *good* about winning the essay contest.
2. I did *well* in the history test.
3. The injured skier needed help *bad*.
4. If you check your answers, you will have *less* errors.
5. I don't like *that* sort of hat.
6. *These* kind is much more practical.
7. This recipe requires *less* milk and *less* eggs.
8. Did you eat *well* at camp?
9. I'd like to have one of *them* pocket calculators.
10. Mindy felt *badly* about quitting the team.

Exercise B: Follow the directions for Exercise A.

1. The bass guitar sounds *well* in that arrangement.
2. I don't play chess very *good*.
3. Nowadays there are *fewer* circuses than there were during the 1950's and '60's.
4. *Those* kinds of remarks never help.
5. *Those* kind of camera is very expensive.
6. The reviewer commented that the book ended *badly*.
7. Where did you get *them* kittens?
8. Our car runs *well* since we had the engine overhauled.
9. *These* kind of exercise is easy to do.
10. *Them* four-cylinder cars are economical to operate.

8.10 Comparative and Superlative

Adjectives and adverbs are used to describe other words. Most adjectives and adverbs have two special forms that are used to compare characteristics. The **comparative** degree is used to compare two things. The **superlative** degree is used to express the highest degree of a characteristic when three or more things are compared.

COMPARATIVE ADJECTIVE:	Steve's jokes are *funnier* than mine.
SUPERLATIVE ADJECTIVE:	Georgette is the *tallest* girl in her class.
COMPARATIVE ADVERB:	Joe pole-vaulted *higher* than Chris.
SUPERLATIVE ADVERB:	Of all the boys in the neighborhood, Sam plays *roughest*.

Adjectives in Comparisons

There are two ways of making the comparative form of adjectives.

1. Most adjectives of one syllable and a few adjectives of two syllables add *-er* to form the comparative.

   cold—colder   sad—sadder
   silly—sillier   warm—warmer
   thin—thinner   wealthy—wealthier

2. Most adjectives of two syllables and all adjectives of more than two syllables use the words *more* and *less* to form the comparative.

   careless—more careless   powerful—less powerful
   quizzical—less quizzical   sanitary—more sanitary
   brilliant—more brilliant   nervous—less nervous

The superlative of adjectives is also formed in two ways. Adjectives that form the comparative with *-er* form the superlative with *-est*. Adjectives that form the comparative with *more* and *less* form the superlative with *most* and *least*.

ADJECTIVE	COMPARATIVE	SUPERLATIVE
straight	straighter	straightest
happy	happier	happiest
fragrant	more fragrant	most fragrant
disastrous	less disastrous	least disastrous
sophomoric	more sophomoric	most sophomoric

Irregular Comparison of Adjectives

Some adjectives form the comparative and superlative with an entirely new word.

ADJECTIVE	COMPARATIVE	SUPERLATIVE
good	better	best
well	better	best
bad	worse	worst
ill	worse	worst
little	less *or* lesser	least
much	more	most
many	more	most
far	farther *or* further	farthest *or* furthest

Adverbs in Comparisons

Adverbs form the comparative and superlative in two ways.

1. Adverbs of one syllable add *-er*.

   fast—faster   hard—harder   long—longer

2. Most adverbs ending in *-ly* form the comparative with *more* and *less*.

   violently—less violently   cautiously—more cautiously

3. The superlative form of the adverb is formed with *-est* or the words *most* and *least*. Adverbs that form the comparative with *-er* form the superlative with *-est*. Adverbs that use *more* and *less* for the comparative use *most* and *least* for the superlative.

ADVERB	COMPARATIVE	SUPERLATIVE
slow	slower	slowest
precisely	more precisely	most precisely
hastily	less hastily	least hastily
ambiguously	more ambiguously	most ambiguously

Irregular Comparison of Adverbs

A few adverbs form the comparative and superlative with entirely new words.

ADVERB	COMPARATIVE	SUPERLATIVE
far	farther, further	farthest, furthest
late	later	latest, last
little	less	least
much	more	most
well	better	best

Exercise A: Find the adjectives and tell whether they are in comparative form or superlative form.

1. I find biography more interesting than fiction.
2. Who is our most likely candidate?
3. The lowest point in the United States is Death Valley.
4. The Sears Tower is taller than the Empire State Building.
5. Chris is the most ambitious person in the class.
6. Dogs have a keener sense of smell than cats.
7. Laura is the fastest runner on the team.
8. The driver chose the route that seemed least dangerous.
9. The amoeba is the lowest of all animal forms.
10. Who is older, Lynn or Randy?

Exercise B: Find each adverb. Tell whether it is in the comparative or the superlative form.

1. You will have to turn the wheels more sharply if you want to get into that parking space.
2. This detergent claims to have the longest lasting suds.
3. Which of the three deserves the Pulitzer Prize most?
4. The weaver handled her yarns less deftly after her automobile accident.
5. If you arrive at the play earlier than we do, save some good seats for us.
6. Medieval craftsmen worked more patiently than modern workers probably because they had fewer distractions.

7. We drove farther than we wanted to before stopping.
8. If you would work less rapidly, you might make fewer mistakes.
9. The Gordons don't like to drive or take the train, but they like flying least of all.
10. Sheila performed the part of Juliet more movingly than her understudy.

Exercise C: Writing Choose two plays, television shows, or concerts that you have seen recently. Write a few paragraphs comparing the two. Use the comparative and superlative forms of modifiers in your paragraphs.

8.11 The Double Comparison

Comparisons of adjectives and adverbs are formed either by adding the *-er* ending or by using the word *more* or *less*. Do not use both.

Superlatives of adjectives and adverbs are formed either by adding the *-est* ending or by using the word *most* or *least*. Do not use both.

NONSTANDARD: We had a more easier time with that test.
STANDARD: We had an easier time with that test.

NONSTANDARD: Speak in a more softer tone.
STANDARD: Speak in a softer tone.

NONSTANDARD: Try to speak more correcter.
STANDARD: Try to speak more correctly.

8.12 Illogical Comparisons

The word *other*, or the word *else*, is required in comparisons of an individual member with the rest of the group.

ILLOGICAL: Our school won more awards than any school in the city. (Our school is also in the city.)
CLEAR: Our school won more awards than any *other* school in the city.

ILLOGICAL: Angela is as bright as anyone on the team.

CLEAR: Angela is as bright as anyone *else* on the team.

The words *than* or *as* are required after the first modifier in a compound comparison.

ILLOGICAL: The begonia is as healthy if not healthier than the cactus.

CLEAR BUT
AWKWARD: The begonia is as healthy *as*, if not healthier than, the cactus.

BETTER: The begonia is as healthy *as* the cactus, if not healthier.

ILLOGICAL: This cake is as good if not better than the one I baked for the County Fair.

CLEAR: This cake is as good *as* the one I baked for the County Fair, if not better.

ILLOGICAL: Al had as many errors if not more than Jan.

CLEAR: Al had as many errors *as* Jan, if not more.

Both parts of a comparison must be stated completely if there is any chance of its being misunderstood.

CONFUSING: I admire her more than Joan.

CLEAR: I admire her more than Joan *does*.

CLEAR: I admire her more than I *admire* Joan.

CONFUSING: Central defeated West worse than East.

CLEAR: Central defeated West worse than East *did*.

CLEAR: Central defeated West worse than it *defeated* East.

ILLOGICAL: The training of a nurse is longer than a technician.

CLEAR: The training of a nurse is longer than *that* of a technician.

BETTER: A nurse's training is longer than a technician's *is*.

Exercise A: Revise the following comparisons.

1. You should try to make your explanation more clearer.
2. Vicki beat me in tennis worse than Chuck.

3. Who is the oldest, you or Frank?
4. Ms. Gerardi likes picnics more than her husband.
5. This model is probably as expensive if not more expensive than that one.
6. Of the two, Leslie seems the most likely to win.
7. This dessert is more tastier.
8. I like Susan better than Charlotte.
9. Pat thinks *People* has better articles than any magazine.
10. The gas mileage of a compact car is much better than a full-size.

Exercise B: Follow the same directions as for Exercise A.

1. W. Somerset Maugham's *Of Human Bondage* is as good or better than any of his other books.
2. It was the most saddest movie I had ever seen.
3. Which of the two hats do you think is the most appropriate?
4. Transferring schools was much more easier than Steve had expected.
5. Of the two exercises, the second is easiest.
6. I like professional hockey better than Harry.
7. The United States is bigger than any country in the Americas.
8. Which of these two trees do you think is healthiest?
9. Strawberries are much more cheaper this week than last.
10. Diamonds are harder than any substance.

8.13   The Double Negative

A double negative occurs when two negative words are incorrectly used instead of one. This situation often occurs in sentences that contain contractions.

NONSTANDARD: He did*n't* ask me *nothing*.
STANDARD: He did*n't* ask me *anything*.

NONSTANDARD: Kindergartners do*n't* have *no* homework.
STANDARD: Kindergartners do*n't* have *any* homework.

Hardly, scarcely, or *barely,* used with a negative word, is nonstandard.

NONSTANDARD: There was*n't hardly* any rain in May.
STANDARD: There was *hardly* any rain in May.

NONSTANDARD: The award did*n't scarcely* cover her expenses.
STANDARD: The award *scarcely* covered her expenses.

Exercise: These sentences cover all of the problems of adjective and adverb usage in this Section. Choose the standard form from those in parentheses.

1. Morris (can, can't) hardly keep up with his work.
2. (Fewer, Less) people shop on Monday than on Tuesday.
3. You (will, won't) get hardly any bad effects from this medicine.
4. The inland route is longer, but it is (safer, more safer).
5. I (can't, can) scarcely believe that such a terrible thing has happened.
6. Please talk as (quiet, quietly) as possible.
7. You'll stay in good condition if you exercise (regular, regularly).
8. We haven't had (any, no) warm weather since August.
9. Do you feel (confident, confidently) about today's game?
10. He (didn't have, had) hardly any money with him.
11. The river has risen (considerable, considerably) tonight.
12. Little Timmy (could, couldn't) scarcely keep his eyes open.
13. Are (them, those) portable typewriters heavy?
14. The hole in the box should be a little (wider, more wider).
15. Instant oatmeal tastes surprisingly (well, good).
16. She ran down the hill as (quick, quickly) as she could.
17. I enjoy (those, that) kind of movie because it is good entertainment.
18. This coat material feels (rough, roughly).
19. The team was not (real, really) interested in the game.
20. Of all the members of the glee club, Ben has the (better, best) voice.

REINFORCEMENT EXERCISES

Adjective and Adverb Usage

A. Use adjectives and adverbs correctly. Rewrite these sentences, correcting errors in the use of modifiers. If a sentence contains no errors, write *Correct*.

1. The attic of the old house smelled mustily.
2. Linda answered happily that she had made the finals.
3. The church bells rang peaceful in the late evening.
4. Sometimes good news is hard to take calm.
5. Mina looked stunningly in her new coat and boots.
6. The bear cub appeared friendly, but the mother bear was dangerous.
7. The capybara, the world's largest rodent, swims good.
8. The defendant spoke quiet and said she had not been in town on the night of the accident.
9. Van cleaned his room thorough before the guests arrived.
10. The smell of fresh bread drifted temptingly in the air.

B. Use troublesome modifiers correctly. Decide whether the italicized words are correct or not. Rewrite any sentences that contain errors. If a sentence contains no errors, write *Correct*.

1. Mark looked *badly* after he rolled down the cliff.
2. *Less* attention should be paid to movie stars and more to musicians and artists.
3. *These* sort of instrument is called a rain gauge.
4. Kyle performs *good* when it matters.
5. Our vet is very familiar with *those* kind of dog.
6. The patient seemed to feel *well* until the medication was changed.
7. *Them* little rolls of film are microfilm.
8. The prospector trudged through Chilkoot Pass with *less* supplies than he had wanted.
9. Pawn to King Four was not a *good* move.
10. My apology was *badly* phrased.

C. Correct improper comparisons. Revise the following sentences, correcting all errors in comparison.

1. Guido's pizza was as delicious if not better than Mama Angelino's.
2. My father trusts chemical fertilizers more than my mother.
3. Witherspoon seems to be the most positive of the two candidates.
4. The dinosaur fossil found in Texas was more older than any previous fossil found there.
5. The tides at the Bay of Fundy are higher than Boston.
6. Which do you like better, mint chip or butter pecan?
7. That is the most silliest joke I have ever heard.
8. Alaska has more acreage than any state in the United States.
9. My dog is more cute than yours.
10. Does a computer work accurater than an abacus?

D. Correct double negatives. Rewrite the following sentences correcting the double negatives. If a sentence contains no errors, write *Correct*.

1. They couldn't hardly fail to notice the neon sign.
2. Nobody on the experimental diet couldn't get enough vitamins.
3. Before the Federal Deposit Insurance Corporation was established, some banks couldn't barely survive hard times.
4. Until she took Ms. McComb's art class, my mother had never done no painting.
5. I would run two miles today, but there isn't no dry trail to run on.
6. Haven't none of the kennel's pups been sold?
7. Unlike rainfall, snowfall is often measured by weight, not depth.
8. The biscuits were baked, but they weren't scarcely edible.
9. There isn't nobody who can master chess instantly.
10. It didn't take long for newspapers to use the telegraph.

MIXED REVIEW

Adjective and Adverb Usage

A. Choose the standard form from those given in parentheses.

1. Of all Hawaiian trees, the monkeypod may be the (more useful, most useful).
2. Bogs (are, aren't) hardly able to survive near construction sites.
3. The square dancers clapped (happy, happily).
4. As he felt himself slip, the mountain climber clung to the rope (tighter, more tightly).
5. An igloo is (good, well) protection against an arctic storm.
6. This novel has (fewer, less) pages than that nonfiction book.
7. The lecture on kites seemed (frivolous, frivolously), but it was in fact quite (serious, seriously).
8. Joan Joyce struck out both Ted Williams and Hank Aaron (easy, easily).
9. (This, These) kinds of paintings are of great historical value.
10. The *Cutty Sark* was more famous than (any, any other) clipper ship.
11. The route through the Suez Canal was (shorter, shortest) and (less costly, less costlier) than the route around Africa.
12. The marching band played (good, well), placing second in the state contest.
13. The professor warned that there shouldn't be (any, no) horseplay in the chemistry lab.
14. A health-conscious cook might use (less, fewer) sugar in a cake recipe in order to cut down on calories and carbohydrates.
15. Jock rows across Puget Sound (more often, most often) than he takes a ferry.
16. I (was, wasn't) barely able to tell the difference between the bisque and the chowder.

17. Stan biked (fewer, less) miles this month than he did last.
18. The mother and father looked (loving, lovingly) at the infant.
19. Is it true that solitaire is the (most popular, most popularest) card game?
20. Who arranged (them, those) flowers?

B. Some of the following sentences contain errors in the use of modifiers. Identify these sentences and rewrite them. If a sentence is already correct, write *Correct*.

1. I would like to own one of them recreational vehicles.
2. Randy can think more quicker on his feet than anyone else I know.
3. The most costliest ingredients are used to make our cookies.
4. Nobody didn't want to leave when the school trip was over.
5. Sharon felt badly about the mistake she made.
6. The combination of voices in the chorus sounded beautiful.
7. You performed your part in the play very good.
8. Laurie likes Michael Jackson more than her mother.
9. The laboratory assistant stirred the mixture cautious.
10. The new year hadn't scarcely begun when the first snow fell.
11. The travelers appeared happy to be home at last.
12. Lionel's second idea was more better than his first.
13. Which city do you like best, New York or San Francisco?
14. These kind of telephones are going out of style.
15. The apple cider tasted like it had turned badly.
16. Rosa finds radio as entertaining if not more than television.
17. Sam spent less actual dollars than Robert but also got less value for his money.
18. The dachshund has shorter legs than any dog.
19. The team played good today.
20. Portia looked well after her operation.

USING GRAMMAR IN WRITING
Adjective and Adverb Usage

A. Rock music has entered an exciting era in which the musical performance of a song is complemented by a video performance. Some rock fans now claim that one cannot truly enjoy a song without seeing its video first. Other listeners disagree and feel that the video portion interferes with their personal reaction to the music. Write an essay in which you give your feelings on the value of rock video. Compare the way you reacted to music before videos became popular and the way you react now. Use at least one specific example of a tune which you liked more or less after you saw the video. Use several comparisons in your essay.

B. Scientific research depends upon the researchers' ability to examine a subject closely and then to describe it accurately. Choose any of the following subjects. In one or two paragraphs, describe what you see. Be as exact as possible by using precise modifiers and by comparing your subject to a similar object or process.

the formation of a crystal	the mixing of oil and water	a type of cloud a spider's web
the body of an insect	the human eye	

C. Satellite communications have made the transmission of news from one part of the world to another almost instantaneous. A century ago, on the other hand, news could take months, or even years, to travel across the globe. The advantages of increased speed in the transmission of news are perhaps obvious. What, however, are some of the disadvantages? Write an essay in which you compare the old, slow forms of news transmission with the superfast modern forms. Cover the advantages in your essay, but do not neglect to mention the disadvantages as well.

9.0 The Right Word

The expressions **standard** and **nonstandard** have been used in previous Sections of this Handbook to alert you to grammatical errors that are common in American English. Standard usages are words and phrases that are acceptable in all situations. Nonstandard usages are words and phrases that are not acceptable in all situations.

Many nonstandard constructions may be familiar to you since they are often used in informal spoken language. However, it is best to eliminate them from your speech because they may brand you as a careless or untrained user of the language. Nonstandard words and phrases are never acceptable in writing unless it is the most informal and personal writing, such as personal letters or diary entries. For more information on the various levels of usage in English, see Chapter 7, "The Process of Writing."

This Section will explain the differences between pairs of words that are commonly misused. Study these pairs to be sure you know how to use each of the words correctly. Refer to the list in this Section when you have questions regarding standard usage. If the answer to your question is not covered here, use a good dictionary.

9.1 Words Commonly Confused

accept, except *Accept* is a verb. It means "to agree or to receive something willingly." *Except* is sometimes used as a verb to mean "leave out; exclude." More often, *except* is a preposition. As a preposition, it means "but" or "excluding."

> Carol *accepted* the school board's offer at once.
> It is unfair to *except* people you do not like from eligibility. (verb)
> Everyone was laughing *except* the driver. (preposition)

adapt, adopt *Adapt* means "to make *apt* or suitable; to adjust." *Adopt* means "to *opt* or choose as one's own; to accept." The second syllable of each of these words will help you remember their meanings.

> Have you *adapted* to your new surroundings in the city?
> The Kinneys *adopted* a puppy from the Humane Society.

advice, advise *Advice* is a noun, and *advise* is a verb. When you *advise* someone, you give that person *advice*.

affect, effect *Affect* is a verb meaning "to influence" or "impress." When *effect* is used as a verb, it means "bring about" or "accomplish." As a noun it is a "result" of action.

> Will the new gas tax *affect* your use of your car? (verb)
> The state legislature *effected* this new tax. (verb)
> Will the tax have an *effect* on the amount you drive? (noun)

agree to, with, on You agree *to* something such as a plan. You agree *with* someone else, or something such as liver does not agree *with* you. You agree with others *on* a course of action.

allusion, illusion An *allusion* is a reference. An *illusion* is a false perception or interpretation.

> The story made an *allusion* to our poor football record.
> Betty had the *illusion* that her work was satisfactory.

already, all ready *Already* is an adverb meaning "even now" or "previously."*All ready* is an adjective phrase meaning "completely prepared."

altogether, all together *Altogether* means "entirely" or "on the whole."*All together* means that all parts of a group are considered.

> The report of the accident is *altogether* wrong. (entirely)
> The crew pulled on the rope *all together*.

alumna, alumnus An *alumna* is a female graduate; the plural is *alumnae*. An *alumnus* is a male graduate; the plural is *alumni*.

among, between Use *between* when you are joining or separating two things. Use *among* when there are more than two.

> NONSTANDARD: Divide the money *between* the three of us.
> STANDARD: Divide the money *among* the three of us.

amount, number *Amount* is used to indicate a total sum of things. It is used to refer to items that cannot be counted. *Number* is used to refer to items that can be counted.

> The *amount* of food consumed was amazing. (*food* cannot be counted.)
> The *number* of hamburgers consumed was amazing. (*hamburgers* can be counted.)

angry at, with You are angry *with* a person and angry *at* a thing.

apt, likely, liable These three words all have probability in common. *Apt* means "having a tendency to." *Likely to* implies "probably going to." *Liable to* implies negative consequences. It means "subject to something usually unpleasant."

> People are *apt* to worry when the economy is bad.
> It is *likely* to rain before nightfall.
> If you speed on this road, you are *liable* to be arrested.

bad, badly See Section 8.7.

being   This completely acceptable present participle is most safely used as part of a main verb. Used as a modifier it creates extremely awkward sentences. *Being as* and *being that* are not satisfactory substitutes for *since* or *because*.

NONSTANDARD: Being that he is the boss, we do what he says.

STANDARD: Because he is the boss, we do what he says.

beside, besides   *Beside* means "at the side of." *Besides* means "in addition to."

Lorne stood *beside* the fallen oak.
Besides good looks, the contestants must have talent.

between   *Between* is not followed by a singular noun or by a singular pronoun.

NONSTANDARD: Between each bite, he sipped his cocoa.

STANDARD: Between *bites*, he sipped his cocoa.

NONSTANDARD: Between every page, Jack inserted a paper.

STANDARD: Between *the pages*, Jack inserted papers.

borrow, lend   *Borrow* and *lend* are verbs. You *borrow from* someone. You *lend to* someone.

NONSTANDARD: Will you *borrow* me your atlas?

STANDARD: Will you *lend* me your atlas?

STANDARD: May I *borrow* your atlas?

bring, take   *Bring* implies movement toward the speaker. *Take* implies movement away from the speaker.

I will *take* this book to school. (*away* from here)
He will *bring* us some milk. (*toward* us)
Sarah will *take* me home. (*away* from here.)

but that, but what   The word *but* has a negative meaning. If it is preceded by another negative, it creates a double negative.

NONSTANDARD: I have *no* doubt *but that* Terri will win.

STANDARD: I have *no* doubt that Terri will win.

can, may   *Can* means "able or having the power to do something." *May* is used to ask or to grant permission. It also expresses the probability of something happening.

> *Can* you solve the first problem? (ability)
> *May* we go to the library? (permission)
> It *may* snow tomorrow. (probability)

Could is the past tense of *can; might* is the past of *may*.

compliment, complement   A *compliment* is praise. A *complement* makes something complete or whole.

continual, continuous   *Continuous* means "without interruption." *Continual* occurs repeatedly, but is interrupted.

> There were *continual* sounds of hammering.
> There is a *continuous* stretch of desert across North Africa.

differ from, with   One thing or person differs *from* another in characteristics. You differ *with* someone when you disagree.

different from, different than   The standard usage is almost always *different from*. Occasionally, you may have to use the phrase *different than* to avoid awkwardness.

> Our new neighborhood is very *different from* the old.
> The job was quite *different than* it had seemed.

disinterested, uninterested   *Disinterested* means "neutral; unbiased by personal advantage." *Uninterested* means simply "having no interest."

> We need a *disinterested* judge to decide who is right.
> The children seemed *uninterested* in the science fair.

Exercise A: Rewrite these sentences to make them follow standard usage. Some of the sentences are written correctly.

1. Pinter adopted *The French Lieutenant's Woman* for the screen.
2. My final examination was different than yours.

3. "Bring this basket of goodies to your grandmother," said
   Red Riding Hood's mother.
4. Harp solos were played between each course.
5. Hal asked Marie to borrow him her book for the night.
6. What is the effect of nuclear wastes on the environment?
7. Consider it a compliment if people imitate you.
8. If we work altogether, we should have a first-rate prom.
9. Samantha was totally disinterested in what he said.
10. Only a small number of stuffed animals was purchased.

Exercise B: Choose the standard form from the words given.

1. Jordan asked, "(Can, May) I use the car tonight?"
2. Rachel found it hard to (except, accept) her good fortune.
3. Cynthia's mother is an (alumnus, alumna) of Vassar.
4. The secret was kept (between, among) the four friends.
5. Faulkner's title *The Sound and the Fury* is an (allusion,
   illusion) to a line in *Macbeth*.
6. Liz was (already, all ready) to greet her new niece.
7. Jessie didn't want anything (beside, besides) sporting
   equipment for his birthday.
8. The equator is an imaginary (continuous, continual) band
   around the middle of the earth.
9. The barbeque sauce tasted (bad, badly).
10. Darrell was angry (at, with) Irene after the debate.

eager, anxious *Anxious* means "experiencing uneasiness
caused by anticipated anger or misfortune." *Eager* means
"longing or enthusiastic."

> The Florios were *anxious* until the plane landed.
> The class is *eager* to begin working on individual projects.

emigrate, immigrate To *emigrate* is to leave one's homeland.
To *immigrate* is to enter a country for the purpose of settling.
An *emigrant* is one who is traveling from a former home. An
immigrant is one who has arrived in a new country.

etc.   The abbreviation *et cetera* means "and others" or "and so forth." Try to avoid using this abbreviation in formal writing. Never precede *etc.* with the word *and*. This is repetitious because the *et* in *et cetera* means *and* in Latin.

fewer, less   See Section 8.9.

formally, formerly   *Formally* means "in a formal manner." *Formerly* means "previously."

further, farther; furthest, farthest   *Farther* is used for comparisons of distance and *further* for any other comparisons.

> Which is *farther* from the equator Rio or Rome? (distance)
> *Further* discussions were held before the two sides agreed. (continuation)

good, well   See Section 8.8.

hanged, hung   *Hanged* refers to the execution of people. *Hung* refers to the placement or suspension of an object on a wall, ceiling, hook, or elsewhere.

> The mob *hanged* its enemy in effigy.
> The mourners *hung* a wreath on the simple grave.

imply, infer   A speaker or writer suggests or *implies* something. The reader, listener, or observer comes to a conclusion, or *infers* something, on the basis of what has been said.

> The author *implied* that war was madness.
> Critics *inferred* that Frost's "Stopping by a Woods on a Snowy Evening" was actually about death.

in, into   *In* means inside something. *Into* tells of motion from the outside to the inside of something.

> NONSTANDARD: The books fell *in* the mud.
> STANDARD: The books fell *into* the mud.

ingenious, ingenuous   *Ingenious* means "clever and resourceful." *Ingenuous* means "frank and honest."

is where, is when   Do not use of *where* or *when* in a definition.

NONSTANDARD: Widdershins *is when* you move in a counter-clockwise direction.

STANDARD: Widdershins is a counterclockwise direction.

it's, its   *It's* is a contraction for *it is*. *Its* is a possessive pronoun meaning "belonging to it."

kind, sort, type   See Section 8.5.

lay, lie   See Section 5.6.

learn, teach   To *learn* means "to gain knowledge or instruction." To teach is "to provide knowledge" or "to instruct."

After we *learn* how to ski, we will *teach* you.

leave, let   *Leave* means "to go away from." *Let* means "permit." The principal parts are *leave, left, left,* and *let, let, let.*

NONSTANDARD: Please *leave* the boy go on with his story.

STANDARD: Please *let* the boy go on with his story.

NONSTANDARD: We should have *left* Sue go.

STANDARD: We should have *let* Sue go.

like, as, as if   In informal English, *like* is sometimes used as a conjunction. Formally, *like* is a preposition and introduces a prepositional phrase.

NOT ACCEPTED: I feel *like* Sally does about swimming.

BETTER: I feel *as* Sally does about swimming.

NOT ACCEPTED: Jeff acted *like* he had heard the story.

BETTER: Jeff acted *as if* he had heard the story.

STANDARD: *Like* all boys, Davy wanted a bike.

most, almost   *Almost* is an adverb meaning "nearly." *Most* is an adjective meaning "the greater part."

NONSTANDARD: *Most* everything I do turns out favorably.

STANDARD: *Almost* everything I do turns out favorably.

of, have   Certain phrases like *could have, might have, should have* are sometimes spoken, and then written, as if they were *could of, might of, should of*. This usage is incorrect.

only   The misplacement of this word can cause confusion in a sentence. For clarity, the word *only* should be positioned before the word(s) it qualifies. Notice the difference in meaning in the sentences below.

> Three people *only* sent cards.
> *Only* three people sent cards.

percent, percentage   *Percent* is correctly used only when preceded by a number. When there is no preceding number, *percentage* is correct.

> About 70 *percent* of the pictures turned out well.
> A large *percentage* of our students go to college.

raise, rise   See Section 5.6.

real, really   In precise usage *real* is an adjective, and *really* is an adverb.

> NONSTANDARD: Homemade ice cream is *real* delicious.
> STANDARD: Homemade ice cream is *really* delicious.

their, they're, there   *Their* is a possessive pronoun meaning "belonging to them." *They're* is a contraction for "they are." *There*, like *here*, refers to a place.

to, too   *To* is a preposition used to introduce prepositional phrases: *to the movies*. *To* is also the sign of the infinitive: *to think*. *Too* is an adverb meaning "overly" or "also."

unique   Unique means "one of a kind." Therefore, it is illogical to qualify the word, as in "somewhat unique." A few other absolute words that do not take comparatives or superlatives are *equal, fatal, final, absolute*.

> NONSTANDARD: This party is *very unique*.
> STANDARD: This party is *unique*.

way, ways   *Ways* is misused when it refers to distance.

NONSTANDARD: We went a little *ways* into the forest.
STANDARD: We went a little *way* into the forest.
STANDARD: There are many *ways* to skin a cat.

Exercise A: Rewrite the following sentences to make them follow standard usage. Some sentences are already correct.

1. The decision of the judges is absolutely final.
2. The crater was further away than we had expected.
3. Marianne is anxious to see what her uncle brought back from Mexico.
4. The children hung tinsel and ornaments on the tree.
5. Leonard could of had that job if he had applied in time.
6. Only a small percent of actors are employed.
7. After Thanksgiving dinner Grandfather lied down.
8. Omphaloskepsis is when you meditate.
9. The alley was filled with bottles, boxes, and etc.
10. It felt good to swim a half mile before breakfast.

Exercise B: Follow the same directions as for Exercise A.

1. The class inferred from the bulletin that the principal was cracking down on unexcused absences.
2. Lloyd asked Judy to learn him how to play the guitar.
3. Most everyone in town turned out for the public hearing.
4. Debra had seen Shawn, but they had never been formerly introduced.
5. The dog was digging holes, looking for its bone.
6. Transportation has come a long ways from the horse-drawn cart.
7. The Olafson's regretted having to emigrate from their homeland.
8. Our team had to let the opposition make it's point before we could reply.
9. The flannel sheets felt real warm and cozy.
10. Aunt Harriet went in the kitchen to check the turkey.

9.2 Words Commonly Misused

a lot   The mispelling *alot* is nonstandard. In addition, the phrase is overused. Vary your writing with other expressions, such as "a great deal."

all of   The *of* is unecessary except before pronouns.

> NONSTANDARD: *All of* the work was above average.
> STANDARD: *All* the work was above average.
> STANDARD: *All of* it was above average.

all right   These two words are sometimes misspelled as one. *Alright* is nonstandard.

anywhere, nowhere, somewhere, anyway   *Anywheres,   nowheres, somewheres,* and *anyways* are nonstandard.

had of, off of   The *of* is unnecessary and nonstandard.

> NONSTANDARD: The cat jumped *off of* the windowsill.
> STANDARD: The cat jumped *off* the windowsill.
> NONSTANDARD: If Tad *had of* been at the party, he would
>   have enjoyed himself.
> STANDARD: If Tad *had* been at the party, he would have
>   enjoyed himself.

kind of a, sort of a   The *a* is unnecessary and nonstandard.

> NONSTANDARD: What kind of a place is this?
> STANDARD: What kind of place is this?

majority   This word can be used only with items that can be counted. It is nonstandard if used in speaking of time or distance.

> NONSTANDARD: The *majority* of the period was spent doing
>   review.
> STANDARD: *Most* of the period was spent doing review.

seldom ever   The *ever* is unnecessary and nonstandard. Use *seldom, very seldom,* or *hardly ever* instead.

Exercise: Rewrite the following sentences, correcting any errors in usage.

1. If I had of only thought of it sooner, I would have brought my camera.
2. There are alot of people going into the computer field today.
3. Tova seldom ever asks her parents for spending money.
4. The majority of Roger's weekend was spent in the workshop.
5. Three heavy volumes toppled off of the shelf.
6. Ernie's glasses were nowheres to be found.
7. All of the kindergarteners were out in the playground.
8. Dr. Fleming asked the driver if it was alright for the students to leave their books on the bus.
9. The kind of a car Dave bought is a 1973 Impala.
10. Somewheres in this big city is a summer job for me.

REINFORCEMENT EXERCISE

The Right Word

A. Use commonly confused words correctly. The following sentences contain errors in word choice. Rewrite these sentences, correcting any errors. If a sentence contains no errors, write *Correct*.

1. A postal letter-sorting case in New York differs with one in Los Angeles.
2. The nurse adviced the accountant to go home and call his doctor.
3. Bring this quart of milk to the customer at the counter.
4. The child's eyes glowed when she saw the large amount of presents.
5. The Grossman family has adapted two Bolivian children.
6. My father was willing to except my weak explanation, but my mother was not.
7. Is it alright to type a thank-you note?
8. Marnie accepted the nomination although she did not want to run for office.
9. Between every word, Dr. Fishbein says "um-ah."
10. Brent had no allusions about the availability of summer jobs.
11. We had no fear but what the pilot would land the plane safely.
12. Nancy's concentration was disturbed by continuous interruptions.
13. The title *Lilies of the Field* is an allusion to the Sermon on the Mount.
14. Mr. Guthrie borrowed Lloyd some skis to use on the trip.
15. That man sunning himself on his yacht was formally a prospector.
16. At the end of twenty-four hours, Diana Nyad had swum further than she had anticipated.
17. The jury stood altogether when the judge entered the courtroom.

18. The driver must of passed the turn-off.
19. Cheddar cheese is traditionally served as a compliment to apple pie.
20. An ultramodern skyscraper was erected besides the cabin.

B. Use commonly misused words correctly. Rewrite the following sentences, correcting any errors in usage. If a sentence contains no error, write *Correct*.

1. The hailstones bounced off the roof and onto the grass.
2. Almost anywheres you go, you will find food franchises.
3. It is all right to have a strong opinion as long as you are willing to listen to those of others.
4. Hank seldom ever goes downtown without running into one of his cousins.
5. Mr. Redpath saved alot of money once he started ordering supplies from a wholesale catalogue.
6. If I had of been born in the 15th century, I would have lived in Italy.
7. That kind of a book is too advanced for our class.
8. All of the paint had worn off the sides of the barn.
9. The majority of Bonnie's time is spent correcting other people's mistakes.
10. The entire school enjoyed the demonstration of Muppets a great deal.
11. The painting fell off of the wall and hit the table, setting off the burglar alarm.
12. People seldom ever get to see a total eclipse of the sun.
13. Alot of people think that our foreign policy is too complicated to understand.
14. The fire marshall inspected all of the exits.
15. What sort of a bird can say fifty words?
16. The majority of the photographs were overexposed.
17. My waterproof wristwatch is somewheres in the pool.
18. If I had of known that January 6 was called Twelfth Night, I would have understood the play better.
19. What kind of a book is the one with a spiral binding?
20. Nowheres did the lease say that we had to pay a deposit.

MIXED REVIEW

The Right Word

A. Rewrite these sentences to make them follow standard usage.

1. When we are young, we often fail to appreciate the advise of our parents.
2. The flag of Ireland differs with the flag of Italy only in one of its vertical bands.
3. Ceylon is further if you do not take the polar air route; that is, there are less miles in the polar air route.
4. After Aunt Belinda crocheted the square, she framed it and hanged it in the hallway.
5. The report inferred that middle management was not delegating work effectively.
6. Darwin studied how various species of plants and animals adopted to their surroundings.
7. The babysitter learned my younger sister to play Pac Man.
8. The forest ranger who took us on a tour would not leave us touch the rare wild flowers.
9. "What kind of a car did Buckminster Fuller design?" Sheila asked.
10. So far, all of the designs have been rejected accept mine.
11. Mr. Farley should not of called our compost heap a "garbage pile!"
12. Priscilla and Rob formerly announced their engagement in the newspaper last week.
13. The five Marx brothers could never decide between themselves which one was funnier.
14. Because he had alot of determination and a strong will, Tim was able to walk again.
15. Seldom ever does a comet with twelve tails appear.
16. The sky turned slate grey in October and stayed that way for the majority of the winter.
17. Their trying to rescue the baby whale that was beached.
18. Brian's parents were hoping that three weeks of survival camping would have a positive affect on his self esteem.

B. Some of the following sentences contain errors in word usage. Rewrite these sentences correcting the errors. If a sentence contains no errors, write *Correct.*

1. What states beside Ohio and Colorado end in *o?*
2. One returning alumna acted like he was still in his teens.
3. The director told us we should learn to except a compliment graciously.
4. Our tour guide decided to leave us travel to the airport alone.
5. One continual line of fans poured into the Astrodome.
6. Between each act of the play, there was a ten-minute intermission.
7. The last piece of evidence was a photograph of a woman walking into the building through a side door.
8. The suburban malls had seldom ever been so crowded as they were that spring.
9. Being one of the contestants, Ira was not allowed to vote.
10. Profits were divided among the corporation's large amount of stockholders.
11. The jury inferred from the testimony that the candidate had accepted illegal contributions.
12. Most of e. e. cummings poems are different than conventional poems.
13. A large percent of accused witches were jailed after their trials.
14. The President made an allusion to the Premier's statement.
15. The Papadapoulos family was anxious to visit their cousins in Athens.
16. The class in French Literature will study Molière, Racine, Flaubert, and etc.
17. When Julie is with Heidi, she acts like she is a two-year-old.
18. Pauline enjoys most everything her parents cook.
19. The next gas station is just a little ways down the road.
20. The judges found the two finalists to be very equal in ability.

USING GRAMMAR IN WRITING
The Right Word

A. Some people believe that women should be drafted into the armed services as well as men. Others believe that it is appropriate for men to be drafted, but not women. What is your opinion on this subject? Express your views in a letter to the editor of a local paper. Use as many of the words covered in Section 9 as possible. When you have completed your essay, go back and underline all of the words that are mentioned in the Section. See if you can use at least one-third of these troublesome words correctly.

B. The words covered in Section 9 are not the only words in American English that are commonly confused and commonly misused. Use a dictionary to look up the following word pairs. Write a definition of each and explain the differences between them. Write a sentence for each word that clearly shows you know how to use it correctly.

adverse / averse	laudable / laudatory
prescribe / proscribe	regardless / irrespective
raze / raise	repertoire / repertory
impassable / impassible	sympathy / empathy
flaunt / flout	reverend / reverent
device / devise	discreet / discrete
judicial / judicious	

C. As you watch TV or listen to the radio, you will hear many examples of the type of nonstandard usages described in this chapter. Record as many of these as you can during one week. Then write a short report in which you describe some of these errors and draw conclusions about where they are most likely to be found.

CUMULATIVE REVIEW
Usage (II)

A. Using the Correct Forms of Words. Choose the correct word from those given in parentheses.

1. After the curtain was (raised, risen), the play began.
2. The plumber looked (disapprovingly, disapproving) at the rusted pipes.
3. None of the farmers (expect, expects) rain soon.
4. I appreciated (him, his) complimenting my serve.
5. Teaching guitar or playing in a band (was, were) his goal.
6. Neither my mother nor my father (was, were) home.
7. Which of the two was the (better, best) President?
8. Everyone improved (his or her, their) grades last semester.
9. (Who, whom) did the reporters interview?
10. The promoters hardly had (no, any) tickets left.

B. Finding errors in usage. Identify the errors of agreement or form in the following sentences. Rewrite each incorrect sentence. Write *C* if a sentence is already correct.

1. A police officer swum out to rescue Juan.
2. There were less people in the audience tonight.
3. The President had spoke to the Soviet diplomat before.
4. We girls hung our supplies from a branch.
5. Here's most of the books you lended me last week.
6. The lecturer inferred that the space program was too expensive.
7. Silvia's new hairstyle looks well.
8. Each of the contestants has practiced for weeks.
9. By afternoon the lake had froze solid.
10. Ethics are a subject taught in college.

10.0 Capitalization

10.1 Proper Nouns and Adjectives

A **common noun** names the general group to which a person, place, or thing belongs. A **proper noun** distinguishes an individual person, place, or thing. An adjective formed from a proper noun is called a **proper adjective.** Proper nouns and proper adjectives should be capitalized.

COMMON NOUN	PROPER NOUN	PROPER ADJECTIVE
book	Talmud	Talmudic
queen	Elizabeth I	Elizabethan
state	Alaska	Alaskan
writer	Kafka	Kafkaesque
city	Rome	Roman
mountains	Alps	Alpine

Proper nouns and proper adjectives are sometimes used in hyphenated words. Capitalize only those words that are capitalized when used alone. Prefixes, such as *pre-, un-,* and *anti-* are not capitalized even when they are attached to a proper noun or adjective.

> anti-American   pre-Christian   pro-French

Questions often arise concerning the use of capitals for proper nouns. The rules given below will help you decide whether a word is a proper noun or a common noun.

10.2 Geographical Names

In a geographical name, capitalize the first letter of each word except articles and prepositions.

Do not capitalize the article *the* before a geographical name. The article is not considered part of the name.

CONTINENTS:	Australia, Africa, Europe
BODIES OF WATER:	the Atlantic Ocean, San Francisco Bay, the Mississippi River, the Great Lakes, Loch Ness
LAND FORMS:	the Gobi Desert, the Rocky Mountains, Crystal Cave, Mount Hood, Shenandoah Valley
POLITICAL UNITS:	the United States of America, the Republic of Texas, the Commonwealth of Massachusetts, the Province of Quebec
PUBLIC AREAS:	Glacier National Park, Mammoth Cave, Big Hole Battlefield
ROADS AND HIGHWAYS:	Fifth Avenue, New Jersey Turnpike, U.S. Highway 1, Twelfth Street

10.3 Common Nouns in Names

A common noun that is part of a name is capitalized. A common noun used to define or refer to a proper noun is not capitalized.

PART OF THE NAME	REFERENCE OR DEFINITION
New York State	the state of Minnesota
New York City	the city of Buffalo
the Western Plains	plains in the West
Hudson Valley	the valley of the Hudson

10.4 Words Modified by Proper Adjectives

The word modified by a proper adjective is not capitalized unless adjective and noun together are a geographical name.

the Indian Ocean   the Indian nation
the Swiss Alps   a Swiss watch
the Irish Sea   Irish songs

10.5 First Words

Capitalize the first word of a sentence, a direct quotation, and a line of poetry.

What brought the man to our hideout?

"I have come," he said, "to repay a debt."

Whenever Richard Cory went down town,
   We people on the pavement looked at him:
He was a gentleman from sole to crown,
   Clean favored, and imperially slim.*

Note: The second part of a divided quotation does not begin with a capital letter unless it starts a new sentence.

10.6 *A.D., B.C., I, O*

Capitalize the abbreviations *A.D.* and *B.C.*, the pronoun *I*, and the interjection *O*.

The abbreviations B.C. and A.D. should only be used with the number of a year: 87 B.C., A.D. 630. The interjection O occurs in poetry, in the Bible, or in prayers or petitions: O Lord, O King.

O is quite different from the explosive interjection *oh*, which is capitalized only at the beginning of a sentence.

---

*From *Richard Cory* by E. A. Robinson, quoted by permission of the Macmillan Company.

Exercise: Copy the following sentences, supplying any necessary capitals.

1. a chief crop of hawaii is pineapples.
2. the british frigate bowed to the american ship.
3. yellowstone national park is in the state of wyoming.
4. st. patrick's day is celebrated differently in ireland.
5. at the mouth of the mississippi lies new orleans.
6. have you visited mt. rushmore in the black hills?
7. saul became the first king of the hebrew nation in 1095 b.c.
8. one-third of the canadian people speak french.
9. glacier bay is located in alaska.
10. the knight said, "hear me, o king, and grant my petition."
11. the canadians were neither pro-russian nor pro-american in the hockey play-offs.
12. the canal links the mediterranean sea and the red sea.
13. the shenandoah river flows into the potomac river.
14. malone is a town in new york near the canadian border.
15. not far from pike's peak lies the city of colorado springs.
16. i want french toast, canadian bacon, and english muffins.
17. the st. lawrence seaway is the largest waterway built since the panama canal.
18. the american continents were named for an italian sailor, amerigo vespucci.
19. nero became emperor of rome in a.d. 54.
20. After the spaniards had conquered the aztec capital, they rebuilt the city and called it mexico city.

10.7 Directions and Sections

Capitalize names of sections of the country but not of directions of the compass.

The climate attracts settlers to the West.
The South is known for the hospitality of its people.
To the north is Sacramento.

We are going south this winter.

St. Louis is east of Kansas City.

The shopping center is west of here.

The East is more densely populated than the Southwest.

Capitalize proper adjectives derived from names of sections of the country. Do not capitalize adjectives derived from words indicating direction.

a westerly breeze a Midwestern university

a northbound flight a Southern state

Exercise: Copy the following sentences, supplying any necessary capitals. If a sentence is correct, write *C* next to the number.

1. Anne has applied to three colleges in the midwest.
2. The Appalachian Mountains are located in the east.
3. It is doubtful that the cold front now in the middle west will reach the eastern states.
4. Read the timetable upward for eastbound trains.
5. At the southern tip is Key West, Florida.
6. Lars went to a vocational school in the southwest.
7. After touring the near east, we flew west to Rome.
8. Our oldest university, Harvard, is an eastern school.
9. The nearest ranger station is a mile south of here.
10. The street on the west side of our school is Mills Street.
11. Our doctor was born and raised in the south.
12. Stratford-on-Avon is northwest of London, England.
13. Fighting was reported in the middle east.
14. Alison traveled westward through four southern states.
15. The mystique of the east lures travelers to the Orient.
16. Are the Watsons going south for the winter?
17. Change from a northwesterly to a northeasterly direction.
18. Do midwestern teams play better football?
19. The Joshua tree grows in the southwest.
20. The north central states are one of our country's chief farming, mining, and manufacturing areas.

10.8 Languages, Races, Nationalities, and Religions

Capitalize the names of languages, races, nationalities, and religions and the adjectives formed from them.

the Spanish language	Buddhism	Jew
Indian	Catholic	Brazilian

Do not capitalize names of school subjects unless they are specific course names. However, always capitalize names of languages.

history	American History III
English	German

10.9 Organizations and Institutions

Capitalize important words in the names of organizations, buildings, firms, schools, churches and other institutions. Do not capitalize *and* or prepositions. Capitalize an article (*a, an,* or *the*) only if it appears as the first word in a name.

Pittsburgh Chamber of Commerce
Library of Congress
Hadley School for the Blind
Metropolitan Museum of Art

Note: In brand names, only proper nouns and adjectives are capitalized: *Chevy van, Buick Century.*

Exercise: Copy the following sentences, supplying any necessary capitals.

1. All science students must take biology I and II before they take a chemistry course.
2. There is a sale on california oranges and chiquita bananas at tony's market.
3. Copies of most new books go to the library of congress.

4. Ship the latin and english books to morris high school.
5. Ms. hovis works for the department of agriculture in a laboratory at beltsville, maryland.
6. Dr. quinn belongs to the american dental association.
7. The new york public library displayed the japanese woodcuts.
8. The guest speaker is a physicist who used to work for the national aeronautics and space administration.
9. Professor saville of oberlin college addressed the league of women voters.
10. The rockefeller institute for medical research is located on york avenue.
11. A graduate of beloit college, elise is now attending the university of illinois school of veterinary medicine.
12. You can get hunt's tomato sauce at hoffman's fine foods.
13. The masterwork chorus will give a concert in the morristown high school auditorium.
14. Have you seen mr. case's new pontiac sunbird?
15. Two new speech electives are oral interpretation I and creative dramatics III.

10.10 Titles of Persons

Capitalize words that show rank, office, or profession when they are used with a person's name.

Doctor Walsh	Sister Mary	Father Flynn
Chief Joseph	Controller Bucklin	Dean Barkan

Capitalize a title used without a name only if it refers to an important government official or person in some other high position.

the President of the United States	the Governor
the Vice-President	the Bishop

The words *ex-* and *-elect*, when used with a title, are not capitalized: *ex-President Carter*, the *Governor-elect*.

10.11 Family Relationships

Capitalize the name of a family relationship when it is used with a person's name.

Aunt Faye   Uncle Abe   Grandma Rial   Cousin Alvin

When words like *mother, father, dad,* and *mom* are used alone in place of a particular person's name, they are capitalized. When modified by a possessive pronoun, as in *your mother,* or when they do not stand for a particular person, they are not capitalized.

Ann asked Dad for the car yesterday.
I saw your mother at the peace rally in Prague.
Roland's sister is Deidre's aunt.

10.12 Titles of Books and Works of Art

Capitalize the first word and every important word in the titles of books, stories, articles, poems, films, works of art, and musical compositions.

A conjunction or an article *(a, an, the)* is not capitalized unless it is the first word in a title. A preposition is only capitalized if it is the first word in a title, or if it has more than five letters.

Go Tell It on the   "I Like To See It Lap the Miles"
  Mountain   *One Flew over the*
the *Mona Lisa*   *Cuckoo's Nest*

Exercise: Copy each word that requires a capital in these sentences.

1. Is mom going to drive judge fuller to the airport?
2. My sister played "tales from the vienna woods."
3. Have dad and mom met lieutenant wickham?

4. My sister saw *rear window* four times and *vertigo* twice.
5. I think aunt dorothy or my mother will drive.
6. At the banquet the governor praised the secretary of state and the vice-president.
7. Aunt ruth's daughter is my cousin, and my mother's aunt is my great-aunt.
8. My favorite overture is beethoven's "egmont."
9. The chief speaker will be fire chief schwenker.
10. Amy asked aunt lois to lend her *rockets, missiles, and space travel*.
11. Have you ever read *a farewell to arms*, mother?
12. Alec's father drove us out to see grandmother stone, who is dad's grandmother.
13. I have read "to a skylark" in shelley's *complete poems*.
14. The mayor introduced senator sitwell as the next president of the united states.
15. Two biographies of ex-president kennedy are *a thousand days* and *kennedy*.
16. uncle robert had an audience with the pope.
17. I would like you to meet ms. gavin, who is senator-elect.
18. My father will talk to dean wood tomorrow.
19. The secretary of housing and urban developing is flying to meet the president-elect.
20. Assistant attorney-general robertson may be the next chief justice of the supreme court.

10.13   The Deity

Capitalize all words referring to the Deity, the Holy Family, and to religious scriptures.

God	the Almighty	the Gospel
the Father	the Lord	the Torah
the Son	Jehovah	the Talmud
the Holy Ghost	Allah	the Koran
the Virgin Mary	the Bible	

Capitalize personal pronouns but not relative pronouns that refer to the Deity.

> May God make His light to shine down upon you.
> Praise God from whom all blessings flow.

10.14 Days, Months, Holidays

Capitalize the names of days of the week, of months, and of holidays. Do not capitalize the names of seasons.

Monday	the Fourth of July	autumn
January	Valentine's Day	spring

10.15 Historical Names

Capitalize the names of historical events, documents, and periods.

Declaration of Independence	the Middle Ages
Battle of the Bulge	the Jacksonian Period

Exercise A: Copy the words that require capitals in these sentences.

1. Margaret's favorite period in history is the age of enlightenment.
2. The boston tea party took place in 1773.
3. The second continental congress lasted for five years.
4. The first shots of the american revolution were fired at the battle of lexington.
5. The nun asked the lord for his guidance.
6. Our town has a parade every spring on memorial day.
7. The bible study class starts in january.
8. The school year starts on the tuesday after labor day.
9. Columbus day is now celebrated on the monday closest to october 12.

10. The victorian era is usually thought of as an age of gentleness and propriety.
11. The period in which shelley, keats, and byron wrote is known as the romantic age.
12. We celebrated new year's eve at sue murphy's house.
13. Some renaissance artists were inspired by the classic works of the ancient greeks and romans.
14. The united states senate rejected the treaty of versailles.
15. Chief sitting bull defeated general custer in the battle of little big horn.

Exercise B: Copy the words that need capital letters.

1. My aunt's interests are music and english literature.
2. I think millet's best painting is "the man with a hoe."
3. The language of the brazilian people is portuguese.
4. The magna carta of england was imposed upon king john.
5. Lucas served us french toast with vermont maple syrup.
6. My mother plays in the boston symphony orchestra.
7. In 1890, the battle of wounded knee was the last major conflict between indians and u.s. troops.
8. The president of the langston literary guild called the meeting to order.
9. The young indian woman saved captain john smith's life.
10. On the first friday in april, the american legion will hold its annual convention in detroit.
11. Confucius, the chinese philosopher, was born in 551 b.c.
12. One of margaret mead's cultural studies was *coming of age in samoa.*
13. Originally, the southern states of south carolina, georgia, alabama, mississippi, and florida formed the confederate states of america.
14. Seldom is there an equal balance of power between republicans and democrats in the united states congress.
15. The poem "the charge of the light brigade" tells of a heroic event in the crimean war.

REINFORCEMENT EXERCISES
Capitalization

A. Use correct capitalization. Correctly capitalize the following.

1. betsy ross and the american flag
2. non-irish people on st. patrick's day
3. constantinople, or istanbul
4. an australian folk singer
5. the marshall islands
6. french perfume
7. a dickens character
8. newark, new jersey
9. an english playwright
10. a shakespearean sonnet

B. Use correct capitalization. Correctly capitalize the following phrases. Then use each phrase in a sentence.

1. uncle mike's favorite newspaper, the sun
2. a.d. 300
3. an ambassador from the united nations
4. the italian painter da Vinci
5. alexander the great
6. known for its southern hospitality
7. sears, roebuck and company
8. "a rose for emily" by william faulkner
9. the mardi gras festival in new orleans
10. organic chemistry 2B

C. Use proper capitalization. Rewrite the following sentences, supplying necessary capitals.

1. I pack boxes at the sturdee container company.
2. "whales," said father, "are the largest living mammals."
3. puerto rico celebrates three kings' day on january 6.

4. *home* is a play about a black man who returns to the south.
5. what poet wrote, "o troy, troy"?
6. ramon made the photocopies at the pioneer trust bank.
7. emmy neother was a german mathematician who taught at gottingen university and bryn mawr college.
8. Dr. Jones agreed to teach the women in literature course.
9. we did not hear cousin eartha say, "never again."
10. after the 7th century a.d. in china, the taoist religion failed to attract as many people as buddhism.

MIXED REVIEW

Capitalization

A. Rewrite the following sentences, supplying the necessary capitals.

1. both the sac and fox indians were members of the algonquian nation; they lived in the great lakes region during the 17th century.
2. while i prefer the design of arena swimming goggles, i find that speedo goggles work better for me.
3. the feast of the pentecost, celebrated on june 7, commemorates the descent of the holy ghost.
4. "please address the letter correctly," insisted ms. rath. "the street name is berry, not barry."
5. shirley jackson wrote the classic horror novel *the haunting of hill house*.
6. the first world series to be televised was the 1947 series between the brooklyn dodgers and the new york yankees.
7. myra was reading *swimming for total fitness*.
8. "i am not going into the water," announced jon, "until I know how to swim."
9. how in the world did nicole know that savo island was part of the solomon islands?
10. alexander james dallas was born in jamaica, the west indies, in a.d. 1759.
11. in jewish homes, the first day of hanukkah is celebrated by lighting one candle.
12. in the u.s.s.r., most major rivers, such as the ob and lena, flow north.
13. the dairy industry in america is big in new england and the upper midwest.
14. hank williams, who died on new year's day of 1953, wrote "jambalaya" and "your cheatin' heart."
15. the dakota territory included the present-day states of north and south dakota, montana, and wyoming.

16. we named our new printing company print-it-now.
17. sidney hillman, a lithuanian-born labor leader, was
   president of the amalgamated clothing workers.
18. by checking a perpetual calendar, the detective learned
   that may 21 was *not* on a tuesday in 1975.
19. of course north africa borders on the mediterranean sea.
20. dorr's rebellion occurred in rhode island in 1842.

B. Rewrite the following sentences, supplying the necessary capitals.

1. the spring dance is scheduled for the saturday after st.
   patrick's day.
2. evan likes polish sausage on french bread.
3. the red cross has local offices on tenth street.
4. our english class read *the grapes of wrath* and *moby dick*.
5. my father took a first aid course at evansville hospital.
6. the pipeline transports oil south from alaskan oilfields.
7. the environmental protection agency banned certain
   dangerous pesticides.
8. the name *susan* comes from the hebrew word for lily.
9. last week aunt stephanie directed a performance of
   madame butterfly at the lyric opera house.
10. every sunday father cunningham reads from the bible.
11. in july grandma grant opened her restaurant, called
   grandma's gastronomy.
12. the parade on memorial day will come south down central
   avenue.
13. students in advanced biology IIB examined the aquatic
   life in glen lake.
14. the league of nations held its first meeting at geneva,
   switzerland, in 1920.
15. we took route 66 west across the mississippi river and into
   the flatlands of the west.

USING MECHANICS IN WRITING
Capitalization

A. In business letters, the "inside address" includes the same information that appears on the envelope. The order of the information begins with the most specific and ends with the most general, as follows:

> Person's Name, Title
> Department, Company
> Building
> Street Address
> City, State, ZIP Code

Write a real or imaginary letter of complaint to a company that has sold you an inferior product or service. Use the specific brand name of the product or service, and be sure to tell when and where you bought it. Include the name of the addressee, that person's title, the company name, and the address in the inside address of your letter.

B. A new high school is about to be constructed in your town. The school board has asked your class to choose items to be placed in the cornerstone of the building. They have asked the students to select a book, a magazine, an album by a popular rock group, an episode from a television series, a movie, a piece of designer clothing, a picture of a movie star, and a picture of a "hero" who best represent the tastes and interests of late twentieth century American youth. Make up a form listing three choices in each of these categories on which members of your class could vote. Then circle your choices, and give reasons for your selection.

11.0 End Marks and Commas

11.1 Periods at the Close of Sentences

Place a period at the close of every declarative sentence and of most imperative sentences.

Sometimes a period is used at the end of a group of words that is not a complete sentence.

> Utah is the Beehive State. (declarative sentence)
> Please pass the butter. (imperative sentence)
> That was a wonderful movie. Truly wonderful. (group of words)

11.2 Periods in Abbreviations

Place a period after every part of an abbreviation.

E. A. Robinson	Edwin Arlington Robinson
A.M.	Ante Meridiem
R.S.V.P.	Répondez S'il Vous Plaît

Since the 1930's it has become the custom not to use periods in abbreviations of certain government agencies and international organizations.

FHA	Federal Housing Authority
FBI	Federal Bureau of Investigation
UN	United Nations
NATO	North Altantic Treaty Organization

11.3   Exclamation Points

Place an exclamation point after an exclamatory sentence and after an exclamation set off from a sentence.

Great! We can't lose now.   Wow! I don't believe it!
What a pass!   Go away!
Hold that line!   Wilson for Senator!

11.4   Question Marks

Place a question mark after an interrogative sentence or after a question that is not a complete sentence.

The question mark is the writer's way of indicating he is asking a question. It sometimes is the only way a reader knows that a sentence is a question, not a statement.

Have they changed premiers?   They have changed premiers?
Do you call this a composition? This is a composition?
The date? January 21.   That's a hat?

Exercise: Copy these sentences, using end marks and punctuation as required for sentences and abbreviations. Use question marks only for sentences in normal interrogative form.

1. Just hand me that pair of pliers
2. What a close call that was
3. Lt Marks asked to be sent overseas
4. Please notify the YWCA of your change of address
5. You could have taken a later flight, couldn't you
6. You can reach me at 208 So King St, Mt Arlington, NJ
7. Down, Rover The idea of your jumping up like that
8. Please send the package C O D to Nashville, Tenn
9. Marcus Aurelius died in A D 180
10. Does the FCC ever censor television programs
11. How kind you are
12. Could I get you a cup of coffee or tea

Uses of the Comma

11.5 Introductory Words

Introductory words such as *yes, no, well, why,* and *oh* are followed by a comma.

> Oh no, not another detour.
> Well, there we were, drifting with the current.
> Why, nobody with any sense would do that.

Adverbs that are used as introductory words are followed by commas. Some examples are *besides, however, furthermore* and, *therefore.*

11.6 Introductory Phrases and Clauses

A participial phrase at the beginning of a sentence is followed by a comma.

An adverbial clause at the beginning of a sentence is followed by a comma.

A succession of prepositional phrases at the beginning of a sentence is followed by a comma.

A single prepositional phrase at the beginning of a sentence may be set off by a comma if it is followed by a natural pause when read.

> *Watching the trail,* we saw the wagon train approach. (participial phrase)
> *On the ledge at the top of the tower,* the princess brushed her long blond tresses. (succession of prepositional phrases)
> *When the prince arrived,* he scratched his bald head and looked up at the tower. (adverbial clause)
> *Through the grimy window,* a single beam of light shone. (optional comma after single introductory prepositional phrase)

11.7   Transposed Words and Phrases

Words and phrases moved to the beginning of a sentence from their normal position are usually set off by a comma.

> He naturally checked the address in the directory. (normal order)
>
> *Naturally,* he checked the address in the directory. (transposed order)
>
> It was obviously a case of mistaken identity. (normal order)
>
> *Obviously,* it was a case of mistaken identity. (transposed order)
>
> You need a guide book to get the most out of the fair. (normal order)
>
> *To get the most out of the fair,* you need a guide book.

Exercise: Copy the following sentences, inserting commas where necessary. Two of the sentences are correct.

1. When the lightning struck our terrier pup dashed under the dining room table.
2. Driving on Dad began to sing.
3. For the best view sit here.
4. If I had moved an inch the boat would have turned over.
5. Well you do seem a little heavier.
6. If your answers are incorrect change them.
7. When Leila has finished the house will look like new.
8. At the bottom of the valley people were walking about.
9. To get a fresh turkey we had to go to a poultry farm.
10. While the fire was burning Otto had to keep getting more and more firewood.
11. Yes I thought Arlene's speech was the best.
12. The show was well received by the critics.
13. Why every picture in my roll of film was spoiled!
14. Speaking in public was a skill he had exhibited since grade school days.
15. While Jay watched Dora played a set of tennis with Mom.

11.8   Appositives

An appositive is set off from the rest of the sentence by commas.

Ms. Clark, *an astronomer,* thinks it's a UFO.
The collector, *Mr. Lisle,* bought the chair at an auction.

11.9   Words of Direct Address

Words of direct address are set off by commas.

Ray, did you buy a season ticket?
My fellow citizens, I ask you to vote—not for me alone—
but for a greater America.

11.10   Parenthetical Expressions

A **parenthetical expression** explains or qualifies what is being
said in the sentence. It should be set off by commas. Sometimes, however, the same words may be important parts of a
sentence. Only use commas to set off the words or phrases if
they are indeed parenthetical; that is, if they could be left out
of the sentence.

Einstein's theory, *I understand,* was challenged by Bohr.
(parenthetical expression)
I understand Einstein's theory of general relativity. (not
parenthetical)
Mort, *of course,* has the key. (parenthetical expression)
Of course we are going. (not parenthetical)

Parenthetical expressions are set off by commas.

Some expressions often used parenthetically are:

of course	as a matter of fact	for example
in fact	I believe (hope, think)	on the other hand
indeed	I suppose	

Conjunctive adverbs (see Section 1.7) used parenthetically within the sentence are set off by commas: *therefore, moreover, nevertheless, however, consequently,* and so on.

> You realize, *therefore,* that you run a risk.
> The coat, *moreover,* does not fit properly.
> The carnival, *however,* was a tremendous success.

Adverbs like *however, therefore,* and *consequently* can be used to modify a verb, adjective, or another adverb in a sentence. In these cases, they are essential to the meaning of the sentence. Therefore, they are not set off by commas.

> My friends insisted that I could not succeed. I was *therefore* determined not to give up.
> The procedure for screening security risks was *consequently* changed.
> My brother can't dance like Michael Jackson *however* hard he tries.

11.11 Dates, Addresses, Geographical Names

In dates and addresses of more than one part, set off every part after the first from the rest of the sentence.

> We visited the baseball museum located in Cooperstown.
> (one part)

> In Cooperstown, New York, we visited the museum.
> (two parts, the second set off by commas)

> The last package mailed from Johannesburg arrived on June 6.
> (one part)

> Wisconsin entered the Union on May 29, 1848.
> (two parts with a comma after the first)

> The letter was addressed to 280 East End Avenue, Pleasantville, Ohio 43148, where he formerly lived.
> (three parts, the second and third set off by commas)

Note: The day of the month and the month are one item. The name of the street and the house number are one item. The name of the state and the zip code are one item.

June 6   240 East Thirty-first Street   California 93921

Exercise A: Copy these sentences, inserting necessary commas.

1. Write to me at 110 North Spooner Street Madison Wisconsin 53705.
2. Would you consider July 4 1776 a more important date than March 4 1789?
3. The affair on the whole came off very successfully.
4. Both athletes and actors it is said are highly superstitious.
5. You bad dog you have chewed my guitar!
6. Ladies and gentlemen of the jury I wish to present Exhibit A.
7. That was as I shall explain a narrow escape.
8. Hans after all is a foreign exchange student and needs time to adjust.
9. Mother have you met Ms. Connors my history teacher?
10. On June 1 1984 the play opened in Chicago Illinois and Los Angeles California.

Exercise B: Follow the same directions as for Exercise A.

1. Lucky the beagle next door barks when the bell rings.
2. If you lower the picture Nancy it will look better.
3. Julia Ward Howe writer of "The Battle Hymn of the Republic" was a prominent worker for world peace.
4. His strange laugh a high-pitched cackle could be heard above the audience.
5. Let me remind you my friends that we simply must sell more tickets for the dance.
6. If you really want to watch this program Lynn stop reading that magazine.
7. George Washington retired from the army at Annapolis Maryland on December 23 1783.

8. The record states that he was born on February 2 1944 at 1091 San Pasqual Street Pasadena California.
9. Send your contributions to Mr. Frank Quinn 1851 West 107th Street Chicago Illinois 60643.
10. I shall be at the Beach Hotel 11 South Kentucky Avenue Atlantic City New Jersey.

11.12   Nonrestrictive Modifiers

A **restrictive clause** is one that restricts, or limits, the person, place, or thing it is modifying. It is essential to the meaning of the sentence. It cannot be separated from the rest of the sentence.

Restrictive clauses are *not* set off from the rest of the sentence by commas.

The biography *that I mean* is the new one about Conan Doyle.
(The clause tells *which* biography.)

Young people need heroes *whom they can imitate.*
(The clause describes essential characteristics of heroes.)

The person *who has a pleasant disposition* attracts friends.
(Without the clause the sentence has no specific meaning.)

A **nonrestrictive clause** does not restrict, or limit, what it modifies. Its information is interesting but not essential. If it were dropped from the sentence, the sentence would still be perfectly clear in meaning.

Nonrestrictive clauses are set off by commas from the rest of the sentence.

The speed limit, *which is rigidly enforced,* helps decrease traffic accidents.

Teachers, *who spend their lives educating young people,* are pleased when their students attain success as adults.

Restrictive clauses that refer to things are introduced by the word *that*. Nonrestrictive clauses that refer to things are introduced by the word *which*.

> The state *that* has under a million people is Rhode Island.
> Rhode Island, *which* was the home of Gilbert Stuart, is where I was born.

Participial phrases are restrictive when they define, or restrict, the person, place, or thing they modify.

> The jet *making a forced landing* has mechanical trouble. (Without the phrase, the sentence loses its specific meaning.)
> The bird *perched on the tree outside the window* awakened me with its chirping. (The phrase identifies the bird.)

Nonrestrictive participial phrases add additional information. They are not essential to the meaning of the sentence. They can be dropped without changing the main idea.

> *Looking back,* we could see the undulating hills.
> The boys, *approaching the clearing,* saw the campfire.

Nonrestrictive participial phrases *are* set off from the rest of the sentence by commas. Restrictive phrases are *not* set off by commas.

Exercise: Number your paper 1–20. Decide whether the adjective clause or the participial phrase is restrictive or nonrestrictive. After each number write *restrictive* or *nonrestrictive*. Copy and insert commas in the sentences in which commas are needed.

1. The train that goes to Philadelphia is on Track 3.
2. Ms. Moss who teaches industrial arts just bought a car.
3. Robyn who is a jockey must keep her weight down.
4. Harold Leach is the boy wearing the green sweater.
5. The rose which had been pressed in a book was gone.
6. Buy the paper that is least expensive.
7. The little girl smiling shyly is my sister.

8. The plane that left Honolulu at noon carried two hundred passengers.
9. Enclosed is ten dollars which is the amount you asked for.
10. This bank established by my grandmother many years ago has grown into a thriving institution.
11. The vacation seemed unreal coming after months of anticipation.
12. Chris's cheesecake of which I ate more than my share is our family favorite.
13. The person receiving the package must sign for it.
14. Michele who is my closest friend would not talk to me.
15. Players who are over six feet tall have an advantage in basketball.
16. Cora's application handed in two weeks ago has not been acted on as yet.
17. All people dream nightly often having several dreams.
18. Renoir is the Impressionist who painted *Luncheon of the Boating Party*.
19. Carolyn who was the first speaker introduced the subject.
20. The girl who was the first speaker is Carolyn Davis.

11.13 Compound Sentences

Place a comma before the conjunction that joins two main clauses in a compound sentence.

You must get your work done on time, *or* you will be fired.

Thomas More hoped to die naturally, *but* he died at the executioner's hand.

Suddenly the thunder rolled, *and* the picnickers scattered in all directions.

I could not remember the title of the book, *nor* could I remember the author.

When clauses are quite short, the comma may be omitted.

She invited me to dinner and I accepted.

I ate shrimp and Jim had clams.

11.14 Series

A **series** is a group of three or more related items.

SERIES OF NOUNS:	*Typewriters, calculators,* and *dictaphones* were ordered for the business office.
SERIES OF VERBS:	The human rights committee *met, discussed* specific proposals, and *adopted* a new constitution.
SERIES OF ADJECTIVES:	Blamed for the loss of the game, Paul felt *embarrassed, bewildered,* and *lonely.*
SERIES OF PHRASES:	Lorna piled the luggage *on the counters, in the corners,* and *outside the doors of the waiting room.*

Commas are used to separate the parts of a series.

A comma should not be used after the last item in a series. A comma is optional before a conjunction that joins the last two items in a series. To avoid the possibility of confusion, however, it is wise to use a comma before the conjunction.

If all items in a series are joined by conjunctions, do not use commas in addition to the conjunctions.

The electric fan whirred and buzzed and oscillated.
A book or a newspaper or a magazine will satisfy me.

11.15 Coordinate Adjectives

Commas are placed between coordinate adjectives that modify the same noun.

The soaring, majestic spire seemed to reach for the sky.
The flashing, blinding, zigzag lightning terrified us.

To determine whether adjectives are coordinate, try placing an *and* between them. If it sounds natural, they are coordinate, and a comma is needed.

PROBLEM:	The soft soothing music relaxed him.
NATURAL:	The soft *and* soothing music relaxed him.
SOLUTION:	The soft, soothing music relaxed him.
PROBLEM:	The tempting delicious aroma made our mouths water.
NATURAL:	The tempting *and* delicious aroma made our mouths water.
SOLUTION:	The tempting, delicious aroma made our mouths water.
PROBLEM:	The small gray car uses less gasoline.
NOT NATURAL:	The small *and* gray car uses less gasoline.
SOLUTION:	The small gray car uses less gasoline.

In general, it is safe to omit the comma before numbers and adjectives of size, shape, and age.

CORRECT:	The little round jug
CORRECT:	A fat old dachshund
CORRECT:	Four local bands

Exercise: Copy these sentences, placing commas where they are needed. One sentence is correct.

1. Elections are open to sophomores juniors and seniors.
2. The house is modern but the furniture is old-fashioned.
3. Please get a pound of butter a loaf of bread and a melon.
4. The rain was gentle warm and spring-like.
5. I like vanilla but maple walnut is my favorite.
6. I did not see the hole in the ice nor did I hear the warning cries.
7. We packed some sandwiches and fruit and then we rode our bikes to the fairgrounds.
8. For breakfast we had ham and eggs toast and jam and coffee.
9. Notice your own mistakes or someone else will.
10. The old dilapidated backless book was finally discarded.
11. Our class baked huckleberry pecan and pumpkin pies to serve at the picnic.

12. I gave up my social life studied hard and passed the exam.
13. The salesperson showed me a tape recorder but it was too expensive.
14. I never saw anyone as inquisitive as persistent or as baffling as Grandpa Larsen.
15. She was a sprightly old woman.
16. That I was weak tired and sick to my stomach made no difference to my boss.
17. It was one of those warm muggy days in early September.
18. Some people prefer traditional names but others favor unusual off-beat names.
19. The legislature passed laws in the areas of education health and welfare.
20. Daniel Boone served well in the American Revolution but we remember even better his courage on the Wilderness Trail.

11.16 Clarity

Use a comma to separate words or phrases that might be mistakenly joined in reading.

There are three common situations in which words may be mistakenly read together. The first occurs when the conjunctions *but* and *for* are mistaken for prepositions.

CONFUSING: No one spoke but Christie looked hopefully at the doctor.

CLEAR: No one spoke, but Christie looked hopefully at the doctor.

CONFUSING: George wrote to the factory for a part was missing.

CLEAR: George wrote to the factory, for a part was missing.

A second source of confusion is a noun following a verbal phrase.

CONFUSING:	Before attacking the soldiers checked supply lines.
CLEAR:	Before attacking, the soldiers checked supply lines.

CONFUSING:	To understand a student must listen.
CLEAR:	To understand, a student must listen.

CONFUSING:	After eating the survivors had renewed strength and hope.
CLEAR:	After eating, the survivors had renewed strength and hope.

A third source of confusion is the word that can be an adverb, preposition, or conjunction at the beginning of the sentence.

CONFUSING:	Below the rocks were sharp and treacherous.
CLEAR:	Below, the rocks were sharp and treacherous.

11.17 Words Omitted

Use a comma when words are omitted from parallel word groups.

Pat sewed the seams, and Leroy, the hem.
I prefer languages; my sister, science.
The eggs were cold; the orange juice, warm.

Exercise A: Copy these sentences, placing commas where necessary to avoid confusion.

1. Inside the fire was burning brightly.
2. The day before he had scarcely spoken.
3. Jeff had to hurry for the clock was wrong.
4. In her Mother has unlimited confidence.
5. To Sally Ray was a faithful friend.
6. Before dressing the little girl ate breakfast.
7. Having ordered Jill studied the faces of the other diners.
8. Joe has read four novels by Charles Dickens; Martha one.

9. Beyond the rainbow glistens with color.
10. Sarah Edmonds served as a soldier for the Union Army in the Civil War; Pauline Cushman as a Union spy.

Exercise B: Follow the same directions as for Exercise A.

1. To prepare each student should review the assigned chapters.
2. Throughout the convention was interrupted by demonstrations.
3. By counting the leaders realized that one camper was missing.
4. Donna is going to the University of Iowa; Star to the Air Force Academy.
5. The swimmer knew all the strokes but the butterfly was her favorite.
6. By criticizing a person often hurts feelings.
7. A copyright is granted for the lifetime of the owner of the copyright plus fifty years; a patent for seventeen years.
8. To Alice Elizabeth sent a handsome gift.
9. *Abraham Lincoln* was written by John Drinkwater; *Abe Lincoln in Illinois* by Robert E. Sherwood.
10. Owen's occupation is carpentry; his hobby fixing old clocks.

REINFORCEMENT EXERCISES
End Marks and Commas

A. Use end marks correctly. Punctuate the following sentences as necessary. Use question marks only for sentences in normal interrogative order.

1. Dorothy Kellman, PhD, explained that the body breaks down some foods into amino acids
2. Did you know that Paul Nipkow contributed to the invention of television
3. Lora was confused by the acronyms I R A, the E R A, and the I R S
4. Do you know what the *T S* in T S Eliot stands for
5. Please give this envelope to Dr William Frye
6. Oh no V. Lynn Sanders is a woman Why did I address her letter to Mr Sanders
7. Don't you think it is rude to call me just to chat at 10:30 P M
8. Ms R F Frankel went to work for N A S A in Houston, Texas
9. The text was compiled by L F Dean, W Gibson, and K G Wilson
10. Wow That's what I call a birthday cake

B. Use commas after introductory words and phrases. Insert commas where needed in the following sentences.

1. However tired you may be you still must wash the car.
2. Of course you could look it up in *The Reverse Dictionary*.
3. After the bitter cacao beans are pressed they yield a chocolate liquor.
4. Well Hurricane Ira hit Hawaii, not the Gulf Coast.
5. No that is not my hat.
6. For the best hamburgers eat at Smather's.

7. Until you have tried to light a fire you may not realize how difficult it is.
8. While she was running Gretchen removed her gloves and threw them into the crowd.
9. Why I can't believe this bill—it must be a mistake.
10. Under the couch with the high wooden legs lay the actor who played the dead body.

C. Use commas correctly. Insert commas where necessary.

1. Naturally Bridgit you may attend any college you wish.
2. Monterrey Mexico has a population of well over a million.
3. Iran, Ireland, and Israel widely different nations might all be classified as church states.
4. When did you pay the library fine Sherry?
5. We believed therefore that Nova Scotia was settled by people from Scotland.
6. Nightcrawlers also called earthworms feed on dead plant material in the soil.
7. Believe me Chris the climb is easy to make.
8. Melvil Dewey founder of the Dewey decimal system was an advocate of phonetic spelling.
9. The Scottish cabinetmaker Duncan Phyfe gave his name to a style of furniture.
10. The distance from Los Angeles California to Memphis Tennessee is nearly two thousand miles.

D. Use commas to set off nonrestrictive modifiers. Identify the italicized phrases and clauses as *restrictive* or *nonrestrictive*. Insert commas where necessary. Remember that commas are *not* used to set off restrictive modifiers.

1. The seeds of coriander *which is one of the oldest known spices* have been found in ancient Egyptian tombs.
2. This is the hat *that Marcia knitted for Robert.*
3. The golf ball hit the runner *jogging on the fairway.*

4. *Bending down to smell the rose* Caleb was stung by a bee.
5. The musician *who composed the piece* took a deep bow.
6. The fossil *that was unearthed in Colorado* was definitely that of a dinosaur.
7. Saber-toothed tigers *which are extinct* could open their jaws at a ninety-degree angle.
8. Those are the t-shirts *on which we silkscreened our club's motto.*
9. The driver *who won the 1977 Indy 500* was A. J. Foyt.
10. John Huston *who directed <u>The Maltese Falcon</u>* played in *China Town.*

E. Use commas correctly. Insert commas in the following sentences as necessary. One sentence is already correct.

1. I looked up the word in a thesaurus but I couldn't find the synonym I wanted.
2. Some early units of measurement were the fathom the hand the span and the cubit.
3. Chris painted the wolf figure black red and blue-green.
4. The scientist plucked the moss with tweezers deposited it in a plastic bag and put the bag in her knapsack.
5. Canandaigua Keuka Seneca Cayuga Owasco and Skaneateles are the six Finger Lakes of New York.
6. Dave knew that the bright yellow berries were poisonous so he avoided them.
7. A huge eighteen-foot wave capsized our boat.
8. Bennet bought his nephew a soft cuddly teddy bear.
9. Supplying us with needles thread and buttons the irritated costume designer told us to make our own costumes.
10. The cold frosty drink of lemonade quenched Melanie's thirst.
11. Aspirin should not be taken by people who must use anticoagulants blood thinners or certain diabetic drugs.
12. Ethan examined all the pennies in the huge vase but he did not find a single rare coin.

13. Malcolm ate popcorn as a high-fiber low-calorie snack but he could not get used to the taste of it without butter.
14. Some holidays that are celebrated in Canada and not the United States are Boxing Day Remembrance Day and Guy Fawkes Day.
15. A wren generally lives about three years but a crow may live as many as a hundred years.

F. Use commas for clarity. Punctuate the following sentences as necessary.

1. The man was a tracker; the cougar a stalker.
2. Inside the plane was decorated in brown leather.
3. After hitting the player ran for first base with all his might.
4. I thought everybody had heard of Typhoid Mary but George hadn't.
5. In order to float wood must be less dense than water.
6. All the tourists visited Rome; some Naples as well.
7. Breaking the waves battered the old rowboat.
8. Below the engine rumbled and roared.
9. Ted exchanged the tent for a mouse had chewed several holes in it.
10. The dog barked for its owner was in danger.

MIXED REVIEW
End Marks and Commas

A. Copy these sentences, inserting the necessary punctuation.

1. Nonsense The Delicious apples which are grown in this orchard are best when eaten raw
2. Lake Windermere praised by poets Wordsworth and Coleridge is no more than two hundred feet deep
3. Frequently we visit our grandparents downstate
4. All of the Westons are our friends but Betty Weston is I feel the best friend of all
5. Yes as many as 35,000 foreign students are enrolled here
6. After biting Carol said that the filling seemed uneven so the dentist smoothed it out
7. Naturally Ms. Ebla we will return the rental skis
8. Diving into the lake feet first the osprey caught the fish in its long sharp claws
9. Katsushika Hokusai was a Japanese painter draftsman and wood engraver who used more than fifty different names to sign his various works of art
10. Jerome Kern who wrote the song "Smoke Gets in Your Eyes" also wrote the musical *Show Boat*
11. Shhhh Somebody will hear us
12. The Romans conquered the Celts in A D 43 and after that the Celts adopted Christianity
13. In fifty-six successive games Joe DiMaggio went to bat 223 times collected ninety-one hits and set a baseball record that still stands
14. Many people consider Fred Astaire a great dancer
15. The doctor advised me to stay home for the rest of my family was sick too
16. Diamond Head Hawaii got its name if I remember correctly when 19th-century sailors mistook the bright crystalline rocks on the mountain for diamonds

17. Believe it or not Beryl won a set of wooden salad bowls
18. Yes the pupil opens or closes to admit more or less light
19. We visited our maternal grandparents Salem and Hosiah Edwards in Butte Montana last July
20. Dr. Fox did you break down the hydrocarbons or did you accept the analysis of your assistant

B. Copy these sentences, inserting the necessary periods, commas, question marks, and exclamation points.

1. Sgt Robinson joined the W A C's on July 17 1950
2. Everyone wanted to play Monopoly but Grover had to go
3. We studied equilateral isoceles and right triangles
4. Yes Bertie the tax laws on interest have changed
5. Is Campbell Hill the highest point in Ohio Mrs Evans
6. No H U D is not responsible for this building
7. J J Rousseau the famous writer and philosopher was born in Geneva Switzerland in A D 1712
8. Hooray Our team took state for the first time
9. After polishing the windows seemed to disappear
10. Three of Shakespeare's most famous heroines are Juliet Desdemona and Portia
11. Swimming in the ocean is in my opinion more exciting than swimming in a pool
12. Help your brother bring the groceries into the house
13. Because an interstate highway was built my uncle's house had to be moved
14. Above the branches looked like a canopy
15. Under the eaves in a little hole in the roof a family of sparrows has made its nest
16. Retrievers for example can do useful work
17. It's a girl
18. Poseidon who carried a trident was lord of the sea
19. Kites which have been used for research as well as for recreation come in many shapes
20. Trenton is the capital of New Jersey; Albany New York

USING MECHANICS IN WRITING
End Marks and Commas

A. Imagine that you have invented a vehicle that can travel over land, sea, and air. Give your invention some other outstanding features, such as the ability to climb trees or use water as fuel. When you have imagined all the features of this dream machine, write a full-page ad for it, informing the public of the revolution that is about to take place in transportation. Like other advertisers, you will probably want to make use of question marks and exclamation points to drive your message home.

B. Numerous popular novels and TV mini-series have chronicled the experiences and adventures of a single family through several generations. Think of one of these novels or movies, or make up a story line of your own. Now assume that you have to write a summary of this story. Briefly describe the triumphs, tragedies, and twists of fate that befall your characters over the years.

For example, you might write a brief history of "your" family from the time their ancestors first came to America. What conditions brought them here? Where did they settle? What occupations did they take up? Be sure to mention any outstanding characters in the family, and use restrictive and nonrestrictive clauses and phrases to describe them accurately. You may have to do some research to do justice to your story.

12.0 The Semicolon, the Colon, the Dash, and Parentheses

12.1 Semicolons Between Main Clauses

A semicolon is placed between the main clauses of a compound sentence when they are not joined by a conjunction.

Two main clauses may be separated by a period. If the clauses are closely related, however, a period might be too severe a separation. To make the relationship between the clauses more evident, they may be joined by a comma with a conjunction or by a semicolon.

> You may approve of the measure, *but* we do not.
> You may approve of the measure; we do not.

12.2 Semicolons and Conjunctive Adverbs

A semicolon is used between clauses joined by conjunctive adverbs or by phrases like *for example, in fact, for instance.*

> The problem of absences has become acute; in fact, it is first on the agenda for faculty consideration.

> Three people had asked me to that movie; however, I had promised Hubert that I would go with him instead.

Sir Walter Scott was only a silent partner in the bankrupt firm; nevertheless, he assumed responsibility for the debts.

Jill has a genius for leadership as well as many other talents; for example, she can play three musical instruments.

Note that the conjunctive adverb or phrase is followed by a comma in the examples above.

12.3 Semicolons Between Word Groups Containing Commas

A sentence may be difficult to read if it has too many commas. A semicolon should be used instead of a comma before a conjunction that joins two main clauses when the clause that precedes the conjunction includes commas.

A semicolon is used between main clauses joined by a conjunction if the clause before the conjunction contains commas.

The train stops at Davis, Foster, and Central Streets; but it does not run at all after midnight.

The camp counselors planned games, races, and a variety show; and everyone helped with the preparations.

Her brother won't clean, cook, or do laundry; nor will he do any other chores around the house.

A semicolon is used between a series of phrases if they contain commas.

This year my sisters will have their birthdays on Saturday, January 7; Saturday, February 4; and Monday, May 14.

The people who influenced Penny's choice of college were Ms. Schmidt, her English teacher; Mr. Benson, her guidance counselor; and Annie Bates, her best friend.

In two weeks the tour group went to London, England; Paris, France; Rome, Italy; and Athens, Greece.

Exercise A: Two of the following sentences need no semicolons. For the other sentences, indicate the point at which a semicolon should replace a comma.

1. If you enjoy hunting and fishing, go to Maine, but if you enjoy crowds and excitement, go to Atlantic City.
2. Linda sang and danced in the school musical, and she won the debate tournament.
3. Inside the old house, it was hot, outside, it was cool.
4. In some ways I like geometry, in other ways I don't.
5. Stop in for your papers on Monday or Tuesday, otherwise, you may have to wait a whole week.
6. Mom would not change her mind and let us go, however, she agreed to our having company for dinner.
7. Thoreau was unlike many of his contemporaries, he would not compromise his convictions.
8. Juanita is as excited as a child when it snows, she never saw a snowstorm until she was twenty.
9. On the night before, Bert had gone to bed early, consequently, he was at his best for the examination.
10. The following officers were elected: Elaine Berek, president, Jane Carrolton, vice-president, George Goodson, secretary.
11. He steeled himself for the jab, but when the nurse injected the vaccine, he scarcely felt any pain.
12. A tragedy often ends with a catastrophe, on the other hand, a comedy ends happily.
13. On his short-wave set, Ed has received stations in Pusan, Korea, Anchorage, Alaska, and Edmonton, Canada.
14. Diane enjoyed the pictures of the Olympic Games, she was a newsphotographer and a track star herself.
15. Every morning he set out to sea, and every evening he returned with a boatload of fish.

Exercise B: Writing Write a paragraph listing your teachers and the subjects they teach. Use semicolons to separate phrases that contain commas.

12.4　Colons to Introduce Lists

A colon is sometimes used to tell the reader to expect an explanation or more detailed information.

A colon is used to introduce a list of items.

A colon is used when an explanatory list is preceded by the words *the following* or *as follows.* Do not use a colon before a series of modifiers or complements that follow the verb.

> We camped out at the following places: Lake Tahoe, Nevada; Jackson's Hole, Wyoming; and Yellowstone.　(list)
> The committee collected money, clothing, and blankets for the victims of the mud slides. (series of complements following the verb)
> Information is available in encyclopedias, in atlases, and in dictionaries. (series of modifiers following a verb)

12.5　Colons with Formal Quotations

A colon is used to introduce a formal quotation.

> The president opened the meeting with these words: "We are beginning a period of expansion in which all of you will play a key role."

12.6 Colons Before Explanatory Statements

A colon is used between two sentences when the second explains the first. The second sentence begins with a capital letter.

> Now I understand what caused his downfall: His failure to admit his guilt and make a public apology turned away those who might have shown him mercy.
> I think I know the cause: I ate six chocolate eclairs and three brownies.

12.7 Other Uses of the Colon

A colon is also used (1) after the formal salutation of a letter, (2) between the hour and minute figures of clock time, (3) in Biblical references, (4) between the title and subtitle of a book.

> Dear Ms. Franklin: *Music: A Design for Listening*
> 10:55 A.M.   Exodus 9:8–13

12.8 The Dash To Show Break in Thought

A dash is used to show an abrupt break in thought.

In dialogue, the break in thought is often caused by uncertainty or hesitancy as in the first example below.

> The trouble is—I suppose he knows it himself—he just can't get along with people.
> We are to meet at Mary's for the surprise—oh, have the plans been changed?
> I am firmly convinced—but what weight do my opinions carry anymore?

12.9 The Dash with Interrupters

A dash is used to set off a long explanatory statement that interrupts the thought.

> Robert Frost—who had to gain his first recognition not in his own country, but abroad—is now considered by many to be America's most distinguished poet.
> There was a feeling of curious anticipation—a feeling shared throughout the world—when Communist China first invited the President of the United States to visit Peking.

12.10 The Dash Before a Summary

The dash is used after a series to indicate a summarizing statement.

Old prints, faded manuscripts, the yellowed pages of books long out of print—these were his special delights.

Simplicity of operation, low cost, assembly-line production—these were the factors that Henry Ford introduced to revolutionize the manufacture of automobiles.

Exercise: Copy the following sentences, inserting semicolons, colons, and dashes where necessary.

1. The plant shop sold only the following varieties English ivy, Swedish ivy, and grape ivy.
2. Jack telephoned to ask me to buy the following whole wheat bread, Swiss cheese, and dill pickles.
3. The train was due at 5 30, but it was not there by 6 15.
4. The title of the book is *Past to Present A World History.*
5. The newsboy gave poor service he was afraid of the dog.
6. Let me explain how I oh, here comes George!
7. My schedule this year includes the following subjects English III, French III, Algebra II, and Physics II.
8. Eliza would not want a kitten for a pet she has a canary.
9. We can summarize Emerson's philosophy in these words "Trust thyself; every heart vibrates to that iron string."
10. Tom Saunders was a model student he made all A's he was a talented football player he was always pleasant.
11. The article you need is in Helicon Volume III pages 2–12.
12. We went down the slope in a hurry slid down, in fact.
13. I know how the accident happened by the way Kate stopped in a few minutes ago and left a messge for you.
14. Ms. Harris began her speech by reading Job 9 1–8.
15. Robert Holt we call him class clown was in the play.
16. In his excitement the dance was our best in years Fred soon forgot he was homesick.

17. Here we are, face to face with a difficult and new problem difficult and new, that is, in the sense that we are strangers to it.
18. The campus was beautifully planted with pin oaks, flowering trees, and a variety of gardens all gifts of former graduating classes.
19. To arrive promptly, to concentrate on his work, to organize these were the things he found difficult.
20. Judge Potter she is a friend of my mother's helped me get a summer job.

12.11 Parentheses To Enclose Supplementary or Explanatory Words

To set off or enclose information that is explanatory or supplemental, you may use commas, dashes, or parentheses. Commas are the best choice when the supplementary material is closely related to the main purpose of the sentence. When the supplementary material is loosely related, dashes should be used. Material that is so loosely related it could be written as a separate sentence may be enclosed in parentheses.

Parentheses should be avoided in high school compositions. Use commas or dashes to enclose explanatory material within a sentence. If the material is so distantly related as to require parentheses, put it in a separate sentence.

COMMAS ADEQUATE: Andy could not use his telescope, which he got in February, until he went to Arizona in April.

DASHES REQUIRED: A meteorite fell through the roof of a house—the Comet Drive-In was only a few feet away—in Alabama in 1954.

PARENTHESES APPROPRIATE: She speaks Arabic (her family has lived in the Middle East), but English is her first language.

PARENTHESES
AVOIDED: She speaks Arabic since her family has lived in the Middle East. Her first language, however, is English.

12.12   Punctuation Within Parentheses

Commas, semicolons, and periods are placed outside the closing parenthesis. The question mark and exclamation point are placed inside if the parenthetical material is itself a question or exclamation; otherwise, outside.

The ballet begins at 8:30 (no seating after the curtain).
Donna has four brothers; Alice, two (counting her step-brother); Ann, three.
I was not interested (why should I be?) in their plans.

12.13   Brackets

Use brackets to make corrections in quoted material. Also use them to add explanations to quotations.

"On the 4th [5th] of March, Hayes took office." (correction)
The letter read: "We have him [Jordahl] at our mercy."
(explanatory word inserted by the writer)

12.14   Ellipses

When you leave a word or several words out of the middle of a quotation, use an ellipsis (. . .) to let the reader know that you have omitted material. If the omitted words are at the end of a sentence, use an ellipsis and a period (. . . .).

"With malice toward none; with charity for all . . . let us strive on to finish the work we are in; to bind up the nation's wounds." —ABRAHAM LINCOLN

REINFORCEMENT EXERCISES

The Semicolon, the Colon, the Dash, and Parentheses

A. Use semicolons correctly. Some of the sentences below contain errors in punctuation. Delete commas and substitute semicolons, if necessary.

1. The victory went to James Knox Polk he was a leading Jacksonian Democrat.
2. A square is an example of a polygon, a cube, however, is an example of a polyhedron.
3. *Epistemology* is a branch of philosophy concerned with the nature of knowledge *logic,* on the other hand, is a branch of philosophy concerned with the process of thinking.
4. Lisa played the fife, the flute, the bagpipes, and the clarinet, but she did not play the harmonica.
5. We drove to Lincoln, Nebraska, Miles City, Montana, Marshall, Minnesota, and Minot, North Dakota.
6. The five-digit ZIP code is used in most correspondence the nine-digit one is used in business.
7. Wilt Chamberlain averaged more than fifty points a game during the 1962 basketball season moreover, he scored one hundred points in one game during that same season.
8. Lorraine Hansberry wrote *A Raisin in the Sun,* the title came from a poem by Langston Hughes.
9. Large sea scallops are bivalves they propel themselves by quickly opening and closing their shells.
10. Harriet loves flutes as a result she owns five of them.
11. A mouthbreeder is a fish that carries its eggs and its young in its mouth, for example, the North African percoid fish is a mouthbreeder.
12. Frank learned to play the glockenspiel and the marimba, both are percussion instruments related to the xylophone.

13. This year the holidays that fall on Tuesdays are Valentine's Day, February 14, Election Day, November 6, and Christmas, December 25.
14. People who fly long distances in planes often feel tired when they land, some of this is caused by the low humidity and air pressure in the planes.
15. Most people have seen a rainbow after a sun shower, few, however, have been lucky enough to see the rare lunar rainbow.

B. Use colons and dashes. Copy the following sentences, inserting colons and dashes where necessary. If a sentence is correct, write *Correct*.

1. The title of the work was *But They Made Us Laugh A History of Vaudeville*.
2. Henry David Thoreau, Ralph Waldo Emerson, Amos Bronson these were three of the most famous Transcendentalists.
3. Among the productions she has directed are the following: *Our Town, Skin of Our Teeth,* and *The Vegetable*.
4. Serena made her announcement She would donate the cabinet to a museum.
5. After we ordered hamburgers, fries, hot dogs, fish, and milkshakes, we—why are you turning green?
6. Aubrey decided on the following agenda begin the meeting at 2 30, discuss proposals for the new building site, and dismiss the meeting at 4 15.
7. When oil workers change a drill bit, they must pull all the pipe sometimes ten thousand feet of it out of the hole.
8. Engraved in the front of the building are the words "Know Thyself."
9. The text for Rev. Ainbinder's sermon was Mark 3 25–26.
10. Finally I understood Maggie Kuhn's purpose she was simply trying to establish rights for the elderly.

The Semicolon, the Colon, the Dash, and Parentheses

A. Insert necessary semicolons, colons, and dashes.

1. Leap years were added to the calendar in order to make the solar year the time required for the sun to pass the vernal equinox twice and the calendar year identical.
2. Alexander not Philip was called "the Great."
3. Damascus is an odd mix of the ancient and the modern it is considered the oldest continually inhabited city.
4. The supervisor gave the order Cut the microfilm strips and insert the frames into cardboard holders.
5. Nekton are water animals fish, eels, whales, lobsters, and so on that move independently plankton, on the other hand, are small plants and animals that drift.
6. Ice such as this can be very Help!
7. North America is the third largest continent Africa and Asia are larger.
8. Bob handed me the turpentine Rebecca, a rag.
9. Jane Pauley, Connie Jung, Barbara Walters these are just a few prominent women journalists
10. She translated the Hawaiian proverb for us It is the space inside that gives the drum its sound.
11. Among the works of Russian composer Sergei Prokofiev are the following *The Love of Three Oranges, Peter and the Wolf,* and *Lieutenant Kije.*
12. Stonewall Jackson killed by his own troops when he was mistaken for the enemy was Robert E. Lee's ablest lieutenant.
13. Most large cities have a bank clearinghouse representatives of local banks gather there to exchange checks.
14. A veterinarian must study several sciences in depth zoology, physics, and chemistry are a few of these.
15. New Yorks nickname is the Empire State its motto, *Excelsior* its flower, the rose its bird, the bluebird.

16. The actress Sarah Bernhardt known as "The Divine Sarah" continued to act even after she lost a leg.

17. Van Wyck Brooks wrote *Makers and Finders A History of the Writer in America*.

18. The gypsy moth is not native to the New World it was introduced into the United States about one hundred years ago and is now a destructive insect pest.

19. The following parts of the sandal were leather the upper sole, the strap, the vamp, and the midsole.

20. Wisdom teeth, second molars, first molars, and second bicuspids they all had cavities.

B. Rewrite the following sentences, inserting semicolons, colons, and dashes where necessary.

1. School clubs are enjoying great popularity in fact, some have doubled their membership.

2. The ice cream shop has the following new flavors fudge brownie, coconut, huckleberry, and bubble gum.

3. Mr. Jonas had a surprise His car had a flat tire.

4. Katie's meeting was at 3 30 however, she arrived at 4 30.

5. Princess Caroline's story is told in Volume 3 pages 90–99.

6. I'm waiting for oh, here she comes now.

7. Jim, our forward, is injured but his substitute is very capable.

8. Deep-dish pizza oh, it's so delicious! originated in Chicago.

9. Gemologists recognize real rubies laypeople often do not.

10. Josh read *Thomas Jefferson An Intimate History*.

11. Funny faces, silly props, and a white suit these are Steve Martin's trademarks.

12. Suffragettes crusaded for women's right to vote consequently, the nineteenth amendment was passed.

13. Culture Club toured the following cities Los Angeles, California Boston, Massachusetts and Chicago, Illinois.

14. Glass, steel, concrete modern architects use them freely.

15. George Benson plays guitar Stevie Wonder, piano and Maynard Ferguson, trumpet.

USING MECHANICS IN WRITING

The Semicolon, the Colon, the Dash, and Parentheses

A. The following paragraph from Thomas Pyles's *The Origins and Development of the English Language* has only four sentences. Pyles packs a lot of information into these four sentences through the use of punctuation: parentheses, semicolons, and a colon. Read the passage carefully and then rewrite it, eliminating the parentheses and using only simple sentences. After you have written the paragraph this way, compare the two and see which style is more effective in communicating the information.

> Slavic falls into three main subdivisions: East Slavic includes Great Russian (or just Russian), the common and literary language of Russia; Ruthenian (or Ukrainian), spoken in the Ukraine; and White Russian (or Byelorussian), spoken to the north of the Ukraine. West Slavic includes Polish, Czech, the highly similar Slovak, and Sorbian (or Wendish), a language spoken by a small group of people in East Germany; these languages have lost many of the early forms preserved in East Slavic. The South Slavic languages are Bulgarian, Serbo-Croatian, and Slovenian. The oldest Slavic writing which we know is in Old Bulgarian, sometimes called Old Church Slavic (or Old Church Slavonic), which remained a liturgical language long after it ceased to be generally spoken.

B. Colons are used to separate the title of a book from its subtitle. The subtitle is often longer than the title, not as catchy, and explains or clarifies what the book is actually about. For example, the title *Makers and Finders: A History of the Writer in America* shows how the subtitle can explain what the reader may expect to find in the book. Take the titles of five of your favorite albums and create subtitles that explain the subject matter contained in them to someone who has never heard them.

13.0 The Apostrophe

An **apostrophe** may be used with a noun to show possession or ownership: *Ted's uniform, Myrna's house, the cat's collar.* It may also be used to show membership, a source or origin, an identifying characteristic, or location.

MEMBERSHIP:	Harry's family, Emma's sorority
SOURCE OR ORIGIN:	France's perfumes, Mike's opinion
IDENTIFYING CHARACTERISTIC:	Mona Lisa's smile, leopard's spots
LOCATION:	Florida's beaches, Canada's highways

The rules given in this Section will help you recognize where apostrophes are needed. Remember to think of these rules when you are proofreading your writing.

13.1 The Possessive of Singular Nouns

The possessive form of a singular noun is usually made by adding an apostrophe and s ('s) to the noun.

boy + 's = boy's   city + 's = city's
school + 's = school's   Ross + 's = Ross's

Note: Some singular proper nouns that end in *s* take the apostrophe alone to form the possessive: *Jesus', Pythagoras'.* In general, however, use the apostrophe and *s* ('s) to form the possessive of singular nouns.

13.2   The Possessive of Plural Nouns

If a plural noun does not end in s, add both apostrophe and s ('s) to form the possessive.

children + 's = children's   people + 's = people's
mice + 's = mice's   women + 's = women's

If a plural noun ends in s, add only the apostrophe to form the possessive.

horses + ' = horses'   waiters + ' = waiters'
Ameses + ' = Ameses'   editors + ' = editors'

Exercise: Write *Correct* for each sentence in which the possessive form is correct. If the form is incorrect, write it correctly.

1. "The Childrens Hour" is one of Longfellows best-known poems.
2. The first witness' testimony greatly impressed the jury.
3. Jess's make-up was like an actress's.
4. Carmels climate is famous for its uniformity.
5. Charles's father was invited to sit at the captains' table.
6. Our Olympic team did well in women's downhill skiing.
7. The Joneses dog barked all night.
8. The dentists' conversation put her patients at ease.
9. The jewels in the duchess' tiara were diamonds.
10. Dad attended the alumnis' annual dinner.
11. Robert Burns's poems are beloved by the Scots.
12. Moses' Ten Commandments are also known as the Decalogue.
13. One birds' song could be heard over the mens' voices.
14. The Burnses farm sits on a knoll between two oak trees.
15. Have you read Henry James's *Washington Square?*
16. Les' sister goes to a girls' preparatory school.
17. The womans' estate was administered by her lawyers.
18. For Bess's birthday her mother gave her a watch.
19. Both editor's arguments influenced the author's decision.
20. Squirrel's tails are not bushy in the springtime.

13.3   The Possessive of Compound Nouns

A **compound noun** is a noun composed of more than one word. Some compound nouns are written with hyphens between the parts.

Only the last part of a hyphenated noun shows possession.

father-in-law + 's = father-in-law's
commander-in-chief + 's = commander-in-chief's
sergeant-at-arms + 's = sergeant-at-arms's

Nouns such as *the Queen of England, the President of the United States, the Secretary of State* form the possessive by adding an apostrophe and *s* to the last word only: *the Queen of England's dynasty*. This awkward phrasing may be avoided, however, by using an *of* phrase.

The dynasty of the Queen of England
the responsibilities of the President of the United States
the salary of the Secretary of State

13.4   Joint Ownership

When the names of two or more persons are used to show joint ownership, only the name of the last person mentioned is given the possessive form. Add an apostrophe or an apostrophe and *s* in accordance with the spelling of that name.

Louise and Tom's family
fathers and sons' banquet
author and critic's correspondence
the judge and jury's decision

The rule applies also to names of firms and organizations.

Clarke and Taylor's sale
Brown, Jackson, and Company's building
The League of Women Voters' pamphlet

13.5   Separate Ownership or Possession

If the names of two or more persons are used to show separate ownership, each name is given the possessive form.

Madison's and Jefferson's careers

This construction may become awkward. It can be avoided by using an *of* phrase.

the careers of Madison and Jefferson

13.6   Possessive of Indefinite Pronouns

Use an apostrophe and *s* to form the possessive of indefinite pronouns.

anybody + 's = anybody's   no one + 's = no one's
everyone + 's = everyone's   something + 's = something's

For compound words like *someone else, anybody else,* and *no one else,* an apostrophe and *s* are added to the last word:

no one else's   anybody else's

The apostrophe is not used to form the possessive of personal pronouns.

NONSTANDARD: their's, your's, her's, our's, it's
STANDARD: theirs, yours, hers, ours, its

13.7   Expressions of Time and Amount

When used as adjectives, words expressing time and amount are given the possessive form.

one hour's work   four minutes' time
a month's delay   four months' delay
a week's vacation   two weeks' vacation

Exercise: Copy the italicized words, changing them to show ownership or possession correctly.

1. Carrie's *sister-in-law* party was a great success.
2. The weather is *nobody* fault.
3. *Jane and Tim* cousin spent the weekend with them.
4. The red scarf is *your's;* the blue one is *her's.*
5. Herb said, "It's a good fifteen *minutes* walk to the bus."
6. The *attorney-general* office is on the tenth floor.
7. The *Senator from Maine* motion was being considered.
8. The *accountant* and *taxpayer* signatures were on the tax return.
9. The *West Side Savings Bank* window was broken.
10. The workers struck for two *week* vacation with pay.
11. I took *someone else* umbrella by mistake.
12. The *Marquess of Queensberry* rules are a code for the boxing ring.
13. The committee heard the *Secretary of Commerce* report.
14. There was a gala opening of *Clayton and Hart* store today.
15. The *catcher* throw cut off the base runner.
16. The Quick Cleaners clean a suit in three *hours* time.
17. If that remark were *anybody else* except yours, I would get mad.
18. *Madison and Jefferson* letters are of great historical interest.
19. The *Governor of Ohio* address was the main speech at the dinner.
20. Those skis are *their's;* these are *our's.*

13.8 Apostrophes to Show Omissions

An apostrophe is used to show the omission of letters or figures.

the Homestead Act of '62	*1862*
the class of '89	*1989*
ne'er	*never*
shouldn't	*should not*

13.9 Plurals of Letters, Words, Numbers, and Signs

An apostrophe is used to show the plurals of letters, words, numbers, and signs used as words.

> How many *s*'s are there in Mississippi?
> Beware of using too many *and*'s in your themes.
> His *7*'s look like *9*'s.

Note: Letters, numbers, signs, and words used as words are italicized in print. They may be underlined or placed in quotation marks in manuscript or typescript. The *'s* that forms the plural appears in regular Roman type in print. The *'s* should not be underlined in manuscript or typescript.

Exercise A: Copy the following sentences, inserting an apostrophe (and *s*) where needed.

1. Shes the best basketball player on the team.
2. Havent you asked for a weeks vacation?
3. I can never distinguish your *is* from your *es*.
4. After ten days delay, the publisher answered my letter.
5. Mother belongs to two womens political groups.
6. Alice's speech had too many *ands* and *buts*.
7. White and Judsons store has just installed escalators.
8. In the spring of 76 we visited Washingtons home.
9. We bought fifty dollars worth of groceries.
10. My brother-in-laws telephone number is unlisted.
11. Venus orbit is between Mercurys and the Earths.
12. Pythagoras theorem is still useful today.

Exercise B: Write the possessive singular and the possessive plural of each of the following words:

1. day	4. principal	7. sister	10. lady
2. city	5. baby	8. son	11. mouse
3. class	6. salesperson	9. country	12. woman

REINFORCEMENT EXERCISES
The Apostrophe

A. Use the possessive form of nouns. Some of the following sentences contain errors in the use of apostrophes. If a sentence contains an error, rewrite it correctly. If a sentence does not contain an error, write *Correct*.

1. The reading list included Henry Jameses novel *A Portrait of a Lady*.
2. Representatives from Newark and New York met to discuss the two cities mutual problems.
3. The chickens were panicked by the foxes cries in the night.
4. A group formed to discuss the creation of a womens' political group for Thompsonville.
5. The farmers goal was to join together and build a cooperative grain elevator.
6. What did Longfellow mean by "the childrens' hour"?
7. Did you see Gwendolyn Brooks's reading of her poetry?
8. These houses heating bills run to about $1,000 per year.
9. We prefer the Collinses landscaping to the Franklins.
10. The books' dust jackets were all torn and shabby.

B. Use apostrophes to show ownership. Rewrite the sentences below using the correct possessive form.

1. My two sister-in-law's families play baseball together on Saturday afternoons.
2. Paul Winchel and Edgar Bergen's ventriloquist acts were extremely popular in the 1950's.
3. We ordered a weeks worth of groceries just before the storm hit.
4. Jim and Sadies' Restaurant features Sadies barbequed ribs.
5. The lion cub had been separated from it's mother.
6. It's anybodys guess as to who the next President will be.
7. The editor's-in-chief hurt the two cub reporters feelings.

8. Maine and Texas' histories were the subjects of two articles in this months *National Geographic*.
9. Donnie's and Marie's home state is Utah.
10. The mens' locker room was remodeled after the fire.

C. Use apostrophes for omissions and plurals. Rewrite the following sentences, inserting an apostrophe, or an apostrophe and *s*, where needed. If a sentence is correct, write *Correct*.

1. Lynette failed to see that the two 4s canceled each other.
2. They did not participate in the 84 Olympics.
3. Sherry and Peter were writing a musical comedy, *Im Rowing As Fast As I Can*.
4. The first page of the document contained thirty-two *therefores*; therefore we wouldnt sign it.
5. Children born in the early 1970s will graduate from high school in the late 1980s.
6. Many business telephone numbers contain 0s as the last two or three digits.
7. Perhaps a dog chases its tail to amuse itself.
8. How many people pronounce both *rs* in *February*?
9. His speech was peppered with *mes*, *mines*, and *mys*.
10. Larry and Joanna's dog wouldnt have barked if the Adamses cat hadnt sneaked onto its porch.

MIXED REVIEW

The Apostrophe

A. Rewrite the following sentences, correcting all errors in the use of the apostrophe.

1. The parents and teachers conference was very successful in improving the schools image.
2. The cowboys speech was full of *yeps* and *nopes*.
3. Does Melvilles use of symbolism center around color in *Moby Dick*?
4. Shell realize that we arent there when nobody answers her knock.
5. Stacys courage and ingenuity enabled the rangers to find the missing plane.
6. Gavins and Hughs younger sister is going to be my roommate in college.
7. Theyre studying the effects of the chemical on insects.
8. Some workers give exactly eight hours worth of work for eight hours worth of pay.
9. The woman in the car did not agree with her sister-in-laws advice.
10. "If theyre home, theyre not answering the phone," commented Ricks uncle.
11. The rubies and diamonds facets reflected the light.
12. Im so tired of books titled *The ABCs of* anything, nor am I happy with all the *All You Need to Know About*s in titles.
13. The Secretary-of-States comments were printed in most major papers.
14. Does each *blip* indicate several seconds radar scanning?
15. The camera is the photographers, but the film is the clients.
16. You can abbreviate 1980 as 80, but you cant abbreviate 2000 as 00!
17. Tennysons poem contains the line, "Our's is not to reason why."

18. This years wheat crop exceeded all expectations.
19. Arent womens running shoes cut on a different last than mens running shoes?
20. No one elses suggestion was as original as Austins.

B. Rewrite the following sentences, correcting all errors in the use of the apostrophe.

1. Margaret's and Don's mother, after two year's work in a bookstore, decided to start her own business.
2. Rutherford B. Hayes term of office was in the late 1800s.
3. Didnt Sarah and Diane's home runs tie the score?
4. Alex said he hadnt read any of Keats poems.
5. Joan begins all her sentences with *and so*s.
6. My sister spent the weekend at her mother's-in-law home.
7. Tim's and Kim's parents car is a 76 Pontiac.
7. Les's sister dots her *i*s with a circle.
9. Wasnt the five oclock bus late tonight?
10. Hanks' cake won a prize at the food fair.
11. Theres your jacket; Ive mended the sleeve.
12. Nobody elses violin was out of tune except Charles'.
13. Green's and Company store was closing just as I arrived.
14. I couldnt read Phils' writing because his *e*s and *i*s look alike.
15. Politician's lives are open to public scrutiny.
16. The dog led it's master to the commander's-in-chief tent.
17. Which came first, Adams's or Jefferson's administration?
18. The dogs hair was all over the visitors suit.
19. Dad didn't see anything funny in Louis and Steves prank.
20. All the employees at Morgan's and Clark's department store get two week's vacation.

USING MECHANICS IN WRITING
The Apostrophe

A. Each of the parent-child pairs listed below has made a contribution to American life in the same field. Do some research into the lives and achievements of one of these pairs and write a report on your findings. Use the plural possessive form of their family name whenever possible to discuss the collective achievement of parent and child in their chosen field.

John Adams and John Quincy Adams
W. C. Wyeth and Andrew Wyeth
Judy Garland and Liza Minelli
Alvan Clark and Alvan Graham Clark
Lucy Stone and Alice Stone Blackwell

B. Do some research on an unusual career field that interests you. Some possibilities appear below. Write an informative article for your classmates that lists several positions available in that field, along with the responsibilities that each one involves. You might also include some of the jargon used in the field, including the nicknames that are used for some of the different job titles (best boy, gaffer). Since the article is informal, you may also feel free to use contractions.

TV or movie production: directors, camera operators, special effects crew, film editor
Music: disc or video jockey, sound engineer, conductors, singer for voice-overs
Research: divers, arctic explorers
Police work: forensics specialist, detective, undercover agent

14.0 Quotations

14.1 Direct and Indirect Quotations

Quotation marks are used to enclose a direct quotation.

A direct quotation repeats the exact words that someone has written or said.

> Montaigne said, "The greatest thing in the world is to know how to be yourself."
> "The horse," Jim said, "is rearing again."

An indirect quotation gives not the exact words, but the general ideas of the speaker.

> INDIRECT: The television announcer warned that a hurricane was approaching.
> DIRECT: "A hurricane is approaching," the television announcer warned.

Quotation marks are not used with an indirect quotation.

14.2 Punctuation of Direct Quotations

The following rules govern the use of punctuation and capitals in direct quotations.

1. **In dialogue, the first word of the quotation is capitalized.** In other situations, material quoted from a written source might use words from the middle of a sentence. When this is true, the first word is not capitalized.

   > Washington considered religion "an indispensable support" of government.

2. **The speaker's words are set off from the rest of the sentence.** Note the placement of commas in these examples:

The reviewer stated, "Doctorow's novel is a masterpiece."
"Doctorow's novel is a masterpiece," the reviewer stated.

3. **When the end of the quotation is also the end of the sentence, the period falls inside the quotation marks.**

Sascha said, "You are all invited."

4. **If the quoted words are a question or an exclamation, the question mark or the exclamation point falls inside the quotation marks. In this situation no comma is needed.**

"How do you like your courses?" Sue asked.
"Don't touch that!" he shouted.

5. **If the entire sentence is a question or an exclamation, the exclamation point or question mark falls outside the quotation marks.**

Wasn't their campaign slogan "Tippecanoe and Tyler, too"?
I deny my opponent's charge that I am "avoiding the issues"!

6. **The colon and the semicolon at the close of a quotation fall outside the quotation marks.**

The governor told his constituents that the following were on his list as "must legislation": a tax cut, aid to education, and subsidy for city transit.
Read A. E. Van Vogt's "The Enchanted Village"; then compare it with Stanley G. Weinbaum's "Parasite Planet."

7. **Both parts of a divided quotation are enclosed in quotation marks. The first word of the second part is not capitalized unless it begins a new sentence.**

"It was a great shock," Harry said, "to hear of his illness."
"I recommend not telling the patient," the doctor said.
"You may alarm him and aggravate his suffering."

8. In dialogue, a new paragraph and a new set of quotation marks show a change in speaker.

"Why do you want to drop out of school?" the counselor asked.

"I've been in school for ten years," Tony said. "I want to get out and earn some money."

"If you check the job market for unskilled workers," the counselor replied, "you'll find you have as much chance to get a job as you would to bat clean-up spot for the New York Yankees."

14.3 Quotations Within Quotations

Single quotation marks are used to enclose a quotation within a quotation.

Gary reported, "When somebody told Churchill not to end sentences with a preposition, Sir Winston replied, 'That is the kind of nonsense up with which I will not put.' "

Sheila asked, "Was it Roosevelt who said, 'The only thing we have to fear is fear itself'?"

14.4 Long Quotations

A quotation may be several paragraphs in length.

In long quotations, begin each paragraph with quotation marks. Place quotation marks at the end of the last paragraph only.

Exercise A: Copy the following sentences, adding the necessary punctuation marks and capital letters.

1. Boonesboro Jack reported is the name of the first American settlement west of the Appalachians
2. Why don't you take your vacation in winter she asked there are many Southern cruises

3. Look out the ranger shouted there are rocks falling from the ledge above you
4. Bill reported that Dick had declared authoritatively there are no trout in this stream
5. Did Mathilda say yes or maybe
6. Did you think Evelyn Waugh was a woman asked Professor McConnell
7. One of Shakespeare's characters said that all the world's a stage
8. Caesar is supposed to have said et tu, Brute?; he could not believe that Brutus was one of the conspirators who plotted to kill him
9. Stuart asked did Anaxagoras or Heraclitus say the same man never steps in the same river twice
10. If the groundhog comes out of his den and sees his shadow on February 2 said Bonnie there will be six more weeks of winter

Exercise B: Copy the following passage, correcting any errors in punctuation, capitalization, or paragraphing.

Hattie recognized the similarity between them. When he came to see her she said Jerry, you're the only one I can really talk to about my troubles. What am I going to do for money? I have Hotchkiss Insurance. I paid eight dollars a month. That won't do you much good, Hat. No Blue Cross? I let it drop ten years ago. Maybe I could sell some of my valuables. What have you got? he said. His eye began to droop with laughter. Why she said defiantly there's plenty. First there's the beautiful, precious Persian rug that India left me. Coals from the fireplace have been burning it for years, Hat! The rug is in perfect condition she said with an angry sway of her shoulders. A beautiful object like that never loses its value. And the oak table from the Spanish monastery is three hundred years old. With luck you could get twenty bucks for it. It would cost fifty to haul it out of here. It's the house you ought to sell.—SAUL BELLOW

14.5 Setting Off Titles

The titles of *whole* works, like books, magazines, and plays, are italicized. Indicate italics in your own writing and typing by underlining.

When indicating the title of a *part* of a book, magazine, or newspaper, use quotation marks.

Use quotation marks to enclose the titles of chapters and other parts of books and to enclose the titles of stories, poems, essays, articles, and short musical compositions.

> In *Literature of America* I read Shirley Jackson's story "The Lottery."
>
> Isaac Asimov's "Anatomy of a Martian" first appeared in *Esquire*.

14.6 Words Used in Special Ways

Words used in special ways or special senses are enclosed in quotation marks.

You may use quotation marks to indicate that you are using a word or group of words in some special way. If, for example, someone has used a word in a way you do not accept, you may indicate this by placing the word in quotes. You may also indicate that you realize a word is a slang word and not appropriate for formal writing by enclosing it in quotation marks.

> The bank teller was immediately called "on the carpet" for a shortage in his accounts.
>
> Social workers now call poor people "the socially disadvantaged."
>
> In the fad language known as Valspeak, impressive things were "awesome"; negative things were "beige" or even "grody."
>
> One reviewer actually wrote that her performance was the "definitive Lady Macbeth!"

Note: When a comma or period immediately follows the quoted word, it falls *inside* the quotation marks. The semicolon falls *outside* the quotation marks. See the third example above. If the quoted word appears at the end of a question or exclamation, the question mark or exclamation point falls *outside* the quotation marks. See the last example above.

14.7 Words Used as Words

In print, a word that is referred to as a word is italicized. In writing or typing, underline such a word.

> In general, avoid using the word *physiognomy* for *face*.
> I dislike the words *oriented* and *orientation*.

When a word and its definition are in the same sentence, italicize the word and place the definition in quotation marks.

> The word *perspicuity* means "clearness of expression."

Exercise A: Copy the following sentences. Insert quotation marks where necessary. Indicate italics by underlining.

1. Mary said that she was reading Stephen Leacock's essay My Financial Career.
2. John asked her if that essay is in Literary Lapses.
3. We asked the candidate what he meant by law and order.
4. Matt uses the word like too much.
5. Did the report say continuously or continually?
6. The Garden Party is a story in Women in Fiction.
7. Letters to the Editor in the May 14 issue of Time is particularly entertaining.
8. Margo ends every sentence with y'know observed Kelly.
9. You will enjoy the chapter called The Long Snowfall in Rachel Carson's interesting volume The Sea Around Us.
10. We will have our first tornado drill this morning, the voice over the loudspeaker announced.

Exercise B: Follow the same directions as for Exercise A.

1. Have you read Shelley's poem To a Skylark?
2. The word enjoin means to command or order.
3. Patrizia once wrote appitamy when she meant epitome.
4. The actor seemed surprised that his fans thought he was a hunk.
5. The word palindrome signifies a word such as noon or a group of words such as Madam, I'm Adam that reads the same backwards or forwards.
6. The city inspectors were on hand to offer helpful suggestions.
7. Claire Boothe Luce called a certain kind of confused thinking about international affairs globaloney.
8. The first chapter of Steiner's After Babel is called Understanding as Translation.
9. Try to eliminate the really's and a lot's from your writing.
10. Frankie called the increased dues getting blood from a turnip.

REINFORCEMENT EXERCISES

Quotations

A. Punctuate direct and indirect quotations. Rewrite the following sentences, inserting proper punctuation and necessary capital letters. If a sentence is correct as it is, write *Correct*.

1. Fish need shade plants said the pet store owner because they have no eyelids.
2. Mr. Walchek replied Louis Vuitton has been making luggage since 1854.
3. The sports announcer said that Erika Hess from Switzerland was the 1982 World Cup slalom champion.
4. Stop shouted the interior decorator. Do not paint over that beautiful oak molding.
5. This article said Ralph defines *vexillology* as The study of the history and symbolism of flags.
6. Was Dr. Tsui the instructor who said By the end of this session, you will understand the appeal of myths.
7. Yes, the defendant distinctly said called on, not called, testified the police detective.
8. Father announced that we would not leave the house until the leaves were raked and bagged.
9. Light a candle advised Mother and listen to the transistor radio until the power is back on.
10. Mrs. Halifax whispered is this speaker really an expert on how to sell your writing? He can't even speak well!

B. Use quotation marks, underlining, and apostrophes. Rewrite the following sentences, correcting any errors in punctuation and capitalization.

1. In Croatian the word hvala, which is also spelled fala, means thanks, said Mr. Dragovich.
2. Art Tatum, the jazz pianist, recorded Tea for Two and Tatum Pole Boogie on the album entitled Piano Starts Here.

3. When the slang known as Valspeak was popular, everything was grody or tubular.

4. Was Mike the chess club member who said I recommend the chapter entitled The Two-Bishop Sacrifice in The Fireside Book of Chess?

5. W. H. Auden used the expression Poetry makes nothing happen in his poem In Memory of W. B. Yeats, said Dr. Gillicut.

6. Ms. Fisher asked Has anyone read Elinor Wylie's poem, The Eagle and the Mole?

7. Did you really believe the product was guaranteed for life? asked my brother.

8. Do not confuse the word humus with the word hummus; one is dirt and the other is food! laughed Mr. Brannigan.

9. Professor Silver said Rembrandt painted a scene that was called The Night Watch for several centuries until it was cleaned in 1947, revealing a daytime scene.

10. The evening of good food and entertainment turned out to be a disaster said Mrs. Cummings.

MIXED REVIEW

Quotations

A. Copy the following sentences, inserting the necessary quotation marks, capitals, and punctuation. Indicate italics by underlining. One sentence is already correct.

1. The French do not capitalize the word vendredi, which means Friday.
2. If the class will pay attention, I will explain the word anagram said the instructor. I think you'll even enjoy the lesson.
3. Alicia remarked my favorite poems by Marianne Moore are Silence, Poetry, and Antique Harvesters.
4. Do you realize, asked the nature guide, that the lovely jack-in-the-pulpit is sometimes called an Indian turnip.
5. Hudson Maxim perfected an explosive called maximite, explained Mr. Ober, which was more shockproof than dynamite.
6. Why didn't you tell me that beaucoup meant much, demanded Chuck I thought beaucoup was a name!
7. Help shouted Alex this fish is pulling me out of the boat.
8. Was it Dorothy Parker or Dorothy Thompson, asked Candace, who wrote the humorous poem Love Song?
9. The article explained that a white dwarf was a small, extremely dense star.
10. Song of the Riders is a small section of Stephen Vincent Benet's epic poem, John Brown's Body.
11. The term publishing means the production of printed materials.
12. William Edgar Borah, a U.S. Senator from Idaho, was often called the great opposer, replied Ms. Hollenbach.
13. Sandra asked who said here's looking at you, kid.
14. The term widget, sighed the proprietor, refers to a hypothetical, not an actual, object.
15. Did Hal say The best chapter in The Iron Heel was called The Beginning of the End.

16. What do you mean by supernova Lisa, asked Ann.
17. We discovered, reported Florence, that the new and improved product was exactly the same as the original.
18. Is Carlo the one student, asked Ms. Quigley, who knows what the word luge means.
19. This is truly a house-warming present, joked my aunt, because I'm going to toss it into the fire.
20. During which war, asked Mr. Benson, did Francis Scott Key write The Star-Spangled Banner.

B. Follow the directions for Exercise A.

1. All aboard shouted the conductor.
2. Whose jeans are these Ryan asked.
3. Your deadline is tomorrow the editor announced.
4. We will soon have the equipment the principal noted for a school radio station.
5. Courtney remarked that the short, severe look is in.
6. Ralph Waldo Emerson defined a friend as the masterpiece of nature.
7. The huge sign said Keep out; we did.
8. How dare you call me a rude dude!
9. Is Coca-Cola's slogan still It's the real thing?
10. Soccer is the newest sport at Taft the coach said let's make it the best.
11. Erin asked did that sign say Dangerous curve ahead?
12. Tony said Dad told us only your best is good enough.
13. Carrie's favorite short story is F. Scott Fitzgerald's Babylon Revisited.
14. W. H. Auden's poem The Unknown Citizen satirizes conformity.
15. The first chapter of The Scarlet Letter, The Prison-door, contrasts the prison with a wild rose bush.
16. Who first recorded Puttin' on the Ritz Francine asked.
17. The coach asked me to relieve the pitcher said Bobbie.
18. The only comment on Judith's test paper was superb.
19. The car salesperson called the 1982 Toyota pre-owned.
20. Nemesis means an avenger or an unbeatable rival.

USING MECHANICS IN WRITING
Quotations

Below is a passage from "The Catbird Seat," by James Thurber. All of the quotation marks have been removed. Although Thurber wrote this dialogue in two continuous paragraphs, rewrite it now, adding proper punctuation and following conventional paragraphing rules.

Mr. Martin got to the office at eight thirty the next morning, as usual. At a quarter to nine, Ulgine Barrows, who had never before arrived at work before ten, swept into his office. I'm reporting to Mr. Fitweiler now! she shouted. If he turns you over to the police, it's no more than you deserve! Mr. Martin gave her a look of shocked surprise. I beg your pardon? he said. Mrs. Barrows snorted and bounced out of the room, leaving Miss Paird and Joey Hart staring after her. What's the matter with that old devil now? asked Miss Paird. I have no idea, said Mr. Martin, resuming his work. . . .

Forty-five minutes later, Mrs. Barrows left the president's office and . . . Mr. Fitweiler sent for Mr. Martin. The head of the filing department, neat, quiet, attentive, stood in front of the old man's desk. Mr. Fitweiler was pale and nervous. He made a small, bruffing sound in his throat. Martin, he said, you have been with us more than twenty years. Twenty-two, sir, said Mr. Martin. In that time, pursued the president, your work and your—uh—manner have been exemplary. I trust so, sir, said Mr. Martin. I have understood, Martin, said Mr. Fitweiler, that you have never taken a drink or smoked. That is correct, sir, said Mr. Martin. Ah, yes. Mr. Fitweiler polished his glasses. He was silent for a moment, searching for the proper words to say to the head of the filing department. Mrs. Barrows, he said finally, Mrs. Barrows has worked hard, Martin, very hard. It grieves me to report that she has suffered a severe breakdown.

CUMULATIVE REVIEW
Capitalization and Punctuation

Using Correct Capitalization and Punctuation. Rewrite the following selection, correcting any errors in capitalization and punctuation.

When westerners think of egypt they almost always conjure up pictures from the past. This arabic speaking nation which is located in the northeastern corner of africa is known primarily for it's ancient wonders including the great pyramid at giza the royal treasures of king tutankhaman and the magnificent temples of karnak and luxor. The egyptian people are extremely proud of their noble heritage but they are equally proud of the strides they have recently taken into the modern age.

From 3100 bc to ad 1952 the land of the nile was ruled by a succession of monarchs. In 1953 a group of army officers that included gamal abdel nasser having overthrown their king ended the monarchy and established a legislative government creating what is now known as the arab republic of egypt. The constitution of this republic provides for a president, one or more vice presidents, a cabinet, a legislature, and courts. The president must be nominated by at least two thirds of egypts legislature and approved by a majority of the countrys voters.

Under its republican form of government egypt has prospered and grown. Elementary education has become mandatory several great Colleges and Universities have been established and the temples and tombs of the pharaohs have given way to such monuments of modern technology as factories television and the aswan dam. While agriculture remains egypts major industry other industries are rapidly emerging. Of particular importance to egypts economy are recent developments in tourism the manufacturing of cement chemicals fertilizers paper and steel and the mining of gypsum iron ore manganese petroleum and salt.

2. **The speaker's words are set off from the rest of the sentence.**
Note the placement of commas in these examples:

The reviewer stated, "Doctorow's novel is a masterpiece."
"Doctorow's novel is a masterpiece," the reviewer stated.

3. **When the end of the quotation is also the end of the sentence, the period falls inside the quotation marks.**

Sascha said, "You are all invited."

4. **If the quoted words are a question or an exclamation, the question mark or the exclamation point falls inside the quotation marks. In this situation no comma is needed.**

"How do you like your courses?" Sue asked.
"Don't touch that!" he shouted.

5. **If the entire sentence is a question or an exclamation, the exclamation point or question mark falls outside the quotation marks.**

Wasn't their campaign slogan "Tippecanoe and Tyler, too"?
I deny my opponent's charge that I am "avoiding the issues"!

6. **The colon and the semicolon at the close of a quotation fall outside the quotation marks.**

The governor told his constituents that the following were on his list as "must legislation": a tax cut, aid to education, and subsidy for city transit.
Read A. E. Van Vogt's "The Enchanted Village"; then compare it with Stanley G. Weinbaum's "Parasite Planet."

7. **Both parts of a divided quotation are enclosed in quotation marks. The first word of the second part is not capitalized unless it begins a new sentence.**

"It was a great shock," Harry said, "to hear of his illness."
"I recommend not telling the patient," the doctor said.
"You may alarm him and aggravate his suffering."

8. In dialogue, a new paragraph and a new set of quotation marks show a change in speaker.

"Why do you want to drop out of school?" the counselor asked.

"I've been in school for ten years," Tony said. "I want to get out and earn some money."

"If you check the job market for unskilled workers," the counselor replied, "you'll find you have as much chance to get a job as you would to bat clean-up spot for the New York Yankees."

14.3   Quotations Within Quotations

Single quotation marks are used to enclose a quotation within a quotation.

Gary reported, "When somebody told Churchill not to end sentences with a preposition, Sir Winston replied, 'That is the kind of nonsense up with which I will not put.' "

Sheila asked, "Was it Roosevelt who said, 'The only thing we have to fear is fear itself'?"

14.4   Long Quotations

A quotation may be several paragraphs in length.

In long quotations, begin each paragraph with quotation marks. Place quotation marks at the end of the last paragraph only.

Exercise A: Copy the following sentences, adding the necessary punctuation marks and capital letters.

1. Boonesboro Jack reported is the name of the first American settlement west of the Appalachians
2. Why don't you take your vacation in winter she asked there are many Southern cruises

15.0 Spelling

There are many peculiarities and irregularities in English
spelling. Words that sound alike are not always spelled alike
(*stuff*, *tough*), and words that are spelled alike do not always
sound alike (*seen*, *been*). People who have trouble with spelling
are understandably frustrated by the seemingly arbitrary varia-
tions between sound and spelling. Yet, there are ways to help
improve spelling.

1. **Proofread all your writing.** Even the best spellers will occasionally write *to* for *too* or *your* for *you're* when writing a
   first draft. Careful proofreading and revision will eliminate these apparent spelling mistakes from your writing.

2. **Learn to look at the letters in a word.** Divide long words into
   parts and notice the arrangement of letters in each part.

3. **Keep a list of your spelling errors.** Most people spell a majority of words correctly. By keeping a list of your own personal trouble spots, you can focus your attention on the
   specific words that you tend to misspell and be alert to
   the correct spelling when you use these words in writing.

4. **Practice on your own spelling problems.** All of us have our
   own spelling problems and we all use individual methods
   to remember correct spellings. One way is to use flash
   cards. On one side of a card, write a word that is troublesome to you. When you have made up a number of cards,
   take one from the pack and look at every letter in the
   word. Pronounce each part of the word. Turn the card
   over and write the word on a separate sheet of paper.
   Check to see if you have written the correct spelling.

5. Memorize and apply the few rules of spelling given below. There are some rules that will help you spell correctly. Be sure you understand these rules because they relieve the necessity of memorizing each word individually.

Exercise: Divide these words into parts so that every word part has a vowel sound. Study the parts for problem spots or helpful patterns.

1. candidate	7. schedule	13. bulletin
2. necessary	8. anonymous	14. ascend
3. disappoint	9. privilege	15, fascinating
4. environment	10. association	16. conscientious
5. indefinitely	11. character	17. inoculation
6. thorough	12. appreciate	18. government

15.1 The Final Silent e

When a suffix beginning with a vowel is added to a word ending in a silent e, the e is usually dropped.

invite + ation = invitation   admire + able = admirable

ice + y = icy   fame + ous = famous

create + ive = creative   imagine + ary = imaginary

When the final silent e is preceded by c or g, the e is usually retained before a suffix beginning with a or o.

courage + ous = courageous   peace + able = peaceable

notice + able = noticeable

When a suffix beginning with a consonant is added to a word ending in a silent e, the e is usually retained.

state + ment = statement   safe + ty = safety

same + ness = sameness

The following words are exceptions: *truly, argument, wholly, awful.*

15.2   Words Ending in *y*

When a suffix is added to a word ending in *y* preceded by a consonant, the *y* is usually changed to *i*.

There are two exceptions: (1) When *-ing* is added, the *y* does not change. (2) Some one-syllable words do not change the *y*: *dryness, shyness*.

merry + ment = merriment	sixty + eth = sixtieth
city + es = cities	hazy + ness = haziness
hurry + ed = hurried	carry + ing = carrying

When a suffix is added to a word ending in *y* preceded by a vowel, the *y* usually does not change.

delay + ing = delaying	employ + er = employer
enjoy + ed = enjoyed	

EXCEPTIONS: day + ly = daily, gay + ly = gaily.

Exercise A: For each sentence below, look at the word given in parentheses. Change it to the necessary form by adding a suffix. Then write the sentence, filling in the blank with the new word.

1. The _____ of spring caused rejoicing in Scandinavia. (arrive—noun)
2. The administration may soon be forced to take _____ action. (discipline—adjective)
3. Brian's costume was _____ ridiculous. (true—adverb)
4. The campers found the early morning swim _____. (exhilarate—present participle)
5. Both sides were hoping to find a _____ settlement. (peace—adjective)
6. The piano, the _____ item, required professional movers. (heavy—superlative)
7. Milk and fresh eggs are delivered from the dairy _____. (day—adverb)
8. Nothing but _____ caused me to miss the concert. (lazy—noun)

9. The character's motives were not _____ understandable.
   (whole—adverb)
10. Believing that the _____ was for her, Joanne accepted.
   (invite—noun)
11. Dara _____ apologized for the mistake she had made.
   (sincere—adverb)
12. The senior class made a group _____ to the Kidney
   Foundation. (donate—noun)
13. Columbus, Indiana, is famous for its _____ monuments.
   (architecture—adjective)
14. Roman soldiers built _____ as far north as what is now
   Great Britain. (fortify—noun)
15. The store offered discounts and prizes for its _____
   anniversary. (fifty—ordinal number)
16. The new line of computer software is _____ easy to use.
   (extreme—adverb)
17. Billie dragged the suitcases _____ down the fire escape.
   (clumsy—adverb)
18. Tolkien's characters, though _____, are thoroughly
   believable. (imagine—adjective)
19. By noon the morning _____ had vanished. (hazy—noun)
20. Members of the team were required to purchase _____
   before they could participate in interscholastic sports.
   (insure—noun)

Exercise B: Add the suffixes as shown and write the new word.

1. negate + ion
2. monotony + ous
3. appraise + al
4. viscose + ity
5. definite + ive
6. quantify + er
7. ray + less
8. hygiene + ics
9. use + age
10. tragedy + an
11. future + istic
12. orate + ion
13. manage + ment
14. pasture + age
15. monument + al
16. create + ion
17. sisterly + ness
18. liquify + er
19. life + less
20. perpetrate + or
21. present + able
22. wavy + ness
23. shapely + er
24. tone + ic
25. service + able
26. rope + y
27. orange + ry
28. eighty + eth
29. alloy + ed
30. precede + ing

15.3 The Suffixes -*ness* and -*ly*

When the suffix -*ly* is added to a word ending in *l*, both *l*'s are retained. When -*ness* is added to a word ending in *n*, both *n*'s are retained.

gradual + ly = gradually   even + ness = evenness
actual + ly = actually   thin + ness = thinness

15.4 The Addition of Prefixes

When a prefix is added to a word, the spelling of the word remains the same.

mis + spell = misspell   dis + similar = dissimilar
im + mobilize = immobilize   trans + ship = transship
il + legal = illegal   re + enter = reenter

15.5 Words with the "Seed" Sound

Only one English word ends in *sede: supersede.*
Three words end in *ceed: exceed, proceed, succeed.*
All other words ending in the sound of *seed* are spelled *cede: secede, accede, recede, concede, precede.*

Exercise A: Correct the spelling errors in these sentences.

1. This faded old map is virtualy ilegible.
2. Kansas is being penalized fifteen yards for ilegal proceedure.
3. The eveness of the two teams made the game unusualy exciting.
4. A re-examination of our foreign policy was requested.
5. Rays from iradiated cobalt or gold have successfully attacked cancerous tissue.
6. Breaking a leg normaly imobilizes a person for months.

7. The captain's sterness caused disatisfaction.
8. The meeting is usualy preceeded by a potluck supper.
9. The SEC investigates iregularities in the stock market.
10. Scientists dissagree as to whether the nosecone actualy re-entered the atmosphere.
11. This exceptionaly brilliant youngster should be unusualy successful.
12. The officer answered civily that driving without a license was iresponsible.
13. Nuclear-powered ships will eventualy supercede conventionaly powered types.
14. The attorney examined the evidence that the judge had ruled irelevant.
15. The judge ruled that the evidence presented was imaterial, and the case proceded.

Exercise B: Add the suffixes and prefixes as indicated. Write the new word.

1. ir + reverent
2. green + ness
3. historical + ly
4. dis + service
5. pre + exist

6. thermal + ly
7. un + nerve
8. mis + fortune
9. im + material
10. re + kindle

11. clean + ness
12. coincidental + ly
13. com + patriot
14. ex + communicate
15. non + native

15.6 Words with *ie* and *ei*

When the sound is long e (ē), the word is spelled *ie* except after c.

I BEFORE E

relieve	priest	shriek
believe	relief	yield
piece	thief	pierce

EXCEPT AFTER C

receive	ceiling	deceit
perceive	conceive	receipt

Exceptions: either, neither, financier, weird, species, seize, leisure. You can remember these words by combining them into such a sentence as: *Neither financier seized either weird species of leisure.*

Exercise A: Copy the sentences, supplying the letters *ie* or *ei*.

1. Americans in the future will have to fill more l___sure time.
2. Is my brother's wife's sister's daughter my n___ce?
3. The th___f pleaded poverty to mitigate his sentence.
4. The outbreak of dysentery was rel___ved by proper hyg___ne.
5. Bowra's book sums up the ach___vement of Greek civilization.
6. Marine biologists studied the spec___s that will y___ld a harvest in underwater farming.
7. W___rd shr___ks from the synthesizer were used as sound effects.
8. The "f___rce animal" outside turned out to be a lost kitten.
9. Holography is a relatively new f___ld.
10. There are still people who bel___ve the world is flat.

Exercise B: Follow the same directions as for Exercise A.

1. The trophy went to n___ther of the top-seeded players.
2. When the water pipe burst, Steve's c___lings fell down.
3. A p___ce of the p___r suddenly collapsed.
4. Chris proved he had paid the bill with his canceled check because he had not gotten a rec___pt.
5. Tom could not be dec___ved by Charlie's tricks.
6. The hikers built a lean-to as a sh___ld.
7. Nonna is irretr___vably committed to the f___ld of medicine.
8. Aunt Susan enjoys Malcolm's misch___vous pranks.
9. It is hard to conc___ve of the world without cars.
10. Lulu wants to be ___ther a physicist or a chemist.

15.7 Doubling the Final Consonant

Words of one syllable, ending in one consonant preceded by one vowel, double the final consonant before adding a suffix beginning with a vowel.

1. The words below are the kind to which the rule applies.

   fat big slug brag

   These words double the final consonant if the suffix begins with a vowel.

   fat + er = fatter   slug + ish = sluggish
   big + est = biggest   brag + ing = bragging

2. The rule does not apply to the following one-syllable words because two vowels precede the final consonant.

   heat sleep near foot

   These words do not double the final consonant.

   heat + er = heater   near + est = nearest
   sleep + ing = sleeping   foot + ing = footing

3. The final consonant is doubled in words of more than one syllable:
   When they end in one consonant preceded by one vowel.
   When they are accented on the last syllable.

   re·fer′ o·mit′ con·cur′

   The same syllable is accented in the new word formed by adding the suffix.

   o·mit′ + ed = o·mit′ted   re·fer′ + al = re·fer′ral

   If the newly formed word is accented on a different syllable, the final consonant is not doubled.

   pre·fer′ + ence = pref′er·ence
   con·fer′ + ence = con′fer·ence

Exercise A: Copy these words, indicating with an accent mark (′) where each word is accented.

1. propel	7. occur	13. limit
2. commit	8. travel	14. prevail
3. prefer	9. concur	15. forget
4. admit	10. reset	16. dismay
5. forget	11. demur	17. permit
6. desist	12. regret	18. deter

Exercise B: Add the ending indicated and write the new word.

1. bed + ing	11. tan + est	21. appear + ance
2. near + est	12. sail + ing	22. pad + ing
3. travel + er	13. remit + ance	23. goad + ed
4. omit + ed	14. impel + ed	24. compel + ing
5. recur + ence	15. demur + al	25. refer + al
6. forget + able	16. resist + ance	26. fur + y
7. lead + er	17. regret + ing	27. differ + ent
8. deter + ence	18. drug + ist	28. limit + ed
9. avail + able	19. patrol + er	29. flat + est
10. fair + est	20. dip + ed	30. shoot + ing

A List of Commonly Misspelled Words

abbreviate	ab-bre-vi-ate	balance	bal-ance
absence	ab-sence	bargain	bar-gain
accidentally	ac-ci-den-tal-ly	becoming	be-com-ing
accommodate	ac-com-mo-date	beginning	be-gin-ning
accompanying	ac-com-pa-ny-ing	believe	be-lieve
achievement	a-chieve-ment	benefited	ben-e-fit-ed
acknowledge	ac-know-ledge	bicycle	bi-cy-cle
acquaintance	ac-quaint-ance	biscuit	bis-cuit
across	a-cross	bookkeeper	book-keep-er
address	ad-dress	bulletin	bul-le-tin
all right	all right	bureau	bu-reau
altogether	al-to-geth-er	business	busi-ness
always	al-ways	cafeteria	caf-e-te-ri-a
amateur	am-a-teur	calendar	cal-en-dar
analyze	an-a-lyze	campaign	cam-paign
annihilate	an-ni-hi-late	candidate	can-di-date
anonymous	a-non-y-mous	cellophane	cel-lo-phane
answer	an-swer	cemetery	cem-e-ter-y
apologize	a-pol-o-gize	certain	cer-tain
appearance	ap-pear-ance	changeable	change-a-ble
appreciate	ap-pre-ci-ate	characteristic	char-ac-ter-is-tic
appropriate	ap-pro-pri-ate	colonel	colo-nel
arctic	arc-tic	colossal	co-los-sal
argument	ar-gu-ment	column	col-umn
arising	a-ris-ing	commission	com-mis-sion
arrangement	ar-range-ment	committed	com-mit-ted
ascend	as-cend	committee	com-mit-tee
assassinate	as-sas-si-nate	comparative	com-par-a-tive
associate	as-so-ci-ate	compel	com-pel
attendance	at-tend-ance	competitive	com-pet-i-tive
audience	au-di-ence	complexion	com-plex-ion
auxiliary	aux-il-ia-ry	compulsory	com-pul-so-ry
awkward	awk-ward	conscience	con-science
bachelor	bach-e-lor	conscientious	con-sci-en-tious

conscious	con-scious	eminent	em-i-nent
consensus	con-sen-sus	emphasize	em-pha-size
contemptible	con-tempt-i-ble	enthusiastic	en-thu-si-as-tic
convenience	con-ven-ience	environment	en-vi-ron-ment
corps	corps	equipped	e-quipped
correspondence	cor-re-spond-ence	especially	es-pe-cial-ly
courageous	cou-ra-geous	etiquette	et-i-quette
courteous	cour-te-ous	exaggerate	ex-ag-ger-ate
criticism	crit-i-cism	excellent	ex-cel-lent
criticize	crit-i-cize	exceptional	ex-cep-tion-al
curiosity	cu-ri-os-i-ty	exhaust	ex-haust
cylinder	cyl-in-der	exhilarate	ex-hil-a-rate
dealt	dealt	existence	ex-ist-ence
decision	de-ci-sion	expense	ex-pense
definitely	def-i-nite-ly	experience	ex-pe-ri-ence
dependent	de-pend-ent	familiar	fa-mil-iar
descent	de-scent	fascinating	fas-ci-nat-ing
description	de-scrip-tion	fatigue	fa-tigue
desirable	de-sir-a-ble	February	Feb-ru-ar-y
despair	de-spair	feminine	fem-i-nine
desperate	des-per-ate	financial	fi-nan-cial
dictionary	dic-tion-ar-y	foreign	for-eign
different	dif-fer-ent	forfeit	for-feit
dining	din-ing	fourth	fourth
diphtheria	diph-the-ri-a	fragile	frag-ile
disagree	dis-a-gree	generally	gen-er-al-ly
disappear	dis-ap-pear	genius	gen-ius
disappoint	dis-ap-point	government	gov-ern-ment
discipline	dis-ci-pline	grammar	gram-mar
dissatisfied	dis-sat-is-fied	guarantee	guar-an-tee
economical	e-co-nom-i-cal	guard	guard
efficient	ef-fi-cient	gymnasium	gym-na-si-um
eighth	eighth	handkerchief	hand-ker-chief
eligible	el-i-gi-ble	height	height
eliminate	e-lim-i-nate	hindrance	hin-drance
embarrass	em-bar-rass	horizon	ho-ri-zon

humorous	hu-mor-ous	mischievous	mis-chie-vous
imaginary	im-ag-i-nar-y	missile	mis-sile
immediately	im-me-di-ate-ly	misspell	mis-spell
incidentally	in-ci-den-tal-ly	mortgage	mort-gage
inconvenience	in-con-ven-ience	municipal	mu-nic-i-pal
incredible	in-cred-i-ble	necessary	nec-es-sar-y
indefinitely	in-def-i-nite-ly	nickel	nick-el
indispensable	in-dis-pen-sa-ble	ninety	nine-ty
inevitable	in-ev-i-ta-ble	noticeable	no-tice-a-ble
infinite	in-fi-nite	nuclear	nu-cle-ar
influence	in-flu-ence	nuisance	nui-sance
inoculation	in-oc-u-la-tion	obstacle	ob-sta-cle
intelligence	in-tel-li-gence	occasionally	oc-ca-sion-al-ly
interesting	in-ter-est-ing	occur	oc-cur
irrelevant	ir-rel-e-vant	occurrence	oc-cur-rence
irresistible	ir-re-sist-i-ble	opinion	o-pin-ion
knowledge	knowl-edge	opportunity	op-por-tu-ni-ty
laboratory	lab-o-ra-to-ry	optimistic	op-ti-mis-tic
legitimate	le-git-i-mate	original	o-rig-i-nal
leisure	lei-sure	outrageous	out-ra-geous
lieutenant	lieu-ten-ant	pamphlet	pam-phlet
lightning	light-ning	parallel	par-al-lel
literacy	lit-er-a-cy	parliament	par-lia-ment
literature	lit-er-a-ture	particularly	par-tic-u-lar-ly
loneliness	lone-li-ness	pastime	pas-time
luxurious	lux-u-ri-ous	permanent	per-ma-nent
maintenance	main-te-nance	permissible	per-mis-si-ble
maneuver	ma-neu-ver	perseverance	per-se-ver-ance
marriage	mar-riage	perspiration	per-spi-ra-tion
mathematics	math-e-mat-ics	persuade	per-suade
matinee	mat-i-nee	picnicking	pic-nick-ing
medicine	med-i-cine	pleasant	pleas-ant
medieval	me-di-e-val	pneumonia	pneu-mo-ni-a
microphone	mi-cro-phone	politics	pol-i-tics
miniature	min-i-a-ture	possess	pos-sess
minimum	min-i-mum	possibility	pos-si-bil-i-ty

practice	prac-tice	specifically	spe-cif-i-cal-ly
preference	pref-er-ence	specimen	spec-i-men
prejudice	prej-u-dice	strategy	strat-e-gy
preparation	prep-a-ra-tion	strictly	strict-ly
privilege	priv-i-lege	subtle	sub-tle
probably	prob-a-bly	success	suc-cess
professor	pro-fes-sor	sufficient	suf-fi-cient
pronunciation	pro-nun-ci-a-tion	surprise	sur-prise
propeller	pro-pel-ler	syllable	syl-la-ble
prophecy	proph-e-cy	sympathy	sym-pa-thy
psychology	psy-chol-o-gy	symptom	symp-tom
pursue	pur-sue	tariff	tar-iff
quantity	quan-ti-ty	temperament	tem-per-a-ment
questionnaire	ques-tion-naire	temperature	tem-per-a-ture
realize	re-al-ize	thorough	thor-ough
recognize	rec-og-nize	throughout	through-out
recommend	rec-om-mend	together	to-geth-er
reference	ref-er-ence	tomorrow	to-mor-row
referred	re-ferred	traffic	traf-fic
rehearse	re-hearse	tragedy	trag-e-dy
reign	reign	transferred	trans-ferred
repetition	rep-e-ti-tion	truly	tru-ly
representative	rep-re-sent-a-tive	Tuesday	Tues-day
restaurant	res-tau-rant	tyranny	tyr-an-ny
rhythm	rhythm	twelfth	twelfth
ridiculous	ri-dic-u-lous	unanimous	u-nan-i-mous
sandwich	sand-wich	undoubtedly	un-doubt-ed-ly
schedule	sched-ule	unnecessary	un-nec-es-sar-y
scissors	scis-sors	vacuum	vac-u-um
secretary	sec-re-tar-y	vengeance	venge-ance
separate	sep-a-rate	vicinity	vi-cin-i-ty
sergeant	ser-geant	village	vil-lage
similar	sim-i-lar	villain	vil-lain
sincerely	sin-cere-ly	weird	weird
sophomore	soph-o-more	wholly	whol-ly
souvenir	sou-ve-nir	writing	writ-ing

REINFORCEMENT EXERCISES
Spelling

A. Add suffixes to words ending in silent e or y. Combine the following base words and suffixes and write the new word.

1. advertise + er
2. examine + ing
3. dirty + est
4. dally + ing
5. pace + ing
6. cry + er
7. manage + able
8. true + ly
9. complete + tion
10. terrible + ly
11. reverse + able
12. vary + able
13. day + ly
14. tarry + ed
15. retire + ing
16. lone + some
17. upheave + al
18. dizzy + est
19. trace + able
20. sensitive + ity

B. Identify misspelled words. Find the misspelled words in the following list and spell them correctly. Two words are correct.

1. accidentaly
2. procede
3. greeness
4. usualy
5. unecessary
6. conceed
7. misunderstanding
8. ilegal
9. suceed
10. imigrant
11. cleanness
12. awfuly
13. fulley
14. dissappointment
15. meaness
16. nonncommittal
17. superceed
18. hopefuly
19. unnable
20. ilogically

C. Spell words containing *ei* or *ie*. Rewrite the following sentences, correcting any errors in spelling. If a sentence is correct as it is, write *Correct*.

1. The theif stole six skeins of biege yarn.
2. The children were up to mischeif at the neighbor's house.

3. Coffee and chocolate contain caffeine, so ignore that peice of coffee-chocolate pie.
4. The stuntwoman feinted to the left, then weilded the sword to the right.
5. The casheir did not beleive that I did not have a receipt.
6. We all crave leisure time, so we must seize it when we can.
7. The artist was famous for her fiery temper and for the wrought-iron chandeliers she created.
8. Mr. McClosky's chief virtue was that he never practiced deceit, but because of this he was unable to percieve it in others.
9. Who first concieved of the idea of building a hot-air balloon?
10. The ceiling yeilded to the wrecker's wieght.

D. Add suffixes. Combine the following base words and suffixes, being careful to spell the resulting words correctly.

1. thrill + ing
2. flop + y
3. trap + ing
4. admit + ance
5. float + ing
6. journal + ist
7. mature + ity
8. revise + ion
9. linger + ing
10. trim + ed
11. refer + ed
12. skim + ed
13. toil + ing
14. propel + ing
15. twitch + ed
16. wrap + ing
17. hold + er
18. control + er
19. dally + ance
20. foot + ing

MIXED REVIEW
Spelling

A. Combine the following words and word parts using the spelling rules presented in this Section.

1. awful + ly
2. sensitive + ity
3. waver + ing
4. hop + ing
5. co + operate
6. sociology + cal
7. paste + y
8. grovel + ing
9. hope + ing
10. trans + continental
11. bat + er
12. serial + ize
13. successful + ly
14. spruce + ing
15. skip + ing
16. plant + er
17. mean + ness
18. wan + ness
19. pace + ing
20. concur + ence

B. Find the misspelled words in the following sentences and spell them correctly.

1. "The temperament of young people is very changable," adviseed the fameous psychologyst.
2. A Supreme Court ruleing superceeds lower-court decisions.
3. Because Hans was used to small black bears, the size of the huge grizzly scarred him.
4. The lieutenant did not realy beleive that the frontier had come to an end.
5. Rachel's explanation immediatly clearred up the confuseion.
6. Blevins shouted across the gayly decorateed gym.
7. Some people are worriing about obeseity while others are freting over thiness.
8. Nutritionists test varyous foods for wholesomness.
9. The secureity guard rang me up in the middle of the night unecessarylly, for no theif had entered the building.

10. Luke did not explain very precisly how we should go about wraping his giant painting.
11. Lowerring the unnemployment rate is one task that Congress is faceing.
12. Mr. Lawson was carring a sixty-pound wieght down the stairs quite casualy.
13. Vicki was voted cheif of staff by the mischeivous students.
14. The quarterback proceded without any noticable injurys.
15. Who could be funnyer or wittyer than Woody Allen?
16. The exploreers looked with amazment at the wierd cliff dwellings.
17. Fans shreiked as Owens was carryed from the feild.
18. Jesse James was an infameous bandit who robed banks.
19. The officer thought we were loiterring, but we were realy waiting for the rest of the swiming team.
20. Creativeity generaly involves comeing up with unnusual and original solutions to problems.

USING MECHANICS IN WRITING
Spelling

A. Look up the twelve labors of Hercules in a mythology book. Write an account of one of the labors as if you were an on-the-spot reporter covering the event live. First write your account in the present tense; then, rewrite the account in the present progressive. Notice how the spellings of words change and how you must remember the rules for adding suffixes. Now rewrite the account again in the past tense. Which version of the story is most vivid?

B. Below is a partial list of *ie* and *ei* words, organized by sound. Use this list to write a limerick with *ie* and *ei* words as the rhyming words at the ends of the lines.

brief	relieve	fierce	conceit	deign
chief	deceive	pierce	receipt	reign
thief	believe	yield	deceit	feign
niece	conceive	field	eight	rein
priest	perceive	wield	weight	vein
piece	receive	neither	sleigh	feint
belief	reprieve	either	neigh	sleight
relief	believe	seizure	weigh	height
grief	retrieve	leisure	inveigh	

C. Many misspellings result from the improper use of words that are commonly confused. A portion of a list of these words is shown below. Write a story, humorous or serious, in which you use one word from each pair. Write another story in which you use each of the remaining words. In both stories, be sure to use the words correctly.

desert	its	principle	their	whose
dessert	it's	principal	they're	who's
hear	loose	stationary	weather	your
here	lose	stationery	whether	you're

16.0 The Plurals of Nouns

16.1 Regular Formation of Plurals

The plural of most nouns is formed by adding -s.

employee + s = employees   door + s = doors
sense + s = senses   badge + s = badges

16.2 Plurals Formed with *es*

The plural of nouns ending in *s*, *sh*, *ch*, *x*, and *z* is formed by adding -es.

fox + es = foxes   church + es = churches
sash + es = sashes   class + es = classes

16.3 Plurals of Nouns Ending in *y*

When a noun ends in *y* preceded by a consonant, the plural is formed by changing the *y* to *i* and adding -es.

city   citi + es = cities
beauty   beauti + es = beauties
company   compani + es = companies
worry   worri + es = worries

When a noun ends in *y* preceded by a vowel, a plural is formed by adding *-s.*

$$play + s = plays \qquad holiday + s = holidays$$
$$galley + s = galleys \qquad turkey + s = turkeys$$
$$delay + s = delays \qquad valley + s = valleys$$

16.4   Plurals of Nouns Ending in *o*

The plural of nouns ending in *o*, preceded by a vowel, is formed by adding *-s.*

$$patio + s = patios \qquad curio + s = curios$$
$$portfolio + s = portfolios \qquad rodeo + s = rodeos$$
$$stereo + s = stereos \qquad kangaroo + s = kangaroos$$

The plural of most nouns ending in *o*, preceded by a consonant, is formed by adding *-s*, but for some nouns of this class the plural is formed by adding *-es.*

$$manifesto + s = manifestos \qquad Eskimo + s = Eskimos$$
$$kimono + s = kimonos \qquad halo + s = halos$$
$$tango + s = tangos \qquad banjo + s = banjos$$

$$tomato + es = tomatoes \qquad torpedo + es = torpedoes$$
$$lingo + es = lingoes \qquad potato + es = potatoes$$

There are some words ending in *o* with a preceding consonant that may form the plural with either *-s* or *-es: motto, mango, mosquito.* The safest thing to do is to memorize the few words that add *-es* and to consult the dictionary about others.

16.5   Plurals of Nouns Ending in *f* or *ff*

The plural of most nouns ending in *f* or *ff* is formed regularly by adding *-s.*

$$waif + s = waifs \qquad proof + s = proofs$$
$$chief + s = chiefs \qquad gulf + s = gulfs$$
$$staff + s = staffs \qquad sheriff + s = sheriffs$$

The plural of some nouns ending in *f* or *fe* is formed by changing the *f* or *fe* to *ve* and adding -*s*.

self—selves	calf—calves	loaf—loaves
half—halves	life—lives	shelf—shelves

Most of the nouns that are pluralized in this way are in common use. The plurals are familiar in both speech and writing. If you have any doubt about how to make one of these nouns plural, look up the word in the dictionary. If the plural is irregular, it will be given immediately after the singular.

16.6 Nouns with Irregular Plurals

The plural of some nouns is formed by a change of spelling.

foot—feet	larva—larvae	man—men
diagnosis—diagnoses	radius—radii	child—children
vortex—vortices	thesis—theses	woman—women
criterion—criteria	opus—opera	medium—media

The plural and singular forms are the same for a few nouns.

species	corps	Japanese	buffalo	scissors

16.7 The Plurals of Names

The plural of a name is formed by adding -*s* or -*es*.

George Wolf—the Wolfs   Joyce Williams—the Williamses

16.8 The Plurals of Compound Nouns

When a compound noun is written without a hyphen, the plural is formed at the end of the word.

nightshirt + s = nightshirts	teaspoonful + s = teaspoonfuls
fingernail + s = fingernails	doghouse + s = doghouses

When a compound noun is made up of a noun plus a modifier, the plural is added to the noun.

> sisters-in-law (the phrase *in-law* is a modifier)
> editors-in-chief (the phrase *in-chief* is a modifier)
> bills of fare (the phrase *of fare* is a modifier)
> courts martial (the word *martial* is a modifier)
> lookers-on (*on* modifies *lookers*)
> lords chancellor (*chancellor* modifies *lords*)

Exercise A: Form the plural of each of the following words. Use the dictionary if necessary.

1. gash	11. corps	21. phenomenon
2. life	12. datum	22. sheriff
3. valley	13. cattle	23. rite of passage
4. belief	14. church	24. teaspoonful
5. worry	15. grief	25. hanger-on
6. laboratory	16. wife	26. bill of sale
7. cupful	17. potato	27. notary public
8. holiday	18. handful	28. writ of protection
9. gulf	19. hypothesis	29. chief of police
10. loaf	20. basis	30. brother-in-law

Exercise B: Find the errors in plural forms in the following sentences. Write the plurals correctly.

1. The northern lights are an unusual phenomena.
2. There are several boxs of matches in the cupboard.
3. Passer-bys admired the photoes.
4. For home economics we bought oranges, potatos, and tomatos.
5. Our allys needed our help against their enemys.
6. The picnickers used dull knifes to cut the loafs of bread.
7. The childrens brought handsful of sand from the beach.
8. I have two sister-in-laws living in Milwaukee.
9. Use two cupsful of flour and two tablespoonsful of sugar.
10. None of the studioes is large enough for two pianoes.

11. There are too many autoes in our citys.
12. Two sopranoes will sing solos.
13. The watchmens were neglecting their dutys.
14. The thiefs covered their faces with handkerchieves.
15. We saw over a dozen deers in the woods and in the vallies.
16. The wolfs have been attacking the sheeps.
17. Both of my brother-in-laws are fishermans.
18. There are still a few wild turkies in these valleys.
19. We are going on a picnic with the Thomas's and the Barry's.
20. The woodes will be filled with jack-in-the-pulpits soon.
21. You must expect delayes in postal service during the holidays.
22. The opposing commander-in-chiefs met with their staffs.
23. The scientists advanced different hypothesises.
24. Shall we plant lily-of-the-valleys in our window boxs?
25. The editor-in-chiefs of several dailys met with their staffes of reporters.

REINFORCEMENT EXERCISES
The Plurals of Nouns

A. Form the plurals of nouns. Complete each of the following sentences with the proper plural form of the noun given in parentheses.

1. Like the main paths in the body's circulatory system, main traffic routes are called _____. (artery)
2. Thousands of men wearing _____ marched down Fifth Avenue during the Shriners Parade. (fez)
3. The team practiced throwing forward _____ all day. (pass)
4. Isn't there a novel about Vietnam entitled the _____ *of Eden?* (*Alley*)
5. My little cousin could not play with his presents because no one had remembered to bring _____. (battery)
6. Six _____, two wizards, and a warlock came trick-or-treating at our house on Halloween. (witch)
7. Dr. Natalie Karakov specialized in building _____. (rookery)
8. The lifespan of some _____ is as little as a single day. (insect)
9. At the experimental farm, Roberta was given the job of overseeing the _____. (hatchery)
10. The best place to study the behavior of _____ is in the wild. (monkey)

B. Form the plurals of nouns. Complete each of the following sentences with the proper plural form of the noun given in parentheses.

1. The Folger Library has more First _____ of Shakespeare's plays than any other library. (Folio)
2. Mrs. Granger bought a bushel of _____ at the farm stand and spent the weekend making tomato sauce. (tomato)

3. Will any new _____ be imposed on imported goods during the coming fiscal year? (tariff)

4. The magician had a huge supply of silk _____ to use in his act. (scarf)

5. Ripley's "Believe It or Not" series explored odd events and people and unexplained _____. (phenomenon)

6. We had to buy seventeen _____ of bread to make enough sandwiches. (loaf)

7. Scientists ranked the active _____ of the world according to likelihood of eruption in the coming year. (volcano)

8. Our cat, Cindy, just used up the eighth of her nine _____. (life)

9. There are many misconceptions about _____, some of which come from fairy tales. (wolf)

10. A remarkable new device allows _____ with spinal defects to "walk" on their own. (child)

C. Correct improper plurals. Rewrite the following sentences, correcting all errors in the formation of plurals.

1. There were more than one hundred Jones' at the reunion.

2. Scientific breaksthrough are often a combination of accident and observation.

3. Aristotle and his followers were mistaken about the basises of matter.

4. Cynthia added three tablespoonsful of salt to the recipe instead of three teaspoonsful.

5. On the quiz, Darian guessed the radiuses of all the circles and consequently got every answer wrong.

6. The biology class was studying the positive and negative effects of bacteriums on the human body.

7. Three bugle corpses marched in the Fourth of July Parade.

8. When we were in Wyoming, we stayed with the Moss's.

9. Dr. Klinger's analysises of the various problems were startlingly insightful.

10. The President-elects from three nations were photographed together.

MIXED REVIEW
The Plurals of Nouns

A. Form the plural of each of the following words. You may need to check a dictionary for the correct spelling.

1. banjo	9. pagoda	17. guppy
2. calf	10. deer	18. trout
3. soprano	11. million	19. alumna
4. sheath	12. ox	20. laurels
5. baseman	13. father-in-law	
6. by-stander	14. humanoid	
7. shelf	15. knife	
8. jack-in-the-box	16. thesis	

B. Complete the following sentences with the proper plural forms of the words given in parentheses.

1. I managed to eat three of the _____ (cream puff) and drink two _____ (glass) of milk.
2. We rode the _____ (burro) down the trail of the Grand Canyon and joked with the _____ (guide).
3. Several women drove the _____ (ox) to market, but the men carried the _____ (goose).
4. Who discovered that _____ (mosquito) spread malaria?
5. The _____ (Ulrich) brought six _____ (cartload) of presents with them.
6. The _____ (staff) of both _____ (agency) were present to distribute the _____ (loaf) of bread.
7. Wilson lost all the _____ (bill of lading).
8. Erika spent several _____ (hour) designing the form for the computer _____ (printout).
9. They had perpetrated several _____ (hoax) before they were caught.
10. Our _____ (brother-in-law) were organizing a game of volleyball, but our _____ (sister-in-law) wanted to play field hockey instead.

USING MECHANICS IN WRITING
The Plurals of Nouns

A. The works of artists are often referred to by the name of the artist instead of the particular name of the work. For example, one might say that a museum owns three Rembrandts, instead of three paintings by Rembrandt. Imagine that you are the curator of a museum of prints and drawings. Below is a list of artists. After each name is a number in parentheses. The number tells how many of the artist's works your museum has in reserve. Write a report for the directors in which you tell how many works you have of each artist.

George Bellows (3)
Kathe Kollwitz (2)
Otto Dix (5)
Pablo Picasso (2)
George Grosz (7)
Morris Graves (2)
Grandma Moses (2)
Giacomo Manzu (5)
Marino Marini (3)
David Siqueiros (2)
Wassily Kandinsky (6)

Juan Gris (3)
William Glackens (4)
Thomas Eakins (5)
Georgia O'Keeffe (3)
Ferdinand Delacroix (2)
Stuart Davis (4)
Jean August Ingres (3)
Joan Miro (2)
Karl Schmidt-Rottluff (3)
Edvard Munch (2)
Jacques Lipchitz (5)

B. Imagine that you have a "Midas touch." Instead of turning to gold, however, everything you touch multiplies. Picture yourself at a dance, a sporting event, cooking a meal, or working on the assembly line of a factory. Write a description of what happens to you, using as many plurals of nouns as you can.

17.0 Good Manuscript Form

The appearance of your written work tells the reader something about you, the writer. If your papers are sloppy or illegible, then your readers may think you did not care about what you were writing or the impression that you would make.

If your school has a standard form for manuscripts, follow the guidelines given there. If not, use the suggestions in this Section to produce a manuscript that will let your readers know that you think what you have to say is important.

17.1 Legible Handwriting

If you can type your papers neatly, do so. A typewritten page is always easier to read than a handwritten one. If you write by hand, use a pen. Only dark blue or black ink is acceptable. Form your letters distinctly so *n*'s will not look like *m*'s, or *u*'s like *v*'s. Be sure you have dotted every *i* and crossed every *t*.

If you must delete material from a typewritten page, strike it out with capital *X*'s or capital *M*'s, or use correction fluid.

17.2   Margins and Spacing

The margin at the top, bottom, and right side of your paper should be one inch wide. Leave a slightly larger margin at the left. The left-hand margin must be perfectly straight for type-written papers and as straight as possible for handwritten papers. Keep the right-hand margin as even as you can without hyphenating too many words at the ends of lines. Try not to hyphenate words at the ends of more than two consecutive lines.

Typed papers must be double-spaced. Indent five spaces for paragraphs. Leave a single space between words and two spaces after end marks.

17.3   Proper Labeling

Follow the instructions given by your teacher for identifying yourself as the author of the paper. Usually, you will be asked to put your name in the top right-hand corner of the first page. Below your name, you will place the name or number of the course. Below that, you will put the date.

The first page is not numbered. Start numbering on page two by putting the number in the top right-hand corner. You may also be required to place your name on each page under the page number.

17.4   Placement of the Title

The title of your paper should appear only once—on the first page. Center the title two lines below the last line of your heading. Leave two lines between the title and the first line of your first paragraph.

The first word of your title must be capitalized. Also capital-ize any other important words in the title (See Section 10.12). Use initial capitals only. Do not capitalize every letter or underline your title. Use quotation marks in the title only if you are quoting some other source.

Teachers sometimes require a separate title page for long papers. A title page contains a heading in the upper right-hand corner and the title centered on the page.

17.5   Preparation of Final Copy

Your first draft should never be your final draft. Leave time to reread your paper carefully and make revisions. Professional writers often do three, four, or five drafts before they produce their final copy, so do not think that the need to write several drafts is a mark of inexperience.

When proofreading your final copy, you may still discover minor errors in spelling or punctuation or a missing word or phrase. Insert missing words by writing them neatly above the line in which they should appear. Use a caret (∧) to indicate where they should be placed in the text. You may make neat corrections by drawing a line through words and writing above them or by deleting a word or phrase with correction fluid and writing in the space. If there are several corrections on a single page, recopy the page.

17.6   Numbers in Writing

Numbers that can be expressed in fewer than four words are usually spelled out; longer numbers are written in figures.

They made a profit of *thirty-one thousand* dollars.
Scott sold 124 boxes of candy this week.
There are only *twenty-four* seats left for tonight's show.
Ms. Blackall wrote a check for $5,450 for a used car.

A number beginning a sentence is spelled out.

Twelve students from our school won scholarships.
Forty-six students saw *Othello* at the Playhouse in the Park.

17.7   Figures in Writing

Figures are used to express dates, street and room numbers, telephone numbers, page and chapter numbers, decimals, percentages, and temperatures.

President Kennedy was assassinated on November 22, 1963.
Send the letter to 5127 Banner Street, Room 492.
Joanne's new telephone number is 786-1905.
The test will cover Chapters 3 and 4, pages 27 through 68.
My temperature was only 98.1 degrees.
Voter turn-out was only 60.4 percent on election day.

Note: Commas are used to separate the figures in sums of money or expressions of large quantities. They are not used in dates, serial numbers, addresses, or telephone numbers.

INCORRECT: Thoreau's *Walden* was first published in 1,854.
CORRECT: Thoreau's *Walden* was first published in 1854.
CORRECT: The fare for the tour was $1,150.50.
CORRECT: The world's population increases by 100,000 people every day.

Exercise: Copy these sentences, correcting any errors in the writing of figures. Four of the sentences are correct.

1. The Library of Congress has almost 400 miles of bookshelves.
2. The library contains nearly 16,000,000 books.
3. The population of Los Angeles is now over 3,000,000.
4. The cost of the house is $47,650.
5. Our telephone number here is 555-7,050.
6. The auditorium has a capacity of 700 people.
7. 5 of the students in my class want to join VISTA.
8. About sixty percent of our high school graduates go to college.
9. Over one hundred thousand people worked on the 1980 census.

10. Questionnaires were mailed to nearly 60,000 households.
11. The first census was taken in seventeen hundred and ninety.
12. My new address is three hundred twenty York Boulevard.
13. Over eight hundred people attended the lecture.
14. Helen's room number at the hospital is three twenty-eight.
15. The highest temperature ever recorded in this country is 134 degrees.

17.8 Abbreviations in Writing

Abbreviations may be used for most titles before and after proper names, for names of government agencies, and in dates.

BEFORE PROPER NAMES:	Dr., Mr., Mrs., Ms., Messrs., Rev., Hon., Gov., Capt.
AFTER PROPER NAMES:	Jr., Sr., D.D., Ph.D.
GOVERNMENT AGENCIES:	FBI, FCC, AEC
DATES AND TIME:	A.D., B.C., A.M., P.M.

There are no periods after abbreviations of government agencies.

The abbreviations of titles are acceptable only when used as part of a name. It is not acceptable to write *The secy. of the club is a dr.* The titles *Honorable* and *Reverend* are not abbreviated when preceded by *the: The Honorable John Ross.* They appear with the person's full name, not just the last name. Abbreviations are not appropriate for the President and Vice-President of the United States.

In ordinary writing, abbreviations are not acceptable for names of countries and states, months and days of the week, nor for words that are part of addresses or firm names.

UNACCEPTABLE:	A new cultural center was built in N.Y.
BETTER:	A new cultural center was built in New York.

UNACCEPTABLE:	Thousands of U.S. troops participated in the maneuvers.
BETTER:	Thousands of United States troops participated in the maneuvers.
UNACCEPTABLE:	Bart works for the Spalding Adv. Co.
BETTER:	Bart works for the Spalding Advertising Company.
UNACCEPTABLE:	School will reopen on Mon., Sept. 3.
BETTER:	School will reopen on Monday, September 3.

In ordinary writing, abbreviations are not acceptable for the following: names of school courses, *page, chapter, Christmas,* and words standing for measurements, such as *bu., in., hr., min., sec.*

17.9 The Hyphen

A hyphen is used at the end of a line to divide a word between syllables.

Hypnosis is increasingly being used in the medical profession to study the human mind, to reduce tension, and to increase motivation.

Note: At least two letters of the hyphenated word should appear on each line. One-syllable words should never be hyphenated.

Many compound words require hyphens. Consult a good dictionary for hyphenation of compound words.

coat-of-arms	double-cross	make-believe
great-aunt	twelve-year-old	has-been
run-through	cross-purposes	looker-on

Sometimes two or more words are used together as if they were a single adjective. When these words appear before a noun, they are hyphenated. They are usually not hyphenated when they come after the noun.

> STANDARD: *Fatuous* is a little-used word that means "fool-
> ish."
>
> STANDARD: The word *fatuous*, which means "foolish," is lit-
> tle used.

seven-year term	slow-acting medicine
well-planned schedule	on-screen personality
deep-rooted fears	light-hearted song
law-abiding citizen	round-the-clock service

Compound numbers between twenty-one and ninety-nine are hyphenated. Fractions, such as *three-eighths* are hyphenated unless either the denominator or the numerator is already a hyphenated word, as in *one forty-eighth* or *twenty-one fiftieths*.

In certain cases, a hyphen is added to a word along with a prefix or suffix. *Co-chairperson* is hyphenated, for example, even though *coauthor* is not. The prefixes *all-*, *self-*, *co-*, and *ex-* often use hyphens. A hyphen is always appropriate when a proper noun takes a prefix or suffix.

self-respect	mid-Victorian	Chaplin-like
de-emphasis	all-embracing	ex-Senator
anti-Marxist	non-Italian	pre-Renaissance

Exercise: Correct the errors in manuscript form in the following sentences.

1. The Arab owned Clarke Chem. Co. is a mfr. of pharmaceutical products.
2. Ms. Hollis and ex Senator Chas. Dutton attended a convention in Butte, Mont.
3. My appointment with Dr. Walsh is on Thurs. at 3:00 P.M.
4. The vice pres. of the club presides in the absence of the pres.
5. Mom's checking account is at the 1st Nat'l Bank.
6. Isn't your father a vice pres. of his co.?
7. My sister has to read two chaps. a wk. in her psych. course.

8. Look at the double spaced chart on the second p. of Chap. 9.
9. In Mar. of 1977 the FDA banned the use of saccharin in food and drink.
10. Dr. Cutler said the median ht. of seventeen year old girls is about 5 ft. 4 in.
11. What day of the wk. does Feb. 14 fall on this yr.?
12. A lt. gen. in the U.S. Army wears three silver stars.
13. Is Great aunt Sylvia treas. of the Forbes Mfg. Co.?
14. The Rev. John Barry will speak at the Norton H.S. graduation ceremony.
15. The 747 flew from Los Angeles, Cal., to New York in 5 hr. and 30 min.

17.10　Italics for Titles

Italics is a printer's term. It refers to a kind of right-slanted type that printers use. When a writer underlines a word, it means the same thing as italics in print.

Titles of books, plays, motion pictures, newspapers, magazines, works of art, and long musical compositions are printed in italics. The names of ships, trains, and airplanes are also printed in italics.

PRINTED FORM:　The orchestra is rehearsing Handel's *Messiah*.

MANUSCRIPT FORM:　The orchestra is rehearsing Handel's <u>Messiah</u>.

PRINTED FORM:　*A Man for All Seasons* is a provocative play about St. Thomas More.

MANUSCRIPT FORM:　<u>A Man for All Seasons</u> is a provocative play about St. Thomas More.

PRINTED FORM:　Look in *The New York Times* for news about the President's arrival.

MANUSCRIPT FORM:　Look in <u>The New York Times</u> for news about the President's arrival.

17.11 Italics for Foreign Words and Phrases

Many foreign words have become so widely used that they are now part of the English language: *siesta, alma mater, bamboo, czar*. Such words are printed in regular type. Foreign words and phrases that have not become part of our language are printed in italics: *voilà, l'chaim, de nada, festina lente*.

The only way to be sure whether a word or phrase of foreign origin should be printed in italics (underlined in manuscript) is to consult the dictionary.

17.12 Italics for Words, Letters, or Figures

Italics are used for words, letters, or figures referred to as such.

In printed works, words, letters, or figures referred to as such are in italics. In writing, they are underlined.

PRINTED FORM:	The *to* should have been written *too*.
MANUSCRIPT FORM:	The <u>to</u> should have been written <u>too</u>.

PRINTED FORM:	In Australia, the long *a* is pronounced as long *i*.
MANUSCRIPT FORM:	In Australia, the long <u>a</u> is pronounced as long <u>i</u>.

17.13 Italics for Emphasis

Italics (underlining) are used to give special emphasis to words or phrases.

Use italics for emphasis sparingly. Try to give emphasis to important words and ideas by writing in a clear, direct style. In high school writing, italics (underlining) should only be used for emphasis when your meaning might not be clear without them.

The writer *implies* a meaning; the reader *infers* it.

17.14   Correction Symbols and Revision

In both high school and college, teachers correct students'
papers by making notes and placing correction symbols in the
margin of the work. These notes and symbols indicate the
errors made both in grammar and in structure. You should take
time not only to read the comments but to correct the errors.
Making such corrections will increase the effectiveness of your
writing.

The following correction symbols are commonly used:

ab   *Abbreviation.* Either the abbreviation is inappropriate or wrong. Consult a dictionary.

agr   *Agreement.* You have made an error in agreement
of subject and verb or of pronoun and antecedent.
Consult Section 6 and Section 7.13–7.16 in your
Handbook.

awk   *Awkward.* The sentence is clumsy. Rewrite it.

cap   *Capital letters.* You have omitted necessary capitals. Consult Section 10 in your Handbook.

cf   *Comma fault.* You have joined two sentences together with a comma. Change the punctuation.

dang   *Dangling construction.* You have written a verbal
phrase in such a way that it does not modify the
word it should. Rewrite the sentence.

frag   *Sentence fragment.* You have placed a period after
a group of words that is not a sentence. Join the
fragment to an existing sentence or add words to
complete the thought.

ital   *Italics.* You have omitted italics that are needed.

k   *Awkward.* See *awk* above.

lc   *Lower case.* Use a small letter, not a capital.

ms   *Manuscript form.* You have not followed the
proper manuscript form. Consult Section 17 in
your Handbook.

no ¶   *No paragraph.* You have started a new paragraph too soon. Join these sentences to the preceding paragraph.

¶   *Paragraph.* Begin a new paragraph at this point.

nc   *Not clear.* Your meaning is not clear. Rewrite the passage to say what you mean.

om   *Omission.* You have left out words that are needed for clarity or smoothness of style.

p   *Punctuation.* You have made an error in punctuation. Consult Sections 11, 12, 13, or 14 in your Handbook for sentences like the one you have improperly punctuated.

ref   *Reference.* There is an error or a weakness in the reference or pronoun to antecedent. Consult Section 7 in your Handbook.

rep   *Repetition.* You have repeated a word too often, or you have repeated something you wrote in preceding sentences.

ro   *Run-on sentence.* You have written two or more sentences as one. Change the punctuation.

shift   *Shift.* You have shifted point of view or tense needlessly.

sp   *Spelling.* You have misspelled a word. Consult a dictionary.

t   *Tense.* You have used the wrong tense form. Consult Section 5 in your Handbook.

tr   *Transpose.* Your meaning would be clearer if a letter, word, sentence, or passage were placed at another point.

wd   *Wrong word.* You have confused homonyms, or you have used a word that does not fit the meaning, or you have used a slang word inappropriately. Consult a dictionary or Section 9 in your Handbook.

REINFORCEMENT EXERCISES
Good Manuscript Form

A. Understand proper manuscript form. The following statements refer to good manuscript form. Tell whether these statements are true or false.

1. The left-hand margin should be somewhat wider than the right-hand margin.
2. Pages are numbered in the lower right-hand corner.
3. Brightly colored inks, such as purple, green, and red, may be used to emphasize important terms or statements.
4. The date appears in the first line of your identifying heading.
5. Use all capitals for the title of your paper.
6. The symbol (∧), which indicates that a word or words should be inserted, is called a *carrot*.
7. Do not underline the title of your paper.
8. The top, bottom, and right hand margins of your paper should all be one inch.
9. The title of the paper is centered on a title page.
10. A carefully written first draft should make proofreading and revision unnecessary.

B. Write numbers and figures correctly. Correct any errors in the writing of numbers and figures.

1. The car cost nine thousand six hundred forty-three dollars and twenty-two cents, without taxes.
2. Steve Goodman begins a song about the twentieth century by referring to the year eighteen ninety-nine.
3. The weather announcer said that we had six point six inches of rain.
4. More than 100 windows fell out of the glass high-rise during the wind storm.

5. 10,000 citizens signed the petition for recall.
6. We moved from six hundred and three Garden Terrace to six hundred and two Garden Terrace.
7. On December twenty-four the temperature was minus forty-eight degrees Fahrenheit.
8. We printed 45 copies of our literary quarterly.
9. The pasteup artist had transposed pages four and five, so the diagram made no sense.
10. 12 seems like a very old age to a 5-year-old.

C. Use abbreviations correctly. Rewrite the following sentences, correcting any errors in the use of abbreviations. If a sentence is correct, write *Correct*.

1. Read chpts. 4 and 5 over the weekend.
2. Tracey works out with ten-lb. dumbbells for twenty minutes each day.
3. The novelist began writing p. 1 on Tues., Apr. 15.
4. On your way to Spotless Linens this Sat., you can drop off a package at the Needham Napkin Co.
5. What were Pres. Johnson's views on the role of the C.I.A.?
6. The team runs 10 km. every Thurs. and Mon. afternoon.
7. The sermon was given by the Rev. Joseph Shepherd.
8. Robert was born in Evansville, Ind., and his sister was born in Evansville, Penn.
9. Pat went to camp in Aug.
10. Dr. Doyle boasted that her daughter had also become a dr. and her son, a gov.

D. Use hyphens correctly. Rewrite the following sentences, correcting any errors in the use of the hyphen. If a sentence is correct, write *Correct*. You may have to consult a dictionary.

1. The actor cultivated a Brandolike mumble.
2. After twenty two rehearsals, the drama club only managed a so so performance.
3. We used a rubber base paint because it made clean-up much easier.

4. The story about a match-maker was based on a reallife character.
5. The mailorder house was offering a two thirds discount on all after-season merchandise.
6. Mr. Poppy is a jack-of-all-trades who lives in a jerry-built house.
7. We were surprised to see a ten year old girl giving our car its tuneup.
8. Mortimer was struggling to remember the names of the first iron-clad war-ships.
9. A well informed antique dealer tried to buy our ladderback chairs for a less-than-equitable price.
10. This source is considered well informed by the media.

E. Understand the use of italics. Rewrite the following sentences, underlining words that would appear in italics if the sentence were printed.

1. Paul Lawrence Dunbar's poetry was collected into a volume called Lyrics of Lowly Life.
2. The critic said that the play was stupendous, not horrendous.
3. Corrie knew that Carmen was a famous opera, but she did not know that Bizet composed it.
4. The Bismarck was a German battleship sunk during World War II.
5. Michael thought the # symbol was to be read as number, but Lilli thought it should be read as pounds.
6. When we visit Aunt Sophie in New Orleans, we read the Picayune Times.
7. Omar Khayyam, an eleventh century Persian poet, wrote the well-known Rubaiyat.
8. Did Wylla say she would or would not accept the nomination?
9. In Japanese, seiko means "success."
10. The rabbi said mazel tov to the families of the bride and groom.

MIXED REVIEW
Good Manuscript Form

A. Rewrite the following sentences, correcting any errors in manuscript form.

1. Roger Bannister was the first man to run the 4 min. mi., and that was way back in the early '50s.
2. The title of The Nothing Book intrigued me until I discovered that the book contained blank pages.
3. 35,000 people lived in the planned community.
4. "Do you even know what jambon means in French?" asked Bryan after I had ordered jambon in the restaurant.
5. Phil writes in such a way that I can't tell the difference between his n's and his r's.
6. When the mist making machine shot out ice instead of mist, the director put on a parka.
7. Bonnie auditioned for A Cry of Players as well as Macbeth.
8. Richard quickly flipped the word a day calendar to his birthdate, and discovered the word fiasco.
9. Texas borders Louisiana, Oklahoma, Ark., New Mex., and, of course, the nation of Mex.
10. A championship baseball team can expect to win about sixty-six percent of its games.
11. "Sometimes, Carl, I think you have the attention span of a four year old child," said Mrs. Ziska to her son.
12. The director of the Met. Opera had great hopes for the young star's Caruso like voice.
13. Felicia signed the agreement on Apr. 30, 1,984.
14. Marcia subscribed to both Personal Computing and Popular Computing; she believed it was de rigeur for a computer novice.
15. A machine with a human like voice told me that the number for Piper's Bowling Alley was 4720948.

16. The capt. of the ship culvitated an Ahab like manner after he read Moby Dick.
17. Everyone was reading What Color Is Your Parachute?, so I borrowed a copy from my editor in chief.
18. Mr. Selby of the F.B.I. was scheduled to speak in N.Y.C. at 9:00 AM on Tues., Jan. 18.
19. Polly has been reading War and Peace in her spare time for 6 months and is now on p. 1,111.
20. Edward put in a 40 hr. work week for Cataline Manu. Co. over spring vacation.

B. Rewrite the following sentences, correcting the errors in the writing of figures and in the use of abbreviations, hyphens, and italics. Indicate italics by underlining.

1. A Concord, N. H., man invented the alarm clock in 1,787.
2. The Rialto Theater at 64 N. Ohio St. charges only $2.
3. 1 state, Wash., and 4 state capitals are named after presidents.
4. The FBI sometimes works with Interpol, an international police organization for over 100 countries.
5. Snow capped Mount Everest is 29,028 ft. high.
6. The self important boxer lost by a K.O. in the 10th round.
7. Only twenty four people entered the contest.
8. The ex Marine stepped on the Portuguese man of war.
9. Prof. Hannah Gray was chosen pres. of the U. of Chicago.
10. On Mon., Feb. 16, at 2:00 P. M., our class will visit the Calif. Ct. of Appeals.
11. The highest R.R. speed in the U.S. was 183.85 m. p. h.
12. Dr. Jekyll and Mr. Hyde were the creations of Robt. Louis Stevenson.
13. I think about ten percent of the clues in the book The Adventures of Sherlock Holmes are misleading.
14. The assignment is to read Ch. 2, pp. 23–28.
15. The story about embezzlement at The Crate Co. is on p. 2 of The New York Times.

USING MECHANICS IN WRITING
Good Manuscript Form

A. Below is part of the first page of an essay that a friend of yours has asked you to criticize for matters of form. Examine the paper carefully and write your friend a note explaining how the paper must be changed to conform to good manuscript form.

```
February 16
Humanities 203
J. J. Purdy


              FOREIGN WORDS IN ENGLISH

        The vocabulary of the Eng. language
   has been enriched over the centuries as
   words were borrowed from many other lan-
   guages. In fact, more than 1/2 of the
   words used by Englishspeaking people
   today were borrowed from French after the
   Norman Conquest of 1,066 ad. Nouns such
   as parliament, religion, biscuit, and
   grammar came into use during this period,
   while such highfrequency words as I, and,
   and because remained in the language from
   the original Anglosaxon or Old Eng.
```

B. You and four of your friends are joint owners of a lottery ticket that wins a million dollars. A newspaper has requested that you write an article explaining how the five of you decide to use your portions of the winnings. Write the article using proper manuscript form, being especially careful to write numbers and figures according to the guidelines in Section 17.

CUMULATIVE REVIEW
Spelling and Manuscript Form

A. Proofreading for Spelling Errors. Correct the spelling errors in the following sentences.

1. Niether of the scientists observed the phenomenons.
2. The computer chips were noticably thiner than a sheet of notebook paper.
3. The druggist repairs pianoes in his liesure time.
4. Two teaspoonfuls of detergent should be enough.
5. Leafs from the Smiths' tree fell on the Barneses' lawn.
6. The scientists proceded to prove their hypothesises.
7. The judgements of the attorney-generals were superceded.
8. Several passer-bys observed the accident.
9. The financeir's company's underwent financial criseses.
10. The new cheif-of-police promised to change the policys of previous chieves-of-police.

B. Using Correction Symbols. Rewrite the passage, correcting the errors indicated by the symbols given in the margin.

sp The word *glamour* is merely a misspronunciation and mis-
sp/cap writting of the word *grammar*. In the middle ages, *grammar*
wd/p meant "the knowledge of how to read and right. Since most
 wd people then could neither read or write, anyone who knew
sp/awk grammer was thought of as possessed of an uncanny range of
lc/shift Knowledge. In other words, this person is a magician. *Gram-*
frag *mar*, or *glamour*, was therefore a special power. Which could
  not be understood by common or ordinary folk. Eventually,
 t the word comes to mean "sorcery" and was used in this sense
cap/frag by the poet Alfred, Lord tennyson. When he spoke of "that
sp maiden in the tale/Whom Gwydion made by glamor out of
lc/ab flowers." In the Twentieth cent., the word *glamour* came
cf into general use in advertising, it now means "a mysterious
tr or alluring charm".

—GILBERT HIGHET

18.0 Outlining

An outline is a helpful tool for organizing material for a composition or speech. The outline is also useful for taking notes on a book or lecture. The outline presents material in skeleton form. It shows what the main points are, how the main points are supported by subpoints and details, and how all of this material is organized. This Section will explain the principles of outlining and give you practice in using them.

18.1 Kinds of Outlines

There are two kinds of outlines in general use. One is the **sentence outline** in which all ideas are expressed in complete sentences. The other form is the **topic outline** in which the ideas are expressed in words or phrases. Both types of outlines are organized in the same way. The main difference is in how fully stated the points for the headings and subheadings are. An example of a topic outline is given on the following page.

How Streets Are Named

The purpose of this composition is to explain the various sources used for naming streets.

I. Geographical Features

    A. Terrain

        1. Prairie Street

        2. Mountainside Avenue

        3. Valley Road

    B. Bodies of water

        1. Ocean Parkway

        2. Riverside Drive

        3. Lake Shore Drive

II. Species

    A. Plant

        1. Maple Street

        2. Hyacinth Boulevard

    B. Animal

        1. Bob O'Link Terrace

        2. Possum Road

III. Notable People

    A. Local celebrities

        1. Dr. Pfingstein Avenue

        2. Paul Holly Drive

    B. National and world celebrities

        1. Lincoln Street

        2. Martin Luther King Boulevard

        3. Copernicus Avenue

IV. Schematic Patterns

    A. Alphabetical

    B. Numerical

A topic outline, such as the one given above, is useful as a reminder of material that you know well and as a guide to organization. A sentence outline, which presents each heading and subheading in sentence form, is useful when the material is complicated or when you must show your plan to someone else. A sentence outline may also be used for note-taking when you will have to refer to the notes several days or weeks later. A sentence outline is given below.

The Structure of the Cell

The purpose of this paper is to explain the various parts of every human cell and to show how they work together.

I. Membranes define cell boundaries.

    A. Membrane has three-layered structure: protein-lipid-protein.

    B. Membranes keep cytoplasm balanced.

        1. Nutrients pass through the membrane.

        2. Wastes exit through the membrane.

    C. Some membranes have surface specializations.

        1. Microvili exist in the reproductive, urinary, and digestive systems.

        2. Cilia exist in respiratory cells.

    D. Membranes exist within cells as well.

        1. The nucleus has its own membrane.

        2. A latticework of intercellular membranes holds the cytoplasm.

II. Organelles provide vital functions within the cells.

    A. Mitochondria produce and store energy.

    B. Endoplasmic Reticulum has several functions.

        1. ER acts as a circulatory system.

        2. Rough ER has ribosomes that make proteins.

        3. Muscular ER carries impulses.

        4. ER forms sacs around cell products.

C. The Golgi Complex helps process cell products.

D. The centriole has two roles.
   1. The centrioles have a role in cell division.
   2. Centrioles affect movements in the cell.

E. Lysosomes act as a digestive system.

F. Vacuoles and vesicles contain chemicals within the cell.

G. Inclusions are particles temporarily suspended in the cytoplasm.

III. The nucleus of the cell controls reproduction.

A. All cells except muscle cells have one nucleus.

B. The nucleus contains important substances.
   1. RNA and DNA are in the nucleus.
   2. Chromatin becomes chromosomes which encode information concerning cell function.

C. The nucleolus controls messages to the cytoplasm.

18.2   Outline Form

For both topic outlines and sentence outlines, you should follow the principles given below.

1. Put the title of your paper at the top of the page. Below it, write a brief statement of your purpose. These are not part of the outline. Your introduction and conclusion are not part of the outline either.

2. Use standard outline form. The order of numerals and letters is given below. Roman numerals are used for main headings and capital letters for subheadings. Arabic numbers are used for points that develop subheadings. As your material breaks down into finer and finer divisions, use small letters, then arabic numbers in parentheses, then small letters in parentheses.

> I.
>> A.
>> B.
>>> 1.
>>> 2.
>>>> a.
>>>> b.
>>>>> (1)
>>>>> (2)
>>>>>> (a)
>>>>>> (b)
>
> II.
>> A.
>> B.
>>> 1.
>>> (and so on)

3. Indent each new division of the outline. Put the letter or numeral directly under the first letter in the first word of the larger heading above.

4. Never divide an idea into a single subdivision. There must be at least two. For example, if there is a *1* under *A*, there must also be at least a *2*. An idea cannot be broken down into fewer than two parts.

5. In a topic outline, headings of the same rank must be worded in parallel form. For example, if *A* is an infinitive, then *B* and *C* must also be infinitives.

6. Begin each heading with a capital letter. Use periods at the ends of lines only in sentence outlines.

Exercise: Complete the topic outline on the next page by inserting the following headings in the appropriate blanks.

Effects of oil on our economy	First refinery	Hydrocarbons
In industry	Synthetic oils	Energy value
	Creates jobs	Uses of oil

Oil and Society

The purpose of this paper is to explore the benefits and dangers of oil use in the modern world.

I. History of oil
  A. First wells
  B.

II. Important facts about oil
  A.
  B. Chemical composition
    1.
    2. Sulphur
    3. Nitrogenous substances
  C. Viscosity

III.
  A. In everyday life
  B. In transportation
  C.
  D. In international trade

IV.
  A. Supports modern technology
  B.
  C. Creates pollution

V. Possible substitutes
  A. Coal
  B. Natural gas
  C.

REINFORCEMENT EXERCISES
Outlining

A. Understand proper outline form. Complete the following statements about proper outline form.

1. A _____ outline uses words or phrases for headings and subheadings.
2. Major headings in an outline are preceded by _____ numerals.
3. The statement of purpose comes immediately after the _____.
4. All ideas in the outline refer back to the _____.
5. A heading can be divided into no less than _____ subheadings.
6. The _____ and the _____ are not parts of the outline.
7. The first letter of each outline entry should be _____.
8. Indent each subheading so the letter or numeral comes under _____.

B. Use correct outline form. Briefly review the following outline and then correct it, keeping in mind the following points: (1) Every topic and subtopic must relate to the controlling purpose. (2) Main topics should be parallel in form; each group of subtopics should be parallel in form. (3) Subtopics should never be fewer than two. (4) Organizational terms should never be used. (5) In a topic outline, complete sentences should not be used.

Life in an Instant City

I. Introduction: The instant city a relatively new phenomenon

II. Profile of typical instant city
   A. Residential area
      1. Single-family dwellings
      2. Contrasting with suburban homes

B. May also include industrial area

C. Commercial areas included by design

III. Describe the population

    A. Economic mix

    B. Backgrounds—blue-collar workers and professionals

IV. These cities are luring people away from suburbs and more established urban areas.

    A. Convenience

        1. Self-contained transportation network

    B. Leisure activities

        1. Boating

        2. Social organizations

        3. Many provide entertainment complexes

    C. They provide some of the advantages of a city with the feeling of a small town.

    D. Education

        1. Centralized schools, for economy

        2. Recruiting teachers

MIXED REVIEW
Outlining

A. Below is an article on percussion instruments. Read it, then write an outline using Roman numerals to list the general categories of percussion instruments. Use capital letters to divide the major headings into particular types of instruments.

A percussion instrument is one that produces a sound when it is hit with the hand or some other instrument. The best known percussion instruments are drums, which are used around the world. Drums are used by primitive peoples as well as by sophisticated symphony orchestras. There are many different kinds of drums, including kettledrums, snare drums, the tom-tom, and tambourines.

The bell is also a percussion instrument. Unlike drums, which consist of some sort of skin stretched and hit, bell instruments are made of some sort of metal and then struck. In addition to the familiar type of bell, there is the glockenspiel and the xylophone. The celesta is similar to the instruments of the bell family, but has some differences. A celesta looks something like a small piano. The steel bars inside the celesta are not hit directly by the player, but are hit by hammers which strike when the player presses the keys.

Last but not least in the percussion family are the striking-sticks instruments. The simplest kind of sticks are just that—two sticks hit against each other. But castanets are part of this same family, as are cymbals and the triangle.

B. Read about the features of each percussion instrument and then expand the previous outline with this information. Use Arabic numbers to subdivide the entries listed beside capital letters. You may also need to use lower case letters to subdivide further.

Glockenspiel—used since medieval times in Europe. Originally bells, later a keyboard with metal bars. Since 19th century, the bars have been struck by hammers.

Kettledrum—a bowl of metal, a membrane stretched over the open end. Kettledrums are the only drums that can be tuned to a definite pitch. Muslims originated the kettledrum.

Triangle—a steel rod bent into a triangular shape, but slightly open at one end. The triangle is struck by a steel rod.

Tom-Tom—Tom-toms are hand drums, usually long, barrel-shaped ones, often with a strap (worn by the player to hold the drum) and usually with membranes on both ends. Originated either with American Indians or in the Orient.

Snare Drum—Most drums have membranes, or drumheads, on both sides, or ends. However, in a snare drum, one head has gut strings twisted with wire stretched across it. When the opposite end of the snare drum is struck, the strings rattle, producing a distinctive snare drum sound.

Celesta—Auguste Mustel, a Frenchman, patented the celesta in 1886. The tone of the celesta has been described as both "delicate" and "ethereal."

USING MECHANICS IN WRITING
Outlining

A. Look at the outline for "Life in an Instant City" in Reinforcement Exercises. Write a short essay developing the ideas in the outline. Although you may not know very much about the subject, you will find that the information and organization presented in the outline is sufficient to guide you in the initial planning of the paper. Do additional research as necessary.

B. Write an outline for a paper that discusses the educational value of various kinds of movies. First, you will want to classify or categorize movies into various types and then discuss the kinds of things the audience can learn from each type. You do not have to use traditional classifications of movies, such as science fiction, horror, documentary, etc. You may classify them any way that is useful to you in order to discuss their educational value.

C. The Table of Contents in a book is often written in the form of an outline, showing major headings that are broken down into subheadings and specific topics. Look through your school textbooks or the books you have at home to see if you can find a Table of Contents that is written in clear outline form. Then use the Table of Contents to write a summary of the content of the book. Your summary should be easy to organize because the subject matter is already organized clearly in the Table of Contents.

Sources of Quoted Materials

Cover

Homage to the Square: Early Diary, 1955. Josef Albers. Nebraska Art Association, Thomas C. Woods Collection.

Editorial Credits

Editor-in-Chief: Joseph F. Littell
Editorial Director, English Programs: Joy Littell
Administrative Editor: Kathleen Laya
Managing Editor: Geraldine Macsal
Director of Secondary English: Bonnie Dobkin
Assistant Editor: Robert D. Shepherd

Associate Designer: Mary E. MacDonald
Handwritten Art: Amy Palmer
Cover Design: Joy Littell, Debbie Costello
Production Assistant: Julie Schumacher

Index

CUMULATIVE REVIEW
Spelling and Manuscript Form

A. Proofreading for Spelling Errors. Correct the spelling errors in the following sentences.

1. Niether of the scientists observed the phenomenons.
2. The computer chips were noticably thiner than a sheet of notebook paper.
3. The druggist repairs pianoes in his liesure time.
4. Two teaspoonfuls of detergent should be enough.
5. Leafs from the Smiths' tree fell on the Barneses lawn.
6. The scientists proceded to prove their hypothesises.
7. The judgements of the attorney-generals were superceded.
8. Several passer-bys observed the accident.
9. The financeir's company's underwent financial criseses.
10. The new cheif-of-police promised to change the policys of previous chieves-of-police.

B. Using Correction Symbols. Rewrite the passage, correcting the errors indicated by the symbols given in the margin.

sp   The word *glamour* is merely a misspronunciation and mis-
sp/cap writting of the word *grammar*. In the middle ages, *grammar*
wd/p meant "the knowledge of how to read and right. Since most
wd people then could neither read or write, anyone who knew
sp/awk grammer was thought of as possessed of an uncanny range of
lc/shift Knowledge. In other words, this person is a magician. *Gram-*
frag *mar*, or *glamour*, was therefore a special power. Which could
    not be understood by common or ordinary folk. Eventually,
t the word comes to mean "sorcery" and was used in this sense
cap/frag by the poet Alfred, Lord tennyson. When he spoke of "that
sp maiden in the tale/Whom Gwydion made by glamor out of
lc/ab flowers." In the Twentieth cent., the word *glamour* came
cf into general use in advertising, it now means "a mysterious
tr or alluring charm".

—GILBERT HIGHET

18.0 Outlining

An outline is a helpful tool for organizing material for a composition or speech. The outline is also useful for taking notes on a book or lecture. The outline presents material in skeleton form. It shows what the main points are, how the main points are supported by subpoints and details, and how all of this material is organized. This Section will explain the principles of outlining and give you practice in using them.

18.1 Kinds of Outlines

There are two kinds of outlines in general use. One is the **sentence outline** in which all ideas are expressed in complete sentences. The other form is the **topic outline** in which the ideas are expressed in words or phrases. Both types of outlines are organized in the same way. The main difference is in how fully stated the points for the headings and subheadings are. An example of a topic outline is given on the following page.

How Streets Are Named

The purpose of this composition is to explain the various sources used for naming streets.

I. Geographical Features

  A. Terrain

    1. Prairie Street

    2. Mountainside Avenue

    3. Valley Road

  B. Bodies of water

    1. Ocean Parkway

    2. Riverside Drive

    3. Lake Shore Drive

II. Species

  A. Plant

    1. Maple Street

    2. Hyacinth Boulevard

  B. Animal

    1. Bob O'Link Terrace

    2. Possum Road

III. Notable People

  A. Local celebrities

    1. Dr. Pfingstein Avenue

    2. Paul Holly Drive

  B. National and world celebrities

    1. Lincoln Street

    2. Martin Luther King Boulevard

    3. Copernicus Avenue

IV. Schematic Patterns

  A. Alphabetical

  B. Numerical

A topic outline, such as the one given above, is useful as a reminder of material that you know well and as a guide to organization. A sentence outline, which presents each heading and subheading in sentence form, is useful when the material is complicated or when you must show your plan to someone else. A sentence outline may also be used for note-taking when you will have to refer to the notes several days or weeks later. A sentence outline is given below.

The Structure of the Cell

The purpose of this paper is to explain the various parts of every human cell and to show how they work together.

I. Membranes define cell boundaries.

    A. Membrane has three-layered structure: protein-lipid-protein.

    B. Membranes keep cytoplasm balanced.

        1. Nutrients pass through the membrane.

        2. Wastes exit through the membrane.

    C. Some membranes have surface specializations.

        1. Microvili exist in the reproductive, urinary, and digestive systems.

        2. Cilia exist in respiratory cells.

    D. Membranes exist within cells as well.

        1. The nucleus has its own membrane.

        2. A latticework of intercellular membranes holds the cytoplasm.

II. Organelles provide vital functions within the cells.

    A. Mitochondria produce and store energy.

    B. Endoplasmic Reticulum has several functions.

        1. ER acts as a circulatory system.

        2. Rough ER has ribosomes that make proteins.

        3. Muscular ER carries impulses.

        4. ER forms sacs around cell products.

Double comparisons, 655
Double negatives, 657–58, 660
  and contractions, 657–58, 660

e, final, in spelling, 758, 760, 770
eager, anxious, 669
Editors
  in bibliography form, 282
  in footnote form, 269
Effect, combining sentences to show,
  31.
Either/or fallacy, 341
Ellipses, 727
Elliptical clauses, 529
emigrate, immigrate, 669–70
Emphasis
  achieving in writing, 138–41
  compound personal pronouns used
    for, 428
  italics used for, 792
Emphatic forms of verbs, 577–79
Empty sentences, 37–39
Encyclopedia articles
  bibliography cards for, 254
  bibliography form for, 286
  footnote form for, 273
Encyclopedias, 314–16
End marks, 550–51, 556, 698–99,
  713, 718–19. *See also*
  Exclamation points; Periods;
  Question marks
English
  formal, 92
  grammar, 421–566
  inflection in, 617
  informal, 92–93
  standard and nonstandard, 92, 93,
    603–04, 606, 621, 628, 630–31,
    649, 655, 657–58, 664–81
  See also Language; Sentences;
  Words
Equivocation, 344–45
-es, forming plurals of nouns, 775–76
et al., 277
etc., 670
et seq., 277
Examples, 94
  in paragraphs, 118
Exclamation points (or marks), 468,
  699, 718

with closing parentheses, 727
with exclamations, 699
with interjections, 449
with quotation marks, 745
Exclamations as quotations, 745
Exclamatory sentences, 468–69, 508–
  09, 516, 699
Explanatory words, parentheses with,
  726–27
Expository writing
  in compositions, 185
  defining, 160–61
  explaining an idea, 159–60
  explaining a process, 159
  to give reasons, 161
  in paragraphs, 158–64

f, ff, fe, plurals of nouns ending in,
  776–77
Fact and opinion, 329–33
  distinguishing, 329–30
  evaluating, 331–33
Facts, 94
  in paragraphs, 118
Fallacies, 340–46. *See also* Critical
  thinking
False analogy, 341
Family relationships, capitalization of,
  689–90
Faulty coordination
  avoiding, 51–52
  coordinating conjunctions in, 557–
  58
Faulty parallelism, 60–61
Feminine gender, 425–28, 630–31
fewer, less, 650
Fiction, library classification for, 306.
  See also Literature
Figurative language, 130
Figures (numbers), 787–88, 795–96
  commas with, 703–04, 787–88
Film titles, as subjects of sentences,
  606
Final copies, 103–04, 786
  of paragraphs, 147
First drafts, 99–100, 129
  of analogy, 175
  of comparison and contrast
    paragraphs, 171
  of compositions, 191–99